REMEMBERING OUR OWN

THE SANTA CRUZ COUNTY MILITARY ROLL OF HONOR 1861-2010

Robert Nelson

REMEMBERING OUR OWN

THE SANTA CRUZ COUNTY MILITARY ROLL OF HONOR 1861-2010

1861 - 2010

ROBERT L. NELSON

The Museum of Art & History @ The McPherson Center

The Museum of Art & History @ The McPherson Center

705 Front Street
Santa Cruz, CA 95060-4508
http://www.santacruzmah.org/

Remembering Our Own

by
Robert L. Nelson

Library of Congress Cataloging-in-Publication Data

Nelson, Robert L., 1937-
  Remembering our own : the Santa Cruz County military roll of honor 1861-2010 / Robert L. Nelson.
    p. cm.
  Includes bibliographical references and index.
  ISBN 978-0-940283-21-3 (alk. paper)
  1. Santa Cruz County (Calif.)--Genealogy. 2. Soldiers--California--Santa Cruz County--Registers. 3. Registers of births, etc.--California--Santa Cruz County. 4. United States--Armed Forces--Registers of dead. 5. Santa Cruz County (Calif.)--History, Military. I. Museum of Art & History @ The McPherson Center. II. Title.
  F868.S3N45 2010
  929'.379471--dc22

                      2010004387

© 2010 by The Museum of Art & History @ The McPherson Center

The opinions expressed by the author are not necessarily those of the publisher.

Printing & Binding Production: Lightning Source, La Vergne, TN 37086
Distributed by: Otter B Books, Santa Cruz, CA 95062

Financial support for this publication provided by
Fred D. McPherson Jr. Publication Fund
of the MAH History Publications Committee

Thanks for financial
contributions from the following donors
Traci Bliss, in memory of Vance Bliss
Harold Anthony Hyde, in memory of Asa Anthony

Thanks for additional financial contributions from
Norman H. Atkins
Stan and Judy Nielson
Ronald Pinkham
and

Daughters of the American Revolution
National Association of Retired Federal Employees
Santa Cruz County Genealogical Society

CONTENTS

Acknowledgments

This work could not have been possible without the efforts and support of the following organizations and individuals:

The History Publications Committee of The Museum of Art & History for their help in publishing this book; committee members who helped included Joan Gilbert Martin for providing many hours of advice and for editing the first draft of the manuscript; Joyce Miller, Stanley Stevens, and Michael Clark for editing the final draft; and Michael Clark for preparing the book for publication;

Amy Dunning of the Archives of the Museum of Art & History for use of material and staff time;

Jane Borg for editing those portions involving Watsonville and Pajaro Valley service personnel;

Marion Pokriots for her review of Santa Cruz and north county biographical sketches;

Pajaro Valley Historical Association for the use of their archival material, staff time, and equipment;

The Genealogical Society of Santa Cruz County for the local records they provided;

Sheila Prader for the invaluable World War I enlistment records that she located;

Mas Hashimoto for stories and records of local casualties of the 100/442nd Regimental Combat Team;

The Watsonville City Library for use of their microfilm and local history files;

Susan Elgin and staff of the Santa Cruz City-County Public Libraries for use of their archival material and workspace;

Brigadier General (ret) Harold Hyde for advice and coordination of veteran support in Watsonville;

Dr. Robert Spencer, MD, who provided the title and veteran support coordination in Santa Cruz;

Mrs. Margaret Penniman who kept my nose to the grindstone to insure that the project was completed.

A special thanks is extended to all the family members and friends of the veterans who shared stories, letters, photos and remembrances of their experiences.

PREFACE

Memorial Day 2002 found an old soldier adjusting his spectacles to read a torn, typewritten roll of honor displayed within a cabinet in the Veterans Memorial Building in Santa Cruz, California. The list of servicemen who had died during the US wars in which Santa Cruz County had participated between 1917 and 1953 included the names of approximately 150 local men who never returned from World War I, World War II, and Korea. Noticeably missing were the names of those who died in the Civil War, Vietnam War, and Middle East wars, along with the names of servicemen representing other areas of the county. Who were those young men and women who had gone off to fight a war and never returned?

In an attempt to solve the mystery, the old soldier decided that he would attempt to identify all of the county's war dead and retell their stories. The United Veterans Council of Santa Cruz County, representing local veterans organizations, also agreed to honor those brothers and sisters in arms on a permanent roll of honor within their building. Out of that six-year research journey an expanded list evolved that contains the names of 461 men and 2 women. As their life stories began to unfold, so also did a picture of a county's youth marching off to war, never to return. It is hoped that by sharing the lives of Santa Cruz County's war dead, the reader will gain a new appreciation of the sacrifice of their forgotten neighbors.

nels

An old soldier
Santa Cruz, California, May 2010

INTRODUCTION

In August 2002 a letter arrived at the Santa Cruz, California, American Legion office from a young Belgian student requesting information about Reuben Wilkinson, a local soldier killed during World War I, who was buried in Flanders Field. In gathering that information it became apparent that few of the 461 men and 2 women from Santa Cruz County who died during the wars of the United States while serving in the military left written accounts of their life. Who were these former members of our county who never returned, and what portion of their life story might be retold in the context of the monumental event in which they participated? The answer to those questions became a six-year quest to honor them and pass their stories on to future generations.

Throughout the county's history, various organizations have recognized their war dead through rolls of honor, plaques and other memorials; however, none of those listings have been complete, accurate or consistent in their criteria for the selection of honorees. The first objective in our story-telling journey was to identify as many previously omitted individuals as possible, correct inaccuracies of earlier lists and establish a consistent standard for recognition.

The US government through its War Department, National Archives Administration, American Battlefield Monuments Commission, and other agencies provided various listings of casualties from World War I through the Vietnam conflict. While significant, each of these honor rolls was limited in their scope, incomplete in number, and inconsistent with other listings in the information they provided.

During and following periods of war, Santa Cruz County high schools, veterans groups and local newspapers created memorials and honor rolls to recognize their war dead. Although these listings were larger and more inclusive than those provided by the government, they were also similarly incomplete and inconsistent from war to war and community to community.

A standard was needed for developing an honor roll that incorporated the requirements of the US government with the subjective desires of the county.

IDENTIFYING WAR DEAD

During the twentieth century Santa Cruz individuals and agencies have attempted to identify residents and former residents who died during wars and to acknowledge them within honor rolls, memorial plaques and special listings.

1. Civil War. "Santa Cruzans of the Civil War," an article by local historian Tom McHugh that appeared in the November 12, 1952, *Santa Cruz Sentinel*, has provided the only known published listing of county individuals believed to have died in the Civil War. After checking its accuracy with Orton's *Records of California Men in the War of the Rebellion,* some names were eliminated. A search of the *Pajaro Valley Times, Pacific Sentinel* and *Santa Cruz Sentinel* during the Civil War period failed to uncover any additional casualty candidates.

2. Spanish American War. No Santa Cruz County service personnel were reported to have died during the Spanish-American War by either government reporting agencies or local newspapers.

3. World War I. In 1921 the California Adjutant Generals office published "Names of Officers and Enlisted Men From California Who Lost Their Lives While Serving in the Armed Forces of the United States During the World War." The list was provided by the US War and Navy Departments; it identified individuals by community.

4. Veteran Memorials. In 1928 local World War I Veterans conducted an extensive search to identify every Santa Cruz County World War I casualty for inclusion on the Victory Byway monument erected at the lower plaza in Santa Cruz.

Pajaro Valley veterans also erected a memorial plaque on an obelisk in the Grove of Remembrance at the junction of Freedom and Buena Vista Roads near Watsonville to honor that region's war dead.

5. High School Memorials. In 1924 Santa Cruz High School installed a plaque at the entrance to its Memorial Field recognizing class members who had died in World War I. The school also installed plaques in the lobby of its main entrance recognizing the same list of World War I classmates. Later they added students who had died in World War II, Korean and Vietnam Wars.

Watsonville High School installed similar plaques on a large memorial stone near the school entrance honoring classmates who had died during World War I, World War II and the Korean War. In 1986 the school unveiled a separate monument in its courtyard recognizing classmates killed in Vietnam.

6. Newspaper Honor Rolls. During World War II rolls of honor were periodically published by the *Santa Cruz Sentinel* and the *Watsonville Register-Pajaronian* listing military service personnel within their circulation area who had died during that conflict. Final updates of these listings were provided at the completion of the war. The *Watsonville Register-Pajaronian* also produced an honor roll listing Pajaro Valley war dead from the Korean War. The *Santa Cruz Sentinel* published a listing on May 24, 2009, that was intended to include all conflicts.

7. US Government Listings. At the completion of World War II the US War Department produced a listing of US Army and Air Force deaths by county. The US National Archives and Records Administration later added a listing of US Navy, Marine Corps and Coast Guard deaths by county. During the Korean and Vietnam Wars, the National Archives and Records Administration (NARA) compiled listings of war dead by county. The US Battlefield Monuments Commission, a government agency responsible for the records and maintenance of overseas American military cemeteries, provided honor rolls of World War I, World War II and Korean War deaths under their jurisdiction. No final government listing for Afghanistan and Iraq War deaths has been released to date.

8. Newspapers. The names of additional Santa Cruz County war dead have been identified in newspapers published in Santa Cruz and Watsonville, California. By reviewing microfilm copies of all the local newspapers during the war years, 109 additional war dead were identified.

ROLL OF HONOR DEVELOPMENT

Previous honor rolls recognizing Santa Cruz County war dead failed to acknowledge a number of individuals and inappropriately included others. This honor roll is intended to correct those errors. To accomplish this a consistent standard was required to insure that the criteria used to honor a casualty residing in one section of the county during one war was applicable to any casualty living in any section in any conflict. To create such a standard three conditions needed to be resolved:

1. What residency connection did the serviceman or woman have with Santa Cruz County?
2. What type or cause of death should be considered for recognition on a roll of honor?
3. What dates accurately represented the various wars or periods of military mobilization?

Residency Criteria

How should Santa Cruz County residency be defined in identifying war its war dead? For the US government the answer was simple. If an individual designated the county as their residence or that of their next of kin at the time of their enlistment, that became their home of record. While objectively simple this poses subjective problems. Should servicemen who were only temporarily assigned in the county be considered residents? Should former residents who were born, educated, worked and lived in Santa Cruz County and moved to another community prior to entry into the armed forces be excluded?

During World War II the *Santa Cruz Sentinel* did not address the questions of when the deceased veterans lived in the community, why or for how long. To be included in their roll of honor they merely solicited the names of "those individuals from northern Santa Cruz County serving in the armed forces of the United States." The *Watsonville Register-Pajaronian,* on the other hand, stipulated that "to be eligible for the Pajaro Valley Roll of Honor the member of the armed forces must have his or her bona fide home in this valley." It was their belief that if a resident moved, the new community would recognize them. To resolve these differences, this updated Military Roll of Honor has combined all of the previously used residency parameters in establishing the following criteria:

1. The state of California defines residency as occurring when an individual makes their home or takes a job in the state. A drivers license application states that "Residency is established by: voting in California elections; paying resident tuition at a California college or university; filing for a home owner's exemption; obtaining a license, or receiving any other privilege or benefit not ordinarily extended to nonresidents." This updated Military Roll of Honor incorporates these parameters and extends the interpretation to include their minor children.

2. The boundaries of Santa Cruz County determine the area of residency for purposes of this roll of honor, with one exception. The Pajaro Valley overlaps into San Benito and Monterey counties and those residents have been considered part of greater Watsonville and included in their honor rolls. This roll of honor continues that practice.

3. If a military casualty had identified Santa Cruz County as his or her residence when enlisting in the armed forces during a period of war, they were included in this roll of honor.

4. If a high school, community memorial, or a newspaper honor roll recognized an individual, they were included in this roll of honor, unless that listing was proven to be incorrect, which occasionally occurred.

5. If through birth, education, employment, marriage, church affiliation, organizational membership, local military association, and so forth, there was evidence that the casualty had a bona-fide residency link with the county, they were included.

6. Service personnel who were temporarily assigned to one of the military facilities in the county were not included unless they specifically chose to be identified as residents.

Type and Cause of Death

The lists of war dead appearing on the United Veterans Council updated Military Roll of Honor represent all the types of death included in previous honor rolls.

Following World War II, the US War Department classified casualty types as Killed in Action (KIA), Died Non Battle (DNB), Died of Wounds (DOW), Finding of Death (FOD) and Missing (M). This system was modified by the National Archives and Records Administration (NARA) during the Korean War and changed again during the Vietnam War. In all of those conflicts only war related and limited service related deaths were included on their listings.

From the Civil War through the Vietnam War, illness and accidents represented a sizeable portion of the military deaths, yet those deaths have frequently been omitted from honor rolls. Local veteran and high school memorials have occasionally included them, though not consistently. Santa Cruz and Watsonville newspapers have similarly been inconsistent at including non-combat related deaths on their honor rolls.

To maintain consistency this memorial will not attempt to differentiate in types of death and will honor all county residents who died in service during a period of war.

Periods of War

The dating of United States conflicts has not posed a significant problem; however, some modifications had to be made. The official listing used by the US government to define war years is the Department of Veterans Affairs (DVA) "Periods of War for VA Benefits Eligibility." The dates for those conflicts are

Indian Wars	January 1, 1817 – December 31, 1898
Spanish American War	April 21, 1898 – July 15, 1903
Mexican Border Period	May 9, 1916 – April 5, 1917
World War I	April 6, 1917 – November 11, 1918
World War II	December 7, 1941 – December 31, 1946
Korean War	June 27, 1950 – January 31, 1955
Vietnam War	
Serving in Vietnam	February 28, 1961 – May 7, 1975
All other VW period vets	August 5, 1964 – May 7, 1975
Middle East Wars	August 2, 1990 – Present

That document will be used in this roll of honor with three exceptions:

1) The DVA listing does not include the American Civil War. April 12, 1861, the firing on Fort Sumter, and April 9, 1865, the surrender at Appomattox, are commonly used to define the beginning and ending of the American Civil War. This roll of honor extends that period into the DVA Indian War period (1817-1898) to accommodate local men recruited during the Civil War and who continued to serve and died at frontier forts.

2) During World War I, three county servicemen died early in 1919 while awaiting discharge. Local honor rolls included them, as will this roll of honor.

3) The attack on Pearl Harbor on December 7, 1941, began the US combat phase of World War II, yet the country mobilized reserves and instituted the draft for the war in early 1941. On May 27, 1941, President Franklin Roosevelt issued a "Declaration of Unlimited National Emergency," which became the starting date for the War Department's World War II Honor list. I have similarly chosen to use that date to include four county veterans who died during that period.

BIOGRAPHICAL SKETCHES

The primary purpose of this work is to provide a memorial obituary for military personnel of Santa Cruz County who died while in the service. Each of these sketches is presented in a similar format with the central focus being on their military experience and subsequent death.

During World War I, World War II and the Korean conflict, information regarding the death of servicemen was frequently late in arriving and masked by military censors. When details were finally received in Santa Cruz, if at all, the death was yesterday's news and not printed. This has necessitated the reconstruction of an obituary or sketch for this publication. In the absence of supporting tales and remembrances, an attempt has been made to draw a picture of what our serviceman's unit was experiencing during the final phase of his life.

Biographical sketches were placed in the chronological sequence of death dates to provide the reader with a perspective of the greater war drama in which the individual was participating.

The intent of these sketches is to provide a snapshot of an individual, not a detailed genealogical document. Most resource material was derived from government agencies, newspaper obituaries, Internet and similar sources, all subject to error. Every attempt has been made to check the accuracy of the facts presented in this book; however, it must be stressed that, as in any reference document, these facts may require additional confirmation.

PHOTOGRAPHS

Photographs, when available, were included to enhance each biographical sketch. Due to the very low quality of many photos, considerable enhancement was required and the results are often of marginal quality.

When photos of individuals were unavailable, a photo of their headstone was substituted when locally obtainable. If neither was available, a cemetery photo was often added when the burial location was known. If no source is credited for the photograph, the photo is by the author.

REFERENCES

Following each of the biographical sketches are locations where the referenced material was obtained. Sources that frequently repeat themselves are only identified by their abbreviations, (i.e. ABMC, NARA, and USDVA etc.) The complete name and e-mail address of those repeating sources may be found on pages 255-257.

ROLL OF HONOR

This Roll of Honor is dedicated to the memory of those former residents of Santa Cruz County, California, who died while serving on active duty in the Armed Forces during a period of war.

CIVIL WAR

Asa Anthony
James M. Atchison
Edward D. Baker
David J. Berry
Alexander Brown

James F. Dolan
Leonard Doty
Christian Foster
James M. Hecox
Ruel W. Kittridge

Lorenzo L. Logan
Donald McCloud
John Myers
Thomas Turk
Eugene Van Asche
Clifford Williams

WORLD WAR I

Vance W. Bliss
Walter F. Brostrom
James A. Brown
Edward H. Carr
Louis D. Chaney
Manuel S. Christodoulon
Ward I. Church
Christ E. Ciges
Leon L. Clarke
Clyde L. Clausen
Clarence L. Corey
Irvin I. Cruts
William F. Devitt
Thomas R. Evans
John E. Feliciano
Frank J. Field
Ernest D. Fitch
Joel Gaba
Charles L. Garretty
Richard B. Haines

Victor H. Handley
Paul M. Herriott
Arthur E. Johnson
Edward H. Lorenson
Evan S. Marlin
John Mickelotti
James W. Nellson
Charles H. Pappassi
Clair C. Parker
Joseph R. Pasha
Albert G. Perkins
Bernard E. Pillsbury
Andrea Pistone
Antone Porta Jr.
Norton Pratt
Floyd E. Reavis
Joseph S. Rebeiro
Kenneth J. Reid
Albert A. Robrecht
Joseph F. Rodriquez

Donald L. Rose
Lester F. Rowe
Fred A. Severance Jr.
Reuben Silva
Sidney W. Simpson
Ernest J. Soria
Thomas J. Sullivan
William A. Sullivan
Silas Totten
Mary Pearl Turner
James L. Warren
Ambrose A. Wass
William J. Weeks
Grayson L. Wilkerson
Reuben M. Wilkinson
Edward L. Williams Jr.
William H. Wood
John W. Wright
Carroll Wyckoff
Fay M. Wyman

WORLD WAR II

Jessie L. Adams
Frederick B. Aldrich
George W. Anthony
Francis E. Aram
Urbano Arrey
Jack B. Averrett
Ernest T. Avila
Vernon C. Baker

Mark R. Graves
Richard Greenwood
Ernest E. Guin
Victor K. Hada
Ralph M. Hameetman
Delford L. Hamrick
Edward J. Hance
James T. Hannay

Donnel A. O'Brien
Charlie Ojeda
Patrick V. O'Leary
Raymond A. Ollestad
George O. Olson
Sidney C. Ormsbee
Melvin L. Orr
Robert E. Overstreet

World War II

Russell C. Barnes
James B. Bean
Lloyd Benson
Manuel L. Bernard Jr.
Esperidion C. Bernido
Leland F. Bias
Floyd W. Bickmore
Orval Blackmore
Richard M. Blood
John A. Bobeda
Albert E. Bode Jr.
Henry J. Boltshauser
William J. Bottero
Arthur R. Boudreau
Lowell A. Bready
Kenneth V. Breeden
Jack D. Brink
Arthur R. Brown
Charles O. Brown Jr.
Wayne E. Bunnell
Robert T. Burke
Lyle L. Burns
William R. Burns
John H. Busby
Curtis C. Bushong
Martin A. Cahill
Gilbert J. Camarlinghi
Salvadore S. Campagna
William H. Carlisle
Glen W. Chamberlain
Opal F. Chilcote
Lester C. Cloud
Paul D. Compton
William L. Comstock
John C. Conley
Harry J. Connolly
Fred H. Cooper
Glenn L. Coquilette
Gilbert B. Cornwell
Serrafine Corrales
Robert Coverstone
William J. Crosetti
John W. Crowe Jr.
Donald G. Dalles
Vernon W. Damm
Lawrence R. Davis
Maurice E. Davis

Svend J. W. Hansen
James C. Harper
Richard L. Harris
James H. Hart
Stanley J. Hart
Henry S. Hayden
Warren R. Hayes
Joseph H. Heatwole
Kenneth A. Hickey
Henry Hicks
Le Roy A. Higley
Edwin C. Hill
Francis E. Hoffman
Leo E. J. Hoffman
Stanley M. Hopkins
Paul F. Horiuchi
Dayton F. Hornor
John C. Humphrey Jr.
Vernon B. Huntsman
Homer W. Ijames Jr.
Henry S. Izumizaki
Hubert C. Jackson
Clifford T. Janz
James B. Jenkins
Raymond J. Jewett
Frank J. Jurach
George D. Kellogg Jr.
William E. Kellogg
Charles V. Kendall
Lewis M. Kerrick
Richard P. Kirby
Robert A. Knox
Kenneth F. Kretsinger
Clemens A. Lambrecht
John C. Lantagne
Kenneth L. Lapham
Harvey A. Larsen
Lawrence W. Lawson Jr.
Paul E. Leach
Edward M. Leonard
Edward B. Lettunich
William E. Littler
Ellsworth W. Lockwood
Gus B. Lofberg Jr.
John M. Lopez
Amedeo L. Lucchesi
Harry F. Madokoro

Leo P. Packham
Charles A. Parmenter
William L. Pate
Lewis R. Payne
Darrell E. Pettus
Charles F. Phillips
Anthony Pike
Walter M. Pimentel
Arthur W. Pinkham
Donald A. Provost
Curtis F. Pullen
Clarence A. Ray
Bill N. Redmon
Daniel J. Remick
James W. Rickel Jr.
Carl N. Riggs
Roy K. Robasciotti
John J. Roche
David M. Rossi
Norman A. Ruddock
Jack W. Rush
Harold E. Rutherford
Carroll G. Sandholdt
Myrl M. Sauers
Dan E. Schiavon
Henry Schipper Jr.
Murl R. Schrock
Herschel A. Schuttish
Everett E. Schwarzmann
Russell B. Scott Jr.
Stanley N. Secondo
Arnold H. Sehestedt
Oscar Silton
Frank Singleton
Phillip L. Skow
William L. Slaughter
Harry L. Smith
Joseph D. Sosbee
Vincent P. Spikula
Desmond E. Spooner
Charles H. Street
Robert W. Struve
Elden D. Stuart
Robert E. Stuck
Ralph B. Sweezey
Ralph W. Thompson
Robert L. Thurman

2

WORLD WAR II

Raymon W. Davis
Edward G. DeLong
Troy V. DeMoss
William M. DeShields
Frederick C. Dodge
Attilio J. Dogliotti
Max E. Dowden
Daniel T. Doyle
Peter Dugger
Arthur J. Earl
Orrin H. Eaton
Charles B. Edwards
George Erbe Jr.
Irwin W. Fernandes
John H. Fitch
Frederice T. Flodberg
William R. Foote
Kenneth E. Fox
Ralph E. Freek
Robert T. Fridley
Boyd W. Friis
Cecil O. Fry
Joe Gillis
Leroy W. Gillman
Albert D. Godfrey
Lawrence E. Goff
Victor L. Gosney

Jack L. Marlow
Joseph C. Marsh
Mahlon A. Marshall
Marvin L. Maul
John E. McCombs Jr.
Melvin G. McCormack
John W. McCullah
Robert E. McCurdy
Eugene E. McGrath
Daren A. McIntyre
Arthur R. McLaughlin
Jack H. McLaughlin
Robert R. McLennan
David B. McQuillen
William Monde
Donald Monroe
Alfred R. Moore
Walter H. Morelli
Francis E. Morgan III
Ralph E. Morrison
George I. Nakamura
Robert L. Napier
Adolph J. Negri
John A. Nelson
Quentin T. Newhart
Kongo Nitta
Ernest J. Novak

Robert L. Toda
William C. Tooze
Harold J. Totman
Vernon E. Trevethan
Eugene V. Upton Jr.
George T. Van Giesen
Earle L. Velasco
Herman J. Vellutini
Thomas H. Verhines
Peter L. Vlasich
Henry C. Voelker
Albert G. Wackermann
Edward L. Walker
LeRoy S. Walton
Marvin A. Walwick
John E. Ware
William M. Weeks
Doak A. Weston
Harold M. Whalman
Kenneth E. Wiley
Robert J. Wilson
Sam Wong
John W. Wood
Charles E. Wright
Douglas W. Young
Dade O. Youngs Jr.
Julio N. Zepeda

KOREAN WAR

Richard A. Anderson
Richard P. Anderson
George Ashton
Ernest D. Bettencourt
Richard A. Boyd
Kenneth J. Cann
Charles R. Compton
James N. Crouch Jr.
Raymond Cruz Jr.
Donald L. Eheler
Alex G. Filomeno
Ralph G. Fisher
Robert Floeck
Donald E. Folk
Melvin L. Forrester
Joseph J. Fugate

Chester C. Johnson
Makio W. Kizuka
Albert J. Kurtz
Leslie W. Lear
Harvey F. Levine
LeRoy W. Machado
Richard R. Mancebo
Gilbert L. Martin
Ernest L. Mathews
Edward L. McCall
Clarence E. McElroy
Charles F. McGuire
Harold E. Mignola
Leslie G. Monroe
Donald S. Moran
Richard Mulholland

Vernon J. Pesenti
Fred N. Petersen Jr.
Orville W. Pierce
Bobby R. Poare
Karl L. Polifka
Guy S. Read Jr.
Wallace Rich
Marion E. Richards
Norman O. Richards
Jules A. Riche
Eugene J. Rogers
Robert H. Searle
James C. Sullivan
Roy Taylor
Robert L. Thorp
John W. Van Ness

KOREAN WAR

Frank R. Gfroerer
Jesse C. Jackson

Daniel P. Murphy
Orville D. Musick

Archie N. Walters
Melvin C. Warwick
William H. Wilner

VIETNAM WAR

Federico Alaniz Jr.
Bruce D. Anderson
LeRoy F. Arellano
Kenneth D. Armstrong
Edwin E. Axton
Daniel J. Barry
James E. Bell
Harold A. Bird
Leo B. Buckholdt
Roy C. Calcote
Richard F. Campos
Gary R. Carpenter
William L. Carter
William D. Choi-Rakofsky
Robert D. Christiansen
Richard T. Christy
Curtis C. Colyear
Mark L. Corrie
Raymond R. Delgado
Robert L. Dinapoli
Mark S. Diorio
Lawrence R. Dodd
Roger G. Dunham
Robert L. Foster
John D. Franks

Eddie D. Gant
Melesso Garcia
Alfred A. Gates
Arthur F. Gleim Jr.
Hervey M. Goold
William H. Haakinson III
Thomas A. Hall
Steven W. Herring
Rocky Y. Hirokawa
Herbert R. Howell
John D. Inguillo
John J. Jennings
Ralph M. Johnson
Ronald J. Johnson
Daryl L. Keen
Terry L. Kelly
Ronald R. King
Welton R. King
Dickie L. Leach
Delbert H. Lint
Vincent Locatelli
Jack W. Marlowe
Jack W. McKinnon Jr.
Louis C. Miller
Warren F. Nickel Jr.

Raymond F. Orr Jr.
Pedro Ortiz
Steven M. Pashman
Marvin R. Pearce
George N. Penniman II
William M. Phinn
Wilton R. Pickett
Melvin L. Pullen
Hildefonso M. Ramirez
Bernardo K. Ramos
Benito B. Rodriguez
Robert Rodriguez
John J. Rogers Jr.
Frank J. Rose Jr.
Richard L. Roy
Lennie H. Scharff
Norman Schmidt
George W. Skakel
Larry E. Sommers
Richard L. St. George
Sherman R. Taylor
Mark H. Thompson
Rainford Tiffin
Steven C. Vandergrift
Jon F. Warmbrodt
Leonard R. White

IRAQ - AFGHANISTAN WARS

Bernard P. Corpuz
Jesus A. Gonzalez
Victor A. Gonzalez

James D. Harris
Jason R. Hendrix
Morgen Jacobs

Kylan A. Jones-Huffman
Andres H. Perez
Jared J. Rossetto
Joseph B. Spence

American Civil War
(1861-1865)

Santa Cruz Military During the American Civil War

At the outbreak of the American Civil War, California sentiment was divided between the North and South. Ultimately the state sided with the Union. The federal government assigned California the responsibility for maintaining coastal artillery posts, manning western forts, keeping communication and supply lines open to the east, and defending against Indians, Confederates and their supporters. To accomplish this, the state authorized the organization of one additional regiment of cavalry and five of infantry. Santa Cruz County provided one company of cavalry and two of infantry. The California 100 and Native California Cavalry, two other military units organized within the state, played a minimal role in local activities during the Civil War.

Albert Brown recruited the local cavalry company in September 1861; they trained in San Francisco until June 1862. The recruits camped on the flat between the San Lorenzo River and Branciforte Creek and on September 22, 1861, left for Camp Alert in San Francisco aboard the schooner *Salinas*. At Camp Alert the company, designated as Company L, 2nd California Cavalry, was expanded with recruits from San Francisco and trained between November 1861 and June 1862.

Company L left Camp Alert in July 1862 and proceeded over the Sierras to Fort Churchill, Nevada Territory, near Carson City. They remained at the post training, guarding and patrolling for the remainder of the year.

In April 1863, Company L was ordered to Bishop, California and later Camp Independence, to assist in rounding up Paiute Indians. During that expedition they were involved in several skirmishes as they pursued and captured a main band of Indians before returning to Fort Churchill in June.

Company L made its way eastward in July 1863 toward Fort Ruby in north central Nevada Territory. Enroute a band of renegade Indians were encountered and its leader captured. In August the company left for Salt Lake City where they were posted for most of the war.

During their stay in Utah, Company L was primarily engaged in a security role. While posted at Camp Douglas in Salt Lake City, they performed military police duty in the city. They were later sent to nearby Rush Valley for a short period to protect the US government cattle herds.

When their term of enlistment expired in October 1864, most of the men of Company L received their discharge at Fort Douglas and returned home. Captain Albert Brown and several other Santa Cruzans re-enlisted and proceeded to Ft. Bridger, Wyoming Territory, and later to Fort Kearney in eastern Wyoming, where they engaged Sioux and Cheyenne Indians in the Powder River Campaigns of 1865-66.

Captain Thomas Tidball enrolled the first infantry company at Santa Cruz in September 1861. Local farmers provided wagons and teams to transport enlistees over the Santa Cruz Mountains to the San Francisco Bay, where they were taken by boat and ferried to Camp Union near Sacramento. On November 22, 1861, the unit, filled out by volunteers from other parts of the state, was designated as Company K, Fifth California Infantry.

During 1862 Company K was involved in fighting floods, guard duty and training in Southern California. Fighting back disastrous floodwaters resulting from the storms of 1861-1862 occupied most of the unit's time while at Camp Union. When Southern troops invaded New Mexico from Texas in March 1862, training was suspended and California infantry regiments were dispatched to Southern California and Arizona to intercept the Confederates. Company K, which had been stationed on Alcatraz, was among the last units to depart for Camp Drum near Los Angles where they trained. Camp Drum was built to expand the capacity of nearby Camp Latham.

Company K moved to Arizona in 1863 where they were used to contain renegade Apache Indians. They left Camp Drum in early 1863 and joined the remainder of the California Column in Yuma, Arizona Territory, on March 31. A month later they marched to Tucson, Arizona, where they were posted.

Containing Apache Indian activity occupied Company K during 1863-1864. While at Tucson they were ordered into Arivaypa Canyon, about ninety miles north of Tucson, to capture marauding Apache Indian bands hiding in the mountains. After capturing a sizeable number of Apaches in a major skirmish, they returned to Tucson and were then sent to Fort Bowie near the New Mexico border to protect the Overland Trail route. They remained in Arizona throughout 1863 and most of 1864 and participated in the Gila River Expedition that attempted to round up bands of Apache Indians.

In October 1864 the company was ordered to Las Cruces, New Mexico, where they were mustered out in November 1864. They arrived back in Santa Cruz in January of 1865.

The second and last infantry company to be recruited in Santa Cruz County was Company A of the 8th California Infantry. This company was raised at Watsonville by Captain Claremont C. Smith and was mustered into the United States service November 17, 1864. It was initially stationed at Fort Point in San Francisco, where it trained until February 1865.

The company left San Francisco on the steamship *Oregon* on February 9, 1865, bound for Cape Disappointment at the mouth of the Columbia River. Arriving two days later they remained at that location guarding the coastal artillery post against potential Confederate naval raids or possible Indian uprisings.

When the Civil War ended in April, the company was found to be surplus and was returned to Fort Point, where they were mustered out October 24, 1865.

(*A Compendium of the War of the Rebellion*, Frederick H Dyer, Des Moines, 1908; "California Regiments;" *Old Soldier*, Robert Nelson, MAH, Santa Cruz, 2004; *Soldiers of the Overland*, Fred B. Rogers, Grabhorn, San Francisco, 1938; Official Records War of the Rebellion, http://www.ehistory.com/uscw/library/or/index.cfm)

BIOGRAPHICAL SKETCHES

1861

*April 12 Fort Sumter fired upon
effectively beginning the Civil War*

EDWARD D. BAKER
(1861/10/21)

(Photo Wikipedia Encyclopedia)

On October 21, 1861, President Abraham Lincoln lost a friend and confidant and Santa Cruz County, California, lost its most illustrious Civil War casualty.

Edward Dickinson Baker was born in London, England on February 24, 1811, immigrated to the United States with his parents in 1815 and settled in Philadelphia, Pennsylvania. In 1825 he moved to Illinois where he practiced law in Springfield. As a Whig politician he became a close friend and neighbor of Abraham Lincoln.

During the Mexican War, Baker was commissioned a colonel and fought at the battles of Vera Cruz and Cerra Gordo. Following the war, he moved to Galena, Illinois, and served a term as a member in the US House of Representatives from that district.

In 1851 the Gold Rush attracted Baker to California and he moved to San Francisco. It was during this period that he became involved in Santa Cruz County. Following statehood in 1850, the southern portion of Santa Cruz County became highly sought after by Americans attempting to acquire rancho tracts from local Californios. In the fall of 1852, Edward Baker was among settlers who "squatted" on the rich lands of the Salsipuedes area of the Pajaro Valley. By subdividing his land Baker helped to open the Pajaro Valley to American settlement. In 1860 Edward Baker moved to Oregon and after a successful election campaign, he became its first US senator.

When the Civil War began, Senator Baker, who was serving in Washington, D. C., raised a regiment of infantry to help meet California's enlistment quota and became colonel of the regiment. He was later given the command of a brigade and promoted to brigadier general. On October 21, 1861, Baker marched off to war and led his 1st California (71st Pennsylvania) Regiment across the Potomac River to attack a Confederate camp at Leesburg, Virginia. After his disastrous defeat, news reached Washington as described by Margaret Leech in her book *Reveille in Washington.*

Near sunset of a lovely autumn day, a newspaper correspondent heard the insistent clicking of the telegraph in the inner room at McClellan's headquarters [in Washington, D. C.] and saw Mr. Lincoln stumble out, with tears rolling down his face. Baker, with that gallantry which effaces a want of discretion, had been killed at the head of his battalion.

Following an elaborate state funeral in Washington, Edward Baker was interred in Washington, D. C. At the end of the Civil War his remains were sent to San Francisco for burial at Laurel Hill Cemetery and in 1940 they were re-interred at the San Francisco National Cemetery in the Presidio. The first Santa Cruz County Grand Army of the Republic post was named in honor of Edward Baker.

(*Santa Cruz County*, Margaret Koch, Valley Publishing, Fresno, 1973, pg. 165; *Historical Times Encyclopedia of the Civil War*, Patricia L. Faust, Editor, Harper's, New York, 1986, pg. 34; *Reveille in Washington*, Margaret Leech, Harpers, New York, 1941, pg. 116; SCSn November 12, 1972)

*September-October Santa Cruz Cavalry and
Infantry companies recruited and sent to training
camps in San Francisco and Sacramento, respectively*

1862
ASA ANTHONY
(1862/01/01)

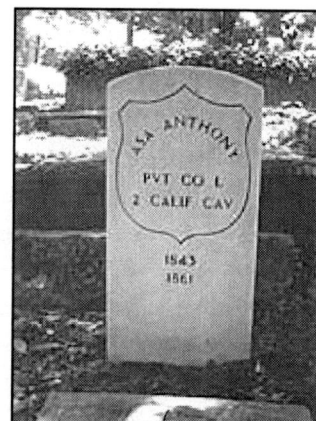

Evergreen Cemetery -- Santa Cruz, California)

A trek across the plains to a new life in sunny California ended in a cold damp army dispensary for Asa Anthony.

Asa Anthony was born May 22, 1842, in Fort Wayne, Indiana, to George and Hannah Anthony. No information is available regarding his early youth. In 1850 George Anthony took his family on an overland trek by wagon to join his brother, Elihu, in Santa Cruz, California. Upon his arrival he found work as a tanner; however, Asa chose to go into farming. On Sundays, Asa regularly attended the First Methodist Church where his uncle served as pastor. Later Asa became active in the Santa Cruz Order of Good Templars, a prohibitionist society.

On September 22, 1861, Asa Anthony enlisted in Company L of the 2nd California Cavalry being formed in Santa Cruz. At the time of his enlistment he was described as being five feet nine inches in height, of a light complexion and with dark hair and dark eyes. Anthony soon earned the respect of his fellow enlistees and prior to the unit's departure from Santa Cruz, was elected as their 4th Corporal. On September 27 Asa and the other local recruits marched to the wharf in Santa Cruz, took the steamer *Salinas* to San Francisco and made their way to Camp Alert located near what is today 25th and Folsom Streets.

The winter of 1862 was one of the coldest, wettest winters in California history and resulted in countless deaths. Attempts were made at Camp Alert to keep men warm and dry by building platforms on which their tents were erected. During this period Asa probably contracted influenza, pneumonia or dysentery, all of which were prevalent in the camp. After becoming ill, Anthony's condition continued to deteriorate and during the last week of December 1861, his condition became critical. During New Years Eve of 1861-62, the young soldier's strength gave out. His body was returned to Santa Cruz for a funeral on January 4, 1862, and burial in Evergreen Cemetery.

(CMWR, Pg. 286; MAHL; SCSn January 2, 1862, January 9, 1862)

March Company K ordered to Camp Latham in Southern California from Sacramento via Alcatraz

---

ALEXANDER BROWN
(1862/03/18)

Alexander Brown was born in Alexandria, Virginia about 1841. No information has been found regarding his formative years. While living in Santa Cruz, he remained single and is believed to have worked as a teamster. Brown also became an active member of Sons of Temperance Lodge # 59 during his stay in the community.

At the time of his enlistment in Company L, 2nd California Cavalry, on September 11, 1861, he was described as being twenty years old, about 5 feet ten inches in height, dark complexioned with dark eyes and hair. Private Brown accompanied the cavalry company to Camp Alert in San

Francisco aboard the steamship *Salinas* on September 27, 1861. During his six months at the camp, his training was minimal and frequently interrupted by inclement weather.

In March 1862, he became ill with "inflammation of the bowels" (dysentery) and on March 18, 1862, he died. The *Pacific Sentinel* of March 27 said "He had by strict attention to his duties and many good qualities, won the respect of both officers and men."

Santa Cruz historian Leon Rowland noted that Private Brown was returned to Santa Cruz for burial and while interment would likely have taken place at Evergreen Cemetery, no record of his funeral or burial exists.

(CMWR, Pg. 287; MAHL; SCSn November 12, 1972, SCR October 19, 1950)

EUGENE VAN ASCHE
(1862/04/10)

Santa Cruz infantrymen lost their first sergeant before a shot was fired.

Eugene Van Asche was born in Belgium; however, the date, place and parentage associated with his birth are not available. Also missing are records of his life in Santa Cruz County.

Van Ashe enrolled as a private in Company K of the 5th California Infantry at Santa Cruz, California on October 21, 1861. He left with the company for Camp Union near Sacramento in November to begin basic training. During his stay at Camp Union he received minimal training while he assisted in flood control during the disastrous floods of 1861-62.

In February 1862 Van Asche traveled with Company K to Alcatraz Island in San Francisco Bay to help guard that post. While at Alcatraz, he was elected first sergeant by the company and was serving in that capacity when the units moved to Camp Drum near Los Angeles in March.

While in training at the Southern California facility, First Sergeant Eugene Van Asche died on April 10, 1862, of an undisclosed illness or condition. The burial location of Eugene Van Asche has not been identified.

(CMWR, Pg. 719; SCSn November 12, 1972)

July 5 Company L departs for Fort Churchill, Nevada

DONALD MCCLOUD
(1862/?)

An unstable mind triggered by unstable weather may have been too much for Donald McCloud.

Donald McCloud was born in Scotland about 1823.

Information regarding his birth, parentage and siblings is not available. Also missing is the date of his arrival in Santa Cruz County. Since he does not appear on the 1860 census his residency in the county was likely of a short duration. McCloud indicated that he was a jeweler on his enlistment forms. Those same records described him as being about five feet nine inches in height, dark complexioned, with hazel colored eyes and dark hair.

Donald McCloud enlisted in Company L of the 2nd California Cavalry on September 15, 1861, and accompanied them to Camp Alert in San Francisco for basic training on September 27.

During the torrential rains and accompanying flooding during the winter of 1861-62 McCloud is reported to have had a nervous breakdown and on March 11, 1862, was given a disability discharge. He was sent to the Insane Asylum in Stockton where he is believed to have died.

(CMWR, Pg. 286; MAHL; SCSn November 12, 1972)

1863

RUEL W. KITTRIDGE
(1863/02/28)

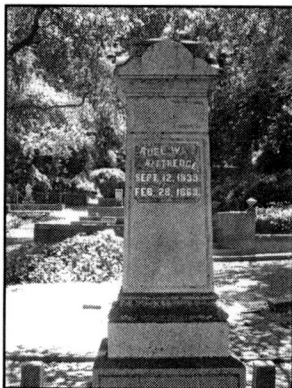

(Evergreen Cemetery Santa Cruz, California)

The "grim reaper" visited the home of Dr. Francis Kittridge and the good doctor could do nothing.

Ruel W. Kittridge, the only son of Dr. Francis M. and Almira Kittridge, was born in Chemsford, Massachusetts, on September 12, 1839.

Prompted by gold and new opportunities, the Kittridge family joined the western migration to California in 1849 and later made their way to Santa Cruz in 1851. After completing elementary school, Ruel worked as a laborer. He was described as being about five feet inches in height; light complexioned with hazel colored eyes and brown hair.

On September 11, 1861, one-day prior to his twenty-second birthday, Ruel Kittridge enlisted in Company L of the 2nd California Cavalry. He accompanied the cavalry

troop to Camp Alert in San Francisco and trained with them for the next six months. While at that location, Kittridge contracted a slight cold caught from exposure during the cold damp winter of 1862. His cold continued to worsen until his prognosis was changed to consumption (tuberculosis).

By July of 1862 Ruel's health had deteriorated to the point where it was necessary to medically discharge him and return him to his home in Santa Cruz where he died on February 28, 1863. Ruel Kittridge was buried in the family plot in Evergreen Cemetery in Santa Cruz

(CMWR, Pg. 289; MAHL; SCSn November 12, 1972)

*March Company K departs for
Yuma and Tucson, Arizona*

*April Company L moved to the Owens Valley,
California, to capture renegade Paiute Indians*

*May 13 Company K campaigns against
Apache in Canyon de Arivaypa, Arizona*

JAMES M. HECOX
(1863/07/20)

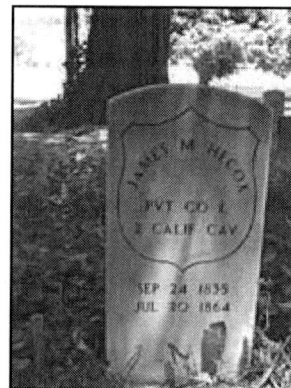

(Evergreen Cemetery Santa Cruz, California)

Hattie Hecox final words to her husband were "we will meet you bye and bye."

James Monroe Hecox, Jr was born on September 24, 1835, in St. Joseph, Michigan, to James and Ida Hecox. No information is available as to his formative years.

In 1852 the Hecox family boarded a covered wagon train bound for California. While traveling across the plains, James Sr. became ill and died, leaving his wife Ida and sons James and Oscar to continue to Santa Cruz. Shortly after their arrival, James, who was seventeen, began seeking work to support his mother and twelve-year-old brother. Lacking a profession or trade, he secured employment in the lumber industry and worked as a woodsman in the nearby redwood forest.

Early in 1861 Hecox, who was twenty-six, married a sixteen-year old Santa Cruz girl, Hattie T. At the time of his marriage he was physically described as being five feet 6 inches tall, with blue eyes and brown hair. The *Santa Cruz Sentinel* also noted "he was so quiet and reserved that the ordinary observer could learn little more of him than his personal appearance indicated."

James Hecox enlisted in Company L, 2nd California Cavalry, in September 1861. The recruits were assembled at a camp on the San Lorenzo River where they remained until September 27. They were then marched through Santa Cruz to the steamship *Salinas* and taken to San Francisco to be trained at Camp Alert. During the next nine months James was given a rudimentary military training course, which was frequently interrupted by the weather.

In late July 1862, Hecox and Company L left San Francisco for Fort Churchill, Nevada. While at that fort, he served as the company blacksmith. Captain Albert Brown, his commanding officer wrote that he was "a good soldier, patient, uncomplaining and always ready and reliable."

During 1862 the Paiute Indians began marauding activities in California's Owens Valley. In April 1863 Company L was sent to Camp Independence located on the eastern slope of the Sierra Mountains to track down the hostile Indians. Captain Brown's "boys" encountered a number of Paiute bands and after defeating them, chased the survivors into the Sierra Mountains.

It is believed that during a mounted patrol into the Sierra Mountains, James Hecox contracted Rocky Mountain spotted fever. After Company L was relieved, they returned to Fort Churchill where James' illness became more severe. By July 1 it was apparent that his medical condition was not improving at the fort and he was sent home on a sick furlough. His mother in a pension affidavit described Private Hecox's final days,

He was sick when he came home and immediately took to his bed. Within one or two days Dr. Bailey, was called in to attend him, but could not stop or stay the disease, and my son grew worse, and died of sickness, and disease within about 12 days after his arriving home.

James Hecox died on July 20, 1863. At his death his wife Hattie's final words to him were, "we will meet you bye and bye." On September 1, 1885, she fulfilled her promise.

(CMWR, Pg. 289; MAHL; NARA Pension Application Mrs. Ida Hecox Miller March 1892; SCSn August 16, 1863, SCSn November 12, 1972)

August Company L at Camp Ruby, Nevada, guarding overland train

August Company K at Camp Bowie, Arizona, guarding Santa Fe Trail

September 14 Company L moves to Salt Lake City, Utah, for provost duty

1864

March 7 Company L guarded cattle in Rush Valley, Utah

LEONARD DOTY
(1864/03/15)

(Photo by Kathy Martin http://www.findagrave.com)

Leonard Doty was born about 1829 in Richland County, Ohio. No information is available as to his parents, siblings or early life. In September 1861 he was working in Santa Cruz as a carpenter. Doty's military records indicate that he was dark complexioned with blond hair, blue eyes and stood five feet six inches in height.

On September 11, 1861, Leonard Doty enlisted in Company L, 2nd California Cavalry, in Santa Cruz. The recruits remained at a temporary campsite in the city until transportation to the training facility in San Francisco could be arranged. Along with other recruits, he boarded the steamer *Salinas* when it departed Santa Cruz for Camp Alert in San Francisco on September 27, 1861. During his nine months at the camp his training consisted primarily of drill, maintenance of equipment and guard duty.

In July 1862, the Santa Cruz cavalry company, enlarged by recruits from other locations, left for Fort Churchill in Nevada Territory. From their arrival at the fort in August until the following spring, Doty performed garrison duty and conducted patrols in the nearby vicinity.

In March 1861, Company L was ordered to the Owens Valley in California to track down renegade Paiute Indians; they remained there until June when they returned to Fort Churchill. Shortly after their return, the company headed east to Fort Ruby, Nevada, where they spent the remainder of 1862.

Company L traveled to Salt Lake City, Utah, in October 1863 to perform provost (MP) duty in the city. Later they guarded government cattle in the nearby Rush Valley until the spring of 1864. It may have been at that location that Leonard Doty contracted an illness or condition that resulted in his death on March 15, 1864. He is buried in the Camp Douglas Cemetery in Salt Lake City, Utah.

(CMWR, Pg. 286; MAHL; SCSn November 12, 1972

May 9-June 3 Company K in Gila River campaign in Arizona

LORENZO L. LOGAN
(1864/04 or 1864/07/17?)

A Santa Cruz sheriff, fireman and collector of port revenues, his trail ended in Missouri, or was it Michigan?

It is believed that Lorenzo Longley Logan was born in Maine about 1822 and relocated to Kentucky before arriving in California. No information is available regarding his family or early life. He first appears in Santa Cruz County, California, in the voter's registration of 1854. From the early 1850s to his departure from Santa Cruz County in 1860 or 1861, he served as a Santa Cruz sheriff, collector for the port of Santa Cruz and was one of the cities first fireman. Logan supplemented his income locally as a woodsman until he left for Nevada City, California about 1860-61.

On August 10, 1861, Lorenzo Logan enrolled as a private in Company G of the 1st California infantry. After a training period at Camp Union, guard duty on Alcatraz Island and training at Fort Drum in Southern California, Company G joined the California Column.

The California Column referred to those military regiments that made their way from Southern California to Arizona and New Mexico during the Civil War to protect those territories against Confederates and Indians. They moved in increments through Southern California to Yuma, Arizona, and on to Tucson. Logan was involved in several engagements with hostile Apache Indians in the Tucson Area during early 1863. In August 1863 he likely took part in the Gila River campaign before being sent to New Mexico.

While in New Mexico, Company G had encounters with Indians living in that territory. During one of these engagements Logan is reported to have suffered arrow wounds

resulting in his being discharged for medical reasons at Fort McRae, New Mexico on April 24, 1864.

Local Santa Cruz historian Tom McHugh provides two possible accounts of the death of Lorenzo Logan. The first indicates that, "he [Logan] died at the hands of Missouri guerillas and was killed at the age of 42 in April 1864." The second suggests that "he [Logan] died in Sylvanus, Michigan July 17, 1864 from a variety of causes originating from arrow wounds inflicted in New Mexico." Future historians may finalize the story of this colorful Santa Cruz resident.

(USCR, 1860 US Census, CA, Santa Cruz; CMWR, Pg. 365; SCSn November 12, 1972)

July Company L at Oquirrah Mountains, Utah

October 10 Company L 3- year volunteers mustered out of federal service in Salt Lake City, Utah

November Company A formed at Watsonville sent to Fort Point, California, for training

November 27 Company K volunteers mustered out of federal service in Las Cruces, New Mexico

---

1865

JAMES M. ATCHISON
(1865/01/05)

Little remains to shed light on the life of James Atchison. It is believed that he was born in Tennessee about 1829. Later he made his way to Watsonville; however, the period of his arrival is unknown.

Enlistment records indicate that James Atchison, age thirty nine, enrolled in Company A of the 8th California Infantry, in Watsonville on November 12, 1864. He enlisted just prior to the company's departure for Fort Point in San Francisco on November 15 and trained with them only until January 1865. During the period of his encampment at Fort Point, the facility was described as being cold, damp and unsanitary, which may have contributed to his medical condition.

On January 5, 1865, James Atchison died of an undescribed illness or condition. His body was not returned to Watsonville and was likely buried at the Presidio cemetery in San Francisco.

(CMWR, pg. 800; SCSn November 12, 1972)

*February 9 Company A departed
for Washington Territory*

THOMAS TURK
(1865/02/10)

Tom chose not to return.

Information relating to Thomas Turk's birth, family and formative years is not available. Also missing are records or narratives regarding his residency in Santa Cruz County.

Turk was recruited as a private in Company K of the 5th California Infantry in Watsonville, California, on October 21, 1861. He enlisted during a later enlistment and accompanied other enlistees overland to San Francisco Bay. After their arrival at an unidentified port, the recruits were taken by boat to Camp Union in Sacramento. After performing flood relief support in that area, they were provided with a basic introduction to military life.

During 1861-62 Turk performed guard duty with Company K on Alcatraz Island in San Francisco Bay. In March 1863 the company was ordered to Camp Drum near Los Angeles where they joined the California Column. After leaving Camp Drum, they traveled to Yuma, Tucson, and later to Fort Bowie, Arizona. Turk most likely participated in the Gila River Expedition and other campaigns against hostile Apache Indians during this period of his enlistment. On November 27, 1864 he was discharged at the expiration of his enlistment at Las Cruces, New Mexico.

According to Santa Cruz historian Tom McHugh, Thomas Turk died in Franklin, Texas of an undisclosed cause on February 10, 1865. The location of Turk's remains is not known.

(CMWR, Pg. 719; SCSn November 12, 1972)

JOHN MYERS
(1865/02/23)

John gave up farming in the Pajaro Valley for a plot in Las Cruces.

According to 1860 US census records John Myers was born about 1834 in Ohio and while residing in Santa Cruz County, worked as a farmer in the Pajaro Valley. No additional information has been found regarding his early life.

On February 13, 1862, at Alcatraz Island in San Francisco Bay, twenty-seven year old Myers enlisted as a private in Company K of the 5th California Infantry Regiment. His enlistment was part of the final recruiting drive in the county by its commander Captain Thomas Tidball.

Myers accompanied Company K in its move to Los Angeles where they joined the California Column enroute to Arizona. While serving in Arizona, he participated in the campaigns against Apache Indians at Arivaypa Canyon

and during the Gila River Expedition of 1864. He was also present at Ft. Bowie, Arizona, where Company K guarded the overland trail.

In November 1864 Company K was ordered to Las Cruces, New Mexico, at the conclusion of their enlistment to be mustered out of service. John Myers was discharged with the remainder of the company on November 28, 1864. He chose to remain in the army and was subsequently transferred into Company F of the 1st Veterans Infantry. According to Santa Cruz historian Tom McHugh "John Myers died at Las Cruces, New Mexico, of an unspecified cause on February 23, 1865." The location of his remains is not known.

(USCR, 1860 US Census, CA, Santa Cruz; CMWR, Pg. 719; SCSn November 12, 1972)

*April 9 Surrender of Lee at Appomattox,
Virginia, ending the American Civil War.*

DAVID J. BERRY
(1865/05/09)

An Indian arrow finally had its intended effect on Captain Berry.

No Information is available regarding David Berry's, birth, family, formative years or residence in Santa Cruz County.

Company L records note that David J. Berry was enrolled as a First Lieutenant in Company L of the 2nd California Cavalry on September 23, 1861, in Santa Cruz, California; however, no personal data regarding him was recorded at that time. Berry served as the executive officer of that company during its training period at Camp Alert in San Francisco and in its movement to Fort Churchill, Nevada Territory, in August 1862.

On October 12, 1862, David Berry was promoted to Captain at Fort Churchill and left Company L to become the commander of Company A.

During January 1863 Captain Berry's company participated in the battle of Bear River in Washington Territory.

Shoshone raids under Chief Bear Hunter during the winter of 1862-63 provoked Federal retaliation. Troops under Col. Patrick E. Connor set out from Ft. Douglas, Utah, in the deep snow of January 1863 towards Chief Bear Hunter's camp, 120 miles north near present-day Preston, Idaho. The Native American camp included about 300 Shoshone warriors defensively placed in the Battle Creek ravine west of Bear River with high embankments in which the Indians had cut access trails. Shortly after dawn on January 29, Connor's troops appeared across the river and began crossing. Before all of the men had crossed and Connor had arrived, some troops made an unsuccessful frontal attack which the Indians easily repulsed inflicting numerous casualties. When Connor took over, he sent troops to where the ravine debauched through the bluffs. Some of these men covered the mouth of the ravine to prevent any escape while others moved down the rims, firing on the Indians below.

During the Battle of Bear River, David Berry was severely wounded in the right shoulder and treated at Camp Douglas in Salt Lake City, Utah. He later returned to Camp Union in Sacramento, where he died on May 9, 1865, from internal ailments resulting from the arrow wound he received at Bear River. The location of his remains is not known.

(CMWR, Pg. 284; MAHL; SCSn November 12, 1972; WSAC, Battle Summaries American Battlefield Protection Assoc. http://www.cr.nps.gov, [16 September 2008])

November 11 Company A mustered out of service and returns to Watsonville

---

1866

CLIFFORD WILLIAMS
(1866/07/30)

(Evergreen Cemetery - Santa Cruz, California)

His ship finally came in; however, it was twenty-two miles short of his destination.

Clifford Williams was born in Philadelphia, Pennsylvania, about 1843. It is believed that members of his family migrated to California prior to, or during the Civil War.

Williams joined the US Navy at an unspecified date and location and in early 1865, was serving as a "coal passer" aboard the *USS Suwanee* in Pennsylvania.

In 1865 the Confederate privateer, *Shenandoah,* was plying Pacific waters in the hope of drawing Union vessels off its blockade of the south. On February 17, 1865, the *Suwanee* received orders to proceed to the Pacific Ocean to search for the *Shenandoah*. After rounding Cape Horn, the

Suwanee steamed up the Pacific coast to San Francisco where it remained until April 1865 when it departed for Puget Sound. The *Suwanee* continued searching up and down the coast for the Confederate raider, not knowing that it had left Pacific waters for England in the fall of 1865.

During one of the ship's visits to Peru or Mexico during the summer of 1866, Clifford Williams contracted "brain fever" (meningitis). His condition continued to deteriorate as the *Suwanee* returned to Northern California. When they arrived at Monterey on July 30, 1866, Williams had died on board the ship. Since the ship was departing for Santa Cruz its Captain allowed Williams to remain on board to finish his voyage home to Santa Cruz.

In Santa Cruz Clifford Williams received a funeral he could never have expected. During the week of the *Suwanee's* arrival the city had been conducting a conference of dignitaries, including Governor Low. The crew planned an elaborate funeral and the ship's captain extended invitations to the officials to join them. *The Santa Cruz Sentinel* reported that a procession including fife and drummers, a hearse, pallbearers, officials, forty members of the ship's crew and presumably, family members made its way to Evergreen Cemetery. A local Episcopal priest conducted the graveside service and marines fired a volley over the grave. The procession reassembled and returned to the ship where officials were entertained. Later Williams received a fitting headstone purchased with the $250 that his crewmates had raised. That headstone still remains in Evergreen Cemetery.

(DANFS, Suwanee; *The Illustrated History of the Civil War* by Henry Steele Commager-, page 260; SCSn November 12, 1972; SCSn August 4, 1866; *Pajaro Times* August 6, 1866; Evergreen Cemetery SCCMAH archives)

CHRISTIAN FOSTER
(1866/10/?)

His killer forgot to look in his boots.

Christian Foster was born in Ohio about 1836. No additional information regarding his birth, family, or early years is available. He was reported to have been raised in Santa Cruz County and in 1861 was working as a farm laborer in the Pajaro Valley near Watsonville.

On October 21, 1861, Captain Thomas Tidball recruited Foster into Company K of the 5th California Infantry. After his enlistment, he proceeded with other newly recruited men to Camp Union near Sacramento to begin training.

When the company arrived at the training facility, their first two months were spent assisting in flood relief resulting from the great storm of 1861-1862. The time that the company remained at Fort Union only provided them with the rudiments of infantry drill, tactics and equipment maintenance.

Foster's company was assigned guard duty on Alcatraz Island in San Francisco Bay in January 1862 and soon after its arrival, Christian Foster was elected as the 2nd Sergeant of the company. After a short stay at the facility, his unit was ordered to report to Camp Latham near Los Angeles. Following the death of Eugene Van Asche on April 10, 1862, Christian Foster was elected First Sergeant of Company K.

Company K formed with other California Column units about May and proceeded to Tucson by way of Yuma Arizona. After completing a series skirmishes with Apache Indians during an expedition out of Tucson, the company was assigned to Fort Bowie near the New Mexico border. In May and June 1864 local infantrymen participated in the Gila River Expedition. The purpose of this campaign was to eliminate, capture or disperse hostile Apache tribes. The only company casualty during this encounter was First Sergeant Christian Foster who was wounded in the knee from a spent musket minie ball.

Company K returned to Fort Bowie and remained there until October 1864 when they were ordered to Las Cruces, New Mexico, to be discharged on November 27, 1864. Rather than return to Santa Cruz, Foster chose to remain in New Mexico. Santa Cruz historian Tom McHugh reported, "Christian Foster was murdered on the streets of Santa Fe, New Mexico, in October 1866. He had been raised in Santa Cruz. Stolen from him after his murder were bounty money and a deed for 160 acres of land, but overlooked was a considerable amount of money hidden in a boot"

(USCR, 1860 US Census, CA, Santa Cruz; CMWR, Pg.716; *Pacific Sentinel* February 8, 1862; Official Record War of the Rebellion Vol. 50, Chapter LXII, page 917; SCSn November 12, 1972)

JAMES F. DOLAN
(1866/)

Brigham Young's secret police may have been his undoing.

James F. Dolan was born in Boston, Massachusetts about 1840. Details regarding his birth, family or early years is not available. He was described in 1861 as being five feet four inches in height, light complexioned, with blue eyes and brown hair. Dolan listed his occupation as a blacksmith, yet the location in the county where he lived and worked is not known.

At twenty years of age James Dolan was enrolled in Company L of the 2nd California Cavalry on September 11, 1861. He traveled with the company to Fort Alert in San Francisco, California, and was trained for the next nine months. While at the camp, he was subjected to the torrential floods of that year, which would have frequently interrupted his training program.

In July 1862 Dolan accompanied his unit on its march over the Sierra Mountains to Fort Churchill. In June 1863 he was serving with his company in the Owens River, California, area where they had been sent to help drive Paiute Indians onto reservations.

The company returned to Fort Churchill, Nevada. Company L was ordered to Fort Ruby in northeast Nevada during July and again encountered additional tribes of Indians during its tour at that outpost. They remained at that post guarding the overland trail and government beef herds

During the middle of 1863 the company was relieved and made its way to Salt Lake City, where they arrived in October and served as military policeman. After his release, Dolan re-enlisted as a veteran volunteer in Salt Lake City, Utah, on August 31, 1864.

In an article entitled "Santa Cruzans in the Civil War" dated November 12, 1972, historian Tom McHugh noted, "James F. Dolan was a corporal in the 2nd California Cavalry and was believed to have been killed by special police at Salt Lake City Utah." The location of James Dolan's remains is not known.

(CMWR, Pg. 287; MAHL; SCSn November 12, 1972)

World War I
(1914-1918)

Santa Cruz County Military During World War I

Military activity in Santa Cruz County California during the First World War era began with the "Punitive Expedition" into neighboring Mexico in 1916 and concluded with the military demobilization in early 1919. At the beginning of World War I local army and naval reserve units were mobilized and later merged into the federal branches. The limited six-month combat exposure of US forces in Europe minimized war-related deaths; however, influenza accounted for a substantial number of these deaths.

The 1916 raid into New Mexico by the Mexican bandit and revolutionary leader Pancho Villa triggered military mobilization in Santa Cruz County. On March 4, 1916, Pancho Villa, with 400 men, crossed the border and raided Columbus, New Mexico, killing sixteen citizens and partly burning the town. The next day President Wilson ordered a force into Mexico to capture Villa and his band. In May 1916, Company L of the Second California Infantry recruited eighty-four men in Watsonville and in June they were sent to Nogales, Mexico, to join General Pershing's Mexican "Punitive Expedition." The local company remained in Nogales until November 16, 1916, when they returned to Watsonville.

The Santa Cruz Naval Reserve was placed on alert from February 1917 until it was mustered into federal service on April 17, 1917. The local reservists were sent from Santa Cruz to San Francisco and sworn into active duty aboard the naval ship *Oregon*. A few members of the Santa Cruz reserve unit refused to be sworn in because a provision had been added to their enlistment agreement increasing the period of active service. They were subsequently discharged, returned home and registered for the draft. Most of the other reservists were assigned to vessels.

A significant number of Santa Cruz County men enlisted in the armed forces during the period; however, specific numbers are not available.

The US Selective Service military draft law, passed on May 18, 1917, served as the main source for raising troops within the county. Registration for the draft began in June 1917 and by September 1918, 5,355 men had been registered in Santa Cruz and Watsonville. The first draft inducted men between the ages of twenty-one and thirty-one and the second from ages thirty-one to forty-five. Of those men registered, 3,462 were enlisted for service in the armed forces.

The first men inducted departed Santa Cruz during September and October 1917 and were sent to training camps located primarily in the western United States. Approximately two-thirds of the recruits received their training at Camp Lewis near Tacoma, Washington, while others acquired basic army skills at Ft. Kearney near San Diego, California. The remainder of the Santa Cruzans entering the service during World War I were assigned to facilities at various army posts throughout the country. Airmen, typically, were trained at Hicks Field and Camp MacArthur in Texas. The US Navy recruits from Santa Cruz were probably trained at the US Naval Training Station, San Francisco. Marines received their basic training at Paris Island, South Carolina.

During World War I, Santa Cruz County lost sixty of its residents or former residents serving in the armed force as a result of the combat, military-related accidents and illness. The first Santa Cruz County serviceman to die during World War I was US Army recruit Andrea Pistone who died on Angel Island in San Francisco Bay while undergoing training. The last known county casualty was Captain E. L. Williams whose plane crashed on March 28, 1919, in Colon, Panama.

(Encyclopedia Britannica; WRP February 14, 2008, pg. 15; "Santa Cruz in the War," SCSf 12/23/18—1/29/1919)

BIOGRAPHICAL SKETCHES

1917

April 6 US declares war on Germany

ANDREA PISTONE
(1917/04/22)

(San Francisco National Cemetery - Internet Photo)

Andrea Pistone was Santa Cruz County's first listed World War I death.

Andrea, the second son of Nichol and Genrichetta Pistone, was born in Pianipaludo, Italy, near Genoa about 1898. He and his brother Giobrata accompanied their parents in the family immigration to the United States in February 1906 aboard the *SS Deutschland* that arrived in New York on February 24. The Pistone family then traveled to Monterey where Nichol worked as a laborer in the lime industry. Andrea likely received some education in Monterey before he and his brother Giobrata moved to Aptos in 1915 to work in the lumber industry. In 1917 the brothers relocated to a residence on Mission Street in Santa Cruz.

On March 14, 1917, Andrea enlisted in the US Army through a program sponsored by the county probation department and was sent to Fort McDowell in San Francisco for training.

Fort McDowell was very active during World War I, serving as a Recruit Depot for men entering the Army. Men drafted in the western states were sent to Fort McDowell and held for about two weeks, during which time they would be given physical examinations, issued uniforms, and given some rudimentary military training. At the same time enlisted men returning from Hawaii and the Philippines for discharge, furlough, retirement or reassignments were being processed at the post. About 4,000 men a month passed through Fort McDowell during this period. Overcrowding became the rule—temporary tent encampments were erected at Point Blunt and on the old Camp Reynolds parade ground in an effort to ease the crush. The war-driven overcrowding was such that the newly completed Post hospital at East Garrison did not serve as a hospital when completed, but became a temporary barracks instead.

Pistone was listed as an unassigned recruit at the time of his death on April 22, 1917. The cause of his death is not available; however, an unusually high number of soldiers (five) died in the Fort McDowell hospital during April 1917. Andrea Pistone's remains were buried at the San Francisco National Cemetery in the Presidio of San Francisco.

CAG; 1910 US Census, CA, Monterey; SCSf, 1917/03/15 2:1; SC Cnty Naturalization, SCCGS Vol. 4 Pg 127; SF Nat'l Cem website http://www.interment.net/data/us/ca/sanfran/sfnat/san_fran_pikpr.htm; Soennichsen, John, Calif. State Military Museum, Historic California Posts: Fort McDowell, http://www.militarymuseum.org/CpReynolds.html [11 October 2009]

GRAYSON L. WILKERSON
(1917/05/18)

(Evergreen Cemetery - Santa Cruz, California)

Grayson Lacy Wilkerson, son of L. A. and Flora Wilkerson of the Vine Hill district of Santa Cruz, was born in Pomona, California, on September 16, 1898. On his mother's side he had descended from the Lacy family who were pioneer residents of Santa Cruz. Young Wilkerson, along with his brother Robert and sisters Bernice, Lois and Helen, accompanied their parents to Santa Cruz where his father became the pastor of the First Christian Church. Grayson spent his formative years in Santa Cruz and attended local elementary schools; however, there is no record of his attending a local high school.

California Adjutant General Office records indicate that when Wilkerson enlisted in the US Army on April 13, 1917, he listed his residence as Keeler, California. He was assigned to the cavalry branch and sent to Fort McDowell located on Angel island in San Francisco Bay for processing.

Possibly it was due to overcrowding, unsanitary conditions or the lack of medical attention at the post that brought about the "pneumatic" illness that Wilkerson contracted. A US Army Surgeon General's report indicated that there were six deaths among recruits at Fort McDowell during May 1917. On May 18, 1917, Private Grayson Lacy Wilkerson died of left lobar pneumonia. His body was returned to Santa Cruz and interred in Evergreen cemetery.

(CAG; Santa Cruz County Burial Permits 1905-1938, Genealogical
Society of Santa Cruz Cnty, 2001; SCSf May 22, 1917 8:3;

JOHN E. FELICIANO
(1917/06/19)

(Pioneer Cemetery - Watsonville, California)

A young army bugler was consumed by the rushing Feather River.

It is believed that John E. Feliciano was born in Watsonville about 1899. No additional information regarding his birth, family or formative years has been located.

John enlisted as a bugler in Company L of the National Guard in the summer of 1917 as its members were returning from Nogales, Arizona, where they had been serving in the 1916 Mexican Incursion.

After their return, the company was sent to Las Plumas, California, on the Feather River to guard the power plant of the Great Western Power Company against possible sabotage.

The *Watsonville Evening Pajaronian* of June 20, 1917, provided details on Private Feliciano's death.

John Feliciano, bugler for Company L of the Second Regiment, was drowned in the Feather River at Las Plumas shortly after noon yesterday. Feliciano and three companions were crossing the river on an improvised raft when it suddenly went to pieces, throwing the guardsmen into the water. Feliciano was swept away and Frank Berden would have suffered the same fate had it not been for William Moore, who managed to get Berden ashore and then went after Feliciano. He was unable to reach the struggling soldier and threw him a board hoping it would hold him up until he could reach him. But Feliciano was swept away and drowned. Lawrence Bisby, the fourth member of the party, managed to reach the shore in safety..

The body of John Feliciano was recovered and returned to Watsonville; his funeral was held at the Christian Church with fellow members of Company L serving as pallbearers. Civil War veterans of the local R. L. McCook Post of the Grand Army of the Republic provided the guard of honor for Feliciano, whose remains were buried in the Watsonville Pioneer cemetery.

When the Victory Byway Memorial obelisk was erected in Santa Cruz, the name "Ferdinand" accompanied his name rather than John. No explanation has been found for that discrepancy.

(CAG; WEP June 19, 20, 21, 1917)

1918

ERNEST D. FITCH
(1918/01/05)

(Arlington National Cemetery - Internet photo)

A Mendocino farmer made his way to Arlington Cemetery by way of Santa Cruz.

Ernest DeMill Fitch was born on June 29, 1892, in the small dairy farming community of Manchester in Mendocino County, California. Information regarding his birth, family and early life are not available. His arrival date in Santa Cruz County is not known; however, in June of 1917 he was living in the San Lorenzo valley community of Zayante and employed by the Hartman and Perry Company as a "die-making laborer."

Ernest Fitch's military experience began on June 5, 1917 when he registered for the draft. At the time of his registration he was described as being single, of medium height and stature with light colored hair and light blue eyes. Ernest Fitch was part of the first draft contingency from Santa Cruz County, primarily made up of men between the ages of twenty-one to thirty-one. On September 22, 1917, the draftees boarded a train in Santa Cruz and were sent to Camp Lewis, Washington.

Upon completion of basic training, Fitch was assigned to Company E, 4th Battalion of the 20th Engineers, located in the Washington, DC area for additional training and deployment to Europe. A unit history indicates that

Hikes, drills, fatigue duty, measles, mumps, changes of living quarters, extremely cold weather, and persistent rumors of departure marked the days of waiting for sailing orders, but a number of items of equipment were delayed, and Christmas came with no definite news. Finally the barrack bags were checked out, visitors were forbidden entrance to camp, and marched out of the University grounds at 12:30 A.M. on the morning of January 3, accompanied by a snowstorm.

Private Ernest Fitch did not accompany his departing comrades on January 3 because of illness and he died two days later. The cause of Fitch's death is not known; however, the measles and mumps outbreak mentioned in the unit history may have been contributing factors. His remains were interred in Arlington National Cemetery across the Potomac River from Washington, DC.

(CAG; WWIDR; 20th Engineers, WWI 4th Btn 20th Engineer, http://www.20thengineers.com/ww1-bn04.html, [16 Sept 2008]); WRP October 8, 1918 4:3; USDVA)

IRVIN I. CRUTS
(1918/01/15)

(Meuse-Argonne - Internet photo)

Mrs. Cruts' soldier boy was buried tenderly "Over There."

Irvin I. Cruts was born in Stewartsville, New Jersey, to Mr. and Mrs. Reuben H. Cruts on August 13, 1888. He remained in Warren County where he spent his formative years and attended local schools. After completing his education, he worked at a cement plant near his home as a craneman on a steam shovel.

Desiring adventure, Cruts traveled through Canada and into the Western United States, finally settling in Santa Cruz, California. In Santa Cruz, Cruts worked on a dairy farm near Arana Gulch. When the dairy went out of business, he found work at the Portland Cement Plant in Davenport as a millwright.

With the outbreak of World War I, Irvin intended to enlist but chose to be drafted with his friends in order that they might remain together. Private Cruts who was described as short and stout with brown eyes and dark hair was sent to Camp Lewis, Washington, for training and then ordered to Camp Mills in Hempstead, New York, for overseas assignment. While awaiting shipment to Europe in December 1917, Cruts visited home for the last time.

Upon arrival in England Irvin wrote his mother indicating that he was feeling well except for a slight cold. When he reached France, that slight cold had developed into pneumonia and on January 15, 1918, Private Irvin I. Cruts was found dead. A newspaper reporter interviewed his mother in New Jersey and she shared a final touching message of his service life and death.

"I'm proud my brave boy was in the service of his country when he died. He was proud of his uniform. He loved his country, and he made himself a good soldier. He told me some of the men hated to be in the army, but he said he found it best to be cheerful, to do everything willingly, and to make the best of a rough life. When he was here in December, he said every American young man must prepare to do all in his power to make America win this war. He didn't grumble when he didn't get his pay on time, when he had to sleep in tents during the cold weather, and when he had short rations, as he often had in traveling and at certain camps. He was a soldier through and through and that's why he was sent abroad ahead of some who were drafted at the same time in Santa Cruz, California. I am sure they will bury him tenderly over there. I'd like him brought back home, but that may not be. He's there for America and that's some consolation."

Mrs. Cruts' "Soldier Boy," Irvin, is buried in the Meuse-Argonne American Cemetery in Romagne, France

(WWIDR; ABMC; SCSn January 31, 1918 8:3)

JAMES L. WARREN
(1918/03/?)

Forgotten among the local World War I soldiers appearing on the county's Victory Byway Memorial was the name of James Warren.

James L. Warren was born in Watsonville, California, December 14, 1888, to William and Elizabeth Warren. He spent his formative years in the family home on Carr Street in Watsonville and along with his brother Thomas, attended local schools. In 1910 James was employed as a machinist in Watsonville and continued to live in the family residence that his brother had acquired. He later moved to San Francisco where he worked as a mechanical engineer for the I. S. Smith Company

On June 5, 1917, James Warren registered for the draft and was described as being single, of medium height and stature, with brown hair and brown eyes. Private Warren was undergoing training at Camp Meade, Maryland, when he contracted the Spanish flu. On March 12, 1918, the *Watsonville Register-Pajaronian* reported:

DIED: At the military Cantonment in Maryland March 1918 of pneumonia James Warren, formerly a resident of Watsonville.

During the time of his death, that cantonment was reporting an increase in the number of influenza cases. The location of the remains of James L. Warren has not been identified.

(CAG; USCR, 1900; 1910 US Census, CA, Santa Cruz; WWIDR; WRP March 12, 1918 page 3:3)

CLAIR C. PARKER
(1918/03/14)

(Santa Cruz Memorial Park - Santa Cruz, California)

"Our first gold star boy" was the title given Clair Parker by his classmates in their 1919 Santa Cruz High School *Trident* yearbook.

Clair Cecil Parker was born in South Dakota about 1896 to Louis and Katie Parker and moved to Santa Cruz with his family about 1902. Clair and his brothers, Earl and Waldo, lived with their mother in the family home on Bellevue Avenue in Santa Cruz. Clair attended local grammar schools and was a member of the Santa Cruz High School Class of 1915. After his school years, the San Vicente Lumber mill employed him as a machinist.

Parker's military service began with his draft registration in June 1917. His draft records describe him as being of medium height with brown hair and blue eyes. Following his entry into the army on December 12, 1917, he volunteered for the Aviation Corps and was sent to Camp MacArthur in Waco, Texas, for training.

Soon after Private Parker arrived at the camp, he developed a case of pleuro-pneumonia requiring hospitalization. During his nine weeks of hospitalization an operation was attempted in order to improve his condition but was unsuccessful. The army then made plans for his return to Santa Cruz for a month's medical furlough; however, his condition worsened before that could occur. On March 14, 1918, a nurse shared with him that his end was near and Parker merely replied, "It is all right," and he passed without fear.

On March 22, 1918, family, friends, city officials and Civil War veterans from the Grand Army of the Republic were on hand to pay their respects to Clair at the First Methodist Church where he had been baptized. Clair Cecil Parker was buried in Santa Cruz Memorial Park (IOOF) cemetery.

(CAG; USCR, 1910 US, CA, Santa Cruz Cnty; SCSn March 16, 1918 4:4; SCSf March 21, 1918 8:5, March 23, 1918 3:4; SCEN May 10, 1924)

WILLIAM H. WOOD
(1918/03/19)

A violent explosion at sea ended the naval service of a Santa Cruz gunner's mate.

William Henry Wood's birth date and place of birth have not been identified. His mother's name was Virginia. William and his sister, Mrs. W. M. Sherer, may have spent a portion of their formative years in the county and attended local schools, but that has not been established. It is also possible that Gunner's Mate Wood was a member of the local naval reserve unit prior to World War I, as a "W Wood" is included in its roster. When he began his active duty service in the US Navy, he was assigned to the destroyer USS Manley.

After fitting out in Boston Navy Yard, Manley *sailed 25 November 1917 to join the convoy escort and patrol forces based at Queenstown, Ireland. On the morning of 19 March 1918, while* Manley *escorted a convoy, a violent explosion, caused by the accidental detonation of her depth charges practically destroyed her stern, killing her executive officer, Lt. Comdr. Richard M. Elliot, Jr., and 33 enlisted men. Fragments pierced two 50-gallon drums of gasoline and two tanks containing 100 gallons of alcohol. The leaking fluids caught fire as they ran along the deck and enveloped the ship in flames which were not extinguished until late that night.*

The Navy department sent a telegram to his mother, Virginia Wood, on March 25 informing her that her son had been a victim of that explosion and that they were unable to recover his body. They further noted, "the bureau is reluctantly compelled to believe that he has lost his life."

In addition to being recognized on the World War I Memorial in Santa Cruz, William H. Wood is included on the Tablet of the Missing at Suresnes American Cemetery in France.

(ABMC; SCSf March 26, 1918 3:1; WIKI, USS Manley)

FRED A. SEVERANCE JR.
(1918/04/16)

(Oakwood Memorial Park - Santa Cruz, California)

Measles and pneumonia ended the life of a caring son, a brother and a Santa Cruz sailor.

Fred Alonzo Severance Jr. was born on November 17,

1888, in Fort Bragg, California, to Fred and Fannie Severance. His sisters Bertha, Edna and another sister rounded out the Severance family. The location where Fred Jr. spent his formative years has not been identified, nor has the date when he arrived in Santa Cruz. By 1917 his parents had divorced. His mother had remarried and moved to Santa Rosa; his father remained in Santa Cruz. In June 1917 Fred Jr. resided on Surfside Avenue in Santa Cruz and was employed as a "woodsman" by the F. A. Hihn Company on Soquel Creek. During this period he also became an active member in the Red Men fraternal organization.

Severance registered for the army draft but served in the navy. His draft registration records describe him as being tall and slender with blue eyes and brown hair. In 1917 Fred Severance Jr. joined the Navy rather than being inducted into the army and was assigned the rank of third class engineer. During his short naval career he received his basic training at Mare Island near Napa, California, and remained at that facility. Duty in Napa provided Fred with an opportunity to visit his mother in Santa Rosa and his father and a sister in Santa Cruz.

In early 1918 Severance contracted measles at the naval base and was hospitalized for a short period. Once his health returned he obtained a leave to travel to Santa Cruz to visit his sister, Mrs. Jordan. While enroute to Santa Cruz, Fred developed a chill that turned into pneumonia. His health continued to fail and on April 16, 1918, Third Class Engineer Fred Alonzo Severance Jr. died at the age of twenty-nine. Following a funeral, his remains were buried in Oakwood Memorial Park in Santa Cruz.

(WWIDR; Santa Cruz County Burial Permits 1905-1938, Genealogical Society of Santa Cruz Cnty, 2001; SCSf April 16, 1918 2:4)

PAUL M. HERRIOTT
(1918/05/02)

(University of California yearbook)

On May 7, 1918, the President of the University of California, the Secretary to the Governor of California, Speakers of the California Assembly and Senate, the District

Attorney of Alameda County, the California State Insurance Commissioner and a representative of California's US Senator Hiram, all came to honor a dead cadet who had been preparing to become a second lieutenant.

Paul Morton Herriott was born in St Paul, Minnesota, about 1886 to Calvin and Mary Herriott. Young Herriott, along with brothers Charles and Clarence and sisters Grace and Mrs. Arthur March, arrived in Santa Cruz in November 1900, where their father became the pastor of a local Presbyterian Church. Paul was remembered as being a "good boy, but not a 'goody-goody' boy," and was referred to as "the playmate of many of the 'class one' young men." He entered Santa Cruz High School with the 1903 class but moved to Portland Oregon during his senior year.

After graduating from Portland Academy in 1904, he enrolled in the University of California at Berkeley where he majored in journalism, played on the football team and joined the Epsilon Psi fraternity. During his college years Paul was said to having done a little "cow punching" on the Miller and Lux cattle ranch.

Following his graduation from UC Berkeley in 1908, the San Francisco Examiner employed Herriott as their Oakland reporter. Later, while working with the *San Francisco Bulletin*, Herriott joined the gubernatorial campaign team of H. W. Johnson. Governor Johnson was impressed with Paul's work and appointed him to the State Board of Control. When Johnson was elected to the US Senate, he took Paul with him to Washington, D.C., as his private secretary.

In 1918 Herriott resigned from Senator Johnson's staff, enlisted in the army aviation service and was assigned to a cadet-training program at Hicks Field in Fort Worth, Texas. On May 3, 1918, the *Santa Cruz Sentinel* reported that "Cadet Paul Herriott of Oakland and Lieut. James Ennis of New York were killed when their machine fell after a 'nose dive.'" The accident occurred while the plane was flying about 150 feet off the ground at Hicks Flying Field, Herriott was scheduled to have received his commission within a few weeks of the crash.

The *Santa Cruz Surf* highlighted the career of Paul Herriott by noting that he "was one of the coteries of young men who in recent years attained high positions in the government of California and was well known in nearly every city and town of the state." Paul Herriott is buried at the Mountain View Cemetery in Oakland, California.

(CAG; USCR, 1910; US Census, CA, Santa Cruz; SCSf May 2, 1918 1:3, May 8, 1918 3:1; SCSn May 3, 1918 1:3; *San Francisco Chronicle* May 3, 1918, pg 11)

ALBERT G. PERKINS
(1918/07/19)

(Aisne-Marne American Cemetery - Internet photo)

Watsonville folks remembered Al as a "light hearted companion and one always ready to accept a dare, or laugh at a jest."

Albert G. Perkins was born in Ohio about 1886. Prior to 1909, he had arrived in California where he met and married Corrie. By 1910 the couple had settled in Butte Township in Siskiyou County where Perkins was employed in a lumber mill. Shortly thereafter the family moved to Watsonville where the Hihn-Hammond Lumber Company employed him. In 1913 Albert, along with his wife and daughter Frances, moved to Santa Clara County to be closer to other Perkins family members. The following year a second daughter, Hazel, was born into the family.

Albert Perkins qualified for a draft deferment; however, he chose to enlist in the army. California Adjutant General records indicate that at the time of his enlistment he was residing in San Francisco. Perkins was assigned to Company D, 12th Machine Gun Battalion, 8th Brigade of the 4th Infantry Division and trained at an unspecified training facility. The division moved to Camp Mills, New York, on April 21, 1918, and throughout May transported its units to Brest in northwestern France.

After a two to three month training period in France, Perkins was committed to the front. The 1918 unit history noted that during July Company D had moved into the area of Reims to stop the last major German offensive of the war at the Second Battle of the Marne.

On July 19, 1918, Private First Class Albert G. Perkins was killed in action and was buried in the Aisne-Marne American Cemetery in France.

(CAG; USCR, 1910; US Census, CA, Siskiyou; ABMC; WIKI, 2nd Battle of the Marne; WRP August 29, 1918 5:2)

ANTONE PORTA JR.
(1918/07/19)

(Internet photo)

An Aptos Druid fell at the Marne.

Antone Porta Jr. was born on October. 25, 1887, in Aptos, California, to Mr. and Mrs. Antone Porta, Sr. Antone, along with his brother Baptista and sisters Katherina and Angelina, grew up on the family ranch in Aptos and attended the local school. Following his school years, Antone continued to farm in the area and became an active member of the Santa Cruz Grove of Druids fraternal society.

Porta's World War I introduction to the army occurred on June 5, 1917, when he registered for the draft. Records of the period described him as being of medium height and build with black hair and brown eyes, and noted that he had suffered from a rupture. His request for draft deferment to support his parents was denied and he was among the first of the Santa Cruz County men inducted into the army.

After basic training, Private Porta was assigned to the 59th Infantry Regiment, 8th Infantry Brigade of the 4th Infantry Division. His unit moved to Camp Mills, New York on April 30, 1918, and was shipped to France on May 23. Porta's unit may have been among those aboard the *SS Moldavia* when it was torpedoed by a U-boat off the English coast and lost 56 men.

Upon arrival in France Porta received a two to three month training period in trench warfare before being transported to the front. The history of Private Porta's division at the time of his death noted.

July 18-22, Div (less Arty) participates in the Aisne-Marne Operation. July 19, 59th Inf attacks, captures Bois de Cassel, Bois de l'Orme, Bois de Leipzig, and reaches the line, Courchamps, Bois de Leipzig, 1 km west of Sommelans.

On November 14, 1918 Antone Porta, Sr. received a telegram from the war department informing him that his son, who had been previously reported as missing in action was killed in action on July 19, 1918. Private Antone Porta Jr. was buried in the Aisne-Marne American Cemetery in Belleau, France.

(CAG; WWIDR; ABMC; SCSn November 17, 1918 5:5; WRP November 18, 1918 2:2, US Army Center of Military History, 4th Div [RA] Record of Events, http://www.history.army.mil/books/wwi/ob/4-ROE-OB.htm, [16 September 2008])

RICHARD B. HAINES
(1918/08/06)

(Oise-AisneAmerican Cemetery - Internet photo)

A Red Cross band on the sleeve is not a guarantee of safety on the battlefield.

Richard B. Haines was born in Santa Cruz, California about 1889 to Mr. and Mrs. W. W. Haines. During his formative years he resided in Aptos with his parents and brother Loyal and probably attended local elementary schools. Following his school years, Haines was employed as a painter.

On January 11, 1910, at the age of twenty-one, Haines enlisted in the US Army at Ft. McDowell, California. After completing basic training, his first assignment was with US Army Ambulance Company 4. When World War I began, he was serving as a sergeant in a sanitation detachment (Medical Corps) of the 125th Infantry Regiment, 32nd Infantry Division. By August 1918 Haines had risen to the rank of sergeant first class and was awaiting deployment to Europe.

The 125th Infantry left Hoboken, New Jersey, on February 16, 1918, and arrived in Brest, France, on March 4. Immediately after their arrival, the regiment served as a temporary labor force in the construction of supply depots. On May 29 they received orders to cross the German frontier at Sentheim in Alsace. By the time the Oise-Aisne Offense began on July 14, they had moved to Massevaux, Alsace, France.

Richard Haines was subjected to the same conditions as combat infantrymen; however, his only protection was the red cross on the band around his sleeve. On August 6, 1918, Sergeant First Class Richard B. Haines was killed in action while aiding troops and was buried in the Oise-Aisne American Cemetery in France.

(CAG; ABMC; 32 Inf Div Vet. Assoc., 32 Inf Div in WWI, http://www.32nd-Division.org/history/ww1/32-ww1.html, [16 September 2008]; WEP November 14, 1918 3:4, SCSf, November 18, 1918 3:1)

THOMAS R. EVANS
(1918/08/9)

(Santa Cruz High School yearbook)

"Tall handsome and good natured, Bob is a combination of football player and actor, and has maintained both roles," stated the 1914 Santa Cruz High School *Trident* yearbook.

Thomas Roy Evans was born in Grants Pass, Oregon, on December 19, 1894, and was nicknamed "Bob" after a famous US admiral. Following a brief relocation to San Jose, the family moved to Santa Cruz where his father worked in the County Assessor's office. Young Evans attended the local Congregational Church with his mother and younger brother Robert; he was active in the Sunday school and the St. Paul's young men's class.

"Bob" Evans was one of the most popular boys to graduate from Santa Cruz High School in the class of 1914, noted the school yearbook. In addition to being a good student he was active in the social affairs of Phi Delta Kappa fraternity and served as the captain of the football team.

After leaving high school, Evans worked with several surveying crews before finding employment with Towne and Dixon in their grocery business. A year before enlisting in the service he decided to take up work in the commercial sign business under the tutelage of sign artist Roy Hammond.

The military entered Evans' life in June 1917 with his draft registration. He was described as being tall, of medium stature with gray eyes and light brown hair. In July 1917 he volunteered for active service, was assigned to the Aviation Corps signal section and sent to Berkeley for his initial training. Upon completing a training course in flying at the aviation grounds at Grand Island in San Diego, he was commissioned a second lieutenant and sent to the Canal Zone. The *Star & Herald* of Colon, Panama, Canal Zone in their edition of August 9, 1918, described the fatal event that claimed Evans life.

Shortly after 9:45 this morning Lieut. Thomas R. Evans and Corporal George E. Semsey left the areo base at Fort Sherman and ascended into the air, flying around and rising to a height of about 3,000 feet. A short while after,

they began circling and descending, and when they were something under 2,000 feet the machine was seen to make a sudden plunge and dived head first into the sea. The machine fell inside the breakwater, about a mile from Fort de Lesseps. No time was lost in sending help from all directions. It was found that the plane had sunk into the sea.

The body of Thomas Roy "Bob" Evans was returned to Santa Cruz for a large funeral held at the Congregational Church on September 10, 1918. Local dignitaries filled the pews and the old Civil War veterans of the community served as an honor guard to say goodbye. The remains of Thomas Roy Evans, age twenty-four, were buried at Santa Cruz Memorial Park.

(CAG; WWIDR; SCSf August 10, 1918 3:4; SCSn Sept 11, 1918 5:4; Santa Cruz County Burial Permits 1905-1938, Genealogical Society of Santa Cruz Cnty, 2001

DONALD L. ROSE
(1918/08/10)

(Pioneer Cemetery - Watsonville, California)

Donald discovered that directing traffic during war includes hazards other than vehicles.

Donald L. Rose was born July 26, 1886, in Howard Springs, Colorado, into the family of Fayette and Dora Rose. The family moved to Santa Cruz where his father was a partner in the firm of McMillen & Rose. After arriving in the county, Donald attended elementary schools before enrolling in Santa Cruz High School. The Rose family was also active in the Christian Church and young Rose served as president of the Christian Endeavor Union during his school years. Following graduation from high school in 1908, Rose attended the Eugene Oregon Bible College for a short period. After returning to Santa Cruz County, he settled at Corralitos.

It is not known when Rose enlisted in the army, but he likely entered the service during the latter half of 1917. California Adjutant General records indicate that, at the time of his enlistment, he was living in Merced, California. Upon completing basic training, he was assigned to Company A of the Fourth Military Police. Private Rose was sent to Europe about May 1918 and arrived in France in June. Soon after his arrival, a fellow soldier accidentally shot him in the leg at one of the American training camps and he was hospitalized until the following July. He returned to duty and was, according to one account, directing traffic at a dangerous cross roads in the Argonne Forrest on August 10, 1918, when an incoming artillery round exploded near him taking his life.

Private Donald L. Rose was initially buried in France; however, in 1921 his body was exhumed and returned to Watsonville. On July 28, 1921, the American Legion reinterred Donald Rose in Watsonville's Pioneer Cemetery.

(CAG; USCR, 1910 US Census, CA, Santa Cruz; SCSf October 15, 1918 1:3; SCSn October 17, 1918 4:4; WRP July 28, 1921 3:2; SCEN May 10, 1924)

VICTOR H. HANDLEY
(1918/08/14)

(Holy Cross Cemetery - Santa Cruz, California)

Vic's life was stopped short by his own machine gun.

Victor Hubert Handley, a descendent of one of the city's older families, was born in Santa Cruz, California, on April 12, 1888. His parents, Mr. and Mrs. Thomas Handley, had been early settlers in the community and his father worked for the High Water Company. Vic, as he was familiarly known, was raised in a family that included a sister and two brothers. Young Handley attended the Christian Brothers School, possessed a musical and dramatic talent and was remembered as a gentle good-natured boy. His quiet personality found an outlet at Holy Cross Church where he served as an acolyte and member of the Sanctuary Society. Prior to the war, Victor Handley was employed as a laborer for the National Tank Company at Fruitvale near Berkeley, California.

When Handley entered military service, his draft records described him as being tall, of large stature with brown hair and blue eyes. After his induction, he was sent to Camp Lewis, Washington, and assigned to California's 40th Infantry Division. When he had completed basic training, he was

posted to Camp Green, North Carolina, where he became a member of a machine gun crew and was shipped overseas.

The unit to which Handley was ultimately assigned has not been identified but was located in the French province of Lorraine. Some time in late July or early August 1918, Handley and his machine gun crew was ordered to the front to participate in what is believed to have been the 2nd Battle of the Marne. While the battle was underway, the recoil of his own machine gun seriously wounded Handley and he was sent to England for hospitalization. He was unable to survive those wounds and died August 14, 1918.

Victor Handley was initially buried in England; however, following the war, his remains were reinterred in a Handley plot of Holy Cross Cemetery on February 26, 1921.

(CAG; WWIDR; Santa Cruz County Burial Permits 1905-1938; GSSCC 2001; SCSf September 02, 1918 1:7)

CHRIST E. CIGES
(1918/08/18)

(Suresnes American Cemetery, France - Internet photo)

"A Greek of Davenport in the Casualty Lists for Today" declared the *Santa Cruz Surf.*

Christ Eustratios Ciges was born in Mythlene Pimpeli, Greece, on February 2, 1889, and remained in that community during his formative years. The date of his departure from Greece is not known, but when he arrived in Santa Cruz County the R.E. Danaher Company employed him as a "Lumber Piler."

When the US entered World War I, Ciges registered for the draft on June 15, 1917. His records at that time described him as being of medium height and build with brown hair and brown eyes. Ciges was a member of the first group of army inductees to be sent from the county in 1918 and following basic training, was assigned to the 109th Infantry Regiment, of the 28th Division.

On August 6, the date which officially marked the end of the Aisne-Marne operation, the First and Third Corps held a continuous front of 11 km. (6.8 miles) along the Vesle. Between that date and the commencement of the Oise-Aisne operation, August 18, there was but small movement of this line, but there were several changes in the composition of the troops holding it. On August 7, the 28th Division relieved the 32d. . . . Between August 6 and 18 many raids were made and withstood by the Third Corps, chiefly in the vicinity of Fismes and Fismette, in attempts by both belligerents to hold the river. Machine Gun opposition was stubborn and sustained, causing a constant stream of wounded.

Private Ciges was possibly wounded during one of these engagements and transported to an army hospital near Paris. On August 18, 1918, Christ E. Ciges died from his wounds and was buried in the American Cemetery in Suresnes located between Paris and Versailles.

(CAG; WWIDR; ABMC; SCSf April 12, 1912 6:4, October 28, 1918 3:1; WEP December 28, 1918 5:7; Editors, Med Dept. US Army WWI, pg. 441, http://history.amedd.army.mil/booksdocs/wwi/fieldoperations/chapter13.htm, [16 September 2008]).

CARROLL WYCKOFF
(1918/09/04)

Native-born sons are not quickly forgotten, even though they adopt new homes.

Carroll Wyckoff, whose parents were Samuel and Pearl Wyckoff, was born in Watsonville about 1899 into a prominent local family. He spent his early years in the Pajaro Valley before moving with his family to Napa, California. Brothers Emory and Shirley joined him in the Wyckoff family along with his grandmother.

After completing his education, Private Wyckoff joined the US Army in Napa in 1918. Following basic training, he was assigned to the new tank training facility at Camp Colt at Gettysburg, Pennsylvania, commanded by Major Dwight D. Eisenhower. During the period of his training the Spanish flu epidemic was rampant. An Internet website in existence in 2007 noted

The first major crisis in the notable career of Eisenhower occurred at Camp Colt in September 1918 and involved Fr. Boyle and SFX [St. Francis Xavier] Parish. It was the development of the most virulent epidemic ever to strike the community – the deadly Spanish Influenza. By September 25th Fr. Boyle offered the army the use of SFX Hall as a hospital (which was already in use as quarters for the men at the government's request) and it was immediately accepted by the now Major Eisenhower. School was closed and the desks and furniture removed thus converting use back to a hospital for the sick and dying soldiers as had occurred 55 years before ...

The entire auditorium of Xavier Hall was converted to hospital wards, but by October 2nd even that 70 patient capacity was reached. The first floor of the building was then

cleared and it too was used for more patients. The Gettysburg Times reported that The cots were placed in rows while the stage was utilized as an office for the doctor and medics in charge.

On October 4, 1918, at the height of the flu epidemic, Carroll Wyckoff died at Gettysburg, Pennsylvania. His burial site has not been identified, but his remains were likely returned to Napa, California for interment.

(CAG; USCR, 1910 Census, CA, Napa; WEP October 5, 1918 3:5; http://www.hancockshakervillage.org/stars_and_stripes/sample6.html (2007)

FLOYD E. REAVIS
(1918/09/05)

(St. Mihiel American Cemetery - Internet photo)

Floyd Ellwood Reavis was born on April 8, 1895, in the small farming community of Midvale in southwestern Idaho. He was the fourth of the nine children of Charles and Belle Reavis. Also joining him in the family were brothers Roy, Herbert, Marion, Norris and Glen and sisters Mabel, Louise and Thelma.

As a young boy, Floyd attended local Midvale schools in addition to working on the family farm. In June 1914 he graduated from Midvale High School and continued working on the farm the following year before securing a position as a rural postal delivery carrier.

Reavis was living in Midvale, Idaho on June 5, 1917, when he registered for the draft; however, he apparently moved to California during the following year. The Battlefield Monument Commission indicated that he entered the service in California and the California Adjutant Generals office noted that his residence was in Santa Cruz. Draft records describe him as being tall, slender with light brown hair and grey eyes.

After entering the US Army, Reavis was likely sent to Camp Lewis Washington, for basic training. At the completion of his training period he was assigned to the 158th Infantry Regiment of the 40th Infantry Division.

Arizona's First Infantry Regiment was drafted into Federal Service for World War I, August 5, 1917 as part of the 40th Division. The Regiment was re-designated as the 158th Infantry Regiment on October 3, 1917, and sent overseas in July and August 1918. In France, the 158th Infantry was assigned to a division, which furnished replacement personnel to other units.

Private Floyd Reavis was serving with that unit in the St. Mihiel battlefield area of France when he contracted an unspecified disease that resulted in his death on September 5, 1918. His remains were buried in the St. Mihiel Cemetery in Thiaucourt, France.

(WWIDR, CAG; 1910 US Census, ID, Washington, Midvale; ABMC; *History of Middle Valley*, by Evelyn Leger, http://74.125.155.132/search?q=cache:oBYmY9TIbq8J:midvale. lili.org/files/midvale/Leger,Evelyn%3BHistoryMiddleValley.doc; Arizona Memory Project http://azmemory.lib.az.us/cdm4/index. php?CISOROOT=/ammbush [12 October 2009])

CLARENCE L. COREY
(1918/09/12)

(Internet photo)

Clarence, the son of former Kansas State Representative A. J. Corey of Fort Worth, Kansas, was born about 1888 and moved to Santa Cruz, California with his family in 1913.

When World War I began, Corey immediately enlisted in the army and was assigned to the Quartermaster Corps. Wanting to see action he requested a transfer and was subsequently assigned as a machine gunner in the Aviation Corps. His correspondence home shared his experiences while serving on the front as he described "the bursting shells and the war activity all around him." During the summer of 1918, he was transferred to the 11th Infantry Regiment of the 5th Division.

The 5th Division had received orders to attack in a sector on the southeast face of the St. Mihiel salient and, commencing on September 4, conducted a series of grueling night marches through mud and cold rain to cover the one hundred kilometers to the assembly areas south of Regnieville. The storm broke before the enemy was prepared. In fact, the Germans had foreseen the operation and had

decided to withdraw; however, the attack came about forty-eight hours before it was expected. It was apparent that the American movement to the front had been accomplished with adequate secrecy. Preceded by a four-hour artillery preparation, the 6th and 11th Infantry Regiments went "over the top" at 5 a.m. on September 12.

On October 4, 1918, A. J. Corey, a Civil War veteran living in Santa Cruz, received a telegram from the war department informing him that his son, Sergeant Clarence L. Corey, had been killed somewhere in France on September 12, 1918. The remains of Clarence Corey were later returned to the United States and buried at Arlington National Cemetery, Virginia.

(CAG; USDVA; Society of the 5th Div, WWI History, http://www. societyofthefifthdivision.com/, [16 September 2008]; SCSf October 5, 1918; SCSn October 6, 1918)

FRANK J. FIELD
(1918/09/21)

A Watsonville sailor had a heart for rendering popular and comedy songs but one that failed him while serving in the navy.

Frank Jay Field was born in La Peer, Michigan, on February 8, 1889. Information regarding his family and the date of his arrival in the Pajaro Valley is not known; however, in 1910 he was living with an aunt in Corralitos. While residing in the county, he was employed by the City Grocery and the A & H Grocery. Prior to World War I, Frank moved to Oakland where he worked as a chauffeur for the Ainsworth Brothers. In Oakland he also became active in the entertainment societies known as Le Tres Jolie Club and the Five Forty-five Club. He was known in the East Bay for "having an unusual talent for rendering popular and comedy songs."

On June 5, 1917, Frank Field reported to the Oakland draft board and registered for service. Enlistment records described him as being tall and slender with brown hair and blue eyes. He applied for a deferment to support his mother and sister, but it was denied and he was drafted. Following his induction he accompanied the first draft contingency to Camp Lewis, Washington. While at the camp, he was found to have a weak heart and was given a medical discharge.

Field returned home and enlisted in the Naval Reserve. Because of his prior machining experience he was promoted to Machinist Mate Second Class. While undergoing training at San Pedro, California, he applied for enrollment in a special submarine chaser class at Columbia University. After completing that program, he was promoted to Machinist Mate First Class and ordered to New London, Connecticut to await a ship assignment.

During his stay at New London, Frank Field contracted the Spanish influenza and died on September 21, 1918. At the military funeral held for him in Oakland, six sailors served as pallbearers, a firing squad presented a salute and a bugler played "Taps." His burial location is unknown.
(USCR, 1910 US Census, CA, Santa Cruz; WWIDR; WRP October 8, 1918 4:3;)

THOMAS J. SULLIVAN
(1918/09/23)

(San Francisco National Cemetery - Internet photo)

The Spanish flu epidemic ended the life of a former Pajaro Valley orphan.

Thomas J. Sullivan was born about 1889 in Salinas; however, because of the absence of his parents he and his brothers James, Edward and Michael were raised and educated in the Pajaro Valley Roman Catholic Orphan Asylum. When he reached adulthood, he was released from the orphanage and worked for a number of years at the Z. A. Hughes ranch in the Pajaro Valley. Later he moved to the Sacramento Valley where he resided prior to World War I.

Sullivan registered for the draft in Sacramento in June 1917. In August 1918 he had relocated to San Francisco where he was inducted. Sullivan was sent to Camp Lewis, Washington, for his basic training and where, during the month of September, he contracted influenza. He remained hospitalized at the Washington facility until his death on September 23, 1918.

His remains were returned to California and were interred in the San Francisco National Cemetery in the Presidio.
(CAG; USCR, 1910 US Census, CA, Monterey; USDVA; WRP September 24, 1918 6:3)

WARD I. CHURCH
(1918/09/24)

(Santa Cruz High School yearbook)

Ward Isaac Church was born on March 7, 1897. Information regarding his birth location, parents or early life has not been located. In the 1914 *Trident* yearbook his classmates commented, "We knew him but slightly, but to his friends the greatness of a man lies within the crust of silence wherein he draws." Comments later shared at the 1924 memorial service indicated that Ward Church was "Not with us very long, but respected and admired for his quiet manliness as a student."

In early 1918, while living in the community of Loyalton in Sierra County, California, he enlisted in the US Army at Sacramento. After his basic training at an unidentified facility, he sailed for France about July 1918. Ward is listed as having served in the army as a "wagoner" during the war. That would suggest that he was probably a truck driver with a quartermaster company dispensing supplies to front line troops.

The Santa Cruz High School 1919 *Trident* yearbook reported that Ward Church died in September of pneumonia and was "buried with all military honors in the American cemetery at Valdahon Doubs, France."

Following the war his remains were returned and reburied in the Loyalton, Cemetery.
(CAG; Santa Cruz High School *Trident*, 1914; SCEN May 10, 1924; USDVA, *Soldiers of the Great War*, Page 142, Haulsee, Howe & Doyle, Google Books 2009; *Sierra County Pioneer Cemetery Historic Survey*, Compiled by Lee Adams, 1997 http://files.usgwarchives. net/ca/sierra/cemeteries/sier-a-c.txt, [July 2009])

EDWARD H. LORENSON
(1918/09/27)

(Watsonville Register-Pajaronian photo)

Ed Lorenson is remembered today by an American Legion post that bears his name.

Edward Hans Lorenson was born March 13, 1889, in San Francisco, California, and raised in the San Joaquin Valley. Later his family moved to San Jose, California, where he graduated from high school in 1906. Following high school, Lorenson joined the *San Jose Mercury* as a reporter and continued there until his relocation to Watsonville in 1908, where he became the city editor of the *Evening Pajaronian*.

Lorenson's work, community activities and marriage helped to cement him to Watsonville. In 1913 Ed married Kate Iverson, a local girl, and the two became popular among the younger set of the period. His career with the newspaper continued to grow and he was active in local baseball and sports.

In 1916 Lorenson helped to form Company L of the 2nd Infantry Regiment of the California National Guard in Watsonville. Later in the year the unit was activated and ordered to the Mexican border. Ed Lorenson resigned his position at the *Evening Pajaronian* to serve as its first sergeant. In early 1917 the company returned home, was mustered out and Lorenson returned to work at the *Evening Pajaronian*.

Although Ed Lorenson's former military service might have exempted him from the draft he saw it as his obligation to serve. At the time of his draft registration in June 1917 he was described as being tall and "stout" with light colored hair and blue eyes. On September 26 he was inducted into the army in the second draft and sent to Camp Lewis, Washington, for training. Upon arrival he was assigned to the 363rd Infantry Regiment of the 91st Infantry Division, promoted to corporal and placed in charge of new recruits. Throughout his stay at the camp Lorenson wrote articles describing camp life that were printed in the Watsonville *Evening Pajaronian*.

In June 1918 the 363rd Infantry Regiment left Camp Lewis and traveled cross-country to Camp Merritt, New Jersey, and on July 6, 1918, departed for France. In September they were ordered to the front to participate in the Meuse Argonne offensive. A letter received by Ed's wife, Kate, from the Red Cross detailed the events leading his death.

Your husband was killed on Sept. 27th, just before dusk probably about 5 o'clock. An account of the circumstances was given me by Captain Frank S. Sever of Company I, who said:

We were a few hundred yards from the village of Eclisfontaine on the afternoon of Sept. 27th. About three o'clock that afternoon the company had its first death when Corporal Otto Blau was killed by a sniper. Corporal Lorenson was the second man killed.

Ahead of us were about 300 Germans who were in the act of surrendering as Companies K and M of our battalion had encircled them. We had advanced across a ravine from where Corporal Blau had been killed and as we were receiving the surrender of these Germans in the ravine, a heavy German artillery fire began to descend in front of us and upon Companies K and M. Our own artillery began to fire there, and so we were between two fires. The 300 Germans began to run and we opened up on them with rifles and automatics. Eighty-one of them surrendered, many were killed or wounded, and the rest escaped.

We fell back to the bottom of the ravine to escape the German barrage. The German artillerymen then raised their range and caught us again so we advanced up the slope to our previous position, so as to be ahead of the barrage. Then the barrage ceased, and we halted and took up a position behind an old German barbed wire entanglement.

It was about five o'clock. The men were told to eat from their reserve rations. As they were eating, the barrage began again, and the company was ordered down a slope toward the ravine. About this time a six-inch German shell struck Corporal Lorenson and killed him instantly.

Edward Hans Lorenson's body was recovered and is buried in the Meuse-Argonne American Cemetery in Romagne, France. Following the war, Watsonville's American Legion post was named in his honor.

(CAG; WWIDR; ABMC; WRP, November 2, 1918; WEP, 1918/11/02)

JOSEPH F. RODRIQUEZ
(1918/09/28)

A gas mask drill failed to produce the training experience that Joe Rodriquez deserved.

Joseph Francis Rodriquez was born February 9, 1891, in California. Early records indicate that he was raised in a family that included at least three sisters. Rodriquez' draft records denote that he attended school for seven years before beginning a life of farming. For a brief period the Sisters of Notre Dame employed him at their Saratoga, California, facility. In 1917 he was apparently residing and working in a Santa Cruz County rural community.

At the time of his draft registration in June 1917, Rodriguez described himself as being five feet four inches in height and weighing 135 pounds. Following his induction into the army, he was sent to Camp Fremont near Menlo Park, California, for basic training. While undergoing gas mask training on September 28, 1918, an unspecified accident occurred that took his life.

His remains were sent to Salinas, California, and following his funeral, were buried at an unidentified location in that community.

(CAG; WRP September 28, 1918; Pajaro Valley Historical Assoc. Archives; WEP October 1, 1918 1:3)

WILLIAM F. DEVITT
(1918/09/30)

(Photo courtesy of the Eaton family)

William was a "splendid" and "likable young fellow among those who knew him."

William Felix Devitt was born in Felton, California, on October 25, 1895, to J. R. and Nellie Soper Devitt, members of a well-known local family. Their other sons Milton, Robert and Arthur and daughters Fleta and Ellen completed the Devitt family. After finishing school, William Devitt was employed as a clerk in the M. E. Dodge Cigar Store and later at the Cascade Laundry in Santa Cruz.

Devitt's association with the armed forces began in 1917 with his draft registration. His draft records described him as being tall and of medium build with light brown hair and blue eyes. Recruit Devitt was inducted into the army and departed Santa Cruz for Camp Lewis, Washington, on October 5, 1917. After completing basic training, he was assigned to the 364th Infantry Regiment of the 91st Infantry Division and shipped to France in July 1918.

In September William Devitt's unit was moved into the Meuse-Argonne sector in the vicinity of Metz to participate in an Allied offensive against the entrenched Germans. On September 26, 1918, the 364th Infantry Regiment was sent up on the line and ordered "over the top" of the trenches in a coordinated Allied movement against the retreating Germans. The fighting that continued through September 30 was successful in driving the Germans back, but during the action, Devitt was killed.

The remains of William Felix Devitt are interred in the Meuse-Argonne American Cemetery in Romagne, France.

(CAG; WWIDR; ABMC; WEP August 31, 1917; SCSf November 27, 1918 8:7; SCSn November 27, 1918 5:2; 91st Div Publication Com., *Story of the 91st Division*, San Mateo CA 1919, books.google. com/books?id=3tIMAAAAYAAJ, [16 Sept 2008])

CLYDE L. CLAUSEN
(1918/10/04)

Clyde Clausen was Santa Cruz County's sole "leatherneck" death in World War I.

Clyde Laurence Clausen was born in Brooklyn, New York, on May 23, 1894. Information regarding his family and connection with the county has not been found. He was described as being of an "adventurous disposition and anxious to see the world and take an active part in the big things that were going on." In 1917, before the US entry into the war, he left the county to travel toward New York with plans to visit family enroute and stop at different points of interest.

On April 26, 1917, while visiting friends at Port Royal, South Dakota, he enlisted in the US Marine Corps. After completing his basic training at Quantico, Virginia, he left for Europe and arrived in France ten days later.

During his wartime service in France, Clausen went "over the top" three times. "The first trip over he was gassed slightly; the second time he met with no hurt, but the third time he gave his life for his country." According to the USMC 6th Regimental history, Clyde's Company M moved up to the front in the Meuse-Argonne area on October 2 and took up positions near Somme-Py. On October 4, 1918, the Germans launched a massive gas attack and artillery barrage upon the marine position that may have resulted in Clyde's death. The official Marine report of his death stated:

Clyde L Clausen October 4- Killed in action by 067[?] South of St. Etienne, Champagne sector, Marne France. Date of burial, location and number of grave unknown. Character that would have been used if discharged...Excellent.

Clyde Clausen's body was initially buried in France, but was returned home following the war and interred in an unidentified Santa Clara County cemetery by the Monaghan Mortuary.

(WEP November 12, 1918 5:5; Santa Clara County Historical & Genealogical Society, Monaghan Mortuary Records; US Marine Corps

Enlistment Records 1798-1940 Amazon.com; Marine Corps in WWI, With the 4th Brigade of Marines, http://www.scuttlebuttsmallchow. com/4brgchron.html, [16 September 2008])

JAMES A. BROWN
(1918/10/01)

(Early postcard of Meuse-Argonne Cemetery, Romagne, France)

Santa Cruz County World War I veterans adopted James Brown as one of their own.

In December 1918 the California War History Committee reported that James A. Brown of Soquel had died of wounds. No reference to his life or relationship with Santa Cruz County has been uncovered other than that appearing in the *Santa Cruz Sentinel* on November 2, 1918,

Killed in France

Mrs. Hannah M. Brown of Soquel has received the sad news of the death of her son James, who was killed in action in France. Left to mourn are his mother and Fat Soquel. The bereaved mother and sister were recent newcomers to Soquel. This young man never lived in this county.

James A. Brown entered the US army in San Francisco, California, and apparently used his mother's address in Soquel. He probably received his basic training at Camp Lewis, Washington, and was assigned to the 363rd Regiment of the 91st Infantry Division. In the summer of 1918 his division was shipped to France and moved into the Meuse-Argonne region in the vicinity of Metz.

In September, James and the 91st Division were engaged in intense combat during the Allied offensive against the entrenched Germans. On October 1, 1918, the day of his death, his unit history recorded that,

Many men were suffering from diarrhea due to exposure for five days without warm overcoats and blankets. Most officers and men had raincoats and some had found German blankets in dugouts. The men built shelter from small arms fire by excavating the northern edges of shell holes. But they were observed by hostile planes and subjected to heavy fire (shrapnel and shell) from German artillery in the Argonne and northeast of Gesnes. Although many casualties resulted the morale was undisturbed.

On October 1, 1918, Private James A. Brown died from wounds he had received earlier. His remains were buried in the Meuse-Argonne American Cemetery in Romagne, France. Although he had never lived in the county, local World War I veterans included his name on the Victory Byway Memorial in 1928.

(CAG; ABMC; SCSn November 2, 1918, 5:3, WRP December 28,1918 5:7; 91st Div Publication Com., Story of the 91st Division, San Mateo CA 1919, page 37-38, books.google.com/ books?id=3tIMAAAAYAAJ, [16 Sept 2008])

JOHN MICKELOTTI
(1918/10/06)

(Internet Photo)

An Italian immigrant made a large down payment on his adopted country, but was unable to reap the full benefit.

Guiseppe "John" Mickelotti was born on March 13, 1896, in the Tyrol province of Austria. Leaving his parents' home he migrated to California and established residence at Sunol in Alameda County. In 1917 he moved to Shasta County where he worked briefly as a miner.

On June 5, 1917, John Mickelotti registered for the draft in Shasta County. He indicated on his enrollment form that he was an unemployed miner and described himself as being tall and slender with black hair and brown eyes. During that summer, he moved to Santa Cruz County, informed the draft board that Bonny Doon was his new residence and shortly thereafter was drafted.

The name John *Mickeletti* of Ben Lomond was included among the county inductees leaving Santa Cruz, on October 5, 1917, for Camp Lewis, Washington. Following a nine- or ten-month training program, he would have likely been shipped overseas during the summer of 1918.

Upon arrival in France, Private Mickelotti reported to the 9th Infantry Regiment of the 2nd Infantry Division serving in the Champagne Ardennes Region and with little additional training, was committed to the Meuse Argonne. During the period of Mickelotti's combat service, the 2nd Infantry Division was heavily engaged in a major offensive in the Meuse Argonne. On October 6, 1918, John Mickelotti was reported killed in action and was buried in the American Cemetery in Romagne, France.

(WWIDR; CAG; ABMC; WIKI, 2nd Infantry Div.; EP August 31, 1917)

WALTER F. BROSTROM
(1918/10/07)

(Early postcard of Meuse-Argonne Cemetery, Romagne, France)

"Corporal Brostrom Dies on Battlefield For Democracy," declared the *Santa Cruz Sentinel*.

Walter F. Brostrom was born September 14, 1893, to Andrew and Gertrude Brostrom in the small Santa Cruz Mountain community of Eccles, located north of Felton on Zayante Creek. Walter, along with three brothers, Emil, Herman and Frederick and a sister, Annie, spent his formative years in Santa Cruz County attending local schools. Sometime prior to 1917, Brostrom left the area and moved to southern California where he found employment. In the spring of 1917 he relocated to Lake Tahoe where he worked as a hotel bellman before returning to Santa Cruz.

On May 28, 1917, Brostrom registered for the draft and was described as being of medium height and stature, with red hair and brown eyes. When his application for an exemption due to poor health was denied, Walter volunteered to be inducted in the first call. He was subsequently drafted in October and probably received his basic training at Camp Lewis, Washington. Upon completion of his infantry instruction he was assigned to the 4th Infantry Division, 58th Infantry Regiment and promoted to corporal.

During the spring of 1918, Walter was shipped to France. In early October his unit was fighting its way through the many forests surrounding the city of Brieulles and had gained a foothold in the area of Bois de Fays. Government records indicate that Brostrom died on October 7, 1918, in the Meuse-Argonne area of France. The cause of his death has not been found and may have resulted from other than combat causes. Walter Brostrom was buried in the Meuse-Argonne American Cemetery at Romagne, France.

(CAG; 1900 US Census, CA, San Lorenzo; WIKI; 4th Infantry Division; SCSn December 6, 1918 2:3, WEP December 09, 1918 3:8; WWIDR; ABMC)

EVAN S. MARLIN
(1918/10/07)

(Santa Cruz Memorial Park - Santa Cruz, California)

School children in Soquel today are reminded of Evan as they have a snack under the shade of trees dedicated to him and Fay Wyman.

Evan Sturgeon Marlin was born on October. 12, 1896, to Abraham and Abbie Sturgeon Marlin in the small Merced County community of Newman, where his mother's family, the Sturgeons, lived. Little is known of his father who had previously resided in Walla Walla, Washington. The Marlin family later moved to Capitola where Evan and his brother Kenneth attended Soquel Grammar School. Evan went on to complete his education at Heald's Business College in Santa Cruz.

On May 12, 1916, Evan Marlin and Grace Crowley applied for a wedding license in Santa Cruz and likely married shortly thereafter.

Evan Marlin may have been working in the Midwest when he registered for the draft on June 5, 1918, in Dayton, Ohio, listing the Chicago Commissary Company as his employer. He was described at the time as being of medium height and stature with dark brown hair and blue eyes.

Marlin returned to Santa Cruz where he was inducted into the army and sent to an unidentified training facility. After completing his initial training, he was assigned to the 151st Brigade and stationed at Camp Grant the home of the 86th Infantry Division in Rockford, Illinois.

During the influenza epidemic of 1918, over 1,400 soldiers at Camp Grant lost their lives from the disease. In September, while awaiting orders there for deployment to France, Evan Marlin contracted the flu. His condition continued to worsen and on October 7, 1918, his family received a telegram reporting his death.

Evan's remains were returned to Newman, California, where his mother, brother and eighty-year-old grandfather lived. His remains were later reinterred in Santa Cruz Memorial Park.

(CAG; 1910 US Census, CA, Santa Cruz; WWIDR; SCSf October

10, 1918 2:3; SCSn October 18, 1918 5:7; November 13,1923 2:1; WIKI, Camp Grant, Cemetery Survey)

CHARLES L. GARRETTY
(1918/10/09)

(1930 postcard of Meuse-Argonne Cemetery, Romagne, France)

"Roy" was unable to send home his promised gifts for everyone.

Charles L. Garretty, the son of Mr. and Mrs. Bernard Garretty, was born in Santa Cruz, California on November 2, 1893. Charles, who soon acquired the nickname "Roy," resided in the family home on Water Street with his three brothers and two sisters. Upon completing his formal education, the San Vicente Lumber Company employed Roy as a "steam engineer" at their logging camp in Swanton.

Garretty's introduction to the army began with his draft registration in June 1917. His induction records described him as being of medium height and stature with brown hair and brown eyes. He was among the last of the county residents to be inducted and left Santa Cruz on Easter Sunday 1918, for Camp Lewis, Washington. While at the camp, he wrote home about his marksmanship and noted that, "out of 60 shots he made 48 good ones."

Private Garretty was assigned to the 361st Infantry Regiment of the 91st Infantry Division and left for France in July 1918. While in France, he sent a brief letter home along with silk handkerchiefs as souvenirs and promised that in his next letter he would include gifts for everyone. In September he participated in the St. Mihiel Offensive and in October his unit moved into the Meuse Argonne Region.

October 9: The 361st Infantry and the 347th Machine Gun Battalion advanced at 9:40 o'clock, October 9, the right assault battalion reaching the base of Hill 255 under heavy artillery and machine gun fire from the two crests north of them. Many casualties were suffered. At 11 o'clock, wounded men from the right flank combat liaison detachment reported that the 125th Infantry (32nd Division), on the right of the 181st Brigade, had not advanced abreast of them. Further advance being impossible the new line was held, the men digging in and waiting until the resistance from Hills 269 and 255 could be reduced by artillery. Meanwhile Hill

269 was reconnoitered by patrols and was attacked by the 1st Battalion, 361st Infantry. The crest was seized and held at 16 o'clock. Under artillery-fire protection the 3rd Battalion, 361st Infantry, seized Hill 255, after fighting all afternoon, about 18 o'clock and dug in.

When the armistice was declared on November 11, there was relief in the Garretty household because they expected that Roy would be coming home; however, on November 23 the family received a telegram informing them that he had been killed on October 9, 1918. Private Charles Garretty was buried in the Meuse-Argonne American Cemetery at Romagne, France.

(CAG; 91st Div Publication Com., San Mateo CA 1919, Story of the 91st Division, books.google.com/books?id=3tIMAAAAYAAJ, [16 September 2008]; WWIDR; ABMC; SCSf November 23, 1918 1:8; SCSn November 24, 1918 5:3)

MANUEL S. CHRISTODOULON
(1918/10/10)

(Meuse-Argonne American Cemetery 2000 - Internet photo)

A Davenport Greek went "Over There" to support his two brothers in the Greek army.

Manuel S. Christodoulon was born on the Greek Island of Samos in August 1887 and came to the United States about 1912. Upon arrival he joined two of his brothers, Cheriokas and Nick, at the Portland Cement Company in Davenport, California. Christodoulon, who was described as being stout in stature, five feet seven inches in height and with brown hair and brown eyes. He worked as a "hoistman" at the cement quarry.

When the US entered World War I, he told friends that he wanted to support his adopted country and in March of 1918 volunteered for the draft. Christodoulon was further motivated to enlist in order to assist two other brothers serving in the Greek army fighting the Turkish allies of Germany. He was first sent to Camp Ord on March 31,1918, and later assigned to the 361st Infantry Regiment of the 91st Infantry Division at Camp Lewis, Washington.

In the summer of 1918 he accompanied the 361st Regiment when it departed for France. In September Christodoulon's regiment encountered the enemy for the first time at St. Mihiel and following that engagement, he wrote friends in Davenport telling of "having the Germans on the run," and commenting on how he enjoyed army life.

The life of Manuel Christodoulon came to an end on October 10, 1918. His unit had just taken the line to participate in the Meuse-Argonne offensive against an entrenched Germans machine gun position when his regiment attacked. During the attack, Private Manuel Christodoulon was killed in action. Following the battle, his remains were interred at the Meuse-Argonne American Cemetery at Romagne, France.

(CAG; WWIDR; ABMC; SCSf November 29, 1918 1:5; SCSn November 30, 1918 5:2; WIKI, 91st Infantry Division)

VANCE W. BLISS
(1918/10/12)

(Santa Cruz High School yearbook)

Dentistry and poetry came to an end for a dedicated young officer from Santa Cruz.

Vance Wilbur Bliss, the youngest of the four children of Dr. and Mrs. F. W. Bliss, was born in Santa Cruz, California, on June 13, 1889. Young Vance was educated at Mission Hill School before entering Santa Cruz High School. There he was remembered as being a popular well-rounded student who was a scholar, poet, sculptor and 100-yard-dash track record holder.

When he graduated from high school in 1909, Vance Bliss made the decision to follow his father, brother and two uncles in the dental profession. He enrolled in the California Dental College affiliated with the University of California and after graduating, returned to Santa Cruz to join his father's dental practice. In addition to pursing his professional career, Vance was involved in various research projects and renewed his earlier interests in poetry and art.

At the outbreak of World War I, Bliss, who was described as being a tall man of medium build with light brown eyes and dark brown hair, volunteered for service and was sent to Camp Fremont near Menlo Park California. Upon completing his training he was commissioned a first lieutenant

in the US Dental Reserve Corps, ordered to New York and shipped to Europe.

In late September 1918, Lt. Bliss' troopship departed New York and arrived in Liverpool, England, on October 10. Vance wired his parents that he had arrived in good health; however, two days later he was admitted to a military hospital in Blundersands, England with respiratory problems.

In October a hospital nurse wrote the Bliss family informing them that Vance had died of pneumonia on October 12, 1918. The body of Vance W. Bliss was later returned to the US and interred in Arlington National Cemetery.

(CAG; WWIDR; SCSf June 3, 1918 3:7; SCSn November 5, 1918, November 14, 1918; SCEN May 10, 1924; USDVA; Photo-SCHS)

JOSEPH R. PASHA
(1918/10/12)

(Internet Photo)

The Christmas Eve story of their Joseph was far different from that of Joseph in the manger for Aptos school children in 1918.

Joseph R. Pasha was born in Santa Cruz County on February 14, 1898. His mother's name was Louisa. The 1910 Census reveals that Louisa Pasha, an immigrant from Italy, was the head of a household that included Joseph, his younger brother John and one of Louisa's younger brothers. Joseph was at that time attending a local Aptos grammar school.

In 1913, when his mother died, Pasha found employment at the St. George Hotel in Santa Cruz. During his leisure time, he participated in the local Aquinas Dramatic Club and began developing his acting skills. Prior to World War I, Pasha moved to Long Beach and worked with a southern California motion picture company.

The absence of draft records suggests that Joseph Pasha may have enlisted in the US Army rather than being inducted. The units to which he was assigned or the camp in which he trained have not been identified, but it is believed that he served with a unit engaged in the Meuse-Argonne offensive in the fall of 1918.

After his arrival in France, Pasha began corresponding with teachers and students at the Aptos School. Newspaper articles of the day noted how much the children looked forward to receiving his frequent letters from Europe. On October 12, 1918, word was received that he had been wounded in action. On Christmas Eve 1918, the students of Aptos School received the sad word that their pen pal Joseph Pasha had died from wounds received in France. His remains were returned following the war and reinterred in the Mt. Carmel Cemetery in Aptos.

(CAG; SCSf December 24, 1918; Cemetery Records of Santa Cruz, Cnty Calif.; 1910US Census, CA, Santa Cruz)

ALBERT A. ROBRECHT
(1918/10/12)

(St. Mihiel American Cemetery Thiaucourt, France - Internet photo)

After having been struck in the face by a piece of shrapnel, Al wanted a "crack at the Huns."

Albert A. Robrecht was born in August 1896, in Louisiana, to John and Mary Rosalie Robrecht. Joining him in the family were brothers John and Gustavus and sisters Elizabeth, Mary, Joanna, Bernadine, Christina and Anna. By 1910 the family had settled in the Larkin Valley area of Santa Cruz County where his father had acquired a farm. After completing some level of elementary school education, Albert worked on the family farm.

Albert Robrecht is reported to have been a member of Company L, 2nd Infantry Regiment of the California National Guard. This likely occurred after its return from the Mexican border and prior to its later merger with another unit. When the guard unit was disbanded in November 1917, Private Robrecht was assigned to Company C 103rd Machine Gun Battalion, 52nd Infantry Brigade, 26th Infantry Division.

The 26th Infantry Division, known as the "Yankee Division" made its way "over there" to France early in 1918 and after a brief orientation period, was sent to the front. Albert was recovering from shrapnel wounds, probably received at the St. Mihiel salient in September, when he contracted an unspecified disease.

On October 12, 1918, Albert A. Robrecht died and was buried at St. Mihiel American Cemetery, Thiaucourt, France.

In 1930 his mother joined other "doughboy" mothers who traveled to France to say goodbye to their sons.

(CAG; USCR, 1910 US Census, CA, Santa Cruz; ABMC; WEP November 26, 1918 5:4)

LOUIS D. CHANEY
(1918/10/15)

(Suresnes American Cemetery France - Internet photo)

Farming failed to earn Louis an exemption, and influenza gave him an unwanted one.

Louis Davis Chaney was born on September 18, 1889, in Dunstable, Massachusetts, to Mr. and Mrs. G. W. Chaney. It has not been established when Louis arrived in Santa Cruz County but in 1917 he was working as a farmer on the Majors Brothers - Enright Ranch on the Coast Road. When he registered for the draft on June 5, 1917, he was single, living on Branciforte Avenue in Santa Cruz and described as being tall, of medium stature, with blue eyes and dark brown hair.

Louis Chaney applied for a draft exemption as a farmer but his request was denied and he was inducted in one of the early drafts. Army life began for him at Camp Kearney near San Diego, California, where he was sent for basic training. Following training, he was assigned as a private in the 145th Field Artillery Regiment of the 40th Infantry Division. In July 1918 his unit traveled to Camp Mills, New York, to await transportation overseas. In August they sailed for Europe and three weeks later arrived in France.

Upon arrival in France the 145th Field Artillery moved to Bordeaux, where they remained for the duration of the war. On October 15, 1918, Private Louis D. Chaney "died of a disease" near Paris. He was buried at the Suresnes American Cemetery located between Paris and Versailles.

(CAG; 145th Field Military.Com, History of the Deuce, http://www.military.com/HomePage/UnitPageHistory/ 1,13506,714176%7C772463,00.html, [16 September 2008]; SCSn December 6 1918; WEP November 7, 1918 3:4; WWIDR; ABMC)

ERNEST J. SORIA
(1918/10/19)

(Santa Cruz Memorial Park - Santa Cruz, California)

Ernest was a naval reservist who contracted his life-ending flu while serving in the army.

Ernest Joseph Soria was born in Santa Cruz on March 7, 1892, to Petronillo and Anna Soria, a family descended from early Californio settlers. Also included in the family were their children, Edward, Carl, Harry, Ada, Richard, William, Frederick and Teresa. After completing his education, Ernest became an apprentice plumber.

The name Ernest Soria appears in a *Santa Cruz Sentinel* article of March 29, 1917, along with other members of the local detachment of naval reservists awaiting muster into federal service. When that unit was called into active duty in April 1917, its members reported to the *USS Oregon* stationed in San Francisco for duty. On September 25, 1917, Ernest Soria was given a medical discharge from the navy and returned to his family home in Santa Cruz.

In September 1918 he registered for the draft and was found fit to serve. His induction records picture him as being tall in height, of slender build with brown hair and gray eyes. During that month, he was inducted into the army and sent to Camp Lewis, Washington.

After completing less than a month of training, Private Ernest J. Soria contracted influenza and died at the camp's medical facility on October 19, 1918. Soria's mother, Anna, had his remains returned to Santa Cruz where they were interred in Santa Cruz Memorial Park.

(USCR, 1910 US Census, CA, Santa Cruz; WWIDR; WEP September 5, 1918; SCSf, October 19, 1918 4:3, December 30, 1918)

CHARLES H. PAPPASSI
(1918/10/20)

A newspaper heading "Dies at Camp Bowie" announced the end of a former local clerk.

Charles Henry Pappassi was born April 13, 1889, in Santa Cruz, California, to Paul and Martha Pappassi. Paul was an orchardist who, with his wife, two sons and two daughters, settled in the Corralitos-Laurel area. Charles spent his for-

mative years in the county and received an education that enabled him to work as clerk in a local store. Sometime prior to June 1917 he moved to San Francisco and while living in that city, commuted to Oakland where he was employed as a carpenter.

Charles Pappassi appeared before the San Francisco draft board on June 5, 1917, where he registered for induction. Records at that time described him as being tall, of medium build with brown hair and brown eyes. California Adjutant General records denote that when Pappassi was inducted into the army in late 1917 or early 1918, he was living in San Jose.

After entering the army, Pappassi received orders to report to Camp Bowie, Texas. Camp Bowie, the home of the 36th Infantry Division, had been established in Fort Worth, Texas in 1917, and served as its main training facility. On October 20, 1918, Charles H. Pappassi died at Camp Bowie from what the California War History Committee described as an "accident or other causes." The location of Charles Pappassi's gravesite has not been identified.

(CAG; WWIDR; SCSf October 23, 1918 2:3; White, Lonnie J, Texas Military Forces Museum, 36th Division in WWI, http://www.texasmilitaryforcesmuseum.org/36division/white.htm [16 September 2008]; WEP December 28, 1918 5:7)

MARY PEARL TURNER
(1918/10/21)

Pearl Turner was the only Santa Cruz County woman, serving in the armed forces, to have died during World War I.

Mary Pearl Turner was born in California about 1892 to Harry and Sarah Turner. Sometime between 1900 and 1910 Pearl, along with her parents and sister Irene, moved to Santa Cruz and settled into a home in the Seabright district. Pearl attended Santa Cruz High School as a member of the class of 1910. While in school, her friends described her appearance as being "most attractive and winsome."

Following the completion of her high school education, Pearl moved into a residence on Union Street in San Francisco and enrolled as a "Nursing Apprentice" in the nursing program at St. Lukes Hospital. After graduating from the program, she joined the St. Lukes staff where she was said to have "gained the respect of the staff and physicians with whom she worked."

When the government put out a call for volunteer nurses prior to the US entry into World War I, Pearl Turner responded and joined the Naval Nurse Corps. During her service, she was assigned to the naval medical facility located at Mare Island near Vallejo California.

With the diagnosis of influenza in the community, Navy

authorities quickly responded. Liberty in the city was canceled and functions involving large groups of personnel were prohibited. On 5 October[1918] the emergency hospitals were opened. The peak of the epidemic among service people in the yard was around 13-15 October, and it was virtually ended by 30 October. There were 1,536 (1,600 predicted) service personnel treated for influenza. An emergency hospital for civilian employees of the yard opened on Navy yard grounds on 3 November and closed 30 November. Two hundred eighty-seven civilians received care.

During this period, Pearl Turner contracted influenza. Her mother traveled to Vallejo to nurse her daughter and remained by her side until her death on October 21, 1918.

The 1919 Santa Cruz High School *Trident*, honoring Pearl and its other war dead, noted, "So hard did she work, and so devoted was she to her duties that she contracted influenza in the hospital in Mare Island and died." Pearl Turner's gravesite has not been located.

(USCR, 1910 US Census, CA, Santa Cruz; St. Lukes Hospital 1914-1915, List of Graduates at the Training School 1890-1913; http://www.sfgenealogy.com/sf/schools/stluke15.htm, (16 September 2008]); SCSn October 23, 1918 4:7; SCSf October 23, 1918 3:1; SCEN May 10, 1924; Snyder, Thomas Naval Historical Center, Great Flu Epidemic at Mare Island Navy Yard and Vallejo, http://www.history.navy.mil/library/online/influenza_mareis.htm [16 September 2008]; CDR)

FAY M. WYMAN
(1918/10/26)

(Photo courtesy of Ted Maddock)

Long time Soquel resident Richard Nutter recalls being instructed as a boy never to violate the sanctity of a small cluster of trees at the Soquel School dedicated to Fay Wyman.

Fay Mudie Wyman was born in Soquel, California, on June 14, 1892, to Adi and Anna Wyman. He was descended from early Soquel pioneers. Fay, along with his brother Rolland and sisters Laura and Ruth, grew up in Soquel where they were members of the local Congregational Church. He was graduated from Soquel Grammar School and Santa Cruz High School.

Following the completion of his formal education, Wyman worked as a salesman/driver for the Associated Oil Company of Madera, California. He continued to maintain his local residence and remained active in the Soquel International Order of Odd Fellows.

In June 1917 Wyman joined other young men of the county and registered for the draft. At that time he was described as being of medium height, slender build with black hair and brown eyes. While he noted that he had "weak arches and weak eyes," he did not apply for a draft exemption. On October 5, 1917, Fay Wyman was inducted into the army and accompanied other draftees from the county to Camp Lewis, Washington. Following basic training, he was transferred to Camp Kearney near San Diego and to New Jersey to await shipment overseas.

Wyman left for France in June 1918 and shortly after his arrival, joined the 59th Infantry Regiment of the 4th Division as it prepared to participate in the Argonne offensive. Fay wrote home describing how he had "been over the top twice, and did not receive even a scratch."

On December 14, 1918, his mother, Anna received the following telegram from the adjutant general at Washington, "deeply regret to inform you that it is officially reported that Private Fay M. Wyman died October 26 from wounds received in action." Ted Maddock, a member of the Wyman-Parrish family, indicated that the family history contained a different version of Fay's death. They were told that he was accidentally shot and killed by a fellow soldier cleaning a weapon.

Fay was initially buried in France but later returned to the US and was interred in Arlington National Cemetery. In recognition of his service the county's first Veterans of Foreign Wars post chose Wyman for their post name.

In 1923 five redwood trees were planted to form a star on the grounds of the Soquel School. In the center of the star is a stone monument with a bronze plaque recognizing Fay Wyman and Evan Marlin of Soquel who lost their lives in the Great War.

(CAG; USCR, 1910 US Census, CA, Santa Cruz; WWIDR; SCSf December 13, 1918 1:5; WEP December 14, 1918; SCEN October 29, 1923 4:4; USDVA)

EDWARD H. CARR
(1918/10/26)

(Santa Cruz Memorial Park - Santa Cruz, California)

In 1918 Ed Carr found himself back in khaki preparing "chow" for doughboys.

Edward Henry Carr was born April 2, 1888, in Santa Cruz, California, to Fred and Ellen Carr. Fred spent his formative years in the family home with brothers Fred Jr. and Victor. He briefly attended a local grammar school before transferring into Christian Brothers parochial school. After completing his formal education, Carr was employed by the California Powder Company in Santa Cruz before moving to Placer County California. There he used his experience in the powder business to obtain employment with the Grant Powder Company at Clipper Gap.

In 1913 Edward Carr joined the US Army and was sent to the Philippine Islands where he served as a cook for two years. Following his discharge, he returned to Santa Cruz and worked as a dairyman on the Wilder Ranch.

In March 1918 Carr, who was described as being tall and slender with brown eyes and brown hair, reported to the local draft board and re-enlisted as a cook. He was assigned to an aviation company at Kelly Field, Texas and left Santa Cruz on March 18. Private Carr had barely settled in to his new location when he was stricken with a severe cold followed by a cough that would not leave. The doctors at Camp Kelly finally released Ed from active duty and sent him home to Santa Cruz to recuperate.

When he arrived home, his mother obtained the best medical assistance locally available and personally nursed him for several months. On Sunday October 26, 1918, all her efforts failed and Private Edward H. Carr died. Following his funeral Edward Carr was buried at the Santa Cruz Memorial Park.

(WWIDR; SCSn October 29, 1918 4:5)

WILLIAM J. WEEKS
(1918/10/27)

(Meuse-Argonne American Cemetery, France - Internet photo)

Four Watsonville brothers went to France, and three returned, leaving William at Verdun.

William J. Weeks was born about 1891 in Santa Clara, California, but spent most of his life in Watsonville. Also included in the Weeks family were his parents, brothers Frank, Mike and Ray and sisters Bebe and Mrs. Al Echeverria.

Details relating to the life of William Weeks are not available; however, his military experiences were chronicled by his brother Mike and given to the Pajaro Valley Historical Association in 1990. Below is an unedited copy of Michael's letter

Watsonville, Cal
To War History committee
Us four brothers enlisted in Company L, 2nd Calif. Inf. March 28 & 30th 1917. Were sent to Presidio S.F. April 5th. Later were split up & sent to different places for guard duty. We mobilized again at Fort Mason July 20th. On October 29th 1917 we entrained for Camp Kearney San Diego. Transferred to Company. G 160th Inf. 40th Division. Went overseas as replacements from Kearney June 13th 1918. Arrived in Camp Merritt N.J. Sailed from New York June 27th on the Nester. British bound arriving in Liver Pool July 10th. Left England Southampton 18th of July arriving in La. Harve [sic, Le Havre] France 19th. Drilled at Port LeRoy and Marcany. Went into the 26 New England Division 103rd Inf. July 28th 1918. Just relieved from the drive at Cheaut Theury. [sic, Chateau Thierry] Went into action Sept. 12 to 13. Captured a town call Billy [sic, Belleau?] that was our objective. Was relieved by 4th Division. Later was sent to Verdun held lines for two weeks and then drove on 8th until the day Armistice was signed 11th 1918.

We left France on the 28th of March, sailed from Breast [sic, Brest]. Arriving at Boston April 5, 1919. Sailed on the USS America. Frank and Mike were discharged at Kearny April 21, 1919.

William Weeks was killed at Verdun October 18, 1918 by shellfire.

Ray was wounded at Verdun November 3rd sent to Hospital, Base 10, Center, Base 54.7. A Base 20. Harrison Base 399. Breast Base 7. New York Fox Hill Camp Kearny Cal Surgical 8.

Yours Truly Mike Weeks

According to the American Battle Monuments Commission, Private William J. Weeks of the 103rd Infantry Regiment, 26th Infantry Division died on October 27, 1918, and is buried in the Meuse-Argonne American Cemetery at Romagne, France.

(CAG; ABMC; WRP December 17, 1918, PVHA Archival Files).

REUBEN M. WILKINSON
(1918/11/02)

(Santa Cruz High School yearbook)

Reuben was a track star in high school, a skill that may have cost him his life.

Reuben Wilkinson, the eldest son of Albert and Lottie Wilkinson, was born in Los Angeles, California, on April 8, 1894. His father was a traveling salesman who moved the family to Santa Cruz sometime after 1910. When the family arrived in the community, Reuben enrolled in Santa Cruz High School located across the street from the family home. High school yearbooks make frequent reference to the academic accomplishments of Reuben Wilkinson and his prowess as a track star.

In 1914 Wilkinson graduated from high school and moved to Needles, California, where the Claypool Company, a large grocery concern, employed him as a clerk.

While residing in Needles, Wilkinson registered for the draft on June 5, 1917. At that time he was described as being tall and slender with brown hair and gray eyes. When inducted, he was sent to Camp Lewis, Washington, for his basic training.

Volunteers were requested to fill the 364th Infantry Regiment of the 91st Infantry Division, and Private Wilkinson was among the first to step forward. In the latter part of June 1918, those volunteer replacements traveled east through Canada, Chicago and on to their debarkation port in New Jersey.

The 91st Infantry set sail for "over there" during June and July and when they arrived in France, they made preparation for what would be the fall Meuse-Argonne offensive. On September 30, 1918, Private Wilkinson wrote home describing his first combat experience.

Dear Mother and Father:

Well, I have a little "blighty" at last, but it is nothing serious, so if you have received word that I am a casualty do not be worried, as everything is O.K.

I was in the first wave of our advance for two days and two nights and than I had to get bumped off. I sure would have liked to stay with the bunch and chased those "boches" clear off the map.

We were advancing in the face of the German rear guard action which consists mostly of machine gun and artillery fire when one of their high explosive shells broke so close to me that the man who was behind me was blown to pieces and the man in front was knocked down and I do not know if he was killed or not; I hope not, because we have been pals from the time we started.

Just before the explosion a machine gun bullet passed through the cuff on my shirt sleeve and when the explosion of the big shell came something hit me on the mouth and in the back of the head and I was thrown about ten or twelve feet and I struck on my knees. Then I got to my feet and went about 450 yards and then fell, to be picked up later, which I do not remember, by the first aid men and here I am now.

Will close for the present hoping all are well, and with love to you both, I remain

Your Son... Reuben M. Wilkinson

Reuben was hospitalized as a result of the wounds that he incurred during the Meuse-Argonne offensive and remained confined for a portion of October. In late October he returned to his regiment to assist in the great Lys-Scheldt battles in Flanders, Belgium. A special eulogy in his high school *Trident* newspaper on May 10, 1919, describes the final episode in Reuben Wilkinson's life occurring on November 2, 1918.

His was the most dangerous of jobs, that of a runner or carrier of messages. His officers and comrades speak of his perfect fearlessness and willingness to volunteer for the most dangerous missions. He was killed by a machine gun bullet while carrying messages in a country literally [alive] with machine gun nests.

Reuben Wilkinson is buried in the Flanders Field American Cemetery among the poppies in Waregem, Belgium.

(WWIDR; ABMC; SCSn November 1918 5:4, December 3, 1918 2:4; SCEN May 10, 1924; Photo-SCHS)

ARTHUR E. JOHNSON
(1918/11/03)

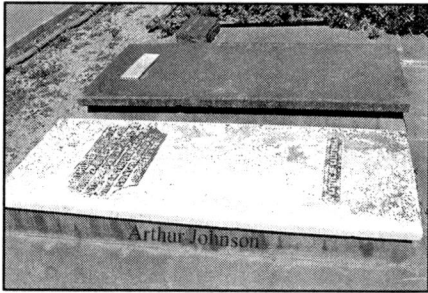

(Pioneer Cemetery - Watsonville, California)

His "friends could hardly believe he had passed into the great beyond as they took a last look at this fine young man's face."

Arthur Edward Johnson was born in San Jose, California, on May 21, 1894, to Nels and Hannah Johnson. Along with two sisters and a brother, Rudolph, he lived with his parents at the family home on Third Street in Watsonville, California. Prior to World War I, Arthur was employed by the firm Iverson and Davis and was a member of the B.R.C.A. (believed to be the Brotherhood of Railway Carmen of America) #765. Johnson's work likely took him to Monterey County, as "auto loads of people from Salinas and Soledad" would later attend his funeral.

California Adjutant General records indicate that when Johnson entered the US Navy he listed San Francisco as his residence. His basic training likely took place at the Naval Training Station - San Francisco, which was located on Yerba Buena Island in San Francisco Bay.

After completing his initial training program, he was assigned to Submarine Chaser #285. That ship was stationed at Colon in the Panama Canal Zone to protect shipping lanes near the canal. While serving aboard that vessel, Arthur contracted malaria and died November 3, 1918.

Arthur Johnson's body was returned to Watsonville and his funeral was conducted in the home of his parents on December 17, 1918. Cadets of Watsonville High School served as his honor guard and later provided a gun salute and played taps at his internment in the Watsonville Pioneer (IOOF) cemetery.

(CAG; Joseph M Radigan, Sub Chaser #285, 1996-2005, http://www.navsource.org/archives/12/150285.htm, [16 September 2008]; USCR, 1900 US Census, CA, Santa Cruz; WRP November 7, 1918 3:2; WEP December 18, 1918 2:4)

__November 11__ World War I Armistice signed on the 11th hour of the 11th day of the 11th month.

REUBEN SILVA
(1918/11/11)

(Watsonville High School yearbook)

On the day that World War I ended Reuben breathed his final breath.

Reuben Silva was born on November 9, 1896, in Watsonville, California, to Mr. and Mrs. M. J. Silva. The Silvas' other children included sons George, Herbert, John, Royal and daughters Mary, Josephine, Emma and Lulu. Reuben spent his formative years in Soquel, Aptos and Watsonville where he entered high school. In 1915 Silva graduated from Watsonville High School and moved to Berkeley to live with a sister. While living in the east bay area, he was employed as a "bolter" at an Oakland shipyard.

In June 1918 Reuben Silva registered for the draft in Albany, California, and in the fall was inducted into the army. At the time he was described as being of medium height and stature with light colored hair and blue eyes. Reuben was assigned to a heavy artillery company at Fort Rosecrans in San Diego where he began his basic training period. He had just completed two weeks of the training course when he contracted the Spanish Flu and was admitted to the fort's medical facility.

On Armistice Day, November 11, 1918, Reuben Silva died of the flu. His sister Mary who was living in San Diego brought his body home to Watsonville for a funeral and burial in Watsonville's Pioneer Cemetery.

(CAG; USCR, 1900 & 1910 US Census, CA, Santa Cruz; WWID WRP November 12, 1918; Photo WHS)

LEON L. CLARKE
(1918/11/12)

(Santa Cruz Riptide photo)

"My daddy is going to shoot the Kaiser. When I grow up I am going to shoot Kaisers too," declared Leon Luther Clarke Jr.

Leon Luther Clarke was born about 1884 in Illinois. Census records indicate that his parents were also natives of that state, but no information regarding his siblings or early life was noted. Leon's formal education prepared him for a career in engineering. This was followed by marriage to Grace in 1906. The couple later moved to Oakland, California, where he found employment as a mechanical engineer in road construction.

During the summer of 1917, Clarke moved with his wife and son to Santa Cruz where he was placed in charge of the California Highway Commission construction program in the county. Military records also suggest that he may have maintained a residence in San Francisco.

Leon Clarke applied for a commission and in the fall of 1918, was designated a Lieutenant, assigned to the Army Corps of Engineers and ordered to report to Washington, D. C., for assignment. Leaving his wife and son in Santa Cruz, he departed on October 23, and headed east.

In Washington, D. C., Lt. Clarke was assigned duty at Camp Humphries, (Ft. Belvoir) Virginia and while at that location, contracted the pneumonia that took his life on November 12, 1918. Leon Luther Clarke's final resting-place has yet to be identified.

Major Leon Luther Clarke Jr. served in World War II and shot at a different breed of "Kaisers."

(CAG; USCR, 1910 US Census, CA, Alameda; SCSf October 23, 1918 3:2; SCSn November 13, 1918 4:5)

LESTER F. ROWE
(1918/11/14)

(Santa Cruz Memorial Park - Santa Cruz California)

A Watsonville business school graduate made an unwelcome contract with the flu.

Lester Frank Rowe was born on October 6, 1897, in Redwood City, California, to Frank and Bertie Francis Rowe. The family moved to the Pajaro Valley while Lester was quite young and settled in the Green Valley area. His brother Phillip and his sisters Marie, Hazel, Ora, Florence and Phyllis joined Lester in the Rowe family. Young Rowe attended local schools and enrolled in the commercial department of Watsonville High School from which he was graduated about 1914.

After graduation Lester accepted a job with the Associated Oil Company of Bakersfield, California, and worked as a storekeeper at the company's facility in the small Kern County community of Reward, California.

Lester registered for the draft in Bakersfield on June 15, 1918, and was described as being tall and slender with brown eyes and brown hair. He was inducted in the fifth draft of 1918 and sent to Camp Kearney near San Diego, California. After completing basic training, he was assigned a clerical position in the camp's dental infirmary. During his military service, Lester rose to the position of chief clerk and was promoted to the rank of sergeant.

On October 28, 1918, Rowe contracted Spanish Influenza, which developed into pneumonia. His parents traveled to San Diego to spend time with him during his last few days and on November 14, 1918, Sergeant Lester Rowe died at the age of twenty-one years. Following a funeral service at the Christian Church in Watsonville on November 16, 1918, Lester Rowe was buried in Watsonville Pioneer cemetery.

(CAG; WWIDR; WRP November 15, 1918 1:7; WEP November 15, 1918 1:2)

WILLIAM A. SULLIVAN
(1918/11/21)

(Watsonville High School yearbook)

County veterans declared a cadet awaiting an active duty commission to be one of them.

William Ambrose Sullivan was born May 23, 1900, in Wisconsin to Mr. and Mrs. E. T. Sullivan. At an early age he accompanied his family to Santa Cruz County where they settled in the Larkin Valley area. Along with brothers Frank and Eugene and sisters Irene and Marie, he attended local schools. Sullivan was a popular student at Watsonville High School and was graduated 1918.

In the summer between high school and college William worked as a farmer on the E. E. Sullivan farm at Cerres, in Stanislaus County. In September he registered for the draft at Modesto, and was described as being tall, of medium stature and with dark hair and brown eyes.

In the fall of 1918 Sullivan enrolled in the University of California at Berkeley and entered the student training corps, a predecessor of the present day ROTC program. In 1918 Sullivan was stricken with influenza and after a long recuperation period, was on the road to recovery when he contracted spinal meningitis.

Cadet William Ambrose Sullivan died at Berkeley, California, on November 21, 1918, and was buried in the Valley Catholic cemetery near Watsonville on November 25, 1918.

William Sullivan was not on active duty in the army at the time of his death; however, because of his active cadet status his name was included on the county's memorial plaques recognizing local World War I deaths.

(WWIDR; WRP November 22, 1918 5:7; WEP November 25, 1918 1:3; Photo-WHS)

JOSEPH S. REBEIRO
(1918/12/29)

(Arlington National Cemetery WWI Section- Internet Photo)

Joe was too young for the draft, but old enough to become a multi-battle combat survivor.

Joseph S. Rebeiro was born about 1898 and is believed to have been a Pajaro Valley resident for most of his life. He was one of the four children of Mr. and Mrs. Joseph Rebeiro Sr. who lived in or near Watsonville, California. Joseph attended local schools and Watsonville High School. After he left school, he was employed as a clerk in the Williams and Biebernach store in Watsonville and was remembered as being "a very pleasant and sociable young man and popular with all our people."

Rebeiro began his military experience with the Army National Guard. He was too young for the June 1917 draft registration, but old enough to enlist in Company L of the 2nd California Regiment of the National Guard. Private Rebeiro was sent to Camp Kearney, near San Diego, for training and was there at the time of his father's death on August 31, 1917.

In October Joseph Rebeiro was reassigned to the Presidio of San Francisco where he remained on temporary duty before joining Company H, 103rd Regiment of the 26th Division (Yankee Division). He accompanied that unit to France where it was assigned to the 1st Infantry Division ("Big Red 1").

During the fighting in France, Rebeiro saw combat in the Aisne-Marne offensive of July, the fighting at Chateau-Thierry and the Meuse Argonne. In December, while awaiting transportation back to the United States, Rebeiro contracted the Spanish Flu and was hospitalized.

On January 1, 1919, family members of Joe Rebeiro received a wire informing them that he had died of influenza on December 29, 1918. The remains of Private Joe S. Rebeiro were interred at Arlington National Cemetery.

(CAG; WEP August 31, 1917; WEP October 18, 1917, November 14,1917 5:6; January 1, 1919 1:5)

SILAS TOTTEN
(1918/12/29)

(Watsonville Pioneer Cemetery – Watsonville California)

Silas was overlooked when memorial plaques were erected in Santa Cruz County.

Silas Totten was born May 10, 1897, in Aromas, California, to Mr. and Mrs. Joseph S. Totten. The Tottens resided in the Pajaro Valley with their children, Flora, Mattie, Ora, Josephine, Myrtle, Reuben, Paul and Silas, until they moved to Turlock, California. Silas Totten remained in the Pajaro valley and lived in the Corralitos area for a number of years.

When Silas Totten registered for the draft on June 5, 1918, he was unemployed and living at the Lincoln Hotel in San Francisco. Induction records describe him as being single, tall in height and of slender build, with brown hair and grey eyes. Totten was inducted soon after his registration and received basic training at an unspecified facility. After completing his training, he was probably stationed near San Francisco and promoted to corporal.

The obituary for Silas Totten appearing in the *Watsonville Evening Pajaronian* noted "Corporal Totten had died in San Francisco on December 29, 1918 following a brief illness." His remains were returned to Watsonville and interred in the family plot in the IOOF Pioneer Cemetery.

(WWIDR; WEP December 31, 1918)

NORTON PRATT
(1918/?)

(Santa Cruz High School yearbook)

"Put me among the girls" was Norton Pratt's request accompanying his photo in the 1914 Santa Cruz High School *Trident* yearbook.

Norton Pratt was born about 1896; however, details pertaining to his early life have not surfaced. He spent part of his senior year at Santa Cruz High School and became "prominent at once in track athletics, football and student affairs." Included among those girls that he wished to be put among was silent screen movie star Zasu Pitts, a member of his 1914 high school graduating class. The school's *Trident* newspaper of May 10, 1919, noted that Norton Pratt "meant much to the school while with us and left a large circle of friends."

After graduation, Pratt enrolled in Cornell University in New York and remained there until his junior year when he left to enlist in the US Navy. He was only in the service a short time before he contracted pneumonia and died in a New York naval hospital. Details regarding Norton Pratt's military service and death have not been located, nor has his place of burial.

(SCHS *Trident* Yearbook, Santa Cruz 1914; SCEN May 10, 1924)

KENNETH J. REID
(1918/?)

From a few references and some speculation a foggy portrait of this soldier can be attempted.

First World War draft records for California note that Kenneth James Reid was born on November 9, 1897, and that his mother's name was Dellie Belle Reid. The location of Kenneth's birth, the names of other family siblings and date of his family's arrival in Santa Cruz have not been discovereds. An article appearing in a 1919 memorial issue of the Santa Cruz High School *Trident* honoring former classmate who had died while in military service noted,

"Kenneth Reid (Class of 1917) was also but a short time with us. His teachers and classmates will remember his

sunny disposition and his unselfish refined manners."

University of California, Berkeley records reveal that Kenneth James Reid served as the freshman class treasurer during 1917-1918. Draft records note that while a student at the University of California, he was living in Oakland, California.

Kenneth Reid was inducted into the US Army on September 12, 1918. At that time he was described as being five feet six inches in height of medium build with blue eyes and brown hair. The 1919 Santa Cruz High School *Trident* article went on to state, "he was killed in a truck accident at a camp in Washington State." That camp would probably have been Camp Lewis. The burial location of Kenneth Reid has not been located.

(WWIDR; University of California, Berkeley Blue & Gold Yearbook; 1918 SCEN May 10, 1924)

1919

BERNARD E. PILLSBURY
(1919/02/04)

(Santa Cruz High School yearbook)

A Soquel youth, with intense spirit and high ideals, gave up his education to support his mother and surrendered his life to his country.

Bernard Pillsbury was born about 1900 and was descended from New England stock. His family originated in Maine and moved to Soquel, California, where his father, a college-educated chemist and paper manufacturer, supervised the installation of machinery in the Hihn-Hammond paper mill. The family were active members of the Congregational Church in Soquel and also participated in the Christian Science movement.

In April 1917, while Bernard was in high school, his father died and shortly afterwards, he was forced to drop out of school to assist with family finances. According to the high school's *Trident* newspaper, Bernard was "full of action and enthusiasm and ability—not strong in body,

but having intense spirit and high ideals." He was also remembered for the cheerful way he gave up his school ambitions after the death of his father to become his mother's support.

In June 1918 Pillsbury enlisted in the Quartermaster Department of the US Army and probably completed his basic training at Camp Lewis, Washington. In January 1919, while serving as a private with Troop C of the 1st Cavalry, he contracted influenza at Camp Harry J. Jones in Snohomish County, Washington. Private Bernard E. Pillsbury died from that disease on February 4, 1919. His burial location is not known.

(SCHS Trident, Santa Cruz May 10, 1919; SCSf June 18, 1918 3:37, SCSn, May 10, 1924; Snohomish County Washington, World War I Roll of Honor; http://www.rootsweb.com/~wasnohom/sc26rofh. htm, [16 September 2008])

JOEL GABA
(1919/02/13)

(Kirk dale Cemetery, Liverpool England - Internet Photo)

A Santa Cruzan who served with the Canadian Army was a different brand of doughboy.

Joel Gaba, the son of Mark and Annie Gaba, was born on August 20, 1880, in South Norwalk, Connecticut. During their stay in Santa Cruz, the Gaba family resided on Otis Street. Also included in the family were their son Sam and daughter Fanny. It is not known how long Joel remained in Santa Cruz, but in September 1917 he was unmarried and working as a watchman in Portland, Oregon.

On September 17, 1917, Joel Gaba reported to a Canadian Overseas Expeditionary Force recruiting office, probably in British Columbia, and enlisted in the Canadian army. At the time of his enlistments Gaba was described as being thirty-seven years of age with a dark complexion, brown eyes and black hair. He also indicated that his religious denomination of preference was the Presbyterian Church.

Joel's initial assignment was with a Canadian Army hospital unit in Victoria, British Columbia. In March 1918 he wrote his parents indicating that he was "being kept busy night and day setting up special tents for the contagious as much of the camp was quarantined for measles." Later in the year Gaba served as a Sapper (combat engineer) in the Canadian Railway Troops, 7th Bn Division, and traveled with that unit to England.

On February 13, 1919, Joel Gaba died in Liverpool, England, of pneumonia and his remains were buried in the Kirkdale Cemetery in Liverpool.

(War Graves Commission, Canadian World War I Enlistment Records and Commonwealth, http://www.collectionscanada.gc.ca/databases/cef/001042-100.01-e.php [16 September 2008]; SCSf March 16, 1918 4:1; WEP March 03, 1919 3:4)

EDWARD L. WILLIAMS JR.
(1919/03/28)

CAP'T E. L. WILLIAMS COM'D 7 TH AERO SQUADR...
BORN NOV. 8, 1892, DIED AT
FRANCE FIELD C. Z. MAR. 28, 1919.

(Santa Cruz Memorial Park - Santa Cruz California)

Chevalier Edward L. Williams never wore the white and gold medal designating him a Knight of the Order of the Crown of Italy.

Edward Williams was born November 2, 1892, to Mr. and Mrs. Edward L. Williams, Sr. The elder Williams was an Englishman who had married a Tennessee belle by the name of Elizabeth Polk; the couple later moved to Chicago, Illinois, where their sons were born. Information regarding Edward's siblings, education and formative years has not been located.

When the US entered World War I, Edward Williams was given a commission as a lieutenant in the US Army Air Service and assigned to their field at Hazelhurst, New Jersey. He was one of six American officers chosen to receive instruction in the use of a Caprini biplane, an Italian aircraft used by Americans during the war. Williams and his instructor, Captain Silvio Resnati, became close friends. Ten days before Lt. Williams was scheduled to make his solo flight in the biplane he watched in shock as Captain Resnati crashed and burned in a similar craft.

Williams became proficient with the Caprini aircraft during the war and was promoted to Captain. According to a *Santa Cruz Evening News* article of January 21, 1921, he was an

outstanding figure in the world war. He became so proficient in the handling of the famous Caprini planes, an

Italian machine, that the Italian government made strong representation to the United States government to send him to Italy. His services were more valuable here however, and he did much in making aviators out of flying recruits for Uncle Sam.

Captain Williams visited family and friends living in Santa Cruz prior to reporting for duty with the 7th Aero Squadron at the Panama Canal. While serving in the Canal Zone, Captain Edward L. Williams Jr. contracted spinal meningitis and died on March 28, 1919.

In 1921 the Italian government posthumously designated Williams as a Knight of the Order of the Crown of Italy, its highest military honor, which gave him the title of Chevalier The remains of Edward Williams were later sent to Santa Cruz and reinterred in the Santa Cruz Memorial Park.

(CAG; Santa Cruz County Burial Permits 1905-1938, Genealogical Society of Santa Cruz Cnty, 2001; SCSf May 29, 1918 3:8; SCEN January 21, 1921 5:4)

JAMES W. NELLSON
(Death date not known)

The name James W. Nellson was included among Santa Cruz men appearing on the California Adjutant Generals 1921 report listing World War I casualties. Nellson's name also appears on an earlier California Adjutant Generals report of 1907 listing soldiers of the Sixtieth Company (depot torpedo) stationed at the Presidio in San Francisco who had been discharged and returned to civilian life. In that list, James W. Nellson was identified as a motorman who had found employment with the United Railway in San Francisco. No other information has been uncovered regarding the life, death and burial location of this soldier.

(http://www.archive.org/stream/circularrelative00unitrich/circularrelative00unitrich_djvu.txt [12 October 2009]; CAG)

SIDNEY W. SIMPSON
(Death date not known)

Local veterans were familiar with Simpson's military service-related death and included him on the Victory Byway Memorial plaque in 1928; however, no other record of that death has been found.

Sidney W. Simpson was born on September 8, 1895, at Wrights [Station], Santa Clara County, California, to Samuel and Mary Simpson. Sidney spent his formative years with his older sister, Ethel, at the family farm in the Highland district north of Soquel. Local grammar schools probably provided him with an elementary education; however, nothing has been located regarding his high school attendance.

Draft records indicate that he was a farmer by occupation and probably worked on the family farm. On June 25, 1917, Simpson completed his selective service registration process at the Highland Precinct. At that time he described himself as being tall, of medium complexion with brown eyes and dark brown hair.

Simpson was likely inducted into the US Army and may have been included among the ninety-five county men that left for training on September 22, 1917. No information has been found regarding his military experience, subsequent death or burial location.

(CAG; WWIDR; USCR, US Census 1900, 1910, CA, Santa Clara)

AMBROSE A. WASS
(Death date not known)

The name Ambrose Allman Wass was included among Santa Cruz war dead on the 1921 California Adjutant Generals list, although it appears that his primary residence was in Berkeley, California.

Ambrose was born in Berkeley California on February 20, 1891, to Frederick and Margaret Wass. Also included in the family was an older brother Royal and sisters Ermine and Ethel.

Wass grew up in the family home in Alameda County where his father worked as a cabinetmaker. The date he arrived in Santa Cruz is not known; however, in June 1917 he was living on Pacific Avenue in Santa Cruz and was self-employed in the auto handling business. His draft records indicate that he was not married and was of medium height and stature with brown hair and brown eyes. At the time of his draft registration, he applied for a service exemption based on "financial matters," but that exemption was not granted. The circumstances of his death and the location of his remains are not known; however, they were probably not combat related.

(WWIDR; CAG; 1910 US Census, CA, Alameda/Berkeley; SOGW; Alameda Cnty WWI Dead, http://saveoaks.com/SaveOaks/Main.html [12 October 09])

JOHN W. WRIGHT
(Death date not known)

The name John W. Wright was included among Capitola men appearing on the California Adjutant Generals 1921 report listing World War I casualties. No other information has been discovered regarding the life, death or burial location of this soldier.

***

World War II
(1941-1946)

Santa Cruz County Military During World War II

Santa Cruz County, California, witnessed more deaths of their residents in military service in World War II than in all other US wars combined. During the Second World War, military reservists in the county were activated, recruiting offices were established and the selective service draft was re-instituted. Local servicemen were dispatched throughout the world and by the war's end, two hundred and forty five of its active duty residents and former residents had failed to return alive.

During 1940 it became obvious to government officials that war was inevitable and plans for US involvement were put into motion. In September the Burke-Wadsworth Selective Service Act was passed requiring young men between the ages of twenty-one to thirty to register with local draft boards, with inductions commencing in October. The initial draft enrollment in October 1940, registered 5,823 county men and concentrated on single men with a classification of class 1- (no deferment). By August of 1942, when manpower needs had increased, the draft board began reducing deferments to include class 2- (limited physical deferment) and class 3- (dependent deferrals). In December of 1943 the records of 4F's (physical deferments) were once again reviewed and by 1945 the Selective Service System was drafting more individuals over twenty-six years of age.

Individuals drafted during World War II were assigned to the various branches according to need, with most of the inductees being sent to the Army and Army Air Force.

The mobilization of reserve units within the state began in late 1940 and continued throughout 1941. In the fall of 1940, Company C of the 194th Tank Battalion increased the recruitment of local men at their Salinas armory. In February 1941 the company was mustered into federal service and sent to Ft. Lewis, Washington, for training. After a six-month training period, they boarded ships in San Francisco bound for the Philippine Islands and arrived at Manila in October 1941.

After the Japanese air attack on Clark Field at Manila on December 8, 1941, and the invasion of the Philippine Islands on December 21, Company C held off the Japanese until forced to surrender in May 1942. The survivors were sent to prison camps during the infamous Bataan Death March, where most remained until the end of the war or where they died.

In January 1942 military recruitment and induction into the armed forces increased significantly. Recruits and inductees from Santa Cruz County were sent to various basic training facilities, usually in the west. Fort Ord, Camp Roberts and Camp San Luis Obispo in California, Camps Adair and White in Oregon, Fort Lewis in Washington, and Camp Joseph T. Robinson in Arkansas are frequently listed among the recruit training centers.

The Army Air Corps trained its recruits throughout the US; however, primarily in the Western states. The AAC established training facilities in Utah, Arizona and Texas and at Hamilton Field, Santa Ana, Merced, and Sacramento California.

The Navy trained most of their new enlistees, called "boots," at San Diego, California, and at Farragut, Idaho, on Lake Pend Oreille. The Marine Corps' basic and school-of-infantry training facility was located at Camp Pendleton, California, and the Coast Guard trainees received their initial instruction in Alameda, California.

Between 1941 and 1946, two hundred and forty five residents and former residents from the county died while in service. Although the war officially ended with VJ Day, September 2, 1945, military demobilization continued throughout 1946. The first Santa Cruzan to die during the World War II period was Opal Chilcote, an army nurse, who died on May 31, 1941. David Rossi, a Merchant Marine, who was drowned on November 19, 1946, was the last recorded death of World War II.

BIOGRAPHICAL SKETCHES

Sept 16, 1940 Congress passes first peacetime draft for a period of one year and activates key reserve units

1941

May 27 Roosevelt declares an unlimited state of national emergency

OPAL F. CHILCOTE
(1941/05/31)

(Morro Rock & Bay, California)

The first Santa Cruz County World War II casualty to be listed in Watsonville's Roll of Honor was a thirty-one year-old army nurse.

Opal Fern Chilcote was born in Hanley, Iowa, on July 21, 1909, to Thomas and Estelle Chilcote. Also included in her family were four brothers, four sisters and a half sister. Opal spent a large portion of her formative years in Cheyenne, Wyoming, where the Chilcote family resided, but returned to Winterset, Iowa, where she graduated from St. Charles High School.

After being employed in a local doctors office for two years, she entered and completed a three-year nurse's training program at Lutheran Hospital in Iowa City, Iowa. She

later left the school's hospital and moved to Fresno where her mother resided. Opal then relocated to Watsonville and for two years was employed in the Third Street Hospital.

When the US began mobilization in early 1941, Opal Chilcote applied for a position in the Army Nurse Corps and was accepted. Commissioned a second lieutenant, Lt. Chilcote was assigned to an army facility in San Luis Obispo, California. On May 31, 1941, while boating in Morro Bay with friends and army associates, the boat in which she was a passenger capsized, throwing the occupants into the water. Opal Chilcote was drowned in the accident. Her body was recovered and sent to Fresno, California, for burial.

Second Lt. Opal Chilcote's death was the first (active duty) military death to be entered into the Pajaro Valley World War II Roll of Honor.

(WRP June 2, 1941 1:2, December 7, 1942; Winterset [Iowa] Madisonian - June 4, 1941)

RICHARD P. KIRBY
(1941/07/18)

(Camp McQuaide Album)

The first recorded death at Camp McQuaide, near Watsonville, California, was of a local youth.

Richard P. Kirby was born in Watsonville to Mr. and

Mrs. Thomas Kirby on November 22, 1922. Included in the Kirby family with Richard were sons Raymond, John and Edwin and daughter Loretta. Richard attended Moreland Notre Dame academy and became active in the Boy Scouts. He later enrolled in Watsonville High School and maintained a newspaper delivery route after school.

In July 1940, while still a student, Richard enlisted in the 250th Coast Artillery National Guard and was federally mobilized with that unit in September. Kirby was forced to leave school, but made plans to return after his tour of duty. Private Kirby was assigned to Battery D at nearby Camp McQuaide and served with that unit guarding Monterey bay for nine months.

On July 7 Kirby began experiencing a lower stomach pain that was diagnosed as appendicitis. An emergency appendectomy was performed; however, complications set in and attempts to save him failed. On July 18, 1941, Richard P. Kirby died at the station hospital.

Following a funeral at St. Patrick's Catholic Church in Watsonville, Private Richard Kirby was given a full military honor funeral and was buried in the Watsonville Catholic Cemetery.

(WRP July 18, 1941 1:3; CDR)

DADE O. YOUNGS JR.
(1941/09/02)

(Santa Cruz High School Service Cardinal)

Dade's date with destiny ended in a car in a garage before he could live out his navy role.

Dade Oliver Youngs Jr. was born to Dade and Christina Youngs on January 29, 1924, in Lemoore, California. When he was still young, the family moved to Santa Cruz, California, where Dade attended Mission Hill Junior High School. In the fall of 1938, Youngs enrolled in Santa Cruz High School where he majored in woodwork and cooking and served on the Junior Traffic Patrol.

Youngs left school early and on February 3, 1941, joined the US Navy. He was sent to San Diego for boot camp and upon completion, was trained as an aviation machin-

ist. Scoring high in his class, he was promoted to Aviation Machinist Mate second class.

While returning to the San Diego, California, naval base on September 2, 1941, Dade Youngs and four companions were passengers in an automobile that went out of control a short distance north of Santa Monica. The vehicle crashed through a fence, clipped off a corner of a house and smashed into a garage, killing Dade. His body was returned to Santa Cruz and buried in the Soquel Cemetery.

(SCSn September 3, 1941 1:5; SCHSC Pg. 21)

HENRY S. HAYDEN
(1941/09/19)

(Camp McQuaide Album)

Accompanying the name "Henry Stokes Hayden" on the December 2, 1942, *Watsonville Register-Pajaronian* Roll of Honor, was the comment, "Missing in Alaska."

Selective Service Records indicate that Henry Hayden was born in New Jersey in 1920. No information is available as to his birth, family or formative years. Enlistment records indicate that he had completed four years of high school, was single and worked as a photographer. It is not known when he arrived in the Pajaro Valley, nor by whom he was employed.

While residing in Santa Cruz County, he enlisted as a private in the 250th Coastal Artillery National Guard. On September 16, 1940, the unit was mustered into federal service and stationed at Camp McQuaide near Watsonville. At the camp Private Hayden was trained to be a coastal artillerymen and/or "army mine planter."

In order to strengthen the defense of the Alaskan coast the army ordered the 250th Coast Artillery from Camp McQuaide to the area of Sitka, Alaska in June 1941. Henry Hayden departed with his battery from San Francisco on September 12, 1941, aboard the *SS Chirkof.* They arrived in Seattle on September 15 and three days later, left for Alaska. During the month of September, his unit was deployed on a windswept island two miles wide and ten miles long, located seven miles across a choppy sea from Kodiak, Alaska.

The circumstances behind Hayden's death are not known, but the American Battlefield Monument Commission records note that on September 19, 1941, Henry Hayden was "Missing in Action or Buried at Sea."

(NARA2; ABMC; SCSn Sept 18 1941, 8:8; WRP December 7, 1942)

December 7 Japanese Bomb Pearl Harbor and destroy US Fleet in surprise attack

---

CLIFFORD T. JANZ
(1941/12/07)

(USS Arizona Memorial – Internet photo)

A world-class event brought an end to the life of a navy lieutenant during a day of infamy.

US Census information suggests that Clifford Thurston Janz was born in New York about 1911. That same 1920 census lists him as a boarder in the household of Frank and Hattie Loomis of Plymouth, Michigan. No record of his formative years or relationship to Santa Cruz County has been found.

The date of his entry into the US Navy is not known; however, casualty records for the *USS Arizona* indicate that he was commissioned on December 10, 1938. Clifford Janz was married during this period; his wife remained in San Diego while he was away at sea.

On December 7, 1941, Lt. Clifford Janz was serving as an engineering officer aboard the battleship *USS Arizona*, which was moored on Ford Island in Pearl Harbor, as Japanese planes flew over the Pali on the island of Oahu. In an official report issued following the war, Ensign D. Hein, a survivor or the attack stated,

At about two or three minutes before 0800 Sunday, I was asleep in my room when I faintly heard a siren. Shortly thereafter I distinctly heard G.Q. I put some clothes on and went up from lower wardroom country to the second deck. Lt. C.T. Janz was sending everyone in the vicinity to shelter below the armored deck. I went down with Lt. Janz and about forty enlisted men. Before we could close the hatch,

there were three violent blasts with flame and powder fumes entering the compartment. I then told all personnel in the vicinity to get out and go topside to avoid the gas. About twenty (20) enlisted personnel and myself went topside. I saw the entire ship forward of #3 turret to be a raging fire."

This explosion likely took the life of Lt. Janz. His remains were never recovered. Janz is memorialized on the Tablets of the Missing at the US National Cemetery in Honolulu.

(http://www.patriotfiles.com/index.php?name=Sections&req=view article&artid=1134&allpages=1&theme=Printer [April 10, 2009)]; USCR, 1920 US Census, MI, Plymouth; ABMC; SCSn November 11, 1944; DANFS, USS Arizona BB-39)

December 8 United States and Britain declare war on Japan.

ROBERT R. MCLENNAN
(1941/12/08)

Robert R. McLennan was born to Mr. and Mrs. William R. McLennan in Texas in 1913. The family later moved to Watsonville, where Robert lived for an undetermined period of time. His enlistment records note that he had graduated from high school, attended a college for one year and in 1940 was living in Stanislaus County, California.

On August 10, 1940, McLennan enlisted in the regular US Army Air Force as a private at the Presidio of Monterey and requested duty in the Philippine Islands. Following his basic training, he was assigned to the 7th Material Squadron, 19th Bomb Group, located in Albuquerque, New Mexico.

In September 1941 the squadron was ordered to San Francisco to join other units bound for the Philippines. They remained at Angel Island until October 4 and then departed for Honolulu. When they arrived at Manila Bay on October 24, they were garrisoned at Clark Field near Manila.

The squadron was completing preparations for a move to Del Monte Airbase on the island of Mindanao, but before that could take place the Japanese attacked. On December 8, 1941, four hours after the Japanese bombed Pearl Harbor, they bombed Clark Field. During that attack, Private Robert R. McLennan was killed and his remains were never recovered.

He is memorialized on the Tablets of the Missing at Manila American Cemetery.

(NARA2: ABMC; *Watsonville Morning Sun* January 1, 1942 1:5; 19th Bomb Group, Clark Field P.I. 1941, http://www.7th-material.org/ (16 September 2008])

WILLIAM R. BURNS
(1941/12/10)

December 24, 1941, was not the joyful holiday that Loiya Burns had prepared for her husband.

William Richard Burns was born about 1906. No information is available as to his parents, place of birth, siblings or formative years.

Burns joined the US Navy in 1925 and throughout his naval career, he served on various ships and at several posts. He continued to advance in rank and by 1941, was a Yeoman first class.

While in the navy, he met and married Loiya Galeener of Watsonville, California. His petty officer rating afforded him an opportunity to have his wife and eleven-year old son, Dennis, accompany him in Hawaii. In June 1941 Loiya and Dennis returned to California and made their home with her parents in the Pajaro Valley.

Petty Officer First Class William Richard Burns was serving in the vicinity of the Philippine Islands on December 10, 1941, when he was killed in action or buried at sea. The telegram notifying his widow of his death arrived at the family home on Christmas Eve.

His body was never recovered and he is memorialized on the Tablets of the Missing at Manila American Cemetery. His awards include the Purple Heart.

(ABMC; Watsonville Morning Sun December 28, 1941 1:2)

RALPH W. THOMPSON
(1941/12/11)

(Santa Cruz High School Service Cardinal)

A quiet country boy from North Carolina with a strong singing voice heard a different sound on December 7, 1941.

Ralph William Thompson was born in Hendersonville, North Carolina, on April 21, 1917, to Frank and Christine Thompson. Two sisters rounded out the family. Christine had moved to Santa Cruz with Ralph and her two daughters; Frank remained in North Carolina. She settled the family into a residence on Berkshire Street and enrolled

Ralph in Mission Hills Junior High School. In 1932 Ralph entered Santa Cruz High School and took a general varied course but his special interest was the choir. After graduating from high school in 1936, Ralph worked as a landscape gardener in Redwood City, California.

In December 1940 Thompson joined the US Navy and entered boot camp in San Diego. Throughout 1941 he attended additional navy schools and served as a Fireman Third Class. In October he received orders to report aboard the *USS Helena* berthed at Pearl Harbor.

When the Japanese attacked on December 7, 1941, Ralph was seriously wounded and hospitalized. He died on December 11 and is buried at the US National Cemetery in Hawaii.

(ABMC; SCR [month/date missing]/1942; SCHSC, Pg. 19; SCSn May 5, 1942 2:6)

HENRY SCHIPPER JR.
(1941/12/25)

(Photo courtesy University of North Dakota Special Collections)

Christmas Day 1941 was long remembered in the Schipper family, but not for bringing good tidings of great joy.

Henry Schipper Jr. was born on January 15, 1910, in Duluth, Minnesota, to Mr. and Mrs. Henry Schipper Sr. The Schipper's later moved to Casselton, North Dakota, with their sons Henry, Ted, Lester, Howard and George and daughters Lois and Geraldine. Henry Jr. attended Casselton High School and after graduation, enrolled in the University of North Dakota, where he majored in commerce.

In addition to his scholastic curriculum Henry joined the Reserve Officers Training Corps and considered a career as an army officer. When he received his degree in 1932, Henry Schipper was also commissioned a second lieutenant in the Army Reserve.

The Schipper family moved to Santa Cruz about 1933. Henry accompanied them and found employment in what was described as the "commercial area." Lt. Schipper continued to remain active in the local army reserve.

In 1933 Henry married Evelyn Lukins, a Santa Cruz

girl, and in 1935 their daughter Judith was born. In the late 1930s, Henry, Evelyn and Judith moved to San Bruno, California, to be closer to the Butler Brothers Store in San Francisco where he was manager of the carpet department.

In 1940, with war clouds gathering in the Pacific, First Lieutenant Henry Schipper was activated by the army and sent to Fort Ord in Monterey. This was followed by a brief assignment at Fort Benning, Georgia. In September 1941 Lt. Schipper was sent to the Philippines and attached to the 72nd Infantry Regiment of the 71st Philippine Infantry Division. In October he was promoted to Captain and assumed responsibility for the training of a battalion of Filipino recruits.

When the Japanese invaded the Philippines in December 1941, Schipper and the recruit battalion he was training on the island of Manbucal were ordered to the defense of Manila. On Christmas Day, 1941, Captain Henry Schipper Jr. was killed in action. His remains were later recovered and interred in the Manila American Cemetery. His awards include Philippines Awards, the Silver Star and Purple Heart.

(ABMC; SCSn December 25, 1941 16:3, January 4, 1942 1:7, January 7, 1942 2:8)

1942

MELVIN L. ORR
(1942/01/04)

(Golden Gate National Cemetery – San Bruno California)

His request for duty in the Philippines was granted and with it, an appointment with death.

Melvin Orr was born on May 25, 1920, to Mr. and Mrs. Mervin L. Orr of Fresno, California. In addition to Melvin, the Orr family included sons Vernon, Myron, Darrell and Kenneth and a daughter Beverly. Melvin spent much of his formative years in Santa Cruz, where his father repaired cash registers and typewriters. While living in Santa Cruz, young Melvin worked in a restaurant at the beach. In 1934 the Orr

family returned to Fresno where he completed three years of high school. He remained in the Central Valley until the time of his enlistment.

On October 3, 1941, Melvin Orr enlisted in the regular US Army Quartermaster Corps and requested assignment in the Philippine Islands. After completing basic training, Orr was sent to the Philippines and posted to Fort Mills.

In December 1941, war was declared and the Japanese began bombing raids on the fort. During a particularly heavy aerial bombardment on January 4, 1942, Private Melvin L. Orr was killed. His commanding officer later wrote to his parents recounting the youth's courage and bravery while under attack.

Melvin was initially buried on the post grounds, but his remains were later exhumed and shipped to the Golden Gate Cemetery in San Bruno, California for reburial in 1949.

(NARA2; USDVA; SCSn April 2, 1942 8:5)

THOMAS H. VERHINES
(1942/01/09)

(Santa Cruz Riptide photo)

Thomas Verhines left a wife and daughter to re-experience a military messenger of death.

Thomas Henry Verhines was born September 9, 1921, to A. C. and Gertrude Verhines in Fresno, California, where his father worked as a building contractor. The family, consisting of sons Kenneth and Clarence and daughter Margaret, moved to Santa Cruz and settled into a home on Windham Street. About 1940 Verhines married Elizabeth Jacobs in Santa Cruz.

Thomas Verhines joined the naval reserve in 1941; it was about this time that the couple's daughter Helen was born. On May 6, 1941, Seaman Second Class Verhines was called to active duty and left immediately for Hawaii where he was assigned to the *USS St. Louis* berthed at Pearl Harbor. While serving aboard that ship, Seaman Verhines developed a tumor in his knee and entered the US Naval hospital to have it removed. His medical condition became more serious than was initially diagnosed and he remained in the hospital in Hawaii for three months.

In October Verhines was returned to California and admitted to the naval hospital in Vallejo for additional treatments. Over the next two months his condition deteriorated and on January 9, 1942, he died. Following a funeral he was buried at Golden Gate National Cemetery in San Bruno.

A sad footnote to the story was the ongoing tragedy encountered by his wife, Elizabeth, who later married Clemens Lambrecht, a soldier who was killed in France, leaving her a widow for a second time. Clemens Lambrecht also appears on the county's Roll of Honor.

(USDVA; SCSn August 30, 1941 5:4, January 10, 1942 1:8; DANFS, USS St. Louis CL-49)

WILLIAM M. DeSHIELDS
(1942/03/01)

William DeShields, the cruiser *USS Houston,* and the Sunda Straits all triangulated at the wrong time.

William Martin DeShields was born in Fresno County California, on June 12, 1912, to Mr. and Mrs. Lewis DeShields. In 1920 he and his sister Mildred were living with their father in Fresno, who was a "packing house" superintendent.

William entered the US Navy sometime in the 1930s and received boot camp training in San Diego. By 1942 he had risen to the rank of quartermaster first class and was serving aboard the heavy cruiser *USS Houston*.

On February 26, 1942 a large Japanese convoy was seen moving toward the Java Sea and the *Houston*, along with Dutch and British vessels under the command of Dutch Vice Admiral Karel W.F.M. Doorman, was ordered to intercept and destroy it. The Japanese fleet was encountered and the Battle of the Java Sea commenced. Following that encounter, the Battle of the Sunda Strait took place on March 1, 1942.

Before losing contact with Perth *and* Houston*, Doorman had ordered them to retire. This was accomplished, but the next day the two ships steamed into Banten Bay, hoping to damage the Japanese invasion forces there. The cruisers were almost torpedoed as they approached the bay, but evaded the nine torpedoes launched by destroyer* Fubuki.

The cruisers then sank one transport and forced three others to beach. A destroyer squadron blocked Sunda *Strait, their means of retreat, and on the other hand large cruisers* Mogami *and* Mikuma *stood dangerously near. The resulting battle was foreordained, but* Houston *and* Perth *could not withdraw.* Perth *came under fire at 23:36 and in an hour had been sunk from gunfire and torpedo hits.* Houston *then fought alone until soon after midnight, when she took*

a torpedo and began to lose headway. During this time Houston's *gunners scored hits on three different destroyers and sank a minesweeper, but suffered three more torpedo explosions in quick succession. Captain Albert Rooks was killed by a bursting shell at 00:30 and as the ship came to a stop Japanese destroyers moved in, machine gunning the decks. A few minutes later the* Houston *rolled over and sank, her ensign still flying. Of the original crew of 1,061 only 368 survived.*

The body of Quartermaster First Class William M. DeShields was never recovered, and the Navy officially declared him dead on December 15, 1945. He is memorialized on the Tablets of the Missing at Manila American Cemetery. His awards include the Purple Heart.

(CBR; USCR, 1920 US Census, CA, Fresno; ABMC; SCSn May 15, 1942 1:2; USNM; WIKI, USS Houston CL/CA-30)

RICHARD M. BLOOD
(1942/05/07)

(Santa Cruz High School Service Cardinal)

Richard awaited rescue from a life raft that arrived too late.

Richard M. Blood was born on January 25, 1922, in San Jose, California, to Mr. and Mrs. (Maude) Blood. Little is known of his parents and siblings. Richard enrolled in Santa Cruz High School in the fall of 1937 and was active in swimming and other sports. The SCHS *Service Cardinal* also noted "On October 26, 1938, Richard Blood moved to Los Angeles where he completed his education."

In 1939 Blood enlisted in the US Navy and began basic training at the US Naval Training Center in San Diego. After additional instruction, he became a Yeoman. By 1942 Richard Blood had risen to the rank of Yeoman Second Class and been assigned to the USS Neosho, a cargo and refueling ship. Petty Officer Blood was with the Neosho when it met its end during the Battle of the Coral Sea.

As the American and Japanese fleets sought each other out in the opening maneuvers of the climactic Battle of the Coral Sea on 6 May 1942, Neosho *fueled* Yorktown *(CV-5) and*

Astoria (CA-34), *then retired from the carrier force with a lone escort,* Sims (DD-409). *Next day at 10:00, Japanese aircraft spotted the two ships, and believing them to be a carrier and her escort, launched the first of two attacks which sank* Sims *and left* Neosho, *victim of 7 direct hits and a suicide dive by one of the bombers. Ablaze aft and in danger of breaking in two, she had shot down at least 3 of the attackers. Superb seamanship and skilled damage control work kept* Neosho *afloat for the next four days. The sorely stricken ship was first located by an RAAF aircraft, then by an American PBY* Catalina. *At 13:00, 11 May,* Henley (DD-391) *arrived to rescue the 123 survivors and to sink by gunfire, the ship they had so valiantly kept alive against impossible odds.*

Richard M. Blood was not among those survivors. He is reported to have died on a sixty-eight-man life raft while awaiting rescue. His body was turned over to the sea and he is memorialized on the Tablets of the Missing at Manila American Cemetery.

(ABMC; SCHSC, pg. 5; WIKI, USS Neosho; Del's Journey.com, USS Neosho at Coral Sea, List of Survivors and Casualties http://www.delsjourney.com/uss_neosho/coral_sea/neosho_at_coral_sea/survivors_and_casualties.htm, [16 September 2008])

JOHN C. LANTAGNE
(1942/05/26)

(Manila American Cemetery circa 1946 - Internet photo)

John Lantagne would be the first of many local GI's to die in a Japanese POW Camp.

John C. Lantagne was born on October 10, 1918, in Santa Cruz, California, to Mr. E. and Rose Lantagne. The family also included sons Joseph and Dore and daughter Mary. John later moved to San Jose where he attended San Jose High School. In 1937 he returned to Santa Cruz and enrolled in Santa Cruz High School, but left after his junior year. John remained in the county after leaving school and worked as a farm hand.

On February 24, 1941, Lantagne enlisted in the US Army and was sent to Fort Lewis, Washington, for basic training. Upon completing the basic course he was assigned to the 194th Tank Battalion. In September 1941 the tank battal-

ion was sent to the Philippine Islands and assigned to Fort Stotsenberg near Clark Field and Manila.

When the Japanese invaded the islands in late December 1941, John's unit defended Manila before retreating to the Bataan Peninsula, where they were ordered to hold the Japanese army as long as possible. When their food and supplies gave out on April 9, they surrendered.

Private John C. Lantagne was included in the infamous Bataan Death March and later housed at the Camp O'Donnell prison. Lantagne was reported to have died May 26, 1942, while imprisoned and was buried at the compound.

At the conclusion of the war his remains were disinterred and reburied in the Manila American Cemetery.

(ABMC; NARA2; SCHSC, Pg. 16; SCSn June 13, 1947)

ORRIN H. EATON
(1942/05/28)

(Watsonville High School yearbook)

Orrin carried the Civil War tradition of his grandfather with him into World War II.

Orrin Henry Eaton, a native of Watsonville, California, was born on April 20, 1918, to Orrin O. and Cecilia Eaton who lived on the San Juan Road in the Pajaro Valley. Orrin and his sisters, Muriel and Katherine, attended local grammar schools. Later he transferred to the Montezuma School for Boys near Los Gatos and graduated about 1936. He then entered the University of California Davis agricultural school.

On December 20, 1940, Orrin joined the National Guard and in February, transferred into Company C of the 194th Tank Battalion in Salinas. He trained with that unit at Fort Lewis, Washington, and accompanied them to Fort Stotsenberg in the Philippine Islands the following September.

In late December, 1941, when the Japanese invaded the Philippines, the tank battalion attempted to defend Manila; however, they were forced to retreat to the Bataan peninsula. During this period, Corporal Eaton served as a tank driver until forced to surrender in April 1942.

Orrin Eaton participated in the Bataan Death March; however, the name of the prison camp in which he was housed is not available. Soon after arrival in that camp, his health gave out and on May 28, 1942, he died. His remains were later recovered and buried in the Manila American Cemetery.

(CBR; NARA2; ABMC; 194TB; WRP June 5, 1945 1:4)

JAMES W. RICKEL JR..
(1942/06/04)

Hanging in the window of the Rickel home in Watsonville was the city's first gold star flag.

James Wilson Rickel Jr. was born about 1919 to Mr. and Mrs. James W. Rickel. James, along with brothers Vernon and Sidney and sisters Opal and Beulah, shared the family Watsonville home and attended local schools. He enrolled in Watsonville High School; however, there is no record of his graduation.

When World War II broke out, James Rickel joined the US Navy and following boot camp in San Diego, received training as an electrician. He was promoted to Electrician's Mate Third Class and assigned to the aircraft carrier *USS Yorktown.*

Quick repairs [following the battle of the Coral Sea] *at Pearl Harbor put* Yorktown *into good enough condition to participate in the Battle of Midway on 4-6 June 1942. During this great turning point of the Pacific War, her air group fatally damaged the Japanese aircraft carrier* Soryu *and shared in the destruction of the carrier* Hiryu *and cruiser* Mikuma. *However, successive strikes by dive-bombers and torpedo planes from* Hiryu *seriously damaged* Yorktown, *causing her abandonment during the afternoon of 4 June. Two days later, while salvage efforts were underway, the Japanese submarine I-168 torpedoed both the damaged carrier and the destroyer* Hammann (DD-412), *sinking the latter immediately and* Yorktown *shortly after daybreak on 7 June 1942.*

Rickel was initially declared Missing in Action; however, a family member confirmed his death. James' uncle was a member of the navy salvage crew that boarded the *Yorktown* after it was first bombed and torpedoed June 4. "Opening the hatch into the compartment where young Rickel was stationed, the salvagers found it filled with water and oil indicating that the men within had all perished."

Petty Officer Third Class James Wilson Rickel was officially declared dead on June 5, 1943, and memorialized on the Tablets of the Missing at Honolulu Memorial Cemetery. His awards include the Purple Heart.

(ABMC; W DANFS; USS Yorktown CV-5; WRP July 11, 1942 1:2, September 16, 1942 1:8)

MANUEL L. BERNARD JR.
(1942/06/11)

(194 Tank Memorial Garden of Memories - Salinas, California)

Manuel L. Bernard Jr. was born in California in 1916 to Mr. and Mrs. Manuel L. Bernard Sr. No additional information is available regarding his siblings or early education; however, his high school education probably took place outside of Santa Cruz County. Bernard's enlistment records indicate that he had completed two years of college (possibly Salinas Junior College), had worked as a bookkeeper and was married.

Bernard probably enrolled in Company C of the 194th Tank Battalion in Salinas, between September 1940 and February 1941, when the company was being formed. He was assigned the rank of staff sergeant and mustered into federal service with the tank company on August 26, 1941, at Ft. Lewis, Washington. In September, Sergeant Bernard and Company C were ordered to Fort Stotsenberg in the Philippine Islands.

When the Japanese invaded the Philippines in late December 1941, Manuel Bernard fought with his tank battalion in the defense of Manila and in its retreat to the Bataan peninsula.

Following the surrender of US forces and the infamous Bataan death march, Sergeant Manuel L. Bernard Jr. was sent to prisoner of war Camp O'Donnell where he died of dysentery on June 11, 1942.

Originally buried at the camp, his remains were later reburied in the Manila American Cemetery at Manila.

(NARA2; ABMC; 194TB)

JACK D. BRINK
(1942/06/15)

(Internet photo)

A Watsonville High School "Wildcat" experienced the Bataan Death March

Jack D. Brink was born in Michigan in 1921, and would have likely attended Watsonville High School between the years 1935 and 1941. His enlistment record indicated that he had completed four years of high school; however, his graduation from a local high school has not been confirmed. Following school Brink went into the entertainment business, remained single and was living in Salinas, California, at the time of his enlistment.

Brink probably joined the National Guard between September 1940, when they were being formed and February 1941, when they departed for Fort Lewis, Washington. Soon after his arrival in the Philippine Islands in the fall of 1941, he was promoted to sergeant. He participated in the defense of the Philippines and his unit's last-ditch stand on the Bataan Peninsula. Sergeant Jack Brink survived the Bataan Death March but died on June 15, 1942, while interned at Cabanatuan Prison Camp.

Brink's remains were never recovered, but his name is recorded on the Tablets of the Missing at Manila American Cemetery.

(NARA2; ABMC; 194TB; http://www.proviso.k12. il.us/bataan%20Web/194_Poster.htm)

EDWARD G. DELONG
1942/07/02)

(US Naval Academy photo)

"Hello Joe," were the sweetest words heard by a local *American Guerilla in the Philippines.*

The small town of Springfield, South Dakota, was the scene of Edward Grover DeLong's birth on August 20, 1915, to Arthur and Sarah Delong. Edward attended local Springfield elementary schools and graduated from the high school in 1932. After a year at the state college, he entered the United States Naval Academy at Annapolis, from which he was graduated in 1937. An assignment on the West Coast took him to Stanford University where he met and married Helen Ris, a Santa Cruz girl.

In 1941 Lt. Delong received orders sending him to sea; and his wife Helen returned to Santa Cruz to live with her mother and father, who managed the local Woolworth store. During 1941, Lt. DeLong served aboard a battleship and destroyer before being transferred to (PT) Motorboat Subchaser, Division 3, in June. Following a month of instruction, Edward DeLong was assigned as an engineering officer with a torpedo boat squadron in the Philippines.

During the Japanese invasion of the Islands in December 1941, Edward's squadron intercepted and destroyed a number of Japanese vessels in Subic Bay. On January 30, 1942, the *Lead Daily Call*, a South Dakota newspaper reported that,

> *Edward DeLong, lieutenant junior grade, from Springfield, S.D., returned with ten naval men from a perilous mission behind Japanese lines on the Bataan peninsula on the night of January 18th, [they had] accomplished their mission and then found themselves faced with the job of returning individually to their base... While trying to get back to base, DeLong encountered a native with a bayoneted rifle. After a moment of startled silence, the native spoke first, saying, "Hello, Joe," which DeLong said, "were the sweetest words I ever heard."*

Following the surrender of American forces at Bataan on

April 9, 1942, a number of Americans continued to resist the Japanese in the islands as depicted in the 1950 movie *American Guerilla in the Philippines*. While attempting to escape in a native boat, Edward DeLong and a fellow officer were captured on the Island of Bangka, North Celebes, and were taken by the Japanese to Manado. In the garden of Lie Boen Yat, Saris, Manado, on July 2, 1942, Lt. Edward Grover DeLong was executed by the Japanese and buried in a common grave.

(SCSn January 27, 1942 1:4, June 30, 1942 1:3, December 17, 1942 1:5, South Dakota State, US Military, Veteran Affairs Fallen Sons Daughters Profiles, plus photo http://www.state.sd.us/military/ VetAffairs/sdwwiimemorial/SubPages/profiles/Display.asp?P=434, [Approx. May 2007])

VICTOR L. GOSNEY
(1942/07/06)

(Courtesy Judy Doering-Nielsen)

Canada sent Watsonville one of her native sons to join the famous Salinas tank company.

Victor L. Gosney was born in Victoria, British Columbia, Canada, in July 1917, to Alfred and Jennie Gosney. The Gosney family also included another son and four daughters. It is believed that the family initially settled in San Jose; however, by 1941 all of their children, including Victor, had relocated to Monterey and Santa Cruz counties. Victor attended Watsonville High School for two years and after leaving school, worked in a service station.

Sometime between September and December 1940 Victor Gosney joined Company C of the 194th Tank Company of the National Guard located in Salinas. Private Gosney accompanied the unit to Fort Lewis, Washington, for training in February 1941. The tank company set sail for the Philippine Islands the following September and by the time they arrived in October, Gosney had been promoted to sergeant. Company C was initially stationed at Fort Stotsenberg with the mission of helping defend Clark Field and the city of Manila.

When bombing attacks by the Japanese began on Decem-

ber 8, 1941, the tank company set up defensive positions and prepared for the inevitable invasion. When the invasion came, they were unable to stop the Japanese and were forced to retreat to the Bataan peninsula. By containing the Japanese for three months, the Bataan defenders enabled allied forces to set up defenses in Australia that were instrumental in preventing an invasion of that country.

After surrendering in May 1942, Sergeant Victor L. Gosney completed the infamous Bataan Death March to Cabanatuan prison camp. It was later reported that he died in the prison on July 6, 1942, from the malaria and dysentery. His body was initially buried at the camp; however, his remains were later removed and reburied in the Manila American Cemetery.

(NARA2; ABMC; WRP June 4, 1945 1:4; http://www.proviso.k12.il.us/bataan%20Web/194_Poster.htm)

RALPH E. MORRISON
(1942/08/03)

(Santa Cruz High School yearbook)

The year and place of Ralph Morrison's birth, his parentage and names of his siblings have not been identified. Ralph came to Santa Cruz High School in the fall of 1924 and served as head coach of the football, track and basketball teams until 1930. While living in the community, he was an active member of the Kiwanis Club.

About 1928 Morrison became interested in aviation and spent the summer in San Diego learning to fly. When he returned to Santa Cruz, he frequently took passengers and students with him on his flights out of the old Capitola airport. Later he obtained a transport license and was one of several pilots hired by William Randolph Hearst to fly guests to and from Los Angeles and San Francisco to Hearst's San Simeon ranch.

In 1942 Ralph entered the Army Air Corps and trained at Santa Ana, California. He was commissioned a lieutenant and stationed at Helena, Montana, before being assigned to a bomber squadron at McDill Field, Florida.

When C. E. "Doc" Fehliman, Santa Cruz High School

teacher and historian, attempted to write to Morrison in early 1943, the letters were returned with the notation "this man is deceased." US Air Force Accident Report records indicate that Ralph E. Morrison was flying an AT-11 aircraft out of Victorville AAF base, California, when it crashed on August 3, 1942.

It is believed that Morrison's remains were not recovered (SCSn March 2, 1943 1:2; AAIR; Photo-SCHS)

ROBERT E. OVERSTREET
(1942/08/05)

(Santa Cruz High School Service Cardinal)

To many Santa Cruzans Bob Overstreet would always be remembered as a fiddle player in a hillbilly band.

Robert E. Overstreet was born in California on September 9, 1922, to Claude and Grace Overstreet. The family, which also included his brother William and sisters Fay and Fern, later moved to Santa Cruz. Upon completing elementary and junior high schools Overstreet enrolled in Santa Cruz High School. To supplement his allowance he worked as a newspaper carrier for the *Santa Cruz Sentinel* and at Miller's hot dog stand on the beach boardwalk. During his high school years, Overstreet was frequently seen playing a fiddle in a local hillbilly band.

Following graduation from high school in 1940, Robert Overstreet attended Salinas Junior College for one semester. It was probably during that period that he enlisted in Company C of the 194th Tank Battalion of the National Guard.

Private Overstreet trained at Fort Lewis, Washington, from February to September 1941, and then shipped out with his company to the Philippine Islands. After arriving at Manila on September 27, 1941, he served at nearby Fort Stotsenburg. While stationed there, he rose in rank to a Technician Fifth Grade.

When the Japanese invaded the island in December 1941, Overstreet helped defend Manila and the Bataan peninsula before being forced to surrender on April 9, 1942. After surviving the Bataan Death March, he was confined to Cabanatuan Prison Camp #1 in the Philippines until his death from unspecified causes on August 5, 1942.

After World War II, the remains of Robert E. Overstreet were exhumed and returned to the US for reburial in Golden Gate National Cemetery in San Bruno, California on July 24, 1950.

(NARA2; SCHSC Pg. 15; USDVA; 194TB; SCSn May 21, 1943 1:5; SCR May 28,1943)

JAMES B. BEAN
(1942/08/07)

A Zayante transplant from Arkansas went down with his ship at Savo Island.

James Buchanan Bean was born January 22, 1917, in Oklahoma. His mother's name was Miranda. In addition to James the family included his brother Raymond and sisters Robbie and Flay. James' father died early in his life and his widowed mother moved into her parents' home in Red Lick, Arkansas. Jim spent his early life in Arkansas before moving to California with his mother and at least one of his sisters, and settling at Zayante in Santa Cruz County.

James returned to Arkansas in December 1936 and joined the US Navy. After completing boot camp in San Diego, he was trained to be a gunner's mate. When Pearl Harbor was attacked on December 7, 1941, James had only three days remaining on his enlistment; however, he re-enlisted for the duration of the war.

Gunner's Mate Second Class James Bean reported aboard an unspecified US navy cruiser (Probably the *USS Vincennes, Astoria* or *Quincy*), which was deployed to the Coral Sea.

Three US cruisers sunk during the one hour 1st Battle of Savo Island by a force of Japanese warships including five heavy cruisers, two light cruisers and one destroyer. The American warships were protecting and escorting US troop transports en route to Guadalcanal. Total losses from the three ships amounted to 1,077 men killed and 709 wounded. On the USS Astoria *216 men were killed. The* Vincennes *lost 332 men and 529 men were lost on the* Quincy. *Many of the blood- and- oil covered survivors, struggling in the water fell victim to the sharks. Japanese casualties were only 58 killed and 70 wounded. The catastrophe at Savo Island was a demoralizing defeat for the Allies and the worst defeat ever suffered by the United States Navy.*

During the action at Savo Island on August 7, 1942, the cruiser on which Bean served was sunk. Petty Officer Second Class James Buchanan Bean was initially listed as Missing in Action, and was officially declared dead on August 10, 1943.

James Bean was awarded the Purple Heart posthumously and memorialized on the Tablets of the Missing at Manila

American Cemetery in the Philippines.

(ABMC; 1920 US Census, AR, Red Lick; SCSn September 17, 1942 1:6, May 21, 1944 5:6; DANFS, *USS Vincennes* CA; Editor, *USS Quincy* at Savo Island, http://www.ussquincy.com/quincyws121200/39_text2.html, [Approx. May 2007])

Aʀᴛʜᴜʀ R. McLᴀᴜɢʜʟɪɴ
(1942/08/09)

(Santa Cruz High School Service Cardinal)

Art applied all his leadership skills in vain in one last effort to assist his damaged ship.

Arthur Richard McLaughlin was born in Berkeley, California, on February 13, 1917, and at a very young age moved with his parents to Soquel, California. The family was later expanded to include a second son, Jack, and a daughter. Arthur remained in Soquel for the next seventeen years, attended Soquel Union Grammar School and in 1930 entered Santa Cruz High School. In addition to achieving scholastic excellence, he played football and served as the school's student body president.

McLauglin graduated from high school in June 1934 and enrolled at the University of California. At Berkeley he played football, majored in commerce and participated in the NROTC program. In 1939 McLaughlin received his BS degree and a commission as an ensign in the US Naval Reserve. From Berkeley he moved to Hawaii where he was employed in his uncle's bank.

In December 1940 Arthur McLaughlin was called into active duty and assigned to the *USS Astoria*. While serving aboard that ship, he was promoted to Lt. (jg). On December 7, 1941, his ship was steaming toward Midway Island, which saved it from the carnage at Pearl Harbor. During the first six months of the war, Arthur's ship was engaged in the battles of the Coral Sea and Midway and he was promoted to the rank of lieutenant. In August the *Astoria* headed for the Solomon Islands and Arthur McLaughlin's final adventure.

On the night of 8 August and 9 August [1942], a Japanese force of seven cruisers and a destroyer under Rear Admiral Gunichi Mikawa sneaked by Savo Island and attacked the American ships. At the time, Astoria *had been patrolling to the east of Savo Island in column behind* Vincennes *and* Quincy. *The Japanese came through the channel to the west of Savo Island and opened fire on the* Chicago *and* HMAS Canberra *at about 01:40 on the morning of the 9th hitting both cruisers with torpedoes and shells. They then divided—inadvertently—into two separate groups and turned generally northeast passing on either side of* Astoria *and her two consorts. The enemy cruisers began firing on that force at about 01:50, and the heavy cruiser began return fire immediately. She ceased fire briefly because her commanding officer temporarily mistook the Japanese force for friendly ships but soon resumed shooting.* Astoria *took no hits in the first four Japanese salvoes, but the fifth ripped into her superstructure turning her into an inferno amidships. In quick succession, enemy shells put her number 1 turret out of action and started a serious fire in the plane hangar that burned brightly and provided the enemy with a self-illuminated target..*

The Santa Cruz High School Service Cardinal reported that McLaughlin met a heroic death, "At the start of the action in which he was killed, Arthur was relieved by the regular sky control officer, then made his own battle station. A violent explosion killed him and all of his men on August 9." His body was never recovered and is memorialized on the Tablets of the Missing at Manila American Cemetery. His awards include the Purple Heart.

(ABMC; SCHSC, Pg. 13; WIKI, *USS Astoria* CA-34; SCSn September 11, 1942, 6:5)

Hᴇʀᴍᴀɴ J. Vᴇʟʟᴜᴛɪɴɪ
(1942/08/09)

(Internet photo)

"Herman Vellutini Now Reported as Killed in Action" confirmed the *Santa Cruz Sentinel*.

Herman Junior Vellutini was born March 9, 1923, in Sonoma County, California, the son of Herman and Esther Vellutini of Healdsburg. In 1938 Herman died and Esther, with her sons, Herman, Frank, Fred and Walter, moved to Santa Cruz. Esther subsequently remarried and acquired the Postal Lunch Restaurant on Water Street. During his brief Santa Cruz residency, Herman found employment at the Washington Market.

In 1940, at the age of seventeen, Vellutini joined the navy and following boot camp in San Diego, was assigned to the destroyer *USS Jarvis*.

Jarvis was employed on patrol and escort work in the south Pacific until mid-July, when she joined the task force that was preparing for the US Navy's first major Pacific War offensive undertaking, the invasion of Guadalcanal and Tulagi. Arriving in the invasion area on 7 August 1942, Jarvis covered the landing forces as they put US Marines ashore. The next day, a torpedo hit her when Japanese aircraft counter-attacked. Though badly damaged and down at the bow, she was still seaworthy enough to proceed independently to Australia for repairs. While steaming past the northeastern end of Guadalcanal during the night of 9 August, she was briefly and ineffectively engaged by Japanese ships during the Battle of Savo Island. Shortly after noon on that day, USS Jarvis was attacked by an overwhelming force of Japanese land-based bombers. Hit repeatedly, she was lost with her entire crew.

The body of Ships Clerk Third Class Herman Vellutini was never recovered and he was officially classified as deceased July 12, 1945.

He is memorialized on the Tablets of the Missing at Manila American Cemetery. His awards include the Purple Heart.

(CBR; ABMC; SCSn August 16, 1945 1:8, DANFS, USS Jarvis)

RAYMON W. DAVIS
(1942/08/27)

(Clark Field Cemetery, Manila PI, 1945 – Internet photo)

Ray requested duty in the Philippine Islands and unfortunately his request was granted.

Raymon Woodrow Davis was born in 1913 in Oklahoma. Nothing has surfaced as to his family; however, he had at least one brother, Lewis, who lived in Watsonville. Raymon Davis attended Watsonville Union High School for two years before dropping out of school. Prior to World War II, he worked as a cook in the Pajaro Valley.

On January 14, 1941, Davis enlisted in the regular US Army at Fort MacArthur in San Pedro, California, and was assigned to the coastal artillery. In March, Private Davis was sent to the Philippine Islands and upon arrival was assigned as a cook with the 808th MP detachment at Port Ava in Manila.

Following the Japanese invasion of the Islands in December 1941, Raymon made his way to Corregidor and fought in the defense of that fortress during the Japanese siege. When Corregidor fell on May 6, 1942, Davis was held as a prisoner of war at an unidentified Japanese prison camp in the Philippines, where he died on August 27, 1942.

He was initially buried near the site of his death; however, his remains were later recovered and reburied in the Manila American Cemetery.

(NARA2; ABMC; WRP June 30, 1943 1:8)

GUS B. LOFBERG JR.
(1942/09/05)

(Santa Cruz Riptide photo)

After Pearl Harbor, Gus Lofberg asked for sea duty, "so that I can take a crack at those tramps." He received his wish which proved to be fatal.

Gus Brynolf Lofberg Jr. was born about 1904 in Racine, Wisconsin. He was the son of Lt. Gus B. Lofberg Sr. who was in charge of the local Coast Guard station from 1903-1914. The Lofberg family included his mother Wilma, brother Ted and sister Rosamund. Gus completed high school in Grand Haven, Michigan, and entered the US Naval Academy in 1923. Upon his graduation four years later, he was commissioned an ensign

In 1927 Gus Lofberg Sr. assumed command of the Coast Guard district that included Santa Cruz and moved his family to California. Ensign Lofberg spent time with the family in Santa Cruz before reporting to his ship.

After several years of sea duty, Gus Lofberg was assigned as an instructor at the US Naval Academy. It was possibly during this period that he married Norma Lynn Costella. In 1935 a daughter was born to the couple.

When war broke out, Lt. Lofberg was on a highly specialized naval assignment with the Bauch and Lomb Optical Company. Desiring to get into the fight and "get a crack at the tramps," he requested and received sea duty. Lofberg, who was then a commander, was assigned command of the *USS Little* and sent his family to live in Santa Cruz near his mother.

[The USS Little*] was transferred to the Pacific Fleet in early 1942 and was sent to the South Pacific in July of that year. On 7-9 August 1942,* Little *took part in the first major Allied offensive of the Pacific War, the operation to seize Japanese facilities on Guadalcanal and Tulagi islands. She [the* USS Little*] remained in the Southern Solomons area for the next month, providing valuable transport services to the Marines fighting on Guadalcanal. She was patrolling off Guadalcanal's Lunga Point with* USS Gregory (APD-3) *on the night of 4-5 September 1942 when the two old ships were attacked by a force of three Japanese destroyers. Overwhelmed by greatly superior enemy gun power,* USS Little *was quickly put out of action and sank soon afterwards.*

Gus Lofberg was posthumously awarded the Silver Star for his actions aboard the *USS Little* that were detailed in the *Santa Cruz Sentinel* of August 8, 1943

Suddenly spotlighted under a flood of illumination from two forces of Japanese destroyers, he fought his ship with courageous determination and grim defiance, well aware that she was unequipped to engage an outnumbering force in battle. Scoring several hits on the enemy while attempting to withdraw before a vigorous curtain of fire, he kept his guns blazing away until the Little *was eventually struck and set aflame.*

Commander Gus B. Lofberg's body was never recovered; he was officially declared dead on September 6, 1943. In addition to appearing on the *Santa Cruz Sentinel Honor Roll*, Gus Lofberg was memorialized on the Tablets of the Missing at Manila American Cemetery. His honors include the Purple Heart, Silver Star and Navy Specialty Meritorious Medal. Later the destroyer *Gus B. Lofberg Jr.* was named for him.

(ABMC; DANFS, *USS Little* DD-79; SCR September 18, 1941 1; SCSn August 8, 1943 2:6)

JACK H. McLAUGHLIN
(1942/09/14)

(Santa Cruz High School Service Cardinal)

Jack McLaughlin and his older brother Arthur led very different civilian and military lives.

Jack Henry McLaughlin was born on February 16, 1923, in Santa Cruz, California. He was raised in a Soquel home that included his parents, brother Arthur and one sister. Jack attended Soquel Union Grammar School and about 1938 enrolled in Santa Cruz High School. He remained in high school only a year before dropping out. After leaving school, he worked briefly as an actor/entertainer prior to World War II.

On March 3, 1941, McLaughlin enlisted as a private in the US Army's infantry branch under the name of Jack W. MacLaughlin and requested duty in the Philippine Islands. Jack was initially sent to Luzon to join Company K of the 31st Infantry Regiment. Following his basic training at Fort Clark, he was re-assigned to the 808th Military Police Company in Manila.

During the Japanese invasion of December 1941, his unit helped to control traffic as the US army moved to defend Manila and Bataan. When American and Filipino forces surrendered to the Japanese on April 9, 1942, Private MacLaughlin was sent to Cabanatuan prison camp. During his confinement, he contracted malaria and died on September 14, 1942. His body was reported as buried on Luzon, but was never recovered.

Private Jack Henry MacLaughlin is memorialized on the Tablets of the Missing at the Manila American Cemetery near his brother Arthur who had been killed two months earlier.

(NARA2; ABMC; SCHSC, Pg.13)

JOHN H. FITCH
(1942/10/14)

The name John Hovey Fitch appears in the National Archives and Records Administration listing of service men who died during World War II and who declared Santa Cruz County, California, as their residence. His link with Santa Cruz was possibly through his wife, Marie Magdalene

Fitch, who lived in Santa Cruz.

The date and place of Fitch's birth, along with his parents and siblings, have not been identified It is believed that he was a resident of Pierce County, Washington.

The date of John Fitch's enlistment in the US Navy has not been established, but it is likely he received training at the US Naval Training Center in San Diego. Following boot camp, he received additional instruction to qualify as a radioman. By the fall of 1942, Fitch had risen to the rank of Aviation Chief Radioman and was serving in the Pacific Theatre.

On October 14, 1942, Chief Radioman John Hovey Fitch was listed as missing in action in the Pacific and on December 4, 1945, he was declared dead.

(ABMC; AAIR, ACGEN;)

RALPH B. SWEEZEY
(1942/10/15)

(Santa Cruz High School Service Cardinal)

Ralph Sweezey felt that relief had arrived when the *Meredith* took him off his damaged ship.

Ralph Beecher Sweezey, the son of Mr. and Mrs. Floyd E. Sweezey, was born on July 31, 1921, in San Jose, California. The family later moved to Soquel, California, where Ralph's father managed the Sesnon properties. Young Sweezey attended Mission Hill Junior High School and enrolled in Santa Cruz High School in 1936. He was graduated from high school with the class of June 17, 1939.

Ralph Sweezey joined the US Navy in July 1941 and was sent to the US Naval Training Center in San Diego for boot camp. After completing his training, he was assigned duty at Pearl Harbor aboard the *USS Vireo*. While serving on board that minesweeping destroyer, he saw action at Pearl Harbor where the ship was credited with shooting down an enemy plane.

Following the battle of Midway, the *USS Vireo* was grounded while attempting to rescue the *USS Yorktown*. It was later salvaged and returned to Pearl Harbor for repairs. After reconstruction was completed, Ralph Sweezey and his ship set sail to assist in the Guadalcanal campaign.

On 15 October [1942], while Vireo *was in a convoy taking vital supplies to the embattled Marines on Guadalcanal, approaching Japanese forces were detected. The rest of the convoy hastily left the area and the destroyer* Meredith *removed the old tug's crew and prepared to sink her to prevent capture by the enemy. However, Japanese planes arrived before this could be done and quickly sank the destroyer, leaving* Vireo *abandoned but undamaged. Though most of her crew had been lost with* Meredith, *the tug was salvaged and served actively for the rest of the Pacific War.*

It is believed that Seaman First Class Ralph Beecher Sweezey died while aboard the *USS Meredith* on October 15, 1942; however, his body was never recovered. He was officially declared dead on October 16, 1943, and appears on the Tablets of the Missing at Manila American Cemetery. His awards include the Purple Heart.

(ABMC; SCHSC, Pg. 19, DANFS, *USS Vireo* AM-52; *USS Meredith*; SCSn February 11, 1943 1:6)

FLOYD W. BICKMORE
(1942/10/27)

(Manila American Cemetery Hall of Missing –Internet photo)

Floyd W. Bickmore was born in California in 1901 to William and Ella Bickmore. In 1910 the Bickmore family was living in Santa Cruz County where William was employed as a mechanic in Felton. Floyd and his sister Esther attended local schools while living in Felton.

Floyd Bickmore is believed to have completed his four years of high school in Berkeley, which later credited him with residency in that community. By 1940 he had returned to the Pajaro Valley and was working as a tinsmith to help support of his parents.

Floyd Bickmore joined Company C of the 194th Tank Battalion of the National Guard at Salinas between September 1940 and February 1941. He was promoted to the rank of Staff Sergeant in October 1941 shortly after his arrival in the Philippine Islands. The unit history of the 194th Tank Company indicates that Sergeant Bickmore was promoted to Master Sergeant while on duty in the islands. He remained with Company C through the defense of the Philippines, the Bataan Peninsula and the infamous Death March.

Floyd Bickmore was confined to Cabanatuan Prison where he remained until his death on October 27, 1942. His body was never recovered; he is memorialized on the Tablets of the Missing at Manila American Cemetery in Manila.

(USCR, 1910 US Census, CA, Santa Cruz; NARA2; 194TB; ABMC; SCSn July 9, 1943)

DONNEL A. O'BRIEN
(1942/11/05)

Donnel O'Brien experienced what the word *affliction* can mean to the human body.

Donnel A. O'Brien was born in Lamont, Iowa, in 1906; however, information regarding his parents and early life is not available. O'Brien had two brothers, Fred and Jack; other siblings have not been identified. In addition to grammar school, Donnel's education included two years of high school, which likely occurred in Iowa. O'Brien subsequently married and the couple had children prior to their divorce. About 1935 Donnel moved to Santa Cruz and for the next six years worked in the local plastering trade.

Following the attack on Pearl Harbor in December 1941, O'Brien registered for the draft and was inducted into the army at the Presidio of Monterey on May 3, 1942. He was assigned to the Army Air Corps and sent to Shepherd Field, Texas, for basic training.

On May 29, while in Texas, O'Brien was stricken with what was described as "an affliction." When the condition became more severe, he was transferred to O'Reilly General Hospital in Springfield, Missouri. During the last four months of his life he was paralyzed with his arms and legs confined within wire splints.

On November 5, 1942, Donnel O'Brien died; his body was sent to Lamont, Iowa, for his funeral and internment arrangements.

(NARA2; SCSn December 14, 1942)

PAUL E. LEACH
(1942/11/8?)

A one-week honeymoon was all that was allotted to Paul Leach before North Africa.

Information relating to Paul Elmo Leach's birth and family has not been located; however, his mother, Mrs. Pearl Kingston, may have raised him in Kansas City, Missouri.

The date he entered the Army is unknown, but in 1942 Corporal Paul Leach was probably a member of the 3rd Infantry Division stationed at Ford Ord, California. He likely met Edna Mae Davis of Santa Cruz during that assign-

ment, and on August 30, 1942, the couple were married in her mother's home. Edna lived with her mother during Paul's absence, and that home became their official residence.

On September 6, 1942, Leach and his unit boarded trains for Camp Pickett, Virginia. After reaching the camp, the 3rd Infantry trained until October 24 and then boarded ships destined for "Operation Torch" in North Africa.

On November 8, 1942, the 3rd Infantry Division stormed ashore at Casablanca supported by 400 ships and 1,000 aircraft. The invasion was a complete surprise and the 3rd Division quickly established their beachhead but the [Vichy]French forces fought back bitterly. For three days, the Americans fought the French forces until finally, the French agreed to a cease-fire and joined the Allied forces. With Casablanca secured, the Allies could now move men and materiel into the Mediterranean Sea without fear of the Straights of Gibraltar being sealed off.

On January 12, 1943, Edna Mae received a telegram from the War Department informing her that her husband was killed in action in North Africa. No record has been found as to his burial location; however, his remains were most likely returned to the United States after the war.

(SCSn December 16, 1942 5:1; Ed, 3rd Inf Div During WWII, http://history-world.org/3rd_infantry_division.htm, [16 September 2008])

FRANCIS E. ARAM
(1942/11/13)

(Santa Cruz Riptide photo)

Father and son sergeants went off to war together, but only the father returned.

Francis E. Aram was born on December 30, 1922. in Fresno County, California, to Lorena and Joseph Aram. The family later moved to the San Lorenzo Valley where Joseph worked as a steam engineer. A subsequent move took them to Salinas where Francis probably completed four years of high school. While living in the Monterey Bay area, Aram earned an income working in the entertainment business.

In September 1940 Francis Aram enlisted in Company

C of the 194th Tank Company and was later joined by his father. The Arams adapted well to the military; both Francis and Joseph rose to the rank of sergeant. In February 1941 the 194th Tank Battalion was inducted into federal service and sent to Fort Lewis, Washington, for training. They remained at that Pacific Northwest camp until September when they reported to San Francisco to be transported to Fort Stotsenburg in the Philippine Islands.

Joseph and Francis Aram were at Clark Field when Pearl Harbor was attacked on December 7, 1941, and when Japanese aircraft bombed Manila the following day. On December 24, the Japanese landed troops at Lamon Bay in the Philippines and Company C was sent to detain them. The Japanese invaders overwhelmed the defenders, forcing them to retreat to the Bataan Peninsula.

On April 9, 1942, US and Philippine forces surrendered to the Japanese. The Arams joined the Bataan Death March at Mariveles at the tip of the Bataan peninsula and marched to Cabanatuan Prison eighty-five miles north without food or water.

During his confinement, Francis contracted beriberi and died on November 13, 1942. Joseph remained in the camp until he was sent to Hoten, Mukden, Manchuria, to work in Japanese mines. He survived the war and returned home.

Francis E. Aram was buried in a shallow grave somewhere in the Philippines. His name is included on the memorial plaque in the Manila American Cemetery.

(CBR; USCR, 1920 US Census, CA, Santa Cruz; NARA2; SCSn December 29, 1942 1:8; 194TB; ABMC; SCR August 6, 1943)

JOE GILLIS
(1942/11/23)

(Internet photo)

While Japanese soldiers marched over and around him, Joe Gillis played dead for twenty-eight hours to avoid capture.

In 1921 Joe Gillis was the last son born in West Virginia to John and Victoria Gillis. The couple, along with their sons John, Frank, Julian and Joe and daughter Ann, moved to Fresno, California. Joe attended Fresno schools until the family relocated to the Pajaro Valley. He continued his education at Notre Dame Academy in Watsonville. When his father died, his mother opened the New York Bakery to help support the family.

After completing high school, Joe worked at the Santo ranch in the Springfield district of the Pajaro Valley. When his mother married Mr. Santo, Emil Morrello, a son of Santo's from a previous marriage, became Joe's stepbrother.

In 1940 Joe Gillis and Emil Morrello joined Company C of the 194th Tank Battalion in Salinas and the following February were sent to Fort Lewis, Washington, for training. In September the company was sent to the Philippine Islands. Following the Japanese invasion of the Philippines and the fall of Manila, the 194th Tank Battalion helped form the Bataan Peninsula's last line of defense.

On Christmas Day 1941, Joe and Emil, along with three other members of a tank crew, found themselves forward of friendly lines and surrounded by Japanese. When their tank became disabled, the crewmen searched for an escape route back to friendly lines. Two of the men chose to strike out alone and arrived safely back within US lines. Joe, Emil and William Hall, all from Watsonville, encountered a large Japanese unit approaching them. The only recourse open to them was to fight, run or play dead. They chose the latter and for twenty-eight hours as Japanese troops moved around them and in some cases stepped over them, they lay on the ground without flinching a muscle. After the last Japanese unit had passed, they got up and quickly made their way back to US lines.

Avoiding capture was only temporary for Joe Gillis; on April 9, 1942, U.S forces on the peninsula were forced to capitulate. Corporal Joe Gillis survived the Bataan Death March and over a year of imprisonment at Cabanatuan Prison, but his end finally arrived on November 23, 1942.

On Wednesday July 28, 1943, Mrs. Victoria Santo received a wire from the Red Cross notifying her that her son Joe had died in a prison camp. Emil Morrello survived the prison camp ordeal and returned to Watsonville. It is believed that the body of Joe Gillis was buried in the vicinity of the Cabanatuan POW Camp.

(NARA2; WRP January 10, 1942 1:7, July 31, 1943; 194TB; http://www.proviso.k12.il.us/bataan%20Web/194_Poster.htm)

DANIEL J. REMICK
(1942/11/30)

In its May 30, 1945 edition, the *Santa Cruz Sentinel* published the name of Daniel Joseph Remick among those local servicemen listed as missing in action. No record of this sailor's life in Santa Cruz County has been located.

It is not known when or where Daniel Remick was born,

nor is information regarding his parents or siblings available. Navy records indicate that he entered the US Navy from California. While in the navy, Remick served as a gunner's mate third class aboard the *USS Northampton,* which was a heavy cruiser serving in the Pacific Theatre. Daniel Remick was reported as having been lost at sea on November 30, 1942, which helps pinpoint the action that resulted in his death.

Northampton *next operated with a cruiser-destroyer force, to prevent the Japanese from reinforcing their troops on Guadalcanal. The Battle of Tassafaronga began 40 minutes before midnight, 30 November [1942], when three American destroyers made a surprise torpedo attack on the Japanese. All-American ships then opened fire, which the startled enemy did not return for seven minutes. Then two of the American cruisers took torpedo hits within the space of a minute, and 10 minutes later, another was hit, and all being forced to retire from the action.* Northampton *and* Honolulu, *with six destroyers, continued the fierce action, scoring many hits. Close to the end of the engagement,* Northampton *was struck by two torpedoes, which tore a huge hole in her port side, ripping away decks and bulkheads. Flaming diesel oil sprayed over the ship, she took on water rapidly and began to list. Three hours later, as she began to sink stern first, she had to be abandoned. So orderly and controlled was the process that loss of life was surprisingly light, and the survivors were all picked up within an hour by destroyers. While three cruisers had been damaged and* Northampton *lost, the Japanese had been denied a major reinforcement, and once again the Navy had given vital support to the Marines fighting ashore."*

The body of Daniel Joseph Remick was never recovered. He is memorialized on the Tablets of the Missing at Manila American Cemetery.

(ACGEN; ABMC; DANFS, USS Northampton CA-26)

RAYMOND J. JEWETT
(1942/12/28)

"Former Santa Cruzan Loses Life in Crash," noted the February 26, 1943, *Santa Cruz Sentinel.*

Raymond J. Jewett was born in Minnesota in 1920 to Mr. and Mrs. Jewett; his mother's name was Gertrude. By 1940 his mother had remarried and was living in Modesto, California. Jewett may also have lived in the San Joaquin Valley and graduated from high school there before moving to Santa Cruz. The *Santa Cruz Sentinel* noted that "Jewett lived and worked in Santa Cruz for some time," and while his employer is unknown, it stated that he had worked as an office clerk or in a similar administrative capacity.

In August 1941 Jewett, who was single and living in Contra Costa County, enlisted in the US Army Air Corps

as a private. After completing basic training, he was accepted into a special program to prepare him to fly or navigate bombers. At the completion of the program, he was promoted to Flight Officer (Warrant Officer) and stationed at the MacDill Air Force Base in Florida.

On December 28, 1942, Raymond J. Jewett and five other officers were aboard a plane flying out of Tampa, Florida, when they encountered unspecified problems forcing them to crash into the Gulf of Mexico. Although the Navy, Coast Guard and Army Air Force searched for five days, neither their bodies nor the plane was located.

(NARA2; SCSn news February 26, 1943 3:8; http://en.wikipedia. org/wiki/Flight_officer;)

1943

HAROLD E. RUTHERFORD
(1943/01/12)

(Santa Cruz High School Service Cardinal)

As Hal Rutherford bailed out of his rapidly descending plane, his body crashed into the tail section.

Harold Erwin Rutherford was born in California on September 8, 1904, to Mr. and Mrs. William T. Rutherford. In addition to his brother Clyde, who died in 1927, he had four sisters Gladys, Pauline, Geraldine and Marguerite and a half brother Harold Van Gorder. Rutherford spent his formative years in Santa Cruz and attended Mission Hill Junior High School. In September 1920 he entered Santa Cruz High School, where he majored in English and took college preparatory courses.

In June 1924 Rutherford graduated from high school and the following October joined the US Navy. He received his basic training at the US Naval Training Center in San Diego followed by specialized courses in aviation mechanics. After completing his four-year tour, he re-enlisted and was sent to the Naval Flying School at Pensacola, Florida. During those years, Rutherford rose in rank to Chief Petty Officer and logged over 6000 hours of flying time.

About 1938 Harold Rutherford was commissioned and began advancing through the officer ranks. While in the Navy, he married Marjorie and they had two sons, George and Keith William. In December 1941 he was at Pearl Harbor during the Japanese attack and later had an opportunity to repay the Japanese during the air battles over the Marshall Islands and Midway. While serving at Guadalcanal in September 1942, Rutherford was promoted to full lieutenant.

Following a mission on January 12, 1943, Lieutenant. Harold E. Rutherford's plane went into an inverted spin at 13,000 feet over the sea and when bailing out at 6000 feet, his body hit the tail of the falling ship, resulting in his death. His body was recovered and buried with full military honors at Noumea, New Caledonia.

In December 1947 Rutherford's remains were returned to San Diego and reburied in the Fort Rosecrans National Cemetery.

(USCR, 1910 US Census, CA, Santa Cruz; SCR January 2, 1943 1; SCHSC, Pg. 17; SCSn January 20, 1943 1:8)

SVEND J. W. HANSEN
(1943/02/01)

(Santa Cruz High School Service Cardinal)

Flying combat missions according to Svend Hansen was, "an emotion similar to playing Watsonville High School in 1936 except the stakes are higher and the results more tangible and long lasting."

Svend J. W. Hansen was born in Santa Cruz, California, on June 30, 1920, to Mr. and Mrs. Svend J. Hansen of Ben Lomond. In 1928 while Svend and his sister Anita were attending Ben Lomond Grammar School, their mother died. In 1934 Hansen entered Santa Cruz High School, where he was active in sports and excelled in football. After graduating from high school in 1937, Svend entered San Jose State College. During his three years in college, Sven helped pay his expenses by working part time as a sales clerk. He also earned a block letter in football.

In December 1941 Hansen enlisted in the US Army Air Corps in Monterey and was sent to MacDill Field, Florida, for basic training followed by radio school. While serving in the army, he wrote several articles for the *Santa Cruz Riptide* weekly newspaper, describing life in an army camp. In May 1942 Svend Hansen was sent to England where he joined a B-17 crew in the 340th Bombardment Squadron of the 17th Bombardment Group.

During the North African campaign, Hansen flew missions as a radio operator and gunner aboard a B-17 named "Flaming Mayme." In November 1942 Svend downed his first German Messerschmitt while flying over Tunis, Tunisia. General James Doolittle later awarded Svend the Air Medal for his North African service.

Hansen continued to fly combat missions with what he described as, "an emotion similar to playing Watsonville High School in 1936 except the stakes are higher and the results more tangible and long lasting." The stakes became much more long lasting for Sergeant Svend Hansen on February 1, 1943, when his bomber was seen to go into a steep dive over Tunisia. Four parachutes were seen leaving the plane; however, Hansen's was not one of them.

Svend Hansen's remains were recovered and returned to Santa Cruz for burial in 1950 in Santa Cruz Memorial Garden Cemetery.

(NARA2 SCHSC, Pg. 10; SCR May 22, 1942 1, November 6, 1942 1; SCSn December 20, 1942 1:4, February 18,1943 1:8)

JAMES T. HANNAY
(1943/03/28)

James T. Hannay was born in the "Garden City" of San Jose on March 27, 1912, to James and Nettie Hannay and spent much of his youth Santa Clara County. He completed grammar school but did not continue through high school. Later James married and the couple settled in Santa Cruz, where he was employed by the Doudell Trucking firm. James and his wife had one son named James.

On June 27, 1942, James Hannay was inducted into the army as a private and sent to Fort Knox, Kentucky, for training in armor. Following his training, he is believed to have joined an armored unit in North Africa. In March 1943 those units were involved in combat operations against German forces under General Rommel. At the time of of Hannay's death, US armored forces in North Africa were fighting in Tunisia. On March 28, 1943, Private James T. Hannay was killed in action.

The burial location of James T. Hannay has not been identified; however, his remains were likely returned to the US following the war.

(CBR; NARA2; SCSn May 3, 1943 2:7, April 29, 1943 1:7)

MARVIN L. MAUL
(1943/04/17)

(Santa Cruz High School Service Cardinal)

A common childhood disease brought an end to the adult life of Marvin Maul.

Marvin Leonard Maul was born in Nebraska on October 29, 1921, to Leonard and Paula Maul. The Maul family, which included two other sons and three daughters, moved from Amherst, Nebraska, to Santa Cruz in late 1937. On January 3, 1938, Marvin transferred into Santa Cruz High School where he served as the business manager of the school paper and appeared in a junior class play. After completing high school in June 1939, Marvin was employed locally as a clerk and for a year, served in the National Guard.

On October 7, 1942, Maul was mustered into federal service as an army private at the Presidio in Monterey. After completing basic training, Private Maul was sent to medical school at Camp Barkley, Texas, for three months. Upon the completion of that training, Maul was posted to Fort Lewis, Washington, where he served as a clerk.

In April 1943, Marvin was admitted to the infirmary with an acute respiratory condition followed by a severe case of measles. On April 17, 1943, Private Marvin Maul died at the Fort Lewis hospital. His body was returned to Santa Cruz and following a funeral on April 24, was interred in Oakwood Cemetery.

(NARA2; SCHSC, Pg. 13, SCSn, April 18, 1943 1:3, SCSn April 21, 1943 6:4)

CHARLES V. KENDALL
(1943/04/29)

(Oakwood Memorial Park - Santa Cruz, California)

Margaret gave her airline seat to Eva so that a mom might spend a few moments with her dying son.

Charles V. Kendall was born in San Francisco, California on July 15, 1921, to Mr. and Mrs. Kendall; his mother's name was Eva. Additional siblings in the Kendall family have not been identified. Charles spent many of his formative years in Santa Cruz, living at the home of his uncle Al Seidlinger. He entered Santa Cruz High School in about 1937 where he spent the next three years. After completing high school, he enrolled in the University of California in Berkeley, where he studied for two years. Prior to entering the service, Charles Kendall met and married Margaret and worked part time as a clerk.

On August 27, 1942, Kendall entered the US Army while still living in Berkeley. After completing basic training, he was assigned to Camp Kearns Air Base near Salt Lake, City, Utah, a temporary facility that trained over 40,000 airmen. It is possible that Private Kendall was used in a clerical capacity during that assignment.

In April 1943 Charles was diagnosed with an unspecified illness or condition that continued to worsen. When his wife and mother were informed of the serious nature of his condition, they attempted to schedule transportation to the base to be by his side. Only one airline ticket was available; Margaret insisted that her mother-in-law fly while she took a train. Eva arrived in time to spend an hour with her son, but Margaret was too late for a final goodbye when her husband Private Charles Kendall passed away on April 29, 1943. His body was returned to Santa Cruz for a military funeral and interment in Oakwood Memorial Park on May 3, 1943.

(CBR; NARA2; SCSn May 4, 1943 2:4; Alexander/Fish, Defense Industry of Utah, http://www.media.utah.edu/UHE/d/DEFENSE. html, [16 Sept. 2008]; Oakwood Memorial Park Survey November 12, 2007)

ATTILIO J. DOGLIOTTI.
(1943/05/08)

(Santa Cruz High School Service Cardinal)

"Tillie's" great ambition was to become a pilot.

Attilio Joseph Dogliotti, the son of Bartolomeo and Maria Dogliotti, was born on November 25, 1920, in Davenport, California, and spent most of his life between Santa Cruz, Castroville and Carmel, California. In 1935 he entered Santa Cruz High School where he took a general and varied course program. The high school yearbooks reveal that Dogliotti was active in athletics and participated in several sports. He graduated with the class of 1939 and prior to the war, worked for the Coast Drum Box Company and the Davenport Portland Cement Company.

On April 22, 1942, Dogliotti enlisted in the Army Air Corps as an Air Cadet. His initial training occurred at Santa Ana, California, followed by flight schools at Blythe, Lemoore and Stockton, California. On January 4, 1943, Tillie received his gold bars and silver wings as a second lieutenant and pilot.

Following his commissioning, Lt. Dogliotti was sent to Tucson, Arizona, and assigned to a B-24 Liberator bomber training school. At its conclusion he flew to Pocatello, Idaho, and became a member of a ten man B-24 crew in the 538 Bomb Squadron of the 382 Bomb Group. After other crews were assembled, they flew to Gibbs Field in El Paso, Texas, to pick up six regular combat duty B-24 Liberators. On their return trip to Idaho on May 8, 1943, they encountered a storm in New Mexico where Dogliotti's plane lost a tail and crashed. "Tillie," who was not flying the aircraft at the time of the crash, and three other crewmembers died instantly. Of the six B-24 Liberators that had left El Paso, four made it to Pocatello safely.

The remains of Second Lieutenant Attilio Joseph Dogliotti were returned to Santa Cruz where a funeral mass was held at Holy Cross Church on May 16, 1943. His remains were buried at the Holy Cross Cemetery.

(SCHSC, Pg. 9; SCSn May 10, 1943 1:1, May 17, 1943)

EDWIN C. HILL
(1943/05/14)

(Santa Cruz High School Service Cardinal)

"Bud" Hill was supplying a lost detachment of soldiers when a mountain got in the way.

Edwin C. "Bud" Hill was born on October 21, 1916, to Mr. and Mrs. Thomas Hill. Bud, along with a brother and sister, grew up in the small mountain community of Ben Lomond in the San Lorenzo Valley and attended local schools. In 1930 he began classes at Santa Cruz High School where he majored in engineering.

Following his graduation in 1934, Hill worked for a short period at a Ben Lomond store. He then enrolled in San Jose State College and graduated with a BS degree in December 1941.

Immediately after his graduation, Hill joined the Army Air Corps's cadet program in Santa Ana. That program included flying school at Visalia, gunnery school in Las Vegas and finally navigator school at Mather Field near Sacramento. In March 1943, Edwin Hill graduated and received his wings with a second lieutenant commission.

When the Japanese invaded Attu, an island in the Aleutian Island chain in Alaska, the US responded. Lt. Hill was sent to the 21st AAF Bomb Squadron that was assisting in its recapture.

On May 14, 1943, Hill's plane was sent to Attu to deliver supplies to a detachment of Americans soldiers that had become separated from their unit. The aircraft was attempting to climb out of a valley when it crashed into the side of a mountain, killing Bud and the other members of the crew.

Lt. Edwin C. (Bud) Hill was posthumously awarded the Air Medal and is buried at the Golden Gate National Cemetery in San Bruno.

(USDVA, SCHSC, Pg. 11; SCSn June 17, 1943 1:7, May 21, 1943 1:3)

Harold M. Whalman
(1943/05/18)

The *Santa Cruz Sentinel* readers of their May 23, 1943, edition were drawn to the headline "Harold M Whalman, Oiler, Santa Cruz Man Killed by Torpedo on Tanker in Pacific."

Harold Myron Whalman was born in California to John and Louisa Whalman about 1901. In 1920 he and his sisters, Annie and Martha, were living with their parents in the family home in Oakland. John Whalman was a mariner by occupation and may have introduced his son to a similar life on the sea. Harold Whalman's relationship to Santa Cruz has not been found beyond the newspaper headline.

During World War II, Harold was an "oiler" aboard an 18,000-ton Standard Oil Tanker that was torpedoed by the Japanese in the South Pacific on May 18, 1943, while returning to its port on the West Coast. The submarine surfaced after its torpedo hit the ship and sank the tanker.

After spending twelve hours in lifeboats, a number of the tanker survivors were picked up by a US destroyer; however, Whalman was not among them. His body was never recovered and he was presumed to have drowned.

(USCR, 1920 US Census, CA, Alameda; SCSn May 23, 1943 1:4)

Joseph H. Heatwole
(1943/05/19)

(Watsonville High School yearbook)

A plane crash in Santa Ana prevented Joe from doing the job for which he had trained.

Joseph Hunter Heatwole was born in Fresno County, California, on March 17, 1918, to Joseph and Harriet Heatwole.

In 1920 the Heatwole family was living in Fresno, California, where Joseph Sr. worked as a carpenter. The family later moved to the Green Valley sector of the Pajaro Valley and Joseph Jr. enrolled in Watsonville High School. In high school he distinguished himself in football, basketball, track and tennis and was graduated in 1936. Following his graduation, he enrolled in San Jose State College where he played on the basketball team.

Heatwole may have received his commission as an ensign in the US Navy prior to January 1942. The *Watsonville Register-Pajaronian* indicated that he had served at Pearl Harbor and Maui in the Hawaiian Islands from January to November 1942. in December 1942 following his Hawaiian assignment, Heatwole married Jean Salmon of San Jose. The couple left immediately for Santa Ana, where he was assigned to a naval aviation unit.

On May 19, 1943, Lieutenant Joseph Hunter Heatwole was killed in a plane crash in the Santa Ana area. His remains were returned to San Jose and following a funeral at the Amos O. Williams chapel, were interred in the Golden Gate National Cemetery in San Bruno, California on May 24, 1943.

(CBR; WRP May 20, 1943 1:2; Williams Funeral Home Book 1943 Pg. 159; USDVA; Photo-WHS)

LeRoy S. Walton
(1943/05/22)

(McQuaide Album)

LeRoy came full circle from McQuaide, to Colorado to a resting place in the Pajaro Valley.

LeRoy Scott Walton was born in San Francisco, California on January 26, 1920 and was the son of Mr. and Mrs. Chester A. Walton of San Carlos, California. The Walton family also included sons Robin and Donald and daughter Susan. LeRoy graduated from Jefferson High School and San Mateo Junior College. Following junior college he enrolled in the School of Engineering at the University of California at Berkeley.

On September 19, 1940 Walton joined the San Francisco Coast Artillery National Guard unit, was given the rank of sergeant and assigned to Camp McQuaide. Later he was accepted for flight training at Roswell, New Mexico and upon completion was awarded his wings and commissioned a second lieutenant. While in New Mexico, he married Carol Light of Watsonville and moved to that community.

While participating in a routine training mission near

Colorado Springs, Colorado, on May 22, 1943, the B-17 which Second Lieutenant LeRoy Walton was co-piloting crashed shortly after take off killing all aboard.

His remains were returned to Watsonville and following a funeral at the All Saints Episcopal Church, were laid to rest in the Pajaro Valley Memorial Park.

(CBR; NARA2; SCSn May 24, 1943 1:3, WRP May 24, 1943 1:2, May 26, 1943 1:1, Headstone-Pajaro Valley Cemetery, Watsonville CA)

WILLIAM E. LITTLER
(1943/05/24)

(Santa Cruz Riptide photo)

"When I have Done My Best" was appropriately sung for Bill at his funeral.

William Eugene Littler was born in Newburg, Missouri, about 1916 to Mr. and Mrs. J. H. Littler. The Littler family, consisting of sons William and John and daughters Roberta, Marjorie and Mary, settled in Turlock, California. William attended elementary and high school in that Central Valley community. After graduating from high school, Littler enrolled in Modesto Junior College. When the family moved to Santa Cruz in the late 1930s, he joined them in their Twin Lakes home and established his residency in the county.

In February 1941 Littler joined the US Navy and was sent to San Diego for basic training. Following boot camp, he was assigned to naval aviation and rose through promotions to air radioman second class. He subsequently joined an air detachment unit in the North Pacific and served with it for over a year.

While flying a mission at an unidentified location over the North Pacific on May 24, 1943, Petty Officer Second Class Littler's plane crashed and he was killed. His remains were returned to California in 1946 for burial in the Golden Gate National Cemetery in San Bruno.

(SCSn May 27, 1943, 1:3, June 3, 1943, 3:5; SCR June 4, 1943; USDVA)

CHARLES B. EDWARDS
(1943/05/28)

"Son of Soquel Man Killed in Training Plane" brought a Memorial Day message home to *Santa Cruz Sentinel* readers.

The United States War Department List of Dead and Missing World War II Casualties for the County of Santa Cruz includes the name of Flight Officer Charles B. Edwards. Nothing, in addition to the below newspaper clipping, has been uncovered regarding this individual.

"Son of Soquel Man Killed in Training Plane"
Flight officer Charles B. Edwards, son of William H. Edwards of Soquel, was killed Friday night in the crash of a cub trainer plane at the army air base at Alliance, Neb., according to an Associate Press report. The cause of the crash, a few miles west of the air base, was not determined, said the statement by the public relations officer. William H. Edwards is a resident of the Monterey Bay Country club tract just east of Soquel."

An Aviation Archeological Investigation and Report confirms that Charles B. Edwards was flying an L-3B aircraft when it crashed at the Alliance, Nebraska Municipal Airport on May 28, 1943, and was totally destroyed. The location of his remains, if recovered, is not known.

(SCSn May 30, 1943 1:2; AAIR)

ERNEST T. AVILA
(1943/05/29)

(St Mary's Catholic Cemetery – Gilroy, California)

A headstone in Gilroy serves as a reminder of an Aleutian Island casualty.

Ernest Avila was born in California on December 29, 1914, to Robert and Lona Avila. He had a younger sister, Lena. In 1920, the family was living in Paraiso, Monterey County, California. Military records indicate that Ernest completed grammar school; however, there is no record of his attending high school. When he registered for the draft, he indicated that he was a single male, living in Santa Cruz County and was employed as a clerk.

On May 20, 1941, Ernest T. Avila joined the US Army in San Francisco and was assigned the rank of private. After completing basic training, he was sent to the 7th Infantry Division, 32nd Infantry Regiment.

In the spring of 1943, Avila's unit was sent to the Aleutian Islands to assist in removing the Japanese who had invaded Kiska Island. By the end of May they had nearly completed their task; however, pockets of resistance still remained on nearby Attu Island.

"On the 29th of May, 1943 at 3:15a.m. [Japanese General] Yamasaki's remaining troops took advantage of the lingering fog and managed to break through the American lines. Ten minutes later, with the artillery battery located on Engineer Hill in sight, the Japanese commander ordered a Banzai attack."

On May 29, 1943, Ernest T. Avila was listed as having been "Killed in Action." His remains were returned to California and buried in Saint Mary's Catholic Cemetery in Gilroy, California.

(ACGEN; 1920 US Census, CA, Monterey; NARA2; Saint Mary's Cemetery Headstone; Editor, World War II In The Aleutians: A Brief History, http://www.hlswilliwaw.com/aleutians/Aleutians/html/aleutians-wwii.htm, [16 September 2008])

RUSSELL C. BARNES
(1943/05/29)

(Santa Cruz High School Service Cardinal)

Russell had to wait until 1948 for a return trip home.

Russell C. Barnes was born in California on October 12, 1906, to Mr. and Mrs. W. J. Barnes and spent his youth in Santa Cruz along with his brother Floyd and a sister. He attended local schools and entered Santa Cruz High School, but left in the spring of 1924 during his junior year. Russell moved to San Jose, found work in a machine shop as a welder and remained at the same shop for the next nineteen years.

On March 6, 1941, Russell Barnes was inducted into the US Army in San Francisco. His unit has not been identified, but it was probably a component of the 17th or 32nd Infan-

try Division. Between May 11 and May 19, 1943, US Forces attacked the Japanese army entrenched on Attu Island in the Aleutian chain.

An Adjutant General Office report forwarded to Private Russell C. Barnes' parents on June 16, 1943, informed them that he was killed in action on May 29, 1943. His body was interred at a temporary location and following the war, his remains were sent to the Williams Mortuary in Santa Clara County for reburial at an unspecified cemetery.

(NARA2; SCHSC Pg. 5, SCSn June 18, 1943 1:6, S Clara Cnty Gen. Soc., http://www.rootsweb.com/~cascchgs/wfh/wfhb1.html, [16 September 2008])

KENNETH F. KRETSINGER
(1943/05/29)

(Golden Gate National Cemetery – San Bruno California)

A posthumous award for "heroic or meritorious achievement in combat" was the last gift that a young lieutenant was able to leave his family.

Kenneth F. Kretsinger was born in Berkeley, California, September 9, 1917, to George and Ethel Kretsinger. The family later moved to Los Gatos where Ken and his sister Jean attended local schools. During his preparatory years, he developed an interest in natural science and was subsequently enrolled in the Montezuma School for Boys on Bear Creek Road near Los Gatos.

Upon completion of high school, Kretsinger enrolled in the University of California Berkeley and majored in zoology. At UCB he entered ROTC and upon his graduation in 1940, was commissioned a second lieutenant in the US Army.

Kretsinger enrolled in a graduate level game management program at Oregon State College but before he could complete it, he was called into active duty. Lt Kretsinger was assigned to the 32nd Infantry Regiment of the 7th Infantry Division at Fort Ord and was sent to Fort Benning, Georgia, and Camp San Luis, California, for additional training.

In 1941 Kenneth Kretsinger married Blanche Hocom, a Santa Cruz girl, and the couple established their residence in Santa Cruz.

In 1942 Kretsinger's division was deployed to the Aleutian Islands; Blanche remained in Santa Cruz where she maintained the family home. Their son Kenneth Dean Kretsinger was born On April 9, 1943.

On May 29, 1943, First Lieutenant Kenneth F. Kretsinger was killed in action by enemy machine gun fire in the Aleutian battle of Attu. For his action he was awarded the Bronze Star. In1948 his remains were re-buried in the Golden Gate National Cemetery at San Bruno.

(CBR; USCR, 1920 US Census, CA, Santa Clara; *Berkley Daily Gazette*, May 30, 1944; SCSn June 18,1943, January 29, 1945 1:4; USDVA)

ARTHUR W. PINKHAM
(1943/06/11)

(Santa Cruz Riptide photo)

A county supervisor's son went to war and ended his life as a prisoner of war.

Arthur W. Pinkham was born on January 27, 1919, in San Francisco, California, to Mr. and Mrs. Charles W. Pinkham. The Pinkhams subsequently moved to Davenport in Santa Cruz County where Arthur attended grammar school. Pinkham entered Santa Cruz High School about 1933 and took courses in trade, industry and carpentry. He left high school on December 2, 1935, to seek employment.

On October 2, 1938, Arthur Pinkham joined the US Navy and following boot camp at San Diego and training in his specialty field, he was sent to Pearl Harbor in July 1939. When he arrived in Hawaii, he reported aboard the *USS Hull* that later departed for the Philippine Islands. In December 1941 Pinkham was serving aboard the *USS Perry*.

During the Japanese, invasion Seaman First Class Pinkham was wounded and taken to the island of Corregidor where the Japanese captured him on May 6, 1942. Mr. and Mrs. Pinkham received word from the Red Cross that their son Arthur had died from peritonitis on June 11, 1943,

while serving as a prisoner of war. His remains were never recovered, but he was memorialized on the Tablets of the Missing at Manila American Cemetery. (*Note: the ABMC's, 26 August 1942 record of his death can not be explained*)

(ABMC; SCHSC Pg. 17; SCSn June 19, 1943; DANFS, USS Perry DD-340)

DAYTON F. HORNOR
(1943/06/30)

(Santa Cruz High School Service Cardinal)

A heart attack failed to prevent Dayton from helping GIs with malaria.

Dayton F. Hornor was born in Tulare County, California, on April 19, 1911, to Dr. D. H. and Mary Hornor. In addition to Dayton, the family included his brothers David, Ralph and Kenneth. After his retirement as a railroad surgeon, Dr. Hornor moved his family to Santa Cruz from the Sacramento Valley. On August 24, 1925, Dayton entered Santa Cruz High School where he majored in chemistry and served as the school's student body president. After graduating in June 1929, Dayton enrolled in an unidentified college where he studied for four years.

At some point during the 1930s, Dayton was married. Two daughters, Sheryl and Carol, were later born to the couple before they were divorced. In July 1942 Hornor was living in Placer County and working for the railroad as a locomotive fireman.

On July 15 1942, Dayton Hornor was inducted into the US Army in San Francisco. When he reported for active duty, his mother assumed the care of his daughters in Roseville. Following his training period, he reported to Camp Shelby, Mississippi, and joined the 727th Engineer Battalion.

While stationed in Mississippi, Dayton suffered a heart attack and was sent to New Orleans for treatment. He was eligible for a medical discharge but chose to remain in the service. Because of his background in chemistry, Dayton continued to serve as a lab technician.

Hornor's training in the field of malaria resulted in his

being assigned to the 9th Malaria Survey unit located in India. While serving in India, Sergeant Dayton Hornor was killed in an unspecified accident on June 30, 1943. The location of his remains is not known but they were possibly returned to the US after the war.

(NARA2, SCHSC Pg. 11; SCSn August 3, 1943 5:6)

ALBERT G. WACKERMANN
(1943/07/04)

(Santa Cruz High School Service Cardinal)

Albert G. Wackermann was born of August 7, 1915, in San Francisco, California, to Theodore and Delia Wackermann. The family also consisted of another son Theodore Jr. and daughters Bertha and Adelene. Theodore later moved his family to Santa Cruz where he worked as a baker. Albert entered Santa Cruz High School in 1929 and took a scientific course of study. He was a member of the Tow Tong Honor Society, Lettermen's Society, Secretary-Treasurer of his sophomore class, boy's athletic manager and manager of the track team.

Wackermann graduated with the class of 1933 and returned to San Francisco where, like his father, he worked as a baker.

Albert served with the Merchant Marines for two years before enlisting in the US Army on September 8, 1942. Private Wackermann was assigned to the Army Air Corps and following basic training, attended the Flexible Gunnery School in Florida and the Radio School in Salt Lake City, Utah. Upon the completion of his training, Albert was posted to Blythe Field, California, Texas and Colorado.

In May 1943 Wackermann was sent to England with the Eighth Air Force. During his service with the 533rd Bomber Squadron, 381st Bomber Group, he flew fifteen missions as a B-17 turret gunner and radio operator.

On July 4, 1943, while flying a mission over LeMans, France, Staff Sergeant Albert G. Wackermann was killed in action. His remains were recovered and buried at the Ardennes American Cemetery in Neupre, Belgium. His awards include the Purple Heart awarded by General H. A.

Arnold, along with a Presidential Citation.

(USCR, 1920 US Federal Census, CA, San Francisco; ABMC; SCHSC Pg. 20)

JOHN E. McCOMBS JR.
(1943/07/05)

(Santa Cruz Riptide photo)

While floating in the South Pacific, John held on to his father's bible as long as possible.

John Earle McCombs Jr. was born on March 11, 1922, in Santa Clara County, California, to Mr. and Mrs. John McCombs. John and his brother, Claude, attended local schools and in September 1937, he entered Santa Cruz High School. In school McCombs specialized in a trade and industrial course, while outside of school his special interest was hunting and fishing. McCombs left Santa Cruz High School in December 1941.

On January 5, 1942, John McCombs joined the US Navy. As a going away present his father gave him the bible which he had carried through World War I to serve as a source of inspiration and safe keeping for his son.

Seaman Recruit McCombs received his boot training at Treasure Island in San Francisco followed by advanced training at another location within California.

In October 1942, John was assigned to the *USS Benham* in Pearl Harbor and was aboard that ship when Japanese surface vessels off of Savo Island bombarded it. When it sank, John was cast adrift in his life jacket with the few items he was able to salvage. When rescue was late in arriving, he found it necessary to begin discarding items in order to save his strength. The last item to sink to the bottom was his father's bible. Shortly afterwards rescue vessels appeared, and he was taken aboard.

After a brief recovery period, McCombs was assigned to the *USS Helena* and returned to duty off the Solomon Islands. While there he saw action at Guadalcanal, Munde and Kula Gulf.

The end of the *Helena* came in July 1943, when it was torpedoed off New Georgia Island in the Solomons and sank. This time, John Earle McCombs Jr. was unable to survive and went over the side to his death. His body was never recovered. He is memorialized on the Tablets of the missing at Manila American Cemetery. His awards include the Purple Heart.

(ABMC; SCHSC Pg. 12; DANFS, USS Helena CL-50; SCR May 7, 1943 –6, July 30, 1943 – 5)

JOHN H. BUSBY
(1943/07/11)

(Santa Cruz High School Service Cardinal)

John possessed a strong heart for others, but a weak heart for himself.

John Harold Busby was born on December 13, 1913, in Meridian, Idaho, to John and Clara Busby. At a very early age, he came to Santa Cruz where his father found work as a carpenter. John, along with his parents, his brothers Vern, Claude and Ralph and sisters Mildred and Elinor, lived in a house on Washburn Street in Santa Cruz. In August 1927 he entered Santa Cruz High School where he was known for his prowess as a golfer.

After graduating from high school in 1931, Busby worked at the Casa del Rey Hotel and served as a bell captain for ten of the twelve years of his employment at that hotel.

When World War II began, John Busby attempted to join the military service but was initially rejected because of a weak heart. On May 29, 1942, he was reclassified as I-A and entered the US Army. After receiving basic training at Camp Callan, California, Private Busby was promoted to private first class and assigned to the 202nd Coast Artillery stationed at Seattle, Washington.

Shortly after breakfast on Sunday July 11, 1943 "Buzz," as his friends affectionately knew him, was stricken with a heart attack. Attempts to save him at the Bremerton Naval Hospital were unsuccessful and his heart gave out. His body was returned to Santa Cruz and following a funeral, was interred in Santa Cruz Memorial Park.

(NARA2; SCHSC Pg. 7, SCSn July 15, 1943 3:1, SCR July 23, 1943 –1)

GEORGE O. OLSON
(1943/07/18)

(US Coast Guard Academy Photo)

Olson's relationship with Santa Cruz County was minimal. He is included in this book edition because of his listing in the *Santa Cruz Sentinel* May 31, 1945, Honor Roll.

Information regarding George Olson's family, birth and early life have not been located; however, it is believed that he was born about 1911. He entered the US Coast Guard Academy and graduated in 1933. Olson completed flight training in July 1937 and was classified as the fifty-third licensed Coast Guard aircraft pilot.

He was married and resided in Santa Cruz with his wife and twelve year old stepson Gerry until his death.

Lt. Commander George O. Olson and Lt. (jg) Joseph D. Sosbee were killed in Alaska when the plane in which they were flying through fog struck a mountainside The plane, with a combined crew of eight Coast Guard and Coast and Geodetic Survey personnel, left San Francisco aboard a PBY 5A Catalina bound for Alaska on a survey mission. The plane had been modified to accommodate a special nine lens aerial mapping camera developed by the Coast and Geodetic Survey. On Sunday morning July 18, 1943, while flying through fog, the aircraft hit Mount Moffett near Adak, Alaska, and all aboard were killed. The disposition of his remains, if recovered, is unknown.

(SCSn July 21, 1943 1:6; Check-Six.Com US Coast Guard Aircraft Accidents, http://www.check-six.com/lib/Coast_Guard_Aviation_ Casualties.htm#1940, [16 September, 2008])

JOSEPH D. SOSBEE
(1943/07/18)

(Internet Photo)

Joseph D. Sosbee's relationship with Santa Cruz County was minimal. He is included in this book because of his listing in the *Santa Cruz Sentinel* May 31, 1945, Honor Roll.

The US Census of 1920 indicates that he was born in Arkansas (possibly Russellville) about 1919 to Joseph A. and Clara Sosbee. A photo suggests that he may have attended a military academy prior to being commissioned in the US Coast Guard. Sosbee was married and had a son Stuart, who was twenty months old when the family moved to Santa Cruz. At the time of his death he had just been promoted to Lt. (jg) and was the head of a photogrammetric mission in defense-related work in the Aleutian Islands. The location of his remains, if recovered, is unknown.

(USCR, 1920 US Census, AR, Russellville; (SCSn July 21, 1943 1:6; Check-Six.Com US Coast Guard Aircraft Accidents , http://www.check-six.com/lib/Coast_Guard_Aviation_Casualties. htm#1940, [16 September, 2008] http://www.history.noaa.gov/ ships/sosbee.html, [21 December, 2009])

ARTHUR R. BROWN
(1943/08/03)

(Santa Cruz High School Service Cardinal)

A misstep and a splash from a gas can united to end the life of a marine cook.

Arthur Raymond Brown was born on August 29, 1923, in Santa Cruz to Raymond and Alice Brown. He had six sisters to watch over him during his formative years. He attended Mission Hill Junior High School and on February 2, 1939, entered Santa Cruz High School where he majored in carpentry.

In December 1941, Brown dropped out of school, entered the Merchant Marine Service and was trained to serve in the engineering department aboard transport and cargo ships.

Desiring more action, Arthur Brown left the Merchant Marines in February 1942, and in March joined the US Marine Corps. After completing training at Camp Pendleton, he was assigned to the 3rd Marine Division and served as a field cook. When he was promoted to chief cook, he became a non-commissioned officer.

While serving on an unidentified island in the South Pacific [probably in the Solomon Islands], he was carrying a can of gasoline past an open fire when some of the gasoline spilled into the blaze and exploded, engulfing him in flames. The attending medical officer noted in a letter to his parents that attempts to save him were unsuccessful. Sergeant Arthur R. Brown died on August 3, 1943.

His body was returned to Hawaii for burial in the National Cemetery at the "Punchbowl" on January 25, 1942.

(ABMC, SCHSC Pg. 6, SCR September 3, 1943 –2)

ROY K. ROBASCIOTTI
(1943/08/06)

(Sicily Rome American Cemetery Nettuno 1945 - Internet photo)

Roy K. Robasciotti was born in San Luis Obispo County, California, in 1910 to Benedetto and Santina Robasciotti. The Robasciotti household also included sisters Oliva and Jeanette and brother Arnold. When Roy was eight years old, his mother died and he lived briefly in the home of Carmella Minetti in Morro Bay, California. Roy later returned to his father's care and moved to the family home on Henry Street in Santa Cruz. It is unclear how long he remained there. After completing grammar school he attended a high school for one year.

Robasciotti enlisted in the regular army at Fort MacArthur at San Pedro California, on November 11, 1940.

When enlisting, he noted that he was single, drove a commercial vehicle for a living and that Santa Cruz was his residence. After completing basic training, Private Robasciotti was assigned to the 15th Infantry Regiment of the 3rd Infantry Division.

The following is a recap of the unit's activities during the period leading up to Roy's death.

[After the North African campaign] The regiment remained on duty in Morocco until March 1943, serving with other divisional units as the honor guard for President Roosevelt during the Casablanca Conference. In March 1943, the 15th moved to Tunisia, where it trained for further amphibious operations until July. The 15th was part of the 3ID's Task Force Joss in the invasion of Sicily on July 1943. The regiment fought with distinction at Palermo, Messina, and elsewhere in the Sicilian Campaign.

On September 8, 1943, Ben Robasciotti received a telegram from Washington, D. C. informing him that his son, Private First Class Roy K. Robasciotti, had been killed on August 6, 1943. Roy is buried in the Sicily-Rome American Cemetery in Nettuno Italy. His awards include the Purple Heart.

(USCR, 1920 US Census, CA, San Luis Obispo; NARA2; ABMC; 15th Infantry Regiment, Lineage and Historical Development, http://www.geocities.com/eureka/plaza/7750/15thinf02.html, [16 September 2008]; SCSn Sept 9, 1943 1:4)

SIDNEY C. ORMSBEE
(1943/08/16)

(Santa Cruz High School Service Cardinal)

Sid's name remains imprinted today in a stained glass panel in St. Johns Episcopal Church in Aptos, California.

Sidney Chase Ormsbee was born in Oakland, California, on April 16, 1916, to Mr. and Mrs. H. N. Ormsbee. He moved to Santa Cruz County as an infant and grew up in Capitola. Sidney attended grammar school in nearby Soquel and in 1932, entered Santa Cruz High School. In high school he took a general varied course, joined the Science Club and played on the basketball and football teams.

Upon graduation in 1936, Ormsbee enrolled in San Jose State College and for the next three years majored in forestry engineering. After leaving school, he worked as a forest ranger at Felton until the war began.

On December 20, 1941, Sidney Ormsbee entered the Army Air Corps as an aviation cadet. He was sent to Kelly Field, Texas, for his initial training followed by schools in Oklahoma City, Houston, and Midland, Texas. On September 3, 1942, he became Second Lieutenant Ormsbee.

While Sidney was undergoing combat training at Columbia, South Carolina, a U-boat menace along the US East Coast diverted him to submarine patrol duty until February 1943.

Upon receiving orders to North Africa, Lt. Ormsbee was assigned to the 487th AAF Squadron and navigated his B-17 Flying Fortress across the Atlantic, by way of Brazil, to Tunis, where he landed February 14. While serving in North Africa, he participated in the Tunisian campaign.

During the invasion of Italy, Ormsbee flew missions over Solerno and Palermo in Sicily, and was cited for bravery on a flight over Naples. After completing a bombing mission on August 16, 1943, Lieutenant Ormsbee's plane was shot down by anti-aircraft fire off Cape Faro. He bailed out of the aircraft, but was killed during his descent or upon landing.

The remains of Sidney Ormsbee were later recovered and returned to California, where they were interred in Oakwood Memorial Park in Santa Cruz.

(NARA2; SCR June 3, 1943 1, SCHSC Pg. 15, SCSn August 25, 1943 1:5}

ALBERT D. GODFREY
(1943/08/17)

(Santa Cruz High School Service Cardinal)

Delos was serving on a "tin can" when it exploded.

Albert Delos Godfrey was born on March 27, 1922, in Soquel, California, to Mr. and Mrs. Albert D. Godfrey. The Godfrey family also included one other son, Herbert, and a daughter, Mrs. Martin Blakemore. "Delos," as he was popularly known, attended elementary school in Soquel until

1937 when he entered Santa Cruz High School. In school he completed a trade and industrial course of study. Following his graduation in 1940, Godfrey went to Los Angeles where the North American Company employed him in their sheet metal department.

In June 1942, Albert Godfrey joined the US Navy, and was sent to boot camp in San Diego. When he completed his introductory and advanced training in early 1943, he was assigned to the Destroyer *Abner Read.*

After two weeks in dry dock at San Francisco, Abner Read *got underway on 14 June for Adak, Alaska. Upon her arrival there, she joined Task Force (TF) 16 and, soon thereafter, began patrolling the waters around Kiska Island. On 22 July, as part of TG 16.22, she took part in a heavy bombardment of Kiska. Between 12 and 15 August, the destroyer again shelled Kiska in support of landing operations on that island. On 17 August, American forces discovered that Japan had removed its forces from the island. While she was patrolling off Kiska that night,* Abner Read *was shaken by an explosion aft at 0150. The exact cause of the blast was unknown, and it was later thought that the destroyer had struck a mine. The concussion tore a huge hole in her stern and ruptured her smoke tanks. Men sleeping in aft compartments suffered from smoke inhalation. In the darkness, a few men fell through holes in the deck into fuel oil tanks below. Soon the stern broke away and sank. Once in the water, the men recovered from the effects of the smoke and could breathe.* Abner Read *was taken undertow by* Ute (AT-76) *at 0355 and was pulled to Adak for temporary repairs. The destroyer lost 70 men who were killed or missing, and another 47 were wounded.*

The explosion aboard the *Abner Read* on August 17, 1943, took the life of Seaman Second Class Albert Delos Godfrey. His remains were never recovered. He is memorialized on the Tablets of the Missing at the Honolulu Memorial. His awards include the Purple Heart.

(ABMC, SCHSC Pg. 10; DANFS, USS Abner Read DD-520; SCSn September 1, 1943 1:4)

BOYD W. FRIIS
(1943/08/25)

(Watsonville High School yearbook)

Two Watsonville High School "Wildcats" climbed into a plane for a final flight.

Boyd W. Friis was born in Sacramento, California, on July 23, 1919, to Mr. and Mrs. Sorn Friis. His family later moved to Watsonville where he enrolled in Watsonville High School. Boyd graduated in June 1938 and shortly thereafter, moved with his parents to nearby Salinas, California. Friis attended college for two years and prior to the war, worked in the entertainment field.

In March 1941, Boyd Friis enlisted in the regular US Army Air Corps Aviation Cadet program at the Presidio of Monterey. Following his training, he was awarded his wings and commissioned a second lieutenant. After a year and a half of service, he was promoted to first lieutenant and assigned to Merced Air Force Base, California.

On August 25, 1943, Friis was piloting an aircraft carrying the Merced AAFB finance officer, Lt. Stanley Secondo (also of Watsonville), to Denver, Colorado, when it crashed. His plane, accompanied by another aircraft, had passed Salt Lake City, Cheyenne and the Rocky Mountains on their way to Denver when he encountered engine trouble. Boyd radioed the companion plane that he was turning around and would attempt a forced landing at an auxiliary landing field he had spotted earlier. He missed that field by five miles and crashed, killing himself and Stanley Secondo. This was to have been Boyd's last cross-country trip before his promotion to captain.

The remains of First Lieutenant Boyd W. Friis were returned to Salinas for a funeral and interment in the Garden of Memories Cemetery.

(CBR; NARA2; SCSn August 28, 1943 1:3, WRP August 28, 1943; Photo-WHS)

STANLEY N. SECONDO
(1943/08/25)

(Courtesy of Diane Secondo Holley)

Stan was Watsonville to the core.

Stanley Norman Secondo was born on July 28, 1913, in Watsonville to Mr. and Mrs. Peter Secondo, whose family has lived in the Pajaro Valley for over one hundred years. Stan attended local schools, enrolled in Watsonville High School and was graduated in June 1933. Following graduation he entered Santa Clara University, where he studied for the next four years.

After completing college, Secondo became active in the Watsonville business and social community. He joined two friends, Marty Franich and Harold Mignola, in the automobile and service station business and was a member of the Elks, Lions, Service, and Rod and Gun Clubs and Native Sons of the Golden West.

When the war began, Stanley volunteered for active duty and on December 13, 1941, was given a commission in the US Army Finance Corps. Secondo was sent to Santa Ana, California, for training and then to the finance school at Fort Benjamin Harrison, Indiana. Following a brief assignment at Bakersfield, California, he was promoted to first lieutenant and appointed as the Finance Officer of the Merced Airbase.

In June 1942, Stanley Secondo married Patti Ann Shaw of Watsonville in the Fort Ord Chapel. After returning to the Merced AAFB, he began making plans for a forthcoming flight to Denver, Colorado, in July for an Army Finance meeting.

Stanley Secondo and Boyd Friis departed on their fatal flight to Denver on August 25, 1943. Following the airplane crash that took his life, the remains of First Lieutenant Stanley Norman Secondo were returned to Watsonville for a funeral and burial in the Valley Catholic Cemetery.

(CBR; SCSn August 28, 1943 1:3, WRP August 28, 1943 1:2, August 28, 1943 1:3)

ROBERT A. KNOX
(1943/08/31)

(Watsonville High School yearbook)

Robert Alvin Knox was born on March 26, 1922, in San Francisco, California, to Mr. and Mrs. R. E. Knox. Along with his sisters Barbara and Marjorie, Bob was raised in the Aptos area of Santa Cruz County. After completing grammar school, he enrolled in Watsonville High School. There Robert played in the band, was in the school orchestra and was a member of the track team. He graduated in June 1940. Upon graduation he moved to San Luis Obispo, California where he worked for Purity Food Stores.

Robert Knox enlisted in the US Navy on June 7, 1942 and was sent to the US Naval Training Center in San Diego. Following boot camp, he attended the navy's aviation radio school in Seattle, Washington, and the aviation gunnery school in Hollywood, Florida.

In January 1943, Knox reported to Floyd Bennett Field in Brooklyn, New York for ship assignment. In June of that same year, he joined the crew of an unspecified ship serving in the Atlantic Theater of the war.

On August 31, 1943, Aviation Radioman Third Class Robert Alvin Knox's plane crashed; he was reported "killed in the line of duty."

His remains were recovered, returned to California and reinterred in the Golden Gate National Cemetery in San Bruno in 1948.

(USDVA; SCSn October 7, 1943 5:7; Photo-WHS)

JAMES H. HART
(1943/09/03)

(Watsonville High School yearbook)

A "shave tail" lieutenant continued to fight.

James Howard Hart was born in Oklahoma in 1918 to Mr. and Mrs. Carmel Hart. Along with his parents and two brothers, Jay and Clarence, he moved to the Pajaro Valley about 1930. He spent his formative years in Watsonville and attended local grammar schools before entering Watsonville High School about 1932.

Following his graduation in 1936, Hart was employed locally in the entertainment field and in 1938, enrolled in Salinas Junior College.

In 1940 James Hart joined Company C of the 194th Tank Company and by 1941 had risen to the rank of corporal. He left Salinas with the tankers when they were ordered to Fort Lewis, Washington, in February 1941, and sailed with them in September aboard the *SS Coolidge* as it passed through the Golden Gate Bridge bound for Manila.

Shortly after arriving in the Philippines, Hart was commissioned a second lieutenant. He remained with the company through the defense of the islands and during its last stand and surrender on the Bataan Peninsula.

After his battalion was forced to surrender on April 9, 1942, Lt. Hart most likely continued to fight on. In 1942 the War Department informed the Hart family that their son James was "Missing in Action." The family waited in vain to hear that he was a prisoner of war. On Christmas Eve 1945, they received a telegram from the adjutant general of the army stating, "An official message has now been received which states that he [Lt. James Howard Hart] was killed in action on Sept. 3, 1943 in Bamban Tarlac, Philippine Islands." This would suggest that he had either escaped from a POW camp, or remained free to fight for a year and five months after his unit had surrendered. Lt. Hart's reported death occurred approximately 100 miles from where his unit had surrendered in 1942. His body was never recovered.

(NARA2; WRP May 26, 1942 1:1, December 26, 1945 1:6; 194TB;

Photo-WHS)

FRANCIS E. MORGAN III
(1943/09/06)

(San Francisco National Cemetery – Internet photo)

A native-born Santa Cruz airman was unable to wear his wings.

Francis Edward Morgan III was born in Santa Cruz, California, on March 8, 1923, to Dr. and Mrs. F. E. Morgan II, a prominent local dentist. The Morgan family also included a daughter and another son. Early in his life his father moved the family to Los Angeles to begin a new practice. After attending Los Angeles elementary and high schools, Francis III enrolled in San Jose State College about 1942.

Morgan left San Jose State College in early 1943 to enter the Army Air Corps cadet program. He completed his initial training in Santa Ana, California, and was then transferred to an Army Air Force facility in King City, California, for additional training.

On September 6, 1943, before Cadet Francis Edward Morgan's commissioning and the issuance of his wings, he was flying a PT-22 training aircraft at King City, when it collided with another aircraft and crashed. Morgan was killed in the crash. Following a funeral, his remains were buried in the San Francisco National Cemetery at the Presidio of San Francisco.

(USDVA; AAIR; SCSn September 9, 1943 1:1)

FRANCIS E. HOFFMAN
(1943/09/23)

(Golden Gate National Cemetery - San Bruno California)

Francis Hoffman was born March 25, 1920, to Mr. and Mrs. Ernest E. Hoffman on his father's ranch in Boulder Creek, California. Francis was raised with his brother Ernest at that ranch located on Bear Creek Road in the San Lorenzo Valley north of Santa Cruz. He attended local schools and entered Santa Cruz High School about 1936. In high school he took college preparatory courses and was a member of the fall class of 1940. After finishing school, he moved to Alameda County where he found employment and was married.

While living in Alameda County, Francis Hoffman registered for the draft and enlisted in the US Army in San Francisco on November 19, 1941. After completing basic training, he received additional instruction as a military policeman. He was then assigned to an MP company [Possibly the 202nd] that participated with the 3rd Infantry Division in the Italian Campaign of 1943.

During fighting at an unidentified location in Italy on September 23, 1943, Private First Class Francis Hoffman was killed in action. His remains were later returned to the United States and buried in Golden Gate National Cemetery San Bruno, California.

(NARA2; SCHSC Pg. 22, SCSn November 9, 1943)

ROBERT J. WILSON
(1943/10/07)

(Photo courtesy Charlyne Carpenter)

Robert Jay Wilson was born about 1925. His mother's name was Annie. The family also included sons Benjamin, Woodrow and Paul and a daughter Bernice. The year the family moved to the Pajaro Valley is not known, but they lived on Bridge Street in Watsonville during a portion of his school years. Robert attended Watsonville High School for about two years. He left in January 1942 to enlist in the US Navy. Following boot camp at the US Naval Training Center in San Diego, he was assigned to the *USS Selfridge* and joined its crew about May 1942.

In May, Selfridge *was reassigned to the 3d Fleet. On the 12th, she arrived at Nouméa. Through the summer, she operated with cruisers of TF 36, later TF 37, and participated in exercises with TF's 38, 39 and 34. In late September, as a unit of the 3d Fleet's amphibious force, she escorted an LST convoy to Vella Lavella, then commenced nighttime patrols up "the Slot" to intercept Japanese shipping.*

On the night of 6 October, Selfridge, O'Bannon, *and* Chevalier *intercepted an enemy force of six destroyers, three destroyer transports, and smaller armed craft some 12 miles off Marquana Bay as it attempted to evacuate land forces from Vella Lavella. In the ensuing Battle of Vella Lavella,* Chevalier *was torpedoed and damaged beyond repair. She was sunk on the 7th by an American torpedo.* Selfridge *and* O'Bannon *were both heavily damaged;* Selfridge *by an enemy torpedo;* O'Bannon *by enemy action compounded by collision with* Chevalier *just after the latter had gone dead in the water.*

Personnel casualties on board Selfridge *amounted to 13 killed, 11 wounded, and 36 missing.*

Seaman Second Class Robert J. Wilson was listed among those killed; however, his body was never recovered. He is included on the Tablets of the Missing at Manila American Cemetery. His awards include the Purple Heart.

(ABMC; WRP October 15, 1943 1:1, November 24, 1943 1:1; DANFS, USS Selfridge DD-357)

Myrl M. Sauers
(1943/11/20)

(Santa Cruz High School Service Cardinal)

A grandmother received the message, "Regret to inform you" announcing the death of her grandson at Tarawa.

Myrl Melvin Sauers was born on December 2, 1923, in Santa Cruz, California. Information regarding his parents is unavailable. Mrs. Hattie Fightmaster, Sauer's grandmother, raised him and his brother Dale in her Santa Cruz home. Melvin (the name he preferred) attended local elementary schools and Chaminade High School until he transferred to Santa Cruz High School in his junior year. In high school Melvin took college preparatory courses, majored in mathematics and played on the high school's basketball and football teams. He left high school in the spring of 1941.

In January 1942 Melvin Sauers joined the US Marine Corps. After completing basic and school-of-infantry training at Camp Pendleton, California, in April 1943, he was designated as a "gunner." Private Sauers was assigned to the 2nd Marine Division as it was wrapping up the Guadalcanal Campaign and preparing for the invasion of Tarawa in the South Pacific.

The Battle of Tarawa was a battle in the Pacific Theatre of World War II, largely fought from November 20-23, 1943. It was the second time the United States was on the offensive (the Battle of Guadalcanal had been the first), and the first offensive in the critical central Pacific region. It was also the first time in the war that the United States faced serious Japanese opposition to a US amphibious landing. Previous landings met little or no initial resistance; Tarawa was to be different. The 4,500 Japanese defenders were well-supplied and well-prepared; they fought almost to the last man, exacting a heavy toll on the American Marines.

Private First Class Myrl Melvin Sauers was one of those marines who paid the heavy toll at Tarawa. On November 20, 1943, Mel Sauers was killed in action. His body was never recovered; however, he is memorialized on the Tablets of the Missing at Honolulu Memorial Cemetery.

His awards include the Purple Heart.

(ABMC, SCHSC Pg. 17, SCR January 28, 1944 –1, WIKI, Tarawa, SCSn March 10, 1944)

David B. McQuillen
(1943/11/30)

David was looking for submarines in Africa when he seems to have vaporized.

David Bernard McQuillen was born about 1922 in the Monterey Bay area. He was the son of Captain Peter L. and Merle McQuillen. Following his father's retirement after serving at the Presidio of Monterey, the McQuillen family continued to live in Watsonville. David attended local schools and about 1936 enrolled in Watsonville High School.

About 1942 David McQuillen enlisted in the US Navy and following boot camp, was assigned to the naval aviation section and sent to radio school. Upon graduation he became a radioman and top turret gunner aboard a B-24 Liberator. McQuillen's unit served in the South Atlantic area and was engaged in patrolling the coast of Africa searching for enemy submarines.

In December 1943, the navy informed the McQuillen family that their son was missing. David's mother wrote for additional information surrounding the "missing status" of her son and in February, received the following reply:

I am able at this time to give you the following additional information on your son's case. He was a radioman aboard a large navy bomber. During the flight in question the plane was engaged in patrol against enemy submarines off the coast of Africa. The plane failed to land at its base upon completion of this flight. Exhaustive search of the area in which the plane was known to be has failed to locate the plane or your son.

The US Navy later officially listed Aviation Radioman Third Class David Bernard McQuillen as "Lost at Sea" on November 30, 1943.

(WRP December 30, 1943 1:1, February 9, 1944 1:1; ACGEN;)

Charles O. Brown Jr.
(1943/12/02)

(Santa Cruz High School Service Cardinal)

High school drama training had not prepared Charles for the real life drama that awaited him over Italy in 1943.

Charles Orville Brown Jr. was born in Santa Cruz, California, on October 16, 1914, to Charles and Mildred Brown. Charles attended local schools with his two sisters, Dell and Velma. In 1929 he entered Santa Cruz High School and was remembered for his amateur theatrical performances.

Following his graduation in 1932, Charles enrolled in San Jose State College and majored in music. After leaving college in 1942, he began a career in the insurance business with the Metropolitan Life Insurance Company. During that same period he was married; however, that marriage ended in a divorce

In February 1942 Charles Brown enlisted in the US Army Air Force and was sent to Shepard Field, Texas, for training. After basic training, he reported to Scotts Field, Illinois, for radio instruction; Boca Raton, Florida, for radar training; and DeRidder, Louisiana, where he was trained to be a bombardier on B25 bombers.

Staff Sergeant Brown was deployed to North Africa in February 1943 and participated in the war in Tunisia. Following the North African campaign, Brown and his crewmembers conducted bombing missions over Sicily.

After Sicily fell to the Allies, the Italian mainland became the Army Air Force's next target. Brown was assigned to the AAF base in Foggia and began flying missions from that location.

On the morning of December 2, 1943, after having completed twenty-eight previous missions, Sergeant Brown's plane was hit and seen falling to the earth. His remains were recovered and buried in the Sicily-Rome American Cemetery at Nettuno, Italy. His awards included the Air Medal with four Oak Leaf Clusters.

(NARA2; SCHSC, Pg. 7; SCSn August 8, 1944 1:3; ABMC)

Lewis M. Kerrick
(1943/12/16)

(Santa Cruz Riptide photo)

Lew Kerrick *[third from left]* and his "Blond Bomber" helped to establish a World War II tradition among GI bomber crews.

Lewis M. Kerrick was born in Santa Cruz, California, on July 8, 1919. No information is available regarding his parents. His grandparents, W. O. Kerrick and his wife, raised Lew. Lewis Kerrick attended local schools and about 1933 began Chaminade High School and graduated in 1937.

Kerrick enrolled in New Mexico Military Academy in Roswell, New Mexico, and while there became a rifleman of national prominence before graduating in 1939. For the next two years, Kerrick worked as a skiing instructor at Donner Summit, California.

On December 12, 1941, Lewis Kerrick enlisted in the Army Air Corps Aviation Cadet program at Moffett Field, California. He completed preliminary instruction at King City, California, and was then sent to Kelly Field, Texas, with the first contingent of cadets entering the program. Upon completion of cadet training, Kerrick received his silver wings and the brass bars of a second lieutenant. Schools in Georgia, North Carolina, Oklahoma and Washington State rounded out his flight training. It is believed that Lew Kerrick was married while in Oklahoma.

Following his stateside training, Lt. Kerrick was promoted to first lieutenant and assigned to the 337th Bomber Squadron, 96th Bomber Group of the 8th Air Force stationed in England. As he flew over Santa Cruz for the last time, Lew circled over his grandfather's laundry business, dipping his wings to say goodbye.

During World War II, naming bombers became an Air Force tradition. Lewis Kerrick had a picture of the movie star Betty Grable, whom he had met in Kansas, painted on the nose of his B-17. With her sponsorship he named it the "Blond Bomber." When he heard that Grable was about to have a baby, Kerrick gained further attention by replacing missions completed insignias with crawling babies on the side of his plane.

On December 16, 1943, during its eighth bombing mission over Germany, the "Blond Bomber" was hit and never returned to base. First Lieutenant Lewis M. Kerrick went down with his plane and was memorialized on the Tablets at Netherlands American Cemetery at Margraten. His awards include the Air medal with Oak Leaf Cluster.

(CBR; ABMC, NARA2; SCSn October 17, 1941 2:3, December 7, 1943 1:4, January 3, 1944 1:6, SCR January 7, 1944-1)

ROBERT L. THURMAN
(1943/12/24)

(Santa Cruz High School Service Cardinal)

Death could not rob Bob Thurman of the commission he had earned.

Robert Lee Thurman was born on April 22, 1923, in Santa Cruz, California, to Ralph and Wilma Thurman. He attended local grammar schools, Mission Hill Junior High School and on September 11, 1939, entered Santa Cruz High School. He took college preparatory courses in high school and was a star center on the Cardlet football team of 1942.

After graduating from high school, Thurman reported to the Mare Island Navy Yard to enlist in the naval air-cadet-training program. On January 14, 1943, Cadet Thurman began a three-month training program at St. Mary's College, followed by additional instruction at Los Alamitos, California. In December 1943 he began the final phase of his cadet instruction at Pensacola, Florida.

On December 21, 1943, during a training flight, Thurman's plane crashed and he was placed in a hospital. On Christmas Eve 1943, Robert Lee Thurman succumbed to the injuries that he had sustained in the crash. His remains were returned to Santa Cruz for a funeral and interment in Santa Cruz Memorial Park.

In March 1944, his mother, Mrs. Wilma Thurman, received a letter from Washington, D.C. informing her that

in recognition of Robert's training service prior to his death, Secretary of the Navy Frank Knox had signed the paperwork commissioning Robert Lee Thurman (posthumously) an ensign in the USNR.

(SCHSC Pg. 19; SCSn December 25, 1943 8:2, December 26, 1943, March 31, 1944 1:6)

1944

RALPH E. FREEK
(1944/01/16)

(Ft. McPherson National Cemetery - Internet photo)

Finding targets for Ralph to photograph was easy; finding Freek proved more difficult.

Ralph E. Freek was born in Montana in 1921. After moving to Santa Cruz at an early age, he probably lived with his grandmother, Mrs. Switzler and aunt, May Aubrey Morse, who resided in Santa Cruz. Ralph Freek was living in the community in the 1930s and finished Mission Hill Junior High School in 1936. Shortly thereafter he left and moved to Siskiyou County where he completed high school. In 1941 Ralph spent a year at Sacramento Junior College taking a civilian pilot training program while working in the entertainment business.

Ralph Freek enlisted in the Army Air Corps' cadet program on April 3, 1942, and was sent to Santa Ana, California for further training. While flying a training exercise at the Visalia Army Air Force base on May 23, 1942, Ralph was involved in a crash; however, he was allowed to remain in the cadet program. After completing his initial training in October 1942 at Stockton Field, California, Freek received his wings and was commissioned a second lieutenant.

In 1943 Lt. Freek was sent overseas and assigned to a photo-reconnaissance group in New Guinea. While flying a mission on January 16, 1944, First Lieutenant Ralph E. Freek was reported missing. The circumstances surrounding his death have not been located, but his remains were later found and interred in the McPherson National Cemetery in Maxwell, Nebraska.

(USDVA; NARA2; SCSn March 18, 1942 5:1, April 07, 1945 1:2;

AAIR)

ARNOLD H. SEHESTEDT
(1944/01/21)

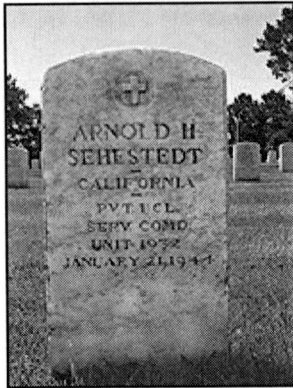

(Golden Gate National Cemetery - San Bruno California)

A runaway truck in San Francisco got in Arnold's way.

Arnold H. Sehestedt was born on January 17, 1907, in California, to Samuel and Emma Sehestedt. Arnold, along with his brother Harold and sister Edna, grew up in a home in the Branciforte district of Santa Cruz. It is likely that he attended local elementary schools, but his high school enrollment has not been confirmed. Later, Arnold and his mother moved to the Granite Creek area of the county where they remained until 1943.

During his residence in the county, Sehestedt was employed as a plumber. He learned that trade while employed by the Santa Cruz Plumbing Service and practiced it working for the firm of Fred Schlichting.

In 1943 Arnold Sehestedt entered the US Army, and his mother relocated to Berkeley, California, to live with her daughter Edna. Sehestedt completed basic training and was assigned to Station Complement Unit 1932, a supply company assigned to Fort Winfield Scott at the Presidio of San Francisco. While working at that fort on January 21, 1944, Arnold Sehestedt was struck and killed by a runaway truck.

Following a funeral at the Halstead and Company Mortuary in San Francisco on January 26, Sehestedt was buried in the Golden Gate National Cemetery in San Bruno, California.

(USCR, 1910, US Census, CA, Santa Cruz; NARA2; ACGEN; USDVA; SCSn January 22, 1944 Page 1, January 23, 1944; CDR)

QUENTIN T. NEWHART
(1944/01/28)

(Santa Cruz High School Service Cardinal)

Quentin hit the silk with "those Devils in Baggy Pants."

Quentin T. Newhart was born in California in 1920 to A. P. and Barbara Newhart. In addition to Quentin, the Newhart family included sons Talbert and Harry and daughter Emma. In 1930 Barbara Newhart moved from San Rafael to Santa Cruz and purchased the local Mode O' Day clothing shop. Quentin entered Santa Cruz High School about 1935 and took college preparatory science courses.

Upon graduation from high school, Newhart enrolled in San Francisco State College, majored in literature and social studies and worked part time as a warehouseman. After completing two years of college, he left to join the Merchant Marine Service and remained with them until October 1942.

Quentin Newhart enlisted in the US Army in San Francisco on October 17, 1942. Following his basic training, he was sent to Fort Benning, Georgia, for paratrooper instruction. In 1943 he became a member of the 504th Parachute Regiment of the 82nd Airborne Division. The division was called "those devils in baggy pants," a name retrieved from a German army officer's diary.

Quentin was with the 504th during the invasion of Sicily in July 1943, and is believed to have jumped on Salerno to help save that beachhead.

While the 504th was fighting near Naples in October 1943, Quentin was wounded and sent to a hospital in North Africa for a one-month recuperation period. The history of the 504th after Private First Class Newhart's return and subsequent death follows:

Finally, the Regiment was pulled back to Naples on 4 January 1944 and rumors of another parachute mission spread. The operation was to be called "Shingle," and it involved an airborne assault into a sector behind the coastal town of Anzio, 28 miles south of Rome. It seemed, however, that even the locals in Naples knew of the operation, so the 504th was glad that the beach would be assaulted from troop-carrying landing craft. The landing on Red Beach went smoothly -- at least until enemy planes started their strafing runs on the landing craft. The unit disembarked under fire and was sent shortly thereafter to patrol in force along the Mussolini Canal. After several days of intense German artillery fire, the enemy launched his main drive to push the Allies back into the sea. The 3rd Battalion was committed with the British First (Guards) Division in the heaviest fighting, with the paratrooper companies reduced in strength to between 20 and 30 men. H Company drove forward to rescue a captured British General and was cut off. I Company broke through to them with their remaining 16 men.

It was probably during this period of fighting in the vicinity of Anzio that Private First Class Quentin T. Newhart was killed in action on January 28, 1944. His body was buried in the Sicily-Rome American Cemetery in Nettuno, Italy. His awards include the Purple Heart.

(ABMC; NARA2; SCHSC, Pg. 14, SCSn February 29, 1944 1:7, SCR March 3, 1944 –1, WIKI, 50504th Infantry Parachute)

JOSEPH C. MARSH
(1944/01/29)

(Watsonville Register-Pajaronian photo)

For almost three months the fate of Joe Marsh remained a mystery.

Joseph Cowles Marsh was born in Watsonville on December 1, 1921, to Lynn and Lillian Marsh of Freedom. Joe and his brother Robert attended local schools and in 1935, he enrolled in Watsonville High School. In high school he played on the football team, was active in the Spanish club and worked on the *Manzanita* yearbook. Outside of school he participated in the DeMolay fraternal organization and earned his Eagle Scout badge. After Joe graduated in 1939, he enrolled in Salinas Junior College and completed that school's two-year program.

In 1941 Joseph Marsh was employed by Pacific Gas and Electric in the maintenance department and became active in the Pajaro Valley community by joining the 20-30 Club and the Masons.

Marsh enlisted in the army's aviation training program on July 23, 1942, and was called into the service in Febru-

ary 1943. Cadet Marsh was sent to Santa Ana, California, for his primary training, followed by advanced training at Visalia and Lancaster, California, and Williams Field, Arizona. He was commissioned a second lieutenant and assigned to a P-38 fighter squadron stationed at Salinas and Santa Maria.

On January 29, 1944, Second Lieutenant Joseph Cowles Marsh and eleven other pilots were returning from Riverside, California, to Santa Maria aboard a bomber when it crashed. Search parties continued to scour the California hills and mountains, but the wreckage was not found until April 19, 1944. The remains of Joseph Marsh were returned to Watsonville, cremated and buried in the Pajaro Valley Memorial Park.

(WRP April 26, 1944 1:4, April 24, 1944)

CHARLES A. PARMENTER
(1944/02/08)

(Santa Cruz High School Service Cardinal)

In 1945 the troop ship *Lawrence Victory* gave Charles a ride home, but not the way he had originally planned.

Charles A. Parmenter was born in Davenport, California, on July 28, 1923, to Arthur M. and Elizabeth Parmenter. He attended local schools and entered Santa Cruz High School about 1938. In high school he followed a trade and industrial curriculum. In February 1942, Parmenter transferred to Oakland Evening School, graduated in June and found employment in Alameda County as a welder.

On February 17, 1943, Charles Parmenter was inducted into the US Army in San Francisco and sent to Camp Wolters, Texas, for basic training. After completing the infantry training program, he was assigned to the Texas 141st Infantry Regiment of the 36th Infantry Division. That summer, he was sent to North Africa and by 1944 was in Italy.

The Germans called the 141st "wild men from Texas, skilled in field craft and fighting." In January and February, 1944 the 141st reached the River Rapido, a name that left a bloody page in the records of the 141st and 143rd. Terrible casualties resulted as the Alamo Regiment attempted to force the stream, lacking boats, bridges and artillery support. The 48 hours at the Rapido River cost the Regiment dearly. And there still was fighting ahead, Monte Cassino. By the end of this campaign, February 27, platoons were reduced to squads, companies to platoon strength and battalions to two hundred men.

It is likely that Private Charles A. Parmenter lost his life while fighting in the area of the River Rapido on February 8, 1944. He was initially buried in Italy, but his remains were returned home in 1945. His final resting place has not been identified.

(NARA2; SCHSC Pg. 15, SCSn March 15, 1944 1:6, November 11, 1948 2:5; Texas Military Forces Museum, 141st Infantry Regiment, http://www.texasmilitaryforcesmuseum.org/36division/archives/141/141lin.htm, [16 September 2008])

KENNETH E. FOX
(1944/02/10)

(Watsonville High School yearbook)

A budding reporter experienced a shocking air crash story but was unable to include a byline.

Kenneth E. Fox was born in Nevada in 1921. No information is available regarding his father. His mother later married Victor J. Petersen, a Pajaro Valley resident and relocated to Watsonville. Kenneth entered Watsonville High School in the late 1930s and while there, served on the school board, Red Cross council and was a sports reporter and business manager for school publications.

After Fox's graduation in 1939, he attended college for a year and the family left Watsonville. When Victor Peterson was transferred to Panama (about 1941), Ken's mother relocated to San Jose and he moved to Gilroy. While in Gilroy, he worked as a reporter for the *Gilroy Dispatch* newspaper.

On September 10, 1942 Kenneth Fox was inducted into the army in San Francisco and in 1943 entered the Aviation Cadet Program.

He was scheduled to complete his flight training in March 1944; however, that never occurred. While flying over George Field near Lawrenceville, Illinois, on February 10, 1944, the plane that Cadet Kenneth E. Fox was flying collided with another aircraft killing him and eight other airmen.

His remains were returned to San Jose for a funeral and burial at Golden Gate National Cemetery in San Bruno, February 18, 1944.

USDVA; NARA2; WRP February 11, 1944 1:4; WRP February 17, 1944, 1:7; Photo-WHS)

JACK W. RUSH
(1944/02/20)

(Santa Cruz High School Service Cardinal)

Sergeant Jack Rush was on hand at Eniwetok for a different kind of blast.

Jack W. Rush was born in California on October 28, 1922, to Charles and Ethel Rush. Jack and his brothers Charles and Robert were raised in Soquel and attended the local grammar school. About 1939 he enrolled in Santa Cruz High School and specified trade and industrial printing as his specific areas of interest.

On April 17, 1941, Jack Rush enlisted in the US Army in San Francisco and was assigned to the infantry. He was sent to Hawaii and was in training at Schofield Barracks when the Japanese attacked on December 7, 1941. In June 1942, Rush was promoted to sergeant and assigned to the Christmas Islands where he remained for the next ten months.

Jack Rush returned to Hawaii in August 1943 to enter a specialized machine gun training program. In January 1944, he was promoted to staff sergeant and assigned to the 106th Infantry Regiment of the 27th Infantry Division. Sergeant Rush was with that unit in their invasion of Eniwetok Island in the Marshall Island chain in February 1944.

Captured documents suggested that the defences on Eniwetok Island would be light, and accordingly there was only a short bombardment on 19 February before the 106th Infantry Regiment went ashore. This was a mistake: the Japanese soldiers had strong positions and the Americans were stopped by heavy automatic fire. The island was not secured until 21 February. 37 Americans were killed; more than 800 Japanese defenders died.

Sergeant Jack W. Rush was one of those thirty-seven Americans killed in action during the invasion. His body was initially buried on the island but was returned to California to be buried in the Golden Gate National Cemetery in San Bruno in1949.

(NARA2; USDVA; WIKI, Eniwetok; SCHSC Pg. 17, SCSn March 16, 1944 1:5, SCR March 24, 1944 –1)

DAREN A. MCINTYRE
(1944/02/24)

(Watsonville High School yearbook)

A local navigator directed his B-17 over Germany but received too much flak to return.

Daren Adrian McIntyre was born on April 1, 1922, in Ojai, California, to Mr. and Mrs. L. O. McIntyre. He came to Watsonville with his parents in 1923 and along with his brother Leslie, attended local schools. Daren enrolled in Watsonville High School in 1936 and was well known among students. In addition to working as a newspaper carrier, he was active in the Watsonville DeMolay organization. In 1940 he graduated from high school and for the next two years worked at the Charles Ford Company and the Watsonville Lumber Company

McIntyre enlisted in the army in September 1942 and was accepted into the Aviation Cadet Program. After training at Santa Ana, California, and Ellington Field, Texas, he completed the navigator school in October 1943 and was commissioned a second lieutenant. After further training at Wendover Field, Utah, he was assigned to the 457th Bomb Group that flew B-17s out of England.

On February 24, 1944, the Flying Fortress in which Second Lieutenant Daren Adrian McIntyre served as navigator was flying a bombing raid over Schweinfurt, Germany, when it was hit by flak. Some of the crewmembers bailed out; however, McIntyre went down with his aircraft as it

crashed in the vicinity of Ostsrands von Emmern, Germany. His body was never recovered His awards include the Air Medal.

(CBR; WRP July 30, 1945, October 16, 1951 1:1; Photo-WHS; Homage to Lilo, Combat Chronology, http://www.chez.com/franckruffino/My-Site/Victory_21.htm, [16 September 2008])

TROY V. DEMOSS
(1944/02/26)

(Pioneer Cemetery – Watsonville, California)

Troy's plane was a half a mile short of a "touchdown" when the lights went out.

Troy Vernon DeMoss was born in Oklahoma in 1924 to Mr. and Mrs. DeMoss, His mother's name was Rose. Also included in the family were brothers Ray, James and Fred, and sisters Edith, Helen, Pauline, Juanita, Lorrette and Geraldine. The family later moved to Watsonville where Troy attended local schools and Watsonville High School for a year.

After finishing his formal education, DeMoss worked for the Postal Telegraph Company in Watsonville as a messenger. During the early 1940s, he married a girl named Jodie, and worked as an assembler at an unidentified aircraft assembly plant.

On March 22, 1943 Troy DeMoss was inducted into the US Army at San Francisco and assigned to its Air Force. After training as an aerial gunner at Las Vegas, Nevada, and Salt Lake City, Utah, he was promoted to sergeant and sent to Alexandria AAFB, Louisiana.

On February 26, 1944 the *Watsonville Register-Pajaronian* reported that Sergeant Troy Vernon DeMoss' plane was "demolished half a mile short of the Alexandria Field runway while coming in for a landing." He was killed in the crash and his remains were returned to Watsonville.

Following a funeral service in the Church of the Nazarene, Troy DeMoss was interred in Watsonville Pioneer Cemetery.

(NARA2; WRP February 26, 1944 1:2, March 2, 1944 1:1)

DANIEL T. DOYLE
(1944/03/?)

(Santa Cruz Riptide photo)

Danny played out his final hand at Cassino.

Daniel Thomas Doyle was born in Santa Cruz, California, on December 19, 1919, to Daniel and Mary Doyle. He grew up in a home on Bay Street in Santa Cruz and attended local schools. About 1933 he enrolled in Chaminade High School, played basketball for the "Panthers" and in the Knights of Columbus basketball league. After three years of high school, Danny left Chaminade to work for the Monterey Bay Lumber Company.

On December 12, 1942, Doyle was inducted into the US Army as a private. He completed basic training at Camp Roberts, California, and was probably assigned to the 36th Infantry Division that shipped overseas in April 1943. After a short tour in North Africa, Private First Class Doyle and his unit were sent to the Italian Front. On September 9, 1943, he fought during the invasion at Salerno, was wounded and returned to North Africa for recuperation.

After forty-five days of hospitalization, Danny Doyle returned to his unit as it was preparing for an assault on Monte Cassino.

On February 15 [1945] the monastery, high on a peak overlooking the town of Cassino, was destroyed by American B-17, B-25, and B-26 bombers. Two days after the bombing, crack German paratroopers poured into the ruins to defend it. From January 17 to May 18, it was assaulted four times by Allied troops, for a loss of over 54,000 Allied and 20,000 German soldiers.

The exact date that Private First Class Daniel T Doyle was killed in action has not been identified. His mother received a telegram from the war department the second week in March notifying her that he was missing. A follow-up telegram on March 17, 1944, confirmed his death.

Following the war, the remains of Danny Doyle were returned to Santa Cruz and buried in the family plot in the Old Holy Cross Cemetery.

(NARA2; SCSn June 9, 1943 2:1, October 10, 1943 2:1, November 21, 1943 4:3, March 17, 1944 1:5; WIKI, Cassino)

WILLIAM L. COMSTOCK
(1944/03/03)

(Golden Gate National Cemetery – San Bruno California)

Listed in the National Archives Records Administration names of Santa Cruz County war casualties is that of William Leo Comstock.

Comstock was born on June 30, 1907, in Oklahoma to Mr. and Mrs. Claude Comstock. No information is available as to his siblings, education or the community in which he spent his youth.

Information relating to his naval career is also missing. William Comstock was a Motor Machinist's Mate Third Class, US Naval Reserve. No additional information regarding his naval service has surfaced. The date and length of his residence in Santa Cruz County have also not been established. His parents, Mr. and Mrs. Claude Allen Comstock resided in Santa Cruz at the time of their son's death on March 3, 1944, and the county was used as the address of his next of kin.

Comstock's remains were recovered and returned to the Golden Gate National Cemetery in San Bruno where they were interred in 1948.

(USDVA; ACGEN)

SAM WONG
(1944/03/04)

(Courtesy John Wong)

Corporal Sam Wong was the only recorded Chinese-American death from Santa Cruz County identified during World War II.

Sam was born in China about 1925, to Mr. and Mrs. Tom Wong. Along with Sam and their other children, John, Jimmy, Lily, Mabel, Hazel and Bess, the Wong family moved to Watsonville in 1942. Tom opened and operated the Star Café and Sam enrolled in Watsonville High School. When not attending classes, he assisted his father at the family café. Prior to World War II, Sam also received instruction as an electronic repair technician.

In July 1943, Sam Wong was inducted into the US Army and assigned to its air force. Following his basic training, he received instruction as an aerial gunner. During his tour in the Air Force, Sam rose to the rank of corporal and served aboard a B-17 Flying Fortress as a belly gunner.

Before departing for the European theater, Wong was sent with his plane to Sioux City, Iowa, to take part in a combat training exercise. While participating in that exercise on March 4, 1944, the four-motored bomber began developing engine trouble. Three of the nine-man crew bailed out, while the remaining six, including Sam, were killed when the plane crashed.

The remains of Corporal Sam Wong were returned to Watsonville where a large funeral was held at the (Chinese) Presbyterian Church, followed by burial at the Watsonville Pioneer Cemetery.

(WRP March 6, 1944 1:4, March 11, 1944 1:1)

KENNETH A. HICKEY
(1944/03/08)

(Santa Cruz High School Service Cardinal)

A wife and fourteen-month-old son awaited a husband and father who never returned.

Kenneth Anthony Hickey was born on June 16, 1920, in Hollister, California, to Edward and Mary Hickey. In 1931 he and his brother Terrance moved to Santa Cruz with their parents. His sister Patricia was later added to the Hickey family. In Santa Cruz Ken attended Mission Hill Junior High School where he met Lela Borden who became his childhood sweetheart. At Santa Cruz High School Hickey excelled scholastically, was a star athlete and a student body leader. Throughout high school his romance with Lela Borden continued.

Following his high school graduation in 1937, Ken and Lela both enrolled in the University of California, Berkeley. During his three years at UCB, he worked part time as a warehouseman and stock clerk. In 1942 Ken and Lela were married.

In April 1942, Kenneth Hickey enlisted in the Army Air Corps Aviation Cadet program and was sent to Santa Ana, California, for cadet training. Additional training assignments followed and upon completion of flight school at Mather Field in Sacramento in August 1943, he was commissioned a second lieutenant. In 1943, their son Kenneth was born.

In November 1943, Hickey bid his wife and nine-month old son goodbye and navigated his B-17 to England as a member of the 338th Bomb Group of the US 8th Air Force. On March 8, 1944, Second Lieutenant Kenneth Anthony Hickey flew off on his eighteenth bombing mission over Germany. He did not return from that mission.

His remains were later recovered, returned to the US and buried in Golden Gate National Cemetery in San Bruno, California in 1950.

(NARA2; USDVA; SCHSC Pg. 11, SCSn March 29, 1944 1:2, SCR April 7, 1944–1)

RUSSELL B. SCOTT JR.
(1944/03/08)

(National Memorial Cemetery Pacific - Internet photo)

"Lieut. Russell Scott Dies in Hawaiian Islands" noted the *Santa Cruz News* article.

Russell B. Scott Jr. was born to Mr. and Mrs. Russell B. Scott, Sr. on July 31, 1921. His place of birth, siblings and information regarding his formative years have not been located, but it is likely that he was raised in Illinois.

Scott, a resident of Chicago, Illinois, entered the army, was commissioned a second lieutenant and assigned to the 54th Coast Artillery at Camp McQuaide near Watsonville. While serving in the county, Lieutenant Scott met and married Dorothy Ross of Santa Cruz, where the couple made their home.

In February 1943, Lt. Scott was transferred to the 55th Coast Artillery located in Hawaii. It is likely that he was assigned to the 2nd Battalion that became attached to the 24th Corps Artillery preparing for the invasion of the Mariana Islands in the Central Pacific. Prior to that invasion, he was serving at an unidentified location in the Central Pacific when he was accidentally wounded in early March. Lt. Scott was returned to Hawaii where he died on March 8, 1944.

He was buried at an unspecified location and later reinterred in the Honolulu Memorial Cemetery on February 17, 1949.

(ABMC, SCSn May 10, 1944)

JACK B. AVERRETT
(1944/03/10)

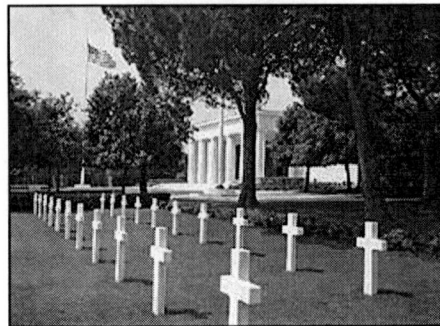

(Sicily Rome American Cemetery Nettuno - Internet photo)

Jack joined his brother Waldo in the army, but the Italian campaign prevented their reunion.

Jack B. Averrett, who was descended from Pajaro Valley pioneer Jacob Blackburn, was born to Mr. and Mrs. Harry Averrett in Watsonville in 1917. His mother died when he was a baby, leaving his father to care for him and his brother Waldo. Harry re-married and provided a home for his sons and second wife until a World War I wound forced his confinement in the VA Hospital at Palo Alto. Jack had only completed one year of high school when he was forced to leave school and seek employment. In January 1943 he was unemployed and living in Carbon County, Utah.

Jack B. Averrett returned to California and on February 6, 1943, was inducted into the army in Sacramento. Following basic training, he was assigned to the 540th Combat Engineers. The 540th regimental history details activities of his unit during the final weeks of his life.

On January 22, 1944, Allied forces landed at Anzio, Italy, in Operation Shingle, a movement to draw German forces away from Cassino and provide the Allies access to Rome. The 540th Engineer Combat Regiment was involved in clearing and maintaining the beach at Anzio as a port of operations for the Allied forces after a heavy bombardment by the German artillery.

On March 10, 1944, while the 540th Combat Engineers continued to fight their way out of Anzio, Jack B. Averrett was listed as killed in action. His body was recovered and buried in the Sicily-Rome American Cemetery in Nettuno, Italy. His awards include the Purple Heart.

(ABMC; NARA2; WRP April 18, 1944 1:4, SCSn July27, 1944; West Virginia Division Culture & History, West Virginia Veterans Memorial, http://www.wvculture.org/history/wvmemory/vets/hughes/hughes.html, [16 September 2008])

WALTER H. MORELLI
(1944/03/13)

(Santa Cruz High School Service Cardinal)

Two Santa Cruz buddies joined the Merchant Marines together; only one returned home.

Walter Henry Morelli was born in Santa Cruz, California, on October 1, 1921, to Olympio and Mary Morelli. He shared the family home with his parents, his brothers Fred and Anthony and his sister Emma. Following grammar school, Walter attended Mission Hill Junior High School before enrolling in Santa Cruz High School in 1937. He only remained at that school for one semester and in the fall of 1937 transferred to Chaminade High School. During his years in Chaminade, he excelled in basketball and also played on the church league teams. Morelli graduated from Chaminade High School with the class of 1940 and remained in the area.

In 1942 Walter and his buddy, Richard Jeantrout, joined the US Merchant Marines. The two young men were sent to a two-month training program at Port Hueneme and in August were assigned as able-bodied seaman aboard the Standard Oil Company tanker *H.D. Collier.* Morelli served aboard the tanker enroute to New Zealand and Australia before returning home for Christmas 1942. In January 1943, the ship made its way back to Australia, India and Arabia, and returned to the US in July.

Walter Morelli and the *Collier* left California in August 1943 for the last time and sailed across the South Pacific carrying oil between Southern Hemisphere countries. Events of March 13, 1944, began the final episode in Morelli's life.

March 13, 1944. The tanker SS H.D. Collier operated by Standard Oil of San Francisco (Chevron) was en route from Iran to Bombay with 103,000 barrels of gasoline and kerosene when it was torpedoed by the Japanese submarine I-26 about 300 miles from Karachi, India. The entire stern immediately caught fire, and the radio aerials were destroyed. The forward gun could not be aimed at the sub, and the stern gun was in flames. The sub surfaced and began shelling the ship as the crew-abandoned ship. 33 members of

the crew and 12 Naval Armed Guard were killed.

Walter Henry Morelli was on watch when the torpedo hit the ship and disappeared immediately. His Santa Cruz buddy, Richard Jeantrout, was rescued from the *Collier* and returned home alone. Morelli's body was never recovered. In 1945 Walter was posthumously awarded the Mariner's Medal.

(Merchant Mariners.org, This Week in the History of the Merchant Marines, http://www.usmm.org/this week .html [16 September 2008]; SCHSC Pg. 13; SCSn March, 1944 2:6, January 30, 1945 1:2, SCR April 21, 1944 –1)

JOHN E. WARE
(1944/03/16)

Watsonville readers of the *Register-Pajaronian* became a part of John Ware's B-17 as he shared his experiences of a bombing mission.

John E. Ware was born in Kern County, California, on May 30, 1924, to Mr. and Mrs. Ralph Ware. The Wares originally resided in Monterey. It was probably in that community that he attended elementary school and three years of high school. After he left high school, he moved to Aptos, where his parents were living, and he worked in the construction trade.

John Ware enlisted in the Army Air Corps on November 20, 1942, and received training in Salinas, California, Buckley Field, Colorado, and Kingman, Arizona, before being shipped overseas. Sergeant Ware served as a tail gunner on a B-17 named *Hangover* that was part of the 711th Bomb Squadron of the 447th Bomb Group of the 8th Air Force stationed in England.

In February 1944 Ware described a bombing mission over France in a letter home to his parents. A portion of that account is taken from a *Watsonville Register-Pajaronian* article that appeared on February 5, 1944.

Press stories, early in January, told the story of the first and last mission of the Flying Fortress, Hangover, in a raid over Cognac, France when three German fighters, and probably four more, were shot down. Staff Sergeant John E. Ware, son of Mr. and Mrs. Ralph Ware, Rt. 1, Box 191, Aptos, was one of the crew members of the bomber which eventually found its way back to its English base, picked with 142 holes, all four engines damaged, the instruments destroyed and out of gas. He wrote home a vivid description of the mission of testing guns over the English Channel, of opening up on two Focke Wulf 190s at 1000 yards. I was really scared, he continues: The flak started then. It sounded as though all hell had broken loose. I hovered over my guns and prayed. The Number 2 engine was hit by flak and caught on fire. His story goes on about bandaging the head of the top turret gunner who had been hit and getting back to his position in time to really start shooting at the swarms of FW 109s and ME 109s which attacked the Hangover.

On March 16, 1944, S/Sgt John E. Ware and the *Hangover* were not so lucky. They departed on their final mission over Augsburg, Germany; however, while over Orconte, France, the *Hangover* crashed and John was killed. The location of his remains is not known.

(NARA2; 447th Bomb Group, Combat Action List, http://www.447bg.com/aclist_2.html, (Approx. May 2007), WRP February 5, 1944 1:1, SCSn November 10, 1944 1:2)

FRANK J. JURACH
(1944/03/18)

(Watsonville Register-Pajaronian photo)

For a year and a half the Jurach family awaited word as to the fate of their son Frank.

Frank Joseph Jurach was born in Sacramento, California, on February 8, 1924, to Mr. and Peter Jurach. Frank's family, which included his brothers Edward and Anthony, moved to the Pajaro Valley where he spent the latter portion of his youth. While living in the valley, he attended Watsonville High School, where he was active in the Latin and Spanish clubs, was a yell leader on the rally squad, was a member of the track team and participated in school plays. Frank graduated in 1941. For five years Jurach delivered newspapers for the *Watsonville Register-Pajaronian* and later became head carrier. Prior to entering the armed forces, he attended Salinas Junior College.

Frank Jurach joined the Army Air Corps in January 1943. His initial training was at Keesler Field, Mississippi, and later he attended the armorer school at Camp Buckley in Denver, Colorado. In January 1944, he came home to Watsonville for the last time before going overseas.

When Jurach arrived in England in February 1944, he was assigned to the 8th Air Force as a B-17 gunner. The unit in which he served has not been confirmed but was likely part of the 303rd Bomb Group.

On March 18, 1944, while on a mission over Germany,

Jurach's Flying Fortress failed to return and the air force notified his parents that he was missing in action. For a year and half knowledge of his fate was unknown. Finally, on September 20, 1945, the Jurach family received a letter from Maj. General Edward F. Witsell acting adjutant general in which he said,

Information in the hands of the war department indicates that your son was a crew member in a B-17 aircraft which departed England on an operational mission to Munich, Germany. Mechanical failure caused the ship to leave the formation and it was trailing approximately 300 yards when it was attacked by six enemy fighter planes that so damaged your son's craft that the crew was ordered to abandon it. During the engagement at least one German fighter was shot down. Seven of the 10-man crew are known to have since been evacuated to the United States. The aircraft crashed in the vicinity of Rottwell, which is approximately 135 miles west of Munich in Southwestern Germany.

The location of the remains of Sergeant Frank Joseph Jurach, if recovered, is not known.

(CBR; ACGEN; WRP September 21, 1945 1:2)

GEORGE D. KELLOGG JR.
(1944/03/19)

(Watsonville Register-Pajaronian photo)

The Watsonville High School Class of 1940 lost one of its own and a young girl lost her fiancé.

George Dewey Kellogg Jr. was born about 1922, to Mr. and Mrs. George D. Kellogg. The location of his birth and early life has not been established. At least a portion of his formative years was spent at the family residence on Brennan Street in Watsonville. Between 1936 and 1940 he attended Watsonville High School and was among the 1940 graduates.

In 1943 George Kellogg joined the US Army Air Force and was assigned to the AAF ground forces technical training command. During this period, he was sent to the armorer school at Buckley Field, Colorado, and later graduated from the gunnery school at Harlingen, Texas.

George announced his engagement to Virginia Rimassa in October 1943, while home on leave before being shipped overseas.

Kellogg was sent to Italy in March 1944 and assigned to a B-17 crew as an aerial gunner. On March 19, 1944, while on a mission over Italy, the Flying Fortress in which Staff Sergeant George Dewey Kellogg Jr. was a crewmember was hit by enemy fire and crashed.

His body was never recovered. He was memorialized on the Tablets of the Missing at Sicily-Rome American Cemetery in Nettuno, Italy. His awards include the Air Medal and Purple Heart.

(ABMC, WRP April 14, 1944 1:2, July 3, 1944 1:2, November 9, 1944 1:3)

ARTHUR R. BOUDREAU
(1944/04/17)

(Santa Cruz High School Service Cardinal)

Art Boudreau enjoyed speed and risk taking during his brief twenty-two year life.

Arthur Raymond Boudreau was born on May 6, 1922, in Chippewa Falls, Wisconsin, to Mr. and Mrs. William Boudreau. The Boudreau family also consisted of two other sons and one daughter. They arrived in Santa Cruz about 1936 and Arthur enrolled in Santa Cruz High School. He graduated in 1939 and worked for some time in the circulation department of the *Santa Cruz Evening News*.

Arthur loved his motorcycle and sports. At one time, he was involved in an accident that resulted in the breaking of both of his arms. Boudreau also enjoyed skiing and won the gold trophy of the Santa Cruz Ski Club.

On March 30, 1943, Art Boudreau enlisted in the US Army. He received his basic training at Camp Cooke in Kearns, Utah and in August was selected for the aviation flying (warrant) officer program being conducted at the Santa Ana, Air Base. After completing that phase of the program, he was sent to the Merced Army Air Base for his final training.

Art Boudreau had over 100 flying hours to his credit when his plane crashed on April 17, 1944, near Highway 140, eleven miles west of Merced, and he was killed. The remains of Cadet Arthur Raymond Boudreau were returned to Santa Cruz and buried in Holy Cross cemetery.

(AAIR; SCHSC Pg 6; SCSn April 18, 1944 1:6, April 22, 1944 8:3, Holy Cross Cemetery headstone)

ALFRED R. MOORE
(1944/04/22)

(Watsonville High School yearbook)

A lake in Florida was the final body of water for this naval airman.

Alfred Raymond Moore was born about 1922, in Cortez, Colorado, to Mr. and Mrs. Raymond Moore. Shortly after his birth, Alfred's family moved to Watsonville where he was raised with his brothers Edgar and Stanley and sister Virginia. Alfred attended local schools and entered Watsonville High School in 1935 where he was active in school affairs. After graduating from high school in 1939, Moore entered Salinas Junior College and worked as a clerk at a Purity store.

In December 1941, Alfred Moore joined the US Navy and was sent to San Diego for boot camp training. After completing basic training, he served as a painter third class in San Diego.

Moore applied and was accepted into the naval air cadet program in January 1943, and was sent to Chapel Hill, North Carolina, for cadet training. Additional instruction at Olathe, Kansas, and Corpus Christi, Texas, followed, and on February 10, 1944, he was commissioned an ensign.

Ensign Alfred Moore was flying over a lake on a training exercise near Sanford, Florida on April 22, 1944, when his plane collided with another aircraft. It crashed into the lake and Moore was killed. His remains may have been interred in Watsonville Pioneer Cemetery, but cemetery records are inconclusive.

(WRP April 24, 1944 1:2)

FREDERICK B. ALDRICH
(1944/05/05)

Fred Aldrich is a *Santa Cruz Sentinel* roll of honor addition for whom there is little available information.

Frederick Bert Aldrich, the husband of a Santa Cruz girl, was born in Ohio on April 8, 1922. No additional information regarding his family or early life is available. He joined the US Navy in 1940 and after basic training and gunnery school, rose to the rank of gunner's mate third class.

Details of his courtship and marriage to Edna Brimblecom, the daughter of Mr. and Mrs. Fred Brimblecom of Santa Cruz are not known. They married and while he was at sea, Edna remained with her parents at their home in Santa Cruz.

In April 1945, Edna Aldrich was notified that Fred had been hospitalized at the Long Beach Naval hospital with an undisclosed medical condition. She went to Long Beach where she found him confined to an oxygen tent in a quarantined area.

On May 5, 1944, Frederick B. Aldrich died. His body was sent to Steubenville, Ohio for burial.

(SCSn May 7, 1944 1:3; CDR; Photo-WHS)

MAX E. DOWDEN
(1944/05/12)

(Santa Cruz High School Service Cardinal)

"Yes, I can say I have walked with heroes,"

Max E. Dowden, the son of Mr. and Mrs. Homer L. Dowden, was born on October 4, 1916, in Albany, New York. He and his brother Charles joined their parents in their move to Santa Cruz, California, in 1930. The family settled into a home on Cedar Street, and in September Max enrolled in Santa Cruz High School. In high school he was an outstanding student, a member of the High Tow Tong honor society and a basketball star who held the city scoring record until 1943. Outside of school, Dowden was active in DeMolay, a young men's Masonic organization.

In 1934 Max Dowden graduated from high school and shortly thereafter enrolled in the University of California.

During his student years, he had learned to fly airplanes. After a brief period at UC Berkeley, he left school and accepted a position in sales with a southern firm headquartered in Memphis, Tennessee.

In 1941 Dowden attempted to join the US Army Air Force but lacked the two years of college education they required at the time, and he turned to Canada.

Because the Royal Canadian Air Force needed pilots to ferry its planes to England, Max Dowden was accepted into their cadet program. He was sent to an air force school in Manitoba for training and late in 1941, received a commission in the Royal Canadian Air Force.

His initial assignment involved shuttling planes from the US to Canada to England. Over the next two years, Max also received specialized training in night bombing techniques aboard British Lancaster bombers.

Wishing to serve in his own country's air force, Dowden requested and received a transfer to the US Army Air Force in 1943. After completing training at US flight schools, he was assigned to the 8th USAAF in England.

In 1944 the Royal Air Force was in desperate need of trained Lancaster pilots to fly night raiding missions; the USAAF loaned Lieutenant Dowden back to them. The final episode in First Lieutenant Max E Dowden's life was described in a letter written to his mother by RAF Warrant Officer Russell E. Rees of Tilsbury, Essex, England.

[On May 12, 1944] We were on the way home after leaving the target, Duisberg. Everything seemed to be going fine. The heavy flak, which has been causing us so much bother, was left far behind. The Belgium coast was 10 minutes flying time ahead. One's thoughts were dwelling upon the sanctuary of home, the hot rum, the interrogation and bed.

Suddenly our little world was shattered. Peace turned into tumult. A night fighter had approached from dead ahead and sprayed the kite with cannon.

Max gave the order to abandon aircraft. The poor old girl was in a sad plight. The navigator, bomb armer, rear gunner and mid-upper baled out. I was the last living member to go. I sat over the hole Mam, and looked at Max and Frank.

The 'kite' was going into an uncontrollable dive and those two men were struggling to hold a semi-useless stick. They held the 'Yokum' up for those extra precious seconds that five comrades might live.

This was a, night which will vividly remain with me for ever.

Yes, I can say I have walked with heroes."

The body of Max E. Dowden was never recovered. He is memorialized on the Tablet of the Missing at Cambridge American Cemetery, Cambridge, England. His awards include Air Medal with two Oak Leaf Clusters, Purple Heart.

(ABMC, SCHSC Pg. 9, SCSn August 23, 1941, June 8, 1944 1:5; SCR July 20, 1945)

JOHN W. WOOD
(1944/05/15)

(Santa Cruz High School Service Cardinal)

An errant mortar round ended the green world of Jack Wood.

John W. Wood was born on July 5, 1921, in Los Gatos, California, to Mr. and Mrs. John A. Wood. The Wood family later moved to Santa Cruz and settled in the Highland District where their sons John, Richard, Ray and daughters Marjorie and Carol were raised. John, or "Jack" as his friends knew him, entered Santa Cruz High School in 1934 and brought his love of science and forestry with him. In high school he majored in science and continued in the 4H program that he had started in 1931.

Jack Wood's education was directed toward a career in forestry. He was instrumental in a special forestry project conducted between the school and the Coast Counties Gas and Electric Company. That program resulted in a nationally distributed movie entitled "A New Dawn in an Ancient Forest," in which he played a major role. After high school, Wood continued his study of forestry at Salinas Junior College for two years.

In March 1943, John Wood enlisted in a coastal artillery unit and in May was transferred, for six months, to an army special training program at UCLA. This was followed by five additional months of study at Texas A & M University.

The wartime needs of the infantry aborted John Wood's special training program, and he was reassigned to the 393rd Infantry Regiment of the 99th Infantry Division stationed at Camp Maxey, Texas. While on maneuvers, his engineering company was under a live mortar barrage when an ill-timed explosion of a mortar shell snuffed out Wood's life on May 15, 1944.

His funeral services were held May 19, 1944, in Los Gatos. He was laid to rest with full military honors in the Golden Gate Nation Cemetery in San Bruno California.

(NARA2; USDVA; SCHSC Pg. 20; SCSn May 18, 1944 1:5, SCR May 26, 1944 1)

GLEN W. CHAMBERLAIN
(1944/05/28)

A retread doughboy returned to "the Corps"

Glen Watson Chamberlain was born in Kansas on July 29, 1893. Details of his family and formative years are unavailable. When World War I began, Chamberlain joined the US Marine Corps and was discharged at its conclusion. After the war, he returned home and married Beatrice. The couple later had two sons.

The Chamberlains settled in Watsonville during the 1920s, and Glen became involved in the business and social life of the community. He acquired the local Chevrolet dealership and was active in the Kiwanis and Breakfast clubs.

About 1934 the Chamberlains moved to Oakland where Glen, acquired another auto dealership and joined the American Legion and the Masonic lodge.

When World War II began, Glen Chamberlain once again volunteered his services to the US Marine Corps; he was accepted and commissioned a Captain. His knowledge of automotives was put to use by the Marine Corps in their transportation section; he was posted to Guadalcanal.

While serving in the South Pacific, Captain Chamberlain contracted a severe case of malaria and was returned home for treatment. Attempts to cure his condition were unsuccessful and he died on May 28, 1944, in Alameda County. The burial location of Chamberlain has not been identified.

(WRP May 1, 1944 1:4; CDR)

VERNON B. HUNTSMAN
(1944/06/03)

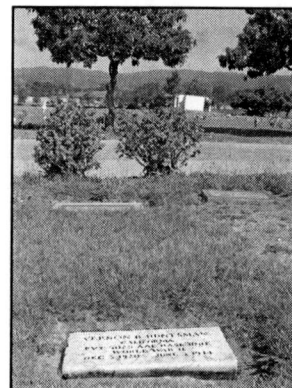

(Pajaro Valley Memorial Park - Watsonville, California)

Vernon B. Huntsman was born in Nebraska on December 3, 1920, to Mr. and Mrs. Huntsman; his mother's name was Hazel. He and his three brothers LeRoy, Luther and Robert and four sisters Viola, Connie, Rosie and Mrs. John Owens later joined their parents in a move to the Pajaro Valley. Vernon lived in Watsonville for three years and briefly attended Watsonville High School. After dropping out of school, he worked locally as a farm hand until the family moved to Niles, California.

Vernon Huntsman joined the US Army in San Francisco on December 22, 1942, and was sent to an unspecified camp for his basic and specialized training. While in the army, Vernon married Mary, who remained in Niles during his absence.

On June 3, 1944, Vernon Huntsman was serving with the 3025 Army Air Force Base Unit at Hicks Field in Fort Worth, Texas, when he was killed in an auto accident. His body was returned to Watsonville and following a funeral service, was interred in Pajaro Valley Memorial Park Cemetery.

(NARA2; WRP May 5, 1944 1:2, May 8, 1944 1:5, Pajaro Valley Cemetery Survey 5/12/08)

JACK L. MARLOW
(1944/06/06)

(Pajaro Memorial Park - Watsonville, California)

"Jack Marlowe Killed in D-Day Invasion" reported the *Watsonville Register-Pajaronian*.

Jack L. Marlow was born in Yuma, Arizona, in 1923, to Mr. and Mrs. R. R. Marlow. His brothers, Wayland and James, and sisters, Bonnie and Opal, joined Jack in the family home. The date of the Marlow family move to Aromas in the Pajaro Valley has not been established. He attended elementary school and two years of high school before leaving school.

After leaving school, Jack married Muriel and later had a son Ronald.

In 1943 Jack Marlow and his family were living in Yuma, Arizona, when he was inducted into the US Army at Phoenix on April 10. Muriel moved back to the family home in Aromas, and Jack reported to Camp Joseph T. Robinson in Arkansas for basic training.

Following paratrooper training at Fort Benning, Georgia, Private Marlow was assigned to the 82nd Airborne Division in training at Camp Mackall, North Carolina. In January 1944, the 82nd were sent to England to prepare for the invasion of France.

The 82nd Airborne was assigned the task of destroying vital German supply bridges and capture causeways leading inland across the flooded areas behind the Normandy beaches where seaborne forces would land to gain control of roads and communications...The poor weather conditions diminished the visibility of the initial "Pathfinder" aircraft. Many were unable to locate their designated drop zones. Some of the Pathfinders that went astray didn't activate their equipment in order to avoid misleading their regiments. In other cases, the presence of enemy troops precluded the use of guidance devices. Consequently, only ten percent of the troopers landed on the proper DZs. This scattering of troopers played to the All-American advantage since they were engaging a force of from 4 to 10 times their number.

On D-Day June 6, 1944, Private Jack L. Marlow was killed in action while serving with his paratrooper unit. His remains were returned to the United States and buried in Pajaro Valley Memorial Park.

(NARA2; WRP August 10, 1944 1:2, The 82nd Airborne, Campaigns During WWII, http://www.ww2-airborne.us/division/campaigns/france.html, [16 September 2008])

LEO P. PACKHAM
(1944/06/06)

(Normandy American Cemetery St Laurent-sur-mer Internet photo)

Included on the list of Santa Cruz County "killed in action" appearing in the *Santa Cruz Sentinel* edition of May 30, 1945, is the name Leo P. Packham. Local record searches have not been able to provide information regarding his connection with Santa Cruz County.

Leo Packham was born in Los Angeles County, California, on November 22, 1921. His parents are believed to have been Mr. and Mrs. Leo P. Packham who were living in San Diego in 1920. It is likely that he was raised and educated in Southern California. No additional information regarding his family is available. After completing four years of high school, he worked in the entertainment field until 1941.

Packham enlisted in the California National Guard in Los Angles on March 3, 1941, and was assigned as a private in the Quartermaster Corps. During his training period, he volunteered for paratrooper duty and after completing "jump school," became a part of the 501st Parachute Regiment of the 101st Airborne Division that jumped on Normandy on D-Day.

In June 1944, the SHAEF decided to drop both the 82nd and 101st Airborne Divisions simultaneously into Normandy. The 501st PIR (less 3rd Battalion) took off for their first combat jump from Merryfield Airport at 2245hrs, 5 June 1944. The 3rd Battalion was to depart at the same time from Welford. All units were to fly across the English Channel and drop into Normandy, five hours prior to the seaborne landing. The 501st drop zones were north and east of the town of Carentan. Two battalions were to seize key canal locks at La Barquette and destroy the bridges over the Douve River, while the third battalion was in division reserve In the predawn hours of D-Day a combination of low clouds, and enemy anti-aircraft fire caused the break-up of the troop carrier formations. Consequently, the sporadic jump patterns caused highly scattered drops. Most of the troopers landed far afield of their designated drop zones. The actions that night bore little resemblance to those so carefully planned and briefed. Amazingly, this unanticipated misstep confused the Germans and allowed the airborne units time to regroup. Unfortunately those who were dropped accurately encountered stiff German resistance.

Technician Fifth Class Leo P. Packham died on June 6, 1944, and is buried in the Normandy American Cemetery, St. Laurent-sur-Mer, France. His awards include the Purple Heart.

(CBR; USCR, 1920 US Census, CA, San Diego; NARA2; ABMC)

CARL N. RIGGS
(1944/06/06)

(Internet Photo [enhanced])

A Watsonville member of the famous "Band of Brothers" now rests in Jefferson Barracks.

Carl Newton Riggs was born in Little Rock, Arkansas, in 1920, to Mr. and Mrs. Riggs. No additional information has surfaced regarding the couple; however, they had two other sons, George and Albert, and two daughters, Katie and Suzi. Carl's older sister Katie raised him from the time he was a baby. Riggs attended schools in Arp, Texas, and Phoenix, Arizona, before arriving in Watsonville.

Carl Riggs studied at Watsonville High School for three years and after leaving school, moved to Salinas. There he worked on a local ranch for five years before becoming a salesman.

On August 9, 1942, Riggs enlisted in the US Army at Salinas and was sent to a basic training facility. After his initial training, he volunteered for airborne infantry and was ordered to Fort Benning, Georgia, for parachute training. At its conclusion, he was assigned to the 506th Infantry Parachute Regiment of the 101st Airborne Division. By the time he departed for Europe, Riggs had been promoted to sergeant.

In 1944 the 506th Regiment was sent to England to prepare for the June 6 invasion of Normandy on D-day.

The 506th PIR took off for their first combat jump at 0100 hrs, 6 June 1944. In the predawn hours of D-Day a combination of low clouds, and enemy anti-aircraft fire caused the break-up of the troop carrier formations. The scattering of the air armada was such that only nine of the eighty-one planes scheduled to drop their men on the Drop Zone (DZ) found their mark. Consequently, the sporadic jump patterns caused most of the troopers to land far afield of their designated DZ. Some of the sticks landed as far away as 20 miles from the designated area. Only the 3rd Battalion landed in close proximity to their designated DZ. However, the Germans had long recognized the area as a likely spot for a parachute assault. The Germans set a strategic trap and in less than 10 minutes managed to kill the battalion commander, Lt. Col. Wolverton, his executive officer Maj. George Grant and a large portion of the battalion.

Carl Riggs and sixteen other members of E Company's "band of brothers" were killed in action on June 6, 1944, in the D-Day invasion when their aircraft was hit and exploded over Ste. Mere-Eglise, Normandy, France.

Riggs remains were later located and returned to the Jefferson Barracks National Cemetery in St. Louis, Missouri, for reburial in a mass grave.

(NARA2; USDVA; 101st Airborne, 506th Parachute Inf. Regiment, http://ww2-airborne.us/units/506/506.html, [16 September 2008] WRP January 31, 1945 1:2, www.506infantry. org/Memorial/personal/tmgrave.htm [April 12, 2009])

LEO E. J. HOFFMAN
(1944/06/09)

(Photo courtesy Pajaro Valley Historical Association)

Leo's second baptism at Anzio was far different from his 1921 Watsonville "sprinkling" experience

Leo Edward Joseph Hoffman was a native of Watsonville, California, and was born on August 18, 1921, to Henry and Celedonia Hoffman. The family also included three other sons: Henry, Robert and Ray. Leo attended local elementary schools and Chaminade High School; he transferred into Watsonville High School between 1936 and 1940.

Leo Hoffman was inducted into the US Army on November 2, 1942, and in January 1943, was sent to Camp White, Oregon, for basic training. Following specialized training, Leo was promoted to Private First Class. In February he was elevated to sergeant and in April rose to staff sergeant. He became a technical sergeant while at Camp Adair, Oregon, in February 1944.

Sergeant Hoffman was assigned to the 361st Infantry Regiment of the 91st Infantry Division and landed in North Africa in May 1944. His unit remained and trained there throughout May for the invasion of Italy. During this period, his brother Henry, who was enroute to India, visited him for the last time. In June 1944, Sergeant Hoffman and his company were ordered to Italy to participate in the Anzio landing.

Having landed at Anzio on 1 June the Regiment took up positions the following night on the ridge four miles northwest of Velletri. On June 3rd at 05:30 they jumped off, and were the first element of the 91st Division to enter combat. Four hours later they received their first baptism of fire.

On June 9, 1944, Technical Sergeant Leo Edward Joseph Hoffman died from the wounds he received during his "baptism of fire." His remains were later returned to Watsonville and interred in the Valley Catholic Cemetery.

(NARA2; WRP July 5, 1944 1:2, July 12, 1944 1:1; Lone Sentry. Com, 91st Infantry Division, http://www.lonesentry.com/91st division/ch2.html, (16 Sept 2008)])

ROBERT W. STRUVE
(1944/06/09)

(Watsonville High School yearbook)

The Pajaro Valley slough that bore his name had little in common with the channel waters he was attempting to cross.

Robert Warren Struve was born in Monterey County, California, on June 5, 1920, to Mr. and Mrs. Hans Struve, a family significant in the wetland development of California's Pajaro Valley. Robert and his three sisters attended local Watsonville schools. In 1935 Bob entered Watsonville High School, where he participated on the archery team and in Future Farmers of America, before graduating in 1939.

In October 1942, Struve joined the US Navy and was sent to the US Naval Training Center in San Diego, California, for boot camp. Upon completion he received orders to Solomon, Washington, for training as a navy quartermaster. Among the duties of navy quartermasters was the maintenance and navigation of barges. Struve provided barge-landing support at Palermo, Naples and Anzio during the Italian campaign.

On June 9, 1944, while twenty miles off the coast of Normandy preparing to assist in his LST's second trip to assist in the landing, Robert's ship was torpedoed. In a letter to the Struve family Robert's captain, Lt. Commander Alvin H. Tutt, described events at Normandy that took the life of their son.

After participating in the initial invasion of France, our ship was beginning its second trip when it was torpedoed by enemy "E" boats, causing great explosions and fires, thereby resulting in its quick loss. Robert was at his battle station performing his duties, with the highest degree of loyalty when the explosion occurred which completely demolished that part of the ship. Since he nor any of the men near there were ever seen again, it must be presumed that he was lost at that time.

The remains of Quartermaster First Class Robert Warren Struve were reportedly buried in Brookwood Cemetery in Surrey, England.

(CBR; SCSn August 12, 1944 5:4, WRP August 11, 1944, March 1, 1945 1:1; Photo-WHS)

VERNON C. BAKER
(1944/06/10)

(Watsonville High School yearbook)

A fighter pilot from Watsonville finished his mission and life in Romania.

Vernon C. Baker was born on July 7, 1921, to Carl and Elizabeth Baker at Reedley, California, a small farming community between Fresno and Visalia. Later the Baker family, which also included another son, Lloyd, moved to Watsonville. Vernon attended Pajaro Valley elementary schools and graduated from Watsonville High School in 1940. Following high school, he attended Salinas Junior College where he took aeronautic courses.

During the prewar years, Baker entered the local business and fraternal community. Watsonville Stationary and Printing Company employed Baker for a short period, as did the Ralph Friend contracting firm. In his youth, Vernon Baker had been active in DeMolay, and he continued to evolve within the local Masonic lodge and ultimately became the "master."

In July 1942, Vernon Baker enlisted in the Army Air Force and was called to duty the following February. After completing cadet training at Santa Ana, Tulare and Marina, California, and Luke Field, Arizona, in December 1943, he was commissioned a second lieutenant. Pursuit pilot training and duty at Mills Field in Marysville and Santa Maria, California, completed his instructional period.

In April 1944, Lt. Baker was sent overseas and assigned to the 71st Fighter Squadron of the 15th Air Force based in Italy. The 71st had established themselves as the first P-38 unit in combat. While flying a mission over Romania on June 10, 1944, Lt. Baker failed to return and was reported missing in action. In March 1945, his parents received confirmation of his death.

Second Lieutenant Vernon C. Baker is buried in Ardennes American Cemetery at Neupre, Belgium.

(CBR; ABMC; 1st Fighter Association, History of 71st Fighter Squadron, http://www.1stfighter.org/history/71sthistory.htm, (16 September 2008; WRP March 12, 1945 1:2, August 30, 1945 2:2; Photo-WHS)

ROBERT T. FRIDLEY
(1944/06/14)

(Santa Cruz High School Service Cardinal)

Two parachutes left Bob Fridley's plane over Yugoslavia; his was not one of them.

Robert Todd Fridley was born on September 6, 1917, in California, to Philip and Ethel Fridley. He was born at the Sycamore Grove Auto Camp owned and managed by his parents. His brothers Vernon, Ernest, Robert and Daniel and his sister Phyllis also lived there. Fridley graduated from Santa Cruz High School in 1936, and for the next two years worked at the Greyhound terminal office in San Francisco. In 1938 he enrolled in Salinas Junior College, studied aviation and obtained his pilot's license.

On January 22, 1942, Fridley enlisted in the US Army Air Force and was accepted into the aviation cadet program. After initial training at Moffett Field, California, he was sent to Sheppard Field, Texas. This was followed by training assignments at Chanute Field, Illinois, Sequoia and Gardner Fields in California, and Marfa Field in Texas. On July 27, 1943, Cadet Fridley earned his wings and commission as a second lieutenant.

Robert Fridley left Texas and made his way to Savannah, Georgia, to join the 775th AAF Bomb Squadron leaving for Foggia, Italy. During the last half of 1943 and the first half of 1944, Fridley flew over 40 missions and was wounded several times in the process.

The final mission of First Lieutenant Robert Todd Fridley was a daylight high-altitude bombing mission over Budapest on June 14, 1944. While over the target, his B-17 was badly damaged; Fridley attempted to "nurse" it back to his base at Foggia but when he reached the Yugoslavian coast near Hvar, the crippled craft was caught in an air down current and crashed into another of the returning planes. Both planes went down and only two parachutes were seen to leave Fridley's aircraft. His was not one of them.

The remains of Robert Fridley were interred in Golden Gate National Cemetery at San Bruno on March 1, 1949. His awards include the Air Medal with two Oak Leaf Clusters.

Note: While DVA records reflect a DOD of 1/14/1944, the June 14 date reported in other publications appears more accurate.

(NARA2; USDVA; SCHSC Pg. 9, SCSn August 15, 1944)

CLARENCE A. RAY
(1944/06/14)

An Air Medal with two oak leaf clusters attested to the metal of a local Safeway clerk.

Clarence A. Ray was born in McKinney, Texas, in 1922, to C. A. & Nora Ray. In 1925 he, along with brothers Curtis and L. C. and sister Euletta, joined the family in its move to New Mexico. Clarence was raised in New Mexico; however, after graduating from high school, he moved to Watsonville. While living there, he worked as a clerk for Safeway Stores and participated in radio theatricals at radio station KHUB. In 1942 he was married and living in Monterey County.

On October 3, 1942, Clarence Ray was inducted into the US Army at Salinas and assigned to the Air Force. Following his basic training, he was sent to radio training school at Truax Field in Madison, Wisconsin, where he graduated with honors.

After completing training, he was assigned to the 8th Air Force and stationed in England. During his time with the Eighth Air Force, Ray served as a lead radio operator on a Flying Fortress and by June 1944, had flown over sixteen missions.

Tech Sergeant Clarence A. Ray flew his last mission on June 14, 1944. While flying over France in support of the Normandy campaign, the Flying Fortress in which Ray served as a crew member was shot down. The location of the remains of Clarence Ray have not been identified.

(NARA2; WRP September 22, 1944 1:2)

JULIO N. ZEPEDA
(1944/06/15)

(Normandy American Cemetery – Internet photo)

A Santa Clara transplant was on hand for the "big one," but was unable to share the tale.

Julio Nevares Zepeda was a Santa Clara County resident who later lived and worked in Watsonville and was included in the *Pajaronian* Roll of Honor. He was born in Ventura County, California, in 1921, to Mr. and Mrs. Frank N. Zepeda. No information regarding his siblings and early life is available. By 1942 the family had relocated to the Green Valley district of the Pajaro Valley. Julio's formal education ceased after he completed grammar school and in 1942 he was working with his father picking fruit on the Dave Mello ranch.

Julio Zepeda was inducted into the US Army as a private on September 26, 1942, and sent to a basic training facility. After completing his basic and special training phase, Julio was assigned to the 120th Infantry Regiment of the 30th Infantry Division.

The 30th Infantry Division arrived in England on February 22, 1944, and trained for the invasion of France until June 11. When Zepeda and his unit landed at Normandy, they found themselves and other US forces contained within a narrow perimeter by the German army. During an attempt to break out of the Omaha Beach sector, Private First Class Julio N. Zepeda was killed in action on June 15, 1944. His body was buried in the Normandy American Cemetery at St. Laurent-sur-Mer, France. His awards include the Purple Heart.

(CBR; ABMC; NARA2; WRP October 7, 1944 1:2)

AMEDEO L. LUCCHESI
(1944/06/20)

An Italian immigrant adopted by Davenport paid his citizenship dues in full at Normandy.

Amedeo L. Lucchesi was born in 1920 in San Marino, Italy, to Mr. and Mrs. Lucchesi. The date the Lucchesi family immigrated to the United States is not known, but they ultimately settled in Sunnyvale, California. Amedeo completed grammar school and two years of high school in Santa Clara County.

Sometime prior to 1943, Lucchesi moved to Davenport in Santa Cruz County and worked on a farm in the north coast area. During this period, Lucchesi met and married Mary Modolo whose family lived in Davenport.

Amedeo was inducted into the US Army on August 6, 1943, and was trained at Camp Gruber, Oklahoma, and Camp Phillips, Kansas. His first assignment was with the 42nd or Rainbow Division, but he was later transferred to the 314th infantry Regiment of the 79th Infantry Division.

On March 22, 1944, Lucchesi and the 314th left Camp Phillips bound for England. They arrived in the British Isles on April 17. The regiment then began a period of intensive training for the invasion of France.

On 19 June, orders came down committing the 314th to its first combat; the 313th /315th were assigned to attack from the north (the former position of the 90th Division) bypassing Valognes to the west, while the 314th night-moved to an area near Binneville. At 0600, 2nd Btn jumped off towards its objective to seize the ridge at Croix Jacob, outside Negreville. They took this position with little trouble.

On June 20, 1944, Private Amedeo L. Lucchesi was listed as Killed in Action. His remains have not been located, but were likely returned to the United States for burial following the war.

(NARA2; 314th Infantry Regiment, WWII History, http://www.lorwings.net/314/outline1.shtml, [16 September 2008]; *SCSn August 10, 1944 1:3*)

CURTIS F. PULLEN
(1944/06/20)

(National Memorial Cemetery Pacific – Internet photo)

The name Curtis F. Pullen appeared on the *Santa Cruz Sentinel* May 30, 1945 Honor Roll, yet his relationship in the county is unknown.

Curtis Faus Pullen was born In Iowa on January 18, 1914, to Keats and Mabel Pullen. He and his brothers, Keats and Robert, were raised and educated in the small community of Onawa, Monona County, Iowa, where their father was in the automobile business.

During the late 1930s or early 1940s, Curtis Pullen married Margaret Holmes. They may have established a residence in Santa Cruz.

When World War II began, Pullen volunteered for the US Navy and following officer training, was commissioned an ensign. Margaret remained in Northern California and established a residence on Sylvan Avenue in San Bruno, California, during his absence.

The place and cause of Lt. (jg) Curtis Pullen's death has not been found. It is possible that his his death, which likely occurred on June 20, 1944, was a result of the major sea battle that took place in the Philippine Sea June 19-20, 1944.

Following his death, his remains were buried at an available US military facility and on January 25, 1949, were rein-

terred in the Honolulu Memorial Cemetery.

(Note: the ABMC gives his date of death as 30 June 1944]
(USCR, 1920 US Census, IA, Monona; ABMC; USNM; ACGEN; Faus Genealogy, Updating the Records of Ruth Lavina Faus, http://freepages.genealogy.rootsweb.com/~piercescga/pdffiles/fausbook1999.pdf, [16 September 2008])

GILBERT B. CORNWELL
(1944/06/21)

(Santa Cruz High School Service Cardinal)

The English had a special honor for "Corni" seven years after his B-24 departed.

Gilbert Brewster Cornwell was born in Santa Cruz County, California, on December 3, 1923. His parents, Mr. and Mrs. Walter Cornwell, lived in the community of Soquel where he and his sister Nan were raised. Brewster, or "Corni" as family and friends knew him, attended the local grammar school before entering Mission Hill Junior High School. In 1939, Brewster Cornwell enrolled in Santa Cruz High School, where he specialized in a trade-industrial program and was active in the Machine Shop Club.

After his graduation in 1942, Corni relocated to San Jose where the Anderson Barngrover Food Machinery Company employed him as a machinist making regulators for submarines.

Gilbert B. Cornwell was inducted into the US Army on January 23, 1943, and assigned to the Air Force. After completing basic training and attending aerial gunnery school in Laredo, Texas, he was promoted to private first class. A radio operator school in Sioux Falls, Iowa, and a combat school in Phoenix, Arizona, followed.

In late 1943, Brewster was sent to England to join the 445th Bomb Group of the 8th Air Force as a B-24 Liberator gunner. While serving with the 445th, Cornwell was promoted to sergeant, and assigned to the 701st Bomber Squadron stationed at Tibenham, England. His squadron flew a variety of missions from bombing fighter production facilities, railroad-marshalling yards, oil refineries, harbor facilities and airfields, to delivering ordinance, fuel and supplies to ground troops.

On June 21, 1944, while returning from bombing oil refineries in Romania, Brewster Cornwell's plane was hit by anti-aircraft fire over Germany. His crippled B-24 was able to make it back across the channel before crashing near Beccles, England. Sergeant Gilbert Brewster Cornwell did not survive that crash and his remains were interred in the Cambridge American Cemetery in Cambridge, England.

In 1951 his sister Nan, along with other American family survivors, were guests of the British government who honored Brewster and the other Americans who died in their defense.

(ABMC; NARA2; SCHSC Pg. 8, 445th Bomb Group, Unit History, http://www.445th-bomb-group.com, [16 September 2008] SCSn July 7, 1944 1:1, SCR July 14, 1944 –1; The Remembrance of Nan [Cornwell] Tunison, 29 September 2008)

LOWELL A. BREADY
(1944/06/24)

(Internet photo)

Bready sacrificed a draft deferrable position to become a "dog face" infantryman.

Lowell A. Bready was born in California on November 3, 1913, yet nothing is known of his parents and siblings. He graduated from the University of California School of Journalism about 1936, and shortly thereafter accepted a newspaper assignment in Pacific Grove.

In June 1937, he joined the staff of the *Santa Cruz Sentinel* where he became county editor. At that newspaper, Lowell also contributed articles to the sports desk during the football and basketball seasons. Bready lived at the Beach Hill Inn during most of his stay in Santa Cruz, and was active in the 20-30 Club, Toastmasters and Junior Chamber of Commerce. Lowell Bready and Elaine McInerney were married in December 1940, and became active socially within the community.

Early in 1941, Lowell was named news editor of the *Sentinel;* however, when that paper merged with the *Santa Cruz Evening News,* he left Santa Cruz to manage publicity

for the Red Cross in San Francisco. Rather than take advantage of the draft exemption that came with the Red Cross position, Bready volunteered for service.

Lowell Bready entered the army officer candidate school (OCS) and underwent training at Camp Roberts, California, and Fort Benning, Georgia, before being commissioned a second lieutenant. In 1943 he was assigned to a replacement battalion at Camp Croft, North Carolina, and promoted to first lieutenant.

In June 1944, Bready was reassigned to the 9th Infantry Regiment of the 2nd infantry Division and posted to England in preparation for the invasion. Lowell's company took part in the invasion at Normandy, and on June 25, 1944, during follow-up action, Lowell Bready was killed in action in France.

He was buried in the Normandy American Cemetery at St. Laurent-sur-Mer, France. His awards include the Bronze Star and Purple Heart.

(ABMC, American Legion Post 184, South Bay Honor Roll, http://post184.com/html/ww2.htm, [16 September 2008], SCSn July 26, 1944 1:5)

PETER DUGGER
(1944/06/29)

(Pajaro Valley Memorial Park – Watsonville, California)

A posthumous Silver Star and a small plot of soil in the Pajaro Valley remind us of Peter.

Peter Dugger was born in Texas on October 26, 1921, to Mr. and Mrs. James Dugger. The family later grew to include another son, Howard, daughters Elsie, Rena and Evelyn and a half brother, Jess McClister. The Duggers arrived in Watsonville during the 1920s, and Peter was enrolled in a local grammar school. After completing elementary school, he attended Watsonville High School for two years.

In the late 1930s, Peter moved to Alameda County where he entered an apprentice program in the building trades. He remained in Alameda County and during the early 1940s, was married to Evelyn.

Peter was inducted into the US Army on November 11,

1942, and sent to a basic training facility. After his departure, his wife moved to Soquel where their son David Charles was born in February 1943. Following basic training, Peter was sent to Camps Adair and White in Oregon for additional instruction. At Camp White, Peter Dugger was assigned to the 361st Infantry Regiment of the 91st Infantry Division.

In May 1943, Private First Class Dugger left for North Africa where he remained until deployed to Italy. During a combat engagement with Germans troops at an unidentified location in Italy, Peter earned the Silver Star. A citation accompanying that award stated:

In an attack up a hill, his platoon was checked by enemy machine gun fire. Maneuvering behind good cover, he reached a vantage point from which he opened fire and killed the entire gun crew. A squad of enemy rifleman then opened fire on him. He returned the fire, killing two and wounding three. The platoon then continued to advance. He crawled to the crest of the hill where he was immediately subjected to an intense mortar barrage... A squad of enemy rifleman advanced to counterattack. He permitted them to advance to within 50 yards of him and then opened fire, killing four and wounding three of the enemy. During the operation, he had wiped out a machinegun crew and six enemy rifleman, wounded six others and had allowed his squad to complete their mission with a minimum of casualties.

Private First Class Peter Dugger died on June 29, 1944, in Italy. Following the war, his remains were reburied in the Pajaro Valley Memorial Park.

(NARA2; WRP August 30, 1944 1:2, February 26, 1945 1:1; Pajaro Valley Cemetery Survey May 12, 2008)

JOHN J. ROCHE
(1944/06/29)

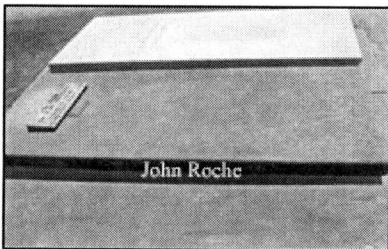

(Watsonville Catholic Cemetery – Watsonville, California)

A heart attack at age thirty-three felled a former construction worker and soldier.

John Joseph Roche was born April 23, 1911. Additional information regarding his parentage, place of birth or siblings has not surfaced. At the time of his enlistment, John lived in San Francisco where he may have attended high school for two years.

After high school, Roche worked as a skilled machinery operator in the construction trades. John married, and he and his wife Louise became active members of All Hallows Catholic Church in San Francisco. The couple later had a daughter, Marie.

On December 29, 1943, John Roche was inducted into the US Army and sent to a basic training facility. During his absence, Louise and Marie moved to the Pajaro Valley where they acquired a home in Watsonville. Following basic training, Private John Roche was stationed at Camp Hulen, Texas, near Palacios.

In January 1944, Camp Hulen was used as a detention center for German prisoners of war and Roche may have been in a unit supporting that operation. While serving at the camp, Private John L. Roche suffered a fatal heart attack on June 29, 1944, and died.

His remains were returned to Watsonville, accompanied by an army buddy, and following a funeral at St. Patrick's Church on July 6, 1944, were interred in Watsonville Catholic Cemetery.

(NARA2; WRP June 30, 1944 1:8, July 5, 1944 1:1)

FREDERICK C. DODGE
(1944/07/03)

(Manila American Cemetery – Internet photo)

Frederick Dodge is another of the casualties appearing in the May 30, 1945, *Santa Cruz Sentinel* Honor Roll with a limited local connection.

Frederick Clarence Dodge was born in 1894 in Washington State, but census records fail to indicate how long he remained in that state. In 1920, he was serving as a boatswain aboard a US steamship sailing out of Brooklyn, New York. He continued to ply the sea for a living and had earned his Master Mariner license and command of his own ship by 1942.

During World War II, his wife Evelyn established residency in Santa Cruz while he served at sea as a Merchant Marine captain.

The American Battlefield Monument Commission records do not specify whether Dodge died on the Philippine Islands or at sea. They only report that he died on July 3, 1944.

The remains of Captain Frederick C. Dodge were buried in the Manila American Cemetery.

(USCR, 1920 US Census, WA; NAR; ABMC, SCSn August 2, 1944 1:3;)

DONALD A. PROVOST
(1944/07/07)

(Golden Gate National Cemetery – San Bruno California)

Donald's terminal condition prevented him, from departing with his jump mates.

Donald A. Provost was born in Fresno, California, on June 17, 1920, and he was the last child born to William and Lillian Provost. Their other children included sons Robert, William and Harold, and daughters Lucille, Pearl and Alice. Provost was raised in Fresno where he completed three years of high school. After high school, he worked as commercial vehicle driver.

Donald Provost enlisted as a private in the regular army at Fresno on October 24, 1940, and requested duty in Hawaii. It is believed that he was then sent there for basic training.

While Provost's initial unit in January is not known, he is likely to have been assigned to an infantry unit serving in Hawaii. His early World War II activities are also unknown; however, he was serving with the 17th Infantry (Airborne) Division in the United States after it was activated on April 15, 1943.

In about the summer of 1944 Donald Provost contracted an unspecified illness or medical condition that prevented him from remaining with his unit when they were deployed overseas in August.

The medical condition affecting Donald Provost was such that he was released to his family's care in their home in Santa Cruz. At this time, his condition worsened and on July 7, 1944, he died. Following an LDS (Mormon) funeral, he was buried with military honors at the Golden Gate National Cemetery in San Carlos July 19, 1944.

(USCR, 1920 US Census, CA, Fresno; NARA2; USDVA; SCSn July 9 1944 8:1, July 20 1944)

JAMES B. JENKINS
(1944/07/09?)

"James Jenkins Killed in Pacific War" noted the *Santa Cruz Sentinel*.

James Bennie Jenkins was born on July 4, 1925, in Tulare County, California, to Mr. and Mrs. Jenkins; his mother's maiden name was Audie Robison. While the *Santa Cruz Sentinel* of May 30, 1945, listed him in its Santa Cruz roll of honor, his California ties appears to be stronger within the state's Central Valley. Jenkins attended grammar and high school in Delano before moving to Santa Cruz with his mother in 1942.

In February 1943, James enlisted in the United States Marine Corps and completed his basic and school-of-infantry training at San Diego.

Private Jenkins was assigned to the 2nd Marine Division in June 1944 as they were preparing for the invasion of the Mariana Islands. His unit invaded Saipan and continued to encounter Japanese resistance through the first week of July. By July 9, the island was declared secure, although isolated pockets of resistance continued to require marine activity until the end of the month.

According to a telegram received by his mother, Audie, on August 1, 1944, Private First Class James B. Jenkins was declared killed in action. The exact date of Jenkins' death and the disposition of his remains have not been identified.

(CBR; SCSn August 1, 1944 1:2; American Memorial Park Saipan, http://www.nps.gov/archive/amme/court_of_honor/court_of_ honor.html, [16 September 2008])

DONALD G. DALLES
(1944/07/19)

(Santa Cruz Riptide photo)

Could the Port Chicago disaster have played a role in Donald's death?

Donald George Dalles was born on October 28, 1926, in Fresno, California, to Mr. and Mrs. George Dalles. The Dalles family also included two daughters, Cecile and Demetris. Donald attended local schools, where he may have met his future wife Louise.

Dalles probably enlisted in the US Navy in 1943 and after completing boot camp, he received additional training to become a coxswain. In September 1943, he was serving at the Oakland Naval Yard when he married Louise Swenson at the First Congregational Church in Santa Cruz.

The *Santa Cruz Sentinel* of July 26, 1944 reported, *Donald George Dalles aged 19 of Santa Cruz, died in Oakland July 19...Dalles, was killed in performance of his duty in a shipyard there.*

The specific cause or event that took the life of Donald Dalles has not been identified. His name is not included among the victims of the Port Chicago disaster that occurred at the same time and in the same vicinity as his death; however, a connection may yet be found.

His body was recovered and his remains were returned to Santa Cruz for a funeral and burial in Oakwood Memorial Park.

(SCR September 24, 1943-4, SCSn July 26, 1944 5:1)

DELFORD L. HAMRICK
(1944/07/22)

(National Memorial Cemetery Pacific – Internet photo)

A Watsonville marine came to grips with his Japanese enemy on Guam.

Delford Louis Hamrick was born in Colorado on January 24, 1923, to Mr. and Mrs. Hamrick. Also included in the family were sons Dallas and Hubert and daughters Lottie, Lucy and Ocle. The Hamricks moved to California in 1930 and settled in Monterey. Later they relocated to Watsonville where Delford attended local elementary schools before enrolling in Watsonville High School.

In September 1942, Delford Hamrick joined the US Marine Corps and was sent to Camp Pendleton near San Diego for basic and school-of-infantry training.

In February 1944 Private First Class Hamrick was ordered to Guadalcanal where he joined the 12th Marine Regiment of the 3rd Marine Division. When he arrived on the island, the 3rd Marine Division was preparing for the invasion of the Mariana Islands.

On 21 July 1944, as a part of the Southern Troops and Landing Force, the Division landed on western beaches of Guam in the vicinity of Asan Point. After twenty days of savage fighting the divisional units reached the northern coast of the island. On 10 August 1944 Guam was declared secure.

Private First Class Delford Louis Hamrick was killed in action on Guam on July 22, 1944. His remains were later returned to Hawaii and buried in the Honolulu Memorial Cemetery on June 20, 1949. His awards include the Purple Heart.

(ABMC, Global Security.org, 3rd Marine Division, http://www.globalsecurity.org/military/agency/usmc/3mardiv.htm. [16 September 2008] WRP October 19, 1944 1:3)

RICHARD L. HARRIS
(1944/07/24)

Richard Lewis Harris was born in San Francisco, California on April 18, 1921, to Mr. and Mrs. L. I. Harris. His brothers Elbert and Lawrence and his sisters Audrey and Emma Mae rounded out the Harris family. Richard grew up in the Pajaro Valley and attended Watsonville High School for three years. The Harris family relocated to San Miguel, California, where he met his future wife, Louise. Prior to the beginning of World War II, Harris was residing in Los Angeles, California and employed as a commercial vehicle driver.

Harris was inducted into the US Army on November 8, 1942, and trained at Fort Knox, Kentucky, and Camp Pickett, Virginia, before being assigned to an unspecified combat unit. In April 1944, Sergeant Harris was shipped overseas to a staging area in England in preparation for the invasion of France.

A September 11, 1944, article appearing in the *Watsonville Register-Pajaronian* noted that Sergeant Richard L. Harris suffered a wound during the invasion at Normandy and on July 24, 1944, he died as a result of that wound. It is believed that Harris' remains were returned to the US for burial, yet the location of his gravesite is not known.

(CBR; NARA2; WRP September 11, 1944 1:2)

IRWIN W. FERNANDES
(1944/08/05)

(Ardennes American Cemetery, Neupre Belgium - Internet photo)

Irwin and his little P38 fighter protected the "heavies" [bombers] on their way to Pilsen.

The name Irwin W. Fernandes appears on the *Santa Cruz Sentinel* May 30, 1945, Roll of Honor, yet his relationship with Santa Cruz County appears to be minimal.

Irwin Fernandes was born in 1921. His mother's name was Catherine. Available records do not indicate his place of birth, his siblings, or information regarding his formative years. In 1942, he was living in Alameda County, had completed two years of college and was working in the entertainment business.

Irwin Fernandes enlisted as a private in the Army Air Force in San Francisco on April 20, 1942, and was sent to an air cadet training facility. In 1943 he had earned his wings, was commissioned as a second lieutenant and assigned to the 77th Fighter Squadron, 20th Fighter Group stationed at March Field, California.

Fernandes' squadron was sent to Europe and arrived in Northamptonshire, England, in August 1943. It was then stationed at Kings Cliff, England. Irwin began flying P-38 fighters on combat missions from Kings Cliff in November 1943 and during one of those missions, was credited with at least one enemy aircraft kill.

During an air engagement on August 5, 1944, the War Department reported that First Lieutenant Irwin W. Fernandes was shot down over Europe and was Killed in Action. His remains were buried in the Ardennes American Cemetery in Neupre, Belgium. His awards included the Distinguished Flying Cross with Oak Leaf Clusters.

(ABMC; NARA2; WIKI, 77th Fighter Squadron; SCSn April 16, 1945 1:1)

CECIL O. FRY
(1944/08/15)

(Golden Gate National Cemetery – San Bruno California)

The fighting in Europe was a far cry from "clerkin" at Watsonville's Busy Bee Market.

Cecil O. Fry was born on August 26, 1908, in Missouri, to Mr. and Mrs. Newt C. Fry. His siblings included a brother Floyd, and four sisters Hazel, Doris, Dorothy and Clara. Later the family moved to Watsonville where he completed grammar school. Watsonville High School lists Cecil among their former students; however, enlistment records suggest that his secondary education was brief.

After leaving school, Fry was employed for a short period as a clerk at the Bumblebee Market in Watsonville and later worked as a farm hand.

Cecil Fry was inducted into the US Army in San Francisco as a private on July 15, 1943. He completed basic and advanced training at Camp Wolters, Texas, before being assigned to the 7th Infantry Regiment of the 3rd Infantry Division. After joining that unit, he was sent to Italy.

In May the Division broke out of the beachhead [Anzio] and drove on to Rome, and then went into training for the invasion of Southern France. On 15 August 1944, another D-day, the Division landed at St. Tropez, advanced up the Rhone Valley, through the Vosges Mountains.

During the action that occurred on August 15, 1944, Private Cecil O. Fry was killed in action. His remains were later returned to the United States and interred in the Golden Gate National Cemetery at San Bruno on November 8, 1948.

(NARA2; USDVA; WRP September 20, 1944 1:6, 3rd Infantry Division, The Third Infantry Division in the World Wars, http://warchronicle.com/units/US/3rd/combat.htm, [16 September 2008])

HARRY L. SMITH
(1944/08/16)

(Forest Lawn Cemetery – Internet photo)

An obituary appearing in the *Watsonville Register-Pajaronian* September 6, 1944, provides the only sketch currently available as to the life of Harry L. Smith.

Lt. Harry Smith Taken By Death

Lt. Harry L. Smith, 44, USNR, former manager of the Watsonville Montgomery Ward Company store, died last August 16 in Brooklyn Naval hospital, New York, of a perforated gastric ulcer, it was learned here Wednesday.

Lt. Smith was a member of the local American Legion post and the Kiwanis club and was widely known. He was manager of the local Ward store from June 1941, to December 1942, and went from here to the Napa store. While there he received his commission in the naval reserve on June 25, 1943. He visited briefly in Watsonville en route to the Babson Institute in Massachusetts for a month's supply corps training. Then he was stationed in the Portsmouth N.H., navy yard as a shipping officer in the supply department from Sept. 12, 1943, to July 2, 1944. He went to Washington, D.C. for special duty, then to New York August 1 to administrative offices for the purpose of an inventory of all naval supplies.

His wife joined him on August 1 in New York and was there when he was stricken. An emergency operation was performed August 5. His daughter Phyllis, PHM3c [Pharmacist Mate third Class] in the WAVES at Pensacola, Fla., naval air station was granted leave to go to New York.

The body of Lt. Harry L. Smith was returned to Los Angeles, where his wife and mother were living, and was interred in Forrest Lawn Cemetery in Glendale.

(WRP September 6, 1944 1:1)

ANTHONY PIKE
(1944/08/22)

(Santa Cruz High School Service Cardinal)

Anthony Pike made contact with a live wire connection.

Anthony Pike was born in Minnesota on March 22, 1918. His mother's name was Mary Lou. In 1924, the family moved to the Live Oak district of Santa Cruz. In addition to Anthony, the family included four daughters. After completing Live Oak Elementary School, he entered Santa Cruz High School. In high school Pike majored in a general varied course of study and played saxophone in the school band. He left high school in the fall of 1935.

Over the next several years, Pike continued to live and work in the county, married Beatrice Olds and joined the local naval reserve unit. A son, Anthony Jr., was later born to the couple.

On June 25, 1942, Pike entered the US Navy Seabees and was sent to Camp Perry, Virginia, for training. In September 1943, he was transferred to Port Hueneme, California, for overseas deployment and shipped out the same month. Seaman Pike saw duty at Pearl Harbor, the Gilbert Islands and at Truk while serving with a navy construction battalion.

Anthony Pike died after he was accidentally electrocuted while on duty at Pearl Harbor on August 22, 1944. His body was returned to Santa Cruz on October 27, 1947, and following a funeral at St. Joseph's Catholic Church in Capitola, was interred in the Mt. Carmel Cemetery in Aptos, California

(SCHSC Pg. 16, SCSn August 28, 1944 1:5)

JOHN C. CONLEY
(1944/08/24)

John Chester Conley was born in 1915, probably in Kansas, to Elsie Mabel Conley. By 1930, when he was fifteen years old, his mother, her husband, Joe Whalin, and a brother, Joseph Whalin, were living in Watsonville. John is included on the Watsonville High School World War II memorial stone, although the years of his attendance are not known.

John Conley was married to Ann, who remained at the family residence in the Pajaro Valley during his military service.

Conley joined the US Navy in June 1942, attended boot camp at the US Naval Training Center in San Diego and volunteered for submarine service. After completing training in New London, Connecticut, he was assigned to submarine patrol duty on the Atlantic coast and promoted to motor machinist mate first class.

During the first part of 1944, Conley was transferred to the Pacific Theater and assigned to the *USS Harder*, which was patrolling in Philippine waters.

Harder and Hake [Harder's sister sub] remained off Dasol Bay, searching for new targets. Before dawn 24 August they sighted a Japanese minesweeper and a three-stack Siamese destroyer. As Hake *closed to attack, the destroyer turned away toward Dasol Bay.* Hake *broke off her approach, turned northward, and sighted* Harder's *periscope about 600 to 700 yards (500 to 600 m) dead ahead. Swinging southward,* Hake *then sighted the minesweeper about 2000 yards (1800 m) off her port quarter swinging toward them. To escape the charging minesweeper,* Hake *started deep and rigged for silent running. At 07:28 she heard 15 rapid depth charges explode in the distance astern. She continued evasive action that morning, then returned to the general area of the attack shortly after noon. She swept the area at periscope depth but found only a ring of marker buoys covering a radius of one-half mile. The vigorous depth charge attack had ended the career of* Harder *with all hands.*

Motor Machinist Mate First Class John C. Conley was one of those hands lost aboard the *USS Harder*. His remains were never recovered, and he was officially declared dead by the US Navy on October 2, 1945. Conley is memorialized on the Tablets of the Unknown at Manila American Cemetery in Manila, Philippines; his awards include the Purple Heart.

(ABMC, WRP January 30, 1945 1:3; 1930 US Census, CA, Watsonville; WIKI, USS Harder SS-257; USS Harder, USS Harder, Crew List, http://navysite.de/crew.php?action=ship&ship=ss_568, [16 September 2008])

SERRAFINE CORRALES
(1944/08/24)

Jerks's Berserk and Serrafine Corrales completed their final mission together.

Serrafine Corrales was a Watsonville boy born in the Pajaro Valley in 1923. Information regarding his birth and parentage has not been located. In addition to his parents, his family included brothers Frank, Manuel and Gaspar, and a sister Andrea. He attended local grammar schools and Watsonville High School for three years. After leaving high school, he was employed as a warehouseman.

Serrafine Corrales was inducted into the US Army in San Francisco on November 1, 1943. He was assigned to the Army Air Force and after completing basic training, he received radio operator and top turret gunner instruction on a B-24 Liberator bomber.

In April 1944, he joined the 4th Bomber Squadron of the 34th Bomber Group posted at Mendlesham, England. Upon arrival, Serrafine was assigned as a crewman aboard a B-24 bomber named *Jerks Berserk*, and for the next five months, he and *Jerks Berserk* flew twenty-four bombing missions over Germany.

On August 24, 1944, came the fateful day of his 25th and final mission. Under the command of Major Joseph Garret, *Jerks Berserk* left Mendlesham and flew to its European target. After completing their bombing run,

[Jerks Berserk] *was hit by flak in #1 engine causing considerable loss of fuel. Engineer reported only three minutes fuel remaining so the crew was ordered to bail out. Nine men did bail out but Major Garrett was unable to leave when the plane went into a spin. He was able to right the plane and decided to fly until the fuel ran out. The plane did reach England and Major Garrett bailed out and the plane crashed into a house at Holt, Suffolk. Fortunately there were no injuries to anyone on the ground.*

Technical Sergeant Serrafine Corrales did not survive the mission of August 24, 1944, nor was his body recovered. He was memorialized on the Tablets of the Missing at Cambridge American Cemetery. His awards include the Air Medal with Oak Leaf Cluster.

(ABMC; NARA2; WRP September 9, 19441:2; Mackey Crew, Mission List, http://valortovictory.tripod.com/crews/Mackey.htm, [16 Sept 2008])

STANLEY M. HOPKINS
(1944/08/25)

(Santa Cruz High School Service Cardinal)

"We have the Krauts pretty much on the run," Stanley told his parents in his last letter.

Stanley M. Hopkins was born in San Francisco, California, on October 13, 1913, to Mr. and Mrs. George Hopkins. His father acquired the Big Tree Park in the San Lorenzo Valley and moved the family to Santa Cruz, where he and his sister Doris spent many formative years. Stanley entered Santa Cruz High School in September 1928 and was a member of the class of 1934. While in high school, he took a general and varied course of study; however, he left school in 1933 before graduating. After leaving school, he worked at the family business in Felton.

Stanley Hopkins enlisted in the US Army in San Francisco on October 22, 1941, and was sent to Fort Knox, Kentucky, to complete basic training. Prior to his being assigned overseas, he became engaged to Lynda Stagnaro in Santa Cruz.

Private Hopkins reported to the 3rd Battalion of the 6th Armored Regiment and was shipped to North Africa, arriving on Christmas Day 1942. In combat during the Bizerte Campaign on April 27, 1943, Private Hopkins was wounded in the back and leg by shrapnel and required hospitalization for several months.

Stanley returned to his unit in time to take part in the landing at Anzio beachhead and later participated in the heavy fighting at Cassino and the capture of Rome. By 1944, he had been promoted to corporal and was preparing for what would become the final episode of his life.

As the 3rd (redesignated 14th Armored Infantry) Battalion, began moving north out of Rome in August 1944, they were confronted with heavy German resistance. The *Santa Cruz Sentinel* of September 26, 1944, later reported,

Hopkins, with a combat infantry battalion of the first armored division saw the necessity of mining a crossroads, but found that no mines were available for this particular spot. Entering a deserted and blasted house, Hopkins pulled a drawer from the dresser, packed it with captured German explosives and placed it on the crossroads.

On August 25, 1944, Corporal Stanley M Hopkins was killed in action somewhere north of Rome. His remains were returned home and interred in the Golden Gate National Cemetery in San Bruno, California, in 1949.

(NARA2; USDVA; SCHSC Pg. 11, SCSn-New May 8, 1943 4:6, September 7, 1944 1:8, SCR September 15, 1944 –1)

HARRY F. MADOKORO
(1944/08/25)

(Courtesy National Japanese American Historical Society)

"We're proud as hell to be in there pitching, doing our share of the work," wrote Harry.

Harry Fumio Madokoro was born in California, in 1912, to Nisaburo and Natsu Madokoro. Harry's only sibling was a younger sister, Yayeko, who died of tuberculosis in 1937. His father was a farm laborer and his mother ran a candy and pastry concession from the front room of their home on Union Street in Watsonville. Harry attended local elementary schools and Watsonville High School for two years in the late 1920s.

During the 1930s, Madokoro worked for several farmers in the Pajaro Valley, and drove farm equipment on the E.H. Spiegl's vegetable farm in San Juan Bautista. When not working, his special interest was his Harley-Davidson motorcycle that he purchased in San Francisco.

In April 1942 the Madokoro family was moved into a relocation center in Salinas and then to a Japanese internment camp in Poston, Arizona. While at Camp II, Harry became the Chief of Police.

In March 1943 an appeal was made to the government by the Japanese American Citizens League to allow Nisei men to form an all-Japanese army unit and Harry Madokoro was the first to volunteer. He and other recruits were sent to Fort Douglas in Salt Lake City, Utah and then to Camp Selby, Mississippi for basic training. It was there that the famous 442nd Regimental Combat Team was organized.

On May 1, 1944 the 442nd boarded ships that transported them to Italy, and on June 2, 1944 arrived in Naples. Madokoro and his unit assisted in the capture of Rome and joined in the pursuit of retreating Germans up the boot of Italy to Livorno, which was captured in July 1944. In July 1944, Madokoro was cited

For extraordinary heroism in action on 7 July 1944 near Molino A Ventoabbto, and on the 16th and 17th of July 1944 in Luciana, Italy. During the final assault on an enemy held hill, Private First Class Madokoro advanced

ahead of his squad to a strategic position from which he could deliver effective automatic rifle fire. Partly exposed to enemy fire, he scanned his sector of the slope for targets. He leveled his automatic rifle on a nest of snipers, forcing them to disperse. Throughout the bitter fight he held his position, neutralizing another enemy nest and pinning down the enemy to enable his platoon to take the hill. Again at Luciana, Italy, Private First Class Madokoro occupied an advanced position and proceeded to fire on the enemy entrenched on the outskirts of the town. With heavy fire directed at him, he stubbornly held his position and provided covering fire when his squad was forced to withdraw because of a concentrated artillery and mortar barrage. The following day, when his squad became separated from the remainder of the company within the town, Private First Class Madokoro provided flank protection against determined enemy attacks. A group of enemy soldiers entered a nearby draw and threw hand grenades into the enemy position. On another occasion he left his position and silenced a machine pistol position with a grenade. Still later in the course of the battle, he approached an enemy machine gun nest and silenced it by firing from a kneeling position. By his stubborn determination, conspicuous devotion to duty and courage, Private First Class Madokoro inspired his squad in preventing the enemy's escape while his company closed in to occupy the town.

Other stories abound of Harry's heroic actions in Italy; however, his date with destiny was rapidly approaching. On August 25, a request was made in Company K for volunteers to go on a night patrol to cross the Arno River on a combat mission; again he was the first to volunteer. The patrol completed the mission; however, while returning, Private First Class Harry Madokoro was killed by a land mine.

Harry Fumio Madokoro's remains were recovered and buried in the Evergreen Cemetery in Los Angeles, California. Madokoro was posthumously awarded the Distinguished Service Cross.

(USCR, 1920 US Census, CA, Santa Cruz; NARA2; WRP September 9, 1944 1:1, Mas Hashimoto, Re-Enactment; Lessons in Loyalty Part 2, 442nd Stories, 2001, http://www. watsonvillesantacruzjacl.org/reenactment/lessons2.htm, [16 September 2008])

CHARLES E. WRIGHT
(1944/09/01)

(Cambridge American Cemetery England - Internet photo)

According to the World War II US War Department records, Charles E. Wright listed Santa Cruz County as his home; however, no records have been found in the county to confirm his residency. Wright's enlistment records indicate that he was born in Oklahoma in 1923, and had attended high school for three years. In November 1942, he was single, unemployed and living in Stanislaus County, California.

Charles Wright enlisted in the United States Army in San Francisco on November 18, 1942, and was assigned to the Air Force. Since death records indicate that he was a first lieutenant, he most likely entered the air cadet program and was trained to serve as a pilot or navigator. At the time of his commissioning Wright listed Santa Cruz County as his residence, but it may have been the residence of his next of kin.

Charles was assigned to the 358th Bomber Squadron of the 303rd Bomber Group, Heavy, of the 8th US Air Force stationed in Moelsworth, England. Most of the bombing missions flown by that squadron were flown over Germany.

On September 1, 1944, the plane in which First Lieutenant Charles E. Wright was a crewmember crashed during a mission, resulting in his death. His remains were recovered and buried in the Cambridge American Cemetery in Cambridge England. His awards include the Distinguished Flying Cross, Air Medal with three Oak Leaf Clusters and the Purple Heart.

(ACGEN; ABMC; NARA2; Hells Angels, 303 Bomber Group, 31 January 1998, http://www.303rdbg.com/, [16 September 2008])

FRED H. COOPER
(1944/09/07?)

The name Fred H. Cooper was included in the US War Department's listing of World War II casualties from Santa Cruz County, California. No information is currently available as to his parents, siblings or connection with the county. March 15, 1942, enlistment records described

Cooper as being a male Caucasion, born in Pennsylvania in 1907. At the time of his selective service registration, he was a resident of Multnomah County, Oregon. Those records also reveal that he had completed four years of high school, was a salesman by occupation and that he was single without dependent children.

Following the completion of his basic and advanced training, it is believed that he was assigned to the 23rd Armored Infantry Battalion of the 7th Armored Division. In early September, his unit was attacking German forces in the vicinity of Metz, France.

Before the battalion succeeded in recovering contact with its column, the column was halted by enemy resistance at Rezonville. Headquarters Combat Command A and Force I pulled off the road, and this battalion was brought forward with all possible speed to clear the route. Five prisoners were taken in the vicinity of Rezonville, and it was decided to by-pass the town and proceed cross-country to locate a bridgehead site on the Moselle River south of Metz. The cross-country movement was made during the night of 6-7 September, and the head of the battalion entered the town of Dornot, on the Moselle River, at about 0400, 7 September 44. During the day, the town was cleared of all enemy troops, with the exception of a few snipers, and an outpost line was established about it. Fire was received from artillery, mortars, flak guns, antitank guns, and small arms ...

Killed in Action Cooper, Fred, H, Private

The date that Fred H. Cooper was killed in action has not been established. His unit history lists him among its September 1944 casualties. It is also not known why his regiment lists him as a private while the War Department lists him as a Staff Sergeant.

The location of his remains, if recovered, has not been identified, but may have been returned to the US.

(ACGEN; NARA2; http://www.7tharmddiv.org/docrep/N-23-AAR. doc)

HENRY C. VOELKER
(1944/09/11)

(Santa Cruz High School Service Cardinal)

Henry's twenty-four year journey took him to a major historical event, but oh at what a cost.

Henry C. Voelker was born in San Francisco, California, on November 5, 1920, to Ferdinand and Frieda Voelker. The Voelker family later moved to Soquel, California, where he attended Soquel Union Grammar School. After completing grammar school, he attended Mission Hill Junior High School in Santa Cruz, which he completed in 1935. In the fall of that year, Henry enrolled in Santa Cruz High School and took a general college preparatory course of study. In high school he became active in the Stamp Club in addition to serving as a sophomore commissioner. Voelker was also a member of DeMolay, a Masonic youth organization.

After graduating from high school in 1938, Henry Voelker attended Salinas Junior College for a short period before returning to San Francisco. While living in the city, he was employed as a plumber. Voelker married and later the couple had a daughter.

On November 27, 1942, Henry Voelker was inducted into the US Army in San Francisco. Following basic training, he underwent desert training exercises in Southern California and in June 1943, was sent to Camp Bowie, Texas. Henry was a member of the 25th Cavalry Recon Squadron (Mech.) of the 4th Armored Division, when it was shipped to England.

During the Normandy invasion in June 1944, the 25th Cavalry was among the first units to be committed. In late August, allied forces had broken out of the Normandy perimeter and by September, Voelker's unit had penetrated deep into France.

On September 11, 1944, near the French town of Vauville, Sergeant Henry Voelker was engaged in a combat mission that earned him the Bronze Star for bravery, but which cost him his life. His remains were returned to the United States and interred in the Golden Gate National

Cemetery at San Bruno November 4, 1948. His other awards include the Purple Heart.

(NARA2; USDVA; 1930 Census, CA, Santa Cruz; SCHSC Pg. 19, SCSn December 11, 1944 1:5)

ARTHUR J. EARL
(1944/09/123)

(Internet photo)

Market Garden was not the pleasant place the name conjured up.

Arthur James Earl was born in Colorado in 1920, to Mr. and Mrs. H. T. Earl. The Earl family also included sons Kenneth and Richard and daughters Anita and Helen. When he was two years old, the family moved into a house on Front Street in Watsonville, California. Arthur attended local elementary schools and about 1934, studied at Watsonville High School for one year. After leaving school, he worked as a painter in the Pajaro Valley for the Speas Company.

On March 7, 1942, Arthur Earl reported to the induction center in San Francisco and was enlisted as an infantry private. His basic training took place at Camp Roberts, California, followed by paratrooper training at Fort Benning, Georgia. During this period, Arthur and Elsie were married.

In January 1944, Earl was assigned to the 501st Parachute Infantry Regiment of the 101st Airborne Division and sent to England. After participating in the Normandy campaign, the 501st Regiment was ordered to Holland for Operation Market Garden.

This was an audacious plan concocted by British Field Marshal Montgomery that would be the first major daylight air assault attempted by a military power since Germany's attack on Crete. Similar to the German assault of four years earlier, the Allies initial plan for September 17, 1944 was to use the paratroopers and glidermen of the 82nd and 101st US Airborne Divisions and England's First Airborne Division in a daring daylight drop into Holland. The airborne Allied troops were to seize roads, bridges and the key communication cities of Eindhoven, Nijmegen and Arnhem, thus cutting Holland in half and clearing a corridor for British armoured and motorized columns all the way to the German border. The 101st mission was to secure the fifteen miles of Hell's Highway stretching from Eindhoven north to Veghel. The 501st was specifically tasked to drop 4 miles south of Veghel and seize railroad and highway bridges over the Aa River and the Willems Canal. Though Lt. Col. Kinnard's 1st Battalion landed wide of their mark, they landed all together and were quickly able to seize two railroad bridges to the west of Veghel. Meanwhile, the other two battalions were able to seize intact the road bridges over the Willems Canal and Aa River.

On September 11, Private Earl jumped with the 2nd Battalion of the 501st Paratroop Infantry Regiment, 101st Airborne Division on Dropzone A near Veghel, Holland. During the succeeding days, his unit engaged in heavy fighting while defending the city.

Arthur J. Earl was killed in action at Veghel on September 23, 1944. His remains were buried in the Netherlands American Cemetery at Margraten, Netherlands; his awards include the Purple Heart.

(ABMC; NARA2; WRP October 11, 1944 1:4; 101st Airborne World War II, 501st Inf Paratroop Regiment, http://www.ww2-airborne.us/units/501/501.html, [16 September 2008])

KENNETH L. LAPHAM
(1944/09/29)

(Golden Gate National Cemetery - San Bruno California)

The Marines learned a lesson in what not to do at Peleliu; however, for Ken Lapham it was a costly lesson.

Kenneth Lloyd Lapham was born on December 29, 1922, in Yuma Arizona, to Mr. and Mrs. Ralph Lapham. No further information is available regarding his family and early life. The Laphams moved to Watsonville in 1939, where Ken worked at the O. O. Eaton lettuce shed.

In January 1942, Lapham enlisted in the US Marine Corps and was sent to San Diego for his basic and school-of-infantry training. He was assigned to the 1st Marine Division and fought with them throughout the Pacific. He was then sent to Peleliu.

[Peleliu was] The site of an important Japanese air base during World War II. Some American war planners viewed the Palaus Island chain as a stepping-stone on the way back to the Philippines; others thought it should be bypassed. The decision was made in mid-1944 to seize three of the southern Palaus. First to be invaded was Peleliu. The US First Marine Division, under Gen. William H. Rupertus, landed early on 15 September 1944. The 10,000-strong Japanese force, strongly entrenched in the island's central ridge system, fought back stubbornly. It took over two months and the addition of an entire regiment to subdue the last Japanese defenders. While nearly 2,000 Americans died in taking Peleliu, some questioned its value. Airfields on Peleliu, it was discovered, could not support the Philippine invasion in the manner expected.

Lapham wrote home to his parents earlier saying that he had encountered some, "pretty close calls." Later he was not so lucky. On September 29, 1944, Private First Class Kenneth Lloyd Lapham died from the wounds that he had received at Peleliu.

The remains of Kenneth Lapham were returned and buried in the Golden Gate National Cemetery at San Bruno, California, in 1948.

(USDVA; WRP October 23, 1944 1:3; Answers.Com, Peleliu; http://www.answers.com/topic/peleliu, [16 September 2008])

CLEMENS A. LAMBRECHT
(1944/10/09)

(Photo Santa Cruz Riptide Newspaper files)

A Santa Cruz wife tearfully had to add a second gold star to the flag in her window.

Clemens A. Lambrecht was born in Oregon in 1912, to Jake and Lena Lambrecht. He grew up on the family farm near Mehama, in Marion County, Oregon, with his brothers Paul, Markus and Miles and sister Opal. Later his parents moved to Washington County near Portland.

Military records indicate that Lambrecht had completed grammar school but there is no record of his completing high school. At the time of his induction in 1942, he was working as a repairman for the Remington Rand Company in Portland.

Clemens Lambrecht was sent to an unspecified camp for his basic and advanced training in June 1941. It is possible that his stateside military assignments also included a local military facility where he met Elizabeth Verhines. On August 24, 1943, he married Mrs. Elizabeth Jacobs Verhines, (see biography of Thomas Verhines) a war widow with a three-year old daughter. Following his marriage, Sergeant Lambrecht joined the 315th Regiment of the 79th Division at Camp Phillips, Kansas, preparing to be deployed overseas.

Lambrecht and his unit left the US on April 7, 1944, arrived in Liverpool on April 17 and began training for the recapture of Europe. On June 13 they were transported to France, where he joined in the pursuit of the retreating Germans. In September 1944,

The division moved forward despite intense attacks from the Forêt de Parroy, the 315th Infantry losing and then recovering part of Lunéville 22 September 44 as the 314th Infantry faced counterattacks at Moncel. The 314th Infantry frontally assaulted Forêt de Monden the following day in heavy combat and the division entered the Forêt de Parroy. The 315th Infantry was temporarily isolated in fighting at the main road junction there on 5 October 44. An all-out divisional assault forced a German withdrawal from the forest with the final capture of the main road junction 9 October 44.

Staff Sergeant Clemens A. Lambrecht was wounded during this action and on October 9, 1944, died from those wounds. Elizabeth Verhines Lambrecht once again found herself a widow, this time with two gold flags hanging in her window.

Lambrecht's body was buried in the Epinal American Cemetery in Epinal, France. His awards include the Purple Heart.

(USCR, 1920 US Census, OR, Marion; NARA2; ABMC; 79th Infantry Regiment, WW II, History, http://home.earthlink.net, [16 Sept. 2008] SCSn October 29, 1944 2:3,

HUBERT C. JACKSON
(1944/10/16)

(Watsonville High School yearbook)

"Wildcats," "Cardinals" and "Packers" helped define "Steamboat Jackson" to Watsonville.

Hubert Curtis Jackson was born in Jasper Alabama, in 1924, to Mr. and Mrs. Lloyd Jackson. The Jackson family moved to Watsonville in 1937, where it expanded to include sons Hubert and Owel and daughters Jeanette and Ollie Lee. Hubert attended a local grammar school and entered Watsonville High School about 1938. Known as "Steamboat" Jackson, he was an all-around athlete and during his two years in high school was captain of its "wildcat" football and baseball teams. After leaving school, he kept up his proficiency in baseball by playing on both the White's Cardinals and Pete's Packer teams of the city league.

Hubert Jackson enlisted in the United States Army Air Force in San Francisco on February 9, 1942. He was trained at Keesler field, Mississippi, Amarillo, Texas, and Wichita Falls, Texas, before being assigned as a nose gunner on a B-24 Liberator bomber. When Private Jackson arrived overseas, he joined the 762nd Squadron of the 460th Bomb Group.

On October 16, 1944, while flying a mission over Yugoslavia, Corporal Hubert Curtis Jackson's plane was shot down and crashed. He was listed as "missing in action" until February 1945, when his parents were officially notified of his death.

His remains were recovered and returned to the United States for burial in the Golden Gate National Cemetery at San Bruno, June 24, 1949.

(NARA2; USDVA; WRP February 2, 1945 1:3; Photo-WHS)

PAUL F. HORIUCHI
(1944/10/19)

(Courtesy National Japanese American Historical Society)

"Go For Broke" designated his unit and defined the intensity of Paul's service.

Paul Fumio Horiuchi was born in Walnut Grove, California, on January 25, 1922, the son of Takeji and Haru Horiuchi. Brothers Tom, Joe, Bill, Ben and Masaru joined Paul in rounding out the family. The Horiuchi family later moved to the Pajaro Valley and resided there until 1940. While in Watsonville, Paul attended Watsonville High School, where he was active on its football and basketball teams and was a member of the nature club. After graduating from high school in 1940, he moved to the Salinas Valley and worked as a pressman for Nichi-Bei, a Japanese language newspaper. Horiuchi was residing in Salinas in the spring of 1942, when Japanese-Americans were moved to the relocation camp at Poston, Arizona.

During a leave from the camp, Horiuchi volunteered for military service and entered the US Army at Salt Lake City, Utah, on December 5, 1943. He was sent to Camp Shelby, Mississippi, for basic training and became a member of Company E, 2nd Battalion, 442nd Regimental Combat Team of the 100th Infantry Division.

Paul Horiuchi and his company boarded troop ships for Italy on May 1, 1944, and arrived at Naples on June 2. He participated in the fall of Rome and pursued retreating Germans up the boot of Italy to Livorno, which was captured in July 1944.

In the fall of 1944, the 442nd was transported to Marseilles, France, and began driving the Germans out of the Rhone Valley. Key to their objective was the recapture of the French town of Bruyeres. The official report of that mission describes Private First Class Paul (Fumio) Horiuchi's last battle.

19 October - The battalions reorganized and attacked again at 1300 with the objective of reaching the railroad embankment 2000 yards East of Bruyeres on the edge of the Forĕt de Belmont. CO's E and G from the 2nd Bn and CO's I and K from the 3rd Bn made the push. Enemy troops dug in behind the embankment held up the advance at 1600, and SP guns from the vicinity of Belmont shelled the forward companies.

Paul Horiuchi was killed in action during this encounter. His remains were later recovered and returned to the United States for reburial in the Golden Gate National Cemetery in San Bruno on January 31, 1949. His awards include the Purple Heart, Bronze Star and Combat Infantryman's Badge.

(NARA2; USDVA; WRP November 11, 1944 1:1; Americans of Japanese Ancestry, WW II Memorial, http://www.ajawarvets.org/campaigns/campaign_06_bruyeres.htm, [16 September 2008])

JOHN A. NELSON
(1944/10/19)

(Santa Cruz High School Service Cardinal)

Davenport folks read in the Santa Cruz Sentinel that one of their own was "Killed in German Clash."

John A. Nelson was born in San Francisco, California, on January 24, 1924. Personal information regarding his parents has not been found. John's early years and education were spent in San Francisco, where he attended local elementary schools and Balboa High School. He and his brother Warren moved to Davenport to live with their aunt and uncle, Mr. & Mrs. John Ferrari, in 1939. In September, John entered Santa Cruz High School, took a general varied course of study and after school worked for the Davenport Bakery. He graduated from high school in 1942 and was employed as a farm hand in the Davenport area until he was drafted.

On December 7, 1943, John Nelson was drafted into the US Army. He trained at Fort Knox, Kentucky, and following training, was assigned to an ordinance battalion attached to an armored division. After spending a ten-day furlough in Santa Cruz, he was shipped to England where he arrived on June 6, 1944.

Nelson's (unidentified) unit took part in the invasion at Normandy France, and in the liberation of Belgium. In his final letter home September 17, 1944, he indicated that he was near Germany.

Private John A. Nelson was reported killed in action on October 19, 1944, during a clash with German forces. The location of his remains has not been identified; however, it is believed that they were returned to the United States.

(CBR; NARA2; SCHSC Pg. 14, SCSn November 07, 1944 1:8)

PETER L. VLASICH
(1944/10/20)

(Holy Cross Cemetery - Santa Cruz, California)

A lonely grave in the Philippines was traded for a place next to his mom and dad.

Peter Louis Vlasich was born in Santa Cruz, California on May 9, 1914, to Martin and Stella Vlasich; he was preceded in the family by his brother Louis, who was two years older. The Vlasich family also included a daughter, Nicki. Peter is reported to have graduated from Chaminade High School in 1933.

After finishing high school, Vlasich enlisted in the US Navy and completed boot camp at an unspecified training facility. Following instruction in naval carpentry, he was stationed at Pearl Harbor, Hawaii and at Mare Island, California. During his period of naval service, Vlasich was promoted through the five enlisted grades to Chief Carpenter's Mate.

When his ship, the cruiser *USS Honolulu*, was at Mare Island near Vallejo for repair and refitting in November 1943, he was granted a twenty-day leave to visit his home in Santa Cruz.

While serving in the navy, Chief Vlasich participated in engagements at Bougainville, the Solomon Islands, Saipan, Guam and Peleliu. His final campaign was in the recapture of the Philippine Islands

The Honolulu *departed from the staging area at Manus Island in the Admiralty Islands on 12 October 1944 and steamed towards the Philippines for the invasion of Leyte. She began a bombardment 19 October from Leyte Gulf, and the next day she began screening the landings. At 16:00 hours, on 20 October an enemy torpedo plane was sighted as it aimed its torpedo at the* Honolulu. *Despite the skill-*

ful maneuvering of Captain Thurber, USN, to evade, the torpedo found its mark on her port side.

Chief Carpenter's Mate Peter Louis Vlasich was one of the casualties of that torpedo and was officially declared dead on October 20, 1944. In a letter to the Vlasich family, one of his shipmates indicated that Peter was buried on Manus, one of the Admiralty Islands.

Following the war, his remains were returned to Santa Cruz and reinterred in the family plot at Holy Cross Cemetery.

(Holy Cross Cemetery Headstone; USNM; SCSn January 4, 1945 1:2; WIKI, USS Honolulu CL-48)

ROBERT COVERSTONE
(1944/10/22)

(Cambridge American Cemetery England - Internet photo)

A heavy English fog eliminated the need for Robert's CPA exam.

Robert Coverstone was born about 1922, to Mr. and Mrs. Virgil Coverstone. Robert spent a portion of his youth in Santa Cruz and in 1939, attended Santa Cruz High School. While in high school, he delivered newspapers for the *Santa Cruz Sentinel.* About 1940 the family moved to Santa Barbara, where he graduated from high school. Coverstone then undertook studies to qualify as a certified public accountant; however, military service prevented him from completing his final examination.

In 1943 Robert Coverstone enlisted in the USAAF. After completing basic training, he entered the air cadet program and took his pre- flight training in Nevada. Upon completion of the advanced pilot training program he was commissioned a second lieutenant and issued his wings.

In June 1944, Lt. Coverstone was shipped overseas as a B-17 pilot assigned to the 422nd Squadron, 305th Bomb Group, 8th Air Force stationed at Chalveston, England. On October 22, 1944, Second Lieutenant Robert Coverstone was the co-pilot aboard the My Achin 'B' Flying Fortress returning to Chalveston from the bombing mission of a tank factory in Hanover, Germany. At the time of his return, the Chalveston area was experiencing heavy overcast and limited visibility. As his B-17 approached the field in the fog, it collided with another returning aircraft

killing both crews.

His remains were recovered and buried in the Cambridge American Cemetery in Cambridge, England. His awards include the Air Medal with two Oak Leaf Clusters.

(ABMC, SCSn December 06, 1944 1:7; 2nd Lt John L Touchett, http://forum.armyairforces.com/m136431-p1-print.aspx [18 April 2009])

MARTIN A. CAHILL
(1944/10/24)

(Internet photo)

An American torpedo sank Marty Cahill.

Martin A. Cahill was born on February 24, 1918, in San Francisco, California, to William and Lena Cahill. His family also included his brothers Anthony and William and his sisters Constance and Mrs. R. Lozier. Martin Cahill attended schools in San Francisco until September 1935, when he enrolled in Santa Cruz High School. After leaving school in 1936, he worked as a commercial vehicle driver.

Martin enlisted in the California National Guard at Salinas on December 6, 1938. He remained active in the guard and was inducted into the US Army on January 29, 1941. In February, his unit was re-designated as C Company, 194th Tank Battalion and was ordered to Fort Lewis, Washington. Martin trained as a cook during the company's seven- month stay at Ft. Lewis. In September the 194th Tank Battalion was transported to the Philippine Islands aboard the *SS President Cleveland* and reached Manila on September 27, 1941.

When the Japanese invaded the Philippines on December 22, Martin's tank company assisted in the defense of Manila. During the next four months, he drove a truck transporting supplies to his unit. Following the surrender of US forces on April 9, 1942, Cahill took part in the Bataan Death March and was confined to the Japanese Prison camp at Cabanatuan, where he remained until the fall of 1944.

In October 1944, Cahill and other prisoners were placed aboard a Japanese vessel bound for Manchuria. A letter from the War Department to his parents in 1945 describes the final episode in the life of Private First Class Martin A. Cahill.

The information available to the war department is that the vessel sailed from Manila on October 11, 1944, with 1775 prisoners of war aboard. On October 24 the vessel was sunk by submarine action in the South China Sea over 200 miles from the Chinese coast, which was the nearest land. Five of the prisoners escaped in a small boat and reached the coast. Four others have been reported as picked up by the Japanese by whom all others aboard are reported lost. Absence of detailed information as to what happened to other individual prisoners and the known circumstances of the incident lead to a conclusion that all other prisoners listed by the Japanese as aboard the vessel perished.

The body of Martin Cahill was never recovered; he was memorialized on the Tablets of the Missing at Manila American Cemetery, Manila, Philippines. His awards include the Purple Heart.

(ABMC; NARA2; SCHSC Pg. 7; SCSn October 26, 1945; (194th Tank Battalion Company C http://www.proviso.w-cook.k12. il.us/Bataan%20Web/194th_C_Co.htm; http://www.proviso.k12. il.us/bataan%20Web/194_Poster.htm)

VERNON E. TREVETHAN
(1944/10/24)

Vernon Ervin Trevethan was born about 1925, in Watsonville, to Edward and Jeanette Trevethan who lived in the nearby community of Freedom. Vernon and his brother Edward were raised and educated in local grammar schools; Vernon attended Watsonville High School.

Trevethan enlisted in the US Navy in October 1942, and probably received his boot camp training at the US Naval Training center in San Diego. Later he received additional instruction at Portsmouth, Virginia, as a machinist mate before being stationed aboard the cruiser *USS Birmingham* serving in the Pacific Fleet.

Assigned to TF 57, she [USS Birmingham] took part in the invasion of Saipan (14 June-4 August 1944); Battle of the Philippine Sea (19-20 June); invasion of Tinian (20 July-1 August); invasion of Guam (21 July); and Philippine Islands raids (9-24 September). She then served with TF 38 during the Okinawa raid (10 October), northern Luzon and Formosa raids (15 and 18-19 October), and the Battle for Leyte Gulf (24 October). During the latter she suffered topside damage from explosions on board Princeton *(CVL-23) while courageously attempting to aid that stricken vessel.*

Vernon Ervin Trevethan, MM3, USN, was listed as a crewmember of the *USS Birmingham* that was Lost at Sea on October 24, 1944. This same action claimed the lives of 230 other crewman of the *Birmingham* who were attempting to save the *USS Princeton* during the battle of Leyte Gulf.

Trevethan was memorialized on the Tablets of the Missing at Manila American Cemetery in Manila. His awards include the Purple Heart.

(ABMC, WRP 1944/12/11, USNM; DANFS, USS Birmingham CL-62)

HOMER W. IJAMES JR.
(1944/10/25)

(Santa Cruz High School Service Cardinal)

Homer was aboard a submarine that was sunk by a torpedo it had just fired.

Homer W. Ijames Jr. was born on October 12, 1926, in Chicago, Illinois, to Homer and Hilda Ijames. The date the Ijames family moved to Santa Cruz is not known. Homer Jr. received his elementary school education at Branciforte School before entering Santa Cruz High School in 1941. He was a member of the school's class of 1944 but left school before graduation to join the navy.

Homer Ijames enlisted in the US Navy on October 13, 1943, and was sent to the US Naval Training Center at San Diego for training. Following boot camp in February 1944, he was sent to the navy's submarine school in New London, Connecticut. Seaman Ijames later received additional instruction at the navy's radar training school at Pearl Harbor. After completing his training phase, Petty Officer Third Class Ijames was assigned to the submarine *USS Tang* in the Pacific Fleet.

The story of Tang's *sinking comes from the report of her surviving Commanding Officer. A night surface attack was launched on October 24, 1944 against a transport, which had previously been stopped in an earlier attack. The first torpedo was fired and when it was observed to be running true, the second and last was loosed. It curved sharply to the left, broached, porpoised and circled. Emergency speed was called for and the rudder was thrown over. These measures resulted only in the torpedo striking the stern of* Tang, *rather than amidships. The explosion was violent, and people as far forward as the control room received broken limbs. The ship went down by the stern with the after three compartments flooded. Of the nine officers and men on the bridge, three were able to swim through the night until picked up eight hours later. One officer escaped from the flooded conning tower, and was rescued with the others.*

The body of Radarman, Third Class Homer W. Ijames Jr. was never recovered; he is memorialized on the Tablets of the Missing at Manila American Cemetery. His awards include the Purple Heart.

(ABMC, SCHSC Pg. 12; COMSUBPAC, USS Tang SS-306, http://www.csp.navy.mil/ww2boats/tang.htm, [16 September 2008])

HARRY J. CONNOLLY
(1944/10/28)

(Santa Cruz High School Service Cardinal)

A Live Oak kid, with all the right moves, met his master in Munster.

Harry James Connolly was born on January 3, 1920, in Santa Cruz, the son of Mr. and Mrs. William Connolly, who lived in the Live Oak district of Santa Cruz County. He and his three brothers, Roy, George and Walter, shared the family home located on lower Capitola Road. Harry attended Live Oak School and entered Santa Cruz High School in 1932. During high school, he was an all- around student. In addition to majoring in mathematics and playing football and basketball, he participated in the band.

Following his graduation from high school in 1936, Harry Connolly enrolled in the University of California at Berkeley. At UCB he remained active in athletics and was a member of the varsity crew that traveled to the East Coast to compete on the Hudson River.

After graduating from college in 1943, Connolly joined the US Army Air Force and was sent to the Utah State Flight Academy at Logan, Utah. His basic training took place at Polaric Flight Academy in Lancaster, California, and his advanced training at Marfa, Texas. Upon the completion of this training in February 1944, he received his pilot's wings

and was commissioned a second lieutenant. B-17 bomber training at Roswell, New Mexico, Alexandria, Louisiana, and Lincoln, Nebraska, rounded out his instruction.

Harry Connelly returned to Santa Cruz for a final visit before joining the 398th Bomb Group of the 8th Air Force located at Nuthampstead, Herfordshire, England.

The 398th Bomb Group (Heavy) was part of the United States Eighth Air Force during World War II. Activated on 1 March 1943, after a period as a Replacement Training Unit in the United States, the 398th Bomb Group moved to England and was stationed at United States Air Force Station 131 at Nuthampstead, Herfordshire from April 1944 until May/June 1945. The Group comprised Group Headquarters and four Squadrons (600th, 601st, 602nd and 603rd). Trained to fly B-17 Bombers (known as Flying Fortresses) the Group completed 195 operations flying from Nuthampstead, mainly attacking strategic targets in Germany such as oil refineries, factories, marshalling yards and aircraft plants.

While flying a bombing mission over Munster, Germany on October 28, 1944, Second Lieutenant Harry James Connolly was killed in action. His parents later received the Purple Heart and the Air Medal that he had been posthumously awarded. His remains were recovered following the war and were reinterred in the Holy Cross Cemetery in Santa Cruz, California.

(CBR; SCHSC Pg. 8; 398th Bomb Group, History, www.398th. org/Research/398th_Preservation, [Approx. 15 May 2007]; SCSn November 13, 1944 1:3)

HENRY S. IZUMIZAKI
(1944/11/02)

(Courtesy National Japanese American Historical Society)

Henry had to avoid detection by some internees at the Poston internment camp in order to join the army.

Henry Sadao Izumizaki was born in Watsonville, California on May 20, 1921, to Kanetsuchi and Fumiyo Izumizaki. In addition to Henry, the Izumizaki family included two other sons, James and Arthur. He attended local schools in the Pajaro Valley and entered Watsonville High School. During his high school years, he played on the football team and was a member of the Block W Society.

Henry, who was described as a quiet and shy person, worked as a farm hand in the Pajaro Valley for the Bronson vegetable farm after graduating from high school. Following the US entry into World War II, the Izumizaki family was moved to the Salinas Rodeo grounds in April 1942 and later relocated to the Japanese-American internment camp at Poston, Arizona. While at the camp, Henry worked as a carpenter with the school construction crew. In 1943 the Japanese American Citizens League (JACL) made a request to the government to create a special army unit made up of Nisei (second-generation Japanese-American) men. He wanted to enlist in the army, but fearing retribution from the camp's pro-Japan element had to sneak out of the camp to enlist.

Henry Izumizaki enlisted in the US Army on May 26, 1943. Following training at Camp Shelby, Mississippi, he was assigned to Company F of the 442nd Regimental Combat Team. The combat team members boarded a troop ship bound for Italy on May 1, 1944, and arrived at Naples, on June 2. Company F participated in the fall of Rome and in the pursuit of retreating Germans up the boot of Italy to Livorno, which was captured in July 1944.

In the fall of 1944, the 442nd was transported to Marseilles, France, to clear the Germans out of the Rhone Valley and recapture French border towns. Mas Hashimoto, a Watsonville historian, shared the final episode in the life of Private First Class Henry Sadao Izumizaki and his role in assisting a trapped Texas Battalion.

During the Battle of the Lost Texas Battalion in early November of 1944, Henry was the Fox Company's runner. The Texas battalion was completely cut off in the Vosges Forest and was destined to be annihilated by the Germans. Several battalions fell short of the rescue operations. A very tired but game 100th/442nd was ordered to rescue of what remained of the Texans. The fighting lasted four more days. Tree bursts from German mortars and artillery filled the sky, and shrapnel rained on the men of the 100th/442nd below. The Germans, who had commanded the high ground, lobbed hand grenades down the hill. No one remembers who called it first but with "Go For Broke!" the men of the 100th/442nd charged. When the hand-to-hand combat ended, the Germans surrendered and 211 Texans were rescued.

Henry sprained his ankle during the steep hillside battle, but he refused to seek medical aid or rest because so many of his comrades were being killed, and there were no

replacements! Henry was one of the 184 killed during that battle. A sliver of shrapnel entered his side and had pierced his heart. Another 600 of the 100th/442nd were badly wounded. Several rifle companies were reduced to less than 10 men.

Henry Izumizaki died on November 2, 1944, and was initially buried in Epinal, France. In 1948, his remains were returned to Watsonville for interment in the Pajaro Valley Memorial Park.

(NARA2; WRP November 24, 1944 1:5, Mas Hashimoto, Re-enactment http://www.watsonvillesantacruzjacl.org/reenactment/lessons2.htm [16 September 2008]; Pajaro Valley Cemetery Headstone 5/12/08)

MARK R. GRAVES
(1944/11/04)

(Epinal American Cemetery France - Internet photo)

The name Mark R. Graves appears on the Watsonville High School World War II Memorial stone. No additional reference to his residence in Santa Cruz County has been found. His failure to appear within the NARA selective service enlistment records suggests that he may have enlisted in the army prior to registering for the draft.

The US War Department listing of World War II dead, credits his service to Lander County, (Austin/Battle Mountain) Nevada, and noted that he died from non-battle circumstances.

The American Battlefield Monument Commission records reveal that Graves was a private, assigned to the 339th Ordnance Depot Company and died on November 4, 1944. Private Mark R. Graves is buried in Epinal, France.

(ACGEN; ABMC)

EDWARD B. LETTUNICH
(1944/11/04)

(Henri-Chapelle American Cemetery, Belgium - Internet photo)

A branch was lopped off an old Pajaro Valley family tree during World War II.

Edward B. Lettunich, a member of an old Pajaro Valley family, was born in Watsonville on November 19, 1913. He was the son of Edward and Stella Lettunich and the brother of George and Ann Lettunich. Edward was raised and educated in the Pajaro Valley, attending local grammar schools and Watsonville High School. Lettunich later transferred to Lowell High School in San Francisco where he graduated in 1931. A *Watsonville Register-Pajaronian* obituary at the time of his death indicated that he was "a graduate of Stanford" and "was at one time an all-American tackle." However, neither of these facts has been confirmed. After leaving college, he re-joined his family in Los Angeles where they had relocated.

When World War II began, Lettunich received a commission in the US Army and advanced to the rank of Captain. He was assigned to the 413th Infantry Regiment of the 104th (Timberwolf) Infantry Division that was formed at Camp Adair, Oregon.

The 104th Infantry Division landed in France on 7 September 1944 and moved into a defensive position in the vicinity of Wuustwezel, Belgium, 23 October 1944...The 104th went over to the offensive on the 25th, soon liberating Zundert, Holland, gaining control of the Breda-Roosendall Road, and overrunning the Vaart Canal defenses. Leur and Etten fell as the Division advanced in a coordinated drive to the Mark River at Standdarbuiten on 2 November 1944 and established a bridgehead. Zevenbergen was captured and the Maas River reached 5 November.

On November 4, 1944, Captain Edward B. Lettunich was killed in action in Holland and his remains were interred in the Henri-Chapelle American Cemetery in Henri-Chapelle, Belgium. His awards include the Purple Heart.

(CBR; ABMC, WRP November 24, 1944; Natl. Timberwolf Org, WWII, 104th Infantry Division, 1999 http://www.104infdiv.org/WORLDWAR.HTM, [16 Sept 2008])

GEORGE T. VAN GIESEN
(1944/11/07)

(Netherlands American Cemetery Margraten – Internet photo)

"George Van Giesen, 26, Killed in France" reported the *Watsonville Register-Pajaronian*.

George T. Van Giesen was born in 1918, the son of Dunn and Alice Van Giesen. He and his sister, Mrs. Bud Silvey, grew up in Watsonville where their father managed the local branch of the Bank of America. Young Van Giesen lived in Watsonville for a number of years and attended local elementary schools until about 1932, when his family moved to San Francisco. While living in San Francisco, George completed his education and married Barbara. The couple remained and worked in the city until the war.

The date of Van Giesen's entry into the US Army is not known; however, he was commissioned as a second lieutenant. Following his training period, he was assigned to the 414th Infantry Regiment, 104th Infantry Division. By the time his unit reached France in September 1944 he had been promoted to first lieutenant.

On November 2, George Van Giesen and the 414th had crossed the Maas River.

The 104th Infantry Division landed in France on 7 September 1944. It moved into defensive positions in the vicinity of Wuestwezel, Belgium, 23 October 1944, and went over to the, offensive on the 26th, taking Zundert, gaining control of the Breda-Roosendaal Road and overrunning Vaart Canal defenses. Leur and Etten fell as the Division advanced to the Mark River, 31 October. A coordinated attack over the Mark River at Standaarduiten, 2 November 1944, established a bridgehead. Zevenbergen was captured and the Maas River reached on 5 November. While the bulk of the Division moved near Aachen, Germany, elements remained to secure Moerdijk before being relieved on 7 November.

First Lieutenant George T. Van Giesen died November 7, 1944, from wounds received in a previous combat engagement. His remains were buried in the Netherlands American Cemetery in Margraten, Netherlands. He was posthumously issued the Distinguished Service Cross; his other awards include the Purple Heart.

(ABMC, WRP December 22, 1944 3:7; 104th Infantry Division, WWII Combat Chronicle, 2003, http://www.army.mil/cmh-pg/lineage/cc/104id.htm, [16 Sept 2008])

JAMES C. HARPER
(1944/11/11)

James C. Harper was born in Georgia in 1920. Information about his parents, siblings or early years has not been located. When he registered for the draft in the fall of 1941, Harper indicated that he was a resident of Santa Cruz County, was single and had completed four years of high school. At that time he was working as a surveyor.

James Harper was inducted into the US Army on October 22, 1941, at San Francisco, as a private in the Army Air Force. After completing basic and advanced training, he was promoted to sergeant and sent to the 744th Bomber Squadron, 456th Bomber Group, (Heavy) of the 15th Air Force in Europe. His unit flew B-24 Liberator bombers and was known as "Steed's Flying Colts" after its commander Colonel Thomas Webster Steed.

The last of 19 missions against Romanian oil production occurred August 18. Missions continued against oil and synthetic oil production facilities at Odertal, Germany; Moosbierbaum and Vienna, Austria; Brux, Czechoslovakia; and Blechhammer, Poland, with 26 bombers lost on 23 missions. Bombing of German lines of communication, particularly marshalling yards and railroad bridges, remained a priority to the end of the war. After August 1944 the 456th did not lose another aircraft to fighter defenses, but losses continued to accumulate from anti-aircraft fire. In the remaining nine months of operations 43 bombers were lost, most to flak. Three or more bombers were lost on five missions, including November 11, when three planes crashed into the Adriatic after being recalled from a mission.

On November 11, 1944, Sergeant James C. Harper was listed as missing in action. He was probably a crewmember of one of the three planes from the unit that crashed into the Adriatic on that day. His remains were never located; he is memorialized on the Tablets of the Missing at Florence American Cemetery, Florence, Italy. His awards include the Air Medal and Purple Heart.

(ABMC, NARA2; WIKI, 456th Bomb Group)

ROBERT L. TODA
(1944/11/12)

(Manila American Cemetery – Internet photo)

"Lieut. Bob Toda Killed on Leyte in Infantry Fight" declared the *Santa Cruz Sentinel*.

Robert Lewis Toda, the son of Mr. and Mrs. Lewis Toda of Farmington, California, was born in San Joaquin County, California, on September 16, 1915. He was raised and educated in the Sacramento Valley where he completed four years of high school. After finishing his formal education, Robert Toda was employed as a commercial vehicle driver.

On March 12, 1941, Toda was inducted into the US Army as a private at Sacramento, California. While undergoing basic training, he was selected for Officer Candidate School and was sent to Fort Benning, Georgia. After graduating from OCS, he was commissioned a second lieutenant and married Arlene. While he was in Georgia, his wife established the family residence in Santa Cruz.

Lt. Toda was assigned to the 381st Infantry Regiment of the 96th Infantry Division that assisted in the invasion of the Philippine Islands.

On October 20, 1944, the Division landed on Leyte above Dulag. By October 30, it had cleared a series of fortified Japanese positions along the Labir-Catmon-San Vicente Hill axis and secured the northern portion of the Corps zone to the Tanauan-Dagami Road. The 96th then made a holding attack to the west from Dagami to permit the 7th Division to cross to the island's East Coast and drive north along Ormoc Bay. This resulted in a series of battalion-sized actions on the Dagami Heights that began on November 3. The 382nd Infantry Regiment assaulted "Bloody Ridge" near Hitomnog, repelled a Japanese attack, and secured "Suicide Ridge" to the north before being relieved by the 381st Infantry on November 20.

First Lieutenant Robert L. Toda was killed in action during the fighting on Luzon on November 12, 1944. His body was recovered and buried in the Manila American Cemetery in Manila. His awards include the Purple Heart.

(CBR; ABMC, NARA2; SCSn January 10, 1945, 96th Infantry Division, Internet History, http://www.geocities.com/Pentagon/Barracks/4096/history.html, [16 September 2008])

LLOYD BENSON
(1944/11/18)

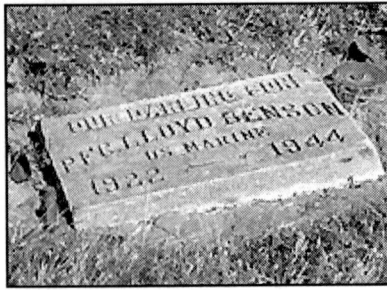

(Pajaro Valley Memorial Park – Watsonville, California)

The cold murky waters of Puget Sound snuffed out the life of a Watsonville marine.

Lloyd Benson was born in Mississippi in 1922. His parents, Mr. and Mrs. L. W. Benson, moved to California about 1934 and settled in the Pajaro Valley. The family ultimately grew to include his brothers Perry, Lewis and Lenwood, and a sister, Mrs. Ray Anderson. Lloyd attended local schools and graduated from Watsonville High School about 1940. Following his graduation, he was employed in the Pajaro Valley until 1943

Lloyd Benson enlisted in the US Marine Corps in September 1943. He received his basic and school-of-infantry training at Camp Pendleton, California, near San Diego and was then posted to the Keyport Naval Torpedo Station near Bremerton, Washington. While at that naval facility, Benson served as a member of the US Marine Corps security force.

On November 18, 1944, while on liberty, Private First Class Benson was driving a car that crashed through a safety gate on the ferry dock at Suquamish, near Bremerton, Washington, and plunged into Puget Sound. Lloyd Benson drowned in the accident. His body was recovered and returned to Watsonville for a funeral service and burial in the Pajaro Valley Memorial Park.

(WRP 1944/11/20 1:2, 1944/12/11?, Pajaro Valley Cemetery Headstone 5/12/08)

ADOLPH J. NEGRI
(1944/11/20)

(Santa Cruz High School yearbook)

A "Railsplitter" from Santa Cruz was posthumously awarded the Silver Star.

Adolph J. Negri was born in Santa Cruz, California on October 1, 1922, to Clem and Mary Negri. The Negri family had moved to Santa Cruz from Italy before Adolph was born. The family included his brother Alfred and sister Eleanor. Adolph's father worked in the limekiln industry.

Adolph spent most of his growing years in Santa Cruz and attended local elementary schools. He entered Santa Cruz High School about 1936 and graduated in 1940. After leaving high school, Negri moved to San Francisco and entered the building trades as an apprentice.

Adolph Negri was inducted into the army as a private at San Francisco on December 15, 1943. He received his basic training at Camp Howze, Texas, followed by advanced instruction at Claiborne, Louisiana. After completing his training schedule, Adolph returned to San Francisco where he was married. A son was later born to the couple. In May 1944, he visited Santa Cruz for the last time to spend a few days with his father before being shipped to Europe.

Upon arrival in France, Adolph Negri was assigned to the 334th Infantry Regiment of the 84th Division known as "Railsplitters." During the last six months of 1944, the 84th Division played a significant role in the liberation of France. By late November, Adolph's regiment had advanced to the North Rhine area of Westphalia Germany, and was called upon to capture the village of Prummern near the city of Geilenkirchen. The Silver Star citation awarded to Negri describes the action that claimed his life on November 20, 1944, at Prummern.

When enemy machine gun fire delayed the advance of his company on a German town [Prummern], Private First Class Adolph Negri, moving forward aggressively with his light machine gun, assaulted the enemy position alone in an effort to enable the advance to continue. He lost his life in this section when fire from several enemy positions was directed upon him.

Adolph Negri was buried in the Netherlands American Cemetery at Margraten, Netherlands. His awards include the Silver Star and Purple Heart.

(CBR; ABMC, NARA2; Lonesentry.com, Railsplitters, The Story of the 84th Infantry Division, [16 September 2008]; SCSn May 13, 1944 10:1, November 26, 1945 1:4; Photo-SCHS)

DONALD MONROE
(1944/12/05)

Included in the *Watsonville Register-Pajaronian* May 25, 1945, listing of Pajaro Valley World War II casualties is the name of Donald Monroe, a resident of San Benito County.

Donald Monroe was born in Illinois in 1924 to Mr. and Mrs. John Monroe, who later moved to the Aromas district of the Pajaro Valley. In addition to Donald, the Monroe family included sons Theodore and John, and daughters Goldie, Bluebell and Rae. Donald completed grammar school, but there is no record of his having attended high school. In early 1943, he was employed by the railroad as a brakeman and was financially assisting his parents.

Donald Monroe was inducted into the army on March 4, 1943, in San Francisco and sent to Fort Rucker, Alabama. While training at Fort Rucker, Monroe was riding a motor-cycle during maneuvers and was involved in an accident that fractured his collarbone. After recovering, he was sent to Camp Van Doren, Mississippi, for advanced training and later attached to an unidentified tank destroyer battalion.

In September 1944, Donald Monroe and his unit were shipped overseas and arrived in France in the late fall of that year. On December 5, 1944, Monroe was reported missing in action and remained in that status until the spring of 1945, when the war department confirmed that he had been killed in action. The location of the remains of Donald Monroe is not known.

(NARA2; WRP May 6, 1944 1:1, January 13, 1945 1:3, unk December, 1945)

GLENN L. COQUILETTE
(1944/12/07)

(Henri-Chapelle American Cemetery, Belgium - Internet photo)

When Glenn Coquilette entered the US Army during World War II, he declared that he was a resident of Santa Cruz County, California. Record of that enlistment or his connection with the county has not been located.

Glenn L. Coquilette, the son of Glenn and Esther Coquilette, was born in McHenry County, Illinois, in the early 1920s. Census records indicate that he may have also had an older sister, Dawn.

The American Battlefield Monuments Commission report reveals that Private Glenn L. Coquilette of the 13th Infantry Regiment, 8th Infantry Division entered the service from California and died on December 7, 1944. The US War Department records add that Coquilette was from Santa Cruz County, California, and was killed in action.

At the period of Glenn Coquilette's death, the German forces in the area where his unit was serving had begun a massive counter-attack. The 13th Division held the area in the vicinity of Kleinhau until relieved by the 121st Regiment. It is likely that it was in these combat engagements that Coquilette was killed.

Private Glenn L. Coquilette is buried at Henri-Chapelle American Cemetery in Henri-Chapelle Belgium. He was awarded the Purple Heart.

(ABMC; ACGEN; USCR, 1920 US Census, IL, McHenry; McHenry County Illinois Genealogy Society, Name Index, May 10, 2003, http://www.mcigs.org/1930_FC_Index/1930_FC_A-C/Co-Cz.htm, [16 September 2008])

MAHLON A. MARSHALL
(1944/12/08)

(Photo courtesy Pajaro Valley Historical Association)

"No one else could have done as well as we did, you can believe it," wrote Marsh's buddy.

Mahlon A. Marshall was born in San Francisco, California, on December 30, 1924, to Dr. O. C. Marshall, a well-known Watsonville physician, and his wife. Raised in the Pajaro Valley, Mahlon attended local elementary schools and Chaminade High School before transferring to Watsonville High School. In high school, he was a member of the track team, on the Student Board, active in the French club and worked on the *Manzanita* yearbook. He also served as president of the local chapter of the California Scholarship Federation. Marshall was an accomplished musician and member of the Musicians Union. Following graduation in June 1942, he enrolled in a pre-med program at San Jose State College, but left before his eighteenth birthday.

Mahlon Marshall enlisted in the US Army in February 1943. After completing basic training, he volunteered for the paratrooper section and in July 1943, earned his silver wings and boots.

"Marsh," as he was known, was assigned to the 511th Parachute Regiment of the 11th Airborne Division and trained at Camp Mackall, North Carolina, and Camp Polk, Louisiana.

His regiment was sent to New Guinea in May 1944 and trained in jungle warfare prior to their departure to Leyte in the Philippine Islands on November 7, 1944. The combat conditions under which Marsh served in the Leyte campaign were described in a letter written to his father by a comrade, which later appeared in the *Watsonville Register-Pajaronian* edition of April 8, 1945.

Five days after landing on Leyte, we were up against our first Japs. Our job was to hold a pass in the mountains so that when the division started pushing on Ormoc, the Japs wouldn't come through into the mountains where it would take years to drive them out. Because the mountains were

so steep and rugged, a company at a time proceeded along the Zaribou trail into the mouth of hell. One company was ambushed...The ambush was wiped out after four days of hard fighting...A small plateau was found in the mountains which we cleared and leveled...

After three days, we moved on. The pass had been taken and held...When we left the strip we didn't have any idea of the kind of hell that was in store for us for the three weeks to come. Our next objective was the Jap main supply trail over the mountains found by one of our combat patrols...We had pushed our way across the island and were now sitting on the Jap supply trail. We could see Ormoc below us and all the Jap controlled country...We almost took the hill to our front when we were recalled and told to hold what we had till troops could relieve us...two battalions were still far behind, but fighting all the way...three days without food because the clouds were stuck on the mountain and planes couldn't get in to supply us...One of our companies during the night had withstood four banzai charges and were isolated on the hill to our rear. Japs in front of us and Japs behind us and no food in sight... And the fourth day rolled by without food...the fifth day; the chaplain had a prayer service. They prayed for the clouds to open and planes to drop food to us. Twenty minutes later, the clouds broke up and planes started to drop food. A lot of Christians were made that day. Wire communications had gone out...This went on for eight more days.

[After describing leading a patrol of volunteers heading toward a division in the rear, of bumping into Japs, of sleeping within a few hundred feed of "God only knows, how many Japs," the paratrooper tells of the reunion with the division which was surprised to see them as they had slipped right through the Jap lines and no man's land]... We found our other company had gone six days without food and watched hundreds of Japs go by within twenty feet of their hiding place...We have about 4000 Japs to our credit in twenty-nine days of the toughest type of fighting in the world. No one else could have done as well as we did, you can believe it."

Private First Class Mahlon A. Marshall died on December 8, 1944, and was buried in the Manila American Cemetery in Manila. Among his awards is the Purple Heart.

(CBR; ABMC; Leo Kocher, Internet History of the 511th Airborne Regiment, http://users.owt.com/leodonna/511thHistory.htm, [16 September 2008]; WRP February 2, 1945 1:2, February 8, 1945 6:5)

ROBERT L. NAPIER
(1944/12/14)

(Santa Cruz High School Service Cardinal)

Bob Napier won a Silver Star for being a "Son of Bitche."

Robert L. Napier was born February 19, 1923, in Monrovia, California, to Robert Henry and Cora Nickels Napier. Early in his life, Robert went to live with foster parents, Mr. and Mrs. Frank Nickels, who resided in Santa Cruz. When he arrived in Santa Cruz, Robert Napier enrolled in Branciforte School and in 1938, entered Santa Cruz High School with the exiting class of 1941.

On August 8, 1941, Robert L. Napier enlisted in the US Army at Hamilton Field, California. Following basic training at Jefferson Barracks, Missouri, he was transferred to Scott Field, Illinois, and then assigned to an Engineering unit at Fort Custer, Michigan. Desiring to be in an airborne unit, he transferred to the 101st Airborne Division, but was injured during a training jump and reassigned to Company M of the 398th Combat Engineers.

In October 1944, Napier's unit was shipped overseas and attached to the 100th Infantry Division in France. In December, after being engaged in heavy fighting in the Vosges Mountains, the 100th attacked the Maginot fortifications near the ancient fortress city of Bitche. During a combat engagement occurring on December 14, Private First Class Robert L Napier was killed in action and posthumously awarded the Silver Star. The accompanying citation read,

For gallantry in action on December 14, 1944 in the vicinity of Bitche, France. During the bitter struggle to take the fiercely defended forts of the Maginot line, Private First Class Napier fearlessly advanced through severe enemy artillery, mortar and small arms fire, in order to get the machine gun into position from which maximum support could be rendered the advancing rifleman. When the intensity of the enemy fire made withdrawal imperative, Private First Class Napier voluntarily remained behind to furnish covering fire. Disregarding his own safety, he manned the gun alone, inflicting great casualties upon the hostile forces until he was

hit and killed by an enemy mortar shell.

Robert L. Napier is buried in the Lorraine American Cemetery in St. Avold, France. In addition to the Silver Star, his awards include the Purple Heart. His division also won a Presidential Citation and the accompanying name "Sons of Bitche."

(ABMC, 1930 US Census, CA Santa Cruz; SCHSC Pg. 14, SCSn November 11, 22 1945 5:4, January 19, 1945 1:1)

ERNEST J. NOVAK
(1944/12/14)

(Jefferson Barracks National Cemetery –Internet photo)

Deserting guards at Palawan prison massacred Ernest.

Ernest Julius Novak was born in Oklahoma City, Oklahoma, on January 9, 1919, to Fabian and Anna Novak. The Novak family was a large family that also included sons Peter, Jacob, Joseph, Nick, Jerry and Fabian Jr. and daughters Anna, Elizabeth, Pauline and Teresa. Ernest attended grammar school in Oklahoma City before moving to Watsonville with his mother and siblings. His father remained in Oklahoma City. While living in Watsonville, Ernest worked for the *Watsonville Register-Pajaronian* as a route man and delivered newspapers.

In San Francisco on April 25, 1941, Ernest Novak enlisted in the US Army, requested duty in the Philippine Islands and was assigned to the Coast Artillery branch. In June of that year he left for the Philippines and upon arrival, he joined the 200/515 Coast Artillery detachments serving one of the forts protecting Manila Bay.

During the Japanese invasion and occupation of Manila in December 1941, Ernest Novak was moved to Corregidor and when that fort fell in May 1942, the Japanese took him prisoner. He continued to remain a prisoner of war until December 14, 1944, when he was brutally massacred by Japanese prison guards at Princesa, Palawan, in the Philippine Islands. The Adjutant General Department provided details of that massacre in a September 1945 letter to Novak's mother.

Private Novak was killed in action December 14 when [he] was "one of a group of 150 members of the US army, navy and marine corps, imprisoned by the Japanese at a camp at Puerto Princesa. This group was attacked without warning by their Japanese guards, who attempted to massacre the prisoners to the last man...Ten of the prisoners succeeded in escaping. These were the only survivors. It has now been officially established by reports received in the war department that all the remaining prisoners, including your son, perished as a result of this ruthless attack.

The body of Private Ernest Julius Novak was initially buried in the Philippines; however, his remains were exhumed and reinterred in the Jefferson Barracks National Cemetery in St. Louis, Missouri, on February 14, 1952.

(NARA2; USDVA; WRP June 17, 1943 1:1, September 1, 1945 1:2; Bataan Corregidor Mem Foundation of NM, A Brief History of the 200th and 515th Coast Artillery http://www.angelfire.com/nm/bcmfofnm/history/briefhistory.html, [16 September 2008])

CHARLES H. STREET
(1944/12/14)

(Santa Cruz High School Service Cardinal)

Charles was indiscriminately slaughtered at Palawan prison.

Charles Hiram Street was born in San Francisco, California, on April 3, 1923, the son of Mr. and Mrs. Eric D. Street. During his early life, the family, which also included sons Eric and Ernest, moved to Whittier, California, where he attended grammar school. In 1939 the Streets moved to Santa Cruz and Charles entered Santa Cruz High School. During the one year that he spent at that school, he played in the band and earned several awards for his music. After dropping out of school, he was employed by the Coast Creamery Company as a waiter.

On June 5, 1941, Street enlisted in the US Army in San Francisco and requested duty in the Philippine Islands. He was assigned to the infantry as a private and shipped to Honolulu in July 1941. In Hawaii he received basic infantry training at Schofield Barracks before continuing on to the Philippine Islands. In September 1941, Street arrived in Manila and joined the 13th Infantry Regiment serving at Fort McKinley.

Following the Japanese invasion of the islands in Decem-

ber, Corporal Street's regiment covered the retreat of American troops fleeing to the Bataan Peninsula. Afer being wounded on Bataan on April 25, 1944, he was sent to the island fortress of Corregidor. When Corregidor fell in May 1942, he was taken prisoner and sent to Cabanatuan Prison where he remained until 1944, when he was transferred to Palawan Prison.

Charles Street was in Palawan prison on that infamous December 14, 1944, day when 140 American prisoners were massacred by their Japanese guards (See biography of Ernest Novak). Following the war, the remains of Charles Hiram Street were exhumed and sent to the Jefferson Barracks National Cemetery in St. Louis, Missouri, where they were interred on February 2, 1952.

(NARA2; USDVA; SCHSC Pg. 18, SCSn October 23, 1945 1:7, WIKI, 31st Infantry Regiment)

CARROLL G. SANDHOLDT
(1944/12/15)

(Photo Courtesy of Pajaro Valley Historical Association)

A Monterey Bay leader and chief boatswain's mate caught a standing streetcar with his car.

Carroll George Sandholdt was born in Monterey, California, on April 29, 1906, to Mr. and Mrs. William Sandholdt, the publishers of the *Monterey Cypress-American* newspaper. He and his brother Wilbur spent their formative years in Monterey and attended local schools until the family moved to Moss Landing in 1922. Sandholdt completed his secondary education at Salinas High School, where he was a member of the football team.

Following his graduation, he enrolled in the University of Southern California, which he attended for three years. After leaving USC, Sandholdt moved to San Francisco and was employed as an automobile salesman. In 1928 Carroll returned to Moss Landing and worked in one of the local Sandholdt business interests.

Carroll Sandholdt married Lucile Calkins of Yreka, California, in 1930 and the couple established their home in Corralitos. The couple continued to reside in that Pajaro

Valley community for several years before moving to Watsonville. Through his membership in the Elks Club and in local dramatic productions with the Carmel Players, he became known within the social community. Sandholdt was an accomplished singer and frequently appeared on radio shows and concerts in San Francisco and Los Angeles.

In September 1943, Carroll Sandholdt joined the US Navy, was given the rank of chief boatswain's mate and was assigned to Treasure Island near San Francisco. In 1944, CBM Sandholdt served a brief tour in Hawaii before returning to Oakland, where he skippered a small harbor craft.

On December 15 1944, while driving a car in Oakland, CBM Carroll George Sandholdt struck a standing streetcar and was killed. Following his funeral on December 18, 1944, he was interred in the Golden Gate National Cemetery in San Bruno, California.

(USDVA, WRP December 16, 1944 1:2,)

VINCENT P. SPIKULA
(1944/12/16)

(Pajaro Valley Catholic Cemetery gravesite photo)

A "Battle Baby" from Watsonville became the county's first death in the Battle of the Bulge.

Vincent Peter Spikula was born in Watsonville, California, on March 4, 1925, to Mr. and Mrs. Martin V. Spikula. The Spikula family also included daughters Mary and Ann. He attended Pajaro Valley elementary schools and enrolled in Watsonville High School in 1939. Vincent graduated from Watsonville High School with the June class of 1943.

Spikula enlisted in the US Army on July 16, 1943, and was sent to Camp Fanning, Texas, for his basic training. He received his advanced infantry training at Camp Maxey, Texas, before being assigned overseas.

In November 1944, Private Spikula joined the 395th Regiment of the 99th Infantry Division that was advancing on the retreating German army.

The inexperienced men of the 99th, dubbed "Battle Babies" by UP War Correspondent John McDermott, were about to receive their baptism by fire in the famous Battle of the Bulge.

On December 16, 1944, "all hell broke loose" on the Belgium-German border when the retreating Germans suddenly turned and counter-attacked. Spikula's battalion has not been identified, but the following 3rd Battalion description of the action is similar to that which he may have experienced.

During the German offensive in the Ardennes, the Third Battalion, 395th Infantry, was assigned the mission of holding the Monschau-Eupin-Liege Road. For four successive days the battalion held this sector against combined German tank and infantry attacks, launched with fanatical determination and supported by heavy artillery. No reserves were available... and the situation was desperate. On at least six different occasions the battalion was forced to place artillery concentrations dangerously close to its own positions in order to repulse penetrations and restore its lines...The enemy artillery was so intense that communications were generally out. The men carried out missions without orders when their positions were penetrated or infiltrated. They killed Germans coming at them from the front, flanks and rear. Outnumbered five to one, they inflicted casualties in the ratio of eighteen to one. With ammunition supplies dwindling rapidly, the men obtained German weapons and utilized ammunition obtained from casualties to drive off the persistent foe. Despite fatigue, constant enemy shelling, and ever-increasing enemy pressure, the Third Battalion guarded a 6000-yard front and destroyed 75 percent of three German infantry regiments.

Private First Class Vincent Peter Spikula was killed in action on December 16, 1944, during the Ardennes offensive. His remains were initially buried in Belgium but were later returned to Watsonville and reinterred in the family vault at Valley Catholic Cemetery.

(CBR; NARA2; Battle Babies, The Story of the 99th Infantry Division, http://www.lonesentry.com/gi_stories_booklets/99thinfantry/index.html, [16 September 2008]; WRP January 5, 1945 1:2, January 26, 1945 1:2; Photo-WHS)

1945

GEORGE ERBE JR.
(1945/01/02)

(Henri-Chapelle American Cemetery- Belgium – Internet photo)

George Erbe Jr. was the son of Mr. and Mrs. George Erbe of the Anzar tract near Aromas in the Pajaro Valley. He was born in San Benito County, California, on February 23, 1923, and had three brothers, Louis, Jack and Lee, along with a sister, Emma. George attended school in Hollister because of its proximity to the Erbe residence near San Juan in the Anzar district.

In March 1943, George enlisted in the US Army and after completing his basic and advanced infantry training, was sent overseas in March 1944 to join the 18th Infantry Regiment of the 1st Infantry Division. That division, known as the "Big Red One," had participated in the invasion of Normandy and

after the beachhead was secured, the Division moved through the Normandy hedgerows. The Division liberated Liege, Belgium and pushed to the German border, crossing through the fortified Siegfried line. The 1st Inf. Div. attacked the first major German city, Aachen, and after many days of bitter house-to-house fighting, the German commander surrendered the city on October 21, 1944. The Division continued its push into Germany, crossing the Rhine River. On December 16th twenty-four enemy divisions, ten of which were armored, launched a massive counterattack in the Ardennes sector, resulting in what became known as the Battle of the Bulge. The Big Red One held the critical shoulder of the bulge at Bullingen, destroying hundreds of German tanks in the process.

On January 2, 1945, Private First Class George Erbe Jr. was killed in action in Belgium during the Battle of the Bulge. His remains were buried in the Henri-Chapelle American Cemetery in Henri-Chapelle, Belgium, and his awards include the Bronze Star and the Purple Heart.

(CBR; ABMC; WRP January 26, 1945 1:2, March 26, 1945 1:6; Society of the 1st Infantry Division, World War II, http://www.1stid.org/history/index.cfm, [16 September 2008])

JOHN M. LOPEZ
(1945/01/03)

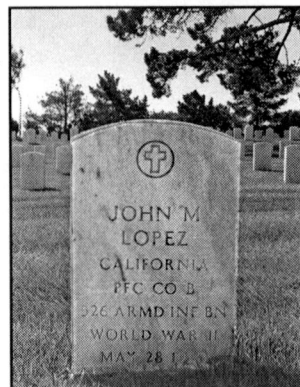

(Golden Gate National Cemetery – San Bruno California)

He followed orders and held at Malmedy, but at a very high cost.

John M. Lopez was born in Santa Cruz, on May 28, 1920, the son of Mr. and Mrs. Joseph Lopez. He and his brother Albert lived with their parents on Myrtle Street and were educated in local schools. About 1935, after completing one year of high school, John left school to begin a career in commercial fishing. By the early 1940s he had married and a son was born to the couple.

John M. Lopez was inducted into the US Army at San Francisco on November 3, 1943, and sent to a Texas facility for basic training. After his departure, his wife and son moved to Oakland. Upon completion of his advanced Infantry training program in 1943 he returned home for Christmas prior to being shipped overseas.

When Lopez arrived in Europe, he was assigned to Company B of the 526th Armored Infantry Battalion serving with the First US Army. The 1st Army had participated in the invasion of Normandy and in the Allied drive to Germany. In late December 1944 the retreating Germans stopped and counterattacked, driving US forces back into Belgium during the Battle of the Bulge. The 526th was rushed to the embattled area and was the first American force to reach the Belgium town of Malmedy, which they were ordered to hold at all costs. In the final two weeks of December 1944, the Germans relentlessly attacked Malmedy; however, the 526th held. By December 31, the German advance had stalled and the offensive stopped.

On January 3, 1945, Private John M. Logan was listed as having been killed in action. His remains were later returned to the United States and on May 3, 1948, were reburied in the Golden Gate National Cemetery at San Bruno.

(NARA2; USDVA; SCSn January 30, 1945; Battle of the Bulge, edited by Ray Merriam, Published by Merriam Press, 1999, Pg. 37, http://books.google.com/books?id=47UGHTrBKPUC&pg, [16 September 2008])

MELVIN G. McCORMACK
(1945/01/07?)

The *Santa Cruz Sentinel* Roll of Honor of May 30, 1945, includes the name Melvin McCormack, USA; however, his county connection is limited.

Melvin G. McCormack was born in Merced County, California, on February 24, 1920. His mother's name was Mildred. No information regarding his birth, family members or early life has been located. Selective Service registration information indicates that he completed four years of high school but the location of his high school is not known.

Prior to their residence in Santa Cruz County, the McCormack family lived in Santa Clara County, where Melvin worked as a farm hand. The family moved to Santa Cruz about 1942 with the intention of making it their permanent residence.

Melvin was inducted into the army in San Francisco on January 10, 1944, and listed Santa Clara County as his residence. He was sent to Fort Benning, Georgia, for basic and advanced training and in the first part of December 1944, was shipped overseas.

The army unit to which Private Melvin G. McCormack was assigned has not been identified but was likely infantry. He was reported as having been slightly wounded in Belgium on January 7, 1945, suggesting the action occurred in the aftermath of the Battle of the Bulge.

In its entirety, the Battle of the Bulge was the bloodiest of the battles that American forces experienced in WWII, the 19,000 American dead unsurpassed by those of any other engagement. For the US Army, the Battle of the Ardennes incorporated more American troops and engaged more enemy troops than any American conflict before WWII. Although the German objective ultimately was unrealized, the Allies' own offensive timetable was set back by months. In the wake of the defeat, many experienced German units were left severely depleted of men and equipment, as German survivors retreated to the defenses of the Siegfried Line.

On April 5, 1945, Mrs. Mildred McCormack was notified that her son Melvin had died from his wounds. The location of the remains of Private McCormack has not been identified, but they were likely returned to the United States following the war.

(CBR; NARA2; WIKI, Battle of the Bulge; SCSn January 30, 1945, April 6, 1945 1:3)

PHILLIP L. SKOW
(1945/01/08)

An air collision and crash in Mexico ended Phillip's family responsibilities.

Phillip L. Skow was born in Dunlap, Iowa, about 1917, the son of Oscar and Mabel Skow. Joining him in the Skow family were brothers Joseph and Raymond and sisters Rosanna and Madeleine (Mrs. E. Norman). Phillip completed his education at St. Joseph school in Dunlap and following the early death of his father, he helped provide financial and physical support for the family.

During this period Skow, found employment with the Southern Pacific Railroad, which sent him to Watsonville. He is reported to have lived in the Pajaro Valley for a number of years and become active in the local Knights of Columbus lodge.

In July 1943, Skow joined the US Army Air Force and was sent to Garden City, Kansas, for basic training, followed by advanced training at Brooks Field, Texas. After completing the air cadet program, he received his wings and was commissioned a second lieutenant.

On January 8, 1945, Second Lieutenant Phillip L. Skow was serving as the co-pilot aboard a Martin B-26, participating in a gunnery practice exercise between Brownsville, Texas, and Matamoros, Mexico. A second B-26 joined Skow's plane to assist in towing targets. During the exercise, the two planes collided and crashed into a lake on the Mexican side of the border killing all crewmembers.

Lt. Skow's remains were recovered and returned to Dunlap, Iowa, for a military funeral and burial.

(WRP 1945/01/?; Anthony J Mireles, Warbird Crash.com 1-8-45 Matamoros, Mexico, http://www.warbirdcrash.com/, [16 Sept 2008])

ELDEN D. STUART
(1945/01/09)

(Santa Cruz Riptide photo)

"Eldon fought a good fight. He finished his course and he kept the faith," noted the *Santa Cruz Riptide*.

Elden Dean Stuart was born on May 10, 1919, in Santa Cruz, California, to Mr. and Mrs. Herbert R. Stuart. The Stuart family was large, consisting of Elden, his brothers Arden, Will, Rolland and Herbert, and sisters Bessie, Laura Bell and Grace Marie. The family lived on Soquel Avenue in Santa Cruz. Elden completed nearby elementary schools and one year at Santa Cruz High School. Upon completion of his formal education, he worked for the Santa Cruz Fruit Packing Company and later joined his brothers working at the cement plant in Davenport.

About 1935 Elden Stuart married Barbara Jean Guyman. A daughter, Bonnie Lee, was born to the couple in 1936 and a son, Arden, in 1940. At this time Stuart was working as a commercial vehicle driver.

Elden Stuart was inducted into the US Army in San Francisco as a private on April 24, 1943. After basic and advanced infantry training, he was assigned to the 163rd Regiment of the 41st Infantry Division serving in the Pacific Theater.

Stuart's division left for Australia on July 15, 1943, and upon arrival made preparations for the Salamaua campaign; its objective being to rid a number a small South Pacific Islands of the remaining Japanese troops. Between 1943 and 1944, Hollandia, Wake and Biak Islands, and other centers of enemy control were liberated.

During 1944, Sergeant Elden Dean Stuart contracted an unspecified jungle disease and after undergoing an infusion of blood plasma that gave him sufficient strength to travel, he was invalided home on December 1, 1944. On December 28, Eldon underwent an emergency operation at Fort Ord, California, from which he died on January 9, 1945.

Following his funeral, he was buried in the Oakwood Memorial Park in Santa Cruz. Eldon was awarded the Infantryman's Medal.

(NARA2; WIKI, 41st Infantry Division SCSn January 10, 1945, SCR February 23, 1945 –6)

HENRY J. BOLTSHAUSER
(1945/01/12)

(Santa Cruz High School Service Cardinal)

The name "chicken" did not describe the fortitude of this quiet Soquel chicken farmer.

Henry J. Boltshauser was born in Santa Cruz, California on July 28, 1914, into the family of Jacob and Amanda Boltshauser. The family also included another son Carl and daughters Alvina, Catherine, Mary, Alice, Grace and Helen. Henry was raised in the Soquel area where he attended local

schools. About 1929 he entered Santa Cruz High School and followed a program designed to prepare him for employment in the carpentry trade. After his graduation in 1933, Henry decided to go into the poultry business and operated a chicken ranch off the Old San Jose Road near Soquel.

Boltshauser was inducted into the army in San Francisco on September 26, 1942, and was sent to Monterey, California, and Camp Blanding, Florida, for training. He remained there from October 1942 until April 1943, and was assigned to the 119th Regiment of the 30th Division.

The 30th Infantry Division shipped out of the US on February 12, 1944, and arrived at Liverpool, England, on February 22. For the next two and a half months Henry and his company prepared for the invasion of Europe. On D-Day, June 6, 1944, the 119th landed on Omaha Beach at Normandy and by June 11 had secured the Vire-et-Taute Canal. In combat action on June 24, 1944, Henry was injured by shrapnel from a German grenade and returned to England.

In October, Henry Boltshauser returned to his unit, battled with them across France and assisted in halting the German Ardennes offensive. On Christmas Day 1944, he was once again wounded. He was sent to a hospital in France and remained there until he succumbed to his wounds on January 12, 1945. He was buried in the Epinal American Cemetery in Epinal, France. Boltshauser's awards include the Purple Heart with Oak Leaf Cluster.

(ABMC; NARA2; 1930 US Census, CA, Santa Cruz; SCHSC Pg. 6; WIKI, 30th Inf Div; SCSn February 23, 1945 1:6; SCR March 2, 1945)

GILBERT J. CAMARLINGHI
(1945/01/29)

(Santa Cruz High School Service Cardinal)

The Coast Guard's most disastrous World War II accident took the life of Gil Camarlinghi.

Gilbert Joseph Camarlinghi was born in Santa Cruz, California, on February 4, 1922, into the family of Mr. and Mrs. Adolph Camarlinghi, a local hotel restaurant owner. A brother, Rudy, also joined Gil in the family. While he was still a child, his family moved to Santa Clara, California.

In 1938 the Camarlinghi family returned to Santa Cruz and Gil transferred into Santa Cruz High School. In high school he followed a general and varied program of study and served as advertising manager on the school's *Trident* newspaper. Following his graduation in 1941, Gil remained in the community until the fall of 1942.

Gilbert Camarlinghi enlisted in the US Coast Guard in October 1942. After completing boot camp at Alameda, Apprentice Seaman Camarlinghi was assigned to patrol duty at Morro Bay, California, followed by duty at the Coast Guard station at Bay and Powell Streets in San Francisco.

In October 1944, Camarlinghi was sent to the South Pacific to join his ship, the *USS Serpens*.

The Serpens *was destroyed on the 29th January 1945, as she was anchored off Lunga Beach, Guadalcanal, in the South Pacific. The commanding officer and seven others, one officer and six enlisted men were ashore. The remaining crewmen were loading depth charges into her holds when the* Serpens *exploded. After the explosion, only the bow of the ship was visible. The rest had disintegrated, and the bow sank soon afterward. 198 Coast Guard crewmen, 57 Army stevedores, and a Public Health Service physician, Dr. Harry M. Levin, were killed in the explosion and another soldier who was ashore was killed by shrapnel. The loss of the USS* Serpens *was the largest single disaster ever suffered by the United States Coast Guard.*

Seaman Second Class Gilbert Joseph Camarlinghi was killed in that explosion and his remains are believed to have been lost with his ship.

(SCHSC Pg. 8, SCSn February 20, 1945 1:2; Wartime History Project, USS Serpens AK-47, 2002, http://www.wartimememories. co.uk/ships/serpens.html, [16 September 2008])

EARLE L. VELASCO
(1945/01/31)

(Manila America Cemetery – Internet photo)

Earle Velasco was descended from Pajaro Valley pioneers and joined them after Luzon.

Earle Leonard Velasco was born in Watsonville in 1919 to Albert and Ethel Velasco. His Velasco and Moot grandparents were pioneer settlers in the Corralitos district of the Pajaro Valley. Earle and his sisters, Melba and Esther, were raised and educated in local schools. Velasco completed one year at Watsonville High School before leaving school to work as a commercial vehicle driver.

Earle was inducted into the US Army at San Francisco on March 3, 1941, and sent to Camp Roberts, California, and Fort Lewis, Washington, for his basic and advanced training. Following his training period, Private Velasco was assigned to the 160th Infantry Regiment of the 40th Infantry Division. Earle received his orders for deployment to the Pacific in the summer of 1942.

During his tour of duty, Velasco's unit performed guard duty in Hawaii, patrolled at Guadalcanal and trained in New Guinea in preparation for the Philippine invasion.

On 9 January 1945, the 160th and 185th Infantry regiments landed in the Baybay-Lingayen area of Luzon, Philippine Islands, and on 9 January seized Lingayen Airfield virtually unopposed. After consolidating in the Dulig-Labrador-Uyong area, the 160th Infantry Battalion began pushing down Route 13 and on 21 January, took Tarlac without resistance. On 23 January, it forced a bridgehead at Bamban and there encountered the main Japanese lines in the Bamban hills.

On January 31, 1945,4 Earle Leonard Velasco was killed in action while fighting on Luzon. He was buried in the Manila American Cemetery in Manila; his awards include the Purple Heart.

(ABMC, NARA2; WRP February 21, 1945 1:2; Global Security. org, 40th Infantry Division, 2000, http://www.globalsecurity.org/ military/agency/army/40id.htm, [16 September 2008])

EDWARD L. WALKER
(1945/02/01)

(Santa Cruz Riptide photo)

Captain Walker survived four years of prison, only to die in Japan as the war was ending.

Edward Leslie Walker, the fourth child of William and Pearl Walker, was born in Santa Cruz in 1911. Joining him in the family were his sisters, Helen and Esther, and his brother, William. Edward received his grammar school education at Holy Cross School and later graduated from Chaminade High School. After high school, he went on to earn a degree from nearby University of Santa Clara.

Edward Walker was commissioned a second lieutenant in 1939 and after completing artillery training at Ft. Bliss, Texas, was sent to Fort Ord, California. In January 1941, First Lieutenant Walker was sent to the Philippine Islands and assigned to the 24th Field Artillery Regiment.

When the Japanese invaded the Philippines in December 1941, Captain Walker was serving in a field artillery unit under the command of a Major King. After the fall of Manila, he and his battery were forced to retreat to the Bataan Peninsula where they continued to fight. With the fall of Bataan, he made his way to Corregidor, but was forced to surrender at the fortress on May 7, 1942. The following December he sent a card home indicating that he was a prisoner of war in the Philippines.

Later in the war the Japanese transferred Walker to a prison camp on the island of Honshu.

The majority of prisoners were put to work in mines, fields, shipyards and factories on a diet of about 600 calories a day. Prisoners were rarely given fat in their diet and all were continuously hungry. The majority survived on barley, green stew, meat or fish once a month and seaweed stew. Red Cross parcels were not distributed to the prisoners.

On February 1, 1945, while a prisoner of war in Japan, Captain Edward L. Walker died of colitis. His remains were later recovered, returned and buried at the Golden Gate National Cemetery in 1948.

(USDVA; SCSn December 16, 1942 1:6, September 16, 1945; History on the Net, WWII, Japan POW Camps, (http://www.historyonthenet. com/WW2/pow_camps_japan.htm, [16 September 2008])

ROBERT E. MCCURDY
(1945/02/04)

(Epinal American Cemetery France – Internet photo)

The name Robert E. McCurdy appears among the US War Department deaths of Santa Cruz County, California; however, his relationship with the county appears limited.

Robert Ernest McCurdy, the son of Mr. and Mrs. Ernest McCurdy, was born in Contra Costa, California, on August 11, 1921. He was raised and educated in Taft, California, before his parents moved to Santa Cruz. At the time of his draft registration in 1942, he indicated that he was single, had completed two years of college and worked as a foreman in a manufacturing facility.

Robert McCurdy was inducted into the US Army on September 10, 1942, and after completing basic training, was selected for armor training at Fort Knox, Kentucky. While at Fort Knox, he married a Kentucky girl. At the completion of his training, Private First Class McCurdy was assigned to the 23rd Tank Battalion of the 12th Armored Division.

McCurdy and his unit sailed for Europe from Camp Shanks, New York, on September 20, 1944, and arrived at Liverpool, England, on October 2. Five weeks later they were sent to France where they joined the 7th US Army. The 23rd Tank Battalion moved into the Alsace Lorraine region of France and during the fighting taking place near Metz on February 4, 1945, Technician 5th Class (Corporal) Robert Ernest McCurdy was killed in action. His body was recovered and buried in the American Cemetery in Epinal France.

(CBR; NARA2, ABMC, SCSn September 30, 1943 4:3, May 12, 1945 1:4; 12th Armored Division History, http://www.12tharmoreddivision.com/history.html, [15 May 2007])

MURL R. SCHROCK
(1945/02/04?)

(Photo Courtesy of U of Nevada Special Collections)

Murl Schrock listed Santa Cruz County as his residence; however, it is possible that it was the residence of his next of kin.

Murl R. Schrock was the second son of Andrew and Elizabeth Schrock and was born on October 2, 1902, in New Plymouth, Payette County, Idaho. Murl was raised with four brothers Milo, Morris, Murray and Marvin. He enrolled in the University of Nevada at Reno and after his graduation in 1926, was employed as a geologist and mining engineer. Schrock began acquiring mining interests in the Philippines and in 1936 moved to those islands.

The Schrock family subsequently relocated to Modesto and then to Santa Cruz, where Andrew Schrock purchased an apartment house. It is unclear whether Murl ever lived in Santa Cruz during his family's residence there.

In 1941 Murl Schrock volunteered in the US Army and listed Santa Cruz, California, as his residence. It is likely that, because of his previous engineering experience, he was commissioned a first lieutenant in the Army Corps of Engineers.

The skimpy, 1500 man US Army engineer garrison in the Philippines was almost evenly divided between Filipino and American personnel. After Japanese forces landed there on December 10, the engineers destroyed bridges from one end of Luzon to the other to slow the enemy's advance. The engineers later erected a series of defensive lines on the Bataan Peninsula and fought as infantry in these defenses before succumbing to superior Japanese forces in April and May 1942.

With the fall of Bataan and Corregidor, Lt. Schrock was captured and confined in prison camp No. 1 at Manila, where he remained until December 13, 1944, when he was placed aboard a ship sending POWs to Japan. The US Navy inadvertently sank the ship; however, Schrock survived, was recaptured and sent to Japan.

On or about February 4, 1945, First Lieutenant Murl R. Schrock is reported to have died in a Japanese prison camp. In 1949 his remains were exhumed, returned to the United States and reinterred at the Jefferson Barracks National Cemetery in St. Louis, Missouri.

(USDVA; David Gratz, Family Genealogy, Schrock, http://davidgratz. com/family/people/p000001u.htm [15 May 2007 approx.]; SCSn Sept. 14, 1945 1:7; Joe N Ballard, Google Books, *History of the US Army Corps of Engineers*, Page 84, http://books.google.com/ books?id=EKieF_-ycGkC&pg=PA84 [16 September 2008])

ROBERT T. BURKE
(1945/02/10)

A Watsonville Air Station ensign and his plane plunged into San Francisco Bay.

Robert T. Burke was born in Pennsylvania in 1923 to Mr. and Mrs. Patrick F. Burke. Robert is believed to have spent his formative years and received his education in the area of Delaware County, Pennsylvania.

After completing high school and possibly some college, Burke entered the naval aviation cadet program, which he completed in 1944.

Following his commissioning, Ensign Burke was assigned to the Watsonville Air Station where he flew training missions and conducted anti-submarine patrols along the California coast. Early in 1945 Burke's wife joined him from Philadelphia and the couple established their residence at the Fan Mar Terrace apartments in Capitola.

On February 10, 1945, Ensign Robert T. Burke was on a routine flight over San Francisco Bay when his fighter plane crashed near the Dunbarton Bridge and he was killed. His remains were recovered, returned to Pennsylvania and interred in the Holy Cross Catholic Cemetery in Delaware County.

(SCSn February 12, 1945; Delaware County, Cemeteries, http:// chestercountygenealogy.com/modules/gengraves/singlelink. php?cid=354&lid=16313, [16 September 2008])

VERNON W. DAMM
(1945/02/15)

Vernon W. Damm's name appears among the War Department's list of Santa Cruz County deaths, yet no record of his residency in the county has been found.

Vernon W. Damm was born in McLennan County, Texas, on October 19, 1924, to Julius and Francis Damm. Vernon was raised and educated in that West Texas county along with his brother, Julius, and sisters, Ruth and Dorothy.

When enlisting in the US Army Air Corps during World War II, Vernon Damm declared Santa Cruz County his place of residence. After completing his basic and advanced training, he was assigned to the 398th Bomber Squadron of the 504th Bomber Group.

From an unofficial Japanese website, details regarding Damm's aircraft and final mission emerge. The plane to which Vernon Damm was assigned was a B-29 bomber nicknamed *Coral Queen*. That aircraft flew bombing missions out of North Field on the island of Tinian in the Mariana Islands. On February 15, 1945, Corporal Vernon W. Damm was listed as the "right crewmember" aboard the plane as it flew its bombing mission targeting the Mitsubishi heavy industry's Nagoya engine factory in Japan. During the mission, the plane was damaged and crashed, killing Vernon and the other nine crew members.

His body was not recovered and is included on the Tablets of the Missing at the Honolulu Memorial in Honolulu. His awards include the Air Medal and Purple Heart.

A memorial stone was later erected in the St. Peters Church Cemetery in Glausner, McLennan County, Texas, in honor of Vernon and his brother Julius who also lost his life during World War II.

(USCR, 1930 US Census, TX, McLennan; NARA2; ACGEN; ABMC; Aoyagi, Aomori, Aomori Air Raids, October 12, 2005, http://translate.google.com/translate?hl=en&sl=ja&u=http: //www10.ocn.ne.jp/~kuushuu, [16 September 2008]); 504th Bomb Group, WWII, http://www.geocities.com/Pentagon/ Quarters/3109/, [16 September 2008]). US Gen Web, McLennan County Texas, Glausner Cemetery List, http://ftp.rootsweb.

com/pub/usgenweb/tx/mclennan/cemeteries/clausne2.txt, [16 Sept 2008]).

NORMAN A. RUDDOCK
(1945/02/18)

(Keokuk National Cemetery DVA Photo)

Included on the War Department's List of Santa Cruz County casualties is the name of Norman A. Ruddock. Information regarding Ruddock's Santa Cruz connection has not been confirmed.

When Norman Ruddock registered for the draft in 1943, he noted that he was born in California in 1924 and was a resident of Santa Cruz County. He also noted that he had completed three years of high school, was single and worked as an auto mechanic.

Ruddock was inducted into the US Army in San Francisco on January 23, 1943, and assigned to the Army Air Force. Following training he was posted to the 5th US Air Force 90th Bomb Group, 319th Squadron, nicknamed the Jolly Roger. His unit flew B-24 Liberator bombers out of Sydney Australia on strikes upon New Guinea and other Japanese military installations in the South Pacific.

In January 1945, Ruddock's B-24 was flying from bases on Mindoro Island in the Philippine Islands and attacking Japanese installations on Luzon. During a mission on February 18, 1945, Technical Sergeant Norman A. Ruddock was killed in action. His remains were recovered and following the war, were reinterred in the Keokuk National Cemetery in Keokuk, Iowa.

(*Note: In 1944 Ruddock listed his address as Route 1, Box 42D Florin, California in his unit personnel records*)

(NARA2; USDVA; 5th AF 90th BG, Jolly Roger Details, 2008, http://www.jollyrogersweb.com/resultDetail.asp?jrID=104, [16 September 2008]); Kensman.com 5th AF, Unit History, http://www. kensmen.com/chronology.html, [16 September 2008])

SALVADORE S. CAMPAGNA
(1945/02/18)

(Watsonville High School yearbook)

"Sam" Campagna was the county's first death in the Iwo Jima campaign.

Salvadore "Sam" Campagna was born in June 1926 at Geneva, New York, to Anthony and Betty Campagna. The Campagna family, which also included daughters Phyllis and Rosemarie, moved to San Jose, California, in the 1930s. Sam received his grammar school education in Santa Clara County. Anthony and Betty later divorced and Betty married a Watsonville man whose name was Arreg. Sam joined his mother, her new husband and his stepbrother Teddy in the Arreg home in the Pajaro Valley and attended Watsonville High School.

In June 1943, on his seventeenth birthday, Campagna enlisted in the US Navy and was sent to the US Naval Training Center in Farragut, Idaho for boot camp. After completing training as a fireman, he was assigned to a ship, believed to have been the destroyer *USS Gamble,* serving in the Pacific Theater. The *Gamble* was primarily used for placing explosive mines at sea and exploding those of the enemy.

In October 1944 the *USS Gamble* returned to California for repairs and Sam visited his family the last time.

After overhaul and refresher training, Gamble *departed San Diego 7 January 1945, en route via Hawaii and the Marshalls to Iwo Jima where she arrived 17 February, to lend fire support to the various sweeping units, and to explode floating mines. During her shelling, a direct hit on an ammunition dump exploded the enemy magazine like a giant firecracker at the foot of Mt. Surabachi. On 18 February 1945* Gamble *was hit just above the waterline by two 250-pound (110-kg) bombs. Both fire rooms immediately flooded and she became dead in the water with two holes in her bottom as all hands fought raging fires, jettisoned topside weight and shored damaged bulkheads. Five men were killed, one missing in action, and eight wounded. As marines stormed the shores of Iwo Jima the next day,* Gamble *was taken in tow by* Dorsey *who turned her over to L8M-126 for passage to Saipan.*

Fireman First Class Salvadore "Sam" Campagna was reported to have died on February 18, 1945, and was buried at sea. Sam's commanding officer later wrote Betty Arreg informing her of the circumstances of his death and indicated that,

It may be of some comfort to know that he died at his job performing it well. So violent was the explosion when we were hit that Salvadore and his buddies in the fire room were killed instantaneously. At least he did not suffer.

A follow-up letter to Sam's mother informed her that a requiem mass was celebrated in the chapel on the island of Saipan for her son, who had been buried at sea with Catholic services and full military honors on the night the ship was hit.

(Note: During the war the name of Campagna's ship was withheld for security reasons. On February 18, 1945 The USS Gamble *was the only US naval vessel reported to have come under enemy attack.)*

(ABMC; WIKI, USS Gamble DD-123; WRP May 18, 1945 1:1)

CHARLIE OJEDA
(1945/02/19)

(Watsonville High School yearbook)

Wounded marines screamed "Corpsman" and Charlie responded.

Charlie Ojeda was born about 1922 in Watsonville to Mr. and Mrs. Manuel Ojeda. In addition to one brother, he shared the family home on Broadis Street with four sisters. He attended local elementary schools and entered Watsonville High School.

After completing his high school education, Ojeda was employed by the local Purity Food Store and later became its assistant manager.

In October 1942 Charlie Ojeda joined the US Navy and was sent to the US Naval Training Center in Farragut, Idaho, for boot camp. After completing the basic course, he was selected for training as a pharmacist's mate and attended schools in San Diego and Long Beach.

Following his military medical training, Ojeda was detailed to the US Marine Corps where he received additional training at Camps Elliott and Pendleton in California. At the completion of those sessions, he was assigned to the 27th Marine Regiment and ordered to the South Pacific.

Ojeda's Regiment was a significant component of the 5th Marine Division's plan for the capture of Iwo Jima. On the 19th of February the

5th Marine Division landed on schedule, overran lightly held beach defenses and progressed inland over numerous mine fields and in the face of moderate fire due to excellent naval gunfire and air preparation of all types. Early progress to the west was relatively easy. Advances to the north and south were heavily contested and we suffered considerable casualties.

The 27th Marines combat assault troops met light resistance from enemy infantry troops on the beach, but found the area being hit repeatedly by enemy mortar and artillery fire. Pharmacist's Mate Second Class Charlie Ojeda was serving as a hospitalman or corpsman with the assault forces on February 19, 1945, when he was killed in action assisting wounded marines.

His body was never recovered and he is memorialized on the Tablets of the Missing at Honolulu Memorial. His awards include the Purple Heart.

(ABMC, Raymond C Backstroke, 5th Marine Div Daily Summaries, http://www.geocities.com/rbackstr2000/aa500219.txt, [16 September 2008]); WRP March 6, 1945 1.2; Photo-WHS)

JOHN W. CROWE JR.
(1945/02/21)

(Santa Cruz High School Service Cardinal)

"I'm allergic to loud and sudden noises," wrote Crowe following the *Lexington's* sinking.

John William Crowe Jr. was born in Santa Cruz, California, on January 29, 1915, to Mr. and Mrs. John W. Crowe. John Jr., the couple's only child, was raised in the community and educated in local grammar schools. At Santa Cruz High School, Crowe majored in science and math and graduated with honors in 1934. Following high school he studied photography at the California Institute of Technology before entering the University of Southern California, where he earned his degree.

With the threat of war growing, John joined the US Navy on April 9, 1941. After completing boot camp in San Diego, he was assigned to the carrier *USS Lexington* as a photographer's mate. Crowe served aboard that vessel through the battles of the Gilbert Islands, Marshall Islands and Coral Sea, where the *Lexington* was sunk.

On May 8, 1942, John Crowe was selected to attend a special naval engineering school at Annapolis, Maryland, to qualify him as a naval engineering officer. After completing the school in January 1943, he was commissioned an ensign and assigned to the *USS Saratoga*. Later he served as a damaged control officer aboard that carrier where he once again heard "loud noises."

On 21 February 1945, Saratoga was detached with an escort of three destroyers to join the amphibious forces and carry out night patrols over Iwo Jima and night heckler missions over nearby Chi-chi Jima. However, as she approached her operating area at 1700 [hrs] on the 21st, an air attack developed, and taking advantage of low cloud cover and Saratoga's insufficient escort, six Japanese planes scored five hits on the carrier in three minutes. Saratoga's flight deck forward was wrecked, her starboard side was holed twice and large fires were started in her hangar deck, while she lost 123 of her crew dead or missing. Another attack at 1900 [hrs] scored an additional bomb hit.

Lieutenant (jg) John W. Crowe Jr. was killed in action during the attack and was buried at sea. He was later memorialized at the Tablets of the Missing at Honolulu Memorial. His awards include the Purple Heart.

(ABMC, SCHSC Pg. 8, SCR June 19, 1942: 3, SCSn March 5, 1945 1:4, SCR March 9, 1945 –1; DANFS, USS Saratoga CV-3)

FREDERICE T. FLODBERG
(1945/02/21)

(Watsonville High School yearbook)

Frederice Theodore Flodberg was born about 1923 to Mr. and Mrs. Fred Flodberg. Information regarding Fred's early life is unavailable. During his years at Watsonville High School, he appears to have been popular. He was in the band, a rally yell leader, a member of the Junior Red Cross, in the French club and was the business manager of the *Manzanita* yearbook. Fred graduated from Watsonville High School in 1941.

In late 1943 or early 1944, Flodberg joined the Army Air Corps Cadet program and was in the advanced stages of the course when he crashed a P38 fighter plane near Santa Rosa, California, on September 22, 1944. Flodberg survived the crash and went on to earn his wings and a commission as a second lieutenant.

After receiving additional training, Flodberg joined the 402nd Fighter Squadron of the 370th Fighter Group. That unit had recently transferred from their Andover-Hampshire base in England to France and was in the process of switching from P-38 to P-51 fighter planes when Flodberg joined them.

In December 1944 through January 1945, Ninth Air Force fighters and bombers were critical in defeating the Wehrmacht during the Battle of the Bulge. There was a noteworthy incident in which American, British, and Canadian air power was grounded by very bad winter weather, but then the bad weather broke, freeing those tactical air forces to help break the back of the Wehrmacht attack.

On February 21, 1945, while flying a support mission, Second Lieutenant Frederice T. Flodberg was killed in action. His body was recovered and buried in the Netherlands American Cemetery in Margraten, Netherlands.

(ABMC, WHS 1941 Yearbook; AAIR; WIKI, 9th Air Force)

PAUL D. COMPTON
(1945/02/23)

(Watsonville High School yearbook)

Elsie drove army trucks while waiting for her sergeant husband who never returned.

Paul D. Compton was born in 1914, to Henry and Data Compton, in Umatilla, Oregon; however, he spent many of his formative years in the Pajaro Valley. His brothers Donald, Philip, Wayne and Max, along with a sister Gwen, joined him in the Compton family. In 1933 Paul graduated from Watsonville High School and was employed by the Granite Construction Company. Compton married and worked as a truck driver in Reno, Nevada, until he entered the plumbing trade.

In January 1943, while living in Nevada, Paul Compton joined the US Army and was sent to Camp Bowie, Texas, for basic training. Advanced training at Camp Claibourne, Louisiana, followed. During his absence, his wife, Elsie, returned to Watsonville, established a residence and obtained employment as a driver in the Camp McQuaide motor pool.

Sergeant Compton was sent to England in April 1944 and joined the 823rd Tank Destroyer Battalion of the 30th Infantry Division. In July 1944 the Battalion was deployed to France to participate in the "Big Push."

Following the Battle of the Bulge in December,

[The 30th Infantry Division] launched a counteroffensive on 13 January 1945 and reached a point two miles south of St. Vith, 26 January, before leaving the Battle of the Bulge and moving to an assembly area near Lierneux, 27 January, and to another near Aachen to prepare for the Roer offensive. The Roer River was crossed, 23 February 1945, near Julich.

It was while fighting on February 23, 1945, that Sergeant Paul D. Compton was killed in action. His remains were buried in the Netherlands American Cemetery in Margraten. His awards include the Purple Heart.

(ABMC; NARA2; 1920 US Census; WRP March 9, 1945 1:3; WIKI, 30th Infantry Division; Photo-WHS)

FRANK SINGLETON
(1945/02/26)

(Santa Cruz High School Service Cardinal)

"Frank Singleton Killed in Battle around Manila" noted the *Santa Cruz Sentinel.*

Frank was born in San Juan Bautista, California, on July 24 1925, to Mr. and Mrs. R. P. Singleton. Frank and his sister were raised in Santa Cruz and attended Live Oak and Branciforte Schools. In 1939 Singleton entered Santa Cruz High School and took courses to prepare him for the carpentry trade. In 1941 he left high school and found employment with the Union Ice Company where he continued to work until he entered the service.

Frank joined the US Army in San Francisco on May 10, 1943, was sent to Camp Roberts and later to Fort Ord, California, for training. After completing training in May 1944, Private Singleton was shipped to a replacement center in New Guinea and assigned to the 5th Cavalry Regiment of the 1st Cavalry Division.

The Division invaded Luzon, landing in the Lingayen Gulf area 27 January 1945, and fought its way to Manila by 3 February 1945. Prisoners at University of Santo Tomas were liberated and the 1st Cavalry had advanced east of Manila by the middle of February before the city was cleared. On 20 February the Division was assigned the mission of seizing and securing crossings over the Marikina River and securing the Tagaytay-Antipolo Line.

Clearing the Japanese out of the city of Manila became a major challenge for the 1st Cavalry Division. On February 26, 1945, the 5th Cavalry Regiment was called upon to assault the Agriculture Building in the heart of Manila. As they advanced, they came under heavy fire from Japanese lodged in nearby apartments and the cavalrymen were forced to withdraw. It was possibly during this encounter that Private First Class Frank Singleton lost his life.

His body was buried in the Manila American Cemetery and among his awards is the Purple Heart.

(ABMC; NARA2; SCHSC, Pg. 18, SCSn March 23, 1945 1:2; WIKI, 1st Cavalry Division, The Battle of Manila by Thomas M. Huber)

KENNETH E. WILEY
(1945/03/15)

(Santa Cruz High School Service Cardinal)

The war began for Ken on a remote Hawaiian island and ended on a motorcycle in South Carolina.

Kenneth Eugene Wiley was born on December 23, 1919, in Washington State to the Reverend and Mrs. Clyde H. Wiley. Reverend Wiley accepted a call to serve a church in Santa Cruz and the Wiley family, consisting of sons Kenneth, Howard and Paul, and daughters Helen and Ella Marie, joined their parents in the move. Kenneth attended local grammar schools and enrolled in Santa Cruz High School, from which he graduated in 1937. From 1936 to 1941 he worked for the Lane Frozen Custard Company at the Santa Cruz Boardwalk.

In the fall of 1941, the US Government hired Wiley as a carpenter on Johnson Island in the Hawaiian Island chain. When the Japanese attacked Hawaii, he volunteered to assist a US Marine Corps detachment stationed there in the event of a Japanese invasion.

On April 7, 1943, Wiley enlisted in the US Army Air Force, which accepted him into the Army Air Force cadet program and assigned him to a special training course at the University of Montana. Additional instruction at Santa Ana, Oxnard, Stockton and Mather Field in Sacramento, California, followed.

Kenneth Wiley graduated from the air cadet program on November 20, 1944 and was commissioned a second lieutenant at Douglas Army Airfield, Arizona. The following March he completed advanced training in South Carolina and was recommended for unlimited flying service in B-25 bombers.

On March 15, 1945, Second Lieutenant Kenneth Eugene Wiley was riding his motorcycle about three miles from Greenville, South Carolina when he was involved in an accident that claimed his life. His body was returned to California and buried in the Liberty Veterans cemetery in Fresno, California.

(SCHSC Pg. 20, SCSn March 21, 1945, SCR March 23, 1945 –1)

STANLEY J. HART
(1945/03/16)

(Santa Cruz High School Service Cardinal)

Jungle disease in the Pacific injured Stanley's body and a car in Modesto destroyed it.

Stanley Jackson Hart was born in Modesto, California on February 7, 1922. He was the only son of Mr. and Mrs. Frank Hart who later moved to Santa Cruz. Stanley attended Branciforte Junior High School and in 1937 entered Santa Cruz High School. In 1938 he left high school and joined the Civilian Conservation Corps of the US Forest Service. In 1940 Hart was working as a commercial vehicle driver.

Stanley Hart enlisted in the Regular US Army on December 23, 1940, and was assigned to the 120th Field Artillery. His basic training took place at the Presidio of Monterey and at Fort Lewis, Washington. When the war began, he was sent to Australia where he volunteered for radio reconnaissance service. This took him to the South Sea island locations of Milne Bay, New Guinea, Goodenough Island, Saidor, Buna, Yammy, Singor, Mott River and Finchaven. During the latter of these engagements, he was blasted from a foxhole and wrote his mother that the muzzle blast from the big guns had caused one eardrum to be broken and an abscess to form in the other ear.

After contracting malaria, Hart was returned to the United States in March 1944 for rest and medical attention at the Hammond Hospital in Modesto, California. On March 16, 1945, while traveling to Santa Cruz on a furlough, Stanley Hart was killed in an automobile accident near Modesto. He was returned home and buried in the Oakwood Memorial Park in Santa Cruz.

(NARA2, SCHSC Pg. 10, SCSn March 27, 1945 1:2)

LELAND F. BIAS
(1945/03/19)

(Santa Cruz High School Service Cardinal)

Crossing the Bridge at Remagen began the final phase of Leland's life.

Leland Floyd Bias was born on December 10, 1924, in Santa Cruz to Mr. and Mrs. Leslie Bias. Leland and his brother, Harold, were raised in a home on Walnut Avenue and educated in local schools. Leland completed Mission Hill Junior High School and enrolled in Santa Cruz High School in the fall of 1940. During his high school years, he also worked part time with the Postal Telegraph Company.

In March 1943, Leland Bias left high school early to enlist in the US Army in Monterey, California. The Santa Cruz High School *Service Cardinal* noted "Private Bias was sent to Fort Leonard Wood, Missouri where he trained with the 75th Infantry Division. After ten months training, that division was sent to Louisiana for maneuvers and then to Camp Breckinridge, Kentucky."

Bias shipped overseas In September 1944 and was assigned to the 1st US Army (Big Red One), 9th Division, 60th Infantry Regiment. While he served with that unit, it was moving through France and preparing to invade Germany. In November and December 1944, the division moved north to Bergrath, Germany, and then launched an attack toward the Roer River.

On December 10 the 9th Division took the towns of Echtz and Schlich and on December 12 Leland received his first wounds.

In February 1945, following the Battle of the Bulge, Bias rejoined his unit as they were beginning their drive toward the Rhine River. On March 10, the Big Red One completed the crossing of the Rhine River at the famous Remagen Bridge. While setting up a bridgehead on the other side of the river, Private First Class Leland Bias was again wounded and on March 19, 1945, succumbed to those wounds.

After the war, his remains were returned home and buried at Santa Cruz Memorial Park.

(NARA2; SCHSC Pg. 5; SCSn April 3, 1945 1:4; WIKI, 9th Infantry Division)

LESTER C. CLOUD
(1945/03/19)

(Lorraine American Cemetery St Avold France – Internet photo)

Lester Cary Cloud was born in Fresno County, in the San Joaquin Valley of California, on September 5, 1912 to Mr. and Mrs. H. R. Cloud. About 1925 the Cloud family, which included sons Lester, Maynard, Carl and Virgil and daughters Opal and (Mrs. W.L. Landis), moved to the Pajaro Valley. Lester may have attended grammar school in Aromas before entering Watsonville High School, where he remained for a very short period of time. After leaving school, he worked in the Pajaro Valley briefly before moving to Alameda County, where he worked as a longshoreman. Prior to 1942, Cloud married; however, that marriage ended in divorce.

Lester Cloud was inducted into the army at San Francisco on July 28, 1942. He was sent to San Antonio, Texas, and Fort Benning, Georgia, for basic and advanced infantry training. Prior to being shipped overseas in September 1943, Lester married his second wife.

Upon arrival in Europe he was assigned to the 142nd Infantry Regiment of the 36th Infantry Division that fought its way from the Mediterranean Sea to the Rhine. In March 1945 the 142nd reached the major German defensive area known as the Siegfried Line.

The day it hit the Siegfried Line [March 19, 1945], the Second Battalion of the 142nd took out eleven pillboxes. The next day it took out twelve more. It was slow, deadly work. Special "knockout" squads of infantrymen and engineers had to drag themselves up to each pillbox under cover of heavy supporting fire. One man would make his way to the rear and plant a "beehive"—a high explosive cone which directed all its force downward into the concrete and steel of the pillbox—to blow out the defenders. Then the squad or another one would go on to the next pillbox. Every pillbox covered the ones around it in a complicated system of interlocking fire. An entire sector had to be knocked out at a time, not merely one fortification or several.

On March 19, 1945, Technician Fifth Class Lester C.

Cloud was killed in action while serving with the 142nd Regiment. He was buried in the Lorraine American Cemetery in St. Avold, France; his awards include the Purple Heart.

(CBR; ABMC; NARA2; WRP April 11, 1945 1:5; Texas Military Force Museum, 36th Infantry Division; http://www. texasmilitaryforcesmuseum.org/36division/archives/france/hyman5. htm, [16 September 2008])

WILLIAM M. WEEKS
(1945/03/19)

Watsonville lost two of its residents, William M. Weeks and Eugene V. Upton Jr. when the *USS Franklin* was bombed.

On November 24, 1921, William Michael Weeks was born in Watsonville to Mr. and Mrs. Michael J. Weeks. The Weeks family also included a daughter, Mildred. His namesake uncle, William J. Weeks, had died in the Argonne in World War I. William attended local schools and graduated from Watsonville High School in 1941.

Weeks enlisted in the US Navy In April 1942 and completed boot camp in San Diego, California, before being sent to radio schools at Oxford, Ohio, and Memphis, Tennessee. Early in 1943 he joined the *USS Franklin* in the Pacific fleet. During Christmas of 1944, he returned home on leave before his ship departed to attack the Japanese homeland.

Before dawn on 19 March 1945 the USS Franklin, *who had maneuvered closer to the Japanese mainland than had any other US carrier during the war, launched a fighter sweep against Honshu and later a strike against shipping in Kobe Harbor. Suddenly, a single enemy plane pierced the cloud cover and made a low-level run on the gallant ship to drop two semi-armor piercing bombs. One struck the flight deck centerline, penetrating to the hangar deck, effecting destruction and igniting fires through the second and third decks, and knocking out the combat information center and airport. The second hit aft, tearing through two decks and fanning fires, which triggered ammunition, bombs and rockets. The* Franklin, *within 50 miles of the Japanese mainland, lay dead in the water, took a 13° starboard list, lost all radio communications, and broiled under the heat from enveloping fires. Many of the crew were blown overboard, driven off by fire, killed or wounded, but the 106 officers and 604 enlisted who voluntarily remained saved their ship through sheer valor and tenacity. The casualties totaled 724 killed and 265 wounded, and would have far exceeded this number except for the heroic work of many survivors.*

Aircraft Radioman Second Class William M. Weeks was one of those sailors killed aboard the *USS Franklin* on March 19, 1945. He was declared missing in action or buried at sea. He is memorialized on the Tablets of the Missing at Honolulu Memorial; his awards include the Purple Heart.

(CBR; ABMC, WRP April 6, 1945 1:3; USS Franklin Association, The Ship that Wouldn't Die; http://www.ussfranklin.org/main.htm, [16 September 2008])

EUGENE V. UPTON JR.
(1945/03/19)

The *Watsonville Register-Pajaronian* Roll of Honor includes the name of Aviation Ordinance Man First Class Eugene Vernon Upton Jr., who lost his life on the *USS Franklin*.

Little information regarding the life of this individual and his residency in Santa Cruz County has been found.

The American Battlefield Monuments Commission indicates that he entered the service from Missouri. An Internet source identified a Eugene V. Upton who lived in Springfield, Missouri who may have been his father. It is likely that Eugene had been stationed at the Naval Air facility in Watsonville prior to joining the *USS Franklin*.

On June 21, 1945, the Watsonville Register- Pajaronian reported:

Eugene V. Upton Listed as Killed
Eugene Vernon Upton Jr. AOM1c, Watsonville, has been listed as killed in the Pacific area by the navy department, according to the Office of War Information.

Mr. Upton's wife was listed as Mrs. Mary Teresa Upton, 24 Front Street this city, but his name has not been on this newspaper's Roll of Honor and efforts to contact the family were unsuccessful.

Aviation Ordnanceman First Class Eugene V. Upton Jr. died on March 19, 1945, aboard the *USS Franklin*; his body was never recovered or was buried at sea. He is memorialized on the Tablets of the Missing at Honolulu Memorial. His awards include the Purple Heart.

(ABMC; USNM; WRP June 21, 1945 1:3; DANFS USS Franklin)

EDWARD M. LEONARD
(1945/03/25)

(Santa Cruz Riptide photo)

March 25 was a special day for Ted as it was both the date of his birth and the date of his death.

Edward M. "Ted" Leonard was born on March 25, 1924, in Santa Cruz, California. He was the youngest son of Mr. and Mrs. John Leonard and the brother of Tom, James, Helen, Rosaria and Catherine Leonard. Ted Leonard attended Holy Cross Grammar School and Chaminade High School before transferring to Belarmine Preparatory School in Santa Clara, California.

After graduation in 1942, Leonard enrolled in the University of Santa Clara with the intent of becoming a chemist; however, after completing one year of college, the war interrupted those plans.

On May 17, 1943, Ted Leonard enlisted in the US Army and was sent to Fort Riley, Kansas for basic training. Because of his education and leadership skills, Leonard was promoted to corporal and remained at the training facility as an instructor.

Corporal Leonard was assigned to the 8th Infantry Regiment of the 1st Cavalry Division and shipped to the Pacific Theater of the war on March 19, 1944. Leonard's first combat exposure was during an amphibious landing at Los Negros Island in the Philippines. A second combat encounter occurred during the attack upon the island of Leyte. Manila lay ahead.

After Manila was captured and mop-up activities completed, Leonard and his fellow infantrymen continued their march to the Luzon town of Tanauan. There, fate and a Silver Star awaited him on his birthday. The *Santa Cruz Sentinel* of June 5, 1945, shared information from Edward Leonard's Silver Star citation.

Cavalry occupation of the important Luzon town of Tanauan was prevented by a heavy concentration of enemy fire. Although he knew the danger involved, Sergeant Leonard crawled beyond the front lines to a point where he could observe for, and direct the fire of his mortar squad. His accurate direction of fire enabled his squad to eliminate the enemy guns. Returning to his own unit, Leonard was fired upon by a hidden enemy machinegun. In his effort to locate the gun, Sergeant Leonard was forced to expose himself. He was killed immediately by an enemy sniper.

Sergeant Edward M. Leonard was also awarded a Bronze Star and Purple Heart posthumously for his action on March 25, 1945. He is buried in the Manila American Cemetery in Manila.

(ABMC; NARA2; SCR October 22, 1943 4, April 20, 1945, April 30, 1948; SCSn April 20, 1945, June 5, 1945 5:7; 1st Cavalry Division, History WWII, http://pao.hood.army.mil/1stcavdiv/about/history/worldwar2.htm, [16 September 2008])

LEWIS R. PAYNE
(1945/03/28)

(Santa Cruz High School Service Cardinal)

Lewis served above and below the ocean's surface, but in the long haul the latter prevailed.

Lewis Roy Payne was born in Ukiah, California, on March 26, 1921, to Lewis B. and Vera Payne. When he was eleven months old, he was brought to Santa Cruz where he spent his formative years. After attending Gault School and Branciforte Junior high school, he enrolled in Santa Cruz High School. In high school Lewis followed a general and varied course of study and in 1938 he graduated at the age of seventeen.

Payne joined the US Navy on November 9, 1938, and was sent to an unidentified US naval facility for boot camp training. After completing basic training in February 1939, he enrolled in the US Navy Ordinance School and graduated third in his class the following June. Payne reported aboard the *USS Hull* and was with that vessel during the Japanese attack on Pearl Harbor and during the Gilbert and Marshal Island campaigns.

In June 1942 Petty Officer Payne was accepted into the navy's submarine training at New London, Connecticut. Prior to attending that school, it is believed that he married and in 1943 became the father of a daughter. He completed submarine training in February 1943 and was assigned to the submarine *USS Poggy*. In March 1945 he was transferred to the *USS Trigger*.

Trigger *(with new skipper Commander David R. Connole) stood out to sea on 11 March to begin her 12th war patrol and headed for the Nansei Shoto area. On 26 March, she was ordered to join a wolf pack called "Earl's Eliminators" and to acknowledge receipt of the message. A weather report came from the submarine that day but no confirmation of her having received the message. The weather report was* Trigger's *last transmission. On 4 April, she was ordered to proceed to Midway Island, but she had not arrived by 1 May and was reported as presumed lost.*

Torpedoman Mate, First Class Lewis Roy Payne was killed in action on March 28, 1945 aboard the *USS Trigger* that was sunk by Japanese aircraft and warships in Nansei Shoto, Ryukyu Islands. He is memorialized on the Tablets of the Missing at Honolulu Memorial; his awards include the Purple Heart.

(ABMC, SCHSC Pg. 16, DANFS; WIKI, USS Trigger SS-237; SCR 1942, unk; SCSn May 17, 1945 1:7,)

ORVAL BLACKMORE
(1945/03/31)

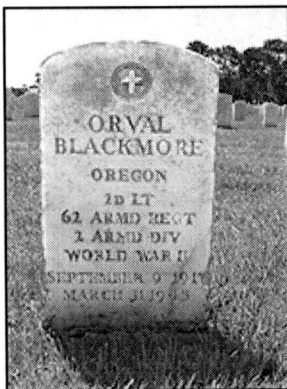

(Golden Gate National Cemetery – San Bruno California)

Alberta waited until 1949 for Orval to return, but for a different kind of homecoming.

Blackmore had a limited relationship with Santa Cruz County but was included on the *Santa Cruz Sentinel* Roll of Honor.

Orval Blackmore was born on September 9, 1917, in Oregon to Orlin and Nellie Blackmore. In the 1920s the family, which included another son Ellis and daughters Maud and Mabel, were living in Cottage Grove City, Oregon, where Orlin worked for the railroad. Orval completed three years of high school in Lane County, Oregon, before leaving to enter the work force as a commercial vehicle driver.

While living in Oregon in 1938, Blackmore enlisted in the US Army. During the next four years, he was promoted

to staff sergeant and served at a number of locations including El Centro, California. In January 1942, while at Imperial, California, Blackmore re-enlisted in the cavalry branch of the army. Shortly thereafter he married Alberta Gruwell of Santa Cruz.

In 1942 Blackmore was serving with the 67th Armored Infantry Regiment of the 2nd Armored Division when it was shipped overseas to participate in the invasion of North Africa. Sergeant Blackmore was wounded during a combat engagement in the Mediterranean sector and awarded a field commission as a second lieutenant.

Following a two months recuperation period, Lt. Blackmore rejoined his unit in Normandy as it was moving across France. When the Germans counterattacked during the Battle of the Bulge in December 1944, his unit fell back in order to help reduce the bulge in the Ardennes forest. In February 1945 the 62nd Armored Regiment resumed its offensive and on March 27 had driven across the Rhine River into Germany.

On March 31, 1945, Second Lieutenant Orval Blackmore was killed in action at an unspecified location in Germany. His remains were returned to California in 1949 and interred in Golden Gate National Cemetery in San Bruno.

(USCR, 1920 US Census, OR, Umatilla; NARA2; USDVA; GGN Cemetery Headstone; SCSn April 15, 1945, 2nd Armored, History of the 2nd Armored Group, http://www.2armorokdday.com/history/, [16 September 2008])

LYLE L. BURNS
(1945/04/03)

Lyle L. Burns was born to Harry S. and Cleona Burns in Nebraska in 1912. It is not known when the Burns family arrived in California; however, Lyle was raised and educated in Los Angeles. After completing three years of high school, he left to enter the work force as a painter.

Lyle joined the regular US Army at Fort MacArthur in San Pedro, California on January 11, 1940, and was assigned to the infantry branch. After basic training, he was stationed at the Presidio at Monterey and it was possibly there that he met and married Illa Foster, who lived in Watsonville. They established a residence in the Pajaro Valley where their daughter Sandra was born. Private Burns was later posted to San Luis Obispo.

Lyle Burns was sent overseas with the 8th Infantry Regiment of the 1st Cavalry Division in June 1943. He remained with the 8th Infantry as it moved through Australia, New Guinea and onto the Admiralty Islands where it saw its first combat.

During the Philippine Island campaign,

The Division invaded Luzon, landing in the Lingayen Gulf area 27 January 1945, and fought its way to Manila by 3

February 1945. Prisoners at University of Santo Tomas were liberated and the 1st Cavalry had advanced east of Manila by the middle of February before the city was cleared. On 20 February the Division was assigned the mission of seizing and securing crossings over the Marikina River and securing the Tagaytay-Antipolo Line. After being relieved 12 March in the Antipolo area, elements pushed south into Batangas and Bicol Provinces. They mopped up remaining pockets of resistance in these areas in small unit actions.

It was possibly while participating in these mopping-up actions that Private First Class Lyle L. Burns was killed or received wounds that resulted in his death on April 3, 1945. He was buried in the American Cemetery in Manila

(ABMC; NARA2; WRP March 2, 1945 1:2)

LAWRENCE E. GOFF
(1945/04/05)

Goff was the first county resident to lose his life in the Okinawa campaign.

Lawrence Eugene Goff was born in 1918 in Benton, Illinois to Dorsia and Delia Goff. He was raised and educated, along with a sister and two brothers in Franklin County, Illinois, where their father worked as a coal miner. After completing grammar school, Goff left school and went to work for an architect.

Lawrence enlisted in the US Army in Chicago on February 14, 1941. At that time he listed Franklin, Illinois, as his residence and noted that he was married. He received his basic and advanced infantry instruction at unspecified training centers. During this period his first marriage ended in divorce.

Following his training period, Goff was likely assigned to the 7th Infantry Division that was based at Fort Ord, California, between 1940 and 1943. He participated in the engagements at Attu and Kiska, Alaska, before returning to Fort Ord. It is possible that Lawrence met and married his second wife, Dorothy Ivey, at that location. The couple established residence in Watsonville where their daughter Joella was born.

Lawrence Goff and his unit were sent to the Philippines and participated in the invasion at Leyte Gulf. In March 1945 the 7th Infantry was moved into position for the invasion of Okinawa.

The attack against Okinawa was launched on Easter Sunday, April 1, 1945. Nobody suspected at the time that it was to be the last beachhead, indeed the last campaign, of World War II...The Division drove down to the hill mass dominated by Hill 178; again the Japanese threw down what seemed to be an impenetrable curtain of fire...After five days of grueling fighting the 184th secured Hill 178 and the

surrounding terrain.

On April 5, 1945 Private First Class Lawrence Eugene Goff, became the first casualty from Santa Cruz County in the Okinawa invasion. The location of his remains are unknown, but may have been returned to the United States about 1949.

(USCR, 1920 US Census, IL, Franklin; NARA2; WRP April 26, 1945 1:1; 7th Inf. Div, History, http://www.carson.army.mil/ UNITS/F7ID/F7ID_Historylong.htm, [16 September 2008])

LEROY W. GILLMAN
(1945/04/05)

Leroy Wayne Gillman was born in Crescent, Oklahoma in July 1922, but no additional information regarding his family or early life is available. It is believed that the family moved to the Pajaro Valley and that Leroy attended Watsonville High School for one or two years between 1936 and 1939 but did not graduate. Following his school years, he moved to Contra Costa County, where he remained single and was employed as an unskilled laborer in the furniture manufacturing business.

Leroy was inducted into the US Army as a private on December 17, 1942. After completing basic and advanced training, he was assigned to an unspecified unit serving in Europe.

Family genealogical records on the Internet indicate that he was killed in action on April 5, 1945, in Germany. The location of the remains of Leroy Wayne Gillman has not been found.

(NARA2; Ancestry.com; WRP May 25, 1945)

VICTOR K. HADA
(1945/04/05)

(Watsonville High School yearbook)

A Silver Star awaited Katsu on Mt. Fologorita.

Victor Katsu Hada was born on July 22, 1921, to Mr. and Mrs. Karoku Hada in Fort Collins, Colorado. The Hada family, which also included another son Susumu, moved to Watsonville, California, where they worked in the local agriculture industry. Katsu attended Pajaro Valley elementary schools and graduated from Watsonville High School in 1941.

Prior to the evacuation of Japanese Americans in February 1942, the Hada family moved back to Colorado. Katsu may also have spent a brief period in Saginaw, Michigan, prior to joining his family in Weld County, Colorado.

Victor Katsu Hada was inducted into the US Army at Ft. Logan, Colorado, on June 9, 1944, and sent to Camp Shelby, Mississippi. There he joined Company K of the 442nd Regimental Combat Team. On October 3, 1944, Katsu married Irene Yonemura at the First Presbyterian Church in Peoria, Illinois. Following a honeymoon, Irene returned to her home in Peoria, Illinois, and Katsu went back to Camp Shelby to prepare for deployment.

Katsu Hada was deployed to Europe in October 1944 and may have joined the 442nd when they were recuperating at the Riviera and receiving much needed replacements. In March 1945, the 442nd proceeded north to the German border. After reaching the German homeland, they received one of their more difficult assignments.

The 100th/442nd had been called to Italy by Gen. Mark Clark for a vital secret mission -- spearheading a diversionary assault on the western sector of the Gothic Line. The 100th/442nd returned to Italy in April 1945 to breach the German Gothic Line, which had blocked the Allied advance for six months...Despite continual bombing, strafing and artillery fire by the Allies, the line seemed impregnable. The task of scaling the 3,000-foot saddle between Mount Cerreta and Mount Folgorita in the dark with full combat gear was given to the 100th Battalion. At dawn on April 5, 1945, elements of the 100th Battalion, supported by artillery fire from the 442nd Regimental Combat Team batteries, began a frontal attack on one of the mountains while other soldiers who had spent the night scaling the 3,000-foot mountain moved in from the top.

On April 5, 1945, Private First Class Victor Katsu Hada and 16 other Nisei members of the 442nd RCT lost their lives. The posthumous Silver Star award describes Katsu's role in that heroic event.

When a member of his squad was wounded in a heavy mortar concentration, Private First Class Hada, motivated by his selfless devotion to his comrades, left his covered position and sought to rescue the man, although he had to crawl through the impact area to do so. In his gallant attempt, he was mortally wounded. His sacrifice of his own life in an attempt to aid his comrade is in the highest tradition of the United States Army and is deserving of highest praise.

The remains of Victor Katsu Hada were buried in Arlington National Cemetery.

(NARA2; Saginaw (MI) May 2, 1945 (1), Saginaw Mourns War Dead; Katherine Baishiki/Kazu Oshima/Geo Oshima. Excerpts from Pacific Citizen and National Japanese American Historical Society 10/20/03 (revised 4/17/04) (revised 9/12/05) Mits Kojimoto; E-mail Remembrances of Shig Kizuka, April 4, 2008; Photo-WHS)

WILLIAM E. KELLOGG
(1945/04/08)

(Watsonville High School yearbook)

Kellog was a Watsonville submariner whose sub unknowingly sank a POW troop ship.

William Ernest Kellogg was born in Watsonville, California, on January 6, 1921, to Bert D. and Blanche Kellogg; his mother's name was Blanche. The family ultimately grew to include two other sons, Robert and Bert. William grew up in the Pajaro Valley and attended Watsonville public schools before entering Watsonville High School. While in high school, he was on the football and track teams and was active in the Future Farmers organization before graduating in 1939. Following his graduation, he went to work at the LaPorte Dairy owned by his stepfather, Adolph LaPorte.

William Kellogg joined the US Navy in 1940 and attended one of its boot camps. Following his basic training, he volunteered for submarine duty and was trained as a torpedoman. By 1943 Kellogg had advanced to the rank of torpedoman second class and after completing specialized training at New London, was promoted to torpedoman first class.

Kellogg was ordered to the *USS Snook* operating in Pacific waters. During its seventh patrol, the *Snook* sunk several Japanese vessels including the unmarked *Airson Maru*, which contained 1800 American POWs. In March 1945 the *Snook* began her ninth and final patrol.

Snook returned to Guam for emergency repairs on March 27th, and departed on March 28th to rejoin her group. The patrol was Snook's ninth. In accordance with her orders, weather reports were received daily from Snook as she proceeded westward until April 1st, when she was told to discontinue the reports. Although the last message received from Snook by shore bases was on April 1st, [a sister submarine]

Tigrone was in contact with her until April 8th. On April 9th, Tigrone was unable to raise her by radio, nor was she ever able to afterwards...When Snook had not appeared or made contact by May 16th, she was reported as presumed lost on her ninth patrol.

Torpedoman First Class William Everett Kellogg's body was never recovered and he was officially declared dead by the Navy on May 6, 1946. He is memorialized on the Tablets of the Missing at the Manila American Cemetery and his awards include the Purple Heart.

(CBR; ABMC; WRP August 11, 1945 1:2; WIKI, USS Snook SS-279; Photo-WHS; COMSUB, USPAC. Fleet, USS Snook, http://www.csp.navy.mil/ww2boats/snook.htm, [16 Sept. 2008])

ROBERT E. STUCK
(1945/04/13)

(Santa Cruz Riptide photo)

Major Stuck made sure that needed troops and supplies got to the field.

Robert E. Stuck was born in North Dakota in 1920 to Mr. and Mrs. Leon H. Stuck. A sister, Marjorie, later joined Bob in the family. Stuck was raised and educated in North Dakota and graduated from Dickinson, North Dakota, High School in 1938. Shortly thereafter the family moved to Santa Cruz, California, and Stuck enrolled in Salinas Junior College. While there, he participated on the track team and in the winter, skied in the Sierra Mountains. From SJC he enrolled in San Jose State College where he joined the Alpha Eta Rho fraternity and took part in track events. During his three years in college, he worked part time in the entertainment field.

Robert Stuck enlisted in the US Army Air Force on December 29, 1941. He qualified for the cadet program and completed training courses at Santa Maria, Lemoore, and Stockton California. At the end the training period, he had earned his wings and a commission as second lieutenant. Lt. Stuck was given additional training at Ft. Wayne, Indiana, and Alliance, Nebraska, and was promoted to first lieutenant.

He was then assigned to the 80th Squadron of the 436th

Troop Carrier Group and in October 1943, was promoted to captain. During July 1944, Robert Stuck was promoted to major and sent overseas.

In Europe Major Stuck's troop carrier unit flew paratroopers over Normandy on June 6, 1944, into Italy in July, and over Holland in September.

[The 436th Troop Carrier Group] Towed gliders to Wesel on 24 March 1945 to provide troops for the airborne assault across the Rhine; carried gasoline to the front lines and evacuated patients, 30-31 March. It flew transport missions almost daily when not engaged in airborne operations; hauled such things as gasoline, ammunition, medical supplies, rations, and clothing; and evacuated the wounded to hospitals in England and France.

While flying an unspecified mission on April 13, 1945, Major Robert E. Stuck was listed as killed in action. He was buried in the Netherlands American Cemetery in Margraten; his awards include the Air Medal with four Oak Leaf Clusters.

(ABMC; NARA2; SCSn September 2, 1942 1:2, April 27, 1945 1:1; 439th Troop Carrier Group; Early History; http://usaaf.com/9thaf/Troop/436TC.htm, [16 September 2008])

WILLIAM H. CARLISLE
(1945/04/14)

(National Memorial Cemetery Pacific – Internet photo)

The Santa Cruz Sentinel article merely said, "Bill Carlisle Killed in Pacific Area."

William H. Carlisle was born in Santa Clara County, California, on February 11, 1920. No other information regarding Carlisle's parentage or place of births is available. An obituary published by the *Santa Cruz Sentinel* on May 17, 1945 noted that he was the grandson of Mrs. Mary A. Carlisle who lived in Aptos; it is possible that he resided with her. Carlisle attended Chaminade High School, where he was described as an outstanding student and star basketball player.

William graduated from high school in 1938 and was employed locally as a farm hand. At this time, he may have also resided in Santa Clara County, as he is listed among the war dead of that county.

Carlisle reported to the Presidio of Monterey and was inducted into the US Army on June 24, 1944. He completed his basic training at Camp Joseph T. Robinson in Arkansas and was then sent to Fort Ord, California. At the completion of his training, he was assigned to the 32nd Infantry Regiment of the 7th Infantry Division.

Private Carlisle joined the 32nd Infantry Regiment in the Philippine Islands between October 1944 and March 1945. In March 1945 the 7th Infantry was sent to Okinawa. The attack on Okinawa was launched on Easter Sunday April 1, 1945 and the 7th Infantry moved inland seizing Kadena airfield and continued across the fourteen-mile wide island to its eastern coast.

> By the 6th of April the first of the infamous ridges such as "Cactus Ridge" in the west and "The Pinnacle" in the east were encountered. From now on the iron defence of Okinawa would be revealed. These first defences would take three weeks to overcome with terrible losses on both sides. On 13th April the Japanese attempted to counterattack but were crushed with heavy losses and ending in total failure.

During the fighting on Okinawa on April 14, 1945, Private William H. Carlisle was killed in action. His remains were reinterred in the Honolulu Memorial Cemetery in Hawaii in 1949. His awards include the Bronze Star and Purple Heart.

(CBR; ABMC; NARA2; SCSn May 17, 1945 1:6; Okinawan Karate and Kobudo Assoc., Battle of Okinawa, 2008 http://www. okka.co.uk/battleokinawa.html, [16 September 2008]) http://www. sfgenealogy.com/santaclara/scww246a.htm. [12 April 2009])

EUGENE E. McGRATH
(1945/04/21)

(Pajaro Valley Memorial Park – Watsonville, California)

Eugene Edward McGrath was born in Watsonville on March 25, 1923, to Mr. and Mrs. Robert E. McGrath, who resided in the Pajaro Valley. He was the oldest of the couple's three sons Eugene, Thomas and James. McGrath spent his formative years in the valley, attended local schools and was graduated from Watsonville High School in 1941. In high school he became a member of DeMolay, a Masonic youth organization and after graduation, he was employed

locally as a welder.

Eugene McGrath reported to the Presidio at Monterey and was inducted into the US Army on May 13, 1944. After completing basic and specialized training in July 1944, he was sent overseas where he joined an unidentified unit in Germany.

Private Eugene Edward McGrath was killed in action at an unspecified location on April 21, 1945. His remains were later returned to Watsonville and reinterred in the Pajaro Valley Memorial Park.

(CBR; NARA2; WRP May 14, 1945 1:2)

JESSIE L. ADAMS
(1945/04/23)

(Golden Gate National Cemetery – San Bruno California)

The *Santa Cruz Sentinel* included the name of Jesse Adams in their Roll of Honor of Santa Cruz War Dead. Jesse Lee Adams, the foster son of Mr. and Mrs. E. A. Parrish of Capitola was born in Oklahoma on December 5, 1918. He received his grammar school education in Texas before moving to Bakersfield, California. It is possible that he lived with the Parrish family in Santa Cruz County during the late 1930s. In the early 1940s, Adams was living in Southern California and working for the Douglas Aircraft Company as a head miller at their Los Angeles facility. While in Southern California, he married a local girl who remained in Santa Monica during his military service.

Jesse Adams enlisted in the US Army at Ft. McArthur on June 10, 1944. Following his basic training at Camp Hood, Texas, he returned to California and was stationed briefly at Fort Ord before being shipped overseas.

Private Adams was a member of the 158th Infantry that served in the Pacific Theater. He took part in the invasion of the Philippines and in late April 1945, was wounded during the capture of the port and city of Legaspi. After a three-day hospitalization period, he returned to duty at Camalig, where his unit was cleaning out Japanese pockets of resistance.

On April 23, 1945, Private First Class Jesse Lee Adams was killed in action. His body was buried in the Philippines but his remains were returned to the United States in 1949 for reburial in the Golden Gate National Cemetery in San Bruno. (NARA2; USDVA; SCSn May 18, 1945 1:4; The Army Surgeon General, Entry 31, Portable Surgical Hospitals - 3d, Box 234, [16 September 2008]; GGNC Survey)

WILLIAM J. CROSETTI
(1945/04/27)

A well-known Pajaro Valley name contributed one of their members to the war effort.

William John Crosetti was born in Watsonville in 1926 to John and Dina Crosetti.

William had two sisters, Grace and Marie Crosetti, a half sister, Nora Bertone, along with three stepbrothers, Roy, Tony and Louis Bertone. Crosetti attended local schools including two years at Watsonville High School. After leaving school, he worked at Coast Line Truck Services.

William Crosetti enlisted in the US Army on September 18, 1944, and was assigned to the Infantry branch. Following his basic and advanced infantry training, he was shipped to the Pacific Theater. While his individual unit has not been identified, it is believed to have been a component of the 1st Cavalry Division.

A wire received by Mrs. Dina Crosetti on May 18, 1945, from the war department informed her that her son, Private William John Crosetti, was killed in action on Luzon on April 27, 1945. The limited enemy activity occurring on Luzon on that date suggests that he may have lost his life near Irisan Gorge, the assault on Baguio, or in action in the Bicol province.

Crosetti's burial location is not known; however, it is likely that his remains were returned to the US following the war. (NARA2; WRP May 19, 1945 1:5)

DOUGLAS W. YOUNG
(1945/04/30)

(Santa Cruz High School Service Cardinal)

Douglas W. Young was born in McKittrick, California, on September 12, 1918, to Mr. and Mrs. C. W. Young. The family, which included another son, moved to Santa Cruz where Doug spent a portion of his formative years. He attended Santa Cruz High School and while in school, was active in the band, the football team and Future Farmers of America.

After graduating in 1936, Young went to work in a small trucking business that his father and brother operated. Later the family moved to Los Angeles where Doug married and started a family that included a son and a daughter.

On November 25, 1943, Douglas Young was inducted into the US Army at Los Angeles and reported to San Luis Obispo, California, for basic training. Later he obtained additional instruction in Texas before being sent overseas. Private Young was assigned to a heavy tank gun crew in Company A, 16th Armored Infantry Battalion, 13th Armored Division of Patton's Third Army, in Southern Germany.

Shifting south to Eschenau, the Division prepared for Bavarian operations. Starting from Parsberg, 26 April, the 13th crossed the Regen River, then the Danube at Matting and secured the area near Dunzling. On the 28th, elements closed in at Plattling and crossed the Isar River.

According to information received by his family, Private First Class Douglas W. Young was killed in action on April 30, 1945, as his unit was crossing the Isar River where it was caught under enemy fire. He was originally buried in a US Military Cemetery in Nuremberg, Germany; however, his remains were later returned and interred in Ft. Rosecrans National Cemetery in San Diego. (NARA2; USDVA; SCHSC Pg. 21, WIKI, 13th Armored Div., SCSn June 5, 1945 1:4; SCR June 1, 1945 –1)

GEORGE W. ANTHONY
(1945/05/02)

(Santa Cruz High School Service Cardinal)

"I'll try to get this [letter] finished if the Nips will let me," but the "Nips" didn't oblige him.

George William Anthony was born in Santa Cruz, California, on August 18, 1925, to Mr. and Mrs. Charles W. Anthony. George attended Branciforte Elementary School and in the fall of 1940. entered Santa Cruz High School. He took a "continuation course" before leaving school in October 1943 to work at the Santa Cruz Freezing Plant where his father was a foreman. Later he relocated to San Joaquin County and was employed as a commercial vehicle driver.

George Anthony was inducted into the service on June 23, 1944, and began his infantry training at Camp Joseph T. Robinson at Little Rock, Arkansas. Upon completion of his basic infantry course, he trained with the 184th Infantry Regiment of the 7th Infantry Division at Fort Ord, California, until December 1944, when the division was ordered to the Pacific Theater. The regiment traveled to Seattle, where he telephoned his parents for the last time.

Private First Class Anthony and his unit were transported to the Philippines and participated in the battles of liberation taking place in early 1945. After a short rest, the 184th was loaded aboard troop carriers to participate in the April 1st invasion of Okinawa. In his last letter he said that he was feeling fine and told his parents not to worry, "I'll try to get this finished if the Nips will let me. I'm in a fox hole trying to scribble." Two days later on May 2, 1945, George W. Anthony died of wounds he received during earlier combat operations.

His remains were later returned to the United States and reburied at the Golden Gate National Cemetery in San Bruno in 1949. His awards included the Bronze Star and Purple Heart.

(NARA2; USDVA; SCHSC Pg. 5; SCSn May 28, 1945 1:6)

OSCAR SILTON
(1945/05/03)

(Santa Cruz High School Service Cardinal)

A German Jewish refugee made a final commitment to his adopted country.

Oscar Silton was born on May 6, 1926, in Cologne, Germany, to Mr. and Mrs. Ernest Silton. Early in his life young Oscar experienced life as a Jew living in Nazi Germany. While he was in school, he saw the concentration camps being built and observed the special work details to which Jews were consigned. He added in an interview for the *Santa Cruz Sentinel* on November 2, 1941,

Full-blooded Jews, he said, were drafted for work under the Nazi German system. Many of them are on airdrome construction projects. The half-Jews, he explained, are drafted for regular army service. Oscar was drafted for military service at age 14 because "I was strong and husky."

In 1941 his father, faced with concentration camp or deportation left Germany with Oscar. The fate of his mother, who may not have been Jewish, is unknown. In September 1941 the Siltons arrived in Santa Cruz where they lived with relatives. Ernest Silton went to San Francisco to attend a special English language course and Oscar remained in Santa Cruz to attend Santa Cruz High School.

While in high school, Oscar learned auto mechanics and after his classes, was employed part time as a mechanic. In 1942 he transferred to Boulder Creek High School where it is believed he graduated. Prior to his military service, he moved to San Francisco and was employed as an auto mechanic.

On September 27, 1944 Oscar Silton was inducted into the US Army in San Francisco. He received his basic training at Camp Roberts, California, and was assigned to the 197th Glider Infantry Regiment. The regiment was serving in "mopping up" operations on Luzon in the Philippine Islands.

Private Oscar Silton was reported killed in action on May 3, 1945, during unspecified action at a yet to be identified location. His remains were later returned to California and reinterred in the Golden Gate National Cemetery at San Bruno.

(NARA2; USDVA; SCSn, November 2, 1941, SCHSC Pg. 18)

CHARLES F. PHILLIPS
(1945/05/04)

(Santa Cruz High School Service Cardinal)

A Greyhound bus canceled the reunion that Charles had planned with his family.

Charles Frederick Phillips was born in Santa Cruz, California, on March 15, 1913. Information regarding his parents and siblings is not available. References to his grandparents, Charles and Mary Stubblefield, in local newspapers suggest that they may have been instrumental in his upbringing. Charles attended Laurel Grammar School before enrolling in Santa Cruz High School about 1928. While in high school, he was active in track, football and basketball.

Phillips left school after two years and was employed by Bibbins Automotive Service as an electrician. He remained with that company for the next ten years. About 1935 Charles Phillips married Vera Hendrix and their family expanded over the years to include a daughter, Barbara Jean, and sons, Frederick Charles and Richard Thomas.

Charles Phillips was inducted into the US Army at the Presidio of Monterey on March 16, 1944, and sent to Fort Knox, Kentucky, for training. Phillips remained at Ft. Knox and for the next fourteen months served as a maintenance man in the tank corps. During that time, he contracted pneumonia requiring his hospitalization for nine months. Following his recovery, he transferred to the Medical Corps and helped organize a machine shop to help rehabilitate returning veterans.

In May 1945 he was scheduled for a promotion to corporal that would have allowed his family to join him in Kentucky. That reunion never occurred. On May 4, 1945 Phillips was riding in a car leaving Ft. Knox that collided with a Greyhound bus. Six of the soldiers in the car, including Charles Phillips, were killed in the crash. His body was returned to Santa Cruz for a funeral and burial in Santa Cruz Memorial Park Cemetery.

(NARA2; SCHSC Pg. 16, SCSn, May 5, 1945 1:7; SCR May 11, 1945–1)

JOHN W. MCCULLAH
(1945/05/04)

(Santa Cruz Riptide photo)

A local naval reservist went down to the sea with his ship.

John W. McCullah was born in Texas about 1915 to John D. and Mary McCullah. By 1920, the family had moved to California, first to Mariposa and then to Hanford. Jack, as he was more commonly known, spent his formative years in Hanford, California, along with his brothers Melvin, Glenn, Robert and Duke. Jack and his brother, Glenn, continued their education in Hanford and graduated from high school prior to the family move to Santa Cruz about 1933.

McCullah joined the Merchant Marines about 1938 and served aboard a tanker. In 1940 he returned to the Bay Area where he was employed by the Coast Counties Gas and Electric Company in Pittsburg, California. In that same year he joined the US Naval Reserve. At this time, Jack married Ethel.

In June 1941, the Navy activated McCullah and assigned him the rank of machinist mate first class. Ethel quit her local teaching job and moved to San Francisco to be closer to Jack when his ship was in port. McCullah was assigned to the *USS Morrison and* served aboard that destroyer throughout its service in the Marshall, Marianas, Carolines and Philippine Island campaigns. The ship's final campaign occurred when

> *On the morning of 4 May [1945],* Morrison *was on station with* Ingraham *and four landing craft. When enemy planes appeared,* Morrison, *as usual, coached her combat air patrol into position to intercept and in an hour-long battle the Corsairs shot down two. Others broke through, however. While* Ingraham *and LCS 31 were hit, LSM(R)-194 was sunk and LCS-21 was also damaged, four suiciders struck* Morrison *in quick succession; three more grazed her and two others narrowly missed. There were also bomb explosions. Ripped apart,* Morrison *sank in fifteen minutes, before there was time to abandon ship.* "Pall bearer" LCS-21 *picked up 179 officers and men, 108 of whom were injured. The remaining 152 shipmates, including most of those stationed below decks, were lost.*

John W. McCullah, along with 151 of his shipmates went down with the ship. His body was never recovered and he is memorialized on the Tablets of the Missing at Honolulu Memorial. His awards include the Purple Heart.

(ABMC; SCSn June 5; SCR June 9, 1944, 1945 1:4, June 15, 1945 –1; Destroyer History Foundation, USS Morrison DD-560, 2008, http://www.destroyerhistory.org/fletcherclass/ussmorrison/index.html, [16 September 2008])

PATRICK V. O'LEARY
(1945/05/04)

(Courtesy Rose Hellier-Dabbs)

A duty officer aboard a cruiser was given a shoebox that provided his link with the future.

Patrick Vincent O'Leary was born September 12, 1917, in West Virginia and educated in the small town of Beckley where he attended high school. Following his graduation, he enrolled in the Colorado School of Mines where he took part in an ROTC program. During the summer, he was employed by the Union Carbide Company in West Virginia.

O'Leary entered the US Navy in 1940 and after completing a special office training program, received additional training in New York City aboard the *USS Prairie State*. On February 28 1941, he was commissioned an ensign and assigned to the naval operations base at Norfolk, Virginia. During this period, he married Edna Mabel Roberts, who was also from West Virginia.

In June 1942 Ensign O'Leary was assigned to the cruiser *USS Birmingham*. He was aboard the *Birmingham* the following year when it left for Sicily to participate in the invasion of July 10-26, 1943. He had now been promoted to Lieutenant.

While serving as duty officer aboard the *Birmingham* one night at a port in Vichy, France, the French underground smuggled a shoebox aboard the ship containing a small Jewish baby girl for safekeeping. Lt. O'Leary took the child aboard, wrapped her in a blanket and obtained permission for her to depart with the ship to the United States. When he returned home, Patrick and Edna adopted the child and named her Rose Erin. When the *Birmingham* was assigned to the Pacific Theater, the family moved to Aptos, California, where Mabel's aunt resided.

In August 1943 Patrick O'Leary left with the *Birmingham* when it departed for Pearl Harbor. He served aboard the ship during the invasion of the Mariana and Philippine Islands. Following the invasion of Iwo Jima, the *Birmingham* sailed for Okinawa. On May 4, 1945, a Japanese Kamikaze plane crashed into the *Birmingham's* deck near the forward gun turret taking the life of Lt. Patrick Vincent O'Leary and fifty other men. Edna Mabel and his adopted daughter Rose Erin (Hellier-Dabbs) continued to make Santa Cruz County their home.

Lt. O'Leary's remains were returned to the United States and buried at the Golden Gate National cemetery at San Bruno in 1949.

(USDVA; DANFS, USS Birmingham CL-62; SCSn June 28, 1945; SCSn May 26, 2003 1)

WILLIAM J. BOTTERO
(1945/05/05)

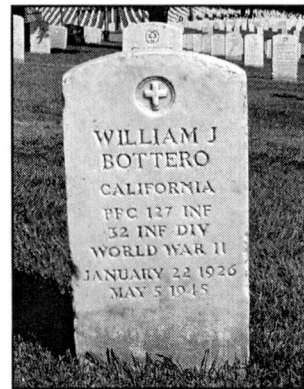

(Golden Gate National Cemetery – San Bruno California)

The Watsonville Register-Pajaronian had but a simple message, "Bill Bottero Luzon Victim."

William Joseph Bottero was born in Watsonville, California, January 22, 1926, to Joseph and Gertrude Bottero. He was raised in the Pajaro Valley and attended Watsonville elementary schools. Later his parents divorced and his father, Joseph, left and moved to Modesto. William entered Watsonville High School and remained there until his junior year. When his mother remarried, the family moved to San Francisco where he completed high school.

In June of 1944, William Bottero joined the US Army. He was sent to Camp Joseph T. Robinson in Arkansas for basic training and to Camp Howze in Gainesville, Texas, for additional instruction. He was then assigned to the 127th Infantry Regiment of the 32nd Infantry Division serving in the South Pacific.

Bottero fought at Buna, survived the Aitape campaign and participated in the attack on Hill 508 at Leyte in the Philippines. On May 5, 1945, Private William Joseph Bottero was killed in action while attacking the Japanese stronghold in Luzon that the GI's had dubbed the "Kongo Fortress." His remains were later returned to the United States and buried in the Golden Gate National Cemetery at San Bruno in 1949.

(USDVA; WRP, June 2, 1945 1:2; Weider History Network, World War II: The US 32nd Infantry Division Battle to Control the Villa

Verde Trail, 2008 http://www.historynet.com/magazines/world_war_
2/3033626.html?page=4&c=y, [16 September 2008]; GGNC Survey)

*May 8 VE (Victory in Europe) Day
ended the war in Europe.*

WAYNE E. BUNNELL
(1945/05/05)

(Manila American Cemetery – Internet photo)

Wayne Bunnell was a former resident of the Pajaro Valley who left the county before World War II. He was born in Washington State in 1908; however, information regarding his family and formative years is not available. He had completed elementary and high school prior to entering the work force about 1926. Bunnell arrived in the Pajaro Valley in 1928, found employment with the Brisco Bros. Trucking Service and married Leta. The couple remained in the county until 1940 when they separated, Leta remained in Watsonville, while Wayne movied to Thurston County in Washington State. There he found work in the lumber products industry in a semi-skilled position.

Wayne Bunnell was inducted into the Army Air Force on March 29 1942, and sent to an unspecified training facility. After completing basic and advanced training, Private Bunnell was assigned to the 199th Anti Aircraft Artillery. The 199th AAA had arrived at Guadalcanal as it was being secured and in November 1943, proceeded to the island of Bougainville. While there, Bunnell manned 50-caliber machine guns to help ward off enemy aircraft.

In October 1944, Wayne's unit moved to New Guinea to prepare for the invasion of the Philippine Islands. Following the invasion at Leyte on October 20, they fought their way to Manila. On May 5, 1945, Private First Class Wayne E. Bunnell died while fighting at an unspecified location in the Philippine Islands. His body was recovered and buried in the Manila American Cemetery in Manila.

NARA2; WRP June 02, 1945; 199 AAA Unit History, http://www.rootsweb.com/~inmarsha/3/warrenkoontz.html, [16 September 2008])

DARELL E. PETTUS
(1945/05/10)

(Golden Gate National Cemetery - San Bruno California)

A soldier left a twin to provide his family with a mirror to the future.

Darell Edward Pettus and his twin brother Harold were born to Mr. and Mrs. Pettus in Hartford, Arkansas, on March 6, 1920. Two older brothers, Carl and Leon, and a sister, Helen, rounded out the Pettus family. The family first moved to Delano, California where Darell completed grammar school. In the mid-1930s, the Pettus family moved to Watsonville and Darell enrolled in Watsonville High School. In school he was affectionately known as Brick because of his red hair and rusty complexion. After school, he delivered newspapers for the *Watsonville Register-Pajaronian*.

Pettus completed two years of high school before dropping out to work in a feed store. Later he obtained employment at the Crowley and Traulsens store. During the early 1940s, Darell Pettus married Helen and in 1942, a son, Billy, was born to the couple. In 1944, the family was residing in Merced where Pettus worked as carpenter.

Darell Pettus was inducted into the US Army in San Francisco in June 1944 and his wife and son returned to his parents' home in Aromas. He completed basic training at Camp Joseph T. Robinson in Little Rock, Arkansas, and in December 1944, was sent to the Philippine Islands. Pettus was assigned to the 96th Division of the 10th Army that participated in the invasion at Leyte and was preparing for the Okinawa campaign.

The invasion of Okinawa began on Easter Sunday, 1 April 1945 ...US forces quickly secured the northern half of Okinawa, but any hope that the campaign would be short was dispelled when XXIV Corps struck the first strong points of the "Shuri Line," a sequence of increasingly more formidable defensive belts in depth, on 9 April. Between 9 and 29 April the Division fought through Cactus Ridge and secured

Tombstone Ridge, Nishibaru Ridge, and the Maeda Escarpment. Its personnel losses were partially replaced before it returned to combat on 10 May.

On May 10, 1945, Private First Class Darell Edward Pettus was killed in action while fighting on Okinawa. His remains were later recovered and returned to California, where they were buried in the Golden Gate National Cemetery San Bruno in 1950.

(NARA2; USDVA; WRP June 8, 1945 1:2; 96th RRC PAO; The 96th Infantry Division, 1918-1945, http://www.usarc.army.mil/96thRSC/History/Command/96th%20Division%20history%20details.htm, [16 September 2008])

CURTIS C. BUSHONG
(1945/05/11)

(Santa Cruz High School Service Cardinal)

Bushong's goal was to buy a farm, but not the variety that was chosen for him.

Curtis Charles Bushong was born on March 7, 1926, in San Francisco, California, into a family that also included two daughters, Erolyn and Muriel. He spent part of his youth in Indiana, but later returned to Los Angeles, California, where he lived with his mother, Mrs. H. P. Quentin. Curtis graduated from junior high school in Los Angeles, and came to Santa Cruz to live with the A. R. Slater family in order to study agriculture. He enrolled in Santa Cruz High School, majored in agriculture and excelled in the school's lightweight athletic programs. After his graduation in February 1944, Curtis planned to study agriculture at Washington State College, but the war brought those plans to a halt.

In March 1944, Curtis Bushong joined the US Marine Corps and began his basic training in San Francisco. On May 29, the marines sent him to Camp Pendleton, California, where he completed his school-of-infantry training. He was then given special instruction at a Japanese language school in San Diego.

Bushong was deployed to the South Pacific on December 14, 1944, and joined Company F, 2nd Battalion of the First Marine Division serving in Guadalcanal. He spent his nineteenth birthday on that island in jungle training exercises. In April 1945, Bushong boarded the *USS Middleton* and sailed for Okinawa, landing there on Easter Sunday.

On April 23, 1945 his company began moving south to assist the 10th Army and on May 11, 1945, during bitter fighting near Shuri, Private Curtis Charles Bushong was killed in action. His remains were later interred in the National Cemetery in Honolulu, Hawaii.

(ABMC, SCHSC Pg. 7, SCSn May 27, 1945 6:4; July 3, 1945 5:4; SCR June 1, 1945)

JOHN A. BOBEDA
(1945/05/19)

(Watsonville High School yearbook)

Nine days after his Watsonville High School buddy Darell Pettus was killed on Okinawa, John joined him.

John Anthony Bobeda was born in 1919 in Watsonville, California, to Antone and Mary Bobeda. The family also included daughters Virginia, Ida and Mary, and sons Pete, Sebastian and Ceferino. John attended local elementary schools before enrolling in high school. While a student at Watsonville High School, he was active on the football and track teams and also worked part time in its maintenance department.

After his graduation from high school in June 1938, Bobeda continued to live and work in the Pajaro Valley. In August 1941 he married, Nickoline Lutich, and was rehired by the high school's maintenance department in a supervisory capacity. A son, John Bobeda Jr., was born to the couple in 1943.

John Bobeda was inducted into the US Army at the Presidio of Monterey in June 1944 and sent to Camp Joseph T. Robinson in Little Rock, Arkansas. Following basic training, he was sent to Fort Ord for additional instruction and deployment orders. Bobeda was then assigned to the 307th Infantry Regiment of the 77th Division conducting mopping up in the Philippines.

In late March 1945, the 307th Infantry Regiment left the

Philippines to participate in the Okinawa campaign. Their initial mission was to capture the neighboring island of IE Shima, made famous as the place of Ernie Pyle's death. Following that island's surrender, they returned to Okinawa to assist in its capture. On May 19, 1945, in one of the closing actions of the campaign, John Bobeda was killed in action.

Bobeda was buried in the US National Cemetery in Honolulu, Hawaii; his awards include the Bronze Star and Purple Heart.

(ABMC; NARA2; Photo-WHS; WIKI, 77 Infantry; WRP July 9, 19451:3)

ALBERT E. BODE JR.
(1945/05/22)

(Watsonville High School yearbook)

A scholarship winner from Watsonville joined the growing Okinawa casualty list.

Albert Ernest Bode Jr. was born in Sacramento, California, on January 31, 1925, and moved to the Pajaro Valley with his parents, Mr. and Mrs. Albert E. Bode Sr. Along with his brother, Stanley, he attended the Roache School and Watsonville High School, where he excelled in scholastic achievements. Albert was a member of the school's scholarship society for four years, the winner of an American Legion scholastic award, played on the school's football team and represented the school at Boys State.

One month prior to his graduation in May 1943, Bode enlisted in the US Marine Corps. After graduating from high school, he was sent to Camp Pendleton for basic and school-of-infantry training. Private Bode then attended the Marine Corps communication schools in San Diego, Camp Pendleton, and Camp Elliott, California. In 1944 Bode was promoted to Private First Class and assigned to the 6th Marine Division, which was preparing for deployment to the South Pacific.

While with the 6th Marine Division, Albert Bode saw action in combat engagements at Eniwetok, Kwajalein, Guam and finally, Okinawa.

On April 1, 1945, the 3rd Amphibious Corps of the 6th Marine Division landed on Okinawa. One of its major objectives was the capture of Sugar Loaf Hill, which they had attacked for two weeks. Private First Class Albert E. Bode was serving as a radio operator in a front line unit during an assault on that hill when he was killed in action on May 22 1945.

His remains were buried at the US Marine cemetery on Okinawa; however, following the war, his remains were returned to the US and reinterred at the Golden Gate Cemetery in San Bruno in 1949.

(USDVA; WRP June 5, 1945 1:2, July 16, 1945 1:1; Photo-WHS)

ESPERIDION C. BERNIDO
(1945/05/?)

The name Esperidion C. Bernido appears on the War Department List of Dead and Missing World War II Casualties for the County of Santa Cruz.

Esperidion was born in 1905 in the Philippine Islands; however, information regarding his parents and siblings is not available. His movements to and within California have been similarly difficult to establish.

Bernido's enlistment records state that he had only completed grammar school. Since his name appears with former students on Watsonville High School's World War II memorial stone, his attendance there must have been brief.

US census records indicate that in 1930 Bernido was living in San Luis Obispo County.

His 1943 enlistment records reveal that at that time he was single, without dependents and working as a farm laborer in Solano County.

Esperidion Bernido was inducted, or enlisted into the US Army at San Francisco as a private on July 29, 1943. Local reference to his military experience and death appears for the first time in 1945. On May 25, 1945, the *Watsonville Evening Pajaronian* included Bernido's name among those Pajaro Valley servicemen killed in action during World War II.

The exact date of his death and location of the remains of Esperidion Bernido has not been identified. The absence of his name among the ABMC foreign casualties and DVA national burials, suggest that his remains may have been returned to the US or the Philippines for private burial.

(ACGEN; NARA2; 1930 US Census, CA, San Luis Obispo; http://search.ancestry.com/cgi-bin/sse.dll?gl=allgs&gsfn=Manuel&gsln=Bernido&gss=seo&ghc=20; [May 16, 2009])

LE ROY A. HIGLEY
(1945/05/23)

(National Memorial Cemetery Pacific – Internet photo)

Okinawa closed the book for a potato farmer from Idaho who had a Watsonville wife.

Le Roy Albert Higley was born in Sugar City, Idaho, on April 28, 1919, to George and Alice Higley. Le Roy's father was a sugar factory engineer in the small community near Rexburg, Idaho. The family was large and consisted of sons George, Howard, Harold, Stephen, Hyman and Le Roy, along with daughters Laverne and Malinda. Le Roy completed grammar school in the Rexburg area prior to his becoming a farmer in Madison County, Idaho. During the early 1940s, he met and married Ruth Velazquez, a resident of the Pajaro Valley and the couple had two children, Melva and Melvin.

On September 23, 1944, Higley entered the US Army and was sent to Fort Hood, Texas for basic training. He was then assigned to duty at Fort Ord, California. During Le Roy's California posting, in December 1944, Ruth and her children returned to Watsonville and established the family residence. In February 1945, Private Higley was sent to Hawaii and in April, joined the 306th Infantry Regiment of the 77th Infantry Division.

The 77th Infantry Division was assigned the task of capturing IE Shima Island three miles west of Okinawa. Between April 16 and April 28 Le Roy Higley's unit helped to secure that island before setting sail for Okinawa. In late May 1945, the 77th Infantry and a US Marine unit joined in an assault on Shuri.

On May 23, 1945 Private Le Roy A. Higley was reported killed in action on Okinawa. His remains were recovered and reinterred in the Honolulu Memorial Cemetery in 1949. Higley's awards include the Bronze Star and Purple Heart.

(USCR, 1920 US Census, ID, Madison; NARA2; ABMC, WRP July 13, 1945 1:2, Global Security. org, 77 Infantry Regiment (RTU), 2000 http://www.globalsecurity.org/military/agency/army/77id. htm) (16 September 2008])

URBANO ARREY
(1945/05/29)

(Golden Gate National Cemetery – San Bruno California)

The country returned the Arrey family's Army and Air Force sons, but buried their Marine.

Included in the *Watsonville Register-Pajaronian* Roll of Honor of December 29, 1945, is the name of Private First Class Urbano Arrey. Arrey, a native of New Mexico, appears to have had a limited connection with Watsonville and Santa Cruz County. He was born in New Mexico January 15, 1927, into the family of Mr. and Mrs. Frank Arrey. His formative years and education took place in New Mexico prior to 1940 when the Arrey family moved to the Pajaro Valley.

During World War II, two of Urbano's brothers also served their country. Thomas served in Germany as a paratrooper and Henry with an army unit in Texas. His brothers Frank Jr. and Robert remained home in Watsonville with his sisters Virginia and Mary.

Urbano Arrey joined the US Marine Corps on September 9, 1943, and was sent to Camp Pendleton, California, for his basic and school-of-infantry training. Arrey went overseas in December 1943 and served with an unidentified regiment of the 6th Marine Division at Guadalcanal, Saipan, Guam and other locations.

During the fighting taking place at Okinawa on May 29, 1945, Private First Class Urbano Arrey was killed in action. His remains were later recovered and on March 11, 1949, reinterred in the Golden Gate National Cemetery in San Bruno California.

(ACGEN; USDVA; WRP June 11, 1945 1:2)

GEORGE I. NAKAMURA
(1945/06/29)

(Santa Cruz High School Service Cardinal)

A building named in his honor was a final tribute to the service of George Nakamura.

George Ichiro Nakamura was born in Mountain View, California, on May 22, 1923, to Mr. and Mrs. George K. Nakamura. Nakamura's father owned and operated the Tourist Hotel on Pacific Avenue in Santa Cruz. The family also included another son Willy and daughters Clara, Dora, Grace, Irene, Mary and Mrs. Bud Nagase.

George attended Mission Hill Junior High School before enrolling in Santa Cruz High School. In high school he took a college preparatory course, worked part time in a warehouse, played clarinet in the school band and was the recipient of a scholarship from the Tong honor society.

After graduation from high school in 1941, he enrolled and attended UC Berkeley where he studied as a pre-med student in 1941 and 1942. When World War II began, the Nakamura family were sent to the Japanese-American internment camp at Tule Lake. On November 28, 1942, while in the internment camp, George Nakamura enlisted in the US Army and was sent to Camp Selby, Mississippi for basic training.

George Nakamura was initially assigned to the 442nd Regimental Combat Team; however, in August 1943 he was transferred to the Military Intelligence System and sent to their translator school in Minnesota. By the end of 1943 he had completed his training and was posted to New Guinea as a translator.

In 1945 Sergeant Nakamura was reassigned to the Philippine Islands to translate and negotiate with Japanese soldiers and prisoners. George was serving at Palawan in the Philippine Islands on June 29, 1945, when he was ordered to attempt to obtain the surrender of a group of Japanese soldiers. According to military historian James McNaughton,

"Nakamura called for them to surrender but to no avail. He then moved within 25 yards of the soldiers, rose up and urged them again to give up. The enemy's response was a

single shot which fatally wounded him."

George Ichiro Nakamura's remains were later returned to the United States and reinterred in the Golden Gate National Cemetery in San Bruno in 1948. His awards included the Silver Star, Bronze Star, Purple Heart and Arrowhead. In 1980, the Defense Linguistic Institute in Monterey added one final tribute to him by naming one of their buildings in his honor.

(NARA2; USDVA; SCHSC Pg. 14; Joint Intelligence Center Pacific Ocean Area, History of the MIS, http://misvets.org/hist.htm, [16 September 2008]; SCSn July 25, 1945 1:5, August 9, 2009 1:1)

MARVIN A. WALWICK
(1945/07/07)

(Manila American Cemetery – Internet photo)

A local chef and Merchant Marine messman ended his cooking days somewhere on Luzon.

Marvin Alfred Walwick was born about 1914 in Nashwauk, Minnesota, to Emil and Nellie Walwick. Marvin's father, a Finnish immigrant, worked as a locomotive engineer in a nearby iron mine. In addition to Marvin, the family included another son, Harding, and a daughter, Hazel. Marvin's formative years were spent in Nashwauk where he attended local grammar schools, Nashwauk High School and Junior College. The time of his arrival in California is not known. While living in Santa Cruz, he married a local girl, Dorothy Rae Wiley, and was employed as a chef at the Casa Del Rey and Palomar Hotels.

During the summer of 1943, Walwick joined the Merchant Marines and after a brief training period, was sent to the South Pacific to serve as a messman. While at Bantangas, Luzon, in the Philippines, Merchant Marine Seaman Marvin Alfred Walwick contracted an undescribed illness and died on July 7, 1945. He was buried in the Manila American Cemetery in Manila.

(USCR, 1920 US Census, MN, Itasca; ABMC; SCSn August 6, 1945 1:5)

WALTER M. PIMENTEL
(1945/07/10)

(National Memorial Cemetery Pacific – Internet photo)

An "Appleknocker" from Santa Cruz proved to be a first class sergeant.

Walter M. Pimentel was born on June 14, 1920, in Santa Cruz, California, to Marion and Theresa Pimental. He and his brother William were educated locally and attended Branciforte Junior High School. Walter enrolled in Santa Cruz High School in September 1936, where he received a general and varied course of instruction with emphasis on farming. He was a member of the exiting class of 1939 but left school after two years. Before the war he worked as a ranch hand in the Los Angeles area.

Walter Pimentel was inducted into the US Army on October 11, 1942, at Los Angeles. After receiving basic training in Hawaii, he was assigned to the 105th Infantry Regiment of the 27th, "Appleknocker," Infantry Division. His promotions came quickly and within three months he had earned his sergeant stripes and after an additional six months, his staff sergeant chevrons. He served as an infantry squad leader and platoon sergeant during the campaigns of the Gilbert and Mariana Islands.

The division set sail from Espiritu Santo in the New Hebrides and arrived at Okinawa on April 9, 1945. During April, it participated in the invasion of the island and secured a dominating ridgeline south of Machinato and Kakazu. On April 28, after a severe struggle, the Machinato Airfield was captured. During this struggle, Staff Sergeant Walter M. Pimentel received shrapnel wounds to his left chest from which he died on July 10, 1945.

Pimentel was initially buried on Okinawa but was reinterred in the Honolulu Memorial Cemetery in 1949. His awards included the Bronze Star with Oak Leaf Cluster and the Purple Heart.

(ABMC; NARA2; SCHSC Pg. 16, SCSn July 25, 1945 1:6; 27th Inf Div http://www.army.mil/cmh-pg/lineage/cc/027id.htm [16 Sept 2008])

RAYMOND A. OLLESTAD
(1945/07/12)

(Santa Cruz High School Service Cardinal)

Rheumatic Fever brought to an end the army and the newspaper career of Ray Ollestad.

Raymond A. Ollestad was born in Alameda County, California, on August 28, 1921, to Mr. and Mrs. August Ollestad. Ray spent his formative years in the family home on Broadway Avenue in Santa Cruz with his parents and sister Wilma. In January 1938 he entered Santa Cruz High School and took a general and varied course of instruction. While in high school, Ollestad also reported sporting events for the *Santa Cruz Sentinel* newspaper. After graduating in February 1942, he worked on the *Sentinel* sports desk.

Ollestad was inducted into the US Army on December 2, 1942. Because of his Norwegian language proficiency he was assigned to a special Norwegian Mountain Infantry unit of the US Army's 99th Infantry Division. After basic training, he was sent to Camp Hale, Colorado, where he received specialized ski instruction. At that location he also edited *The Viking*, the battalions newspaper.

In early 1943 Ollestad contracted a severe case of rheumatic fever that required hospitalization at the Fitzsimmons Army Hospital in Denver, Colorado. After seven months of treatment, he failed to regain his strength and was given a medical discharge.

Upon returning home, the *San Francisco News* hired him as a reporter, but his employment was short lived. The symptoms of rheumatic fever reappeared, his health began deteriorating and on July 12, 1945, former Private First Class Ray Ollestad died at Ft. Miley Hospital in San Francisco. Following a military funeral by the American Legion, he was buried at Oakwood Memorial Park Cemetery in Santa Cruz.

(NARA2; SCHSC Pg. 15; SCSn July 13, 1945 1:1)

KONGO NITTA
(1945/07/14)

(Courtesy of his sister, Mary Meifu)

Kongo Nitta was born on May 13, 1923, in Los Angeles County, California, to Toichi and Chika Nitta, who had emigrated from Japan. The Nitta family also included five daughters, Yoshiko, Mary, Betty, Lorraine and Fugie and three other sons, Noboru, Mas and Sus. Kongo completed grammar school and attended Watsonville High School for three years until the war interrupted his education.

In the Spring of 1942 the Nitta family was moved from their Watsonville home to a temporary facility in Salinas and then sent to the permanent relocation camp in Poston, Arizona. The Nitta family occupied two rooms in Barrack 12, block 216, of Camp II at the facility.

Kongo Nitta enlisted in the US Army in March 1945 and was assigned to Camp Maxey, Texas, for basic training. In July 1945, while undergoing a training exercise at that camp, Private Kongo Nitta was accidentally drowned. His body was recovered and sent to Denver, Colorado, where funeral services were conducted. The family later had his remains reinterred in the Pajaro Valley Memorial Park in Watsonville.

(CBR; NARA2, Internment Record; Mas Hashimoto Watsonville JACL, email (13 April 2008]); Poston Newsletter Prepared for AJA WWII Memorial Alliance by Mits Kojimoto and Lisa Terao Blum)

LAWRENCE W. LAWSON JR.
(1945/07/17)

(Manila American Cemetery – Internet photo)

Appearing in the December 29, 1945, *Watsonville Register-Pajaronian* honor roll is the name of Second Lieutenant Lawrence W. Lawson Jr. What is known regarding this officer is derived from a few shards of information and supposition.

Lawrence W. Lawson Jr. was born in Sonoma County, California, on June 16, 1923, to Lawrence Lawson, Sr. and his wife Isabell. At some period Lawrence moved to West Virginia and at the time of his entry into the armed forces declared that state as his residence.

Given his rank of 2nd Lieutenant, Lawson was commissioned about 1944 and assigned to the Marine Air Force serving in the South Pacific.

During the period of Lawson's service in the Philippine Islands, where he died, the USMC Air Corps was providing close support for the US Army's assault on Zamboanga, Mindanao. After that invasion was completed, "Missions continued to be flown in support of operations at Davo, Malabang and Saragani Bay on the Island of Mindanao, as well as on the island of Jolo." For his service Lt. Lawson earned an Air Medal with two gold stars.

The American Battle Monument Commission indicated that he died on July 17, 1945, in the Philippine Islands; however, the cause of his death was not noted. Lawrence W. Lawson Jr. was buried in the Manila American Cemetery in the Philippines.

(CBR; ABMC; NARA2; USNM; WRP December 29,1945; Naval Aviation in World War II, http://www.history.navy.mil/download/ww2-35.pdf [19 July 2009])

WILLIAM R. FOOTE
(1945/07/21)

(Santa Cruz High School Service Cardinal)

Bill Foote was scheduled for a promotion and rotation home when he ran into Biak Island.

William R. Foote was born on November 29, 1922, in California, to Mr. and Mrs. O. K. Foote. He and his brother Ronnie grew up in Santa Cruz and attended Branciforte Junior High School. In 1937 Foote entered Santa Cruz High School where he was an outstanding basketball star of that school and of the Central Coast league. In addition to establishing scoring records in basketball, he also excelled in softball.

After graduating from high school in 1940, Foote enrolled at San Jose State College, where he continued playing basketball. After a year and a half, he left San Jose State and moved to San Francisco, where he was employed by the Kaiser Shipyards. During that period, he and Doris Collings, a local Santa Cruz girl, were married.

In February 1943, William Foote enrolled in the US Army Air Cadet program and was sent to Buckley Field in Denver, Colorado. After additional training at Fort Sumner, New Mexico, he earned his wings and commission as a second lieutenant. He was then assigned to the Merced Airbase in California that brought him closer to Doris and their newborn daughter, Judy Ann. A short course at Kerns, Utah, provided him with the final training he required to qualify as a copilot of C-47 transports.

In November 1944 Lt. Foote was assigned to the 13th Air Force serving in the South Pacific. His assignment included flying supplies to the front and returning with wounded troops. In July 1945 while flying a mission on Biak Island in the Schouten Island group northeast of New Guinea, Second Lieutenant William R. Foote's C-47 crashed. On July 21, 1945 he died from the wounds sustained during that crash. His remains were returned home in 1949 and interred at the Golden Gate National Cemetery at San Bruno.

(NARA2; USDVA; SCHSC Pg. 9, SCSn August 7, 1945 1:1, SCR August 10, 1945–1)

EDWARD J. HANCE
(1945/07/31)

(Fayetteville National Cemetery - Internet photo)

The name Edward Hance appears in the War Department's listing of Santa Cruz County residents who died during World War II.

Alameda County induction records indicate that Edward J. Hance was born in Montana on June 3, 1903. His failure to appear on the Montana census of 1910 suggests that the family may have moved. Local records have failed to confirm his presence within Santa Cruz County. Prior to August 1942, he was single, had completed two years of high school and was employed in what his enlistment records describe as "building of transportation equipment--not automobile or aircraft."

Edward Hance was inducted into the Army Air Corps in San Francisco on August 31, 1942. Information regarding his military training or the units to which he was subsequently assigned has not been located.

The US Department of Veterans Affairs indicates that Army Air Force Private First Class Edward J. Hance died as a result of non-battle circumstances on July 31, 1945. His body was interred in the Fairmount National Cemetery in Fayetteville, North Carolina.

(ACGEN; NARA2; USDVA)

BILL N. REDMON
(1945/07/31)

(Santa Cruz Riptide photo)

"*Four months after he had gone to the Pacific, and less than three weeks before cessation of hostilities, Lieutenant Bill Redmon took off in his B-25 on a mission that proved to be some place 'Beyond the Blue Horizon,'*" noted a Santa Cruz Riptide *news article.*

Bill N. Redmon was born in Iowa on September 23, 1917, to Mr. and Mrs. George Redmon. In addition to Bill, the other Redmon children included sons George and John and daughters Mary Lou, Jane, Betty and Lois. After he had completed high school in about 1934, Bill moved with his family to Santa Cruz. Upon his arrival he was employed by the Coast Counties Gas and Electric Company and remained with that utility firm for nine years.

In the early 1940s Bill Redmon married Natallia Music of Santa Cruz. The year 1943 found the Redmons living in Contra Costa County, where he was working in a clerical capacity, when their daughter Eileen was born.

In March 1943, Bill Redmon enlisted in the Army Air Corps and after basic training, was sent to Merced, California for cadet training. This was followed, in 1944, by advanced instruction at Luke Field, Arizona. In June of that year he earned his wings as a B-24 Liberator pilot and a commission as a second lieutenant.

In April 1945, Lt. Redmon was sent to the Philippines to join the 345th Bomb Group of the 5th Air Force. Luzon served as his home base for bombing missions on Okinawa and Japan. On July 31, 1945, Second Lieutenant Bill N. Redmon was sent on what would be his final mission. His commanding officer later described that mission in a letter to Bill's wife.

Bill was the co-pilot of a B-25 Mitchell type airplane which was participating in an operational mission against the enemy over Marushima, Kyushu, Japan, on 31 July, '45. As Bill and his crew were making their bombing and strafing run over the target, his plane was suddenly hit by enemy anti aircraft fire, causing the left engine to catch fire

as he pulled off the target and headed toward the sea. Witnesses state that his plane ditched about five miles off shore in Vatsushiro bay... the plane broke apart on ditching and almost instantly the entire plane was alive with flames. Your sorrow may be lessened by the knowledge that he was spared from suffering, and that death came instantly.

The remains of Bill Redmon were recovered and interred in the Golden Gate National Cemetery at San Bruno on February 15, 1950.

(NARA2, USDVA; SCSn April 16, 1944 4:6, August 15, 1945, September 6, 1945 5:1, SCR August 17, 1945)

MAURICE E. DAVIS
(1945/08/14)

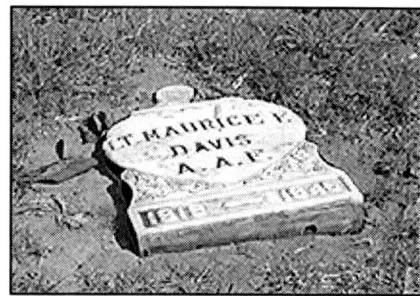

(Pajaro Valley Memorial Park – Watsonville, California)

Saving a drowning boy cost Maurice his life.

Maurice E. Davis was born in Missouri on September 19, 1919, to Luther and Hattie Davis. Maurice spent his early years in Missouri where he was educated. Later he moved with his aunt Mrs. C. R. Farrar to Watsonville, where they maintained a residence on High Street. Sometime prior to August 1941, he relocated to Santa Clara County and registered for the draft. At the time of his registration, Davis had completed one year of college and was working in a service station.

Maurice Davis was inducted into the US Army on August 10, 1941, and sent to Camp Roberts for basic training. Following his advanced training at Camp San Luis Obispo, he was accepted into Officers Candidate School at Fort Benning, Georgia. In December 1942 he graduated from OCS, was commissioned a second lieutenant and assigned to Fort Leonard Wood, Missouri. During this period, he met and married Alma Lee and their son, Robert Edwin, was born.

During his tour at Ft. Leonard Wood, Lt. Davis applied for a transfer and was accepted into the Army Air Corps. He received flight training at Santa Ana, Stockton and King City, California, with specialized training in Chicago, Illinois. In January 1944 he earned his wings and was certified as a multi-engine pilot. Davis was then sent overseas and probably assigned to the 15th Air Force in Bari, Italy.

By March 1945 Maurice Davis had completed thirty bombing missions, been promoted to first lieutenant and had earned the Distinguished Flying Cross, the Air medal with three oak leaf clusters and a unit citation for bombing the Ploesti oil fields in Romania. Lt. Davis returned to the United States and assignments at Santa Monica, California, Williams Field, Arizona, and Keesler Field, Mississippi.

It was at Ocean Springs, Mississippi on August 14, 1945, that First Lt. Maurice E. Davis met his death. While fishing on a nearby lake, Maurice saw a small boy in another boat fall into the water and he jumped into the lake to rescue him. After placing the boy in a boat, he attempted to swim to shore but drowned in the process. His body was recovered and returned for burial in Pajaro Valley Memorial Park.

(NARA2; WRP August 16, 1945 1:3, August 21, 1945 1:5; Pajaro Valley Cemetery headstone)

HERSCHEL A. SCHUTTISH
(1945/08/15)

(Photo courtesy Norman Atkins)

One day separated the WW II deaths of Herschel and his cousin Stony Spooner.

Herschel A. Schuttish was born about 1910 in Pacific Grove, California, to T. J. and Jennie Atkins Schuttish. Along with his two brothers, Clayton and Rolland, he spent his formative years in Monterey County. After graduating from Pacific Grove High School in the 1930s, he moved to Watsonville and lived with his aunt, Christine Spooner and her family. He married while living in Watsonville, and worked as a plasterer for Clark Bros., Espindola's and Granite Construction Company

Hershel was inducted into the US Army in San Francisco on March 3, 1941. Following his basic and advanced training at Fort Ord, he was assigned to the Army Chemical Corps. Schuttish was placed in the 181st Chemical Service Platoon that serviced flame-throwing equipment. During the campaigns of the South Pacific, flame-throwers were used extensively, and servicing them took Herschel Schuttish to the New Hebrides, Guadalcanal and other islands.

Schuttish wrote to his aunt describing his impression of the South Sea Islands. noting that, "It's all O.K down here, hot and rains all the time, mud knee deep, but all those tropical islands are that way." Frequently he would include photographs of the natives, who he described as being "friendly and good people -- like us Yanks 100 per cent."

Hershel Schuttish was sent to the Philippine Islands during their recapture in late 1944. On August 15, 1945, he was killed in an undescribed accident. His body was buried in the Manila American Cemetery.

(NARA2; ABMC; WRP May 1, 1944 1:1, September 7, 1945 1:3)

DESMOND E. SPOONER
(1945/08/16)

(Photo courtesy of Norman Atkins)

The wounds he received on Okinawa proved too much for Stony Spooner.

Desmond E. Spooner was born in Watsonville, California on November 27, 1925, to Harry and Christine Spooner. Stony, as he was nicknamed, grew to adulthood, along with his brother Andrew, in the family home on Marchant Street in Watsonville. Spooner attended local grammar schools and studied at Watsonville High School for three years. He worked in the local canning and food preserving industry after leaving high school.

Desmond Spooner was inducted into the US Army in San Francisco on October 14, 1944, and sent to Camp Roberts and Fort Ord, California, for basic and advanced infantry training. In February 1945, he was shipped to Hawaii and began training with a unit, which is believed to be the 32nd Division of the 7th Infantry Division. Spooner also trained in the Philippine Islands prior to the Okinawa campaign.

On April 1, 1945, the 32nd Regiment took part in the landing at Okinawa and was deployed in the area of Duck Hill.

Decisive action in the Japanese holding battle took place in the vicinity of Duck and Mabel Hills, east of Chan. Here, on 26 May, the 32d Infantry tried to break the enemy resis-

tance, but in a fierce encounter on Duck Hill it was thrown back with heavy casualties. In the withdrawal from Duck Hill the dead had to be left behind. No gain was made on the 27th, and on the 28th there was no activity other than patrolling.

During patrolling activities on May 28, Desmond Spooner received a wound to the abdomen by a sniper, for which he was posthumously awarded the bronze star. The accompanying citation stated,

"As acting squad leader PFC Spooner led his carrying party over a route covered by enemy small arms, machine gun and mortar fire and rendered further dangerous by the presence of a sizeable mine field.... continued to carry supplies after other men of his squad were forced to rest... led a demolitions patrol in reducing by-passed enemy position... volunteering to accompany his platoon leader on a reconnaissance...information thus secured enabled another battalion to fill a dangerous gap."

Stony was evacuated to a military hospital on Saipan and died there on August 16, 1945. An army chaplain later wrote to his mother sharing details of his wounding and death.

"During the fighting on Okinawa, his [Stony's] buddy was wounded first and fell to the ground some distance from Private First Class Spooner. He called Desmond to come and help him. In the attempt to reach his buddy, Desmond received the severe wounds, which finally resulted in the giving of his life."

The remains of Desmond "Stony" Spooner were initially buried on Saipan, but were later returned to Watsonville and interred in the Pioneer Cemetery.

(CBR; NARA2; ACGEN; Spooner Family History by Chris Huntze, November 2, 2009; US Army WWII, Okinawa the last Battle, http://www.history.army.mil/books/wwii/okinawa/ 382,index.htm#contents, Pg. 382, [16 September 2008]); WRP September 5, 1945 1:3, September 7, 1945 1:1)

***September 2** Japanese sign the surrender agreement creating V-J (Victory over Japan) Day.*

RALPH M. HAMEETMAN
(1945/09/04)

"Freedom Man Dies in Navy Plane Crash" noted the *Watsonville Register-Pajaronian.*

Ralph Martin Hameetman was born in New Jersey on November 7, 1920, to Mr. and Mrs. Louis Hameetman. At some time the Hameetman family settled in Freedom, California. Information regarding his family, early life, or the date of his arrival in the Pajaro Valley has not been located.

At an unspecified location and date Ralph Hameetman enlisted in the US Navy. Following completion of boot camp, he was trained as an aviation ordnanceman.

On September 4, 1945, AOM First Class Ralph Martin Hameetman was one of six navy men from the naval auxiliary air station at Oxnard who were on a routine flight when their plane was involved in a mid air collision near El Rio in Ventura County. The two planes, both US Navy TBM-3s carrying three-man crews collided, burst into flames and crashed into a lemon orchard. His remains were turned over to Monterey County; however, the location of his burial has not been identified.

(WRP September 8, 1945 1:4; CDR)

HENRY HICKS
(1945/09/15)

(Pajaro Valley Catholic Cemetery – Watsonville, California)

Henry Hicks has been included among local servicemen who died while on active duty during a war period based upon a *Watsonville Register-Pajaronian* obituary dated September 22, 1945.

Military Rites for Staff Sergeant Henry Hicks
Acting as pallbearers and participating in a full military burial service, 18 members of the US Marine Corps from Moffett field were here Saturday morning for the last rites for Staff Sergeant Henry Hicks, 39, marine who died at Oak Knoll hospital, Oakland, Sept. 15. Also present were marines from the western procurement division with whom sergeant Hicks worked.

From Mel's chapel, the cortege went to St. Patrick's church where Low Mass of requiem was celebrated by the Rev. Fr. James Maroon. Burial was in the family plot in the Valley Catholic cemetery where military honors were given Hicks. The simple headstone above his plot provides no additional information regarding this marine.

The Valley Catholic Cemetery on Hecker Pass Road in Watsonville confirms the burial of Henry Hicks; however, no additional information regarding his life or death has been found.

(WRP September 22, 1945 1:1)

HAROLD J. TOTMAN
(1945/09/17)

(Santa Cruz Riptide photo)

Mr. and Mrs. Frank Totman learned of their son's fate when their letter was returned marked "*DECEASED.*"

Harold James Totman was born in 1923 in California to Mr. and Mrs. Frank. H. Totman and moved to Santa Cruz with his parents the following year. Harold attended Holy Cross School through the fifth grade before the family moved to Patterson, California. He completed grammar and high school in Patterson and two years at Modesto Junior College. During this period, he also worked as a welder.

Harold Totman enlisted in the US Army on December 12, 1942, at the Merced Air Force base and entered the Army Air Corps cadet program. He trained in Lincoln, Nebraska, Cedar Rapids Iowa, and at Santa Ana, King City and Chico, California. Following advanced training at Douglas, Arizona, and Randolph Field, Texas, he was commissioned a second lieutenant.

In 1944 Lieutenant Totman was assigned to the 11th Airborne Division as a C-47 pilot and flew paratroopers to jump sites on Leyte, Luzon and Corregidor in the Philippine Islands. He later had the distinction of carrying the first US occupation troops to Japan. While on a routine flight to the Japanese Island of Honshu on September 17, 1945, First Lieutenant Harold William Totman's plane failed to return. Before his family could officially be made aware of his death, an army clerk mistakenly returned one of their letters marked DECEASED. Later his commanding officer provided his parents with the details accompanying Harold's death.

Harold was pilot of a plane that departed September 17 from Motobu strip, Motobu, Okinawa, Ruyukus on a routine cargo flight to Atsugi airdrome. Prevailing weather conditions at his destination forced Harold to descend on instruments through the overcast, and in doing so his plane crashed into the mountains south of Atsugi. Death came instantly.

Harold's remains were returned to California and are buried in the Holy Cross Mausoleum in San Francisco.

(SCSn October 16, 1945, December 14, 1948 1:6; SCR October 26, 1945 –10)

DOAK A. WESTON
(1945/09/24)

(Santa Cruz High School Service Cardinal)

Doak's name joined Sid Ormsbee's on a stained glass panel in a church in Capitola.

Doak A. Weston was born on May 1, 1918, in Fairbault, Minnesota, to William and Eleanor Weston. At a very early age, Doak accompanied the family in their move to Soquel, California, where he and his younger brother, John, attended school. About 1932 Doak entered Santa Cruz High School and graduated in 1936. The following fall he enrolled in the University of California at Berkeley and graduated about 1940.

Following college Weston married Barbara Peekema and went into the ranching business near Richmond, California. In the succeeding years, the couple had three sons.

In May 1941, Doak Weston entered the US Army Air Force cadet program and began training at Hamilton Field, California. This was followed by additional instruction in Mississippi and Columbus, Ohio, before he earned his wings and commission on December 12, 1942.

In January 1943, Weston reported for duty at the Columbia Army Airbase, South Carolina, and was assigned to a medium bombardment group as a pilot. In February, during a routine training flight, his plane went into an uncontrolled 100-foot plunge into nearby Lake Murray. Out of a crew of six, he was the sole survivor. Following the crash, Weston was found wandering along the shore in a dazed condition and was unable to give any details of the accident.

After his recovery, First Lt. Weston was assigned to the 30th Weather Reconnaissance Squadron in Presque Isle, Maine. Later he was posted to the 31st WRS that flew weather-gathering missions between Grenier Field in Manchester, New Hampshire, and Sornoway, England. During the next two years, he was promoted to captain and then major.

On September 24, 1945, while conducting a B-25 test flight

near Grenier Field, Doak Weston's plane encountered mechanical problems. He held the aircraft on course long enough for his crew to safely bail out; however, he was killed in the crash. If his remains were recovered their burial location is not known.

A stained glass memorial panel was erected in the Episcopal Church of St. John the Baptist in Capitola honoring Doak Weston and Sid Ormsbee, two of their former members.

(USCR, 1920 US Census, MN, Fairbault; SCHSC Pg. 20, SCSn September 25, 1945 1:6)

WILLIAM L. SLAUGHTER
(1945/10/05)

(Santa Cruz High School Service Cardinal)

A football game prevented a merchant mariner from rejoining the civilian community.

William LeRoy Slaughter entered the world on May 2, 1927, in Fresno, California, the son of Mr. and Mrs. James E. Slaughter. His brothers William, Jerry, James, Francis and his sister Nancy joined him in the family. The Slaughter family later moved to Los Gatos, California where he entered high school.

In 1942 James Slaughter Sr. acquired the Log Cabin Restaurant on Soquel Avenue and moved his family to Santa Cruz. William transferred into Santa Cruz High School in the spring of 1942 and began a general and varied course of study. He also played on the high school football team and started a dance band that performed throughout the area.

In November 1944, William Slaughter joined the Merchant Marines and was sent to Avalon, California for training prior to being shipped to the South Pacific. In 1945, Able-bodied Seaman Slaughter's ship transported men and materials to the Marshall Islands, the Carolines, Saipan, Tinian and Okinawa.

On October 5, 1945, while home on leave in Santa Cruz, Slaughter borrowed his father's convertible coupe and headed to Monterey with friends for a nighttime football game. About a mile south of Castroville, the car he was driving crashed head on into another vehicle and he was killed. Following a funeral service, his remains were buried in Oakwood Memorial Park.

(SCHSC Pg. 18, SCSn October 7, 1945 1:3, SCR October 12, 1945 –1)

WILLIAM C. TOOZE
(1945/10/20)

William Tooze was a turn of the century Santa Cruzan who was active in the county for ten years.

William C. Tooze was born in Newberg, Oregon, to a Mr. and Mrs. Tooze about 1881. The Tooze family, consisting of two sons and two daughters, later moved to San Jose, California. Following the completion of his formal education in 1900, William was employed by the Sperry Flour Company and became their Santa Cruz agent. While in Santa Cruz, he was active in the local Masonic Lodge, the First Presbyterian Church and served as president of the local Christian Endeavor Society. He also participated in community athletic programs including the all star baseball team and the relay races between Santa Cruz and Watsonville. During this period, William Tooze married and a daughter, Nancy, was later born to the couple.

About 1910 William Tooze left Santa Cruz and returned to San Jose. During World War I, he was commissioned a Lt. (jg) in the California Naval Militia (Reserve). In 1917 he served as a navigation officer with the first battalion of that organization stationed in Oakland and later as a deck officer aboard the cruiser *USS Pueblo*. Following the war, Tooze remained in the Navy and advanced in rank.

When World War II began, Commander Tooze served aboard the battleship *USS Oregon* until he was promoted to captain and transferred to the 12th Naval District staff. As a staff officer he was subjected to an extremely heavy workload during the latter part of the war. When his health failed, he was hospitalized at Camp White in Medford, Oregon. Following two weeks of treatment, Captain William C. Tooze died on October 20, 1945. His body was sent to San Jose for a funeral and burial; however, the cemetery in that city where he is buried has not been identified.

(SCSn October 21, 1945 1:3)

EVERETT E. SCHWARZMANN
(1945/11/01)

(Santa Cruz Riptide photo)

Everett just wanted to get back to teaching music when his body gave out.

Everett Edward Schwarzmann was born in San Francisco, California, January 2, 1912, to Edward and Minnie Schwarzmann. Everett and his younger brother Robert spent their formative years and received their education in San Francisco. Following high school, Schwarzmann attended the University of California at Berkeley and after graduating, enrolled in a Master of Arts music program at the University of Southern California, where he received his MA degree in 1939.

After leaving USC, Everett Schwarzmann moved to Santa Cruz, where he was hired as a music teacher at Mission Hill Junior High School. He became active in the local community and joined the First Congregational Church where he sang in the choir. He also became a member of the Toastmasters, Monday Music Club, Phi Delta Kappa fraternity and a local singing quartette. Schwarzmann married and was frequently accompanied by his wife on the piano during his singing performances.

In late 1942, Everett Schwarzmann received a commission in the US Navy and was sent to a special training school at Harvard University. Advanced training in radar at Mare Island and Treasure Island, California followed. In 1943 a son, Richard, was born to Everett and his wife in Santa Cruz during his absence.

Ensign Schwarzmann's first ship assignment was in the Atlantic Theater aboard a destroyer escort serving in the Mediterranean Sea. During the last six months of the war, he was transferred to the Third US Fleet in the Pacific theater and assigned to the battleship *USS Wisconsin* for the remainder of the war.

On October 26, 1945, on terminal leave and accompanied by his wife and son, Schwarzmann returned to Santa Cruz. The next day he was stricken with an undisclosed illness and on October 29, he was taken to Oak Knoll Naval Hospital in Oakland. On November 1, 1945, Lt. Everett Edward Schwarzmann died. Following a funeral in Oakland, his body was interred in the Golden Gate National Cemetery in San Bruno.

(USCR, 1920 US Census, CA, San Francisco; CDR; USDVA; DANFS, USS Wisconsin BB-64; SCR November 9, 1945 1; SCSn November 3, 1945 1:7)

JOHN C. HUMPHREY JR.
(1945/11/04)

(Santa Cruz High School Service Cardinal)

"Humphrey was killed in Auto Crash," reported the *Santa Cruz Sentinel.*

John Charles Humphrey Jr. was born on February 11, 1926, in San Francisco, California, to John and Eloise Humphrey. Along with his brother Cyrus and his sister Mary, he spent his formative years in San Francisco. The Humphrey family later moved to Fontana, California, where he enrolled in high school. In 1943 the family relocated to Santa Cruz and John transferred into the junior class of Santa Cruz High School. During his year at Santa Cruz High, he took a college preparatory course and majored in mathematics. After leaving high school, he moved to San Bernardino County.

John Humphrey joined the Army Air Force Reserve and on August 23, 1944, was called to active duty at the Presidio of Monterey and sent to Randolph Field, Texas. After receiving specialized training at other locations, he served as a ground crewman.

Prior to being shipped overseas, Humphrey was given a military leave and returned to spend it in Southern California. While near Fontana, California, he was killed when a train hit the automobile in which he was a passenger. His remains were buried in the Holy Cross Cemetery in Los Angeles.

(NARA2; SCHSC Pg. 12; SCSn November 7, 1945 1:7)

HARVEY A. LARSEN
(1945/11/?)

(Watsonville High School yearbook)

A polio bug in China prevented Harvey Larsen's return home.

Harvey A. Larsen, the only child of Mr. and Mrs. Atwill H. Larsen, was born in Monterey County, California on June 8, 1925. The family lived in in the Interlaken district of the Pajaro Valley, where Harvey attended local elementary schools. He studied at Watsonville High School for three years. In June 1943 he left high school to work for the Levi Zentner Company in Watsonville.

Harvey Larsen enlisted in the Army Air Force on December 15, 1943, and completed his basic training at Shepherd Field, Texas. The following year he was sent to a cargo carrier command unit at Malden Army Airfield in Missouri. In March 1945, he was serving at Fort Wayne, Indiana, when his unit received orders sending them to India.

In June 1945, Sgt. Larsen was transferred to Burma where he served as a crew chief on a C-47 aircraft in a combat cargo squadron. Later in the year he was transferred to a cargo plane unit operating out of China. In the middle of November 1945, while serving in China, Sergeant Harvey A. Larsen contracted an acute form of polio that took his life. The date of his death and the location of his remains have not been identified.

(NARA2; WRP November 24, 1945 1:7; Photo-WHS)

WARREN R. HAYES
(1945/12/20)

(Oakwood Memorial Park – Santa Cruz, California)

An accident prevented Warren from making it home to spend Christmas with his mom.

Warren Roger Hayes was born in Illinois on September 28, 1926; his mother's name was Blanche. Information regarding his early family life is not available. His enlistment records indicate that his education was limited to grammar school. Following school Hayes worked on farms until he and his mother moved to Santa Cruz County, where they resided on 41st Avenue. It is likely that he found employment in one of the local farms prior to his entry into the service.

Warren Hayes was inducted into the US Army at Camp Beale at Marysville, California, on August 24, 1945. During World War II, Camp Beale was used as a training site for the 13th Armored, the 81st and 96th Infantry Divisions. Warren was assigned to an Army [Special] Service Force unit in an unspecified capacity.

At noon on December 20, 1945, Private Warren Roger Hayes was killed near Woodland in an automobile accident, while driving to Santa Cruz to spend Christmas with his mother. His body was returned to Santa Cruz for a funeral and he was buried at Oakwood Memorial Park.

(NARA2; CDR; Global Security.Com; Camp Beale, http://www.globalsecurity.org/military/facility/beale.htm, [16 September 2008] SCSn December 26, 1945 1:5)

DAN E. SCHIAVON
(1945/12/24)

(Courtesy of Eunice Sears)

Dan loved poetry and music but a vehicle mishap in Calcutta put an end to his avocation.

Dan E. Schiavon was born to Mr. and Mrs. Tony Schiavon at Coalinga, California, on March 10, 1922. In the 1930s the family, which also included sons Mario and Louis and daughter Eunice, moved to the Pajaro Valley. Dan finished eighth grade at Roache Road School in Freedom before entering Watsonville High School about 1936. While in high school, he taught himself to play the guitar and entertained audiences at the Fox Theater in Watsonville during intermission. He also developed a love of poetry, which began in high school and continued while serving in the army. Schiavon left high school after completing three years. He remained in the area and was employed as a commercial vehicle driver.

Dan Schiavon reported to the induction center in San Francisco, where he was drafted into the US Army, on October 16, 1942. Following basic training, he received advanced instruction at Camp Howze, Texas, and was stationed with an infantry unit.

In May 1943 Schiavon returned home on a week's leave before joining the 145th Quartermaster Truck Company in India. He was posted to Calcutta, India and served as a truck and jeep driver at the US Army Quartermaster installation. By the end of 1945 Dan was becoming tired of the army and wanted to return home. During one of his despondent moments, he wrote the following poem.

> It's no use to Live
> What's the use of living
> Things are being the way they are
> I think I'll find me a new land
> If it isn't too far
>
> I've searched the world over,
> But nothing could I find,
> To reconstruct my feelings,
> Or make me change my mind.
>
> I've tried it every way I could,
> But it wouldn't work at all.
> Just what would you do if
> It were to be your fall
>
> We've all got our troubles and cares,
> That we've got to expect,
> So lets forget the whole damn thing,
> And break all our necks
>   Yours truly
>   Despondency.

On Christmas Eve 1945, Private First Class Dan E. Schiavon was suffering from a headache that prevented him from driving his jeep and he asked another soldier to drive while he rested in the back seat. The new driver was unfamiliar with the vehicle and rolled it over breaking Dan's neck. His remains were returned home and interred in the Watsonville Catholic Cemetery.

(NARA2; Cemetery Survey; WRP June 4, 1943 1:1, August 4, 1945 1:1, Remembrances of Eunice (Schiavon Sears)

WILLIAM MONDE
(Circa 1945)

Monde was a "Mustang" artillery lieutenant with an address in Santa Cruz.

Second Lieutenant William Monde was born in Idaho in 1910. Later he declared Santa Cruz County, California, as his residence. Information regarding his parents, siblings, life in Idaho or in Santa Cruz has not been found. He completed grammar school but did not continue with his formal education. In December 1940, he was single, living in Kern County, California, and working as a brakeman on a railroad.

William Monde was inducted into the US Army as a private in Los Angles, California, on January 21, 1941. It is likely that he married in the early years of his enlistment, and that his wife established a residence in Santa Cruz. After completing basic training at Camp White, Oregon, Monde was assigned to the 242nd Field Artillery. On January 13, 1943, that unit moved to a firing range in Yakima, Washington. Following a short tour, they were transported to Fort Sill, Oklahoma.

On March 4, 1943 Monde arrived at Fort Sill, Oklahoma, and entered Officers Candidate School. In early June he graduated, was commissioned a second lieutenant and assigned to Battery B, 242nd Field Artillery Battalion. Lt. Monde's unit

> remained at the Field Artillery School and Officer Candidate School until March 11, 1944 when they convoyed to Camp Howze, Texas. At Camp Howze, Army Ground Force Tests were taken preparatory to going overseas. All equipment was turned in. The troops boarded a train on June 21, 1944, arriving at Camp Shanks, NY June 24, 1944. On July 1, 1944, the men of the 242nd boarded a ship (the Thomas H. Barry, formerly the cruise ship, Orienta) in Brooklyn in the largest convoy ever to cross the Atlantic. They arrived at the Firth of Clyde, Scotland, then went by train to Camp Blackbirds in South Wales. All new equipment was issued and the 105mm cannon were test fired. On August 19, 1944, the battalion convoyed to South Hampton, England, and boarded ship to cross the English Channel, landing on Utah beach.

While in France, Second Lieutenant William Monde was reported to have been involved in a jeep accident that claimed his life after the war. His body was initially buried in France; however, his final resting-place has not been identified.

(ACGEN; NARA2; 442nd Field Artillery Battalion WWII http://www.242nd-field-artillery.com, [16 September 2008]; email dated 6/7/2007 from E.V. Walsh)

1946

RICHARD GREENWOOD
(1946/01/24)

(Santa Cruz High School Service Cardinal)

With his discharge certificate in hand, Richard was almost a civilian until a train got in the way.

Richard Greenwood was born on January 16, 1925, in Capitola, California, to Mr. and Mrs. Fred Greenwood. His brother Ernest and his sister Beatrice rounded out the family. Greenwood attended Holy Cross Grammar School and Mission Hill Junior High School before entering Santa Cruz High School in 1940.

After the Japanese attacked Pearl Harbor in December 1941, Greenwood dropped out of high school and on January 16, 1942, enlisted in the US Navy. Upon completion of training at San Diego he was assigned to the Pacific Fleet to serve aboard a navy landing ship. Landing ships were created during World War II to support amphibious operations by carrying significant quantities of vehicles, cargo and troops directly onto an unimproved shore location. Greenwood served as ship's cook first class aboard LSM-435 (Landing Ship Medium) and participated in several Pacific Theater campaigns, including Kwajelein.

Richard Greenwood returned to California and was discharged on January 16, 1946. Before returning to Santa Cruz, he visited his father, then living in Santa Clara County. On January 24, 1946, Richard and his father were riding together on a motorcycle that was hit by a train at the Saratoga-Sunnyvale Road crossing. In the crash he was killed and his father was injured.

Richard Greenwood's remains were returned to Santa Cruz for a funeral at St. Joseph's Church in Capitola and burial at Holy Cross Cemetery.

(SCHSC Pg. 10; SCR February 8, 1946 – 1; WIKI, LSM-435)

WILLIAM L. PATE
(1946/02/22)

(Santa Cruz High School Service Cardinal)

An Old Salt's long fight to recover his health finally came to an end.

William Lloyd Pate was born in Ukiah, California, on July 17, 1916, to Joseph and Phoebe Pate. His family, which also included sons William and Thomas and daughters Marian and Leafy, moved to Santa Cruz about 1918. Pate attended local elementary schools, Mission Hill Junior High and enrolled in Santa Cruz High School in the fall of 1932. During his high school years, he majored in art before leaving in the spring of 1934.

William Pate enlisted in the US Navy on September 17, 1934, and was sent to boot camp. During his naval career, he served aboard the *USS Omaha*, the *Concord*, the *Calioka* and the *Meade*, with shore assignments in navy yards at Mare Island, California, Brooklyn, New York, and Charleston South Carolina. From May 1943 until the end of the war, he saw duty aboard the *USS North Carolina* that sailed out of Pearl Harbor, Hawaii.

In November 1943, North Carolina assisted in capturing enemy positions in the Gilbert Islands. This began a pattern of operations for her that lasted for the rest of World War II: serving in the anti-aircraft screen of aircraft carrier task forces and occasionally using her heavy guns to bombard Japanese-held islands. In these roles, during 1944 she was involved in the Marshalls operation in January-February, attacks on Central Pacific targets through the late winter and spring, the Marianas invasion and Battle of Philippine Sea in June, and Western Pacific carrier strikes in November and December.

On June 14, 1944, William Lloyd Pate entered the Veterans Hospital in Corona, California, with an unspecified medical condition. He remained confined to the hospital for twenty months prior to his death on February 22, 1946. His body was later returned to Santa Cruz and following a funeral, was interred in Santa Cruz Memorial Park.

(SCHSC Pg. 16; DANFS, USS North Carolina; SCSn February 28, 1946 8:3)

ELLSWORTH W. LOCKWOOD
(1946/03/19)

(Santa Cruz High School Service Cardinal)

Ellsworth fought the good fight for eleven months before a virus joined to defeat him.

Ellsworth William Lockwood was born on August 31, 1924, in San Francisco, California, to Mr. and Mrs. Ellsworth A. Lockwood. Later the family moved to Santa Cruz and he enrolled in a local grammar school. Ellsworth completed Mission Hill Junior High School before entering Santa Cruz High School in September 1939. In high school, Lockwood majored in science and was active in the BAA, Science Club and the Tong honor society. Following his graduation in June 1942, the Lockwood family moved to Alameda where he remained until he entered the armed forces.

Ellsworth Lockwood was inducted into the US Army on March 8, 1943, and sent to Camp Bowie, Texas, for basic training followed by advanced training at Camp Howzie, Texas.

In September 1944 Lockwood joined the Seventh U.S Army in Europe as an artillery forward observer.

Hard-fought battles were waged in the Alsace and Lorraine during the winter of 1944-45, in which Seventh Army played a major role. In the spring of 1945, Seventh Army crossed the Rhine River into Germany itself. Parts of the Black Forest and Bavaria were captured by Seventh Army, including Hitler's alpine residence, the Berghof.

While serving at an undisclosed German location in April 1945, Corporal Ellsworth Lockwood was wounded and in July, he returned to the United States for treatment. During the next nine months, his condition prevented his release and in March he acquired a virus that required twenty-four blood transfusions. On March 19, 1946, Technical Sergeant Ellsworth W. Lockwood died while at Dibble General Hospital in Palo Alto, California.

The location of his remains is unknown.

(SCHSC Pg. 12; NARA2; WIKI, 7th Army)

KENNETH V. BREEDEN
(1946/03/30)

(Santa Cruz High School Service Cardinal)

Ken's World War II adventure ended in Mobile Bay.

Kenneth V. Breeden was born in Fort Branch, Indiana on May 29, 1918; his mother's name was Gladys V. Breeden. He moved to Santa Cruz County with his mother and sister, Mary, in 1922. Kenneth attended local schools and entered Santa Cruz High School, where he followed a general and varied course of instruction. He graduated with the June 1937 class. Following his graduation, Western Union and later the Stagnaro Company employed him.

Kenneth Breeden enlisted in the US Air force on February 28, 1940, and received his basic training at Moffett Field, California. Following his instruction period, he remained there for a year as a guard. In 1941 he was promoted to corporal and transferred to Hamilton Field, California, where he performed clerical work.

In August 1941 Breeden volunteered for service in China and was sent to Burma to become part of General Clair Chennault's famous Flying Tigers. The Flying Tigers were a group of volunteer American airmen hired by China prior to the US entry into World War II to man Chinese air bases in its war against Japan. While Ken was engaged in clerical activities, he occasionally drove trucks from Rangoon, Burma, over the precarious Burma Road to the air base in China.

Upon his return to the United States in 1942, Breeden was discharged. He immediately re-enlisted in the US Army Air Force and was promoted to technical sergeant. After receiving training in aircraft gunnery, he returned to the Pacific Theater and flew over fifty missions as a tail gunner against Japanese targets.

On September 25, 1945, Sergeant Breeden was discharged for a second time and joined the US Merchant Marines. While returning to his ship in Mobile Bay, Alabama, on March 30, 1946, he fell overboard and was drowned. His body was recovered and returned to Santa Cruz for burial in Oakwood Memorial Park on April 12, 1946. His awards include Air Medal with one Oak Leaf Cluster.

(NARA2; SCHSC Pg. 6; SCR December 4, 1942, April 19, 1946 -9

DAVID M. ROSSI
(1946/11/19)

(Santa Cruz Riptide photo)

The last documented Santa Cruz serviceman to die during World War II was David Rossi.

David Mario Rossi, better known as Scotty to his friends, was the son of Mario J. and Suzanne Scott Rossi. He was born in San Francisco, on December 21, 1927, and at an early age moved into the Santa Cruz home of his grandparents. He completed Branciforte Junior High School and during the summer, worked for the Beach and Boardwalk Company. In January 1944 Rossi enrolled in Santa Cruz High School, took a continuation course of study and was said to have been very popular. He left high school in the spring of 1944 and never returned.

In April 1945 David Rossi joined the Merchant Marines and following his initial training, was assigned to the victory ship *SS Clarksburg Victory*.

During World War II, 534 Victory ships were constructed and manned by the Merchant Marine Service. Victory Ships were designed and built to carry ammunition and supplies, and had the advantage of traveling at a speed of 15 knots, making them less prone to submarine attack than other transports. They were also equipped with a 5-inch stern gun, a 3-inch bow gun and eight 20-mm machine guns for protection. The first of the Victory ships were named for allied countries and later versions for cities. The Clarksburg Victory *# T-AG-183 was laid down on July 9, 1945, at Suisun Bay California, by the California Shipbuilding Corporation of Los Angeles and delivered to the Maritime Commission on October 15, 1945."*

Able Seaman Rossi's final voyage aboard the *Clarksburg Victory* was to the Mariana Islands in the Pacific in the fall of 1946. On November 19, 1946, the ship was in Guam Bay when a violent storm hit the island and Rossi was washed overboard and drowned. His body was later recovered and given a military burial on the island of Guam.

(SCHSC Pg. 274; USMM.Org, American Merchant Marine at War, http://www.usmm.org/victoryships.html, [16 September 2008]; SCR January 4, 1947? -2)

UNDATED WORLD WAR II DEATHS

LAWRENCE R. DAVIS
(Death Date Unknown)

The name Lawrence R. Davis (Serial No. 39837684) was included in the US War Department's listing of World War II casualties from Santa Cruz County, California. No information is currently available as to his family or connection with the county.

Lawrence Davis was born in Oklahoma in 1912. In addition to finishing elementary and high school, his military enlistment records indicate that he had completed two years of college. Those same records noted that in January 1942, he was a resident of Santa Cruz County, single and was employed as a vegetable farm hand.

Davis was inducted into the army in San Francisco on April 14, 1942, and assigned the rank of private. No information has surfaced as to his training or unit assignment. The US War Department's casualty list indicated that Davis was a private first class at the time of his death and that his death was of a non-battle related nature. The date of death and the location of the remains of Private First Class Lawrence R. Davis have not been found.

(ACGEN; NARA2)

ERNEST E. GUIN
(Death Date Unknown)

The name Ernest E. Guin (Serial No. 39096232) was included in the US War Department's listing of World War II casualties from Santa Cruz County, California. No information is currently available as to his family or physical connection with the county.

Enlistment records reveal that Ernest Guin was born in South Carolina in 1921 and had completed grammar school and one year of high school. At the time of his induction into the service, he indicated that he was a resident of Santa Cruz County, was single and employed as a commercial vehicle driver.

Ernest Guin was drafted into federal service in San Francisco on July 19, 1942. The branch of Army was not designated and he was assigned the rank of private. No information has surfaced as to his training or subsequent unit. The US War Department's casualty list indicates that Guin was a private at the time of his death and that his death was of a non-battle related nature. The date of death and the location of the remains of Private Ernest E Guin have not been identified.

(ACGEN; NARA2)

***

Korean War
(1950-1954)

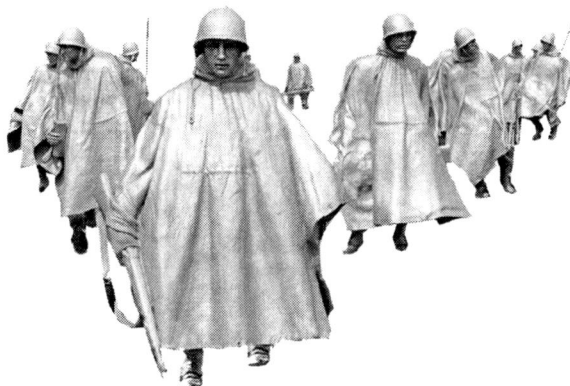

Santa Cruz Militry During The Korean War

Only World War II surpassed the Korean War in the number of Santa Cruz County military deaths occurring over a three-year period. Between 1950 and 1954, fifty-four Santa Cruz County and Pajaro Valley servicemen died while serving on active duty.

During the Korean War period, the Selective Service draft and armed forces recruiting were the main sources for meeting the manpower requirements demanded of the county.

In 1951 The Universal Military Training and Service Act was enacted requiring American males eighteen to twenty-six years old to register for the draft and making them liable, until they reached the age of twenty-six, for up to twenty-four months of active service. On July 9, 1950, the Selective Service board in San Jose began to coordinate the calling up of the 32,000 eligible men from Monterey, San Benito and Santa Cruz Counties who would be drafted during the war. Local boards were established in Santa Cruz and Watsonville to implement the process.

During the war, an Army National Guard Armored (Tank) Company operated in Watsonville and a US Naval Reserve Surface Division trained in Santa Cruz. Both of these units were kept at near full strength, but were never activated as units. A significant number of veterans who had remained in the reserve after World War II were reactivated during the Korean War. The veterans recalled were primarily those with critical military-occupation-specialty (MOS) designations.

High school ROTC units trained students in both Watsonville and Santa Cruz, but played no direct military role during the war.

Watsonville High School honored Lt. Colonel Harold E. Mignola, killed in an air crash on March 23, 1950, as its first Korean War era death; however, Corporal Edward McCall holds the distinction of being the first county combat death. Former Santa Cruz High School student Seaman LeRoy W. Machado, who died on December 4, 1954, was the last county service death recorded.

BIOGRAPHICAL SKETCHES

1950

HAROLD E. MIGNOLA
(1950/03/23)

(Courtesy of Harold E. Mignola Jr.)

Included on the Watsonville High School Korean War Memorial Plaque is the name of Harold Mignola. While his death occurred three months prior to the beginning of hostilities in Korea, it is felt that 90 days should not diminish the intent of his high school classmates in honoring him.

Harold Edward Mignola was born in Salinas, California on January 24, 1914; however, his formative years and education are believed to have taken place in Watsonville, California. His biological father's name is not available, but his mother later remarried George Wale Jr. who introduced him to the automobile business.

During the late 1930s, Mignola, along with Marty Franich and Stanley Secondo (see World War II honor roll) formed a partnership and acquired a service station and automobile agency on East Lake Avenue in Watsonville. In 1940 Harold Mignola and Virginia Phillips of Watsonville were married and a son, Harold Edward Mignola Jr., was born to them.

In 1940, Harold Mignola entered the Royal Canadian Air Force and was trained as an officer. After commissioning, he served as an instructor at their bomber-gunner station at MacDonald, Manitoba, for two years.

Mignola applied for and received a commission in the US Army Air Corps in June 1942 and was sent to Randolph Field, Texas, for an orientation course. After completing that program, he instructed aviation cadets in interception and pursuit at Moore Field, Texas. Mignola continued to serve as a pilot instructor during 1943 and 1944.

In 1945 Harold Mignola served in the Philippine Islands and at the end of World War II, was assigned to Japan as a major. He chose to remain in the US Air Force and by 1950 had risen to the rank of Lt. Colonel.

Lt. Colonel Mignola commanded the 65th Bomber Squadron of the 43rd Bomb Wing at Davis-Monthan Air Force Base stationed in Tucson, Arizona, in 1950. In his new assignment Mignola flew B50 Bombers similar to the B-29 that had bombed Hiroshima and Nagasaki in 1945. The plane he was aboard, as an instructor pilot, was nicknamed the Long Ranger and was capable of flying around the world.

An *Oakland Tribune* article dated July 16, 2005, by Malaika Fraley described the fateful March 23, 1950, day on which Lt. Colonel Mignola was killed.

The Long Ranger had just taken on 870 gallons of fuel mid-air from a tanker plane and was on its way to simulate a bombing strike on Phoenix at 25,000 feet. According to the accident report, the plane was at 17,000 feet when a gunner reported to the pilot that the No. 3 engine was on fire. Within four seconds, fuel tanks exploded, the right wing dove to the ground, and the plane blew apart. There were 14 people aboard and two members of the crew survived by using their parachutes: a bombardier who was thrown out of the nose section and the co-pilot, who climbed out the window

Lt. Colonel Harold E. Mignola's remains were recovered and interred in the Golden Gate National Cemetery in San Bruno, California.

(USDVA; WRP; June 2, 1942 1:2, March 30, 1943 1:1, March 23, 1950 1:6, Oakland Tribune, July 16, 2005)

June 25 *North Korea invades South Korea; Seoul is overrun two days later.*

June 27 *President Truman orders US troops in the Far East to resist aggression; UN demands North Korea withdraw.*

EDWARD L. McCALL
(1950/07/14)

(Watsonville Register-Pajaronian photo)

McCall was the first Pajaro Valley combat death to occur in the Korean War.

Edward Leonard McCall was born in Seminole, Oklahoma, in 1929, to Edward and Opal McCall. At an early age his mother married Willis Troutt, a railroad fireman and the family moved to Campbell, California, where he and his brother James attended school. The Troutt family later moved to Watsonville.

Edward McCall enlisted in the US army in 1948. After completing basic training at Fort Ord, he was sent to Japan where he joined the 24th Infantry Division. McCall was promoted to corporal and assigned as a truck driver for the 63rd Field Artillery Battalion.

When the Korean War began in June 1950, Edward's unit was sent to South Korea with the initial US contingent. During the UN retreat to Taejon in July 1950, the 63rd FA came under intense attack by the North Korean 16th Regiment at the Kum River.

McCall's unit history chronicles the final period in his life

Enemy reconnaissance obviously had located the support artillery and had bypassed the river line rifle companies to strike at it and the line of communications running to the rear. Now came enemy mortar fire. The first shell hit Headquarters Battery switchboard and destroyed telephone communication to the other batteries. In rapid succession mortar shells hit among personnel of the medical section, on the command post, and then on the radio truck. With the loss of the radio truck all means of electrical communication vanished. An ammunition truck was also hit, and exploding shells in it caused further confusion in Headquarters Battery ... [The] enemy machine guns put bands of fire across both the front and the back doors of the building, which held the Fire Direction Center. The men caught inside escaped to a dugout, crawled up a ravine, and made their way south toward Service Battery. In the excitement of the moment,

apparently no one saw Major Dressler. More than two and a half years later his remains and those of Cpl. Edward L. McCall were found together in a common foxhole at the site.

The remains of Edward L. McCall were identified and returned to the United States where they were interred at Jefferson Barracks National Cemetery in St. Louis, Missouri in March 1953. His awards include the Purple Heart awarded posthumously.

(NARAK; ABMC, WRP July 22, 1950 1:2, March 4, 1953 1:8, March? 1953, May 15, 1953 2:5; 24th Div WD, Disaster at the Kum River Line, Pg. 127 http://www.army.mil/cmh-pg/books/korea/20-2-1/sn10.htm, [16 September 2008])

JULES A. RICHE
(1950/07/21)

(Golden Gate National Cemetery – San Bruno California)

"Son of Local Woman Listed as Casualty" noted the *Santa Cruz Sentinel* article.

Jules Augustus Riche was born to Mrs. Rose C. Riche in New Orleans, Louisiana on April 14, 1923. No additional information regarding his father, siblings or early life is available. His formative years and education, including two years of college, are believed to have taken place in Louisiana. Prior to World War II, Riche worked in the entertainment field.

Jules Riche enlisted in the US Army on June 14, 1942. Following his basic training, he was assigned to an unspecified Philippine scout unit. During or after the war, he was commissioned a second lieutenant, either on the battlefield or through the Officer Candidate School program.

When the Korean War began in June 1950, Riche was serving as a First Lieutenant with the 24th Infantry division, 34th Infantry Regiment stationed in Japan. His mother, Rose, moved to Santa Cruz, was employed by the telephone company as an operator and established residence in the community. Jules apparently listed his mother's address as his residence, although he was reported to have only visited Santa Cruz once before joining his unit in Japan.

When General MacArthur ordered United States ground

troops to Korea after the invasion of South Korea by the Communists in June 1950, the 34th was one of the first units to strike back against the aggressors. The regiment arrived at Pusan on July 2d, and three days later was engaged in combat against the North Korean 4th Division. The 34th Regiment assisted Task Force Smith (Lt. Col. Charles B. Smith), consisting of elements of the 24th Division, in their withdrawal from Osan, where the first ground action between United States and Communist troops took place. On the 7th of July the 34th and other elements of the 24th Division were forced to withdraw from the Pyongtaek and Ansong area. By the 11th, the 34th had fought its way back to the Kum River, three miles north of Kongju, where the 3d Battalion, which had suffered a large number of casualties, was reorganized as a single company. The 34th Infantry participated in the bitter fighting around Taejon for five days and was finally forced to withdraw to the vicinity of Kunwi, on July 23, 1950.

On July 21, 1950, in fighting near Taejon, First Lieutenant Jules Augustus Riche was killed in action. His remains were recovered and returned to California where he was interred in the Golden Gate National Cemetery in San Bruno. His awards include the Purple Heart.

(NARA2; USDVA; ABMC, SCSn August 24, 1950 1:8; NARAK; Corregidor Historic Society, Thirty Fourth Regiment in Korea, 2008 http://www.corregidor.org/rock_force/taromen/history.html, [16 September 2008].)

ROBERT H. SEARLE
(1950/08/10)

(Santa Cruz Sentinel photo)

From the time he was ten years old, Bobby Searle dreamed of attending the US Naval Academy and becoming a naval officer.

Robert Howland Searle was born in Santa Cruz on February 5, 1925, to Dan and Mary Carroll Searle. He attended local schools and in 1938 entered Santa Cruz High School. While in high school, he played on both the basketball and baseball teams and was admitted into the Tong honorary

society. At the time of his graduation in 1942, Searle was offered appointments to both the US Naval Academy and the US Military Academy.

After high school graduation, Searle enrolled in Rutherford Preparatory School in Long Beach followed by the University of California in Berkeley. While at Berkeley, he earned starting positions on the varsity baseball and basketball teams. He entered the US Naval Academy in 1945 and in addition to his midshipmen studies, was a member of the academy's varsity basketball and baseball teams.

Following his graduation from Annapolis in 1949, Searle was commissioned an ensign; he selected naval aviation as his branch. He attended flight school, earned his wings and was assigned to carrier duty. On August 10, 1950, while simulating a carrier landing at Barin Field in Foley, Alabama, Ensign Searle's plane crashed into a group of flight student spectators. Robert Searle was killed instantly and three of the spectators were injured by the crash. His remains were recovered and sent to Golden Gate National Cemetery in San Bruno, California where they were interred.

(USDVA; SCR November 17, 1944 –4, SCSn August 10, 1950 1:1, SCSn August 24, 1950 1:2)

GILBERT L. MARTIN
(1950/08/19)

(Watsonville Register-Pajaronian photo)

"Another Watsonville Man Wounded, Army Casualty List Shows," noted the local press.

Gilbert L. Martin was born in 1924 to Mr. and Mrs. James Martin of Wilson, Oklahoma. Gilbert was raised and educated in that community prior to enlisting in the US Marine Corps during World War II. Following his discharge, he returned to Oklahoma and remained there until the Korean War.

When the Korean War began, Martin enlisted in the US Army and was sent to Fort Ord, California, for training and unit assignment. Being stationed at Ft. Ord provided Gilbert with frequent opportunities to visit his uncle Arthur's family, who lived in the Pajaro Valley community of Freedom. It is likely at this time that he met Gladys, a single mother with two daughters. The couple married and established their home in Freedom.

After completing his Fort Ord training, Private First Class Martin was assigned to the 35th Infantry Regiment of the 25th Infantry Division and was sent to join that unit in Japan.

On 13 July 1950, the 35th Infantry Regiment landed at the southern port city of Pusan, Korea. Commanded by Colonel Henry G. Fisher the Regiment initially set up defensive positions with one battalion near Kyong-ju and the other at Pohang Dong. In August the 25th Division was given the assignment to defend the southwestern sector of the 140-mile Pusan perimeter. The Cacti Regiment was ordered to hold the Chung-ni-Masan route into the Pusan Perimeter. On the 18 August a strong communist attack at 0430 hours hit the 1st Battalion, 35th Infantry. A North Korean battalion struck Company A pushing it back, but reinforced by Company C the battalion line was restored.

On August 19, 1950, Private First Class Gilbert L. Martin was killed in action on the Pusan Perimeter of Korea. When a reporter for the *Watsonville Register-Pajaronian* attempted to interview Gladys for a story about Gilbert, he was refused admittance by her employer, Western Frozen Foods Company in Watsonville and told, "we're short-handed now. I can't take her off the line."

The location of the remains of Gilbert L. Martin has yet to be identified. His awards include the Purple Heart

(ABMC, NARAK, SCSn September 6, 1950; WRP September 7, 1950 1:5; 25th Infantry Division Assoc., 35th Infantry Regiment in Korea, 2005, http://www.25thida.com/35thinf.html#Korea, [16 September 2008])

BOBBY R. POARE
(1950/09/01)

Bobby Ray Poare was born November 9, 1932, in Santa Cruz County to Mr. and Mrs. Clarence Poare. Information regarding his birth, family and early life is not available. Poare spent his formative years in the Pajaro Valley and attended local elementary schools; however, because his home was located on the Monterey County side of the Pajaro River, he attended Salinas High School. Later the family moved to Salinas.

About June 1950, Poare enlisted in the US Marine Corps and was sent to Camp Pendleton to complete his basic and school-of-infantry training. After completing training in August 1950, he was promoted to Private First Class and assigned to Company B, 1st Battalion, 5th Marines of the 1st Provisional Marine Brigade.

Poare's unit sailed from San Diego July 12-14, 1950, arrived

in Japan July 31 and was deployed to Korea upon arrival. On August 2, 1950, the unit experienced combat for the first time while defending the Pusan Perimeter at Masan.

On the first of September, during the North Korea Peoples Army (NKPA) final push, the marines were sent to assist the US Army 9th Infantry in the vicinity of Yongstan. During the fighting that occurred on September 1, 1950, Private First Class Bobby Ray Poare was killed in action.

The location of his remains has not been identified. His awards include the Purple Heart.

(CBR; WRP July 11, 1952 1:1, December 1, 1950 1:5 ABMC, the Korean War Almanac, 5th Marines, 1st Provisional Brigade)

KENNETH J. CANN
(1950/09/02)

(Santa Cruz Sentinel photo)

Kenneth James Cann was born on October 3, 1930, to Mr. and Mrs. Norman Cann in Santa Cruz, California. Kenneth spent his formative years in Santa Cruz. About 1945 he entered Santa Cruz High School and remained at the school for the next two years. After leaving school, he was employed in Santa Cruz by the Birds Eye Frozen Food Plant and at the Casa del Rey Hotel.

In 1948 Kenneth Cann enlisted in the US Army and after completing basic and engineer training, was assigned to the 2nd Engineer Combat Battalion of the 2nd Infantry Division at Ft. Lewis, Washington. When the Korean War began, his battalion was rushed to Korea and arrived on July 23, 1950. Their mission was to hold the North Korean army at the Pusan perimeter line until additional troops could arrive. Cann's battalion provided engineering support for the 2nd division; however, in September, during fierce fighting at the Naktong River, their primary function changed from engineers to infantrymen.

The savage battle raged throughout the day and night of 1-2 September and by 2400 hours on the 1st, the entire Division reserve had been committed including the 2nd Engineer Combat Battalion which saw its first action about 2400 hours on 1 September. Time and time again the engineers were to prove as good at combat as they were in engineering activities.

During the fighting occurring on September 2, 1950, Corporal Kenneth James Cann was killed in action. His body was recovered and interred in the Golden Gate National Cemetery in San Bruno. His awards include the Purple Heart.

(USDVA; ABMC; NARAK; Korean War Veterans Alliance 2nd Infantry Division During the Korean War, 1991, http://www.2id.org/naktongriver.htm, [16 September 2008], SCR September 28, 1950 1:5; SCSn September 14,1951 1:5)

JAMES C. SULLIVAN
(1950/09/19)

(Watsonville Register-Pajaronian photo)

Sullivan wrote his mother after being wounded, "Not to worry, I'll be home by Christmas."

James C. Sullivan, the only child of Mr. and Mrs. J. R. Sullivan, was born in Arizona in 1932. The family later relocated to Fresno in 1943, where he attended Washington Junior High School. Sullivan's parents divorced and James was sent to Watsonville in 1946 to attend St. Francis School. He remained at that school for the next two years, graduated and returned to Fresno where he was employed until the Korean War.

In February 1950, James Sullivan enlisted in the US Army. After completing basic and advanced infantry training, he was assigned to the 29th Regimental Combat Team (RCT) serving on Okinawa. When South Korea was invaded, the 29th RCT was ordered to Korea and arrived there on July 24, 1950. Sullivan's unit's was ordered to contain the North Korean Army (NKA) before it reached the vital port of Pusan. Between July 25 and July 28, they were driven back by the NKA to a point twenty-five miles west of Chinju. By September they had contained the NKA in their sector and were rushed into the Masan corridor.

In the fighting that occurred on September 9, 1950, Private First Class James C. Sullivan was wounded and placed in a hospital in Taegu. On September 19 he died

from his wounds. His body was returned to Watsonville and interred in the Pajaro Valley Memorial Park. His awards included the Purple Heart.

(ABMC; NARAK; WRP September 30, 1950 1:5, December 4, 1951, US Army Center of Military History, Fact Sheet, http://korea50.army.mil/history/factsheets/army.shtml, [16 September 2008] Cemetery Survey May 12, 2008)

GEORGE ASHTON
(1950/09/19)

(Watsonville Register-Pajaronian photo)

George couldn't get the army out of his blood until Korea, where he lost his blood.

George Ashton was born on February 9, 1914, in New Mexico, to Mr. and Mrs. George Ashton. He remained in that state with his parents and brother during his formative years. The family later moved to the Pajaro Valley where George attended Watsonville High School for three years.

Shortly after leaving high school in 1932, Ashton joined the US Army and remained in the service until 1935. After his discharge he returned to Watsonville, married Margaret and was hired by the Watsonville Lumber Company. The couple had two children George Jr. in 1937 and Emilie in 1939.

On July 27, 1942, George re-enlisted in the army in Monterey and served throughout World War II in the Persian Gulf and India. When the war ended, he returned to Watsonville and to his job as a foreman at the lumber company.

In the late 1940s Ashton decided to make the military his career and re-enlisted in the US Army at Fort Ord. He was assigned to the 3rd Engineer Combat Battalion of the 24th Infantry Division and sent to Japan. When the North Koreans attacked South Korea in June 1950, elements of the 24th Infantry Division were the first to arrive in Korea. Their mission was to fight a delaying action against the invading North Koreans.

By the middle of September 1950, UN forces had contained the NKA and were ready to break out of the Pusan Perimeter. The 24th Infantry crossed the Naktong River near Waegwan and during that crossing, which cost him his life, Sergeant First Class Ashton earned a Silver Star. The *Watsonville Register-Pajaronian* issue of May 2, 1951, provided the details of the citation.

The award was made for distinguished action against an armed enemy near Waegwan Korea, Sept. 19, 1950.

The general orders told how Sergeant Ashton, while serving as a boat guide in the assault crossing of the Naktong River, saw that two of his boat crews had been killed or wounded and braved heavy enemy fire to retrieve the boats which were drifting downstream, the citation said. After getting these boats back into operation he observed another boat with a wounded soldier in it drifting downstream. He got two men and went into the river under heavy enemy fire and brought this boat to the friendly shore. Since there were no litter bearers on the beach Sergeant Ashton carried the wounded men across 300 yards of beach, swept by enemy fire, to a point of safety. After returning to the beach and placing four more boats in operation, Sergeant Ashton saw that one of the boat leaders had been wounded. He immediately took his place in the boat and started across the river with a load of infantrymen. A mortar shell struck and exploded in or near the boat fatally wounding Sergeant Ashton and seriously wounding 11 others aboard the boat. Disregarding his wounds, Sergeant Ashton called for aid from the beach for the other wounded men, before losing consciousness.

The remains of Sergeant First Class George Ashton were returned to the United States and buried in the Golden Gate National Cemetery in San Bruno. His other awards included the Purple Heart.

(NARA2; NARAK; ABMC; WRP October 3, 1950 1:6, May 2, 1951 1:1, USDVA)

ROBERT FLOECK
(1950/09/23)

His family dwelling was in Los Angeles, but Robert's home remained in the Pajaro Valley.

Robert Floeck was born on October 13, 1918, in Contra Costa County, California to a Mr. and Mrs. Floeck. Floeck's mother later married Allison Gilbert whose family lived in the Pleasant Valley district of the Pajaro Valley. No additional information is available regarding that family. Robert is said to have spent much of his early life in Santa Cruz County and chose to adopt it as his home.

During World War II, Floeck joined the US Marine Corps where he earned a commission and was trained as a fighter pilot. After the war, he married Patricia and acquired a home in Los Angeles, near his parents, where the couple had a child.

When the Korean War broke out, Robert Floeck had risen to the rank of major and was flying F42-4B Corsair fighters with Marine Fighter Squadron 214. During the war, his unit served aboard the aircraft carrier *USS Sicily*. When the Allies landed at Inchon on September 23, 1950, Major Floeck was ordered to fly a mission from the carrier to Wolmi-do at the entrance to the harbor at Inchon.

The Marines, after the planting of the Stars and Stripes atop Wolmi, worked their way downhill and southward through the thickets and shale cliffs toward the stubborn promontory of Sowolmi-do. Here a die-hard group of North Koreans still held out, using their big guns against Wolmi. On Wolmi's crest Lt. Col. Taplett talked by VHF radio to Strike Charlie, a flight of eight Marine Corsairs led by Maj. Robert Floeck from the jeep carrier Sicily. Taplett requested that the Sowolmi-do lighthouse area be hit. Floeck's planes bore down on the area, and five 500-pound bombs and many rockets showered down into the area.

While flying over nearby Seoul, Major Robert Floeck's aircraft received a direct hit by anti-aircraft fire, burst into flames and crashed. His remains were never recovered. He was awarded the Distinguished Flying Cross with two Gold Stars, the Air Medal with eight Gold Stars and the Purple Heart among other honors.

(CBR; ABMC; NARAK-Casualty List; Wolmi-Do Assault, The Taking of Wolmi-Do, 9/25/2007, http://www.kmike.com/wolmi.htm [16 September 2008]; WRP September 30, 1950 1:5)

JESSE C. JACKSON
(1950/11/15)

(Watsonville Register-Pajaronian photo)

Folks in the Pajaro Valley opened their daily paper on December 6, 1950, to read the news "San Juan Road Soldier killed in Korean War."

Jesse C. Jackson was born in 1927 to Mrs. Nobie Jackson. Jesse grew up in a rural San Juan Road residence and attended school in the Springfield district of the Pajaro Valley.

About 1945 Jessie joined the US Navy and after completing boot camp in San Diego, was assigned to the Pacific

Fleet, where he participated in the Bikini atomic bomb test. After three and a half years of naval service, Seaman Jackson was discharged and returned to the Pajaro Valley.

In 1949 Jesse Jackson enlisted in the US Army. After receiving basic and engineer training, he was assigned to the 2nd Engineer Combat Battalion of the 2nd Infantry Division stationed at Fort Lewis, Washington. When the Korean War began, his unit was rushed to Korea and placed in defense of the Pusan Perimeter. The 2nd Infantry Division was the first to break out of the perimeter and the 2nd Engineers Combat became part of the 9th Regimental Combat team as they moved north across 38th parallel.

The History of the 2nd Infantry Division during the Korean War documents the role of Jackson's unit at the time of his death.

> The 9th RCT, attached to the 1st Cavalry Division, was ordered to capture the city of Pugwon and the high ground west of the Chongchon River on 11 November. It moved out the following day and moved into the toughest battle it had faced since its fight for Hill 201 down on the Naktong River. The fighting raged for three days with Pugwon falling late on the 14th with the 9th then crossing the river and attacking north and west where it established contact with other friendly elements attacking north.

During the fighting on November 15, 1950, Private First Class Jesse C. Jackson was killed in action. The location of his remains has not been identified. Jackson's awards include the Purple Heart.

(ABMC; NARAK; Korean War Veterans Alliance, 2nd Infantry Division During the Korean War, 1991, http://www.2id.org/naktongriver.htm, [16 September 2008]; WRP December 06, 1950)

ERNEST D. BETTENCOURT
(1950/11/27)

(Watsonville Register-Pajaronian photo)

For three years Juanita Bettencourt waited to hear what had become of her husband Ernest.

Ernest David Bettencourt was born in Santa Cruz County, California on May 21, 1928, to Edmond and Evan-geline Bettencourt. During his two years at Watsonville High School, Ernest lived in the rural Interlaken district with his mother and her second husband, Ray Cantonwine. After leaving school, Ernest was employed at a local mortuary.

On February 7, 1946, Bettencourt enlisted in the regular army and was assigned to the Military Police Corps in Hawaii for training. Following basic training, he transferred to the Army Medical Corps and after receiving instruction as a medic, he was stationed in Japan for the next four years. In 1950 he was reassigned to a medical unit attached to the 2nd Engineers Combat Battalion of the 2nd Infantry Division stationed at Fort Lewis, Washington. On July 17, 1950, he and Juanita Churchill of Watsonville were married in Olympia, Washington.

Ernest Bettencourt's unit was shipped to Korea on July 20, 1950. In November the 2nd Engineer Combat Battalion, supported by A Battery of the 503rd Field Artillery Battalion, was fighting on the high ground near the Kunu-ri Anju-Sinanju road in North Korea. It was near that location that Ernest Bettencourt earned his Silver Star. The citation accompanying the award noted that

> On November 27, 1950, Sergeant Bettencourt, a medical corpsman, volunteered for a scouting patrol in enemy territory. While on high ground in the vicinity of Wollyong-ni, Korea, the patrol was attacked by small arms and machine gun fire. The two lead scouts were wounded and five other men in the patrol hit. Sergeant Bettencourt exposed himself to the hail of fire, gave first aid to the men and then supervised their evacuation when the patrol was ordered to withdraw.

In 1951 Juanita received notification that Ernest had won the award and awaited his return to share her excitement, but that would not occur. Soon afterward she received notification that he was missing in action. For the next three years Ernest's fate was unknown. Not until January 1954 did the army confirm his death to Juanita. His body was never recovered. In addition to the Silver Star, Ernest D. Bettencourt was posthumously promoted to Sergeant First Class and awarded the Purple Heart.

(CBR; NARA2; NARAK; ABMC, Korean War Almanac Pg. 242, WRP July 27, 1950 3:4, January 8, 1954 1:5)

DONALD S. MORAN
(1950/11/29)

(Santa Cruz Sentinel photo)

"Felton Soldier Recommended For Promotion For His Action Under Fire In Daring Raid Against Reds" noted the *Santa Cruz Sentinel*.

Donald Stewart Moran was born in Cleveland, Ohio, in 1929, to a Mr. and Mrs. Moran. No information has surfaced as to Donald's childhood or possible siblings. His mother later married Ward Bourgeois, and Donald joined them in their Los Angeles home.

About 1946, Donald Moran enlisted in the US Army, completed basic training and remained in uniform for the next two years. Upon his discharge he moved to the Boulder Creek-Felton area of Santa Cruz County, where his parents had relocated. During the ensuing years, he lived and worked in the San Lorenzo Valley.

Donald Moran re-enlisted in the US Army during the late 1940s. Upon his reentry into the military he was given the rank of corporal and assigned to the 38th Infantry Regiment of the 2nd Infantry Division stationed at Fort Lewis, Washington. His fiancée, Sally Daley of Felton, joined him in Seattle, where the two were married. Moran was sent to Korea in late July 1950 and Sally returned to Felton where she worked at a local bakery.

When the 2nd Infantry Division arrived in Korea on August 4, 1950, the 38th Regiment was ordered to hold a portion of the Pusan Perimeter on the Naktong River. It was at this location in September that Donald Moran earned the Silver Star for action under fire. Moran had earned the award for helping "cover four daring infantrymen with accurate fire that were attempting a swimming raid against barges on the Naktong River." In addition to the award, Moran was promoted to Sergeant.

By November 1950, the 2nd Infantry Division had broken out of the Pusan Perimeter and advanced to within 30 miles of the Yalu River border between North Korea and China. During this period, Donald Moran was promoted to Sergeant First Class.

The Chinese Communist Army officially entered the Korean War on November 29, 1950, and attacked UN forces with an army consisting of 380,000 troops. While attempting to hold off this onslaught near Kunu-ri on November 29, 1950, Sergeant First Class Donald S. Moran became Missing in Action. That classification was officially changed to Presumed Dead on December 31, 1953. For his service in Korea he was posthumously promoted to master sergeant and awarded the Purple Heart with Oak Leaf Cluster. His remains were never recovered.

(ABMC; NARAK; SCSn August 18, 1950 1:2, SCSn January 12, 1951 1:6; 2nd Infantry Division, Korean War Veterans Alliance, Inc, Kunuri, http://www.2id.org/kunuri-history.htm, [16 September 2008])

ROBERT L. THORP
(1950/12/07)

(Santa Cruz High School yearbook)

The body of a local athlete and sailor gave out just as his marriage plans were falling into place.

Robert Lawrence Thorp was born in Santa Cruz, California on January 12, 1929, to Mr. and Mrs. Lawrence J. Thorp. He, along with his brother Wayne and sisters Dorothy and Margaret, spent their formative years in the family home on Stanford Street. Local schools provided him with his elementary education. During his youth, he was an active member in the First Baptist Church. In 1943 Robert Thorp entered Santa Cruz High School, where he was remembered for his athletic ability. He was a member of the high school football team for three years and served as its captain. Thorp graduated from high school in 1947 and was employed as a mechanic by the Santa Cruz Lumber Company in its Felton facility. He kept his football skills honed by playing as a quarterback on the Santa Cruz Seahawks team during their first two seasons.

In May 1948, Robert Thorp enlisted in the US Navy and was sent to San Diego to complete his boot camp training. He was then assigned to the naval air section and received training as an engine repairman. At the completion of his training he reported for duty to the Alameda Naval Air Station.

Thorp was diagnosed with an unspecified medical condition in June 1950, which forced cancellation of his September wedding date with Audrey Thuringer. He was admitted into the Oak Knoll Naval hospital in Oakland where he underwent treatment for his condition. On December 7, 1950, Robert Thorp succumbed to that condition and died. His remains were returned to Santa Cruz for a funeral and interment in Oakwood Memorial Park.

(SCSn December 10, 1950 8:1)

MARION E. RICHARDS
(1950/12/12)

(Santa Cruz High School Service Cardinal)

Eddie went back into the army for one more war, but cancer had other plans for him.

Marion Edgar Richards was born in Santa Cruz, California, on September 17, 1910, to Edgar Allen and Mabel Richards. The Richards family also included another son Clarence and daughters Mildred, Esther and Ferne. Later Mabel remarried and a stepson, Eldred Colwell, was added to the family. Eddie, Marion's nickname, attended local schools and graduated from Santa Cruz High School with the class of 1928. He remained and worked in the county and in the middle 1930s, managed the Mission Drive-In in Santa Cruz.

Richards enlisted in the US Army on June 18, 1942, and was trained at Camp Callen in San Diego County and at Camp McQuaide near Watsonville. During World War II, he also served at Fort Jackson, South Carolina, Fort Bragg, North Carolina, and Camp Gordon, Georgia. On October 9, 1945, after thirty-nine months of service, he was discharged at Camp Gordon, Georgia, as a staff sergeant.

Following his discharge, he returned home where he remained until 1947 when he re-enlisted. During Eddie's second tour, he served in the US Army Ordinance Corps at posts in Adak, Alaska, Japan and Korea, prior to being diagnosed with a brain tumor. When that condition was discovered, Richards was sent to an army hospital in Japan, where he remained until his death on December 12, 1950.

The body of Marion Edgar Richards was returned to the United States and following a local funeral, was interred in Golden Gate National Cemetery in San Bruno.

(USCR, 1920 US Census, CA, Santa Cruz; SCHSC, page 67; USDVA; SCSn December 14, 1950 1:3)

1951

ORVILLE D. MUSICK
(1951/02/06)

"Aromas GI's Body Returned," noted the news article; the tug of his roots pulled him home to Iowa.

Orville D. Musick was born in Des Moines, Iowa, in 1930. His mother's name Gertrude.. While living in Des Moines, the family expanded to include sons Russell, Clifford, William and James and a daughter, Joyce. Sometime during the 1940s, Gertrude moved to Aromas, California, with her sons Orville, William and James. While in the area, she married A. B. Ellison, and Orville acquired two stepbrothers, Robert and Lawrence Ellison. After completing elementary school, Orville enrolled in Salinas High School.

About 1948 Orville Musick enlisted in the US Army. After finishing basic and advanced training, Private Musick became a member of the L Company, 21st Infantry Regiment of the 24th Infantry Division serving in Japan. Over the next two years he rose to the rank of sergeant.

When South Korea was invaded in June 1950, the 21st Infantry Regiment was dispatched to Pusan on July 1-2 1950. Throughout July his division was virtually decimated by the North Koreans at Osan, Cho'nan, Choch'iwon, the Kum River and Taejon. Orville's regiment and the remainder of the division then were regrouped and assigned to the defense of the Naktong Perimeter. For his service during the perimeter defense, breakout and the invasion of North, Korea Musick was awarded the Bronze Star.

When his division advanced into North Korea in the fall of 1950 and reached a point eighteen miles from the Yalu River, they came under heavy attack by the Chinese Army. Over the next two months Musick's regiment was forced to withdraw to the south. On February 6, 1951, his company found itself fighting in the Chonyang area of South Korea. The log of his first sergeant, Howard R. Lumsden, records the final day in the life of Orville Musick.

6 Feb 51 Company began receiving small arms & mortar fire 2130 hrs 5 Feb 51 followed by attempt of enemy to infiltrate. All attacks repulsed until heavy attack supported by automatic weapons & mortar fire forced company to withdraw 0430 hrs 6 Feb 51. Company counter attacked at

0900 hrs & 1030 hrs repulsed by heavy enemy fire Reorganization & counter attacking 1230 hrs supported by heavy FA & mortar fire Company regained positions. Enemy withdrew leaving 50 dead.

Listed among the dead on Sergeant Lumsden's log was the name of Sergeant Orville D. Musick.

On August 21, 1951, the transport *Provo Victory* arrived in San Francisco with 502 bodies of Americans who had lost their lives in Korea. Among them was that of Orville Musick. His remains were sent on to Des Moines, Iowa for burial in his hometown. In addition to the Bronze Star, he was awarded the Purple Heart.

(ABMC; NARAK; *Korean War Almanac* Pg. 181-182, WRP November 13, 1950 2:6, August 28, 1951 1:7; *Lum's Little Black Book*, Morning Report Extract by Jim Fine, http://www. lovecompany.org/extracts.htm, [16 September 2008])

GUY S. READ JR.
(1951/02/19)

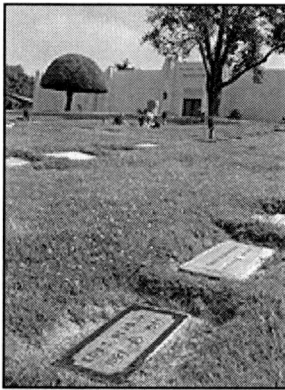

(Pajaro Valley Memorial Park - Watsonville, California)

Guy returned to a home in Watsonville, but it was far different from the one he had left.

Guy Smith Read Jr. was born to Guy and Marie Read in 1921. The location of his birth or information regarding his early life has not been found. He had at least one brother, Richard, living in Cleveland, Ohio, and a stepbrother, Laughlin Rhodes, living in Florida. During World War II, Guy Read served in the regular navy for six years and upon his discharge, settled in Watsonville.

Read was active in the life of the Watsonville community while residing in the Pajaro Valley. He began his career in finance and was employed by the local branch of the Bank of America. Guy and his wife, Marguerite, acquired a home in rural Aromas and in December 1949, a son, Geoffrey, was born to the couple. During his stay in Watsonville, he affiliated with the Watsonville Masonic Lodge and remained active in the US Naval Reserve.

In October 1950, Read was recalled to active duty and sent to the Hawaiian Islands, where he was assigned to a naval finance group. While serving in Hawaii, Tellerman Second Class Guy S. Read Jr. contracted an undisclosed disease or condition that took his life on February 19, 1951. His body was flown home and following a Masonic funeral in Watsonville, was buried with military honors at Pajaro Valley Memorial Park.

(WRP February 22, 1951, March 12, 1951 2:3; Pajaro Valley Cemetery headstone)

ORVILLE W. PIERCE
(1951/04/02)

In 1952 the Ford Ord community began asking itself, "what ever happened to that young officer who helped design Stillwell Hall?" In 1953 they got their answer.

Orville W. Pierce was born in St. Clair County, Illinois, in 1916, and spent most of his early life in that state. He entered the University of Illinois about 1935 and graduated about 1939. While in college, he was probably an ROTC cadet, as he was commissioned a second lieutenant in artillery upon his graduation.

Oroville was stationed with the 74th Field Artillery at Fort Ord, California in 1940 and became one of the designers of Stilwell Hall. Following World War II, he returned to Fort Ord and Watsonville became home to the Pierce family.

In 1950 Major Pierce was sent to Korea to serve as a battery commander of the 503rd Artillery of the 2nd Infantry Division. His family remained in the Pajaro Valley. Upon arrival in Korea, his unit was assigned to the defense of the Pusan perimeter. Following the invasion at Inchon and the subsequent withdrawal of the North Korean Army, his battalion was in the vanguard as US forces made their way to the Yalu River.

On November 30, 1950, the Chinese communist army attacked UN forces with overwhelming force and Major Pierce's battalion was ordered to retreat. The 503rd FA Battalion was assigned to the high ground near Kunu-ri Anju-Sinanju Road to support the retreating division. On December 1, the 503rd FA Battalion was cut off from the division several miles behind enemy lines near Ch'ongnyongch'am. They were surrounded, attacked from all sides and Major Pierce was forced to surrender.

On August 16, 1953, Mrs. Pierce was informed that her husband, Orville, had died on April 2, 1951, while a prisoner of war. The location of the body of Orville Pierce has not been identified.

(NARAK; ABMC; Fort Ord California, History, http://nimst.tripod. com/cgi-bin/FtOrd.html, [16 September 2008] Combat Leadership. com, Maj. Franlich, John US Army, http://www.combatleadership. com/Heroes_Results.asp?MedalID=2376, [16 September 2008]; WRP August 17, 1953 1:1, September 15, 1953 1:1,)

WILLIAM H. WILNER
(1951/06/01)

(Watsonville Register-Pajaronian photo)

Wilner survived the Tiger's March, but in the end the Tiger prevailed.

William Harmon Wilner was born in 1931 to Mr. and Mrs. Charles Wilner. In 1932 Charles moved his wife, son William and daughter Nora to Watsonville, California where he found employment with the Watsonville Laundry and Dry Cleaning Company. William attended local elementary schools and later enrolled in Watsonville High School. His mother died in 1946 while he was still a high school student. Wilner remained in school for the next two years before dropping out.

William enlisted in the US Army on August 7, 1948. After completing basic and advanced training, he was assigned to Company I, 3rd Battalion, 21st Infantry Regiment, 24th Infantry Division serving in Japan. In July 1950 when South Korea was invaded, his unit was rushed to Korea to hold the perimeter line protecting Pusan. William's battalion was located near Chochiwon, South Korea, and during the fighting on July 11, 1950, the North Koreans captured him.

Wilner and the other prisoners were moved from one location to another until October 31, 1950, when they began the infamous Tiger Death March. The march, named for a brutal North Korean major whom the prisoners called the "Tiger" was one in which prisoners were forced to march 108 miles through the mountainous regions of Korea with no heat, food or medical attention. Some of the prisoners were sent to a camp at Hanjang-ni, while William and others continued on to another camp at An-Dong.

During the winter of 1950-51, over 300 of the prisoners died of malnutrition and dysentery and were buried in mass graves in the prison camps near the Yalu River. Included among them was Corporal William Harmon Wilner who died on June 1, 1951. His body was never recovered.

(ABMC; NARAK; US POWs in Korea - Johnson's List: Readers Digest Magazine - by Malcolm McConnell, http://www.lordhenry. com/johnson.htm, [16 September 2008]; WRP August 28, 1950 1:8)

KARL L. POLIFKA
(1951/07/01)

(Internet photo)

No other Santa Cruz County war casualty equals Karl Polifka in national recognition.

Karl Lewis Polifka entered the world in Blessing, Texas, on December 1, 1910. He was the son of Charles and Pauline Polifka, who had moved to South Texas from New Mexico in October of that year. The Polifka family also included sons Leo, Joseph, Karl and Frank and daughter Helen.

About 1919, Charles Polifka moved his family to Watsonville, California and settled into a home on the Santa Cruz highway. During the early 1920s, Karl completed his elementary school education in the Pajaro Valley and entered Watsonville High School. Throughout his high school years he excelled on the school's football team, performed well scholastically and worked part time for the local newspaper. Polifka graduated from high school about 1929.

After high school, Karl studied pre-medicine for the next three years at the University of California and at the University of Texas. At this time, he became interested in flying and was known in the Watsonville area for his daredevil antics.

On October 18, 1931, Karl Polifka married Helen Elizabeth Gregg. Over the ensuing years Karl and Helen resided and worked in Santa Cruz County before moving to Oregon. During their two years in the Pacific Northwest, he was employed in the construction business.

In 1938 Polifka was accepted into the Army Air Corps cadet training program. After completing basic and flight instruction, he was commissioned a second lieutenant and awarded his wings. In 1940 the Army Air Corps sent him to its photography school to prepare him for air reconnaissance. From 1940-1942 Karl was stationed at Moffett Field, California, Fort Lewis, Washington, and Fort Richardson, Alaska, where he mapped air routes in Alaska and Western Canada. During this period, a son, Karl Lewis Polifka Jr., was born to Karl and Helen.

Polifka gained national fame in 1942 while flying an

unarmed P-38 over the Pacific to obtain photos of enemy naval activities. On one occasion he spotted a number of Japanese vessels that turned out to be the main Japanese battle force steaming across the Pacific. That fleet was defeated at the Battle of the Coral Sea as a result of the information that he provided. He continued to defy enemy aircraft in order to take over 1500 photographs of their activities at Guadalcanal.

On several occasions local residents found Polifka's name appearing in such journals as the *New York Daily News*. In January 1943, an article by correspondent James Cullinane recounted one of Polifka's exploits.

"Pop" Polifka, as he was now called, was sent to North Africa and then assigned to Italy where he headed up the Mediterranean Allied Photo Reconnaissance Command. While in Italy, another article, this time in *Time* magazine reported:

"Pop" Polifka was grounded. He fought like a stuck pig to dice Cassino, said an officer on Lieut. General Ira Eaker's staff in Italy, "but the General just wouldn't let him go on another mission." Pop, who is 33-year-old Colonel Karl L. Polifka, had been "dicing" (mapping territory by aerial photography) for years, had flown 125 missions over enemy-held territory, both German and Jap. Eaker figured Pop was too valuable to lose, thought he had better ground him before Pop's luck ran out.

During World War II, Karl Polifka ran up the exceptional total of 173 missions from bases in Australia, New Guinea, North Africa, England and Guam and became Watsonville's most decorated war hero. He was the holder of the Distinguished Service Cross, Silver Star, Legion of Merit, *Croix de Guerre* with gold star and palm, the presidential unit citation with five oak leaf clusters and others; eventually, he received every US award for valor except the Congressional Medal of Honor.

In February 1945, Karl returned to the Pacific Theater as an air intelligence officer for the 10th Army in Okinawa and following VJ Day, was sent to Washington, D. C., to serve on the army-navy operational review board and at the Navy Staff College.

When the Korean War began, Polifka was given command of the 67th Tactical Reconnaissance Wing, which by April 1951, had flown over 3000 missions.

On July 1st, 1951, Colonel Karl L. Polifka was flying an F-51 near Kaesong, Korea, just south of the 38th Parallel. He sighted some enemy ground activity and descended to take a closer look. He circled the area keeping a keen look out and mentally recording all he saw. He noticed the flashes of the small arms fire; but paid it no particular heed until he felt his Mustang shudder with the impact of several bullets.

He fought with the controls as the aircraft began to fall out of the sky; but it was no use. He had to bail out. He released his canopy and exited the spinning aircraft. Unfortunately, his opening parachute caught on the fuselage and he went down with the aircraft, impacting with the ground and dying instantly. The following day air rescue recovered his body."

At the time of his death, Polifka's promotion to brigadier general was before President Truman for approval.

In 1997, forty-six years after his death, a special honor was prepared for Karl Polifka. A new three-million-dollar headquarter building at Kelly Air Force Base in Texas was dedicated in his honor. A special portrait of him was completed and was hung inside the building. Unveiling the portrait of his father during the ceremony was Retired Colonel Karl L Polifka Jr.

Colonel Karl Lewis Polifka is buried at Golden Gate National Cemetery in San Bruno, California.

(ABMC; USDVA; WRP May 19, 1942 1:1, January 26, 1943 1:3, July 6, 1951 1:1; Mary E R Bell Deutchburg History. Polifka' http://www.rootsweb.ancestry.com/~txmatago/deutschburg_hist7. htm, [16 September 2008]; The 67th Tactical Reconnaissance Wing in Korea 1951 - 1954 by Doug Gordon, 2002 http://www.cottonpickers.org/the_67th_tactical_reconnaissance_ wing_in_korea,_1951-1954.htm, Global Security.org, Air Force News, http://www.globalsecurity.org/intell/library/news/1997/ n19970819_971030.html, [16 September 2008])

MELVIN C. WARWICK
(1951/08/17)

(Santa Cruz Sentinel photo)

Mel found the Texas heat was indeed very hot.

Melvin C. Warwick was born in Fresno, California, on January 23, 1931, to Mr. and Mrs. Clarence Elmo Warwick and was raised and educated in California's Central Valley. After Melvin graduated from high school in Fresno, the Warwick family moved to Santa Cruz County and settled in the San Lorenzo valley community of Felton.

In mid July 1951, Warwick enlisted in the US Air Force, was sent to Lackland Air Force Base in San Antonio, Texas, and assigned to the basic military training group. Melvin, who was a large man standing 6 feet in height and weighing 220 pounds, wrote home that he was well, liked service life and the training schedule, but found the temperature very hot.

On August 17, 1951, Melvin Warwick's training company was scheduled to undergo a four-mile march at the Lackland facility; however, he only made it half way through the exercise before complaining of feeling dizzy. He was taken to the base hospital where they attempted to lower his temperature from 107 degrees, but Warwick failed to respond and died from heat stroke.

His remains were returned home and following his funeral service, were interred at Golden Gate National Cemetery in San Bruno.

(USDVA; SCSn August 19, 1951 1:6)

RICHARD R. MANCEBO
(1951/08/31)

(Felton Cemetery – Felton, California)

Although he never returned, Richard's memory is preserved in the Felton Cemetery.

Richard Rodney Mancebo was born in Santa Cruz, California, on March 12, 1928, and is believed to have been the son of Mr. & Mrs. John V. Mancebo, who had immigrated from St. George in the Azores. Nothing has been uncovered relative to his siblings or the formative years of his life. At the time of his draft registration in March 1946, he was living in San Diego, California. Mancebo indicated on his enlistment forms that he was single, had completed three years of high school and was employed in the metal finishing trade.

On March 15, 1946, Richard enlisted in the regular army in Los Angeles and requested duty in the Field Artillery branch in Hawaii. Following his basic training, he was assigned to Company B, 38th Infantry Regiment, of the 2nd Infantry Division stationed at Fort Lewis, Washington. Records at the Felton Cemetery in California suggests that during this period he may have married Jean and that a daughter was born to the couple in 1948.

Following the invasion of South Korea in June 1950, the 2nd Infantry Division was hurriedly dispatched to

Korea and arrived at Pusan on July 23, 1950. The division relieved the 24th Infantry Division on the Naktong River line and remained there until the breakout in late August 1950. When UN forces moved into North Korea, the 2nd Infantry advanced to Kunu-ri near the Yalu river boundary between Korea and China.

When the Chinese entered the war in November 1950, Mancebo's unit began retreating south and during April and May 1951, was located near the Chuchon Basin on Hill 1051.

During the Chinese Spring offensive May 17, 1950, Sergeant Richard R. Mancebo was captured by the Chinese and held in a prisoner of war camp until his death on August 31, 1951. His remains were never recovered.

A headstone in the Felton California cemetery was later erected in the family plot to remember him.

(CBR; ABMC; NARA2; NARAK; 2nd Inf Div, 38th Inf Regt. Korea,
http://www.2id.org/may-massacre.htm, http://www.2id.org/2-38-m.htm, [16 September, 2008]; Rootsweb.com, Felton Cemetery http://ftp.rootsweb.com/pub/usgenweb/ca/santacruz/cemeteries/felton.txt, [16 September 2008])

DANIEL P. MURPHY
(1951/09/03)

(Watsonville Register-Pajaronian photo)

"He was a MAN beyond a doubt."

Daniel Patrick Murphy was born in Watsonville, California, on October 21, 1927, to Mr. and Mrs. M. M. Murphy. He shared the Murphy home with his parents, a brother and three sisters. Murphy spent his formative years in Watsonville and attended local schools. In 1945 he graduated from Watsonville High School and enrolled in Santa Clara University. While at SCU, he entered the ROTC program and upon his graduation was commissioned a second lieutenant. In 1949 Murphy enrolled in Hastings Law School in San Francisco; however, before he could complete the program the Korean War began. He was called to active duty on November 4, 1950, and sent to Fort Sill, Oklahoma, where he was trained as an artillery officer. On February 19, 1951, while stationed at Fort Sill, Daniel married Marjorie Bakich of Watsonville.

Lt. Murphy arrived in Korea on July 12, 1951, and was assigned as a forward observer with the 49th Field Artillery Battalion of the 7th Infantry Division. At the time he joined his unit they were serving in the central front of Korea in the Yangu-Ije-Hwachon area.

On Sept 3, 1951, Second Lieutenant Daniel P. Murphy was attached to Company I, of the 17th Infantry at a time when it was were experiencing an intense mortar barrage by the Chinese. For his part in the ensuing action he was awarded the Silver Star. The accompanying citation read:

Immediately, Lt. Murphy exposed himself to the bursting rounds to move to a position that afforded better observation and from where he could direct accurate counter fire. When forward elements of Company I were overrun by the enemy and his position endangered by infiltration, Lt. Murphy refused to leave and remained in his position until his radio was destroyed by an enemy grenade.

Forced to abandon his position, Lt. Murphy, armed with a carbine, offered his services as an infantryman and while fighting in the command post area, was mortally wounded by an exploding grenade.

The body of Lieutenant Murphy was returned home accompanied by his brother-in-law Capt. Frank Osmer. Following its arrival in December 1951, a funeral was held at St. Patrick's church in Watsonville and Daniel was interred in the Valley Catholic cemetery in the Pajaro Valley.

In February 1952 a letter arrived in the Murphy home from Sergeant Robert W. Turek, Lt. Murphy's reconnaissance sergeant, who was with him when he died. Sgt. Turek wrote,

I was his recon sergeant, and believe me I was proud to be with him wherever we went. Yes, I was with him when he got killed...In the evening after the sun had gone down, we used to talk of home and all our loved ones...Please accept this letter as a token of a guy I'll never forget. He was a MAN beyond a doubt.

In addition to the Silver Star, Daniel Murphy was awarded the Purple Heart and other awards.

(CBR; ABMC; NARAK; WRP February 27, 1951 3:1, September 21, 1951, 1:1 December 1, 1951, February 4, 1952)

CHARLES R. COMPTON
(1951/09/12)

(Pajaro Valley Memorial Park – Watsonville, California)

"Strawberry Valley Youth Dies in Korea," reported the Watsonville *Register-Pajaronian.*

Charles R. Compton was born in Fresno, California, on December 2, 1928, to Mr. and Mrs. J. E. Compton. The Compton family later moved to the Strawberry Valley portion of the Pajaro Valley where he and his sisters, Lucille and Helen, were raised. Compton attended the Lake Elementary School followed by Salinas High School. After leaving Salinas High School, he joined the state division of forestry and for the next seven years served at the Castroville, Moss Landing, Carmel Hill and Alma forestry stations.

Charles Compton was drafted into the US Army on December 20, 1950, spent his first three weeks of basic training at Ford Ord and completed his training at Camp Roberts, California. After a short leave at home, he was shipped to Japan on May 21, 1951. Two days after his arrival he was deployed to Korea. Compton was assigned as an automatic rifleman with the 27th Regimental Combat Team of the 25th Infantry Division assigned to Kumwha in what was referred to as the "Iron Triangle" sector.

When armistice negotiations began on 10 July 1951, the war entered a new stage. The lines became static, with limited objective attacks and probing tank-infantry patrols replacing sweeping offensives. In mid-July the 25th Division returned to the front line, and by the end of the month was in its previous positions in the Ch'orwon-Kumhwa area. The division occupied these positions until mid-December, conducting frequent patrols and several company-sized raids to destroy enemy bunkers. The division also improved its own defensive positions. Artillery bombardments of enemy lines and ambushes of enemy patrols were also common activities.

On September 12, 1951, while fighting in North Korea, Private Charles R. Compton was killed in action. His body was recovered, returned to the US and following a funeral, was interred in the Pajaro Valley Memorial Park.

His awards include the Purple Heart.

(ABMC; NARAK; WRP September 25, 1951 1:1, WRP December

1, 1951 1:1; History.Army.Mil, 25th Infantry Division in Korea, http://www.army.mil/cmh-pg/documents/Korea/25id-KW-IP.htm, [16 September 2008])

ALEX G. FILOMENO
(1951/09/17)

(Co E 2nd Btn 5th Rgt. 1st Marines - Internet photo)

Alex Filomeno was a member of Company E, 2nd Battalion, 5th Regiment of the 1st Marine Division, pictured above, which is the most highly decorated battalion in the history of the US Marine Corps.

Alex Garcia Filomeno was born in Salinas, California, on March 17, 1928, to Mr. and Mrs. Alex G. Filomeno. Young Alex, along with his brother Robert and sisters Helen and Esther, was raised in the Pajaro Valley and attended local schools. Filomeno enrolled in Salinas Union High School but left before graduating.

In 1946 Alex enlisted in the US Marine Corps. While serving with the Marines, he continued his studies and received his Salinas High School diploma in 1948. On March 4, 1949, Filomeno was discharged from the marines and immediately re-enlisted.

In June 1950 Private First Class Filomeno was assigned as a rifleman in Easy Company, 2nd Battalion of the 5th Marine Regiment of the 1st Marine Division stationed at Camp Pendleton, California. In July, E Company shipped out aboard the transport *USS George Clymer* that was quickly dubbed "Greasy George" when it arrived in Pusan Korean on August 2, 1950.

During the Korean War, Alex Filomeno and his unit were exposed to numerous combat engagements. They assisted in holding the Pusan perimeter, participated at the famous landing at Inchon and fought at places called No Name Ridge, Naktong Bulge and hills merely identified by numbers. Their grueling experience at the Chosin Reservoir earned them a place in Marine Corps history. Robert Highland, a fellow 'E' company member, shares what Alex Filomeno experienced at that famous location,

> At the Reservoir on November 27th, and 28th, of 1950, all hell broke loose as the Chinese Army hit us with 120 Thousand Troops, we the Marines numbered fifteen Thousand. This was nine enemy Divisions against one Marine Division. My platoon led by Second Lieutenant Jack Nolan was right in the middle of their charge, somehow our company held that charge and later it was to be named after our company "Easy Alley." During the breakout from the reservoir the 2nd Bn. 5th Marines was given the rear guard.

After fighting their way out of the Chosin area, E company moved to the Masan area where they were engaged at the battles of Hwachon and the Hook before being placed in reserve.

On September 13, the battalion was ordered to take part in Operation Windmill in the Punchbowl Sector of South Korea. In fighting at that location on September 17, 1951, Private First Class Alex Garcia Filomeno was killed in action. His body was buried in the Golden Gate National Cemetery at San Bruno. Included among his awards are the Silver Star and the Purple Heart.

(ABMC; USDVA; Robert Highland, Easy Company, 2nd Battalion, 5th Marine Regiment, 1st Marine Division, USMC http://members.aol.com/famjustin/Highlandbio.html, [16 Sept 2008]; WRP October 1, 1951 1:4, December 26, 1951 1:5)

ARCHIE N. WALTERS
(1951/09/23)

(Santa Cruz Sentinel photo)

An unplanned stop in George L. White's grazing field kept Archie from flying in Korea.

Archie Norman Walters was born on April 3, 1926, in Fresno County, California. His mother's name was Viola Walters. The town of his birth or information regarding his parents and siblings is not available. Walters completed elementary and secondary schools presumably in the Fresno area. He was only able to complete one year at Fresno State College before World War II called him to service.

Archie enlisted in the US Army at San Pedro, California, in 1944. After his discharge in 1945, he and his mother moved to Santa Cruz, established a residence on Fairview Avenue and were living there prior to the Korean War.

Walters entered the US Air Force Air Cadet program and completed basic instruction in 1950. After finishing advanced pilot training, he was commissioned a second lieutenant and sent to Reese Air Force Base near Lubbock, Texas, for additional instruction.

On September 23, 1951, Second Lieutenant Archie N. Walters and Second Lieutenant William H. Malone of Pasadena, California were on a routine training mission when their aircraft developed engine trouble and plowed into George White's ranch field eleven miles northwest of Levelland, Texas. Both officers were killed in the crash. Archie's remains were recovered and following a funeral service in Santa Cruz, were buried in Oakwood Memorial Park.

(CBR; NARA2; SCSn September 24, 1951 1:5; Oakwood Cemetery headstone)

JOSEPH J. FUGATE
(1951/10/17)

(Santa Cruz Sentinel photo)

Jesse was one battle short of a rotation home.

Joseph Jesse Fugate was born in Fresno, California, on December 24, 1929, to Mr. and Mrs. Archie B. Fugate. The Fugate family also included a son Edward and a daughter Grace. He and his siblings were raised and attended school in California's Central Valley. The Fugate family later moved to Santa Cruz in order to live closer to Mrs. Fugate's parents.

In March 1951, Jesse received his induction notice and returned to Fresno where he enlisted in the US Army. After completing basic and advanced training, he was shipped to Korea on August 6, 1951, to join the 8th Cavalry Regiment

of the 1st Cavalry Division.

When Private Fugate joined his unit, it had been in Korea for 500 days and was in a reserve position preparing to move against Line Jamestown.

On 05 October, the 8th Cavalry recaptured Hill 418, a flanking hill on which the northern end of Line Jamestown was anchored. On 10-11 October the Chinese counterattacked twice, unsuccessfully against the 7th Cavalry. Two days later, the 8th Cavalry took the central pivot of the line, Hill 272. The southern end of Line Jamestown, along with a hill called "Old Baldy" [Hill 341], eventually fell to the determined 8th Cavalry troopers. The troopers did not know it, but Line Jamestown would be their last major combat of the Korean War.

On October 17, 1951, Private First Class Joseph Jesse Fugate was killed in action while fighting the enemy near "Old Baldy" [Hill 346]. His body was recovered and returned to Fresno for burial. His awards include the Purple Heart.

(CBR; ABMC, NARAK; SCSn February 3, 1952 2:3; History. Army.Mil, .25th Infantry Division in the Korean War

http://www.first-team.us/journals/8th_rgmt/8thndx03.html)

VERNON J. PESENTI
(1951/11/07)

(San Lorenzo High School yearbook)

Vernon missed celebrating his twenty-second birthday by one week.

Vernon Joseph Pesenti was born in San Francisco, California, on November 24, 1929, to Mr. and Mrs. Anthony Pesenti. His sister Phyllis and brothers Victor and Norman joined him in the family. Vernon was raised in the San Lorenzo Valley where he attended San Lorenzo Valley High School and was a member of the Cougar football team.

Following his graduation from high school in 1948, Pesenti joined the US Air Force. After completing basic and advanced training at Lackland AFB, Texas, Airman Pesenti was assigned to a radar post in Alaska. During his USAF tour, he was promoted to the rank of Staff Sergeant.

While flying aboard a C-47 out of Elmendorf AFB, Alaska, on November 7, 1951, Staff Sergeant Vernon J. Pesenti was killed when the plane crashed. His remains were returned to California and following a military funeral, were interred in Golden Gate National Cemetery in San Bruno.

(CBR; SCSn November 9, 1951 1:4, USDVA; SLVHS Yearbook)

EUGENE J. ROGERS
(1951/12/09)

Eugene Rogers was a US Marine who declared Santa Cruz to be his home; however, record of his residency has not been confirmed. California birth records indicate that Eugene Jerome Rogers was born on May 3, 1930, in Sacramento County, California. Information regarding his birth, family, formative years or military career is not available.

The American Battlefield Monument Commission records indicate that Rogers listed Santa Cruz, California, as his residence when he enlisted in the US Marine Corps. Those records also revealed that "Corporal Rogers was a member of a 4.2" Mortar Company, 7th Marines, 1st Marine Division" and that he was killed in action while fighting the enemy in Korea on December 9, 1951.

All that can be added to this fact is a brief synopsis of the activities of that unit at the time of his death.

On August 17, 1950 the 7th Marines were again activated for service. On September 15, the 1st Marine Division, with the 7th Marines in Reserve, landed at the port city of Inchon. Once the port was secured, the 7th Marines landed and took over the drive for Seoul. For 5 days, the 7th Marines fought against the communist North Korean forces and entered the capital city of Seoul. In bitter house-to-house fighting, the city quickly fell to the Marines and the communists were driven north. In October the 1st Marine Division landed at Wonson. After liberating the port, the Marines began their drive north to the Chosin Reservoir to either capture or destroy a key hydroelectric plant. By November 15, the Marines had reached the southern tip of the reservoir. Then all hell broke loose. Eight Chinese communist Divisions stormed out of the mountains and attacked the 1st Marine Division. The Marines began to withdraw just as winter set in. For four weeks, the Marines fought through seventy-eight miles of mountain roads in icy winter conditions all the while battling the Chinese forces.

The location of the remains of Eugene Jerome Rogers is not known. His awards include the Purple Heart.

(ABMC, Baker-one-seven.com, History of the 7 Marine Regiment

http://www.bakeroneseven.com/7thregiment.htm, [16 Sept. 2008])

ERNEST L. MATHEWS
(1951/12/27)

(Watsonville Register-Pajaronian photo)

"'Bobo' Mathews, Who Never Lost Hope, Succumbed" noted the local newspaper.

Ernest L. Mathews was born in the Pajaro Valley in 1929, to Mr. and Mrs. Frank Mathews. He was raised in a family that included one sister and three brothers. Bobo, as he came to be known, spent his formative years in the rural community of Aromas and attended local schools. About 1942 he entered Watsonville High School; however, record of his graduation has not been confirmed. After leaving high school, he was employed by the Granite Construction Company in Watsonville where he continued to work until 1951.

In early 1951 Ernest Mathews was inducted into the US Army. After completing basic training, he received instruction as a light weapons infantryman at an unspecified camp.

Corporal Mathews was sent to Korea during the summer of 1951. Upon arrival he was assigned to the 7th Cavalry Regiment of the 1st Cavalry Division. To his surprise Bobo discovered that Peter Vojvoda, an old friend from Watsonville, was also a member of that unit. In July 1951 the 1st Cavalry was located in the hills of North Korea a few miles north of the 38th Parallel. During this period, the regiment fought a month-long series of engagements in an area known as the Punchbowl, that included battles at places with names like Pork Chop Hill, Old Baldy and Heartbreak Ridge.

On October 3, 1951, in action taking place near Heartbreak Ridge, Ernest and Peter were sharing a foxhole when a mortar shell exploded nearby. Mathews instinctively shielded Vojvoda from the blast and although both were injured, Peter was able to carry Ernest back to the American lines.

Mathews was hospitalized in Japan and later flown to Letterman hospital in San Francisco. At the hospital doctors informed him that shrapnel had severed his spinal cord and that there was little chance that he would walk again. Throughout December Bobo's condition worsened and sfter Christmas dinner with his parents at the hospital on December 27, 1951, Corporal Ernest L "Bobo" Mathews died. His body was returned to Watsonville and following a funeral, was interred in Watsonville Catholic Cemetery.

(NARAK; WIKI, Battle of Heartbreak Ridge, WRP December 28, 1951 1:1, December 29, 1951 2:4)

RICHARD J. MULHOLLAND
(1951/12/30)

(Watsonville Register-Pajaronian photo)

Two pals joined a third buddy after serving as his pallbearers during a Christmas holiday.

Richard James Mulholland was born in Watsonville, California, on August 26, 1928, to Mr. and Mrs. Maurice J. Mulholland. Richard spent his formative years in the Pajaro Valley and attended Watsonville elementary schools. At an early age his parents divorced and his father remarried providing him with two half sisters and a half brother. During his high school years, Mulholland moved to Carmel where he attended Carmel High School and played on the football team.

In 1948 Richard Mulholland enlisted in the United States Navy for a three-year hitch that was extended to four due to the Korean War. The naval vessel or facility to which Richard Mulholland was attached is not known. During his naval service, he attained the rank of petty officer third class.

Petty Officer Mulholland returned home in December 1951 for the Christmas holidays and was looking forward to spending time with his family and his Carmel High School buddy, Nelson S. Byers, an Annapolis midshipman. During that leave, the two friends were called to serve as pallbearers at the funeral of Dennis MacKenzie, a friend who had been a West Point cadet.

When the time came for the two young men to return to their respective naval units, Byers arranged a flight for both

of them aboard an army C-47 transport. On December 30, 1951, the plane crashed into the Superstition Mountains of Arizona and all aboard were killed. The location of Richard Mulholland's remains has not been identified.

(CBR; WRP, January 7, 1952 9:1)

DONALD L. EHELER
(1951/12/31)

"Army Reports Donald Eheler died in Red Hospital," announced the *Santa Cruz Sentinel.*

Donald LeRoy Eheler was born on November 2, 1928, in Alameda County, California, to Clarence and Bertha Eheler. During the 1930s, Bertha, accompanied by Donald and his brothers Glenn and Ralph, moved into the home of her parents, Mr. and Mrs. Ralph Nakken, in Santa Cruz. Don grew up in Santa Cruz in the late 1930s, attending Gault Elementary School and Branciforte Junior High School. While he was at Santa Cruz High School, his mother remarried and Don moved to Coulee City, Washington.

After leaving high school in that Eastern Washington community, Eheler went to Oregon and worked for two years before moving to Kitsap County, Washington, near Seattle.

In the fall of 1950 Donald Eheler was drafted into the US Army and sent to a basic training facility. After completing training as a light weapon infantryman, Corporal Eheler was sent to Korea and assigned to Company B, 1st Battalion, 5th Cavalry Regiment of the 1st Cavalry Division. When he joined his unit following the 1951 Chinese spring offensive, it was located near the 38th parallel.

In September 1951, the Fifth Cavalry Regiment moved into the Punchbowl area just across the North Korean border. On the night of October 7, 1951, Corporal Donald L. Eheler volunteered for a reconnaissance and raiding party into enemy lines and never returned. It was later discovered that he had been captured, imprisoned in a POW camp and died on December 31, 1951. His body was never recovered.

(ABMC; NARAK; The Korean War Almanac Page 120, SCSn November 30, 1951, January 28, 1954 1:4)

1952

CHESTER C. JOHNSON
(1952/01/14)

(Watsonville High School yearbook)

A World War II pilot returned with his flying skills to a navy plane that let him down.

Chester C. Johnson was born on March 19, 1921, in Santa Clara County, California, to Mr. and Mrs. Hans P. Johnson of the Springfield district of the Pajaro Valley. Hans owned a farm and Chester and his brother, Mervin, performed chores while attending local schools. Chester enrolled in Watsonville High School about 1935. During his high school years, Chester was on the archery team, in the scholarship club and served as drum major for the band before graduating in 1939.

In September 1942, Chester Johnson was drafted and went into the US Navy where he was trained and commissioned an ensign. He then received additional instruction that qualified him to fly navy Liberator bombers. During World War II, Lt. (jg) Johnson flew as a co-pilot on a Liberator during the campaigns at Iwo Jima, Okinawa and the Philippines. For his services he was awarded the Distinguished Flying Cross.

Following the war, Chester Johnson returned to the Pajaro Valley where he married Clara Schmiel, also of the Springfield district. In 1949 the couple had a daughter, Susan. His parents and brother moved to Venice, California, and it is believed that Chester and his family joined them in Southern California.

Johnson remained in the Naval Reserve and when the Korean War began, was recalled to active duty. Lt. Johnson reported to the navy patrol squadron VP-871 stationed at the Alameda Naval Air Station; and his wife and child joined him in the bay area.

In early January 1952, Lt. Johnson received orders assigning him to Patrol Bomber Squadron 772 based at Asugi, Japan, and he departed about January 10, 1952. On January 14, 1952, Chester Johnson was a crewmember aboard a PB4Y-2S Privateer patrol bomber flying out of the naval station when the aircraft developed double engine failure and crashed four miles east of Asugi. The crash killed Lieutenant Chester C. Johnson and the other eleven crewmembers. The location of his remains, if recovered, has not been identified.

(CBR; ABMC, WRP January 17, 1952 1:4)

MAKIO W. KIZUKA
(1952/02/12)

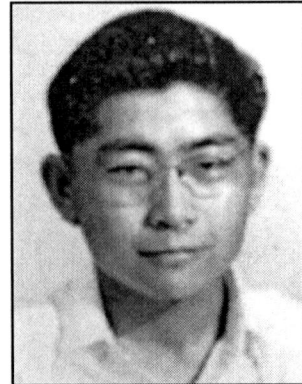

(Watsonville High School yearbook)

"Bill Kizuka Dies at Naval Hospital" announced the *Watsonville Register-Pajaronian*.

Makio William "Bill" Kizuka was born in Watsonville, California, on April 22, 1931, to Mr. and Mrs. T. Kizuka. His parents had emigrated from Japan and his father worked in the Pajaro Valley as a farm operator-manager. Also included in the Kizuka family were his brother Shige and sister Lillian. In the spring of 1942 he was evacuated with his family to the Japanese-American internment camp near Poston, Arizona. Following the war, the family returned to the Pajaro Valley and Kizuka entered Watsonville High School, where he graduated in 1949. After high school, he enrolled in Hartnell College in Salinas, completing its two-year program in 1951.

In June of 1951, Makio joined the US Navy and attended boot camp at the US Naval Training Center at San Diego. After completing basic training, Seaman First Class Makio "Bill" Kizuka remained at the naval facility in San Diego where he suffered a heart attack that took his life on February 12, 1952.

Makio "Bill" Kizuka's remains were returned to Watsonville and following a funeral service at the Westview Presbyterian Church, were buried in Pajaro Valley Memorial Park.

(CBR; NARA2, WWII Japanese Internment Records; WRP February 16, 1952 1:1, Pajaro Valley Cemetery headstone)

RICHARD A. BOYD
(1952/02/15)

(Watsonville High School yearbook)

The "Gun Wound Caused Korea Vet's Death" heading in a local news article alerted Watsonville of the death of "Tex."

Richard Allen Boyd was born on March 3, 1933, to Mr. and Mrs. William E. Boyd. Also sharing the family home on Palm Avenue in Watsonville were his sisters Dorothy Jean and Sue Carole, a brother William Jr. and a stepbrother, Henry Campbell. His father was employed as a pressman by the *Watsonville Register-Pajaronian* newspaper. Boyd attended local elementary schools and about 1948 entered Watsonville High School.

In April 1951 Richard Boyd left high school to enlist in the US Army. "Tex" Boyd, as he was familiarly known, received his basic training at Fort Ord, California and later received instruction qualifying him as a member of a heavy mortar team. In September 1951, he was assigned to Company H, 2nd Battalion, 35th Infantry Regiment of the 25th Infantry Division serving in Korea.

Boyd arrived in Korea just as the armistice was getting underway.

When armistice negotiations began on 10 July 1951, the war entered a new stage. The lines became static with limited objective attacks replacing major offensives. In mid-July the Tropic Lightning [35 Regiment] returned to the front line in its previous positions in the Ch'orwon-Kumhwa area. In October 1951 the 35th Infantry was pulled off the line for rest and training that lasted until 7 November 1951 when the 35th moved back to the front line. In mid-December 1951 the 2nd Division relieved the 25th Division which then moved into reserve near Kapyong.

On February 25, 1952, Mr. and Mrs. William Boyd received a telegram from the Defense Department informing them of the death of their son, Private First Class Richard Allen Boyd, on February 15, 1952. The message indicated that Boyd had been killed by an accidental gunshot wound at the hands of another soldier near Hwachon North Korea.

The body of "Tex" Boyd was returned to the US and is buried in the Golden Gate National Cemetery in San Bruno.
(ABMC; USDVA; WRP April 26, 1951 16:1, February 25, 1952 1:1, February 26, 1952 1:5, April 17, 1952 2:5; 25th Infantry Division, 35th Infantry Regiment (the Cacti) The Korean War, http://www.25thida.com/35thinf.html#Korea, [16 Sept. 2008])

NORMAN O. RICHARDS
(1952/03/26)

(Watsonville Register-Pajaronian photo)

Norman Richards was one of the few men in history to survive a prolonged free fall from an airplane and live to tell about it.

Norman Orin Richards was born on December 4, 1918, in Alameda County, California. His parents, Mr. and Mrs. Roy I. Richards, lived in the Green Valley sector of the Pajaro Valley before moving to Los Gatos. The Richards family also included two daughters, Joan and Edie. Norman grew up in the San Francisco Bay area and before the war, lived in Berkeley and attended the University of California for a year.

On November 5, 1942, Richards entered the US Army as a private and was assigned to the Army Air Force. He was accepted into its aviation cadet program and at its conclusion was commissioned and assigned to a bomber squadron in Europe. When a plane he was piloting over Vienna exploded, Lt. Richards fell several thousand feet without a parachute and after landing in a tree, received only minor injuries. Subsequently he was captured and spent sixteen months in a German POW camp.

Following World War II, Richards returned to California and settled in the Pajaro Valley community of Corralitos. Norman married Betty and the couple had a son, Warren, prior to their divorce. After Betty and Warren moved to Palo Alto, he remained in the Pajaro Valley working as the appliance department manager for Freiermuth Hardware and Plumbing. Later he operated the Coffee Cup Restaurant at the Town and Country shopping center in Watsonville. While living in Corralitos, he was the local grange master, active in the Baptist Church and a member of the

Country Cousins Folk Dance Club.

When the Korean War started, Norman Richards was recalled to active duty and assigned to the 43rd Air Refueling Squadron stationed at Davis Monthan AFB near Tucson, Arizona. On March 26, 1952, Captain Norman Orin Richards was flying a modified B-29 Superfortress in a refueling operation near Tucson when engines number three and four failed and the plane crashed into the desert, killing him and eight others. His remains were recovered and returned to California for a funeral in Los Gatos followed by interment in the Golden Gate National Cemetery.

(CBR; USDVA; NARA2; Warbird Central.Com, B-29 Serial 87782, http://warbird-central.com/american/bombers/B-29/B-29_serials. html [16 September 2008]; WRP March 28, 1952, March 31, 1952 2:5)

LESLIE G. MONROE
(1952/05/19)

(Watsonville Register-Pajaronian photo)

A Watsonville newspaper reported, "Leslie Monroe, 22 Former Resident Dies in Air Crash."

Leslie Glenn Monroe was born in Washington State on October 10, 1929, to Mr. and Mrs. L. G. Monroe. At an early age he accompanied his parents to the Pajaro Valley where they settled in the Amesti district near his grandparents, Mr. and Mrs. A. L. Sweet. He and his brothers Gerald and Delbert attended local elementary schools and in 1943 Leslie enrolled in Watsonville High School. After completing his junior year, the Monroe family moved to Medford, Oregon, and in 1947 Leslie graduated from Central Point High School.

Leslie Monroe entered the naval air cadet program in 1951. After completing that program at Pensacola, Florida, in December 1951, he was commissioned an ensign in the US Navy. Following additional training at Corpus Christi, Texas, Ensign Monroe was attached to a Corsair Squadron at Miramar Naval Air Station in San Diego.

On May 19, 1952, Ensign Leslie Glenn Monroe was on a routine training flight aboard his plane when he was forced to ditch at sea and was killed in the crash. His remains were recovered and returned to Oregon where he was buried in the Eagle Point National Cemetery in Oregon.

(USDVA; WRP May 28, 1952 1:3)

FRED N. PETERSEN JR.
(1952/05/25)

(Watsonville Register-Pajaronian photo)

A Danish born Watsonville photographer marched off to war, never to march home.

Fred N. Petersen Jr. was born in Copenhagen, Denmark, in 1916, to Mr. and Mrs. Fred N. Petersen, Sr. The Petersen family, which also included another son Eric, immigrated to the US and settled in Great Neck, Long Island, New York. Fred later moved to Orange County, New York. After completing three years of high school, he left school to become a photographer. At this time, he married Evelyn.

On January 31, 1941, Fred Jr. enlisted in the US Army at Albany, New York and after completing basic training, spent the next year serving in an artillery unit. He applied for and was accepted into the Officers Candidate School program at Fort Sill, Oklahoma in April 1943. After his graduation in July, he was commissioned a second lieutenant and trained as a pilot for artillery spotting work. The next two years of his military tour were spent in a field artillery unit in the South Pacific. His final World War II assignment was at Fort Sill where he served as an instructor.

After the war, Petersen left active duty, moved to Watsonville and entered into the life of the community. While living in the Pajaro Valley, he worked as a commercial photographer and he and his wife had a son, Fred III, in 1948.

Peterson kept his reserve commission active and served as commander of the local Army National Guard Company. In July 1951 Captain Fred Petersen was recalled to active duty and reported to Fort Sill, Oklahoma. After completing a refresher course, he was ordered to Korea and in November 1951, reported to Headquarters Battery of the 25th Infantry Division Artillery.

During his assignment in Korea, Captain Petersen served

as an artillery observer/pilot and in January 1952, had flown twenty combat missions and earned the Air Medal. By the end of May, he had posted over 150 total missions in Korea while serving in the Iron Triangle sector. On May 25, 1952, with less than a month remaining on his tour he flew a mission into the Iron Triangle area that would be his last. During that mission, his plane was shot down and Captain Fred N. Petersen Jr. was killed.

His remains were recovered and returned to Watsonville, where a funeral was conducted and he was buried in the Pajaro Valley Memorial Park. His awards also include the Purple Heart.

(NARA2; ABMC; NARAK; Kinquest, Danes in the US Army 1940-1946 http://www.kinquest.com/dkgenealogy/wwiidanes.php, http://ftsillocsphotoproject.com/1940sOCSClassRosters.PDF , [16 September 2008]; WRP April 4, 1952 10:4, May 30, 1952 1:1, July 22, 1952 2:2)

JOHN W. VAN NESS
(1952/06/07)

(Santa Cruz Riptide)

"When a pilot heads his plane directly into a withering antiaircraft fire, skimming over the waves at an altitude of 30 feet, he is too busy, and to intent upon sinking his 'pickles' into the belly of an enemy ship to be scared. But after the 'pickles' have been released within 500 yards of the target and the plane is flipped up and away out of danger, then one's mouth fills with cotton and the strength flows out of his knees.'"... John Van Ness

John Wesley Van Ness was born in Fairbury, Nebraska, on March 25, 1918, to F. W. and Myra Van Ness. In the early 1920s, the family moved to Capitola, California, and he and his four sisters enrolled in the elementary school in nearby Soquel. In 1931 Van Ness began Santa Cruz High School and was graduated in 1935.

After completing high school, John Van Ness immediately enlisted in the US Navy. He was sent to San Diego for basic training and later to Pensacola, Florida. The navy discovered that he had an unusual aptitude in mathematics

and mechanics and in 1937 he entered a special program that trained enlisted men as pilots. After his graduation, he was sent to Pearl Harbor, Hawaii, where he served as an air chief petty officer.

When the Japanese attacked on December 7, 1941, Chief Van Ness was manning a machine gun when fragments of a Japanese bomb hit him in the chin and knocked him into the water. In November 1942, he returned to the mainland and served as a navy instructor in Georgia, Texas, and at Pensacola Florida. Van Ness spent the remaining sixteen months of World War II in the Pacific Theater.

John Van Ness and Helen Shaw were married about 1943, and on January 1, 1945, their first son, John, was born. Later a second son, James, was added to the family. After World War II, Van Ness remained in the navy and served aboard the *USS Curtis*.

When the Korean War began, Van Ness was sent to the war zone and remained there until September 9, 1951. Upon his return, he was assigned to the Alameda Naval Air Station. In the spring of 1952, Chief Aviation Pilot John Wesley Van Ness was admitted to the Oak Knoll Naval Hospital in Oakland with an unspecified physical condition from which he died on June 7, 1952. His body was returned to Santa Cruz and following a funeral, was buried in Oakwood Memorial Park.

(SCR November 11, 1942; SCHSC, Page 218; SCSn June 8, 1952 12:4)

RALPH G. FISHER
(1952/06/23)

(Golden Gate National Cemetery – San Bruno California)

Ralph George Fisher was born in Oregon on July 12, 1927. Little information regarding his parentage, place of birth or formative years has surfaced; however, his draft records indicate he was a resident of Wasco County, Oregon.

When he enlisted in the US Army at Portland on November 26, 1946, he declared that he was single, had completed two years of high school and was employed in the sheet metal trade.

The *Watsonville Register-Pajaronian* issue of July 11, 1952, noted that, "Cpl. Fisher was the husband of Mrs. Consuelo Fisher who formerly lived at 3 Linscott court, Alexander Street. [Watsonville]." It is likely that after marrying Consuelo, Ralph Fisher established Watsonville and Santa Cruz County as his residence.

During the Korean War, Ralph G. Fisher was trained as a light weapons infantryman and assigned to the 35th Infantry Regiment of the 25th Infantry Division serving in Korea. In June 1952, Fisher's unit was serving at an area in Korea referred to as the Punchbowl.

By June Communist guns were hurling over 6,800 shells a day at UN positions. During particularly hotly contested actions, Communist gunners occasionally fired as many as 24,000 rounds a day. UN artillerists repaid the compliment five, ten, and sometimes even twenty-fold, and still not a day went by when Communist and UN soldiers did not clash somewhere along the front line. Then on 15 June 1952, the 35th Infantry Regiment relieved the 27th Regiment from their responsibility of the line. All through the remainder of the month, the 35th "Cacti" Regiment conducted raids on enemy positions in the hope of capturing prisoners of war in order to identify units in contact.

During this action at the Punchbowl, Corporal Ralph George Fisher was seriously wounded, evacuated and treated, but succumbed from those wounds on June 23, 1952. His body was recovered and returned to the United States for burial at the Golden Gate National Cemetery in San Bruno California. His awards include the Purple Heart.

(NARA2; NARAK; ABMC; WRP July 11, 1952 1:1;USDVA; 35th Inf Reg History [16 September 2008] http://www.cacti35th. org/regiment/history/korea/1952-01-12.htm)

LESLIE W. LEAR
(1952/06/25)

(Internet photo)

"No Longer a Forgotten Warrior"

Leslie Wayne Lear was born on March 20, 1925 in Santa Cruz, California, to Mr. and Mrs. Leslie I. Lear. He and his sister Barbara attended local elementary schools and in 1939, he entered Santa Cruz High School. Wayne, as his high school classmates knew him, was an all-around student. He was active in sports and played on the football, baseball and the 1941 champion basketball teams. Lear was accepted into the Hi Tow Tong honor society and also served as the 1943 senior class president. He was a member of the June 1943 graduating class.

Leslie Wayne Lear enlisted in the US Army in June 1943 and was immediately singled out as a potential officer candidate. The Army Air Force sent him to Cole College in Cedar Rapids, Iowa for college training prior to his entry into the air cadet program. Upon completion of the course Wayne attended AAF schools at Santa Ana Air Base in Southern California, Ryan Field California and advanced training at Minter Field, California. Following his commissioning as a second lieutenant, he was sent to Douglas, Arizona, for training on B-17 bombers and to Roswell, New Mexico, for B-29 training. At the completion of his training, Lt. Lear went to Lincoln, Nebraska, to assemble a crew. His aircraft traveled from El Paso, Texas, to Seattle, Washington, before making its way to Japan in December 1945.

During this period of his life, Wayne Lear was married and his wife later joined him in Japan. While in Japan, he was promoted to first lieutenant and assigned to the 89th Bomb Squadron of the 38th Bomb group at Osaka, where he served as Communications officer.

When the Korean War began in June 1950, Lear began flying helicopters and was promoted to captain. About June 1952 he reported for duty as a H-5G helicopter pilot for the US Air Force 3rd Air Rescue Squadron in Korea.

On June 25, 1950, Ensign Ronald Dow Eaton USN had flown off of the US carrier *Bon Homme Richard*. It was during his mission that his plane was shot down. Captain Lear was sent to retrieve the downed navy pilot. The official report of the incident noted:

Capt. Leslie W. Lear and A1C Bob D. Holloway, both recently arrived in Korea, were to pick up a downed pilot. Approaching the pickup area in his H-5, Lear requested ResCAP fighters to make a pass and check for ground fire. The fighters did so and received no enemy fire. Well before this time, the enemy had learned to wait until the rescue helicopter arrived before opening fire. Captain Lear began his approach and was fired upon. Breaking off the approach, he called for the fighters to strafe the area. They did so. The H-5 made a run-in, picked up the downed pilot, and began to depart the area while receiving heavy machine gun fire. About six miles from the pickup area, the fighter pilots reported seeing pieces falling from the helicopter, which was flying at an altitude of about 1,200 feet. Bailing out at approximately 800 feet, Hol-

loway was taken POW and was returned alive. Lear and the rescued pilot also bailed out, but they exited at lower altitudes and were presumed to have died upon impact.

The body of Captain Leslie Wayne Lear was never recovered and he was officially listed as missing in action and presumed dead. His awards include the Purple Heart.

(NARA2; ABMC, SCHSC, Page 125; US Air Force Rotorheads, http://www.rotorheadsrus.us/documents/331.html, [16 Sept 2008]; SCSn September 24, 1953 2:5, Korean War Veterans Honor Roll, http://www.koreanwarvetsmemfnd.org/HonorRoll/LWLear.htm, [16 September 2008])

MELVIN L. FORRESTER
(1952/08/15)

(Watsonville Register-Pajaronian photo)

Melvin's navy career and life ended on the streets of San Diego.

Melvin Lee Forrester was born on September 17, 1923 in Fresno California to Mr. and Mrs. Willis Forrester. When Melvin was a young boy, the Forrester family moved to the Pajaro Valley and settled in the community of Freedom. Over the years the family grew to include sons Donald, Alfred, Harry and Ronald and daughters Marilyn and Patricia. Melvin was educated in local schools; however, his graduation from Watsonville High School has yet to be confirmed.

Melvin Forrester joined the US Navy on October 27, 1941. He attended boot camp and was trained as a metalsmith. During World War II, he served in both the European and Pacific Theaters.

Shortly after the war, Melvin married Lois Farris and the couple established residence in Freedom where their children Melvin Jr., Michael and Kathleen were born. He remained in the navy and rose to the rating of metalsmith petty officer first class.

During the Korean War, Melvin Forrester was assigned to the *USS Hampton County LST 803.*

This LST was used primarily for transporting tanks, wheeled and tracked vehicles, and artillery along with construction equipment and military supplies to the combat zone.

Melvin Forrester was crossing a downtown San Diego street on August 15, 1952, when he was hit by a vehicle that killed him. His body was returned to Watsonville and after a funeral at St. Patrick's church, he was interred in the Golden Gate National Cemetery in San Bruno.

(USDVA; DANFS, LST 803 USS Hampton Court; WRP August 18, 1952, August 21, 1952 2:6)

DONALD E. FOLK
(1952/09/30)

(Golden Gate National Cemetery – San Bruno California)

Donald's navy leave was permanently cancelled by a crash on Highway 9.

Donald Eugene Folk was born in Lemoore, King County, California, on January 13, 1931, to Cecil W. and Viola Folk. At a later date the Folks moved to Santa Cruz County with their seven children, Donald, Robert, Marjorie, Sara Jane, Cora Sue, Lorraine and Bonnie. Information relating to the life of Donald prior to his entry into the service has not been located.

About 1949 Donald Folk enlisted in the US Navy and received his boot camp training at the US Naval Training Center in San Diego. He received additional training at a navy school qualifying him as an Interior Communication Electrician (IC) and was assigned to the Landing Ship Transport (LST 1073) *USS Outagami County.*

LST-1073 was recommissioned in early November 1950, some months after the outbreak of the Korean War prompted by a great expansion of US Navy force levels. This LST was used primarily for transporting tanks, wheeled and tracked vehicles, and artillery along with construction equipment and military supplies to the combat zone.

When his ship returned to San Diego during the summer and fall of 1952, Folk received a leave to visit his family in Santa Cruz. On the night of September 30, 1952, IC3 Donald Eugene Folk was a passenger in a car traveling on Highway 9, a mile and a half north of Ben Lomond, when it went out of control and crashed, killing him and injuring the driver. Following his funeral, the body of Donald Folk was interred in

the Golden Gate National Cemetery in San Bruno.
(USDVA; DANFS, USS Outagami County LST-1073; SCSn October 1, 1952 1:5)

RAYMOND CRUZ JR.
(1952/10/18)

(Fairhaven Cemetery, Santa Ana CA – Internet photo)

Little information is available regarding the life of Raymond Cruz. He was born about 1934 in Watsonville to Mr. and Mrs. Raymond Cruz, Sr. He, along with brothers James, Juan, Inez and Robert and sisters Mercy, Beatrice and Lillie, is believed to have spent his formative years in the family residence on Wall Street in Watsonville. The family also resided periodically with members of their extended family in Santa Ana, California.

Raymond Cruz joined the US Marine Corps in 1951 or 1952 and received his basic and school-of-infantry training at Camp Pendleton, California. Following his graduation, he was assigned to the marine guard contingent stationed in the US Naval Air Station at Kodiak, Alaska. While serving at that post, Private First Class Raymond Cruz Jr. was the victim of an accidental gunshot wound on October 18, 1952, that proved fatal. The details of the shooting are unavailable.

His body was returned to California and following a funeral on October 28 at Our Lady of Guadalupe Catholic Church in Santa Ana, Raymond Cruz Jr. was interred in Fairhaven Cemetery in that city.

(WRP October 31, 1952 2:2)

CLARENCE E. MCELROY
(1952/10/31)

(Golden Gate National Cemetery – San Bruno California)

The life of a Bronze Medal recipient ended at the rear of a lumber truck.

Clarence Edward McElroy, the son of Morris and Nellie (Wilheit) McElroy, was born in Texas on September 4, 1932. In addition to Clarence, the McElroy's had two daughters, Christine and Pauline, before they separated. Nellie, Christine and Clarence moved to Santa Cruz, California, and Morris and Pauline remained in Texas. Information is unavailable as to what local schools he may have attended.

Clarence McElroy enlisted in the US Army in the last half of 1950 and after completing basic and advanced training, was sent to Korea where he served with the Seventh Infantry Regiment. During his army service, he earned the Bronze Star.

Five years after the end of WWII, the 7th Infantry was deployed from Fort Devens, Massachusetts to action in Korea where it rejoined the other elements of the 3rd Infantry Division. Landing at Wonsan, North Korea on 17 November 1950, the Cottonbalers took up positions between Wonsan and Hamhung where they fought a courageous rear guard action receiving elements of the First Marine Division as it withdrew from the Chosin Reservoir. They controlled the escape route to Hamhung and the sea for UN forces who had been mauled by the entry into the war by the Chinese.

Corporal McElroy returned home from Korea in December 1951 and at that time, may have married Ethel. In November 1952, Ethel was living with Clarence's mother in Pasadena, while he was stationed at Fort Ord. During his Fort Ord, tour Clarence frequently stayed with his sister in Santa Cruz.

On October 31, 1952 Clarence was a passenger in a vehicle that crashed into a lumber truck in Santa Cruz. Corporal Clarence Eugene McElroy was killed instantly and his two companions were critically injured in the accident. McElroy's body was interred in the Golden Gate National Cemetery in

San Bruno.

(USDVA; SCR August 1, 1952 6:4; 7th Inf Regt. Assoc., History http://www.cottonbalers.com/history/history.asp, [16 September 2008]); SCSn November 2, 1952 1:6, November 3, 1952; CDR)

HARVEY F. LEVINE
(1952/11/02)

(Courtesy of the Levine Family)

"Mom, I might as well give you the straight scoop on things so that if you do worry it will be for something," Harvey wrote to his mother.

Harvey Franklin Levine was born in Brooklyn, New York, on July 30, 1932, to Charles and Rose Levine. In 1947 the Levine family, which also included sons Arnold and Saul, moved to Santa Cruz where Charles had opened the Arnold's Surf Court Motel. Harvey enrolled in Santa Cruz High School and soon had acquired the nickname "Brooklyn" from his fellow students. While in high school, Harvey performed well academically, played on the lightweight football team and became a popular cheerleader. After graduating from high school in 1950, he enrolled in the College of the Pacific in Stockton and remained there until April 1951, when he enlisted in the US Marine Corps.

After completing basic and school-of-infantry training at Camp Pendleton, Private Levine was shipped to Korea in December 1951, where he joined Company A, 1st Battalion, 7th Marine Regiment of the 1st Marine Division. After his arrival, Harvey Levine was immediately thrust into combat and fought at the Hwachon Reservoir. During the Chinese spring offensive, Harvey Levine earned a Bronze Star.

In a letter to his family in October Levine shared his impressions of the conditions at the front:

October 31, 1952

Dear Mom and Dad:

I guess that I can start calling myself a short timer now that the 15th draft has been relieved of duty and is due to leave Korea in about five days. That gives me anywhere from 30 days down to about 20 days left, its all up to which

rumor you want to believe.

Mom, I might as well give you the straight scoop on things so that if you do worry it will be for something.

I have been back in Able company since last August and have been on the line since September 6, steady. You have probably read of The Hook, and of Warsaw where the fighting has been going on.

Well, Mom, you can thank God that I'm alive cause the whole machine gun section and third platoon that was on Warsaw was killed. We still haven't found all the bodies, so we have 'em down as missing. They left three 16th drafters behind because we were so short, but when it hit the fan, we went up and took back the Hook and Ransom. We are still on the line, even though it has quieted down and we got out looking for bodies. No one knows how many men were killed or missing so many were buried under, and have to be dug out. Able company and Charley company have joined together to make one company and together we are still under strength.

The Scotch "Black Watch" is coming up in a couple of days to relieve us. Someone has to. The regiment has been on the line for 60 days with no reserve time and tax on casualties.

But I'm still all right. I had a little concussion, but not enough to bother me or to cause me to turn in, not when you seen men ripped in half by 76's or mortars. They sure throw a lot of Chinks at us.

All for now. By the time you get this we ought to be in the rear.

Love Harvey

On November 2, 1952, while fighting in an area of Korea known as The Hook and Warsaw, Private First Class Harvey Franklin Levine was killed in action by an incoming mortar round. His remains were initially buried in the Golden Gate National Cemetery in San Bruno but were later moved to the Home of Peace Cemetery in Santa Cruz. In addition to the Bronze Star his awards include the Purple Heart.

(ABMC; USDVA; Baker-one-seven.com 7th Marine Regiment History, http://www.bakeroneseven.com/7thregiment.htm [16 September 2008], SCSn November 9, 1952, January 2, 1953 1, December 26, 1952 1:4)

FRANK R. GFROERER
(1952/11/14)

(Watsonville High School yearbook)

Boxes of Christmas presents were found strewn on a hilltop in Korea after the crash that took Frank's life.

Francis Roallen Gfroerer was born in Watsonville, California on January 26, 1931, to Mr. and Mrs. Emmett Gfroerer. Frank, as he chose to be called, was raised in the family home on Bockius Street with his older brother Emmett Jr. and sisters Rosemary, Catherine and Margaret. He attended Moreland Notre Dame Academy and later enrolled in Watsonville High School. Gfroerer played on the high school baseball team during his school years. Following graduation from high school in 1950, he worked at the Service Printing Company and attended Hartnell College in Salinas.

Frank Gfroerer was drafted into the US Army on June 11, 1951. After completing his army training courses, he was ordered to Korea in November 1951, where he joined Company A of the 1092nd Engineer Combat Battalion. The exact location in Korea where he served has not been identified; however, it is likely to have been in the vicinity of the Punchbowl near the 38th Parallel in Eastern Korea. During his tour in Korea, Frank was promoted to corporal and qualified for a five-day leave to Japan. While in Tokyo, Frank intended to acquire Christmas presents to bring to his family upon his rotation home later in the month.

On November 14, 1952, Corporal Frank Gfroerer was returning from Japan aboard a C-119C Flying Boxcar with forty-three other servicemen when it crashed into Mt. Yebong, a 2000-foot peak only a few minutes away from its Seoul destination. One reporter visiting the scene commented that many of the bodies were charred; indicating the plane had burned on crashing. "As I walked through the wreckage," she said in a pooled dispatch, "I found Christmas presents that the men had bought on R and R in Japan."

The remains of Corporal Gfroerer were recovered and returned to San Francisco aboard the troopship *Iran Victory* in February 1953. Following a High Mass of requiem, Frank was buried in the family plot in Valley Catholic cemetery.
(ABMC; WRP November15, 1952 1:3, November 17, 1952 1:1, February 3, 1953 2:3, February 5, 1953)

ALBERT J. KURTZ
(1952/11/28)

(Arlington National Cemetery - Internet photo)

Arlington National Cemetery had a special plot reserved for Al Kurtz.

Albert J. Kurtz was born on February 17, 1907, in Indiana to Harry and Louise Kurtz. Albert, along with three brothers and four sisters, was raised and educated in Jackson County, Indiana. After graduating from a Jackson County high school, Kurtz became a member of the United States Border Patrol Service and remained with that organization until the 1930s when he joined the US Army.

While in the Army, Kurtz served with artillery units in the eastern United States and in Venezuela where he rose to the rank of first sergeant. In 1942 Kurtz was accepted into the Officers Candidate School program at Fort Sill, Oklahoma, and after completing the course, was commissioned a second lieutenant. The units and locations of his service during World War II are not known.

Albert Kurtz was married during the war years and he and his wife, Utha, had two sons, James Albert and Richard.

In May 1952 Kurtz received orders to Korea and was assigned to the 45th Infantry Division. Prior to his departure, the Kurtz family moved to Santa Cruz, where they had acquired a residence on Meder Street. James, the oldest son, was enrolled in Mission Hill Junior High School and Richard in Bay View School.

During his tour in Korea, Chief Warrant Officer Kurtz was diagnosed with cancer and when the condition became acute in late October 1952, he was evacuated from Seoul. He was admitted to Letterman Army Hospital in San Francisco where he remained until his death on November 28, 1952. His body was shipped to Virginia and following a military funeral, was interred in Arlington National Cemetery.
(NARA2; USDVA; 45th Museum.com, History, http://www.45thdivisionmuseum.com/History, [16 September 2008]; SCSn December 1, 1952 10:2; OCS Roster, [16 September

08] http://ftsillocsphotoproject.com/1940sOCSClassRosters.PDF)

1953

ROY TAYLOR
(1953/04/13)

(Watsonville Register-Pajaronian photo)

Lt. Taylor's after burners failed to re-ignite.

Roy Taylor was born on August 22, 1929, to Mr. and Mrs. William H. Taylor. His birth location has not been identified. The Taylor family, which also included their son William, lived in Corralitos and was active in the All Saints Episcopal Church in Watsonville. Roy spent his formative years in the Pajaro Valley, was educated in local schools and graduated from Watsonville High School in June 1947. He enrolled in Hartnell College in Salinas in the same year and remained there until 1950.

In April 1950, Roy Taylor entered the naval air cadet program. When he graduated from the pre-flight training program at Pensacola, Florida, in August 1950, he was named the outstanding student and judged, "the best all around man of his class in the academic, military and physical courses." He continued his naval cadet education until October 1951 when he was commissioned an ensign and received his wings.

Taylor was then sent to advanced flight training at Corpus Christi, Texas, carrier training at Pensacola Florida, and jet aircraft instruction at Kingsville, Texas. In March 1952 Ensign Taylor was assigned to Miramar Naval Air Station in California.

Roy arrived Korea in September 1952 and served as a F9F-5 Pantherjet fighter pilot with Fighter Squadron 122 aboard the *USS Oriskany*.

On April 13, 1953, Lt. (jg) Roy Taylor was returning to the *Oriskany* after escorting a photography airplane on a mission in Korea, when his plane went down. Lt. Cmdr. J.W. Wyrick, his commanding officer, provided details on the accident.

They commenced their letdown at 14,000 feet over the ship preparing to land and at 11,000 feet Roy called the photo pilot, on his radio and told him his engine had flamed out. The photo pilot asked Roy where he was and Roy told him that he was just behind and above him. The photo pilot, Lt. J.F. Grosser, then swung out and followed Roy down. Roy made no further radio transmissions, apparently having turned his radio off in order to conserve its energy for his attempted restarts. From 11,000 feet he had ample time to air restart and then use the cartridge igniter for two more attempts. We do not know why the engine flamed out or why it failed to restart. We are sure that he attempted both means of restarting however. He jettisoned his cockpit canopy at about 1,000 feet preparatory to a water landing. He apparently handled his landing well as he flared out just above the water and let the plane settle in as it slowed down. When he hit the water the fuselage of the plane broke off just forward of the wing, skipped across the water a short distance and sank immediately. The shock of hitting was sufficient at least to have rendered Roy unconscious. The remainder of the plane floated for about a minute, but the two planes that followed him down could find no sign of Roy as the cockpit was in the part that sank.

Destroyers and helicopters were immediately dispatched to rescue Roy but there was no sign of his plane or body. Lt. (jg) Roy Taylor was officially listed as missing and presumed dead. His awards include the Air Medal. with two Gold Stars.

(ABMC; DANFS, USS Oriskany CV-34; WRP August 28, 1950 1:6, October 3, 1951 10:3, January 3, 1952 9:3, March 27, 1952 16:1, April 14, 1953 1:1, April 29, 1953 10:1)

JAMES N. CROUCH JR.
(1953/06/18)

(Hambey Cemetery – Aromas, California)

A "Flying Box Car" ended James' eight-day leave in Japan, his tour in Korea and his life.

James N. Crouch Jr. was the only son of Mr. and Mrs. James N. Crouch, who were natives of the Aromas area of the Pajaro Valley. He was born in Santa Cruz County on

September 18, 1930, and attended elementary school in Aromas and high school in Salinas, California. After leaving school, he worked in the area and married Sally Milner of Manteca, California.

James Crouch was inducted into the US Army on February 29, 1952, and sent to army training facilities for basic and advanced instruction. In August he was shipped to Korea and Sally moved into the home of her in-laws on the San Miguel Canyon Road near Watsonville. Upon arrival in Korea, Private First Class Crouch was assigned as a cook in Company C of the 802nd Engineer Aviation Battalion. The 802nd was an army unit attached to the US Air Force to enlarge and expand Korean airfields.

In June 1953 Crouch received an eight-day leave in Japan. At the conclusion of his leave he boarded a C-124A Globemaster Transport at Tachikawa Air Base in Japan for his return flight to Korea. Shortly after takeoff on June 18, the plane developed engine trouble and crashed into a rice field killing Private First Class Crouch and the other 128 passengers. Newspaper accounts noted, "Most of the victims were still strapped to their seats indicating they were either stunned or killed by the crash impact."

The remains of James Crouch were returned to Watsonville and following a service conducted by the local VFW post, were interred in the Hambey Cemetery near Aromas.

(CBR; ABMC; Sarge USA.com, 802nd Engineer Aviation Construction Battalion http://www.sargeusa.com/pennyshort/main-roots.htm, [16 September 2008]; WRP June 18, 1953 1:8, June 20, 1953 1:3, September 19, 1953 2:5)

CHARLES F. MCGUIRE
(1953/07/07)

CHARLES
FREDERICK
McGUIRE

CALIFORNIA

CAPTAIN
US AIR FORCE
WORLD WAR II
KOREA

SEPTEMBER 7 1921
JULY 7 1953

(Golden Gate National Cemetery – San Bruno California)

The connection between Charles McGuire and Santa Cruz County is unclear; however, during his Korean War service, he designated it as his county of residence.

Charles Frederick McGuire was born on September 7, 1921, in California. In 1945 he was living in Fresno and working as an elevator operator when he enlisted in the US Army. He indicated on his enlistment form that he had completed one year of college and had been married and divorced. He apparently had served in World War II and following the war, joined the National Guard as a master sergeant.

On December 20, 1945, Charles McGuire was recalled into the US Air Force and received training qualifying him for a commission. It is possible that McGuire used the Santa Cruz residence of his wife Rita on his air force entry forms. When he was sent to Korea, Captain McGuire was assigned to the 28th Bomb Squadron of the 19th Bomb Wing.

Immediately after the communist invasion of South Korea, the 19th BG moved from Guam to Okinawa. Initially under the operational control of Twentieth AF, after July 8, 1950, it was attached to FEAF Bomber Command (Provisional). The first B-29 unit in the war, the group on June 28 attacked North Korean storage tanks, marshalling yards, and armor. In the first two months, it flew more than six hundred sorties, supporting UN ground forces by bombing enemy troops, vehicles, and such communications points as the Han River bridges. In the north, its targets included an oil refinery and port facilities at Wonsan, a railroad bridge at Pyongyang, and an airfield at Yonpo. After UN ground forces pushed the communists out of South Korea, the 19th BG turned to strategic objectives in North Korea, including industrial and hydroelectric facilities. It also continued to attack bridges, marshalling yards, supply centers, artillery and troop positions, barracks, port facilities, and airfields.

On July 7, 1953, Captain Charles Frederick McGuire was serving as a crewmember of a B-29A Superfortress bomber that was returning from a bombing mission. The bomber crashed during the landing approach to Pohang Air Base. His remains were recovered, returned to California and interred in the Golden Gate National Cemetery in San Bruno.

(NARA2; ABMC; USDVA; Cemetery headstone inscription; AFHRA/IT, 19th Medium Group, http://afhra.maxwell.af.mil/korean_war/usaf_organizations_korea/medium_bombardment.html, [16 September 2008])

1954

RICHARD A. ANDERSON
(1954/05/24)

(Santa Cruz Sentinel photo)

After three tours, Richard was no stranger to Korea, but the third go round was not the best.

Richard A. Anderson was born on March 5, 1930, in Jamestown, North Dakota, to Mr. and Mrs. J. R. Anderson. Accompanying Richard and his parents on their move to California in 1940, were his brothers James and John and sisters Ramona, Penny and Rita. Upon arrival in California the family settled in Richmond, California, and about 1945 moved to Santa Cruz. Richard entered Santa Cruz High School where he remained for the next two years. During his high school years, he worked part time while learning the sheet-metal trade.

Anderson left high school on August 13, 1946, and joined the US Air Force. After completing basic training, he received additional instruction as a radioman and earned his high school diploma. Over the ensuing years Anderson re-enlisted in the air force and married Sarah. In 1953 the couple's daughter Elizabeth was born.

In December 1953, Sergeant Anderson began his third tour in Korea and while he was stationed in the Far East, Sarah maintained the family residence on Portola Drive in Santa Cruz. By 1954 he had risen to the rank of Staff Sergeant and was serving as a radioman aboard a B-26.

On May 24, 1954, Staff Sergeant Richard A. Anderson, along with his fellow crew members were aboard their aircraft over Cheju-Do Island, sixty miles off the southern tip of Korea when it crashed into the side of a mountain. His remains were recovered and returned to California where they were interred in the Golden Gate National Cemetery in San Bruno.

(NARA2; USDVA; SCSn August 8, 1954)

WALLACE RICH
(1954/05/26)

(Santa Cruz Sentinel photo)

As a "Blue Angel" Buddy Rich helped to inspire American youth.

Wallace Rich was born in Los Angeles, California on February 8, 1926. He was the son of Wallace and Lola Rich who, along with their other son Charles, later moved to Santa Cruz.

"Buddy," as Wallace was nicknamed, attended Santa Cruz High School and graduated in 1944.

Soon after completing high school, Rich enlisted in the US Navy and was accepted into the Naval Air Cadet Program at Pensacola, Florida. In 1947, following the basic and advanced phases of that program, he was commissioned an ensign. Upon completion of additional training, he was assigned to the *USS Princeton* bound for the Korean War zone. Wallace Rich was promoted to Lt. (jg) and flew support missions off the carrier in Korean waters.

When he returned to the United States, Rich was sent to Corpus Christi, Texas, for special flight training and invited to join the renowned Blue Angels. The Blue Angels was a naval aerial acrobatic team with the purpose of promoting interest in naval aviation and precision flying. They were reported to have "performed every aerial acrobatic maneuver in the books in formation at more than 500 miles per hour."

In May 1954 Wallace Rich was promoted to lieutenant and assigned to the aircraft carrier *USS Bennington*. During his tour on the *Bennington,* his career came to an end.

On the 26th of May 1954 the Bennington *was steaming off the Atlantic Coast in Naragansett Bay preparing for carrier qualifications. Last minute preparations for flight trials were being made, and plane crews were busy making final checks. The ship's log indicates that the first evidence of trouble was noted at 0610 hours when there was a report of smoke. At 0611 hours there was a notation of two or three explosions taking place. The ship suffered massive damage in the forward third, with sheets of flame rising during the explosions. 102 men lost their lives within seconds of the explosion and over one hundred others were seriously injured.*

The cause of disaster was later attributed to a launching catapult that exploded. The remains of Lt. Wallace Rich were recovered and returned to California for a funeral and interment in the Golden Gate National Cemetery in San Bruno.

(ABMC; USDVA; SCSn June 17, 1952 1:7, June 2, 1954 14:3; DANFS, USS Bennington CV-20)

LEROY W. MACHADO
(1954/12/01)

(Santa Cruz Sentinel photo)

LeRoy was the last Santa Cruz County serviceman to die during the Korean War period.

LeRoy William Machado was born October 28, 1931, in Santa Cruz to Joseph and Ruth Machado. He was the only son of the couple, who appear to have separated during his youth. LeRoy lived with his mother, but maintained contact with his father and grandparents who also lived in Santa Cruz. Machado attended local schools and entered Santa Cruz High School, where he was active in sports. While in high school, he joined the US Army Reserve's 422nd MP Company and served in that unit for two years. Machado graduated from Santa Cruz High School with the February 1951 class.

LeRoy enlisted in the US Navy in July 1951. He was sent to San Diego for boot camp and after completing his basic and advanced training, was assigned to the US Naval Base in Sasebo, Japan. He remained at that station performing administrative work for the next fifteen months. After completing his far eastern tour, LeRoy returned to California and on February 20, 1954, reported to a naval facility at Treasure Island in San Francisco Bay.

In March 1954, Machado was sent to Bainbridge, Maryland, where he entered a twelve-week training program at the navy's personnel school. Following completion of that school, he returned to Santa Cruz for a thirty-day leave before reporting aboard the *USS Hooper Island* in Southern California.

On the night of December 1, 1954, while in San Gabriel, California, LeRoy Machado drove a vehicle into the rear of a truck laden with potatoes and was killed in the ensuing crash. His body was returned to Santa Cruz for a funeral and interment at Oakwood Memorial Park.

(SCR August 22, 1952 4:3; SCSn March 5, 1954 3:1, December 5, 1954 1:3, Oakwood Cemetery Survey)

RICHARD P. ANDERSON
(Death Date Unknown)

(Santa Cruz High School yearbook)

The name Richard P. Anderson tops the memorial list of Santa Cruz High School students who lost their lives during the Korean War, yet nothing has been uncovered regarding his service record or death. The only information available is an article appearing in the *Santa Cruz Sentinel* at the time of his enlistment in the US Air Force.

Joins Air Force

Richard Paul Anderson 1107 Seabright Avenue has enlisted in the United States Air Force for four years. He will be assigned to Parks air force base at Pleasanton for the airman indoctrination course.

Anderson is the son of Mrs. Lenora Anderson of Route 1, Felton, has lived with his aunt here, Mrs. Rebecca Pacini. He was graduated from Santa Cruz high school in 1951, and was a member of the local National Guard unit before enlisting.

(SCSn November 6, 1952 3:5)

The cause of the death of Richard P. Anderson has not been found, nor has the location of his remains.

***

Vietnam War
(1964-1972)

Santa Cruz County Military During the Vietnam War

Seventy-five Santa Cruz County servicemen lost their lives between 1965 and 1972, countless were injured, and local residents found themselves torn between support for and opposition to the conflict.

The Selective Service draft and military branch enlistments filled the manpower quotas required of Santa Cruz County during the Vietnam War. Both the Army National Guard Company in Watsonville and the Naval Reserve Surface Division in Santa Cruz trained and remained in a state of readiness for the Vietnam War, yet were never required. Company B, 4th Battalion, 149th Armored Division of the California National Guard met and trained one weekend a month at the Watsonville airport and spent two weeks every summer at Camp Irwin in Southern California. Surface Division No. 38 of the 12th Naval District, trained weekly at its center near De Laveaga Park in Santa Cruz. During the summer, its reservists completed boot camp in San Diego, attended classroom training in San Francisco or served aboard naval vessels. When the Santa Cruz facility closed, the unit was trained in Monterey once a month.

Of the seventy-five Santa Cruz County Vietnam War dead, two-thirds had enlisted in the various branches and twenty-four had been inducted into the army.

Local Army recruits typically completed their basic and advanced training at Fort Ord near Monterey, California, or at Fort Lewis, Washington. Fort Ord became the major processing center for Vietnam deployment and over a million men passed through it during the course of the war. The US Navy conducted its boot camp at San Diego, the Coast Guard at Alameda, the US Marine Corps utilized Camp Pendleton, California, for both basic and school-of-infantry training, and the US Air Force trained recruits at Lackland Air Force Base in San Antonio, Texas.

Of the seventy-five recorded deaths of local servicemen during the period, two thirds were directly attributable to the war. The first recorded death of a local GI between 1965-1975 was that of Private Herbert R. Howell, a Pajaro Valley resident who drowned while serving in Germany on March 21, 1965. The last known death of a Santa Cruz County serviceman during the Vietnam era was that of Sergeant Hervey M. Goold of Watsonville who died of leukemia at McCord Air Force Base in Tacoma, Washington, on November 10, 1972.

BIOGRAPHICAL SKETCHES

1964

August 7 the North Vietnamese attacks US destroyer Maddox in the Gulf of Tonkin.

US president Lyndon B. Johnson orders retaliatory attacks.

US Congress approves the Gulf of Tonkin resolution, authorizing authority to wage war.

1965

HERBERT R. HOWELL
(1965/03/21)

(Mission Memorial Park – Seaside, California)

Santa Cruz County's first war casualty of the Vietnam War period was not from Santa Cruz County, was not a war casualty, nor did his death occur in Vietnam, yet Watsonville designated him as one of its own. On March 23, 1965, the *Watsonville Register-Pajaronian* declared "Watsonville Youth Drowns in Germany."

Herbert R. Howell, one of the ten children of Mr. and Mrs. Lon W. Howell, was born in Clovis, New Mexico, July 2, 1946. Later the Howell family, that would grow to include seven boys and three girls, moved to the Pajaro Valley. Herbert was raised in a rural residence on Strawberry Canyon Road located between Watsonville and Moss Landing, California. While Watsonville was his urban center, his education took place at Elkhorn Elementary School and Salinas High School in Monterey County.

With his parent's permission Herbert left high school in the early part of 1963 at age seventeen to enlist in the US Army. After Private Howell completed his basic and advanced individual training in November, he was assigned to Company D of the 703rd Maintenance Battalion of the 7th Army in Europe. While serving at an undefined unit and location in Germany, Private Herbert R Howell was accidentally drowned in the Main River on March 21, 1965.

His body was returned to California and following a funeral service in Pacific Grove on April 1, 1965, was buried with full military honors in the Mission Memorial Park in Seaside California.

(WRP March 23, 1965, WRP March 30, 1965 2:3)

DARYL L. KEEN
(1965/07/16)

(Santa Cruz Sentinel photo)

"We are sitting in the Chu River that goes through Da Nang right now," Daryl Keen wrote home from Vietnam on July 14, 1965. "We are going to load supplies and take them to a base down the coast." This would be the last that his fiancée and family would hear from him as he prepared to move down the river to supply a US Marine detachment.

Daryl La Verne Keen was born on June 8, 1944, to Kermit and Helen Keen. Daryl, along with his brothers, Don, Eugene, Jerold and James, and his sister, Sandra, grew up in the family home on Laurel Street in Santa Cruz. He was described as "a quiet, shy, good-looking blonde young man with bright blue eyes that saw a future as an architect or construction engineer."

At Santa Cruz High School Keen excelled academically and was admitted to the Hi Tow Tong boy's honor society. In addition to being a surfer and strong swimmer he was also a member of the school's undefeated wrestling team. Following his graduation from high school in June 1962, he enrolled in Cabrillo College to continue his technical studies.

In the latter part of 1962 Daryl Keen enlisted in the US Navy and after completing boot camp in San Diego, was trained as a quartermaster. In 1963, he and Susan Riep, a local Santa Cruz girl, announced their plans to marry following his discharge in June 1966.

Quartermaster Third Class Keen was sent to Da Nang where he was assigned to Assault Craft Squadron 1, Division 12. His vessel, the *USS LCU 1493* based in Da Nang, supplied ammunition to US Marine units fighting in the area. While serving in Vietnam, Keen wrote home to share his impressions of the conditions he experienced.

It is hard keeping the writing paper clean. If I take a shower, I am covered with sweat before I dry off. I guess you will have to settle for a grubby letter. The temperature must be a least 110 degrees in the middle of the day...We got a surprise and a let-down this afternoon... It looks like we won't be relieved and sent back to the states like we were supposed to be. I can say for certain we will be over here at least until September.

Daryl also described the deep weariness of marines leaving after months of battling the Viet Cong, "they only sent the marines home who were just too worn out to fight any more."

Appreciating the problem of over-taxed sailors and marines, Daryl volunteered to extend his service time in Vietnam by an additional year to help relieve manpower shortages.

Daryl Keen was drowned on July 16, 1965, while moving ammo down a river in Quang Tin province of South Vietnam to the US Marine's Chou Lie base camp. His body was recovered and returned to Santa Cruz. Father Donald E. Strano, a close family friend, conducted a memorial service for Daryl; his remains were buried in Golden Gate National Cemetery in San Bruno.

(USDVA; VVMW; VVVW; SCSn July 18, 1965 Mobile Riverine Forces Association-Vietnam, Assault Squadron #1, ACD 12, www. mrfa.org/Individual.Units.htm [16 September 2008])

HAROLD A. BIRD
(1965/09/18)

(Santa Cruz Sentinel photo)

Harold was a corpsman who watched out for his marines during the attack on Da Nang.

Harold Alvin Bird was born to Mr. and Mrs. Maurice A. Bird on August 5, 1943, in Clymer, New York. He and his

brothers, Maurice Jr., Eugene and John, joined their parents in the family move to Lompoc, California; however, his sister Nancy remained in New York. Harold completed the first two years of high school at Lompoc in Santa Barbara County. After the family resettled in Boulder Creek in 1960, he enrolled in San Lorenzo Valley High School and graduated with honors in 1962.

Harold Bird enlisted in the local US Naval Reserve Surface Division and went on active duty in 1962. After completing training at the US Naval Training Center in San Diego, he was sent to a hospitalman school to become a navy hospitalman or marine corpsman. Bird, who considered making the navy his career, was promoted to hospital corpsman third class and sent to Camp Pendleton for field training. After graduation he was sent to Vietnam.

Harold arrived in Vietnam on August 5, 1965 and was assigned to Charlie Company of the 1st Regiment, 1st Battalion of the 1st Marine Division. He had only been in Vietnam five weeks when Viet Cong guerillas attacked the Da Nang air base that his unit was guarding. In a predawn hand-to-hand assault on September 18, 1965, Hospitalman Third Class Harold Alvin Bird was shot and killed while attending to wounded marines.

His body was recovered and returned to California where he was buried in the Golden Gate National Cemetery at San Carlos.

(USDVA; VNMW; SCSn September 21, 1965 1:1, September 26, 1965 10:5)

VINCENT LOCATELLI
(1965/11/17)

(Santa Cruz Sentinel photo)

A fellow soldier, Fred Owens, tells this story of Vincent's final battle, "Company Commander Forrest said, 'Who you got KIA?' I said, 'Locatelli.' Forrest said, 'Shit.' Locatelli was the youngest guy in the company."

Vincent Locatelli was born in Italy on March 27, 1945, to Mr. and Mrs. Adolpho Locatelli. In addition to Vincent, the Locatelli family included sons Salvatore, Adolph, John,

Joseph and Mario and daughter Angela. In 1950 the family moved to Santa Cruz, California and settled into a home on Younglove Street. Vincent attended local grammar schools and later studied at Santa Cruz High School. Upon completion of his education, he found employment at the Santa Cruz Portland Cement Company, where he worked until 1963.

Vincent Locatelli was drafted into the US Army during the fall of 1963. After basic training, he was sent to Fort Carson, Colorado, for advanced training. In the early part of August 1965, he was assigned to A Company, 1st Battalion of the 5th Cavalry Regiment in the 1st Cavalry Airmobile. After a brief orientation program at Fort Benning, Georgia, his unit left for Southeast Asia on September 20, 1965.

Upon their arrival in Vietnam, the 1st Cavalry was sent to the Central Highland sector to prevent incursion by the Viet Cong and Viet regular units. Between September and November, Locatelli's unit was engaged in several combat encounters with the enemy, but none of the magnitude of the combat in the La Drang Valley.

On November 16, 1965, the 5th Regiment moved into the La Drang Valley in what was to become the first major US engagement of the Vietnam War. Along the route, the 550-yard column was brought to a halt and company commanders were ordered forward for consultation. During this period, the enemy ambushed the column in several locations. The fighting took place in three- to five-foot elephant grass that prevented either side from seeing the other and during the wild shooting melee, friendly fire casualties frequently occurred.

In the A Company sector, "Charley" as VC soldiers were dubbed, hurled grenades and on November 17, a grenade exploded near Private Vincent Locatelli taking his life. Vincent Locatelli's remains were returned to Santa Cruz and following a funeral service at Holy Cross Church, were entombed in the Holy Cross Mausoleum.

(VNMW; U of Tennessee, Fred Owens Part 1, Oral History Project https://my.tennessee.edu/portal/page?_pageid=91,150490&_dad=portal&_schema=PORTAL, [16 September 2008]; SCSn November 19, 1965 1:7, November 28, 1956 14:7; Cem Survey)

1966

STEVEN M. PASHMAN
(1966/01/25)

(Santa Cruz Sentinel photo)

When Steven boarded a US Air Force C123, little did he realize that he would be involved in one of the worst air disasters in the war.

Steven Mark Pashman, the second son of Mr. and Mrs. John R. Pashman, was born in Topeka, Kansas, on September 25, 1944. He and his two brothers, John and David, attended local Topeka schools until 1960 when the family moved to Santa Cruz, where their father had acquired the Villa Del Mar Motel. The Pashman family moved into a residence on the motel grounds, and Stephen entered Santa Cruz High School.

After graduating from high school in June 1962, Steven enrolled in Cabrillo College. Later he obtained employment at the California Tube Lab in Santa Cruz. Pashman was an avid sports enthusiast and soon became president of the Santa Cruz Sports Club.

Steven Pashman entered the US Army in the fall of 1965 and was sent to a training facility. After completing basic and advanced individual training in late 1965, he was assigned to the 7th Cavalry Regiment of the 1st Cavalry Airmobile Division serving in Vietnam. Pashman arrived in the central highland area of Vietnam on December 13, 1965, with transportation to his unit to be provided by plane.

On the morning of January 25, 1966, Private First Class Steven Mark Pashman and forty-one other troopers of the 7th Cavalry boarded a Fairchild Provider aircraft to be transported to a combat zone in the highlands. The lumbering C123 troop transport had just taken off from the An Khe staging area of the US 1st Cavalry Airmobile Division 250 miles north east of Saigon on the morning of January 25, 1966, when problems were encountered. A low 300-foot cloud cover had hidden a looming mountain in their path and before the pilot could maneuver the craft to avoid it the plane smashed into the hillside. The sound caused by the crash of the explosion shattered the early morning silence. The name Steven Pashman and the names of the other troopers aboard would be etched into the Vietnam Memorial Wall.

The remains of Private Steven M. Pashman were recovered and returned to Santa Cruz where a memorial mass was conducted at Holy Cross Church. Steven's remains were sent to Topeka, Kansas and interred in the Mt. Calvary Cemetery.

(VNMW; SCSn January 25, 1966 1:2, January 27, 1966 1:4, February 4, 1966)

MARK L. CORRIE
(1966/06/07)

(Golden Gate National Cemetery – San Bruno California)

Mark Lane Corrie was born on January 5, 1948, in Los Angeles County, California; however, information regarding his family and pre-military life has not been located.

The name Mark Corrie Fraser is listed among the Vietnam War casualties of Kern County, California, with a corresponding reference to Aptos suggesting a possible connection.

Mark Corrie was apparently living in Aptos, California, when he enlisted in the US Marine Corps in the late spring or summer of 1965. Because he was seventeen at the time of his enlistment, parental permission would have been required for him to enter the US Marine Corps. His age would also suggest that he might have left high school without finishing his senior year. Mark Corrie would have been sent to Camp Pendleton, California, to begin the twelve-week boot camp course that was the first phase of his training to become a marine. After a ten-day leave, likely at his home, Mark returned to Camp Pendleton to undergo the phase II, fifty-two-day school-of-infantry training.

At the completion of his training period, about March 1966, he was sent to Vietnam and assigned as a mortarman within an unidentified regiment of the 3rd Marine Division.

On June 7, 1966, Private First Class Mark Lane Corrie was a passenger in a vehicle involved in a non-hostile acci-

dent in the province of Thua Thien, Vietnam. He was killed in the crash and his body was returned to California where it was interred in the Golden Gate National Cemetery in San Bruno California.

(CBR; VVMW; USDVA; Ancestry.Com, Kern County War Memorial; http://boards.rootsweb.com/topics.Military.wwii. memorials/360/mb.ashx, [16 September 2008])

LEO B. BUCKHOLDT
(1966/06/16)

(Internet photo)

"You will remain in the door of our minds till we meet again on the other side," wrote former marine Randy Kendall about Buddy.

Leo Buddy Buckholdt was born on January 28, 1946, in Oklahoma to Mr. and Mrs. Leo Buckholdt. The Buckholdt family, consisting of Buddy and his brothers Rodney, Bruce, Troy and Ricky and sister Bonnie, later moved to Livermore, California. In the early 1960s the Buckholdt family settled in Santa Cruz and Buddy enrolled in Santa Cruz High School.

In December 1964, following his high school graduation, Leo Buddy Buckholdt enlisted in the US Marine Corps and was sent to Camp Pendleton, California, for his basic training. After completing school-of-infantry training, he was assigned as a helicopter door gunner in VOM Squadron 2 of MAG 16 and he departed for Vietnam.

Upon his arrival in Vietnam Buckholdt was immediately introduced to combat activity. During the month of March 1966, he was involved in a firefight that earned him a recommendation for the Naval Commendation Medal with combat distinguishing device, the Air Medal, First Award and the Air Medal with Gold Star.

Buckholdt's unit was later operating out of Chu Lai, Vietnam, when it was called upon to support marines fighting a battalion of North Vietnamese Army Regulars. During the early hours of June 16, 1966, the eighteen men of the 1st Platoon of C Company of the 1st Recon Marines, who had been placed on Hill 488 (Nui Vu), were attacked by the communist troops of the NVA.

The platoon had received casualties during the initial assault and sent out a call for Medical Evacuation choppers from Ky Ha.

At 0300, four UH-34D's from HMM-363 escorted by 2 UH-1E's from VMO-6 and 2 A-4's departed from Chu Lai to attempt to retract the team. Enemy fire was so intense in the zone that the flight had to wave off. One of the H-34s took seven hits from an automatic weapon.

One UH-1E from VMO-2 was also hit and forced down at BT 195222. The gunner, Private First Class Leo B. Buckholdt, was killed by hostile fire.

Buckholdt's body was removed from the door in the chopper and returned to his home in Santa Cruz. Following a memorial service, Private First Class Leo Buddy Buckholdt was interred in the Golden Gate National Cemetery in San Bruno.

(USDVA; VVMW; VVVVW, SCSn June 20. 1968 1:1; USMC Combat Helicopter Association, 660616 VMO-2 Vietnam, http://www.popasmoke.com/kia/incidents.php?incident_id=48&conflict_id=24, [16 September 2008])

RAINFORD TIFFIN
(1966/07/21)

(Internet photo)

As William Tiffin lay dying, the fate of his son Ray remained unknown.

Rainford "Ray" Tiffin was born on March 4, 1938, in San Francisco, California, to William and Alice Tiffin. In addition to Ray, the Tiffin family included an older son, William. Ray grew up in a home on Anderson Street in Santa Cruz, attended a nearby elementary and junior high school and in 1952, entered Santa Cruz High School. In addition to his studies and student activities, he worked at a local Chevron service station. Upon graduation from high school Tiffin began a two-year program at Monterey Peninsula College.

In 1961 Rainford Tiffin was accepted into the US Air Force air cadet program and was sent to Webb Air Force Base in Big Springs, Texas, where he began pilot training.

After graduating, he was awarded his wings and commissioned a second lieutenant.

While stationed at Luke AFB in Phoenix, Arizona, in 1962, Ray married Judith Woodley. Following additional training, he was assigned to the US airbase at Itazuki Japan, and began ferrying jets from the US to the Far East. Judith joined him and it was at this location that their two sons were born.

In 1965, as a member of the 388th Tactical Fighter Wing, 12th Tactical Fighter Squadron, Tiffin was placed on temporary duty at the Korat Royal Thai Air Force Base. Korat, located approximately 157 miles northeast of Bangkok, became his home for the next year. During that period, his squadron flew strikes against North Vietnamese and Viet Cong installations.

While flying a strike on the La Banh POL storage site, ten miles north of Cho Ngoc, Yen Bai, in North Vietnam, on July 21, 1966, Captain Rainford Tiffin's plane was hit by anti-aircraft fire. Other planes accompanying him on the mission reported that they did not observe an ejection from his plane before it crashed near the village of Cam Nhan. Rainford Tiffin was initially classified as MIA/POW and later promoted to the rank of Major.

With the absence of his body or prisoner of war status by the North Vietnamese, Tiffin was re-classified as killed in action in 1973. His remains have never been recovered.

(CBR; VVMW; Polk's Santa Cruz Directory 1957, 1956 Santa Cruz HS, Cardinal Yearbook, Ejection History.org.uk The Year 1966; Personal remembrances of Judith Tiffin Alpers, May 5, 2009 (Tiffin's widow); SCSn December 31, 1971; http://www.ejection-history.org.uk/PROJECT/YEAR_Pages/1966jul-sep.htm, [16 September 2008] WIKI, Royal Thai Air Base;)

RICHARD F. CAMPOS
(1966/12/06)

(Watsonville Register-Pajaronian photo)

A gray metal coffin containing the remains of an unclaimed GI drew national attention to the plight of a Pajaro Valley orphan.

Richard Frederick Campos was born at the Amador County railroad siding of Carbondale, California, on September 15, 1940, to Neva Campos, an unwed seventeen year old. His father, Albert Salazar, had deserted her and never reappeared. In 1942, while she lay dying of tuberculosis in a public hospital, Neva made arrangements for Richard to live with her sister Maria in San Francisco. He never saw his mother again. His aunt cared for him until 1947 when she also died, leaving the eight-year-old a ward of the court. In 1948 a foster home was found for Campos in San Leandro, California; however, after four years of failing health, his foster mother had to give him up.

Catholic Social Service heard of the orphan's plight and found a home for Richard in their Salesian Order St. Francis School in Watsonville. In a newspaper article appearing in the *Watsonville Register-Pajaronian* on December 22, 1966, Father Pratte recalled Campos, who lived at the school for five years. The priest described him as a good-looking boy with wavy hair and a pleasing smile who adapted well to the school and made many friends. Although he was scholastically described as an average student, he excelled in competition and played on the school's championship eighth grade basketball team. Richard also had the distinction of winning the Watsonville city marble championship.

When he reached his seventeenth birthday, Campos and his best friend, Paul Rivera, left the school for San Francisco. Lacking the necessary funds for housing, they voluntarily housed themselves in a detention center where they were given three meals and a cot each day. He only remained in San Francisco a brief period before entering the armed forces.

In 1958 Richard Campos enlisted in the US Army and after completing basic and advanced training, was assigned to an infantry regiment in Korea. Campos apparently found a home in the army and by 1965 was serving as a sergeant in Company C, 8th Infantry Regiment of the 4th Infantry Division stationed at Fort Lewis, Washington.

In September 1966 Campos' division was sent to Vietnam and assigned to the central highland area in the province of Pleiku. While on a search and destroy patrol on December 6, 1966, a Viet Cong sniper's bullet snuffed out his life. His body was recovered and returned to Oakland to be claimed by a relative and released for burial. No relative could be found to claim the body of Richard Campos and it sat unclaimed in an Army warehouse.

Newspapers began publishing stories of the army's search for a relative to sign the necessary approval to bury Campos. St. Francis School immediately requested permission to bring his body to Watsonville for burial in the Valley Catholic Cemetery, but their request was withheld. When the National Commander of the Veterans of Foreign Wars heard of the situation, his organization began applying pressure on the army to have Campos buried at Arlington National Cemetery.

James Campos, an uncle who Richard had not seen for fifteen years, was finally located. He claimed Richard's remains and made arrangements for his burial

On December 31, 1966, people began arriving early at the Army's Chapel of Our Lady at the San Francisco Presidio for Richard Campos' funeral. The 200 available seats were quickly occupied, standing room only areas were filled, and the remaining attendees congregated outside to listen to the funeral mass. After the funeral, the cortege containing the remains of Richard Campos made its way along the ten-mile route to Golden Gate National Cemetery in San Bruno, where he was laid to rest.

After hearing the story of Richard Campos, Barbara Dane, a folksinger and peace activist, wrote the "Ballad of Richard Campos," an ironic ending for this professional soldier.

(VVVW; VVMW; USDVA; WRP December 22, 1966 1:1, December 30, 1966 1:7; SCSn January 1, 1967 31:4; Philadelphia Inquirer December 23, 1966 Barbara Dane, Songs of Protest, The Vietnam Songbook, http://www.barbaradane.net/billboard3403.html, [16 September 2008])

RONALD J. JOHNSON
(1966/12/17)

(Santa Cruz Sentinel photo)

Christmas Eve 1966 was a sad occasion in the Harold Johnson household; they had just buried their son Ronald.

Ronald Joe Johnson was born in Kings County, California, on September 24, 1947, to Mr. and Mrs. Harold J. Johnson. Ronald's family included brothers Douglas, Gary and Mark and sisters Victoria and Jill. Ronald was raised in Soquel, California, attended local schools and was active in little league baseball. He and his teammates prided themselves in having won the 1960 little league championship for their community. In 1962 he entered Soquel High School, where he was remembered by one of his classmates as being a "nice person and a friend that loved cars." It may have been the love of cars that influenced his after-school employment at a local Chevron service station.

In early 1966 Ronald Johnson enlisted in the US Army and received basic and advanced individual training at an unspecified camp. After completing his training, Johnson was sent to Vietnam. Upon his arrival on April 8, 1966, he was assigned to A Company, 12th Cavalry Regiment of the 1st Cavalry Division.

In June, the army began Operations Irving and Thayer to clear the North Vietnam Army from Binh Dinh Province, and Johnson found himself in the thick of the fighting. The 1st Cavalry's Internet history recalls that,

In the opening phases of Operation "Thayer I," enemy elements of the 7th and 8th battalions, 18th North Vietnamese Army Regiment had been reported in the village of Hoa Hoi [Binh Dinh Province]. The 1st Battalion, 12th Cavalry Regiment, in the face of strong heavy resistance, deployed to encircle the village. On 02 October, B Company was the first to be air assaulted into the landing area 300 meters east of the village. Immediately, the units came under intense small arms and mortar fire. A Company landed to the southwest and began a movement northeast to the village. In the meantime, C Company landed north of the village and began moving south. By this time A and B Companies had linked up and established positions which prevent the enemy from slipping out of the village during the night. [The12th Cav remained in that area until approximately December 27th]

During the fighting that ensued on December 17, 1966, Specialist Fourth Class Ronald Joe Johnson was killed by small arms fire. His body was recovered, returned to Santa Cruz and buried in Holy Cross Cemetery on Christmas Eve Day, 1966.

(CBR; VVVMW; Holy Cross Cemetery headstone; VVVW; SCSn December 19, 1966 1.3, December 22, 1966 20:6; 1st Cav History y http://www.first-team.us/journals/1stndx06.html, [16 Sept 2008])

1967

PEDRO ORTIZ
(1967/05/01)

"Don't come outside to the car, and don't cry, mother," Pedro remarked as he was about to leave Watsonville for the last time, "I want to remember you in your own living room like this."

Pedro Ortiz was born in Fresno County, California, on January 31, 1946, to Raymond and Gloria Ortiz. Over the next several years the couple lived in several communities before divorcing. In addition to Pedro, the Ortiz family consisted of sons Frank and Reynaldo. Later Gloria remarried and brothers Richard and Manuel and sisters Jenny and Lupe Platero were added to Pedro's family.

During the mid-1950s, Pedro was sent to live with his grandparents in the Pajaro Valley where he attended the Pajaro Elementary School for two years.

In the late 1950s Ortiz moved to Calexico where he completed his elementary school education. A final move took him north to Selma, California, where he graduated from Selma High School in 1964.

After spending a year at Reedley College, Ortiz enlisted in the US Army in 1966 and was sent to Fort Ord, California, for basic training. He was then ordered to Fort Campbell, Kentucky, where he received instruction as a helicopter gunner. In December 1966 Ortiz returned to Watsonville to visit his mother for the last time. He also shared with her his dream of finishing college, becoming a social worker and of making Watsonville his home.

When Pedro Ortiz arrived in Vietnam on January 14, 1967, he was assigned to the 335th Assault Helicopter Company serving in the Saigon area. On May 1, 1967, Pedro was involved in a crash that took his life.

The 335th Assault Helicopter Company was tasked with providing airlift for a combat assault being conducted by the 9th Infantry Division operating out of Bear Cat base. Nine aircraft departed Bien Hoa, climbed to 1500 feet, and proceeded toward Bear Cat in a left-staggered trail formation. While enroute the pilot of the #3 aircraft noted that #2 was in very close formation with the lead aircraft and did not appear to be adjusting his position appropriately when lead maneuvered. When lead began a gentle right turn his blade tips struck those of the #2 aircraft. Both aircraft broke up in flight. Eight men died as a result of the mid-air collision.

The body of Pedro Ortiz was returned to Selma, where his father and his two Vietnam veteran brothers were living, for final burial. Specialist Fourth Class Ortiz later was posthumously awarded the Purple Heart and Air Medal with five Oakleaf clusters.

(CBR; VVMW; VVVW; WRP August 17, 1967 1:4, May 13, 1967 1:5)

LAWRENCE R. DODD
(1967/05/26)

(Watsonville Register-Pajaronian photo)

Classmate Donald Hansen remembered Larry as someone who "had a smile that would light up any overcast day in Monterey Bay."

Lawrence Rudin Dodd was born on April 2, 1946, in Watsonville to Mr. and Mrs. Harold Dodd. Larry and his sisters Catherine, Sherrie and Carrie grew up in Aromas, California, and attended local Pajaro Valley schools. In 1960 Dodd enrolled in Watsonville High School and remained there for the next four years. During that period, he played on the football team and was remembered by his friends as being a good-natured individual who was known for truthfulness and dependability. After graduating from high school in 1964, he enrolled in nearby Cabrillo College and followed a course of study to prepare him for the School of Forestry at the University of California at Davis. In December 1965 Larry married Jean Fowler.

Larry Dodd was drafted into the US Army in January 1966 and the following February was sent to Fort Lewis, Washington, to train as an infantryman. After completing basic and advanced individual training, he was assigned to Company C, 3rd Battalion, 8th Infantry Regiment of the 4th Infantry Division preparing for departure to Vietnam. In September 1966, Larry said goodbye to his wife and family for the last time.

Upon arrival in Vietnam Larry's company was deployed to the central highland area where they conducted patrols in search of Viet Cong and North Vietnamese units. His spirits were particularly high on May 26, 1967, as he began the day's patrol. Dodd had just heard that his wife had given birth to their daughter Ladean. He expected to join them in three more months when he rotated home. As Company C was moving along a jungle trail near the Cambodian border at Plei Doc in the central highlands it became strung out and was ambushed by North Vietnamese troops. Larry's company commander was the first to be killed in the firefight and Specialist Fourth Class Lawrence Rudin Dodd

soon joined him.

The body of Larry Dodd, Watsonville's first Vietnam War combat casualty, was recovered and returned home for a funeral and internment in the Golden Gate National Cemetery in San Bruno.

At a later ceremony at Fort Ord Larry's widow, Jean, received the Bronze Star and Purple Heart that were awarded to him posthumously.

(VVMW; WHSM; VVVW; USDVA; WRP June 1, 1967 1:3, June 3, 1967 2:2, September 29, 1967 9:1; Cem Survey)

WELTON R. KING
(1967/06/01)

(Santa Cruz High School yearbook)

Welton taught Santa Cruz High School cadets how to be soldiers and then set the example.

Welton Roger King was born on September 12, 1924, in Amity, Arkansas, to Mr. and Mrs. C. F. King. The King family also consisted of a younger brother Ronald [who also appears on this honor roll] and his sisters Jo Ann and Jane. The family later moved to the California central valley community of Merced. Welton is believed to have graduated from Merced High School prior to the family's move to Santa Cruz. While living in Santa Cruz, he attended San Jose State College and became an ROTC cadet.

After serving in World War II, King returned to Santa Cruz and during the years 1947-1948, taught band and ROTC at Santa Cruz High School. Desiring a career in the US Air Force, Welton re-entered the armed forces during the Korean War and continued to serve throughout the Cold War era. During this period, Welton married Mary Lou and had two sons, Ronald and Douglas, along with a daughter Kathy.

By the time of the Vietnam War, Welton had risen to the rank of Lt. Colonel and continued to fly. The type of aircraft or the Air Wing to which he was assigned has not been identified; however, B29, B52 bombers and other aircraft were being flown out of Okinawa in 1967. On June 1, 1967, while taking off on a mission, Lt. Colonel Welton R. King's aircraft crashed at Kadena AFB on Okinawa. His remains were recovered and returned to California for burial in the Golden Gate National Cemetery in San Bruno, California.

(USDVA, SCSn June 4, 1967 37:7, October 5, 1967 1:4; Photo-SCHS)

RICHARD L. ST. GEORGE
(1967/07/05)

(Watsonville High School yearbook)

Lt. St. George was being prepared to "slay the Soviet dragon" when his twentieth-century steed went down.

Richard L. St. George was born September 9, 1940, in Los Angeles County, California, to Mr. and Mrs. Reginald St. George. In 1954 Richard, along with his brother James and sister Judy, accompanied his parents in the family move to Watsonville. Reginald obtained employment at the Watsonville Press and moved his family into a home on Amesti Road half way between Watsonville and Corralitos. During their Pajaro Valley residence, the St. George family was active in All Saints Episcopal Church where young Richard served as an acolyte (altar boy). After completing grammar school, he entered Watsonville High School and graduated about 1958. During the following three years, St. George completed college programs at Cabrillo and Hartnell Colleges.

In 1963 St. George joined the US Air Force and entered an officer-training program to qualify as a navigator. At the completion of the program he was commissioned a second lieutenant and assigned to the 72nd Wing. While serving in that unit, he received further training as an electronic warfare officer, qualifying him to arm nuclear warheads aboard intercontinental bombers. Throughout his tour of service, St. George flew countless "fail safe" missions over the globe in the event of the need for a nuclear retaliation against the Soviet Union.

On July 5, 1967, while awaiting his promotion to Captain, St. George's plane departed from Ramey AFB in Puerto Rico on a routine training mission. In flight, the aircraft developed mechanical problems over the north coast of the island that the pilot was unable to correct and the B-52 plunged into the sea. Three of the crewmen were able to parachute to safety; however, First Lieutenant Richard St. George and the remainder of the crew sank to the bottom of the sea with the plane. His body was never recovered.

A memorial service with an air force honor guard was conducted at his family church in Watsonville. A headstone in his remembrance was installed in Pajaro Valley Memorial Park.

(CBR; WRP July 6, 1967 1:5, July 12, 1967 2:4, July 17, 1967 2:4; Cem Survey headstone; Photo-WHS)

FRANK J. ROSE JR.
(1967/07/12)

(Watsonville High School Memorial Project)

Two guerrilla's ended Frank Rose's Vietnam experience and his life.

Frank James Rose Jr. was born in Hayward, California, on August 6, 1941, to Mr. and Mrs. Frank James Rose. While he was still an infant, his family relocated to Watsonville where his maternal grandmother was living. Later, before Frank's parents divorced, several siblings joined him in the Rose household. Others were later added when his mother married William Serpa of Watsonville. Rose attended local schools and in 1955 entered Watsonville High School. He enjoyed renovating old cars, which led him into employment as a spray painter at a local paint and body shop. Prior to the Vietnam War, Frank married Claudia Jean, who also lived in the Pajaro Valley.

Frank Rose was drafted into the US Army on October 20, 1966, and sent to Fort Lewis, Washington, for basic and advanced individual training. On April 16, 1967, he was deployed to Vietnam where he joined HQ Company, 35th Engineer Battalion that served as a combat engineer unit. During his tour in Vietnam, Frank's company was engaged in highway maintenance. His unit also provided support for the 1st Cavalry Division (Airmobile) unit in the Bong Son plains during the Loa valley operations.

On July 12, 1967, while working in his company compound area, Specialist Fourth Class Frank James Rose Jr. was shot and killed by two Vietnamese youths, said to be members of a Viet Cong guerilla unit. His body was returned to Watsonville and after a funeral at Valley Catholic Church, was interred in the adjoining cemetery.

(VVMW; WHSM; WRP July 15, 1967, July 17, 1967 1:5 1:1; 35th Unidentified Website, Battalion of Engineers in Vietnam http://stinet.dtic. mil/oai/oai?verb=getRecord&metadataPrefix=html&identifier=AD08244 96 [15 May 2007 Approx].)

NORMAN SCHMIDT
(1967/08/31)

(Internet photo)

"It broke my heart to see him climb into that airplane," Norm's wife said after seeing him off for the last time.

Norman Schmidt was born on July 7, 1926, in Los Angeles County, California, to Mr. and Mrs. H. H. Schmidt, and was raised in the small community of Ben Lomond in Santa Cruz County. During the late1930s, he attended local elementary schools and in 1944 graduated from Boulder Creek High School. Following high school, he enrolled in nearby San Jose State College where he graduated about 1948.

Norman Schmidt entered the US Air Force about 1948 and following training, earned his wings. In the early 1950s Lt. Schmidt completed pilot training at Luke Field, Arizona, and was assigned to a fighter squadron in Korea. During the Korean War, he flew a number of combat missions and on one occasion his plane was shot down.

When the Vietnam War began, Schmidt had risen to the rank of Lt. Colonel and was testing jet fighters at George Air Force Base in Mojave, California. In July 1966, he received orders assigning him to the 435th Tactical Fighter Squadron of the 8th Tactical Fighter Wing, which was flying F105D fighters out of Ubon Air Base, Thailand.

In an article appearing in the *Washington Post* issue of March 26, 2005, Schmidt's daughter, Janet Schmidt Zupan, described her father's last mission, captivity and death.

On Sept. 1, 1966, his F-104 was hit by flak during a mission, and the plane went down. My dad bailed out, drift-

ing toward his last 364 living days, days that separated him so utterly from his life as a son, husband, father and career test pilot. In his final months he was deemed a war criminal, beyond our desperate love and worry, beyond the protection of the country he served, and excluded from the regard for human safety, dignity and life inherent in the articles of the Geneva Conventions.

In a 1974 audiotape, Cmdr. Robert Shumaker shared recollections of my dad. They were in a nine-foot-square cell with two other POWs in the Little Vegas section of the Hanoi Hilton in the summer of 1967. It was a harrowing period for the prisoners, in the wake of a communications purge. Shumaker described an incident on August 21: "After Norm had finished washing he was peeking out (a) crack and trying to get a look at some of the other prisoners. Wouldn't you know it, a guard caught him." For this offense, my dad's legs were locked in stocks attached to his bed. Ten days passed before guards released him from this confinement and took him away for interrogation. He was never seen again. Shumaker concluded that "(Norm) was subjected to torture and succumbed in the process." Other prisoners, in cells down the hall from the interrogation room, reported hearing the "sounds of torture ... a loud scuffle and then silence." My father's remains were disinterred from the Ba Huyen Cemetery in Hanoi in 1974 and returned to us.

The location of Norman Schmidt's grave has not been identified.

(CBR; VVMW; SCR October 05, 1951 6:1, SCSn September 5, 1966 1:4; Task Force Omega, Norman Schmidt, http://www. taskforceomegainc.org/s091.html, [16 Sept 2008] Article By Janet Schmidt Zupan, For The Washington Post, March 26. 2005 7:36PM, http://www.cmonitor.com/apps/pbcs.dll/article?AID=/20050326/ REPOSITORY/503260334/1028/OPINION02, [16 Sept 2008])

RONALD R. KING
(1967/10/03)

Four months after the death of their son Welton, the King family received another jolt.

Ronald Runyan King was born on November 1, 1926 , in Amity, Arkansas, to Mr. and Mrs. C. F. King. The King family consisted of another son, Welton (who was also among the county's war dead) and daughters Jo Ann and Jane. The family later moved to the California central valley community of Merced, where Ronald attended local schools.

Following graduation from Merced High School in 1945, Ronald King entered the US Army and served until the conclusion of World War II. After he was discharged, he returned to his parent's home in Santa Cruz, California, and enrolled in nearby San Jose State College.

After graduating from college, about 1950, King entered the US Air Force and was commissioned a second lieutenant. Following the Korean War, he attended the Air Force Command and Staff College at Maxwell Air Base, Alabama, and then served in England for the next three years. Upon his return to the United States, King completed an advanced training program at McConnell Air Force Base, Kansas, and then received orders to Southeast Asia.

After Major King departed for Thailand in 1967, his wife Margaret and their four sons John, Richard, William and Robert moved into a home in San Jose, California. Upon his arrival at the Takhli Royal Thai Air Base, King was assigned to the 333rd Tactical Fighter Squadron of the 355th Tactical Fighter Wing.

On October 3, 1967, Ronald King had just completed a reconnaissance mission to North Vietnam aboard his F105D fighter when he ran out of fuel over the Gulf of Tonkin. He was reported to have ejected from the aircraft, parachuted into heavy seas and drowned by waves that reached twenty feet in height. His body was never recovered. Major Ronald Runyan King was posthumously promoted to Lt. Colonel and a memorial service in his honor was conducted at the Golden Gate National Cemetery at San Bruno on October 8, 1967.

(VVMW; VVVW; SCSn October 5, 1967 1:4, October 8, 1967)

MELESSO GARCIA
(1967/10/17)

(Internet photo)

Private Melesso Garcia shared misgivings with his comrades about going into combat on October 17, 1967.

Melesso Garcia listed Santa Cruz County as his residence; however, the location of his birth, family members and his life in the community have not been established. He was born on October 18, 1946, and while some portion of his education may have taken place in Watsonville, Watsonville High School did not include him among their students who died in Vietnam.

Garcia enlisted in the regular US Army in the fall of 1966

and received training at Fort Lewis, Washington. He was assigned to Company D, 2nd Battalion (Black Lion Battalion) of the 28th Infantry Regiment and on July 16, 1967, began his Vietnam tour.

On October 17, 1967, Garcia's company was in a jungle area near Ong Thanh (about fifty miles from Saigon) when they were ambushed by approximately 1200 Viet Cong troops. The two US companies (A&D), totaling about 120 men, were pinned down as snipers opened fire from all directions. Pulitzer Prize winning author David Maraniss, in his book *They Marched into Sunlight: War and Peace Vietnam and America, October 1967,* detailed the end of the life of Private First Class Melesso Garcia.

To his left [SP4] Troyer saw Melesso Garcia behind a log, gesturing. It seems that Garcia wanted to say something. He turned on his side and pushed his body up with one hand and at that moment was shot. A look came over his face that Troyer had not seen before. For two days Garcia had been haunted by premonitions that he should not be out there, and now the realization of his foreboding registered on his face.

Melesso Garcia died one day short of his twenty-first birthday. His remains were recovered and returned to Houston, Texas, where they were buried in the Houston National Cemetery.

(VVMW; USDVA Answers.com Battle of Ong Than, *They Marched into Sunlight" War and Peace Vietnam and America, October 1967,* by David Maraniss, Simon & Shuster NY Pp. 250, 272-273, http://www.answers.com/topic/battle-of-ong-thanh, [16 Sept 2008])

LOUIS C. MILLER
(1967/11/06)

(Watsonville Register-Pajaronian photo)

David De Lapena remembered how his friend Louie "always stuck up for the underdog."

Louis Charles Miller was born in Watsonville, California, on December 24, 1948. His parents later divorced and his grandparents, Mr. and Mrs. Charles Burnett, who lived in nearby Corralitos, raised him. Louis received his primary school education at Corralitos Elementary School. One childhood friend reminisced of their "playing in the woods down by the creek and shooting [basketball] hoops at the school." Louis Miller enrolled at Watsonville High School in September 1963, where he was remembered as an average student who was not involved in many extra-curricular activities. Miller appears to have been an outdoors kind of guy who enjoyed activities such as hunting.

High school education came to an end for Louis Miller in January 1967, when at the age of seventeen, he left school to join the US Army. After completing basic training at Fort Ord, California, he was sent to Fort Benning, Georgia, for advanced infantry and paratrooper training. Private Miller was then assigned to B Company, 503rd Regiment of the 173rd Airborne Infantry Division.

On July 2, 1967, Louis Miller arrived in Vietnam. While in "Nam," he served at An Khe, Plieku, and Landing Zone English, among other locations. In September 1967, he was involved in an undisclosed firefight, was wounded and awarded the Purple Heart.

Increased activity by the North Vietnamese army began occurring in the central highlands near Kontum in November and Company B was sent to the area in what was known as Operation MacArthur or the Battle of Dak To.

To expand the coverage of supporting artillery fires, the 4th Battalion of the 173rd was ordered to occupy Hill 823, south of Ben Het, for the construction of Fire Support Base 15. Since the rest of the battalion's companies were already deployed elsewhere, the 120 men of Bravo Company would combat assault onto the hilltop by helicopter alone. After several attempts to denude the hilltop with air strikes and artillery fire, Bravo Company landed unopposed that afternoon, but the hill was not unoccupied. 15 minutes later, contact was made with the North Vietnamese. The battle that ensued raged at close quarters until early the following morning when elements of the 66th PAVN Regiment withdrew, leaving behind more than 100 bodies. Nine Americans of Bravo Company, 4/503 also lay dead and another 28 were wounded.

Included among the names of those nine Americans of Bravo Company killed on November 6, 1967, was that of Louis Charles Miller. His body was recovered and returned to Watsonville for burial in Pajaro Valley Memorial Park.

(VVMW; WHSM; WIKI, Battle of Dak To; WRP November 11, 1967; November 24, 1967)

1968

JACK W. MCKINNON JR.
(1968/01/03)

(Golden Gate National Cemetery – San Bruno California)

Jack McKinnon's life in Santa Cruz County, California, remains a mystery. He was born on March 9, 1948, in Santa Cruz; however no record of his family, formative years or life in the county has been located.

During the early part of 1967, McKinnon was apparently living in Santa Cruz County and was drafted into the US Army. As an entering recruit he would likely have spent the eight-week basic training course at Fort Ord, California, or Fort Lewis, Washington, with an additional five weeks of advanced individual training to prepare him as an infantryman.

Private McKinnon arrived in Vietnam on April 13, 1967, and joined Company D, 4th Battalion of the 31st Infantry Regiment. That unit was in the process of moving from Tay Ninh to Chu Lai on the South China Sea to participate in Operation Oregon, which was a sweep into Binh Son Province.

About 1967 McKinnon was promoted to specialist fourth class and likely participated in additional combat operations in Quang Ngai, Chu Lai, and Que Son Valley. It was probably at one of these locations that Specialist Fourth Class Jack Wiley McKinnon Jr. was killed in action on January 3, 1968, while attempting to prevent Viet Cong guerillas and the North Vietnamese Army from capturing the coastal lowlands.

His body was recovered, returned to California and was interred in the Golden Gate National Cemetery.

(CBR; VVMW; Global Security.org, 4th Battalion 31st Infantry Regiment http://www.globalsecurity.org/military/agency/army/4-31in.htm, [16 September 2008], 196th.Org, Untitled Document, http://www.196th.org/guestbook/Guestbook2005/Guestbook2005archive.htm, USDVA)

WILTON R. PICKETT
(1968/01/09)

(Santa Cruz Sentinel photo)

Wilton Ray Pickett, the only son of Mr. and Mrs. Ray S. Pickett, was born in Los Angeles, California, on July 23, 1941. Wilton grew up in Southern California, attended LA County schools and graduated from Anaheim Union High School in 1959. In 1964 the Pickett family, which also consisted of daughters Judy and Betty Jean, moved to Santa Cruz County where Wilton and his father worked in the heating and sheet metal business. He also found employment in the crop dusting industry. His constant movement from one job to another delayed his being drafted.

In February 1966 Wilton Pickett was inducted into the US Army. Following basic and advanced training, he was assigned to Company B, 815th Engineer Battalion of the 935th Group at Fort Belvoir, Virginia. On March 23, 1967, Pickett and his unit flew to California and upon arrival boarded the troopship *USNS General Walker* for Vietnam.

Upon arrival in Vietnam April 15, 1967, Pickett was transported to his base at Engineer Hill near the central highland town of Pleiku. In Vietnam he drove a dump truck for the construction of bases, structures, roads, airfields, facilities, bridges and other building projects.

On January 9, 1968, at a location identified as Connell Quarry, Specialist Fourth Class Wilton Ray Pickett was killed by small arms gunfire while moving towards a bunker following an explosion. His remains were returned home and following a funeral service on January 22, 1968, were interred in Oakwood Memorial Park in Santa Cruz.

(VVMW; 815th Engineers, History Vietnam Tour, http://groups. msn.com/815thEngineers/inmemoryof.msnw, [15 May 2007 Approx.]; SCSn January 12, 1968 1:7, January 24, 1968 C4: 8; Oakwood Cemetery Survey)

ROBERT L. FOSTER
(1968/01/22)

(Santa Cruz Sentinel photo)

Visions of the movie *Bridge Over the River Kwai* may have entered Robert's mind as he stepped into that river to go bathing.

Robert L. Foster was born in Colorado on January 6, 1941, to Mr. and Mrs. Clyde Foster. He was raised and lived in that state until about 1962 or 1963 when he arrived in Santa Cruz County, California. He and his wife, Betty, moved into the Live Oak district of the county and settled into a residence on 34th Avenue near Pleasure Point by the ocean.

It is not known when Robert Foster entered the US Army; however, by 1967 he had completed his initial training and risen in rank to specialist fifth class. Foster was assigned to the 44th Engineering Group (Construction) at Kanchanaburi, Thailand.

In the jungles of Thailand, the US Army supported major activities for both the Vietnam War and the secret war in Laos. The 44th Engineer Group was assigned the task to build roads and a support (logistics) network based in the plateau region of central Thailand known as Korat.

On January 22, 1968, Robert Foster's wife received news from the Sixth US Army Headquarters in San Francisco that her husband had drowned while bathing in a river near Kanchanaburi, Thailand. That river is likely the River Kwai that runs through Kanchanaburi.

Foster's body was recovered and returned to Santa Cruz where a funeral with full military honors was conducted followed by interment in Oakwood Memorial Park.

(SCSn January 25, 1968 1:7, Oakwood Memorial Park records; http://www.geocities.com/koratmahknut/44thengrgp/historical. htm [29 May 2009], 44th Eng History,)

GARY R. CARPENTER
(1968/01/30)

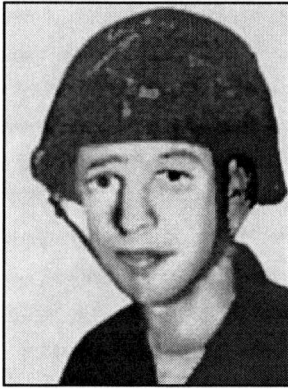

(Watsonville Register-Pajaronian photo)

"I can't smile, I'm supposed to look like a bulldog," was Gary Carpenter's comment to his aunt when she asked him to smile for a picture."

Gary Ralph Carpenter was born on July 6, 1949, in Fresno, California, to Ralph and Jewel Carpenter. At an early age he and his brother Lauren moved to Watsonville where his uncle and aunt, Mr. and Mrs. Roy Carpenter, raised them. Gary attended Freedom school and in 1963 enrolled in Watsonville High School. He was remembered as a cheerful industrious student who enjoyed sports, but because of an outside job was unable to participate on the school's teams. Later he joined DeMolay, an organization affiliated with the Masonic lodge, and belonged to the First Methodist Church youth group.

In June 1967, Gary Carpenter graduated from high school and six days later enlisted in the US Marine Corps. Following basic and school-of-infantry training at Camp Pendleton, Private Carpenter returned home on leave. In an interview with a *Watsonville Register-Pajaronian* reporter, Gary noted that over the past five months he had acquired, "a partiality for burgundy cherry ice cream and a respect for the training administered by the Marine Corps."

On Thanksgiving Day 1967, Gary Carpenter left home for the last time. After arriving in Vietnam, he was assigned to Company H, 2nd Battalion, 3rd Marines of the 1st Marine Division stationed near Da Nang in Quang Nam province. He was immediately subjected to combat and wrote home that the "Gosses" (term used for Communists) had hit his unit. "I had to run 100 yards to get to my foxhole and get my rifle. When I got to it, a friend was hit and bullets were going around us and I started to pray."

On January 30, 1968, while on a patrol in the Quang Nam Province near the DMZ, Private First Class Gary Ralph Carpenter was killed in action when he was shot in the head by a sniper.

His body was returned to California and was buried at Memorial Park in Selma near his birthplace of Fresno.
(VVMW; WHSM; WRP February 2, 1968 1:1)

LENNIE H. SCHARFF
(1968/02/21)

(Santa Cruz Sentinel photo)

High School classmate Dallas Wolf described Lennie Scharff as a "Fine guy, super athlete, good looking...the whole package."

Lennie Harold Scharff was born on August 31, 1948, in Fort Dodge, Iowa, to Mr. and Mrs. Walter Scharff. The Scharff family, which also included his brother Dennis, resided in Iowa until 1961, when they moved to Ben Lomond, California. Scharff finished grammar school and enrolled in nearby San Lorenzo Valley High School. In high school he was remembered for his football ability and gutsy endurance under adversity. On one occasion he continued to play in a football game with a painful shoulder injury without a complaint.

Lennie Scharff enlisted in the US Marine Corps on September 26, 1967. After completing basic and school-of-infantry training at Camp Pendleton, he was assigned to H&S Company, 1st Battalion, 5th Marine Regt. in the 1st Marine Division stationed in Thua Thien Province of Vietnam. During the 1968 Tet New Year Offensive, his battalion was engaged in the heavy fighting near the ancient city of Hue.

On February 21, 1968, Private First Class Lennie Harold Scharff was killed in action by small arms fire. The final chapter in his story is best recounted by his friend Dennis Belville who shared his recollection of Lennie's death and funeral on the Internet web site, Remembrance from the Wall.

I remember that cold winters night when a hush went over the gym. So very strange, the utter silence, the sobbing cheerleaders the shocked disbelief on the faces of the parents. The thought that one of ours has died on the battlefield was a crushing blow. My brother and I were asked to be pallbearers at his funeral. Both of us in our dress navy uniforms proudly put

Lenny to rest that day. I can still hear the single bugler playing taps as it drifted through the redwoods. He gave everything he had on the gridiron for the SLV Cougars and he ultimately gave his life for his country. 'Red right 33 Red' 'break'."

Lennie was buried in the Felton Cemetery on March 9, 1968.

(VVMW; VVVW; SCSn February 24?, 1968 1:3, March 6, 1968 12:2; Street Fighting Lessons Learned from the Battle for Hue for 21st Century Urban Warfare, By Edward J. O'Neill, IV B.A., Kent State University, 1989 May 2003, http://etd.lsu.edu/docs/available/etd-0128103-183352/unrestricted/O'Neill_thesis.pdf, [16 September 2008])

WILLIAM D. CHOI-RAKOFSKY
(1968/02/26)

(Watsonville Register-Pajaronian photo)

After only twenty days of duty in Vietnam, the tour and life of William Choi came to an end.

No information has been found to explain the hyphenated surname of Choi-Rakofsky. Military service records list him as William David Choi, whereas the surname Rakofsky is the name he shared with his brothers, Jack and Glenn.

William David Choi was born in Honolulu, Hawaii on September 7, 1947. His mother's grandparents, Mr. and Mrs. H. B. Yu, lived in Hawaii and his mother's parents, Mr. and Mrs. Welch, resided in Soquel, California. While he was quite young, his mother brought William, his two brothers and one sister to Watsonville, where she married Jack C. Tindle. William attended Mintie White and E.A. Hall elementary schools in Watsonville before entering Soquel High School. After his graduation from high school in 1965 and prior to 1967, William was married to Anita Winifred.

William Choi-Rakofsky entered the army in August 1967 and after completing basic and advance training, was assigned to the 60th Infantry Regiment of the 9th Infantry Division.

On February 8, 1968, Private Choi joined his unit serving in the Phong Dinh Province of Vietnam. At that time the 60th Infantry Regiment was committed to the fighting in the Mekong Delta during the Tet New Year Offensive. "Jitterbug tactics," in which airmobile units were deployed within a dozen meters of the enemy with split second timing, were being used to help deter the communist offensive. It may have been during such an operation that Private First Class William David Choi-Rakofsky was killed in action on February 26, 1968. His body was recovered and returned to Santa Cruz for burial within the Oakwood Memorial Park.

(VVMW; SCSn March 3, 1968 1:4; Global Security.Org, 2nd Battalion 60th Infantry Division "Scouts Out" http://www.globalsecurity.org/military/agency/army/2-60in.htm, [16 September 2008])

GEORGE W. SKAKEL
(1968/03/06)

(Internet photo)

George went to war with a wealth of life experiences and left them in Vietnam.

George Walter Skakel entered the world on January 12, 1946, in Moab, Utah. The names of his parents or details relating to his formative years have not surfaced. The family, which also included his sisters Nancy and Sally, likely relocated to Ojai, California, where George attended Nordhoff High School. After his graduation in June 1964, he hit the road and traveled throughout France, Spain, Germany and England. After completing a class at Oxford, he worked as a merchant seaman earning his passage to India, Thailand, Saigon and Northern Australia, where he worked in a uranium mine. Skakel returned to the US and entered the University of California, Santa Cruz, with its pioneer class of 1965, but only remained through his freshman year. The UCSC newspaper *City on a Hill* later noted that he was drafted because he had not made "normal educational progress" when he dropped out of school for a year and a half.

George Skakel entered the US Army about February 1967. Following basic and advanced training, he was sent to

Vietnam on May 6 and assigned to D Company, 1st Squadron of the 7th Cavalry Regiment, which was serving in the Bong Son Plain district in northern Binh Dinh Province. While in Vietnam, Skakel submitted articles to the UCSC newspaper *The City on a Hill* under the pen name CPL Callibernus.

Following the Tet New Year Offensive in January 1968, his unit was moved to Hue. At that time he was leading a squad of what he described as "Two old-timers and nine college kids." Dick Miller, a former platoon member, shared his remembrance of George Skakel on the Vietnam Memorial Fund Internet Website:

> I didn't like him at first. He was too aggressive for me, always looking for trouble and poking into things on patrol that I preferred to ignore or avoid. Later, when I got to know him better, I came to appreciate his attitude and we became friends. He was an energetic, assertive, and tough trooper, yet he maintained his compassion for everyone and his examples of humanity and morality were inspiring. I was next to him when he was hit and with him when he died, which was almost instantly. Clarence Young and I recognized the mortal nature of his wound, and lay next to him and spoke to him constantly until there was no doubt of his demise. We didn't know if he could hear us, but we wanted him to know that he was not alone and was being tended to by those who loved him.

The body of Sergeant George Walter Skakel was recovered; however, his gravesite has not been located.

(VVMW; VVVW; 7th Infantry "First Team," 7th Cavalry Regiment-Vietnam War http://www.first-team.us/journals/7th_rgmt/7thndx04.html; Skakel-"Callibernus" Killed in Action, UCSC City on a Hill Press, 1968, http://www.nordhoff64.com/class_profile.cfm? member_id=233053, Nordhoff HS Memorial [April 5, 2009])

EDDIE D. GANT
(1968/03/18)

(Watsonville Register-Pajaronian photo)

On March 18, 1968, Eddie's journey back to his southern roots became permanent.

Eddie Dean Gant was born on the second day of the year 1949, in Covington, Tennessee. His mother's name was Margaret. Eddie, his brother Thomas and sister Gwendolin grew up in the greater Memphis area until 1959, when his parents relocated to Watsonville. Eddie attended local Pajaro Valley grammar schools and in the fall of 1963, enrolled in Watsonville High School. While in high school, he became an active member of the Future Farmers of America. In 1966 Gant moved to Grenada, Mississippi, where his grandparents lived, and transferred into Grenada High School.

Eddie Gant left high school in March 1967 to enlist in the US Marine Corps. His basic training took him to Paris Island, South Carolina, followed by additional instruction at Camp Pendleton, California, and Camp Jejune, North Carolina. In October 1967 he completed his marine rifleman training and was sent to Vietnam.

Upon arrival in Vietnam Private First Class Gant was assigned to Company C, 1st Battalion, 1st Marine Regiment of the 1st Marine Division, which was stationed near Da Nang.

> By fall of 1967, the 1st Marines were operating permanently in the northern sector of the I Corps tactical zone. The following winter the communists launched their all-out Tet New Year Offensive. Hue, the old imperial capital, was overrun by the enemy. Between 31 January and 2 March 1968, and elements of the 1st Marines, along with other US Marine and South Vietnamese units, fought to regain control of the city. The battle was characterized by bitter street fighting and hand-to-hand combat.

On March 18, 1968, Lance Corporal Eddie Dean Gant, fighting in the vicinity of Hue in Thua Thien Province, was killed in action. Eddie's remains were returned to Grenada, Mississippi, and buried in Woodlawn Cemetery.

(VVMW; VVVW; WHSM; WRP March 23, 1968; Global Security. Org, 1st Marine Regiment 1st Marine Division http://www.globalsecurity.org/military/agency/usmc/1mar.htm, [16 September 2008])

George N. Penniman II
(1968/03/26)

(Photo courtesy of Margaret Penniman)

George Naylor Penniman II, the son of Mr. and Mrs. John K. Penniman, was born February 9, 1946, in Santa Cruz California, a third generation Santa Cruzan. His early years were spent growing up in Santa Cruz; however, when his father accepted a teaching position in Santa Clara County, the family moved to Los Gatos, California. Although George's new home was twenty miles distant, he and his family considered Santa Cruz their hometown.

George attended schools in Los Gatos until his graduation in 1964, and involved himself in as much school and other activities as his study time would allow. During those years, he was enthusiastic about sports and spent his free moments with friends and family bicycling, skiing, swimming, playing tennis, fishing or camping. Outdoor activities led George to the Boy Scouts, which were an especially enjoyable experience for him. His exposure to music in the lower grades inspired him to continue participating and studying in high school, where he became proficient in the saxophone. He was a member of the Los Gatos High School orchestra, the dance band and for three years, student coordinator and drum major for the marching band. In 1964, George was the recipient of the John Philip Souza Band Award for outstanding achievement.

Immediately after finishing high school in June 1964, George enlisted in the US Navy and following boot camp, was assigned to the *USS Bennington*. He remained as a member of the crew until his death in March 1968. Between December 1966 and April 1967, George was assigned to Task Force Seventy-Seven Kitty Hawk during its highly effective combat operation in Vietnam. Following that tour, he returned to the *USS Bennington* and his squadron, Helicopter Anti-submarine Squadron Eight. It was during this period that the *Bennington* became the primary ship in the Pacific assigned to the Saturn V-501 recovery operation for the Apollo 4 landing, November 9, 1967.

In 1968 the *Bennington* was preparing to re-deploy to Vietnam for the third time; however, due to the few months remaining prior to his discharge, George's deployment was cancelled. In March he selected a college to attend and had begun the process of completing entrance requirements when the fateful accident occurred.

On March 26, 1968, while participating in helicopter recovery maneuvers alongside the *Bennington* in American waters, George was lost at sea. His family and many close friends remember George for his warm, fun-loving personality, his engaging smile, his honesty and loyalty, and cheerful willingness to help others. His assigned duties in the Navy fulfilled this propensity. As Emiddio Massa, his commanding officer, noted in a personal letter to the family, "His [George's] personal contributions will live in the performance of the men he personally guided and trained and in those who had the opportunity to observe and benefit by his example."

(The remembrances of his mother, Mrs. Margaret L.B. Penniman December 2006)

Benito B. Rodriguez
(1968/03/18)

(Watsonville Register-Pajaronian photo)

After three months in Vietnam, Rodriguez considered himself an "old timer."

Benito Bobo Rodriguez was born on April 1, 1948, in Blythe, California, to Bocanegra and Betty Rodriguez. At an early age he moved with his family to Freedom, California, where he and his brothers Charles, Joe and Sandy attended Freedom Elementary School. Young Rodriguez also became involved in the community through the Valley Catholic Church and later served as an altar boy at Sunday mass. During his pre-teen years, he was a pitcher on the church-sponsored Padres little league baseball team. In the fall of 1963 Benito enrolled in Watsonville High School and remained there until January 1966 when he dropped out during his junior year.

Following his eighteenth birthday in April, 1966, Benito

Rodriguez enlisted in the US Army. He completed basic training at Fort Ord, California, advanced infantry training at Fort Gordon, Georgia, and sniper school and paratrooper training at Fort Benning, Georgia. As a 101st Airborne, "Screaming Eagle," sniper he was posted to Fort Campbell, Kentucky, before leaving for Vietnam in January 1968.

When Rodriguez arrived in Vietnam, he joined Company C, 1st Battalion (Airborne), 501st Infantry Regiment of the 101st Airborne Division, serving in the central highlands. The 501st Infantry Regiment's primary mission was to intercept and destroy supplies arriving through the Ho Chi Minh trail.

On April 6, 1968, five days after his twentieth birthday, Sergeant Benito Bobo Rodriguez was on a search and destroy mission in Thua Thien Province when an enemy anti-tank round exploded near him taking his life. His body was returned to Watsonville and buried in Pajaro Valley Memorial Park. Benito was awarded the Bronze Star and the Purple Heart, in addition to service awards.

(VVMW; WHSM; WRP April 8, 1968 1:6; April 20, 1968 2:1; http://www.lzsally.com/sally2/archives/history_of_the_101st_airborne_di.htm, [16 September 2008] 101st Airborne, History)

JACK W. MARLOWE
(1968/04/16)

(Internet photo)

Jack's productive life unraveled with only thirty days remaining in his Vietnam tour.

Jack William Marlowe was born to James and Patricia Marlowe on May 1, 1946. Along with brothers James and Jay, he was raised and attended school in nearby Gilroy, California. During his formative years, Marlowe was active in Little League, the Boy Scouts and the youth activities of the First Baptist Church in Gilroy. When he entered high school, he affiliated with DeMolay, a Masonic youth organization and became a life member.

Upon graduation from Gilroy High School in 1964, Marlowe enrolled in the two-year business program at Cabrillo College in Aptos. While in college, he joined the

Circle Y business fraternity. After completing his Associate of Arts program, he was employed by the County Bank of Santa Cruz.

In February 1967 Jack Marlowe received his draft notice and entered the US Army. Following his basic and advanced infantry training in the summer of 1967, he was assigned to the 199th Light Infantry Brigade of the Americal Division in Vietnam.

When the Tet New Year Offensive began in January 1968, Jack's unit secured the main infiltration routes into and around Saigon against Viet Cong attacks. In mid-February, while in the process of stopping the heavy Viet Cong assaults, Marlowe was wounded and hospitalized at Cam Ranh Bay for twenty-one days. Upon his release he rejoined his unit.

On April 16, 1968, with less than thirty days remaining on his Vietnam tour, Specialist Fourth Class Jack William Marlowe was killed in action from multiple fragmentation wounds in Long An Province. His body was recovered and returned to Watsonville for a full military funeral and burial in Pajaro Valley Memorial Park. His awards include the Bronze Star and Purple Heart.

(VVMW; VVVW; SCSn April 23, 1968 1:7, April 25, 1968 20:1)

WARREN F. NICKEL JR.
(1968/05/03)

(Watsonville Register-Pajaronian photo)

Warren had little time to enjoy his new home in the Pajaro Valley before Vietnam beckoned.

Warren F. Nickel Jr. was born on January 6, 1943, in Marionette, Wisconsin, to Mr. and Mrs. Warren F. Nickel, Sr. The family, which also consisted of sons Dennis and Mark and daughter Sharon, moved to California and settled in San Rafael where Warren attended elementary school. After graduating from San Rafael high school about 1961, he entered Marin Junior College. Later he transferred to Humboldt State College in Arcadia, California where he met and married Mary Jane Westfall of Watsonville in 1966. In 1967 Warren graduated with a BA degree in game management and he and Mary Jane moved to Watsonville.

In October 1968, Warren was drafted into the US Army. He attended basic and advanced individual training programs and at their completion, was assigned to the 5th Infantry Division serving in Bihn Duong Province of South Vietnam.

Private Nickel's tour of duty in Vietnam began on March 28, 1968, during the final phase of the Tet New Year Offensive

The mission of the 25th Infantry Division was to conduct armed aerial reconnaissance of 1st Brigade, 25th Infantry Division to locate VC/NVA forces, enemy logistical bases, and interdict enemy lines of communications. The division had to provide a counter-mortar aero weapons team for Dau Tieng Base Camp during the hours of darkness. It was also required to conduct route reconnaissance and security between Tay Ninh and Trang Bang.

While on a mission near Dau Tieng, a village north of Saigon, Private First Class Warren F. Nickels was killed by a sniper's bullet. His body was recovered and returned to Watsonville. Following a requiem mass at Valley Catholic Church on May 11, 1968, Warren was buried in the adjoining cemetery.

(VVMW; WRP May 7, 1968 1:2, SCSn May 8, 1968 14:8, Adj. Gen. Office 1968, Lessons Learned, Oper. Wilderness, http://stinet.dtic.mil/oai/oai?verb=getRecord&metadataPrefix=html&identifier=AD0390871, [15 May 2007 Approx].)

STEVEN C. VANDERGRIFT
(1968/05/19)

(Santa Cruz Sentinel photo)

Steven Carl Vandergrift was the son of Mr. and Mrs. Richard Vandergrift and was born in Santa Cruz on March 14, 1950. His maternal and paternal grandparents, along with several aunts, uncles and cousins were residents of the county, which provided him with a large extended family. Also included in the Vandergrift household were his brother David and sisters, Debra and Victoria. Steven Vandergrift attended Soquel High School and graduated in June 1968.

In the summer of 1968 Vandergrift joined the US Navy and trained at the US Naval Training Center in San Diego. Following boot camp and advanced training, he was assigned to a US Navy aviation facility in the Philippine Islands. While working at that station on May 3, 1968, Steven Carl Vandergrift was accidentally run over by a tractor and killed. His body was returned to Lake Tahoe, California for burial.

(CBR; SCSn May 27, 1969)

JAMES E. BELL
(1968/06/03)

(Ft. Rosecrans National Cemetery – Internet photo)

When Washington Post Staff Writer Bill Turque was walking near the Vietnam Wall on Memorial Day 2006, he spotted a letter written by a thirteen year old California boy that had been placed in Panel 61, Row 20, addressed to James Everett Bell. It merely said, "I know you were from Watsonville, California, and you were born on January 24, 1948.... A brave soldier like you didn't deserve to be drowned."

Little information is available regarding James Bell and his connection with Santa Cruz County. James Everett Bell was born to Mr. and Mrs. Bell, on January 24, 1948, in Madera County, California. His mother's maiden name was Evelyn Britten. A cousin reported on the Internet that the Bell family had a number of relatives living in Oklahoma, suggesting some relationship with that state. His siblings included at least a brother, Bobby, who was much younger. James Bell related to a navy buddy that in the summer of his teen years he had worked at his uncles' farm "bucking hay."

In 1966, James Bell joined the US Navy and was sent to the US Naval Training Center in San Diego for boot camp. After completing boot camp and fireman training, he was assigned to the 7th (Pacific) Fleet as a fireman aboard the *USS Vega*, a store (supply) ship sailing between "Yankee Station" (San Francisco) and "Market Time" (Vietnam).

On June 3, 1968, while operating in the Gulf of Tonkin off the North Vietnam coast, Fireman Third Class James Everett Bell fell overboard and was drowned. His body was recovered, returned to California and buried in the Fort Rosecrans National Cemetery in San Diego.

(VVMW; USDVA; DANFS; Meganet.Net, Com7th Fleet Vietnam

Ship Casualties http://web.meganet.net/kman/7thfleet, [15 May 2007 Approx.]; Bill Turque, "Four Memorials, Countless Memories-Visitors Grieve Privately and Together," Washington Post Tuesday, May 30, 2006; Page B01)

LEONARD R. WHITE
(1968/06/13)

(Watsonville Register-Pajaronian photo)

Remembrance

By Marie Harris (Leonard's Mother)

I wonder how many mothers have made this wish,
That their sons hadn't wanted to enlist.
But off they go to do their job to fight in Vietnam.
They hug your neck and say don't cry.
I'll see you mom, by and by.
You wait for a letter every day,
and "Oh my God" how we pray.
But instead we receive another kind,
Sorry your son was killed by a hostile mine.
You hope and pray that it's not true,
For you want him home with you.
I realize now that he is gone,
But my love for him lingers on and on.
I lost my son in a far off place.
I pray to God, but it's so hard to face.
Times I am afraid,
but in God I have put my faith.

Leonard Ray White was born on June 2, 1947 in Watsonville, California to J. H. and Marie White. With his brother Gilbert and sisters, Joyce and Linda, he attended local schools in the Pajaro Valley. Leonard was a student at Watsonville High School between 1962 and 1965 and was described by his teachers as being "pleasant, friendly and courteous." Baseball and football were Leonard's favorite sports during his high school years.

On August 29, 1967 Leonard White joined the US Army and completed basic training at Fort Bliss, Texas, followed by airborne training at Fort Benning, Georgia. In February 1968, two months prior to his being deployed to Vietnam, he married Kathy.

On April 6, 1968, Pfc. White reported to Company D, 2nd Battalion of the 173rd Airborne Brigade, serving in Binh Dinh Province in South Vietnam. Shortly thereafter he was promoted to corporal. His paratrooper friend Charles Dewes remembered White:

> Leonard was an airborne infantry soldier! He ... went on aerial combat assault missions ... pulled point ... went on night-time ambushes ... he had to be careful of deadly boo-b-traps ... he had to look out for snipers ... he went on search and destroy missions ... and slept and ate in a hot brutal jungle. Leonard was always willing to do his share and more under sustained fear and enormous physical demand. A young man willing to perform all these dangerous duties in a life and death environment and to be brave daily is no less than heroic. On June 13, 1968 Leonard White relieved another soldier of his position as R.T.O. because that soldier had succumbed to malaria. While on a search and destroy mission this outstanding (Sky Soldier) was caught in the center of a Viet Cong ambush and killed fighting his way out.

Leonard's body was returned to Watsonville and following a funeral, was buried with full military honors at the Pajaro Valley Memorial Park.

(VVWM; WHSM; WRP June 17, 1968 1:4, June 20, 1968 2:5; Charles De Wees Website, Leonard White Remembrance, http://www.173d.com/memorial/white.htm; [15 May 2007 Approx])

RICHARD T. CHRISTY
(1968/06/14)

(Golden Gate National Cemetery San Bruno-Internet photo)

Richard Thomas Christy was born on December 5, 1946 in San Francisco, California. No additional information has been located regarding his family, early years or life within Santa Cruz County. Military records indicate that he was a member of the Jehovah's Witnesses religion and may have attended a Kingdom Hall of that faith in Santa Cruz.

He was drafted into the US Army in 1967 and listed Boulder Creek, California as his residence. After completing basic and advanced individual training, he was assigned to the 2nd Brigade of the 1st Infantry Division serving in Binh Duong Province in Vietnam.

Christy arrived in Vietnam on November 19, 1967, and by early 1968 had risen to the rank of specialist fourth class. During his service with the 1st Infantry Division, it was attempting to stop the Tet New Year Offensive of the North Vietnamese Army.

On 31 January 1968 during the Vietnamese celebration of the Lunar New Year (Tet), the Viet Cong launched a series of simultaneous ground and mortar attacks against most of South Vietnam's major cities and allied military installations. In response to the attacks, the Division was summoned to help secure the sprawling Tan Son Nhut Air Base. By 13 February, units of the Big Red One had engaged and defeated numerous Viet Cong and North Vietnamese soldiers...On 7 April 1968, the Division embarked on the largest operation of the Vietnam War: Operation Toan Thang (Certain Victory), which involved all allied troops throughout the III Corps Tactical Zone. One of the primary missions of this two-part operation was to stop the infiltration of the enemy into the Saigon area.

On June 14, 1968, while participating in Operation Toan Thang II, Specialist Fourth Class Richard Thomas Christy was killed in action by small arms fire. His body was recovered and returned to Golden Gate National Cemetery for burial.

(CBR; VVMW; USDVA; 1st Infantry Division, Vietnam History. http://www.1stid.org/history/index.cfm, 16 September 2008])

LeRoy F. Arellano
(1968/06/22)

(Santa Cruz Sentinel photo)

Sergeant Arellano extended his tour in Vietnam at the cost of his life.

LeRoy Fred Arellano was born on August 5, 1947, in Ely, Nevada. His mother's name was Lucy Arellano. Joining him in the family were his brothers Richard and Robert and his sister, Barbara. He spent his formative years in Ely, where he completed elementary school and entered high school. In 1964 the Arellano family moved to Santa Cruz and LeRoy transferred into Santa Cruz High School. He only attended classes at SCHS for about a year.

In 1965 LeRoy Arellano enlisted in the US Army. Following his basic and advanced individual training, he served tours of duty in Germany and Korea. In 1967 he received orders assigning him to Company C, 1st Battalion, 12th Cavalry Regiment of the 1st Cavalry Division serving in the Bong Song Plain of Binh Dinh Province of Vietnam.

Arellano arrived in Vietnam on May 17, 1967, and joined his regiment that was engaged in Operation Pershing. When the Tet New Year Offensive began, the 12th Cavalry Regiment moved to Quang Tri Province in the northern sector of South Vietnam. The regimental history of the 12th Cavalry chronicles the period of Arellano's service with it in Vietnam.

On April 19 1968, Operation Delaware was launched into the cloud shrouded A Shau Valley, near the Laotian border and 34 kilometers west of Hue. None of the Free World Forces had been in the valley since 1966, which was now being used as a way station on the supply route known as the Ho Chi Minh Trail. The first engagement was made by the 1st and 3rd Brigades. Under fire from mobile, 37mm cannon and 0.50 caliber machine guns, they secured several landing zones. For the next month the brigades scoured the valley floor, clashing with enemy units and uncovering huge enemy caches of food, arms, ammunition, rockets, and Russian made tank and bulldozers.

During the first quarter of 1968, Arellano made the fateful decision to extend his Vietnam tour for an additional twelve months. On June 22, 1968, while wrap-up operations were still underway, Sergeant LeRoy Fred Arellano was killed in action. His body was returned to Santa Cruz and buried in Holy Cross Cemetery. He was posthumously awarded the Silver Star and Purple Heart in military ceremonies conducted at Fort Ord on February 13, 1969.

(VVMW; SCSn June 28, 1968 1:1, February 13, 1969 22:2; First Team. US, 12th Cavalry Division History, http://www.first-team. us/journals/12thrgmt/12_ndx05.html, [16 September 2008])

Robert Rodriguez
(1968/07/05)

(Watsonville Catholic Cemetery - Watsonville, California)

A different messenger of death cut the military career of

Robert Rodriguez short.

Robert Rodriguez was born on April 16, 1931, in Watsonville, California, to Mr. and Mrs. David Rodriguez. Robert was raised in a large household, which included his brothers Edward, David, Richard, Daniel, Gilbert and Tone, along with sisters Angela, Helen, Amelia, Aurora and Patricia. He attended local schools in the Pajaro Valley before entering the US Air Force during the Korean War. While serving in the Air Force, he married Maria. During their marriage, a daughter Terry and son Manuel were born to the couple.

During his seventeen years in military service, the family lived at a number of Air Force facilities, but intended to retire in Watsonville. Early in 1968 Rodriguez was diagnosed as having leukemia, which moved up the Rodriquez family retirement plans. Maria and the children settled into a home on Amesti Road in Watsonville and Robert began treatment at Letterman Hospital in San Francisco.

On July 5, 1968 Sergeant Robert Rodriguez lost his fight and succumbed to cancer. He was returned home and buried in the Watsonville Catholic cemetery.

(CBR; WRP July 6, 1968 2:3)

KENNETH D. ARMSTRONG
(1968/07/11)

(Santa Cruz Sentinel photo)

Kenneth Daniel Armstrong was born on September 5, 1948, to Mr. and Mrs. Kenneth Armstrong whose family also included sons David and Rodney and a daughter Gayle. Danny, as family and friends knew him, grew up in Santa Cruz and attended Branciforte Elementary School.

After completing Branciforte Junior High School, he enrolled in Soquel High School near his parents' home. In high school he was popular with the girls who remember him as a quiet, shy and handsome boy with a smile that seemed to have a giggle to it. During his high school years and following graduation in 1967, he worked for the John Bull Motor Company, the DISCO service station and a service station owned by his parents.

In September 1967, Armstrong enlisted in the US Army

and received basic and engineer individual training. In February 1968, he was assigned to A Company, 92nd Engineer Battalion, 159th Engineer Group, of the 20th Engineer Brigade stationed at Long Binh, Vietnam. Armstrong arrived in Vietnam on February 13, 1968, and shortly thereafter was promoted to corporal. His abilities were soon recognized and he became his company commander's driver and radio operator. Captain Roy Williams later recalled, "He [Armstrong] was a quiet, and unassuming young man, and very good at his job."

On July 6, 1968, Corporal Kenneth Daniel Armstrong dropped Captain Williams off at his office and was driving on a courier assignment along the main supply route to Saigon when he was forced to swerve to avoid a cyclist. In the process he collided with an oncoming vehicle resulting in a crash that threw him from his vehicle causing extensive injuries. During his recovery period, Armstrong contracted pneumonia that hastened his death on July 11, 1968. His body was returned home and he was buried at Oakwood Memorial Park.

(VVMW; VVVW; SCSn July 16, 1968, July 22, 1968 12:7; Cemetery Survey)

DICKIE L. LEACH
(1968/08/08)

(Golden Gate National Cemetery – San Bruno California)

Dickie Lynn Leach was born in Aptos, California on September 17, 1945, to Mr. and Mrs. Clarence Leach, who were newcomers to the community. The Leach family also included sons Clarence, Melvin, Calvin and Michael and daughters Mary and Patricia. Dickie grew up in Santa Cruz County and attended elementary school in Aptos until 1957, when his family moved to Alameda, California. He continued grammar school in Alameda and presumably also attended high school in that community.

In March 1964, Leach enlisted in the US Army and upon completion of basic and advanced individual training courses was assigned to duty in Vietnam. During a combat engagement at an unidentified location in July 1966, he was wounded and hospitalized. Following a year's recuperation in an army hospital and with his tour coming to an end, he re-enlisted and was assigned to Germany for a year.

Leach returned to Vietnam in April 1968 and joined the 101st Air Cav Division aerial weapons Company B as a helicopter gunner. On August 8, 1968, Gunship #66-15277 flew into the A Shau Valley in Thua Thien Province and was brought down by an NVA rocket-propelled grenade, killing Specialist Fourth Class Dickie Lynn Leach and fellow crewmembers.

His body was recovered and returned to Alameda for a funeral and burial in Golden Gate National Cemetery in San Bruno, CA.

(VVMW; USDVA; Army Air Crews.Com, AWC #66-15227 http://www.armyaircrews.com/huey_nam_68.htm, [15 May 2007, Approx].)

MARK H. THOMPSON
(1968/08/24)

(Golden Gate National Cemetery – San Bruno California)

The only information available regarding the life and death of Mark Henry Thompson is a brief newspaper notice, an inscription on a headstone in Golden Gate National Cemetery in San Bruno and a partial death certificate.

Mark Thompson was born on May 4, 1947 in Santa Clara County, California to Mr. and Mrs. Henry J Thompson. His father, a former marine, died in September 1957 and was buried in Golden Gate National Cemetery.

The *Santa Cruz Sentinel* of August 25, 1968 noted,
SC Serviceman Dies in Crash
A soldier identified as Mark Henry Thompson of Santa Cruz was one of two GI's reported killed yesterday in a two-car collision in El Paso Texas.

Thompson and Jimmie L. King of Rochester N.Y. were killed in the crash Associated Press reported. They were attached to the same medical company at White Sands, New Mexico.

No information on age or address was available at press time.

An Internet partial death certificate for Thompson indicated that he was married; however, additional information regarding his spouse has not been found.

Mark Thompson's headstone denoted that he was a corporal in the US Army. He was buried next to his father at the Golden Gate National Cemetery in San Bruno, California.

(CBR; USDVA; SOS August 25, 1968 8:4)

MARVIN R. PEARCE
(1968/08/25)

(Santa Cruz Sentinel photo)

"Follow me," was Marvin's motto as he and his dog moved into the point position with his Paw Power platoon.

Marvin Robert Pearce (Thornburg) was born on March 18, 1949 in Santa Cruz, California, and was raised by Arlee and Francis Pearce. (The name Thornburg, appearing in the obituary of Marvin Pearce, has not been identified).

Marvin spent his formative years in the Live Oak section of Santa Cruz County where he and his sisters, Julie and Margaret, attended elementary school. He continued his education at Santa Cruz High School and remained there until 1967.

Marvin Pearce enlisted in the US Army in early 1967. Following basic and advanced individual training, he was accepted for airborne training at Fort Benning, Georgia. Upon completion of jump school he was assigned to the 101st Airborne, (Screaming Eagles) Division. Unique among 101st airborne units was the 47th Infantry's Scout Dog Platoon to which Marvin Pearce was assigned as a dog handler in early February 1968. After completing a special twelve-week training course, he returned home in early May for a two week leave prior to departing for Vietnam.

After his arrival in Vietnam on May 27, 1968, Pearce was sent to Landing Zone Sally, located thirty miles northwest of Hue. The unit's history describes the activities of Pearce's final four months.

The Platoon supported ground infantry missions of the 101st Division. Scout dogs and their handlers walked point on patrol and utilized silent alerts to detect mines, booby traps, snipers and other enemy personnel. The months of July and August 1968 were difficult ones. Within six weeks, five handlers had been wounded in a variety of combat missions. Handler Marvin R. Pearce became the first platoon member to be killed as the result of a shrapnel wound to the back of the skull.

Specialist Fourth Class Marvin Robert Pearce's body was recovered and returned to Santa Cruz and following his funeral, was buried in Oakwood Memorial Park.

(VVMW; VVVW; 101stt Airborne, 47th Inf (Scout Dog Platoon) http://www.47ipsd.us/47hist.htm#vn, [16 September 2008]; SCSn August 30, 1968 1:3; Cemetery Survey)

RAYMOND F. ORR JR.
(1968/11/02)

(Santa Cruz Sentinel photo)

Ray Orr provided a unique service for the Vietnamese people during his tour in Vietnam.

Raymond Franklin Orr Jr. was born on July 22, 1947 in Klamath Falls, Oregon, to Raymond and Margaret Orr. The Orr family also consisted of his sisters Corrine, Jeannie, Ruby and Sandra and his brother, Roy Rusk. Ray attended elementary school in Klamath Falls, but finished high school at nearby Weed High School in California.

Upon his high school graduation in 1965, Orr moved to Santa Cruz where his mother, Mrs. Margaret Shelvock had relocated. While living in Santa Cruz County, Ray may have worked in the local logging industry.

Raymond Orr enlisted in the US Marine Corps in Santa Cruz on January 21, 1966, and began a four-year tour. After completing basic and school-of-infantry training at Camp Pendleton, California, he remained at that Oceanside facility until March 31, 1967, when he reported for duty in Vietnam. Upon arrival in Southeast Asia, Corporal Orr was assigned to a Combined Action Platoon (CAP) in the Quang Tin province in the northern section of South Vietnam.

The CAP program placed a squad of Marines and one Navy Corpsman in villages from Chu Lai to the DMZ

in South Vietnam from 1965 to 1971. The Marines and Corpsmen of the CAC/CAP units attempted to isolate the people of select villages from the ravages of the war. CAP villages were no longer targets of the indiscriminate Search and Destroy mentality so prevalent during the Vietnam War.

Ray, an avid outdoorsman and sportsman, shared with his mother his desire to go deer hunting in Siskiyou County California, upon his return later in November. He also hoped to acquire water-front property in Montana after his enlistment ended. Those goals would never be realized. On November 2, 1968, while on a patrol, Corporal Raymond Franklin Orr Jr. was killed in action by enemy small arms fire. His body was recovered and returned to the US in November. Following a funeral his remains were interred in the Golden Gate Nation Cemetery in San Bruno.

(VVMW; USDVA; SCSn November 7, 1968 1:2; CAP Marine. com, US Marines Combined Action Platoons (CAC/CAP) http:// www.capmarine.com/, [16 September 2008])

LARRY E. SOMMERS
(1968/11/12)

(Watsonville Register-Pajaronian photo)

"He was a very loving man, a very religious individual who loved his family and country," wrote his cousin Janette Miksik.

Larry Eugene Sommers was born in Redlands, California on October 28, 1948, to Eugene and Marilyn Sommers. In 1960 the family, which also included sons Richard and Ronald and daughter Melanie, moved to the Pajaro Valley. After completing elementary school, Larry entered Watsonville High School where he played baseball and other sports. The next year he transferred to Monte Vista Christian School and remained there for the final three years of his secondary education. While in high school, Sommers supplemented his allowance by working at a local Christmas tree farm. After graduating from Monte Vista in 1966, he enrolled in nearby Cabrillo College where he studied for a year.

Larry Sommers was inducted into the US Army on May 6, 1968. He completed his basic and advanced individual training at Fort Lewis, Washington and on September 13th returned home on a twenty-one day leave. On September 23, 1968, while still on leave, he married Donna Burnham in Carson City, Nevada. Eleven days later he was enroute to Vietnam.

When Sommers arrived in Vietnam, he was assigned to Company A, 4th Battalion of the 47th Infantry whose base camp was located at Dong Tam on the Mekong delta. His unit was part of the Mobile Riverine Force, which was a joint army-navy venture designed to clear the Viet Cong from the waterways of the delta. During a patrol in early November, the man in front of Summers stepped on a booby trap mine detonating it and resulting in Larry suffering major wounds to his scalp and legs. He was removed to a hospital in Saigon and on Tuesday November 12, 1968, Private First Class Larry Eugene Sommers died from his wounds.

His remains were returned to Watsonville, accompanied by an army buddy escort and following a military funeral, he was buried in Pajaro Valley Memorial Park. His awards include the Bronze Star and Purple Heart.

(VVMW; WIKI, Mobile Riverine Force; WHSM; WRP November 20, 1968)

1969

JON F. WARMBRODT
(1969/01/25)

(Ft. Rosecrans National Cemetery – Internet photo)

He went to war wearing a uniform that had belonged to the chancellor of the University of California, Santa Cruz.

Jon Frederick Warmbrodt was born on April 2, 1946, to Mr. and Mrs. Godfried J. Warmbrodt. Information regarding his family and early life is not available; however, it is believed that he spent a portion of his formative years in Santa Monica, California. Following high school, Warmbrodt enrolled in the University of California in Santa Cruz with the Pioneer Class and graduated from Cowell College in 1968.

While an undergraduate, he became a friend of UCSC Chancellor Dean McHenry, who in a 1987 interview, recalled his former student:

He [Jon] joined the Marines, went through boot camp, and despite a slight physical disability, a kind of club foot, a slightly club foot, he managed to get an exemption and went to Quantico [Virginia Marine Corps Training Center], and graduated a second lieutenant, [through] platoon leader's class. He was here Thanksgiving and visited with us [and] we took him out to dinner one night... [Before being shipped to Vietnam] He came by and picked up my last set of Marine uniforms; we're the same size.

Lt. Jon Warmbrodt entered the service from Santa Monica, California and after completing the USMC platoon leader school, received orders to Southeast Asia. Jon arrived in Vietnam on December 3, 1968, and was assigned to L Company, 3rd Battalion, 26th Marines serving in Quang Ngai province. When he joined his company, it was participating in Operation Bold Mariner, a sector sweep to locate enemy troops, equipment caches and to clear booby-trapped tunnels.

In January Second Lieutenant Jon Frederick Warmbrodt led his platoon into one final operation. For his leadership in that action he was posthumously awarded a Silver Star with a commendation that stated:

On 25 January 1969, elements of Company L were operating in Quang Ngai Province when the Marines moved into an enemy minefield. Observing that the unit had sustained several casualties in the initial explosions, Second Lieutenant Warmbrodt fearlessly rushed across the hazardous minefield to assist the wounded men. Realizing the necessity for removing the injured as soon as possible, he immediately requested medical evacuation aircraft and commenced directing corpsmen to treat the more seriously wounded. Prior to the arrival of the evacuation aircraft, he established a landing zone and disregarding the dangers involved, personally cleared a path to it, enabling the safe extraction of the seriously injured. Concerned with the safe removal of the remainder of his men from the minefield, he was directing a tank in clearing a path from the hazardous area when he was mortally wounded by the detonation of an enemy explosive device.

His body was returned to California and following a military funeral, was interred in Fort Rosecrans National Cemetery in San Diego.

(VVMW; VVVW; USDVA; WRP May 7, 1970 2:3; SC Guard. com, Vietnam Weekly Casualties January 2, 1969 http://www. scguard.com/museum/docs/vietnam/1969/January1969. Dean McHenry, Vol. III, UCSC Early Campus History 1958-59, http://library.ucsc.edu/reg-hist/McHenryvolume3.pdf, http:// siris-artinventories.si.edu/ipac20/ipac.jsp?uri=full=3100001~!

HILDEFONSO M. RAMIREZ
(1969/01/31)

(Watsonville High School 1987 Vietnam Memorial Program)

"This man was a very gentle man. His sense of humor
kept our hearts light when they would otherwise be very
heavy," recalled Michael Siddall.

Hildefonso M. Ramirez was born on June 28, 1942,
in Big Springs, Texas, to Mr. and Mrs. Federico Ramirez.
The couple later divorced and his mother and her children
moved to Watsonville, California. There she married A. P.
Asunsion and the family grew to include four boys and five
girls. Hilde, as he was called, attended local schools and in
1956 entered Watsonville High School. In high school he
was described by one of his teachers as "a very likeable boy-
-who gets along in a group. He has ability." Hilde was also
remembered for his skill on the football field.

After his graduation in 1960, he was hired by the Bud
Antle produce-distributing company in Salinas, California.
In 1962 Hilde became a father with the birth of his daugh-
ter Lisa; however, the name of his wife has not been found.
Two years later a second daughter, Gina, was born.

Ramirez was inducted into the US Army on January 18,
1964. Fort Lewis, Washington, provided Private Ramirez
with his basic training followed by an advanced individual
training course at Fort Sill, Oklahoma, that qualified him
as a cannoneer. After a short leave spent at home, he was
ordered to Vietnam.

When Hildefonso Ramirez arrived in Vietnam on July
26, 1968, he was assigned to Battery D, 3rd Battalion, 319th
Artillery Regiment of the 173rd Airborne Division station,
northwest of Saigon. Later in the year he became the recipient of the Bronze Star for exposing himself to enemy fire
when calling in artillery strikes.

In January 1969 Ramirez was awarded the Silver Star for
action that led to his death. The citation accompanying the
award read:

*On January 31, 1969 Private Ramirez's company came
in contact with an entrenched element of North Vietnamese.
An enemy sniper remained in the trench, providing cover
for his withdrawing element. After a member of his platoon
was wounded by the sniper, Private Ramirez was among
those who rose through the intense fire to attack the position.
He continually exposed himself in the advance, engaging
the enemy with rifle and hand grenade fire. His actions
encouraged others in the unit, and the position was overrun.
Immediately after crossing the objective, two members of
the company were again pinned down. Private Ramirez,
oblivious to the intensity of the enemy fire, exposed himself
to lay down a heavy base of fire. Disregarding a wound
in his leg, Private Ramirez advanced to a better vantage
point and continued to fire on the enemy, allowing a rescue
force to come to the aid of the entrapped men. At this time
Private Ramirez was wounded in the chest. He told the
medic coming to his aid to stay back because of the danger,
then died of his wounds. Private Ramirez's actions were an
inspiration to all who fought beside him.*

Ramirez' body was returned to Watsonville and buried in
Pajaro Valley Memorial Park.

(VVMW; VVVW; WHSM; WRP February 7, 1969 2:3, February
17, 1969 2:2)

ROBERT L. DINAPOLI
(1969/02/01)

(Santa Cruz Sentinel photo)

A ride home to the air base turned into disaster.

Robert L. Dinapoli was born in New York to Mr. and
Mrs. Sal Dinapoli on June 19, 1947. At an early age Robert,
along with his parents, his brother Ted and his sister Sally
Ann, moved to San Jose, California. The family remained in
San Jose until about 1958 when they moved to Santa Cruz
and settled into a home on Branciforte Avenue. Dinapoli
completed the remainder of his elementary education
locally and in 1961 enrolled in Santa Cruz High School.

After his high school graduation in 1965, Robert Dinapoli enlisted in the US Airforce for a four-year tour. His basic training took place at Lackland Air Force Base in Texas. In 1966 he was assigned to the 69th Recon Tech Squadron stationed at Yakota Air Base west of Tokyo.

After his arrival in Japan, Dinapoli began working in the classified information section and by the end of 1968, had risen to the rank of sergeant. On February 1, 1969, Sergeant Robert L. Dinapoli, along with two other airmen went into Tokyo for an evening liberty. After returning by train to Yakota, they were offered a ride back to the base by a young Japanese boy. Enroute, the teen-age driver hit a utility pole killing Robert and his companions.

Sergeant Dinapoli's body was returned to Santa Cruz and buried in Oakwood Memorial Park.

(SCSn February 2, 1969 31:6, February 5, 1969, Oakwood MP headstone)

ALFRED A. GATES
(1969/02/07)

(Santa Cruz Sentinel photo)

Alfred Alan Gates was born in San Jose, California, on September 26, 1948, to Alfred and Jean Gates. His siblings included brothers Bill, Tim, and Gary and sisters Paula and Alana. The date that the Gates family moved to Santa Cruz County is not known, but in 1966 Alfred was a student at San Lorenzo Valley High School. Following graduation in 1967, Gates married and moved to San Jose with his wife, Glenda. In San Jose he entered a sheet metal apprenticeship program.

In May 1968, while living in Sunnyvale, California, Alfred Gates received his draft notice. Following basic and advanced training, he returned home for a brief leave before being deployed to Southeast Asia.

On October 7, 1968, Alfred was sent to Vietnam and assigned to Company A, 1st Battalion, 6th Infantry Regiment, which was part of the 198th Light Infantry Brigade serving in Quang Tin province.

During the 1968 Tet New Year offensive, the 6th Infantry was moved to the northern portion of the province to assist the US Marine Corps in containing the insurgents. According to Gates' platoon leader, Norm Boxly,

Company A was assigned to patrols of the Rocket Pocket off Chu Lai to try and find the VC and/or NVA 22mm rocket squads. We ran day patrols very seldom and night ambushes all the time. At resupply in the afternoon we would get an overlay showing our ambush for the night or get it called in code over the radio.

During a patrol that Company A was undertaking on February 7, 1969, Private First Class Alfred Alan Gates was killed in action by small arms fire. His body was recovered and returned to California where he was buried in the Golden Gate Cemetery in San Bruno. Gates was posthumously promoted to corporal and received the Purple Heart.

(VVMW; USDVA; SCSn February 14, 1969; 1:6; Company A, 1st Battalion, 6th Infantry, Memories Norm Boxly, http://www.a-1-6.org/Story-Boxley_Memories.htm, [16 September 2008])

WILLIAM L. CARTER
(1969/02/16)

(Internet photo)

A soldier survived the jungles of Vietnam only to be brought down on the streets of Roy.

William LeRoy Carter was born on July 10, 1949, in Bakersfield, California, to William and Dulcie Carter. The Carter family also consisted of sons Ronald, Donald, Gary, Thomas, Gerry and daughters Leta Fay, Cora Wyonia, Sondra and Pamela. At a very early age the family moved to the Pajaro Valley where they settled and where William attended local schools.

In 1966 William Carter joined the US Army and after receiving basic and advanced individual training, was sent to Vietnam. His unit has not been identified; however, upon completing his tour in January 1967, he rotated back to Fort Lewis, Washington.

William Carter was killed when he was struck by a car at Roy, Washington, near Ft. Lewis, on February 16, 1969. His body was returned to Watsonville where full military honors were conducted over his gravesite in the Pajaro

Valley Memorial Park.

(WRP February 19, 1968; Find a Grave. Com William Carter, http://www.findagrave.com/cgi-bin/fg.cgi?page=gr&GScid=8248& GRid=23148128&)

ROBERT D. CHRISTIANSEN
(1969/02/21)

(Golden Gate National Cemetery – San Bruno California)

Robert remained close to his brother John in death as well as in life.

Robert Douglas Christiansen was born in Santa Cruz, California, on May 3, 1949, to Mr. and Mrs. Gerald B. Christiansen. He was raised in the family home on Pine Flat Road in nearby Bonny Doon, California. It is unclear whether his brothers John, Michael, Bruce and Richard and sisters Mary, Donna and Janet all lived together at that location at the same time. He attended local elementary schools and may have attended San Lorenzo Valley High School in Felton. During his time in Santa Cruz County, Christiansen worked at Spivey's, a popular local restaurant, and at the Dream Inn Hotel.

About 1968, Robert Christiansen moved to Oklahoma City, Oklahoma, where he joined the US Marine Corps. He received his basic and school-of-infantry training at Camp Pendleton, California and qualified as an infantry rifleman.

Lance Corporal Christiansen arrived in Vietnam on January 11, 1969, and was assigned to Company A, 1st Battalion, 9th Marine Regiment of the 2nd Marine Division stationed at the Da Krong Valley base in Quang Tri Province. After only a month with his unit, Robert's company received orders to participate in Operation Dewey Canyon.

Operation Dewey Canyon was the last major offensive by the United States Marine Corps during the Vietnam War. It took place from January 22 through March 18, 1969 and involved a sweep of the North Vietnamese Army (NVA) dominated A Shau Valley by the 9th Marine Regiment reinforced by elements of the 3rd Marine Regiment.

On February 21, 1969, while on a patrol thirty-four miles south of Vandergrift Combat Base near Ca Lu, Lance Cor-

poral Robert Douglas Christiansen suffered fatal wounds to the head from enemy mortar fire. His body was recovered and returned to California where he was buried in the Golden Gate National Cemetery in the plot next to his brother, former Army Private John Todd Christiansen, who had died July 18, 1966, after leaving the service.

(VVMW; UDVA; WIKI, Dewey Canyon; US Marines Combined Action Platoons CAC/CAP, Vietnam 1965-1971 http://www.capmarine.com/, [16 September 2008]; SCSn February 28, 1969)

RAYMOND R. DELGADO
(1969/03/01)

(Watsonville High School 1987 Vietnam Memorial Program)

In 2007 Ray was still remembered by his Brownwood buddy, Alan Hawkins, who continues to tend his grave.

Raymond Rodriguez Delgado was born on December 28, 1949, to Nicolas and Inez Rodriguez in Brown County, Texas. The names of Raymond's siblings are not known. He was raised in the community of Brownwood, where he attended elementary and high school. In the spring of 1967 he moved to Watsonville, California, and enrolled in Watsonville High School. In November of that year Delgado dropped out of school.

Raymond Delgado enlisted in the United States Marine Corps in January 1968, following his eighteenth birthday. He received his basic and school-of-infantry training at Camp Pendleton near San Diego and in June, qualified as a marine rifleman. On July 14 he joined Company C, 1st Battalion, 4th Regiment of the 3rd Marine Division located at the Vandergrift combat base near Ca Lu, Quang Tri Province.

In January 1969 the 3rd Marine Division reinforced the 9th Marine Division in Operation Dewey Canyon, a final push to break up North Vietnamese supply lines and installations in the A Shau Valley. Company C participated in the many sweeps that took place through March.

Delgado, who had moved up from rifleman to team leader, was on a search-and-clear patrol on March 1, 1969, when his unit was attacked and came under heavy mortar fire. A fragment of a mortar round struck Lance Corporal Raymond Rodriguez Delgado in the head resulting in his death. His body was recovered and returned to Brownwood, Texas, for burial.

(VVMW; WHSM; Brown County Texas Birth Certificate Info))

WILLIAM M. PHINN
(1969/03/18)

(Santa Cruz Sentinel photo)

"A horrible day, I was there that day," wrote Rick Lose, describing Phinn's death.

William Mark Phinn was born to Mr. and Mrs. William A. Phinn on June 25, 1948. Information regarding his early life, education or arrival in Santa Cruz County is not known.

In 1968 Phinn's family, which also consisted of his brother Michael, was living near the Capitola Mall in the mid-county area.

William Phinn enlisted in the US Marine Corps in May 1968, and was sent to Camp Pendleton, California for his basic training. While there a fellow recruit, Herb Grimaud, recalled that:

Bill, me and 70 odd other civilians were brought together at MCRD [Marine Corps Recruit Depot] San Diego, April 1968 thru June 1968. It was Platoon 279 and we were the Series Honor Platoon. That means that out of three other platoons in our company that went through boot camp at the same time, we won almost all of the final competitions it took to graduate. Things like drill, rifle range, physical fitness, academic, first aid, etc. We "smoked" everybody. We were pretty raggedy when we first started but we were really squared away by the last few weeks of boot camp.

Following basic training, Private Phinn completed school-of-infantry training at the San Diego facility and after graduating, returned home for a short leave before departing for Vietnam.

William Phinn arrived in Vietnam on October 5, 1968, and likely was assigned to the 3rd Battalion, 26th Regi-

ment of the 3rd Marine Division in Quang Nam province. He participated in a number of sweeps during Operation Dewey Canyon prior to his final patrol.

Squad Leader, Rick Lose, recalled the events of March 18, 1969, the day of Phinn's death on the Vietnam Wall Internet Website.

A horrible day, I was there that day. We were on a search and destroy mission all day [and] were hit hard [but] we did not take any losses. When we returned that afternoon LCpl Phinn was removing his frags [fragmentation grenades] from his ammo bag and it happen[ed] [that] a frag lost its pin and exploded killing four Marines. Phinn did not suffer at all he went peacefully to Jesus. He was a good marine and loved his country.

Lance Corporal William Mark Phinn's body was recovered and returned to California for burial in the Golden Gate National Cemetery in San Bruno.

(VVMW; USDVA; SCSn March 21, 1969 1:1; Operation Dewey Canyon, http://recruitknowledge.com/pages/history/mch5.htm [16 September 2009])

STEVEN W. HERRING
(1969/06/05)

(Watsonville Register-Pajaronian [enhanced] photo)

"A mothers heart cannot be still" began a poem to Steven by his mother before his death.

Steven Wayne Herring was born in Watsonville, California on August 5, 1948, to Ruth and Cecil Herring. Along with sisters, Gail and Joyce, he attended local elementary schools and later enrolled in Watsonville High School. He was remembered in school as loving to fish; he would do anything to be able to go fishing. He also enjoyed riding horses and the thrill of the rodeo. On one occasion he was even known to have ridden a bucking bull. Herring left high school before graduating.

In July 1967, Steven Herring enlisted in the US Army where he earned his high school diploma. He completed basic training at Ft. Bliss, Texas, and advanced individual training at Ft. Huchuca, Arizona, where he qualified as an aircraft maintenance apprentice.

On January 6, 1968, he was sent to Vietnam and assigned as a door gunner on an UH-1C (Huey) helicopter. During his tour Steven received the Air Medal, which read:

Private First Class Herring distinguished himself by exceptionally valorous actions while serving as a door gunner on a UH-ld helicopter involved in the insertion of elements of a Special Forces unit near Song Be. On the initial lift into the landing zone, a successful landing was made in spite of extreme natural hazards. On lift off from the landing zone, the flight began receiving heavy automatic weapons fire. Private First Class Herring began placing highly accurate suppressive fire on the enemy positions. His accurate and aggressive fire protected his aircraft and enabled it to fly to safety.

Herring's helicopter was providing support to elements of the 25th Infantry Division and on June 5, 1969, while flying behind enemy lines at about 150 feet, was hit by small arms fire and "went in" [crashed]. One of the craft's crewmen [believed to be Steven] was killed in the crash and the remaining three were killed by enemy troops. For his part in the action, Specialist Fourth Class Steven Wayne Herring was posthumously awarded the Air Medal with 24 Oakleaf clusters and the Purple Heart. A month before the fateful mission his mother had written the following poem and sent it to her son:

> *My Son in Viet Nam*
> *A mother's heart cannot be still,*
> *Until she sees her boy climb o'er the hill.*
> *In the bed at night I lie*
> *And see you, son, in the bunker, fire lighting the sky.*
> *I pray for God to keep your way clear,*
> *For a worried mother is waiting for you, Dear.*
> *We miss you, Son, and wait for the day you will return.*
> *With boys like you around, those Charleys soon will learn.*
> *Don't those Charleys know that they can't win?*
> *Our boys don't mess around, they really dig in.*
> *Take care, Son, in that land of Viet Nam,*
> *For back here, we're all waiting, Dear, especially your Mom.*
> *To Steve, with love, from Mom*

Steven Herring's body was recovered and buried in the Pajaro Valley Memorial Park.

(VVMW; VVVW; WHSM; WRP, June 11, 1969; Vietnam Helicopter Pilots Association, Helicopter UH-1C 66-00552, http://www.bluemax-ara-assoc.com/aircraft/66-00552.HTM, [16 September 2008]; Starlight Café; My Son in Vietnam, http://thestarlitecafe.com/poems/50/poem_8203039112.html, [16 September 2008])

JOHN D. INGUILLO
(1969/06/06)

(Watsonville Register-Pajaronian photo)

Sergeant Inguillo gave new meaning to the term Shake-and-Bake.

John Deogracias Inguillo, the son of Mr. and Mrs. Deogracias Inguillo, was born in Phoenix, Arizona, on August 10, 1947. His brothers Carlos and Stephen and sisters Dora, Dorothy, Raquel and Yolanda joined him in the Inguillo family. The family later moved to Watsonville, California, and in September 1961 he entered Watsonville High School. After graduating in 1965, he enrolled in Cabrillo College and supplemented the cost of his education by working at the local Value Giant store.

In February 1968, Inguillo was inducted into the US Army and sent to Fort Lewis, Washington, for basic training, and later to Fort Polk, Louisiana, for advanced individual training. The army saw leadership potential in Inguillo and selected him for their Non-Commissioned Officer's Course at Fort Benning, Georgia. This course, commonly referred to as shake-and-bake because of the accelerated nature of the program, was designed to turn the most qualified enlisted men into NCOs in the shortest possible period. On September 24, 1968, Inguillo graduated with other members of Class 41-68, 76th Company and was promoted to sergeant.

Following a leave and a temporary stateside assignment, John Inguillo left for Vietnam on January 8, 1969. On his arrival he became a squad leader in B Company, 4th Battalion of the 23rd Infantry Regiment serving in Tay Ninh Province. During his tour in "Nam," he was involved in a number of combat operations, was wounded and was awarded the Purple Heart. His leadership also earned him a promotion to staff sergeant and he became a platoon sergeant.

On June 6, 1969, while on a patrol near the Nu Ba Den Mountains in Tay Ninh Province, Staff Sergeant John D. Inguillo's platoon came under enemy fire and he responded immediately. According to the official report accompanying his Silver Star award,

While on a reconnaissance in force mission, Company B encountered an enemy force of unknown size. In the initial exchange of fire, several men were wounded and pinned down in the enemy kill zone. Realizing the gravity of the situation, Sergeant Inguillo braved the intense hostile fire as he made his way to the wounded men. With complete disregard for his own safety, Sergeant Inguillo began placing effective fire upon the hostile positions. As the battle progressed, Sergeant Inguillo began treating the seriously wounded. He continued to aid the trapped men until he was fatally wounded.

Sergeant Inguillo's body was recovered and returned to Watsonville for a military funeral and burial in the Pajaro Valley Memorial Park.

(VVMW; VVVW; WHSM; WRP May 23, 1969 8:1, June 13, 1969 2:2,)

EDWIN E. AXTON
(1969/06/11)

(Santa Cruz Sentinel photo)

Sergeant Axton was the boss "from the back of the pilot's head to rear of the bird."

Edwin Everette Axton was born on April 13, 1948. The location of his birth and the names of his parents have not been found. Edwin had a sister, Gail; however, if he had other siblings, their names are not known. Robert Carter, living on Plateau Avenue in Santa Cruz, was identified as his stepfather and Robert Carter Jr. as his stepbrother. Axton attended local schools and entered Santa Cruz High School with the exiting class of 1966, but left school early. During the years prior to his entry into the service, Edwin married Karon and was employed by Pacific Cabinets and Granite Construction Company.

In April 1968 Axton was drafted into the US Army. He received basic training and advanced individual training that qualified him as a helicopter airframe repairman. Following a leave in Santa Cruz, he was sent to Vietnam on November 3, 1968, and arrived in Tay Ninh province where he joined HCC, 2nd Brigade of the 1st Cavalry Division.

Axton was initially assigned as a gunner aboard a Huey helicopter, but soon advanced to the position of crew chief. As crew chief he became the senior guy in the back that make all decisions from the back of the pilot's head to the rear of the bird. Floyd Holbrook, who served with Edwin later noted, "It was a privilege to fly with Axton. He taught me the ropes of becoming a crew chief. I will always remember him." Another individual who had reason to remember him was his pilot. When their helicopter crashed at Landing Zone Jamie in March 1969, Axton, who had escaped from the craft, went back to rescue the pilot.

On June 6, 1969, Specialist Fourth Class Edwin Everett Axton's helicopter was flying near the Cambodian border in support of 1st Cavalry ground operations when it was shot down. Axton was pulled from the craft and airlifted to Japan for medical attention; however, on June 11, 1969, he died from his wounds. His body was returned to Santa Cruz and following a military funeral, was interred in Santa Cruz Memorial Park. Edwin Axton was posthumously promoted to Sergeant and his other awards include the Air Medal and Purple Heart.

(SCSn June 13, 1969, September 24, 1969, VVMW; Becoming an Aerial Gunner, Navigator, or Crew Chief; http://www.brunkco. com/articledetail.php,[16 September 2008])

FEDERICO ALANIZ JR.
(1969/06/13)

(Watsonville Register-Pajaronian photo)

Federico's plans to return to Watsonville and marry were never realized.

Federico Alaniz Jr. was the oldest of the six children of Federico and Juanita Alaniz. Born in Mercedes, Texas, on March 11, 1948, Federico Jr. spent his first seven years in Texas with his brother Robert and sisters Esmeralda, Teresa, Rosa and Leticia, before moving to Watsonville in 1955. Upon arrival in the Pajaro Valley he was enrolled in the E. A. Hall School where he remained until 1964 when he entered Watsonville High School as a freshman. Federico did not finish high school but chose instead to enter the work force. He was employed by a local nursery and in the fields driving a truck.

Alaniz received his draft notice in April 1968, and in May reported to Fort Lewis, Washington, to begin his basic and advanced individual training. On September 22, he reported to Fort Riley, Kansas, where he joined the 21st Infantry Division as a senior wireman. He was then assigned to a brief tour of duty in Germany before being deployed to Vietnam.

Private Alaniz reported to Company B, 1st Battalion, 46th Infantry Division on April 27, 1969, and was attached to the 196/198 Lt. Infantry Regiment stationed in Quang Tin province. In March 1969, his unit moved to Landing Zone Professional in the mountains southwest of Tien Phuoc. There they conducted patrols in the vicinity of Firebase Maryann. During a patrol on June 13, 1969, Company B came under small arms gunfire that took the life of Private First Class Federico Alaniz Jr.

His body was returned; however, his final resting-place has not been identified. His awards include the Bronze Star and Purple Heart.

(VVMW; VVVW; WHSM; WRP June 18, 1969 1:2, June 19, 1969 2:4)

DANIEL J. BARRY
(1969/07/14)

(Soquel High School yearbook)

Barry was a cavalryman who guarded the German border against Ivan's threats.

Daniel J. Barry was born in Minneapolis Minnesota on February 1, 1947. His mother's name was Elaine. His early years were spent with his brother William and sisters Benita and Cynthia in Minnesota before moving to Soquel, California, in 1954. His mother remarried a Mr. Kelliher and her new husband brought his son Charles into their family. During his early years, Daniel attended local grammar schools and became active in St. Joseph's Catholic Church in Capitola. In 1965 he graduated from Soquel High School and was employed locally.

In November 1967 Daniel Barry entered the US Army.

His basic training location is not known; however, his advanced individual training likely took place at Fort Knox, Kentucky. At the conclusion of his training he was assigned to I troop, 3rd Squadron, of the 3rd Armored Cavalry Regiment. At the time that Barry joined his squadron, they were stationed at Kaiserlautern, Germany, and were patrolling the German border of the Iron Curtain to curtail anticipated Soviet action.

In July 1968, the 3rd ACR Regiment was redeployed to the United States and assigned to Fort Lewis, Washington. While his unit was preparing for potential re-deployment to Germany, Daniel Barry was promoted to Sergeant. On July 14, 1969, Daniel J. Barry was killed in an automobile accident in Bremerton, Washington. His body was returned to Santa Cruz and on July 19, following his funeral service, he was interred in Oakwood Memorial Park.

(SCSn July 15, 1969 18:4, July 17, 1969 13:4, Oakwood MP headstone; 3rd Armored Cavalry, Regimental History Pages 24-25 http://www.hood.army.mil/3d_ACR/docs/history_2.pdf, [16 September 2008])

DELBERT H. LINT
(1969/11/15)

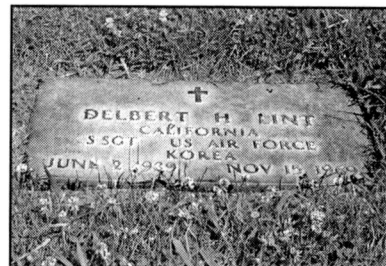

(Pajaro Valley Memorial Park – Watsonville, California)

Sergeant Lint served in the Armed Forces as a soldier, marine and airman.

Delbert Henry Lint was born on June 2, 1929, in Seaside, California. His mother's name was Mary Russell Lint. At an early age he and his brothers, Robert, Fred and James, and sisters, Maryann, Betty and Shirley, were brought to the Pajaro Valley by their parents. Delbert was educated in local schools in the Pajaro Valley before entering the service in 1945. His twenty-two-year military career included service in the US Army, US Marine Corps and the US Air Force. During those years, he married and had two daughters, Karon and Sharon, who continued to reside with their mother in Alabama.

On November 15, 1969, Staff Sergeant Lint was serving in the Philippine Islands when he died at a railroad site. Newspaper accounts of the day attributed his death to a train wreck. The remembrance of family members however, is that he was killed by an individual attempting to steal his groceries. His body was returned to Watsonville and after a military funeral provided by Castle Air Force Base at Whites Chapel, he was interred in Pajaro Valley Memorial Park.

(WRP November 22, WRP November 24, 1969, Pajaro Valley MP headstone)

1970

MARK S. DIORIO
(1970/02/26)

(Soquel High School yearbook)

Mark earned his high school diploma to prepare for life and a Silver Star while ending it.

Mark Steven Diorio, the son of Charles and Lois Diorio, was born in Salinas, California on November 21, 1950. His siblings included his brothers Glenn and Brian and his sister Kim. Salinas provided Mark with his education through the eleventh grade; however, in the fall of 1967 he transferred to Soquel High School in Santa Cruz County to complete his senior year. Mark Diorio graduated in June 1968 and was employed by the California State Division of Forestry.

In February 1969, Mark Diorio enlisted in the US Army. After completing basic training, he was sent to helicopter crew training school where he became a helicopter door gunner. On August 3, 1969, Private First Class Diorio was assigned to Vietnam and joined Company A, 1st Battalion, 9th Cavalry Regiment of the 1st Cavalry Division serving in Tay Ninh province. He continued to fly missions in that area until February 15, 1970, when he flew his last mission. The citation accompanying his Silver Star award for that mission notes:

....Specialist Four Diorio distinguished himself by exceptionally valorous action of February 15, 1970, while serving as a door gunner during a visual reconnaissance mission...

...Diorio's aircraft started receiving fire from an enemy bunker complex. With complete disregard for his own safety, he leaned precariously out of the aircraft to place fire on the hostiles, enabling the pilot to make several passes and mark

the positions for air strikes. Specialist Diorio was severely wounded but bravely continued to engage the enemy until he passed out from his injuries...

Mark Diorio died of his wounds on February 26, 1970. His body was recovered and returned to Salinas for a funeral on March 10, 1970, followed by his burial in the Garden of Memorial Park cemetery.

(VVMW; SCSn March 5, 1970 1:3, March 9, 1970 16:6, August 21, 1970 1:1)

RICHARD L. ROY
(1970/03/03)

(Santa Cruz High School yearbook)

Richard L. Roy was born in San Francisco on October 15, 1949, to Richard and Jacquelin Roy. He was joined in the family by his brother Ronald and sisters Regeanne, Yvette and Yvonne. Richard (Jr.) was raised and educated in San Francisco and Santa Cruz. He attended Santa Cruz High School and was a member of the graduating class of 1967.

In 1968 Richard Roy joined the US Air Force and probably received his basic training at Lackland Air Force Base in San Antonio, Texas, followed by additional training at other Air Force facilities. During this period, he married Rosalinda; later the couple established their residence in Santa Cruz. Airman Roy was subsequently promoted to sergeant and assigned to the US Air Force Europe.

While serving in Holland in 1970, Sergeant Richard L. Roy was diagnosed with an undisclosed illness or condition that resulted in his death on March 3, 1970. His remains were returned to Santa Cruz and following a funeral on March 12, 1970, were interred in Oakwood Memorial Park.

(SCSn March 10, 1970 18:6, Oakwood MP headstone)

ROCKY Y. HIROKAWA
(1970/03/08)

(Watsonville High School yearbook)

Rocky was one month short of a leave in Japan when his firebase was overrun.

Rocky Yukio Hirokawa, the only child of Mr. and Mrs. Ichiro Hirokawa, was born on May 6, 1949, in Denver Colorado. His father, who was in the farming and poultry business, moved the family to Torrance, California, where Rocky entered high school. Ichiro's work brought the Hirokawa family to the Pajaro Valley in March 1966 and Rocky enrolled in Watsonville High School. In high school his friends remembered him "as a very quiet and helpful student," and "as a person easy to get along with and nice to be around." His father's work caused his parents to move to Gardena, California, during his senior year; however, Rocky remained at the Watsonville home of his aunt in order to finish school. Following graduation from high school in June 1967, he re-joined his parents in Southern California.

Hirokawa was drafted into the US Army in September 1968 and sent to Ft. Lewis, Washington. During his basic and advanced training, the army detected leadership potential in him and sent him to their NCO Candidate School at Ft. Benning, Georgia. A Combat Leadership NCO Course at Fort Ord, California, followed.

On September 2,1969, Rocky was sent to Vietnam and assigned as a squad leader in Company A, 2nd Battalion, 8th Cavalry Regiment of the 1st Air Cav. Division. He participated in a number of patrols and missions and earned his first Bronze Star on January 9, 1970, in Phuoc Long Province. The citation read:

When his unit became engaged, with a determined enemy force, with disregard for his own safety, he [Hirokawa] exposed himself to the hostile fire as he moved forward to the point of heaviest contact. He then began placing a heavy volume of suppressive fire on the enemy positions, to cover the medics while they treated the wounded.

On March 8, 1970, Hirokawa and his platoon were participating in the Parrot's Beak March in Tay Ninh Province when they were ambushed.

Sergeant Hirokawa immediately and with complete disregard for his own safety, charged through the intense enemy fire, setting up his machine gun and directing the suppressive fire of his men on the enemy positions. Although wounded, he courageously moved on, issuing orders and supervising his men. When another barrage of enemy mortar rounds landed near him, he received several pieces of shrapnel, but continued to lead his men on the attack.

Over half of Company C was med-evacuated but it was too late for Rocky. His friend Robert (Cowboy) Estep, who was also wounded, moved over and offered comfort to Sergeant Hirokawa before he died.

His body was recovered and following a funeral service in Gardena, was buried in San Pedro, California. In addition to receiving a second Bronze Star, Rocky Hirokawa received the Purple Heart for this action.

(VVMW; WHSM; WRP March 16, 1970)

THOMAS A. HALL
(1970/03/22)

(Soquel High School yearbook)

A $2000 college scholarship disappeared in a bunker explosion in Vietnam.

Thomas Allen Hall was born in Phoenix, Arizona, in 1951, into the family of Mr. and Mrs. William Hall. He did not lack siblings as the Hall family also included sons Gary, Randall, Norman and Robert and daughters Carol, Cynthia, Tracy and Kelly. In 1962 the family moved to Santa Cruz County and acquired a residence on Vine Hill Road. Thomas attended Happy Valley Elementary and Branciforte Junior High School before enrolling in Soquel High School in the fall of 1965. Thomas Hall was a well-rounded student, a member of the cross-country team and active in the local Church of Christ. His academic record earned him membership in the California Scholarship Federation and a $2000 college scholarship that he planned to use at Stanford University in 1972.

Following his high school graduation in June 1969, Hall enlisted in the US Army for three years. The location of his basic training is not known, but he likely received his advanced individual training at Fort Sill, Oklahoma, which qualified him as an artillerymen.

About January 1970, Thomas Hall was assigned to an artillery unit in Vietnam. While serving with that unit on March 22, 1970, he was killed when an explosion occurred in a bunker. His body was recovered, returned to Santa Cruz and following his funeral, was interred in Oakwood Memorial Park.

(SCSn March 29, 1970, April 1, 1970 14:4)

WILLIAM H. HAAKINSON, III
(1970/04/18)

(Watsonville High School yearbook)

With cheeks the size of basketballs, "Chowbag" ran down the court.

William Herbert Haakinson III was born on January 24, 1945, to Dr. William and Eloise Haakinson in San Jose, California. A sister, Julie, joined him in the family. Herb, as he came to be called, was raised and educated in San Jose elementary schools and Bellarmine college preparatory school. In 1961, prior to beginning his senior year, he moved to Aptos and enrolled in Watsonville High School. In high school Herb was remembered as an average student, excellent basketball player and very popular. He was also remembered for his sense of humor. Friends recall his habit of blowing up his cheeks with air until they were of a huge size. In an issue of *Life* Magazine, a photographer captured him running down the basketball court during a high school game with his cheeks blown up to almost basketball size.

Following his graduation, Haakinson entered Cabrillo College and later attended San Francisco State College, where he graduated in 1969 with a degree in psychology. During this period of his life, Herb may have married. He fathered a daughter Kelly, who lived with her mother in Sunnyvale, California.

In the summer of 1969, Haakinson was drafted into the

US Army. He completed his basic training at Fort Ord, California, followed by paratrooper training at Ft. Benning, Georgia. On November 11, 1969, he arrived in Thua Thien province, Vietnam, and was assigned as a rifleman with Company A, 1st Battalion, 506th Regiment of the 101st Airborne Division. While serving in that unit, he was remembered by his company commander as Chowbag Haakinson because of the amount of food he carried with him and as Hackerson by his gin rummy-playing buddies. He was later promoted to specialist fourth class and assigned as an automatic rifleman.

On April 18, 1970, while participating in a sweep patrol in the A Shau Valley area, Specialist Fourth Class William Herbert Haakinson III stepped on a land mine that took his life. His body was recovered and returned to San Jose for burial in the Oakhill Memorial cemetery. For his actions he was posthumously promoted to Sergeant and awarded The Bronze Star and Purple Heart.

(VVMW; WHSM; WRP April 20, 1970 1:7)

MELVIN L. PULLEN
(1970/06/26)

(Santa Cruz Sentinel photo)

Too many mortars were just too much for this "Black horse" cavalryman.

Melvin Lewis Pullen was born on March 28, 1951, in Oregon. His mother's name was Wilma. Sharing the Pullen family home were his brothers, Leonard, Michael and Leslie, and sister, Ardell. The Pullens moved to the San Lorenzo Valley of Santa Cruz County in the early 1960s where Melvin attended local elementary schools. In September 1964 he entered San Lorenzo Valley High School with the exiting class of 1969; however, he left prior to graduation.

Melvin Pullen enlisted in the US Army in April 1969. He completed basic training at Fort Ord, California and advanced individual training at Fort Knox, Kentucky qualifying him as an armored reconnaissance specialist. Following his training period, Pullen served short tours of duty in Germany and at Fort Lewis, Washington. On March 10,

1970, he returned home and married Winifred in Carson City, Nevada.

Private First Class Pullen arrived in Vietnam on May 2, 1970, and was assigned as a half-track gunner in Company K of the 3rd Squadron, of the 11th Armored Cavalry serving in the Third Corps area.

From well-established bases inside Cambodia, the communists would strike out into South Vietnam and then return across the border to resupply and regroup. On 1 May 1970, the 11th Armored Cavalry Regiment participated in an operation known as the Cambodian Excursion in which they penetrated into Cambodia to a location called the Fish Hook. The mission's intent was to deny the enemy safe havens and stop operations at their Parrot's Beak area resupply area.

While Pullen's unit was in Cambodia on June 26, 1970, they came under a heavy enemy mortar attack that claimed his life and that of three other members of his company. His body was recovered, returned to Santa Cruz and following a full military funeral, was buried in Oakwood Memorial Park.

(VVMW, Oakwood MP headstone; SCSn July 7, 1970 1:7 July 7, 1970 22:2; 1 How, Black horse in Vietnam, http://www.1how.net/3-1how.htm, [16 September 2008])

JOHN D. FRANKS
(1970/07/16)

(Santa Cruz Riptide photo)

A Santa Cruz park named in his honor reminds the community of John Franks.

John David Franks, one of the seven children of W. T. and Marguerite Franks, was born on February 26, 1925 in Spokane, Washington. His brothers Charles, William, Steven and James and sisters Rita and Mary rounded out the Franks family. John attended Santa Cruz High School in 1941-42 where he played football. He was graduated from Holy Cross High School in 1943.

Following his graduation, Franks enlisted in the Merchant Marines. He completed his basic training in San Mateo followed by programs at the USMM Academy in Kings Point, New York, officer training at Alameda California, and turbo electric school at UC Berkeley. During World War II, he served in the Atlantic, Mediterranean and Pacific Theaters and earned a Purple Heart.

When the war ended, he accepted a position as engineering officer on the *President McKinley* of the Matson Shipping Lines. During this period, John married Sally Jane Work, also of Santa Cruz, and the couple moved to San Francisco. Soon their family had grown to include sons John Jr. and Eric and daughters Carolyn and Dorothy.

In 1951, Franks volunteered his services during the Korean War to the US Coast Guard and received a commission He continued to move up the ranks and by 1967, was a full Commander stationed in Jacksonville, Florida.

During the Vietnam Conflict, Commander Franks was posted to San Francisco and served as the Chief of Law Enforcement and Intelligence to the commander of the 12th Coast Guard District. In that capacity he was responsible for criminal investigations, personal background checks, the collection and analysis of intelligence data and for providing personal protection services to high-ranking Coast Guard officials and VIPs. Franks also became a member of the Marine Square club and remained active in Masonic activities.

In 1970 Commander John David Franks was diagnosed with an undisclosed illness or condition from which he died on July 16, 1970. Following his cremation and funeral at the Coast Guard Training and Supply Center chapel on Government Island in Alameda, his ashes were scattered at sea. His hometown of Santa Cruz remembered him by naming a park in his honor.

(SCSn July 19, 1970 25:5; SCSC page 267; CGVA, US Coast Guard Ratings, 2006, http://cgsva.lbbhost.com/ratings.html, [16 September 2008])

ARTHUR F. GLEIM JR.
(1970/08/04)

(Palo Alto High School yearbook)

The Vietnam tour of a member of an old Palo Alto watchmaking family was one month too long.

Arthur Frederick Gleim Jr. was born to Mr. and Mrs.

Arthur Gleim in Palo Alto, California, on October 2, 1945. Along with his brother Bruce and sister Georgie, he grew up in Palo Alto and attended local schools. Fred, as he was known, went on to enroll in Palo Alto High School where he was active in audio visual programs, taught Sunday School on weekends, enjoyed aeronautics and had hopes of working at a mission upon graduation. After graduating from high school in June 1963, he entered an unspecified college and earned a business degree to prepare him for entry into the family watch and jewelry business. During or at the completion of his college education, he married Dagmar Ochenkirchen of Aptos, California, and the couple established their residence in Santa Cruz County.

Arthur Gleim was drafted into the US Army about September 1969, and after completing basic and advanced individual training, was ordered to Vietnam. He arrived in Quang Tin province on March 3, 1970 and was assigned to A Company 1st Battalion, 46th Infantry Regiment of the 196th Light Infantry Brigade (Americal Div.).

The battalion operated from LZ [Landing Zone] Professional until August of 1970. In February of 1970, the battalion established a temporary firebase at LZ Mary Ann, at a remote mountain site near Hau Duc, Quang Tin Province. The battalion returned to Mary Ann in the summer of 1970 and operated from there and LZ Young, which was between Tien Phuoc and Tam Ky, during 1970 and 1971.

While serving in the field on August 4, 1970, Specialist Fourth Class Arthur Frederick Gleim Jr. was killed by a sniper's bullet. His remains were returned to Aptos and following a funeral at St. Stephens Lutheran Church in Santa Cruz, were buried in Pajaro Valley Memorial Park.

(VVMF; VFMW; SCSn August 9, 1970 1:1, August 11, 1970 20:4, Sue Dremann, Palo Alto Weekly April 02, 2003, With Love and Remembrance, http://www.paloaltoonline.com/weekly/morgue/2003/2003_04_02.remembrance02.html, [16 September 2008])

CURTIS C. COLYEAR
(1970/08/17)

(Santa Cruz Sentinel photo)

Friendly fire can be anything but friendly, as Curtis would discover.

Curtis Craig Colyear was born in a tent on July 18, 1950 at Sequoia National Park, California, while his parents, Mr. and Mrs. Charles Colyear, were camping. He grew up in Santa Cruz County with his brothers Colburn and Charles and sisters Rosalind, Roberta and Karen. Curt attended Capitola and Soquel elementary schools before enrolling in Santa Cruz High School in September 1963. While in high school, he played on the football team. Following his graduation in 1968, he was employed at a Standard Oil station.

Colyear enlisted in the US Marine Corps in June 1969 and completed his basic and school-of-infantry training at Camp Pendleton, California. During this period, he became engaged to Patty Perry and the couple made plans for a wedding to take place upon his discharge.

In July 1970 Curt Colyear received orders sending him to Southeast Asia, and he arrived in Vietnam on July 20th. He was assigned to Company M, 3rd Battalion, 7th Regiment 1st Marine Division serving in Quang Nam Province.

During the summer [1970], elements of the 7th Marine Regiment entered two major large-scale operations. Pickens Forest, a search and clear mission which centered in the Thu Bon River valley, generated little reaction from the enemy and ended on 24 August. Imperial Lake was undertaken a week later. The 2nd Battalion and elements of the 3rd Battalion, 7th Marines, combed the central Que Son Mountains, looking for the evasive enemy. Units of the 7th Marines captured a NVA battalion command post and found the bodies of four senior commanders in a destroyed bunker. Imperial Lake, as it turned out, was the last operation of the war for the regiment.

When fragments of allied mortar rounds struck him on August 17, 1970, Corporal Curtis Craig Colyear became a Non-Hostile, Ground Casualty caused by Accident. His body was recovered and returned to Santa Cruz for a funeral and burial at Oakwood Memorial Park.

(VVMW; SCSn August 21, 1970 1:8; August 25,1970; 7th Marines
History http://www.marzone.com/7thMarines/Hst0004.htm, [16
Sept 2008])

RALPH M. JOHNSON
(1970/08/24)

Ralph's two-year wait for death finally ended.

Ralph M. Johnson was born on October 10, 1946. His mother's name was Charlotte Johnson. A sister, Adele, joined him in the family. During his formative years, Ralph lived in Santa Cruz County where he attended Live Oak and Santa Cruz schools. After leaving Santa Cruz, he is believed to have lived briefly in Sunnyvale, California, where his stepbrothers, Robert and William Antonelli, resided. In the early 1960s, Johnson was living in San Francisco.

Ralph Johnson enlisted in the US Marine Corps about 1964 and received his basic and school-of-infantry training at Camp Pendleton, California. By 1968 he had risen in rank to become a non-commissioned officer, had married Nancy and established a residence in Millbrae.

Shortly after their marriage, Johnson was assigned to Vietnam. He was participating in the post Tet New Year Offensive operations in the summer of 1968 when a piece of shrapnel struck him. He was evacuated in an unconscious state and taken to Oakland Veterans Hospital where he remained in a coma until his death on August 24, 1970. The location of Ralph Johnson's gravesite has not been identified.

(VVMW; SCSn August 26, 1970, August 26, 1970)

JOHN J. ROGERS JR.
(1970/08/28)

(Santa Cruz High School yearbook)

A young lieutenant returned to Santa Cruz from Germany by way of Los Gatos.

John Joseph Rogers Jr. was born in Alameda County, California, on February 9, 1942, to John and Vera Rogers. John spent his formative years in Santa Cruz County where he attended local schools. He graduated from Santa Cruz High School with the class of 1960. He later attended Cabrillo College.

Rogers entered the US Army in the mid 1960s and completed basic and advanced training. It is believed that he attended the Officer Candidate School program in the army that qualified him for a commission as second lieutenant. He was assigned to the 24th Infantry Division that served in Germany during the Vietnam War era. John married Vera and the couple had two children, Teresa and David.

In August 1970, John Rogers was serving as a first lieutenant in the 24th Infantry Division when it returned from Germany to Fort Riley, Kansas for deactivation. On August 28, 1970, Rogers died from an unspecified cause. At that time, the Rogers family were living in Los Gatos, California.

First Lieutenant John Joseph Rogers Jr. was buried in Oakwood Memorial Park on August 31, 1970.

(CBR; SCSn August 30, 1970 39:6; Oakwood MP headstone;
WIKI, 24th Infantry Division)

ROGER G. DUNHAM
(1970/12/17)

(Santa Cruz High School yearbook)

Roger was born on April Fool's Day but was anything but a fool.

Roger G. Dunham was born on April 1, 1948, in Santa Cruz, California to Richard and Dorothy Dunham. He and his brother Larry attended local schools prior to beginning high school. In September 1962, Dunham entered Santa Cruz High School with the graduating class of 1966. During his high school years, he was an excellent student and avid surfer. After graduating with honors, he enrolled in Stevenson College at the University of California, Santa Cruz. His college education at UCSC was interrupted by military service.

In the late 1960s Dunham entered the US Army. His basic training took place at Ft. Lewis, Washington, where he earned recognition for outstanding leadership and was selected for training in the army's Military Intelligence branch. Following training he was assigned to Detachment B, 2nd Military

Intelligence Section, Ramstein AFB in Germany.

While serving in Germany, Specialist Fourth Class Roger G. Dunham died of an undisclosed illness or condition on December 17, 1970. His body was returned home and was buried at Santa Cruz Memorial Park on December 28, 1970.

(SCSn December 21, 1970 1:4, December 24, 1970 30:7)

1971

JOHN J. JENNINGS
(1971/02/23)

(Watsonville High School yearbook)

John Joseph Jennings was born in 1950 in Salzburg, Austria, to Mr. and Mrs. George Jennings. The Jennings family also included two daughters, Linda Sue and Carolyn. John was raised in Watsonville and attended Pajaro Valley elementary schools. His parents later divorced and his father moved to South Lake Tahoe, California. His mother remarried Charles Jack and remained in Watsonville. John entered Watsonville High School in 1964 and graduated in 1968.

After graduation, Jennings enlisted in the US Navy and was sent to the US Naval Training Center in San Diego for boot camp. Following advanced training in his specialty area, Jennings was assigned to the crew of the cruiser *USS St. Paul.* During his tour aboard the vessel, it was deployed with the Seventh Fleet off the coast of South Vietnam and provided gunfire support to allied troops.

Early in 1971, Jennings was diagnosed with infectious hepatitis and admitted into the US Naval Hospital in Bremerton, Washington. On February 23, 1971, John Joseph Jennings succumbed to the disease. His body was returned to Watsonville and following a funeral, was interred in Pajaro Valley Memorial Park.

(WRP, February 25,1971, Pajaro Valley MP headstone; DANFS, USS St. Paul CA-73)

SHERMAN R. TAYLOR
(1971/02/26)

(Santa Cruz Sentinel photo)

Sherman Ray Taylor was born on October 9, 1952, in Poplar Bluff, Missouri, to Mr. and Mrs. Herman E. Taylor. In addition to Sherman, the Taylor's had five other sons Elmer, Marvin, Harold, Larry and Rand, along with two daughters, Mary and Ann. At an early age the family moved to Santa Cruz County where Sherman attended local schools. He possibly attended Santa Cruz High School; however, there is no record of his completing secondary education at that school.

In 1969 Taylor enlisted in the US Army and after receiving basic training, he obtained additional individual training to qualify as an electronic maintenance specialist. The army facilities where he served prior to being sent to Southeast Asia are not known. On January 19, 1971, Sherman arrived in Vietnam and was assigned to a unit serving in the Ninh Thuan province.

Military records are incomplete as to the cause of Sherman Taylor's death, which occurred on February, 26, 1971. His body was returned home and following a military funeral, was buried in Watsonville's Pioneer cemetery.

(VVMW; SCSn March 7, 1971 36:4)

BERNARDO K. RAMOS
(1971/03/24)

(Watsonville High School yearbook)

Grenades pinned down a Watsonville track star leaving him nowhere to run.

Bernardo Kealoha Ramos was born on November 6, 1950, in Honolulu, Hawaii, to Bernardo and Maria Ramos. Bernardo Sr. had migrated from the Philippine Islands to Hawaii. In Hawaii he married Maria and the couple had five sons: Bernardo, Mario, Benedict, Florentino and Jamie. The family later moved to Watsonville and established their residence on Doering Avenue. Bernardo Jr. entered Watsonville High School and was remembered as being an all around good student and tireless worker who excelled in football, track and karate. After his graduation, he enrolled in Cabrillo College where he majored in math and science.

In 1970 Ramos enlisted in the U.S Army and was sent to Fort Lewis, Washington for basic training. Following his advanced individual training, he was deployed to Vietnam on October 20, 1970. Upon arrival he was assigned as a rifleman in Company D, 4th Battalion, 3rd Brigade of the 23rd Infantry (Americal) serving in Quang Tri Province.

On March 24,1971, Ramos' platoon was conducting a search and destroy mission in a mountainous area and was split into two squads. The previous day they had seen foxholes, fortifications and other evidence of considerable NVA activity and were alert to the possibility of an ambush when they were hit. His squad was attacked and pinned down while grenades were thrown at them over the crest of the hill and AK-47 fire intensified. During the ensuing firefight, Bernardo and three of his fellow platoon members were killed and most of the remainder of the squad was wounded.

Ramos' body was recovered and returned to Watsonville for a requiem mass at Valley Catholic Church and burial in the Pajaro Valley Memorial Park.

(VVMW; WHSM; WRP March 22, 1968 2:1, March 31, 1971, April 2, 1971 2:4; VVVW, Douglas Ayers Site posting by James D. Ronan, (Ramos platoon leader) May 31,1999, http://www.vvmf.org//index.cfm?SectionID=110&anClip=7770, [16 September 2008])

ROY C. CALCOTE
(1971/04/10)

(Courtesy of Shaundra Calcote-Ferrari)

Sergeant Calcote survived four tours as a Green Beret in Vietnam only to suffer an accidental gunshot wound when he came home.

Roy C. Calcote was born in Santa Cruz, California, on March 24, 1943, to Mr. and Mrs. David Calcote. The Calcote family also included another son, David Jr., and a daughter, Ruby. Roy, who was also known as Cim, grew up in Santa Cruz County and was educated in local elementary schools. During his high school years, he attended both Santa Cruz and San Lorenzo Valley high schools.

In 1960 Calcote left school early, enlisted in the US Navy and received boot camp training at the US Naval Training Center in San Diego. At the completion of his four-year tour he was honorably discharged from the Navy.

After briefly returning to civilian life, Roy enlisted in the US Army. During basic training, he volunteered for Special Forces training. With the successful completion of that program he was issued his Green Beret.

The United States Army Special Forces, known in the United States simply as Special Forces or SF, and informally known as 'Green Berets,' is an elite special operations force of the US Army trained for guerrilla warfare, unconventional warfare, and special operations. Its primary mission is to train and assist foreign indigenous forces.

The main SF unit in South Vietnam was the 5th Special Forces Group (Airborne) [it] earned seventeen Congressional Medals of Honor in Vietnam, making it the most prominently decorated unit for its size in that conflict. Special Forces personnel also played key roles in the highly secret Military Assistance Command Vietnam (MACV) Studies and Observation Group.

During the Vietnam War, Roy Calcote was the recipient of two Bronze Stars for bravery and three Purple Hearts. When he returned, he married Elaine and they had two daughters, Cimberly and Shaunda. The family later established their permanent residence in Porterville, California.

On March 27, 1971, while he was still serving in the army, Calcote was the victim of an accidental gunshot wound that required hospitalization. While being treated at Letterman Hospital in San Francisco on April 10, 1971, Staff Sergeant Roy Calcote died. His remains were brought to Santa Cruz for a funeral and burial in Oakwood Memorial Park.

(SCSn April 13, 1971 26:6; WIKI, US Army Special Forces)

BRUCE D. ANDERSON
(1971/05/10)

(Santa Cruz Sentinel photo)

Bruce D. Anderson was born on November 17, 1950, in Detroit, Michigan, to Dr. Gordon and Zola Anderson. His brother Vance and sisters, Linda and Kathy joined him in the family. The Anderson family moved to Santa Cruz in 1955 where Bruce attended local elementary schools prior to entering Mission Hill Junior High School. Later he also attended Virgil Hauselt Junior Academy. During his youth, he was described as active in Pony and Little League baseball, an expert swimmer and an avid outdoor sportsman. Bruce was also active in the Boy Scouts of America. Anderson graduated from Santa Cruz High School in 1968 and enrolled in Cabrillo College.

The date Bruce Anderson entered the US Army is not known, nor is the level of training that he had achieved. On May 4, 1971 Private Bruce Anderson was a passenger in a vehicle with two companions traveling on Highway 17 when their car was struck head on by a pickup truck. He was taken to a San Jose hospital where he died the following week on May 10. Following the funeral, his body was interred in Oakwood Memorial Park.

(SCSn May 4, 1971 1:1, May 13, 1971 18:3, Oakwood MP headstone)

TERRY L. KELLY
(1971/06/17)

(Soquel High School yearbook)

Terry was the last county resident to have his name inscribed on the Vietnam Wall.

Terry Leon Kelly was born in Tennessee on October 28, 1950. His obituary listed his parents as Walt Autry of Santa Cruz and Margie Autry of Sweet Home, Oregon. His brothers, Bill and Rick Autry, and sisters, Lynn and Theresa Autry, continued to live in Santa Cruz. In 1968, while a student at Soquel High School, he won the American Legion oratorical contest. He went on to graduate in June 1969.

Kelly enlisted in the US Army in 1969 and upon completion of his basic training received advanced individual training as a medic. On July 18, 1970 he arrived in Vietnam and was assigned to Company D, 1st Battalion, 12th Cavalry Regiment of the 1st Cavalry Division operating in Phuoc Tuy province.

On June 17, 1971, Private First Class Terry Leon Kelly was killed by what the military described as accidental self-destruction. While the details surrounding Terry's death are not available, this term typically describes accidental deaths that occur when troops fire their weapons or set off explosives by accident. Terry's body was recovered and returned to Florida for burial.

(VVMW; SCSn June 24, 1971 1:3)

1972

Hervey M. Goold
(1972/11/10)

(Watsonville High School yearbook)

Hervey M. Goold was born in Concord, California on May 11, 1945, to James J. and Helen E. Goold. The Goold family also included another son, James. Later the family moved to Watsonville where Hervey was educated in local schools. He enrolled in Watsonville High School and during his school years was a member of the photo club and served on the football, swimming and track teams. He also became active in the Civil Air Patrol.

Following his graduation from high school about June 1963, Hervey Goold joined the US Air Force and completed basic training at Lackland AFB in San Antonio, Texas. This was followed by a technical training course in his specialty field.

Goold remained in the US Air Force for four years and by the time of his last assignment at McCord AFB near Tacoma, Washington, he had reached the rank of sergeant. During his air force career, he retained membership in the Watsonville IOOF Pajaro Lodge and also was active in the Durham post of the American Legion.

In 1972 Goold was diagnosed with leukemia, which necessitated his admission into the Madigan General Hospital in Tacoma. On November 10, 1972, Sergeant Hervey M. Goold died of the cancer and his remains were returned to Watsonville. Following a service at the First Baptist Church on November 15, 1972, Hervey was buried in the Pajaro Valley Memorial Park. His name was not added to the Vietnam Wall.

(WRP November 14, 1971 2:4; PVMP Headstone)

1973

January 27 Paris Peace Accord signed bringing US troops home from Vietnam

AFGHANISTAN – IRAQ WARS

(2001-2010)

SANTA CRUZ COUNTY MILITARY DURING THE AFGHANISTAN - IRAQ WARS

During the Afghanistan-Iraq wars of the early twenty-first century, Santa Cruz County's military involvement was limited.

The elimination of the draft and the restructuring of the armed forces into a professional army of volunteers eliminated the compulsory service obligation that residents faced during previous wars.

During the period of this conflict, there were no state or federal military reserves operational in Santa Cruz County. While there may have been county residents affiliated with units that were called to active duty during the conflict, information regarding them is not available at this time.

All of the major military branches maintained recruiting offices within Santa Cruz County and enlisted a significant number of residents for federal service.

The US Army conducted an eleven-week basic training course at Ft. Benning Georgia, Ft. Jackson, South Carolina, Ft. Leonard Wood, Missouri, Ft. Sill, Oklahoma, and Ft. Knox, Kentucky. The thirteen-week US Marine Corps basic training program was held at Camp Pendleton for recruits living in the western states. The US Navy eight-week boot camp took place at the Great Lakes Naval Training center near North Chicago. The US Air Force conducted an eight-and-a-half week program for its trainees at Lackland AFB near San Antonio, Texas. The US Coast Guard eight-week training session took place at Cape May, New Jersey. All of the service branches conducted advanced training programs lasting up to one year.

The professional military establishment created in 1971 developed comparable career advantages for both men and women in the armed forces. This opportunity also introduced the greater potential for women to become casualties during combat operations.

The first serviceman to die in the Iraq/Afghanistan wars was Jesus A. Gonzalez, a former resident of the Pajaro Valley who died in Iraq on April 12, 2003. As of this writing the last casualty was James Harris who died in Boulder Creek while on medical leave from the US Marine Corps.

http://en.wikipedia.org/wiki/Recruit_training, [09 July 2009]

BIOGRAPHICAL SKETCHES

2003

---

*March 21 The US and its allies launched
a massive aerial assault against Iraq*

JESUS A. GONZALEZ
(2003/04/12)

(Internet photo)

The first Santa Cruz County former resident to lose his life in the Afghanistan-Iraq War called Indio California his home. Jesus Gonzalez shares an honored place among Watsonville's war dead in its Veterans Park.

Jesus A. Gonzalez was born about 1980 in Nuevo Leon, Mexico. His mother's name was Sylvia. The family later moved to Indio, California, where Jesus was raised and educated. Following his graduation from Indio High School, Gonzalez attended the College of the Desert in nearby Palm Desert. His mother married Leopoldo G. Trevino and moved to Watsonville, where she worked for Salud Para La Gente and where Leopoldo became an organizer for the United Farm Workers in the Salinas and Pajaro Valley strawberry fields.

Jesus moved to Watsonville in about 2000 and assisted his stepfather in the labor movement. He married and in 2001, his wife gave birth to a daughter.

Gonzalez had been fascinated by the military as a young boy and about 2002 enlisted in the US Marine Corps. Following his basic and school-of-infantry training at Camp Pendleton, he was assigned to the 1st Marine Division's 1st Tank Battalion stationed at Twenty-nine Palms, California. Lance Corporal Gonzalez accompanied that unit in its movement to Iraq and was later posted at Baghdad.

On April 12, 2003, while manning a checkpoint in Baghdad, Lance Corporal Jesus A. Gonzalez was shot and killed. His body was recovered and returned to California for burial in the Riverside National Cemetery in Riverside.

(WRP, Volunteers plant trees in memorial grove to honor fallen soldiers by David Carkhuff, Posted: Monday, November 12th, 2007, http://www.register-pajaronian.com/fe_view_article.php?story_id=2392&heading=0, [16 September 2008]; Military Times, Honor the Fallen http://www.militarycity.com/valor/256634.html, [16 Sept 2008])

KYLAN A. JONES-HUFFMAN
(2003/08/21)

(Santa Cruz Sentinel photo)

"It's a god damn waste," exclaimed James Huffman in describing the death of his son to a *Santa Cruz Sentinel* reporter.

Kylan Alexander Huffman was born in Santa Cruz, California, in 1972 to James and Dagmar Huffman. Kylan's father, a career army officer, took his family, which also consisted of another son, Niko, and a daughter, Alexia, with him on his assignments in Germany and the United States. Kylan's German born mother introduced her son to her native language and it became the second of his languages. Over the years he also became fluent in French, Arabic and Farsi.

In 1980 Colonel Huffman was reassigned to Fort Ord and the family moved into a home in Aptos, California. Kylan was enrolled in local schools and briefly attended a school for gifted children before transferring into the York School in Monterey. At York, a former teacher described him as, "a brilliant student fascinated with military history," and by others as being "a warm disciplined person with a captivating smile who accepted challenges without a murmur."

In 1990 Kylan graduated from York Academy and was appointed to the US Naval Academy at Annapolis. Following his graduation in 1994, he enrolled in a master's program at the University of Maryland, which he completed the following year. In 1995 he married Heidi Lynn Jones who had been his sweetheart since high school and the two adopted the hyphenated surname of Jones-Huffman. In that same year he attended the Surface Warfare Officers School in Newport, Rhode Island. and at its completion was assigned to the fleet.

Lt. (jg) Jones-Huffman served aboard the *USS Raven* and *USS Ingraham* prior to his release from active duty in 2001. He returned to Washington DC where he was employed by the Navy's Criminal Investigation Department. Kylan also taught the history of ancient Greece and Nazi Germany at the nearby US Naval Academy. During these years, he acquired a love for the Haiku style of Japanese poetry and soon became proficient in its use.

Because of his expertise in Middle Eastern affairs Jones-Huffman, was recalled to active duty in 2002 and assigned to Bahrain. On August 21, 2003 he was stalled in traffic in the southern Iraqi city of Hila when an Iraqi gunman approached and took his life with a bullet. His body was returned to the United States. The burial location of Kylan Jones-Huffman has not been identified.

(Fallen Heroes of Operation Iraqi Freedom, Remembering the Service Members Who Died in the Service of their Country, http://www.fallenheroesmemorial.com/oif/profiles/joneshuffmankylana.htmlr, [16 September 2008]; SCSn 8/23/2003 1:1)

2004

MORGEN JACOBS
(2004/10/07)

(Santa Cruz Sentinel photo)

For Morgen it was all about country and fighting for freedom.

Morgen Jacobs was born on May 14, 1984, in Santa Cruz, California, to Cindy and Michael Cummings. Shortly after Morgen's birth, his parents divorced and his mother remar-

ried Todd Jacobs, who adopted him. A sister, Austin, joined him in the family. Jacobs attended elementary school at Capitola and Santa Cruz Garden schools before entering New Brighton Middle School. Later he enrolled in Soquel High School. As a growing boy he was often found working on model airplanes or building with Legos. In high school Morgen was a popular youth who enjoyed reggae music, mountain biking, softball, golf and skimboarding. After graduating from Soquel High, he planned on enrolling in nearby Cabrillo College. When the terrorist flights into the World Trade Towers occurred on 9/11, Morgen declared his intent to join the army, "to go over to protect America and fight for freedom."

Jacobs enlisted in the US Army in the fall of 2002 and was sent to Fort Benning, Georgia, for basic and advanced individual training. At the completion of his training, he was sent to Schweinfurt, Germany, to join Company B, 1st Battalion, 18th Infantry Regiment of the 1st Infantry Division.

In January 2004 his unit was deployed to Iraq and assigned to the Bayji area ninety miles south of Baghdad. Staff Sergeant Shane Biehl recalled the fateful day on which Morgen was killed.

I was with Jacobs throughout the Iraq deployment. I was in the vehicle behind him when he was killed. I saw the explosion engulf his vehicle. I then jumped out of my vehicle and ran up to help, but we were engaged by AK-47 fire. I then shot and killed (later on we found out) the man who detonated the IEA that killed SPC Jacobs. I helped in pulling Jacobs out of the vehicle. It was the worst day of my life. I always think about that day.

After being wounded by the explosion of his patrol vehicle at Aaliyah, Iraq, on October 6, 2004, Specialist Fourth Class Jacobs was taken to Tikrit, Iraq where he died the next day. His body was returned to Santa Cruz and following a full military funeral, was buried in Santa Cruz Memorial Park.

(Fallen Heroes of Operation Iraqi Freedom, Remembering the Service Members Who Died in the Service of their Country, http://www.fallenheroesmemorial.com/oif/profiles/jacobsmorgenn.html, [16 September 2008]); Chicago Times, Soldiers Story, http://legacy.suntimes.com/ChicagoSunTimes/Soldier/Story.aspx?PersonID=3098099, [16 September 2008]; SCSn October 13, 2004 1, SCSn October 24, 2004 1:1)

VICTOR A. GONZALEZ
(2004/10/13)

(Internet photo)

Victor awaited the time when he could replace his Marine Corps uniform for one of policeman blue.

Victor A. Gonzalez was born on December 29, 1984, in Salinas, California, to Sergio and Amalia Gonzalez. The Gonzalez family, which also included another son, Oscar, and daughters, Edenia and Myrna, later moved to the small community of Pajaro. Gonzalez was educated in Pajaro Valley elementary schools and in September 1999 entered Watsonville High School. While in high school, he was described as being an above average student who appeared to have his life under control. Because of his dependability he was selected to work as a messenger in the principal's office. In sports Victor played on the school's soccer team and ran cross-country. His main interest however, was the cadet program conducted by the Watsonville Police Department where he became a cadet lieutenant.

After Gonzalez graduated from high school in 2003, he enlisted in the US Marine Corps. He completed his basic and school-of-infantry training at Camp Pendleton, California, and returned home on leave prior to deployment to Iraq. During that leave, he confided with police officers that becoming a policeman was his chosen career and that he "couldn't wait to put on his blue police uniform."

Private First Class Gonzalez arrived in Iraq in the spring of 2004 and was assigned as a rifleman in the 2nd Battalion, 5th Marine Regiment of the 1st Marine Division serving in Anbar province. On October 13, 2004 his battalion was part of a convoy destined to secure a hot spot in the province when they came under attack. In the ensuing firefight Lance Corporal Victor A. Gonzalez was killed.

His body was recovered and returned to Watsonville. Following a funeral at St. Patrick's Church on October 22, 2004, he was buried in Valley Catholic cemetery.

(SCSn October 15, 2004 1, SCSn October 23, 2004 1:1)

ANDRES H. PEREZ
(2004/11/14)

(Santa Cruz Sentinel photo)

Andres Perez joined the US Marine Corps for discipline, camaraderie and as a means of obtaining a college education.

Andres Hilarioestra Perez was born in Santa Cruz, California, on July 1, 1983, to Hipolito and Yolanda Perez and was raised in the Live Oak district of the county along with his sisters, Sandra and Elvira. He attended local elementary schools and entered Harbor High School in the fall of 1997. His large stature provided the football team with the extra strength they required to reach the 2000-01 playoffs. Perez' teachers found him to be a well-grounded youth with a wide range of friends. Andres took pride in his Latino heritage and loved to sing the traditional ranchera music of Mexico.

Following graduation from high school in 2001, Andres Perez enlisted in the US Marine Corps and completed his basic training and school-of-infantry training at Camp Pendleton, California. Upon completing his training he was posted as a security guard at a naval facility in Norfolk, Virginia. After two years of barracks duty, he was reassigned to the 3rd Battalion, 1st Marine Division of the 1st Marine Expeditionary Force at the USMC base camp in Iraq.

On November 14, 2004, during the fighting at Fallujah, Iraq, Lance Corporal Andres Perez was killed in action. His body was recovered and returned to Santa Cruz and following a funeral, was buried in Holy Cross Cemetery.

(CBR; Fallen Heroes of Operation Iraqi Freedom, Remembering the Service Members who died in the Service of there Country, http://www.fallenheroesmemorial.com/oif/profiles/perezandresh. html, [16 September 2008]; SCSn November 16, 2004 1. Holy Cross Cemetery headstone)

JOSEPH B. SPENCE
(2005/01/26)

(Santa Cruz Sentinel photo)

Iraq was not comfortable, was not safe, but it was where Joey Spence wanted to be.

Joseph B. Spence was born on June 18, 1980 in Santa Cruz, California to Jim and Becky Spence. Joey, as he was called in the family, had the companionship of his two brothers Tommy and Roger, as he grew up in the family home in the northern portion of the county. His high school years were spent at the Wes Beach High School, a small school located off the Old San Jose Road in Soquel. During his high school years, Spence could frequently be found playing guitar in a garage band and four-wheeling in the Santa Cruz Mountains. After graduating in 1998, he was employed by Central Home Supply Company in Santa Cruz and began setting up a landscaping and construction business. Spence also remained active in the Gateway Church of Scotts Valley.

In December 2001 Joseph Spence enlisted in the US Marine Corps and was sent to Camp Pendleton for his basic and school-of-infantry training. Following their completion, he was assigned to the Marine base in Kaneohe Bay, Hawaii. While home on leave at Thanksgiving, he proposed to Elisabeth Bertsch, whom he had dated since he was sixteen; the couple were married on December 28, 2002.

Spence and his marine unit were engaged against Islamic terrorists in both the Philippine Islands and Iraq. In 2003, while serving as a marine rifleman in the 1st Battalion, 3rd Regiment of the 3rd Marine Division, he fought against the Abu Sayyaf militants in the southern Philippines. When the Iraq War began, his unit was deployed to the Middle East. In a *San Jose Mercury News* interview with his mother she noted that:

He felt he had a mission to help the Iraqi people. When they were clearing out the houses in Al-Fallujah, his mother said, he said the Iraqi people were grateful for the Marines' presence and the Iraqi soldiers don't want them to leave. He said that America has no idea -- no idea -- what our military is doing over there and how grateful the people are....It's

not comfortable. It's not safe. But it's where he wanted to be.

On January 26, 2005 Lance Corporal Joseph B. Spence and his unit were given the mission of providing security for the first elections of the new Iraqi government. He and twenty-four other members of his company boarded a CH-53 Super Stallion marine helicopter in Western Iraq. Soon after the aircraft had begun its flight, it encountered a sandstorm and while attempting to fly through it, went down killing the twenty- five marines, one sailor and five crewmembers. His body was recovered and returned to Santa Cruz for a funeral and burial in Oakwood Memorial Park.

(Marine Chat.Com, "Scotts Valley Marine loved Corps- Copters," David L. Beck *San Jose Mercury News*, http://www.marinechat. com/forums/showthread.php?t=8826, [16 September 2008]; SCSn January 28, 2005 1:1, SCSn February 9, 2005)

2005

JASON R. HENDRIX
(2005/02/16)

(Santa Cruz Sentinel photo)

Staff Sergeant Hendrix was a professional soldier watching out for his men when a roadside bomb ended his career.

Jason R. Hendrix was born on October 26, 1976, in Watsonville, California, to Russell and Renee Hendrix. Within a few years the family moved from their Watsonville apartment to a home in the community of Freedom where Jason, his brother Justin and sister Amanda were raised. Young Jason attended the Salsipuedes Elementary School before continuing into E. A. Hall and Rolling Hills Junior High schools. Jason grew to become a stocky boy and loved sports, especially basketball and bodybuilding. In 1989 Jason's parents divorced with his father moving to Oklahoma, and his mother obtaining temporary custody of him. In 1991 custody of Jason was awarded to his father and after spending two years at Aptos High School, he transferred to Sequoia High School in Claremore, Oklahoma, where his father lived. During his final two years of high school, he became an avid hunter and joined the Army Reserve.

Following his graduation in 1994, Hendrix went on active duty in the army. After receiving additional training, he was assigned to an infantry unit in South Korea where he spent two tours. Jason chose the army as his career and over the next eleven years advanced to the rank of Staff Sergeant. During the Iraqi Freedom War, S/Sergeant Hendrix was assigned to the 1st Battalion, 9th Infantry Regiment of the 2nd Infantry Division serving west of Baghdad in the Sunni Triangle sector.

On February 16, 2005, Staff Sergeant Jason R. Hendrix was chosen to lead a twenty-five-man squad to serve as decoys for a marine unit attempting to knock out a rebel insurgent stronghold in Ramadi. His squad came under heavy artillery fire followed by a small arms firefight. While he was in the process of pulling his injured men out of burning armored vehicles, a roadside bomb exploded, taking his life.

Jason's body was recovered and returned to Oklahoma where he was buried in the Calvary Cemetery in Tulsa. His awards include a Bronze Star and Purple Heart.

(SCSn February 18, 2005 1, February 19, 2005 1; Military Times, Honor the Fallen, January 2003, http://www.militarycity.com/valor/675442.html, [16 Sept 2008])

2006

BERNARD P. CORPUZ
(2006/06/11)

(Santa Cruz Sentinel photo)

On June 10, 2006 Bernard Corpuz had a premonition of his death and asked his aunt to care for his mother.

Bernard P. Corpuz was born on August 16, 1977, in Kings County, California, to Bernaldo and Margaret Corpuz and spent his formative years in Southern California. Bernaldo worked for the US Navy and because of his frequent moves, sent his wife, son and daughter to Watsonville to live closer

to his brothers. Margaret settled in the Royal Oaks area of the Pajaro Valley, acquired a mobile home and sent her son to Palma Catholic High School in Salinas. At Palma Bernard became a well-rounded student with a love for history, heavy metal, and soccer. It was in track as a sprinter and hurdler that he excelled. After his graduation in 1995, he received a track scholarship to Hartnell College where he supplemented his expenses by working in a coffee shop and bagel bakery. After two years at the junior college, Corpuz transferred to the University of LaVerne in Southern California where he majored in political science.

In July 2004 Bernard Corpuz enlisted in the US Army and after completing basic training, was selected to attend the prestigious Defense Language School in Monterey. For the next six months he concentrated upon developing a proficiency in French and was graduated in April 2005. He was then assigned to the 303 Military Intelligence Battalion of the 504 Military Intelligence Brigade stationed at Fort Hood, Texas. There he was trained to function as a detective and criminal investigator.

Shortly after completing the training program, Corpuz was assigned to Ghanzi, Afghanistan. On this assignment, he collected intelligence for Army Rangers, interrogated Afghan militants and debriefed fellow soldiers. On June 11, 2006, Corporal Bernard P. Corpuz died from wounds he received when the convoy in which he was traveling came under enemy small arms fire. During the firefight, an improvised explosive device took his life.

His body was recovered and escorted back to the United States by a girl friend who was also serving in the army in Afghanistan. Corpuz was buried at Arlington National Cemetery. His awards included the Bronze Star and Purple Heart.

(CBR; SCSn June 14, 2006 1:1, June 15, 2006, June 21, 2006, June 26, 2006 1:1; Arlington National Cemetery, Bernard Paul Corpuz, http://www.arlingtoncemetery.net/bpcorpuz.htm, [16 Sept 2008])

2007

JARED J. ROSSETTO
(2007/05/07)

(Santa Cruz Sentinel photo)

Jared John Rossetto was born on February 28, 1983, in Palo Alto, California, to Karen and Jerry Rossetto. In 1987, the family moved to the Pajaro Valley and acquired a home in Corralitos. A sister, Tara, joined Jared in the Rossetto household. Jared attended the Bradley Elementary School before going on to Aptos Junior High School and later Aptos High. In high school he was described as "an athlete who made the honor roll, loved Seinfeld jokes and was kind to new students." In addition to participating on the schools football and track teams, Rossetto also loved golf, body boarding on local beaches and snowboarding in the Sierra Mountains. After graduating from high school in 2001, he worked locally at a pizza parlor and before entering the military, was employed at a local resort restaurant.

In 2002 Jared Rossetto joined the US Navy. After completing boot camp in San Diego, he received naval aviation training as a helicopter crewman. During the ensuing years, he continued to progress in rank, ending as an aviation warfare systems operator 2nd class aboard a SH-60 Seahawk in Helicopter Anti-submarine Squadron 7 in Carrier Air Wing 3. His unit was based in Jacksonville, Florida, and when at sea, he served aboard the *USS Harry S. Truman*.

On May 7, 2007, Rossetto's helicopter was flying at low altitude in a simulated nighttime combat search and rescue exercise near Fallon, Nevada, when it flew into a transmission line and crashed. Jared and his fellow crewmembers were killed in that accident. His body was recovered and returned to Corralitos for a funeral on May 24, 2007.

(SCSn May 10, 2007, May 23, 2007)

2010

JAMES D. HARRIS
(2010/4/6)

(Santa Cruz Sentinel photo)

James Dundee Harris achieved much in his thirty-year tenure on earth.

He was born to Donald and Sylvia Harris on July 14, 1979, in Santa Clara, California. Sharing the family home with him were his brother Kyle and sister Emma. Later his parents divorced and the children moved with their mother to Boulder Creek, California. Upon his mother's subsequent marriage to Jack Kunz, the family expanded to include two brothers and a sister, Joseph Woods, Alicia Rollins and Jackson Kunz. James began elementary school in Boulder Creek and completed his high school education at San Lorenzo Valley High School, where he played on the football team. After his graduation in 1998, the Boulder Creek Fire Department employed him for the next eleven years. On July 31, 1999, he married Margaret Cannelora and they had three daughters, Lorianne, Natalie and Emilee. While living in Boulder Creek, Harris took advantage of the county's great outdoor environment and became an avid hunter and fisherman.

In December 2005, James fulfilled another of his goals by enlisting in the United States Marine Corps. Harris was sent to Camp Pendleton, California, for his initial training and to Camp Lejeune, North Carolina, for his advanced MOS training. After completing his training, he was assigned as a Marine Support Landing Specialist in San Jose, California. During his Marine Corps tour, James Harris rose to the rank of Lance Corporal.

In 2008, James Harris developed medical complications arising from previous back injuries. While attempting to recuperate at home on medical leave in 2009, his physical condition deteriorated and on April 6, 2010, he died at his home in Boulder Creek.

(Santa Cruz Sentinel April 13, 2010 A9:4; interview with Margaret Harris April 14, 2010)

Sources

A variety of research outlets were incorporated in this work. Local newspapers, high school publications and remembrances located on the Internet served as the main resource. The Santa Cruz Public Library and Pajaro Valley Historical Association served as physical research locations.

Santa Cruz County newspapers provided the major source of biographical material in the form of wartime letters, photographs, training vignettes, commendations, newspaper articles and remembrances. Obituaries, when available, served as the single most significant source of biographical material. The *Pacific Sentinel, Santa Cruz Sentinel, Santa Cruz Surf, Santa Cruz Evening News, and the Santa Cruz Riptide,* a weekly magazine, provided the most complete coverage for the northern and central county. The *Pajaro Times* and the *Watsonville Register-Pajaronian* and the *Watsonville Evening Pajaronian* covered information relative to the southern county and the Pajaro Valley in greater detail.

High School publications provided a wealth of information on their former students serving in the armed forces from World War I through the Vietnam War. Copies of the Santa Cruz High School *Trident* and *Cardinal* frequently contained articles and remembrances of students who died during war along with a number of graduation photographs. Foremost of the Santa High School publications was the *Service Cardinal,* a special Second World War edition produced by the students in 1948 recognizing all their students who served in the military with photographs and biographical sketches.

Watsonville High School provided similar assistance in telling the stories of their former students who died during the 20th century wars. The *Manzanita,* their yearly annual, was the main source for photographs of classmates who lost their lives during periods of war. A special 50-year edition also highlighted World War I and II activities. Of special importance was the Watsonville High School Vietnam War Dead Memorial documentation prepared for a special memorial program conducted on April 24, 1987.

The Santa Cruz Public Library and Pajaro Valley Historical Association served as the main sources for acquiring information within the community. City and telephone directories, local census, voter records, vital statistic information and similar research aids were found in the Santa Cruz Public Library. The Pajaro Valley Historical Association provided family histories and historical documentation relevant to local military installations.

Source Acronyms

The following acronyms apply to references in the biographical sketches; the website names, article names, dates if applicable, URL addresses, and dates observed in parentheses complete the references.

AAIR Aviation Archaeological Investigation & Research, AAIR Air Force Accident Report Search <http://www.aviationarchaeology.com/src/dbaf.htm> (16 September 2008)

ABMC American Battlefield Monument Commission, World War I, II, Korean War, Listing, no date referenced, <http://www.abmc.gov/search/wwii.php> (16 September 2008)

CAG California Adjutant General Honor Roll, Names of officers and enlisted men from California who lost their lives while serving in the armed forces of the United States during the World War [One] <http://www.archive.org/stream/namesofofficerse00caliiala/namesofofficerse00caliiala_djvu.txt> (16 March 2009)

ACGEN Access Genealogy, World War II Casualties, [Department of the Navy] 1999-2008, <http://www.accessgenealogy.com/worldwar/> (16 September 2008)

CBR Family Tree Legends, California Birth Records 1905-1995 <http://www.familytreelegends.com/records/calbirths> (7 December 2009)

CDR Vital Search-California, California Death Records and Certificates, 1999, <http://www.vitalsearch-ca.com/gen/ca/_vitals/cadeathm.htm> (16 September 2008)

CSMM California State Military Museum, California Military History, <http://www.military museum.org/history.html> (16 September 2008)

CWNPS National Park Service, [Civil War] Soldier Sailor System, 2004 <http://www.itd.nps.gov/cwss/> (16 September 2008)

DANFS Naval Historical Center, Dictionary of American Naval Fighting Ships, <http://www.hazegray.org/danfs/> (16 September 2008)

DPMO Defense Prisoner of War/Missing Personnel Office, Service Personnel Not Recovered Following WWII, 15Aug 2007 <http://www.dtic.mil/dpmo/WWII_MIA/MIA_MAIN.HTM> (16 September 2008)

NARA2 The National Archives, World War II Army Enlistment Records, 6/01/2002-9/30/2002, documenting the period ca. 1938-1946 Record Group 64 <http://aad.archives.gov/aad/series-list.jsp?cat=all> (16 September 2008)

NARAK The National Archives, Records on Korean War Dead and Wounded Army Casualties, created, 1950 - 1970, documenting the period 2/13/1950 - 12/31/1953 <http://aad.archives.gov/aad/series-description.jsp?s=531> (16 September 2008)

NARAV The National Archives Vietnam War Records California, Listed by Hometown- then name, <http://www.archives.gov/research/vietnam-war/casualty-lists/ca-by-town.html> (16 Sept 2008)

USCR Heritage Quest Online, Search Census, [Federal census images 1790-1930] <http://scplweb.santacruzpl.org:2281/hqoweb/library/do/census/search/basic> (16 September 2008)

USDVA United States Department of Veterans Affairs, Burial & Memorials - Nationwide Gravesite Location, (2 June 2008]), <http://gravelocator.cem.va.gov/j2ee/servlet/NGL_v1> (16 September 2008)

USNM U S Navy Memorial, The Navy Log Search, 2007, <http://www.navylog.org/> (22 December 2009)

VVMW Vietnam Veterans Memorial - The Wall UUSA, Search the Wall, 1996 <http://thewall-usa.com/> (16 September 2008)

VVVW Vietnam Veterans Memorial Fund, The Virtual Wall Search, 2008, <http://www.vvmf.org/index.cfm?SectionID=2> (16 September 2008)

WIKI Wikipedia, The Free Encyclopedia Search, <http://en.wikipedia.org/wiki/Main_Page> (16 September 2008])

WWIDR Ancestry.Com, Search Military Records, US WWI Draft Registration 1917-1918, 2008, <http://landing.ancestry.com/military/titles.aspx?html=ww1draft> FEE SITE (16 September 2008)

194TB 194th Tank Battalion, Personnel of Company C, <http://www.proviso.k12.il.us/Bataan%20Web/194th_C_Co_Roster.htm> (16 September 2008)

Text References

CMWR Record of California Men in the War of the Rebellion, Orton, Sacramento, 1890.

MAHL Company L, 2nd CA Cav. Enlistment Roll, Santa Cruz County Museum of Art & History Archives,

SCHSC *Santa Cruz High School Service Cardinal*, Editors, Santa Cruz, 1948.

SCSn (Newspaper) *Santa Cruz Sentinel*

SCEN (Newspaper) *Santa Cruz Evening News*

SCSf (Newspaper) *Santa Cruz Surf*

SCSn (Newspaper) *Santa Cruz Sentinel-News*

SCR (Newspaper) *Santa Cruz Weekly Riptide*

SOGW (WWI Photos) *Soldiers of the Great War*, Haulsee, Howe and Doyle, Soldiers Record Publishing Assoc., Harvard University Press, 1920.

WHSM (Program Script) Watsonville HS Vietnam War Dead Memorial, April 25, 1987, *Our Classmates Remembered Vietnam*, R.O.P. Processing Class, 1986-87.

WEP (Newspaper) *Watsonville Evening Pajaronian*

WRP (Newspaper) *Watsonville Register-Pajaronian*

A number of texts were utilized in preparation for writing this book; however, since this study was not intended to be the history of wars, I purposely avoided including a long list of military histories available at any library. Below are those texts that served as reference sources in *Remembering Our Own*, as well as those I found useful in drawing an image of the broader conflict.

AFTER TET The Bloodiest Year in Vietnam, Ronald H. Spector, Free Press, New York, 1993.

American Heritage History of World War I, Editors, Bonanza Books, New York, 1982.

American Heritage World War II, C. L. Sulzberger, Crown Publishing, New York, 1966.

A Short History of the Korean War, James Stokesbury, Wm. Morrow, New York, 1988.

Eagle Against the Sun, The American War against Japan, Ronald H Spector, Free Press, New York, 1985.

Historical Times Illustrated Encyclopedia of the Civil

War, Patricia Faust Editor, Harper, New York 1996.

Korean War Almanac, Harry G. Summers, FactsOn-File, New York, 1990.

Over There, by Frank Freidel, Bramhall House, New York, 1964.

Records of California Men in the War of the Rebellion, Richard H. Orton, Sacramento, 1890.

Soldiers of the Overland, Fred B. Rogers, Grabhorn Press, San Francisco, 1938.

Vietnam, A History by Stanley Karnow, Viking Press, New York, 1983.

World Almanac of the Vietnam War, John Bowman, General Editor, Bison Books, New York, 1985.

INDEX

Breinigsville, PA USA
12 May 2010
237815BV00002B/2/P